Lecture Notes in Computer Science 13372

More information about this series at https://link.springer.com/bookseries/558

Sharon Shoham · Yakir Vizel (Eds.)

Computer Aided Verification

34th International Conference, CAV 2022
Haifa, Israel, August 7–10, 2022
Proceedings, Part II

 Springer

Editors
Sharon Shoham
Tel Aviv University
Tel Aviv, Israel

Yakir Vizel ⓘ
Technion – Israel Institute of Technology
Haifa, Israel

ISSN 0302-9743   ISSN 1611-3349 (electronic)
Lecture Notes in Computer Science
ISBN 978-3-031-13187-5   ISBN 978-3-031-13188-2 (eBook)
https://doi.org/10.1007/978-3-031-13188-2

This Springer imprint is published by the registered company Springer Nature Switzerland AG
The registered company address is: Gewerbestrasse 11, 6330 Cham, Switzerland

Preface

It was our privilege to serve as the program chairs for CAV 2022, the 34th International Conference on Computer-Aided Verification. CAV 2022 was held during August 7–10, 2022. CAV-affiliated workshops were held on July 31 to August 1 and August 11 to August 12. This year, CAV was held as part of the Federated Logic Conference (FLoC) and was collocated with many other conferences in software/hardware verification and logic for computer science. Due to the easing of COVID-19 travel restrictions, CAV 2022 and the rest of the FLoC were in-person events.

CAV is an annual conference dedicated to the advancement of the theory and practice of computer-aided formal analysis methods for hardware and software systems. The primary focus of CAV is to extend the frontiers of verification techniques by expanding to new domains such as security, quantum computing, and machine learning. This puts CAV at the cutting edge of formal methods research, and this year's program is a reflection of this commitment.

CAV 2022 received a high number of submissions (209). We accepted nine tool papers, two case studies, and 40 regular papers, which amounts to an acceptance rate of roughly 24%. The accepted papers cover a wide spectrum of topics, from theoretical results to applications of formal methods. These papers apply or extend formal methods to a wide range of domains such as smart contracts, concurrency, machine learning, probabilistic techniques, and industrially deployed systems. The program featured a keynote talk by Ziyad Hanna (Cadence Design Systems and University of Oxford), a plenary talk by Aarti Gupta (Princeton University), and invited talks by Arie Gurfinkel (University of Waterloo) and Neha Rungta (Amazon Web Services). Furthermore, we continued the tradition of Logic Lounge, a series of discussions on computer science topics targeting a general audience. In addition to all talks at CAV, the attendees got access to talks at other conferences held as part of FLoC.

In addition to the main conference, CAV 2022 hosted the following workshops: Formal Methods for ML-Enabled Autonomous Systems (FoMLAS), On the Not So Unusual Effectiveness of Logic, Formal Methods Education Online, Democratizing Software Verification (DSV), Verification of Probabilistic Programs (VeriProP), Program Equivalence and Relational Reasoning (PERR), Parallel and Distributed Automated Reasoning, Numerical Software Verification (NSV-XV), Formal Reasoning in Distributed Algorithms (FRIDA), Formal Methods for Blockchains (FMBC), Synthesis (Synt), and Workshop on Open Problems in Learning and Verification of Neural Networks (WOLVERINE).

Organizing a flagship conference like CAV requires a great deal of effort from the community. The Program Committee (PC) for CAV 2022 consisted of 86 members – a committee of this size ensures that each member has a reasonable number of papers to review in the allotted time. In all, the committee members wrote over 800 reviews while investing significant effort to maintain and ensure the high quality of the conference program. We are grateful to the CAV 2022 PC for their outstanding efforts in evaluating the submissions and making sure that each paper got a fair chance. Like recent years in

CAV, we made the artifact evaluation mandatory for tool paper submissions and optional but encouraged for the rest of the accepted papers. The Artifact Evaluation Committee consisted of 79 reviewers who put in significant effort to evaluate each artifact. The goal of this process was to provide constructive feedback to tool developers and help make the research published in CAV more reproducible. The Artifact Evaluation Committee was generally quite impressed by the quality of the artifacts. Among the accepted regular papers, 77% of the authors submitted an artifact, and 58% of these artifacts passed the evaluation. We are very grateful to the Artifact Evaluation Committee for their hard work and dedication in evaluating the submitted artifacts.

CAV 2022 would not have been possible without the tremendous help we received from several individuals, and we would like to thank everyone who helped make CAV 2022 a success. First, we would like to thank Maria A Schett and Daniel Dietsch for chairing the Artifact Evaluation Committee and Hari Govind V K for putting together the proceedings. We also thank Grigory Fedyukovich for chairing the workshop organization and Shachar Itzhaky for managing publicity. We would like to thank the FLoC organizing committee for organizing the Logic Lounge, Mentoring workshop, and arranging student volunteers. We also thank Hana Chockler for handling sponsorship for all conferences in FLoC. We would also like to thank FLoC chair Alexandra Silva and co-chairs Orna Grumberg and Eran Yahav for the support provided. Last but not least, we would like to thank members of the CAV Steering Committee (Aarti Gupta, Daniel Kroening, Kenneth McMillan, and Orna Grumberg) for helping us with several important aspects of organizing CAV 2022.

We hope that you will find the proceedings of CAV 2022 scientifically interesting and thought-provoking!

June 2022   Sharon Shoham
                                                                                       Yakir Vizel

Organization

Steering Committee

Aarti Gupta   Princeton University, USA
Daniel Kroening   Amazon, USA
Kenneth McMillan   University of Texas at Austin, USA
Orna Grumberg   Technion, Israel

Conference Co-chairs

Sharon Shoham   Tel Aviv University, Israel
Yakir Vizel   Technion, Israel

Artifact Evaluation Co-chairs

Maria A. Schett   University College London, UK
Daniel Dietsch   University of Freiburg, Germany

Publicity Chair

Shachar Itzhaky   Technion, Israel

Workshop Chair

Grigory Fedyukovich   Florida State University, USA

Proceedings and Talks Chair

Hari Govind V. K.   University of Waterloo, Canada

Program Committee

Aina Niemetz   Stanford, USA
Alastair Donaldson   Imperial College London, UK
Alessandro Cimatti   FBK, Italy
Alexander Ivrii   IBM, Israel
Alexander J. Summers   University of British Columbia, Canada
Alexander Nadel   Intel, Israel
Alexandra Silva   Cornell University, USA

Ana Sokolova	University of Salzburg, Austria
Anastasia Mavridou	KBR Inc., NASA Ames Research Center, USA
Andreas Podelski	University of Freiburg, Germany
Andrei Popescu	University of Sheffield, UK
Andrey Rybalchenko	Microsoft Research, UK
Anna Lukina	TU Delft, The Netherlands
Anna Slobodova	Intel, USA
Antoine Miné	Sorbonne Université, France
Armin Biere	University of Freiburg, Germany
Azalea Raad	Imperial College London, UK
Bor-Yuh Evan Chang	University of Colorado Boulder and Amazon, USA
Caterina Urban	INRIA, France
Corina Pasareanu	CMU/NASA Ames Research Center, USA
Dana Drachsler Cohen	Technion, Israel
Daniel Kroening	Amazon, USA
David Jansen	Institute of Software, Chinese Academy of Sciences, China
Deepak D'Souza	Indian Institute of Science, India
Dejan Jovanović	Amazon Web Services, USA
Derek Dreyer	MPI-SWS, Germany
Elizabeth Polgreen	University of Edinburgh, UK
Elvira Albert	Complutense University of Madrid, Spain
Erika Abraham	RWTH Aachen University, Germany
Grigory Fedyukovich	Florida State University, USA
Guy Avni	University of Haifa, Israel
Guy Katz	Hebrew University of Jerusalem, Israel
Hadar Frenkel	CISPA, Germany
Hillel Kugler	Bar Ilan University, Israel
Hiroshi Unno	University of Tsukuba, Japan
Isabel Garcia-Contreras	University of Waterloo, Canada
Ivana Cerna	Masaryk University, Czech Republic
Jade Alglave	University College London and Arm, UK
Jean-Baptiste Jeannin	University of Michigan, USA
Joost-Pieter Katoen	RWTH Aachen University, Germany
Josh Berdine	Meta, UK
Joxan Jaffar	National University of Singapore, Singapore
Kenneth L. McMillan	University of Texas at Austin, USA
Klaus V. Gleissenthall	Vrije Universiteit Amsterdam, The Netherlands
Konstantin Korovin	University of Manchester, UK
Krishna Shankaranarayanan	IIT Bombay, India
Kuldeep Meel	National University of Singapore, Singapore

Artifact Evaluation Committee

Guy Amir	Hebrew University of Jerusalem, Israel
Muqsit Azeem	Technical University of Munich, Germany
Kshitij Bansal	Meta, USA
Tianshu Bao	Vanderbilt University, USA
Fabian Bauer-Marquart	University of Konstanz, Germany
Anna Becchi	Fondazione Bruno Kessler, Italy
Ranadeep Biswas	Informal Systems, France
Christopher Brix	RWTH Aachen University, Germany
Marek Chalupa	IST Austria, Austria
Kevin Cheang	University of California, Berkeley, USA
Lesly-Ann Danie	KU Leuven, Belgium
Kinnari Dave	Certified Kernel Tech, LLC, USA
Simon Dierl	TU Dortmund, Germany
Florian Dorfhuber	Technical University of Munich, Germany
Benjamin Farinier	Technische Universität Wien, Austria
Parisa Fathololumi	Stevens Institute of Technology, USA
Mathias Fleury	University of Freiburg, Germany
Luke Geeson	University College London, UK
Pablo Gordillo	Complutense University of Madrid, Spain
Manish Goyal	University of North Carolina at Chapel Hill, USA
Akos Hajdu	Meta Platforms Inc., UK
Alejandro Hernández-Cerezo	Complutense University of Madrid, Spain
Jana Hofmann	CISPA Helmholtz Center for Information Security, Germany
Miguel Isabel	Universidad Complutense de Madrid, Spain
Martin Jonáš	Fondazione Bruno Kessler, Italy
Samuel Judson	Yale University, USA
Sudeep Kanav	LMU Munich, Germany
Daniela Kaufmann	Johannes Kepler University Linz, Austria
Brian Kempa	Iowa State University, USA
Ayrat Khalimov	Université libre de Bruxelles, Belgium
Nishant Kheterpal	University of Michigan, USA
Edward Kim	University of North Carolina at Chapel Hill, USA
John Kolesar	Yale University, USA
Bettina Könighofer	Graz University of Technology, Austria
Mitja Kulczynski	Kiel University, Germany
Thomas Lemberger	LMU Munich, Germany
Julien Lepiller	Yale University, USA
Sven Linker	Lancaster University in Leipzig, Germany
Kirby Linvill	University of Colorado Boulder, USA
Y. Cyrus Liu	Stevens Institute of Technology, USA

Tianhan Lu   University of Colorado Boulder, USA
Enrico Magnago   Fondazione Bruno Kessler and University of
                                Trento, Italy
Tobias Meggendorfer   IST Austria, Austria
Fabian Meyer   RWTH Aachen University, Germany
Stefanie Mohr   Technical University of Munich, Germany
Raphaël Monat   LIP6, Sorbonne Université and CNRS, France
Felipe R. Monteiro   Amazon, USA
Marcel Moosbrugger   Technische Universität Wien, Austria
Marco Muniz   Aalborg University, Denmark
Neelanjana Pal   Vanderbilt University, USA
Francesco Parolini   Sorbonne University, France
Mário Pereira   Universidade NOVA de Lisboa, Portugal
João Pereira   ETH Zurich, Switzerland
Sumanth Prabhu   Indian Institute of Science and TCS Research,
                                India
Cedric Richter   University of Oldenburg, Germany
Clara Rodríguez   Complutense University of Madrid, Spain
Bob Rubbens   University of Twente, The Netherlands
Rubén Rubio   Universidad Complutense de Madrid, Spain
Stanly Samuel   Indian Institute of Science, India
Daniel Schoepe   Amazon, UK
Philipp Schröer   RWTH Aachen University, Germany
Joseph Scott   University of Waterloo, Canada
Arnab Sharma   University of Oldenburg, Germany
Salomon Sickert   Hebrew University of Jerusalem, Israel
Yahui Song   National University of Singapore, Singapore
Michael Starzinger   University of Salzburg, Austria
Martin Tappler   Graz University of Technology, Austria
Michael Tautschnig   Queen Mary University of London, UK
Mertcan Temel   Intel Corporation, USA
Saeid Tizpaz-Niari   University of Texas at El Paso, USA
Deivid Vale   Radboud University Nijmegen, The Netherlands
Vesal Vojdani   University of Tartu, Estonia
Masaki Waga   Kyoto University, Japan
Peixin Wang   University of Oxford, UK
Tobias Winkler   RWTH Aachen University, Germany
Stefan Zetzsche   University College London, UK
Xiao-Yi Zhang   National Institute of Informatics, Japan
Linpeng Zhang   University College London, UK
Đorđe Žikelić   IST Austria, Austria

Additional Reviewers

A. R. Balasubramanian
Aaron Gember-Jacobson
Abhishek Rose
Aditya Akella
Alberto Larrauri
Alexander Bork
Alvin George
Ameer Hamza
Andres Noetzli
Anna Becchi
Anna Latour
Antti Hyvarinen
Benedikt Maderbacher
Benno Stein
Bettina Koenighofer
Bruno Blanchet
Chana Weil-Kennedy
Christoph Welzel
Christophe Chareton
Christopher Brix
Chun Tian
Constantin Enea
Daniel Hausmann
Daniel Kocher
Daniel Schoepe
Darius Foo
David Delmas
David MacIver
Dmitriy Traytel
Enrique Martin-Martin
Filip Cano
Francesco Parolini
Frederik Schmitt
Frédéric Recoules
Fu Song
Gadi Aleksandrowicz
Gerco van Heerdt
Grégoire Menguy
Gustavo Petri
Guy Amir

Haggai Landa
Hammad Ahmad
Hanna Lachnitt
Hongfei Fu
Ichiro Hasuo
Ilina Stoilkovska
Ira Fesefeldt
Jens Gutsfeld
Ji Guan
Jiawei Chen
Jip Spel
Jochen Hoenicke
Joshua Moerman
Kedar Namjoshi
Kevin Batz
Konstantin Britikov
Koos van der Linden
Lennard Gäher
Lesly-Ann Daniel
Li Wenhua
Li Zhou
Luca Laurenti
Lukas Armborst
Lukáš Holík
Malte Schledjewski
Martin Blicha
Martin Helfrich
Martin Lange
Masoud Ebrahimi
Mathieu Lehaut
Michael Sammler
Michael Starzinger
Miguel Gómez-Zamalloa
Miguel Isabel
Ming Xu
Noemi Passing
Niklas Metzger
Nishant Kheterpal
Noam Zilberstein
Norine Coenen

Omer Rappoport
Ömer Şakar
Peter Lammich
Prabhat Kumar Jha
Raghu Rajan
Rodrigo Otoni
Romain Demangeon
Ron Rothblum
Roope Kaivola
Sadegh Soudjani
Sepideh Asadi
Shachar Itzhaky
Shaun Azzopardi
Shawn Meier
Shelly Garion
Shubhani
Shyam Lal Karra
Simon Spies
Soline Ducousso
Song Yahui
Spandan Das
Sumanth Prabhu
Teodora Baluta
Thomas Noll
Tim King
Tim Quatmann
Timothy Bourke
Tobias Winkler
Vasileios Klimis
Vedad Hadzic
Vishnu Bondalakunta
Wang Fang
Xing Hong
Yangjia Li
Yash Pote
Yehia Abd Alrahman
Yuan Feng
Zachary Kincaid
Ziv Nevo
Zurab Khasidashvili

Contents – Part II

Synthesis and Concurrency

Contents – Part I

Software Verification and Model Checking

Hyperproperties and Security

Formal Methods for Hardware, Cyber-physical, and Hybrid Systems

Probabilistic Techniques

PAC Statistical Model Checking of Mean Payoff in Discrete- and Continuous-Time MDP

Chaitanya Agarwal[1], Shibashis Guha[2(✉)], Jan Křetínský[3],
and Pazhamalai Muruganandham[4]

[1] New York University, New York, USA
[2] Tata Institute of Fundamental Research, Mumbai, India
Shibashis@tifr.res.in
[3] Technical University of Munich, Munich, Germany
[4] Chennai Mathematical Institute, Chennai, India

Abstract. Markov decision processes (MDP) and continuous-time MDP (CTMDP) are the fundamental models for non-deterministic systems with probabilistic uncertainty. Mean payoff (a.k.a. long-run average reward) is one of the most classic objectives considered in their context. We provide the first algorithm to compute mean payoff probably approximately correctly in unknown MDP; further, we extend it to unknown CTMDP. We do not require any knowledge of the state space, only a lower bound on the minimum transition probability, which has been advocated in literature. In addition to providing probably approximately correct (PAC) bounds for our algorithm, we also demonstrate its practical nature by running experiments on standard benchmarks.

1 Introduction

Markov decision process (MDP) [7,30,32] is a basic model for systems featuring both probabilistic and non-deterministic behaviour. They come in two flavours: *discrete-time* MDP (often simply MDP) and *continuous-time* MDP (CTMDP). While the evolution of MDP happens in discrete steps, their natural real-time extension CTMDP additionally feature random time delays governed by exponential probability distributions. Their application domain ranges across a wide spectrum, e.g. operations research [10,16], power management and scheduling [31], networked and distributed systems [19,22], or communication protocols [28], to name a few. One of the key aspects of such systems is their performance, often formalized as *mean payoff* (also called long-run average reward), one of the classic and most studied objectives on (CT)MDP [30] with numerous applications [17]. In this context, probabilistic model checking and performance evaluation intersect [5]. While

This work has been partially supported by the DST-SERB project SRG/2021/000466 *Zero-sum and Nonzero-sum Games for Controller Synthesis of Reactive Systems* and by the German Research Foundation (DFG) projects 427755713 (KR 4890/3-1) *Group-By Objectives in Probabilistic Verification (GOPro)* and 383882557 (KR 4890/2-1) *Statistical Unbounded Verification (SUV)*.

S. Shoham and Y. Vizel (Eds.): CAV 2022, LNCS 13372, pp. 3–25, 2022.
https://doi.org/10.1007/978-3-031-13188-2_1

the former takes the verification perspective of the worst-case analysis and the latter the perspective of optimization for the best case, they are mathematically dual and thus algorithmically the same.

The range of analysis techniques provided by literature is very rich, encompassing linear programming, policy iteration, or value iteration. However, these are applicable only in the setting where the (CT)MDP is known (*whitebox* setting). In order to handle the *blackbox* setting, where the model is unknown or only partially known, *statistical model checking* (SMC) [37] relaxes the requirement of the hard guarantees on the correctness (claimed precision) of the result. Instead it uses *probably approximately correct* (PAC) analysis, which provides essentially a confidence interval on the result: with probability (confidence) at least $1 - \delta$, the result of the analysis is ε-close to the true value. This kind of analysis may be applicable to those systems for which we do not have exclusive access to their internal functionalities, but we can still observe their behaviour.

In this paper, we provide the *first algorithm with PAC bounds on the mean payoff in blackbox MDP*. We treat both the discrete-time and continuous-time MDP, and the SMC algorithm not only features PAC bounds (returning the result with prescribed precision and confidence), but an anytime algorithm (gradually improving the result and, if terminated prematurely, can return the current approximation with its precision and the required confidence).

The difficulty with blackbox models is that we do not know the exact transition probabilities, not even the number of successors for an action from a state. The algorithm thus must simulate the MDP to obtain any information. The visited states can be augmented to a model of the MDP and statistics used to estimate the transition probabilities. The estimates can be used to compute mean payoff precisely on the model. The results of [12] and [33] then provide a method for estimating the number of times each state-action pair needs to be visited in an MDP to obtain a PAC bound on the expected mean-payoff value of the original MDP. However, notice that this requires that the topology be learnt perfectly, for which we either need some knowledge of the state space or recent development in the spirit of [3]. On the one hand, this simple algorithm thus follows in a straightforward way from the recent results in the literature (although to the best of our knowledge it has not been presented as such yet). On the other hand, the required number of samples using these bounds is *prohibitively large*, and therefore, giving guarantees with such analysis is not feasible at all in practice. In fact, the numbers are astronomic already for Markov chains with a handful of states [13]. We discuss further drawbacks of such a naïve solution in Sect. 3. Our main contribution in this paper is a *practical algorithm*. It takes the most promising actions from every state and uses the *on-demand value iteration* [2], not even requiring an exhaustive exploration of the entire MDP. Using techniques of [3,13], we can show that the partial model captures enough information. Most importantly, instead of using [12,33], the PAC bounds are derived directly from the concrete confidence intervals, reflecting the width of each interval and the topology of the model, in the spirit of the practical SMC for reachability [3].

Our contribution can be summarized as follows:

- We provide the first algorithm with PAC bounds on the mean payoff in black-box MDP (Sect. 4) and its extension to blackbox CTMDP (Sect. 5).
- We discuss the drawbacks of a possible more straightforward solution and how to overcome them (in Sect. 3 on the conceptual level, before we dive into the technical algorithms in the subsequent sections).
- We evaluate the algorithm on the standard benchmarks of MDP and CTMDP and discuss the effect of heuristics, partial knowledge of the model, and variants of the algorithms (Sect. 6).

Related Work. SMC of unbounded-horizon properties of MDPs was first considered in [23,29] for reachability. [20] gives a model-free algorithm for ω-regular properties, which is convergent but provides no bounds on the current error. Several approaches provide SMC for MDPs and unbounded-horizon properties with *PAC guarantees*. Firstly, the algorithm of [18] requires (1) the mixing time T of the MDP (2) the ability to restart simulations also in non-initial states (3) visiting *all* states sufficiently many times, and thus (4) the knowledge of the size of the state space $|S|$. Secondly, [9], based on delayed Q-learning [34], lifts the assumptions (2) and (3) and instead of (1) requires only (a bound on) the minimum transition probability $p_{\min}$. Thirdly, [3] additionally lifts the assumption (4), keeping only $p_{\min}$, as in this paper. In [13], it is argued that while unbounded-horizon properties cannot be analysed without any information on the system, knowledge of (a lower bound on) the minimum transition probability $p_{\min}$ is a relatively light and realistic assumption in many scenarios, compared to the knowledge of the whole topology. In this paper, we thus adopt this assumption.

In contrast to SMC that uses possibly more (re-started) runs of the system, there are *online learning* approaches, where the desired behaviour is learnt for the single run. Model-based learning algorithms for mean payoff have been designed both for minimizing regret [4,36] as well as for PAC online learning [25,26].

Due to lack of space, the proofs and some more experimental results and discussions appear in [1].

2 Preliminaries

A *probability distribution* on a finite set X is a mapping $\rho : X \mapsto [0,1]$, such that $\sum_{x \in X} \rho(x) = 1$. We denote by $\mathcal{D}(X)$ the set of probability distributions on X.

Definition 1. (MDP). *A Markov decision process is a tuple of the form* $\mathcal{M} = (S, s_{init}, \mathsf{Act}, \mathsf{Av}, \mathbb{T}, r)$, *where* S *is a finite set of states,* $s_{init} \in S$ *is the initial state,* Act *is a finite set of actions,* $\mathsf{Av} : S \to 2^{\mathsf{Act}}$ *assigns to every state a set of available actions,* $\mathbb{T} : S \times \mathsf{Act} \to \mathcal{D}(S)$ *is a transition function that given a state* s *and an action* $a \in \mathsf{Av}(s)$ *yields a probability distribution over successor states, and* $r : S \to \mathbb{R}^{\geq 0}$ *is a reward function, assigning rewards to states.*

For ease of notation, we write $\mathbb{T}(s,a,t)$ instead of $\mathbb{T}(s,a)(t)$. We denote by $\mathsf{Post}(s,a)$, the set of states that can be reached from s through action a. Formally, $\mathsf{Post}(s,a) = \{t \mid \mathbb{T}(s,a,t) > 0\}$.

The choices of actions are resolved by strategies, generally taking history into account and possibly randomizing. However, for mean payoff it is sufficient to consider *positional* strategies of the form $\pi : S \to \mathsf{Act}$. The semantics of an MDP with an initial state s_{init} is given in terms of each strategy σ inducing a Markov chain $\mathcal{M}^{\sigma}_{s_{init}}$ with the respective probability space and unique probability measure $\mathbb{P}^{\mathcal{M}^{\sigma}_{s_{init}}}$, and the expected value $\mathbb{E}^{\mathcal{M}^{\sigma}_{s_{init}}}[F]$ of a random variable F (see e.g. [6]). We drop $\mathcal{M}^{\sigma}_{s_{init}}$ when it is clear from the context.

End Components An *end-component* (EC) $M = (T, A)$, with $\emptyset \neq T \subseteq S$ and $A : T \to 2^{\mathsf{Act}}$ of an MDP $\mathcal{M}$ is a *sub-MDP* of $\mathcal{M}$ such that: for all $s \in T$, we have that $A(s)$ is a subset of the actions available from s; for all $a \in A(s)$, we have $\mathsf{Post}(s, a) \subseteq T$; and, it's underlying graph is strongly connected. A *maximal end-component* (MEC) is an EC that is not included in any other EC. Given an MDP $\mathcal{M}$, the set of its MECs is denoted by $\mathsf{MEC}(\mathcal{M})$. For $\mathsf{MEC}(\mathcal{M}) = \{(T_1, A_1), \ldots, (T_n, A_n)\}$, we define $\mathsf{MEC_S} = \bigcup_{i=1}^{n} T_i$ as the set of all states contained in some MEC.

Definition 2. (continuous-time MDP (CTMDP)). *A continuous-time Markov decision process is a tuple of the form* $\mathcal{M} = (S, s_{init}, \mathsf{Act}, \mathsf{Av}, \mathsf{R}, r)$, *where* S *is a finite set of states,* $s_{init} \in S$ *is the initial state,* Act *is a finite set of actions,* $\mathsf{Av} : S \to 2^{\mathsf{Act}}$ *assigns to every state a set of available actions,* $\mathsf{R} : S \times \mathsf{Act} \times S \to \mathbb{R}_{\geq 0}$ *is a transition rate matrix that given a state s and an action $a \in \mathsf{Av}(s)$ defines the set of successors t of s on action a if $\mathsf{R}(s, a, t) > 0$, and $r : S \to \mathbb{R}_{\geq 0}$ is a reward rate function, assigning a reward function to a state denoting the reward obtained for spending unit time in s.*

A strategy in a CTMDP decides immediately after entering a state which action needs to be chosen from the current state. For a given state $s \in S$, and an action $a \in \mathsf{Av}(s)$, we denote by $\lambda(s, a) = \sum_t \mathsf{R}(s, a, t) > 0$ the *exit rate* of a in s. The *residence time* for action a in s is exponentially distributed with mean $\frac{1}{\lambda(s,a)}$. An equivalent way of looking at CTMDP is that in state s, we wait for a time which is exponentially distributed with mean $\lambda(s, a)$, and then with probability $\Delta(s, a, t) = \mathsf{R}(s, a, t)/\lambda(s, a)$, we make a transition to state t. The reward accumulated for spending time t in s is $r(s) \cdot \mathsf{t}$.

Uniformization. A *uniform* CTMDP has a constant exit rate C for all state-action pairs i.e., $\lambda(s, a) = C$ for all states $s \in S$ and actions $a \in \mathsf{Av}(s)$. The procedure of converting a non-uniform CTMDP into a uniform one is called *uniformization*. Consider a non-uniform CTMDP $\mathcal{M}$. Let $C \in \mathbb{R}_{\geq 0}$ such that $C \geqslant \lambda(s, a)$ for all $s \in S$ and $a \in \mathsf{Act}$. We can obtain a uniform CTMDP $\mathcal{M}_C$ by assigning the new rates.

$$\mathsf{R}'(s, a, t) = \begin{cases} \mathsf{R}(s, a, t) & \text{if } s \neq t \\ \mathsf{R}(s, a, t) + C - \lambda(s, a) & \text{if } s = t \end{cases} \tag{1}$$

For every action $a \in \mathsf{Av}(s)$ from each state s in the new CTMDP we have a self loop if $\lambda(s, a) < C$. Due to a constant transition rate, the mean interval time between two any two actions is constant.

Mean Payoff. In this work, we consider the (maximum) *mean payoff* (or *long-run average reward*) of an MDP $\mathcal{M}$, which intuitively describes the (maximum) average reward per step we expect to see when simulating the MDP for time going to infinity. Formally, let S_i, A_i, R_i be random variables giving the state visited, action played, and reward obtained in step i, and for CTMDP, T_i the time spent in the state appearing in step i. For MDP, $R_i := r(S_i)$, whereas for CTMDP, $R_i := r(S_i) \cdot T_i$; consequently, for a CTMDP and a strategy π, we have $\mathbb{E}_s^\pi(R_i) = \frac{r(S_i)}{\lambda(S_i, A_i)}$.

Thus given a strategy π, the n-step average reward is

$$v_n^\pi(s) := \mathbb{E}_s^\pi \left(\frac{1}{n} \sum_{i=0}^{n-1} R_i \right) = \frac{1}{n} \sum_{i=0}^{n-1} \frac{r(S_i)}{\lambda(S_i, A_i)}.$$

with the latter equality holding for CTMDP. For both MDP and CTMDP, the *mean payoff* is then

$$v(s) := \max_\pi \liminf_{n \to \infty} v_n^\pi,$$

where the maximum over all strategies can also be without loss of generality restricted to the set of positional strategies Π^{MD}. A well-known alternative characterization we use in this paper is

$$v(s) = \max_{\pi \in \Pi^{\mathsf{MD}}} \sum_{M \in \mathsf{MEC}(\mathcal{M})} \mathbb{P}_s^\pi[\lozenge \square M] \cdot v_M, \tag{2}$$

where $\lozenge$ and $\square$ respectively denote the standard LTL operators *eventually* and *always* respectively. Further, $\lozenge \square M$ denotes the set of paths that eventually remain forever within M and v_M is the unique value achievable in the (CT)MDP restricted to the MEC M. Note that v_M does not depend on the initial state chosen for the restriction.

We consider algorithms that have a limited information about the MDP.

Definition 3. (Blackbox and greybox). *An algorithm inputs an MDP or a CTMDP as* blackbox *if*

- *it knows s_{init},*
- *for a given state,[1] an oracle returns its available actions,*
- *given a state s and action a, it can sample a successor t according to $\mathbb{T}(s, a)$,*
- *it knows $p_{\mathsf{min}} \leqslant \min_{\substack{s \in \mathsf{S}, a \in \mathsf{Av}(s) \\ t \in \mathsf{Post}(s,a)}} \mathbb{T}(s, a, t)$, an under-approximation of the minimum transition probability.*

When input as greybox*, it additionally knows the number $|\mathsf{Post}(s, a)|$ of successors for each state s and action a. Note that the exact probabilities on the transitions in an MDP or the rates in a CTMDP are unknown for both blackbox and greybox learning settings.*

---

[1] In contrast to practical setups in monitoring, our knowledge of the current state is complete, i.e., the previously visited states can be uniquely identified.

3 Overview of Our Approach

Since no solutions are available in the literature and our solution consists of multiple ingredients, we present it in multiple steps to ease the understanding. First, we describe a more *naïve* solution and pinpoint its drawbacks. Second, we give an *overview* of a more sophisticated solution, eliminating the drawbacks. Third, we fill in its *details* in the subsequent sections. Besides, each of the three points is first discussed on discrete-time MDPs and then on continuous-time MDPs. The reason for this is twofold: the separation of concerns simplifies the presentation; and the algorithm for discrete-time MDP is equally important and deserves a standalone description.

3.1 Naïve Solution

We start by suggesting a conceptually simple solution. We can learn mean payoff MP in an MDP $\mathcal{M}$ as follows:

(i) Via simulating the MDP $\mathcal{M}$, we learn a model $\mathcal{M}'$ of $\mathcal{M}$, i.e., we obtain confidence intervals on the *transition probabilities* of $\mathcal{M}$ (of some given width ε_{TP}, called *TP-imprecision*, and confidence $1 - \delta_{TP}$, where δ_{TP} is called *TP-inconfidence*).

(ii) We compute the mean payoff $\widehat{MP}$ on the (imprecise) model $\mathcal{M}'$.

(iii) We compute the *MP-imprecision* $\varepsilon_{MP} = |\widehat{MP} - MP|$ of the *mean payoff* from the TP-imprecision by the "robustness" theorem [8] which quantifies how mean payoff can change when the system is perturbed with a given maximum perturbation. Further, we compute the overall *MP-inconfidence* δ_{MP} from the TP-inconfidence δ_{TP}; in particular, we can simply accumulate all the uncertainty and set $\delta_{MP} = |\mathbb{T}| \cdot \delta_{TP}$, where $|\mathbb{T}|$ is the number of transitions. The result is then probably approximately correct, being ε_{MP}-precise with confidence $1 - \delta_{MP}$. (Inversely, from a desired ε_{MP} we can also compute a sufficient ε_{TP} to be used in the first step.)

Learning the model, i.e. the transition probabilities, can be done by observing the simulation runs and collecting, for each state-action pair (s, a), a statistics of which states occur right after playing a in s. The frequency of each successor t among all successors then estimates the transition probability $\mathbb{T}(s, a, t)$. This is the standard task of estimating the generalized Bernoulli variable (a fixed distribution over finitely many options) with confidence intervals. We stop simulating when *each* transition probability has a precise enough confidence interval (with ε_{TP} and δ_{TP} yielded by the robustness theorem from the desired overall precision).[2] The drawbacks are *(D1: uniform importance)* that even transitions with

---

[2] Several non-trivial questions are dealt with later on: how to resolve the action choices during simulations; when to stop each simulation run and start a new one; additionally, in the black-box setting, when do we know that all successors of each transition have been observed. In particular, the last one is fundamental for the applicability of the robustness theorem. While the literature typically assumes the greybox setting or even richer information, to allow for such an algorithm with PAC bounds, our approach only needs p_{min}.

little to no impact on the mean payoff have to be estimated precisely (with ε_{TP} and δ_{TP}); and *(D2: uniform precision required)* that, even restricting our attention to "important" transitions, it may take a long time before the last one is estimated precisely (while others are already estimated overly precisely).

Subsequently, using standard algorithms the mean payoff $\widehat{MP}$ can be computed precisely by linear programming [30] or precisely enough by value iteration [2]. The respective MP can then be estimated by the robustness theorem [8], which yields for a given maximum perturbation of transition probabilities (in our case, $\varepsilon_{TP}/2$) an upper bound on the respective perturbation of the mean payoff $\varepsilon_{MP}/2$. The drawbacks are *(D3: uniform precision utilized)* that more precise confidence intervals for transitions (obtained due to D2) are not utilized, only the maximum imprecision is taken into account; and *(D4: a-priori bounds)* that the theorem is extremely conservative. Indeed, it reflects neither the topology of the MDP nor how impactful each transition is and thus provides an a-priori bound, extremely loose compared to the possible values of mean payoff that can be actually obtained for concrete values within the confidence intervals. This is practically unusable beyond a handful of states even for Markov chains [13].

For CTMDP $\mathcal{M}$, we additionally need to estimate the rates (see below how). Subsequently, we can uniformize the learnt CTMDP $\mathcal{M}'$. Mean payoff of the uniformized CTMDP is then equal to the mean payoff of its embedded MDP[3]. Hence, we can proceed as before but we also have to compute (i) confidence intervals for the rates from finitely many observations, and (ii) the required precision and confidence of these intervals so that the respective induced error on the mean payoff is not too large. Hence all the drawbacks are inherited and, additionally, also applied to the estimates of the rates. Besides, *(D5: rates)* while imprecisions of rates do not increase MP-imprecision too much, the bound obtained via uniformization and the robustness theorem is very loose. Indeed, imprecise rates are reflected as imprecise self-loops in the uniformization, which themselves do not have much impact on the mean payoff, but can increase the TP-imprecision and thus hugely the MP-imprecision from the robustness theorem.

Finally, note that for both types of MDP, *(D6: not anytime)* this naïve algorithm is not an anytime algorithm[4] since it works with pre-computed ε_{TP} and δ_{TP}. Instead it returns the result with the input precision if given enough time; if not given enough time, it does not return anything (also, if given more time, it does not improve the precision).

3.2   Improved Solution

Now we modify the solution so that the drawbacks are eliminated. The main ideas are (i) to allow for differences in TP-imprecisions (ε_{TP} can vary over

---

[3] An embedded MDP of a CTMDP is obtained by considering for every state s, actions $a \in \mathsf{Av}(s)$, and transitions $t \in \mathsf{Post}(s,a)$, such that $\mathbb{T}(s,a,t) = \Delta(s,a,t)$, and by disregarding the transition rate matrix.

[4] An anytime algorithm can, at every step, return the current estimate with its imprecision, and this bound converges to 0 in the limit.

transitions) and even deliberately ignore less important transitions and instead improve precision for transitions where more information is helpful the most; (ii) rather than using the a-priori robustness theorem, to utilize the precision of each transition to its maximum; and (iii) to give an anytime algorithm that reflects the current confidence intervals and, upon improving them, can efficiently improve the mean-payoff estimate without recomputing it from scratch. There are several ingredients used in our approach.

Firstly, [2] provides an anytime algorithm for approximating mean payoff in a fully known MDP. The algorithm is a version of value iteration, called *on-demand*, performing improvements (so called Bellman updates) of the mean-payoff estimate in each state. Moreover, the algorithm is simulation-based, performing the updates in the visited states, biasing towards states where a more precise estimate is helpful the most ("on demand"). This matches well our learning setting. However, the approach assumes precise knowledge of the transition probabilities and, even more importantly, heavily relies on the knowledge of MECs. Indeed, it decomposes the mean-payoff computation according to Eq. 2 into computing mean payoff within MECs and optimizing (weighted) reachability of the MECs (with weights being their mean payoffs). When the MECs are unknown, none of these two steps can be executed.

Secondly, [3] provides an efficient way of learning reachability probabilities (in the greybox and blackbox settings). Unfortunately, since it considers TP-inconfidence to be the same for all transitions, causing different TP-imprecisions, the use of robustness theorem in [3] makes the algorithm used there practically unusable in many cases. On a positive note, the work identifies the notion of δ_{TP}-sure EC, which reflects how confident we are, based on the simulations so far, that a set of states is an EC. This notion will be crucial also in our algorithm.

Both approaches are based on "bounded value iteration", which computes at any moment of time both a lower and an upper bound on the value that we are approximating (mean payoff or reachability, respectively). This yields anytime algorithms with known imprecision, the latter—being a learning algorithm on an incompletely known MDP—only with some confidence. Note that the upper bound converges only because ECs are identified and either collapsed (in the former) or deflated [24] (in the latter), meaning their upper bounds are decreased in a particular way to ensure correctness.

Our algorithm on (discrete-time) MDP $\mathcal{M}$ performs, essentially, the following. It simulates $\mathcal{M}$ in a similar way as [3]. With each visit of each state, not only it updates the model (includes this transition and improves the estimate of the outgoing transition probabilities), but also updates the estimate of the mean payoff by a Bellman update. Besides, at every moment of time, the current model yields a hypothesis what the actual MECs of $\mathcal{M}$ are and the respective confidence. While we perform the Bellman updates on all visited states deemed transient, the states deemed to be in MECs are updated separately, like in [2]. However, in contrast to [2], where every MEC is fully known and can thus be collapsed, and in contrast to the "bounded" quotient of [3] (see Appendix A of [1]), we instead introduce a special action stay in each of its states, which simulates *staying* in the (not fully known) MEC and obtaining its mean-payoff estimate via reachability:

Definition 4. (stay-augmented MDP). *Let* $\mathcal{M} = (\mathsf{S}, s_{init}, \mathsf{Act}, \mathsf{Av}, \mathbb{T}, r)$ *be an MDP and* $l, u : \mathsf{MEC}(\mathcal{M}) \to [0,1]$ *be real functions on MECs. We augment the* stay *action to* $\mathcal{M}$ *to obtain* $\mathcal{M}' = (\mathsf{S}', s_{init}, \mathsf{Act}', \mathsf{Av}', \mathbb{T}', r')$, *where*

- $\mathsf{S}' = \mathsf{S} \uplus \{s_+, s_-, s_?\}$,
- $\mathsf{Act}' = \mathsf{Act} \uplus \{\mathsf{stay}\}$,
- $\mathsf{Av}'(s) = \begin{cases} \mathsf{Av}(s) & \text{for } s \in \mathsf{S} \setminus \bigcup \mathsf{MEC}(\mathcal{M}) \\ \mathsf{Av}(s) \cup \{\mathsf{stay}\} & \text{for } s \in \bigcup \mathsf{MEC}(\mathcal{M}) \\ \{\mathsf{stay}\} & \text{for } s \in \{s_+, s_-, s_?\} \end{cases}$
- $\mathbb{T}'$ *extends* $\mathbb{T}$ *by* $\mathbb{T}'(s, \mathsf{stay}) = \{s_+ \mapsto l(M), s_- \mapsto 1 - u(M), s_? \mapsto u(M) - l(M)\}$ *on* $s \in M \in \mathsf{MEC}(\mathcal{M})$ *and by* $\mathbb{T}'(s, \mathsf{stay}, s) = 1$ *for* $s \in \{s_+, s_-, s_?\}$.
- r' *extends* r *by* $r'(s_+) = r'(s_?) = r'(s_-) = 0$.[5]

Corollary 1. *If* l, u *are valid lower and upper bounds on the mean-payoff within MECs of* $\mathcal{M}$ *then* $\max_\sigma \mathbb{P}^{M^\sigma}[\lozenge\{s_+\}] \leqslant v(s_{init}) \leqslant \max_\sigma \mathbb{P}^{M^\sigma}[\lozenge\{s_+, s_?\}]$[6] *where,* $\max_\sigma \mathbb{P}^{M^\sigma}[\lozenge S]$ *gives the maximum probability of reaching some state in* S *over all strategies.*

This turns the problem into reachability, and thus allows for deflating (defined for reachability in [3]) and an algorithm combining [3] and [2]. The details are explained in the next section. To summarize (D1) and (D2) are eliminated by not requiring uniform TP-imprecisions; (D3) and (D4) are eliminated via updating lower and upper bounds (using deflating) instead of using the robustness theorem.

Concerning CTMDP, in Sect. 5 we develop a confidence interval computation for the rates. Further, we design an algorithm deriving the MP-imprecision resulting from the rate imprecisions, that acts directly on the CTMDP and not on the embedded MDP of the uniformization. This effectively removes (D5).

4   Algorithm for Discrete-Time MDP

Now that we explained the difficulties of a naïve approach, and the concepts from literature together with novel ideas to overcome them, we describe the actual algorithm for the discrete-time setting. Following a general outline of the algorithm, we give detailed explanations behind the components and provide the statistical guarantees the algorithm gives. Detailed pseudocode of the algorithms for this section is provided in Appendix B of [1].

Overall Algorithm and Details. Our version of an on-demand value iteration for mean payoff in black-box MDP is outlined in Algorithm 1. Initially, the input MDP $\mathcal{M}$ is augmented with terminal states ($\{s_+, s_-, s_?\}$) to obtain the

---

[5] A higher transition probability to s_+ indicates that the MEC has high value, a higher transition probability to $s_?$ indicates high uncertainty in the value of the MEC, while a higher transition probability to s_- indicates that the MEC has low value.

[6] For simplicity of the presentation, we assume the rewards are between 0 and 1, for all states. If they are not, we can always rescale them to [0,1] by dividing them by the maximum reward observed so far and correspondingly adjust $\mathbb{T}(\cdot, \mathsf{stay}, \cdot)$.

stay-augmented MDP $\mathcal{M}'$. We learn a stay-augmented MDP $\mathcal{M}' = (S', s_{init}, Act', Av', \mathbb{T}', r')$ by collecting samples through several simulation runs (Lines 5-8). Over the course of the algorithm, we identify MECs with δ_{TP} confidence (Line 13) and gradually increase precision on their respective values (Lines 9-11). As stated earlier, these simulations are biased towards actions that lead to MECs potentially having higher rewards. Values for MECs are encoded using the stay action (Line 12) and propagated throughout the model using bounded value iteration (Lines 14-19). In Line 14, we reinitialize the values of the states in the partial model since new MECs may be identified and also existing MECs may change. Finally, we claim that the probability estimates $\mathbb{T}'$ are correct with confidence δ_{MP} and if the bounds on the value are precise enough, we terminate the algorithm. Otherwise, we repeat this overall process with improved bounds (Line 20).

Simulation. The SIMULATE function simulates a run over the input blackbox MDP $\mathcal{M}$ and returns the visited states in order. The simulation of $\mathcal{M}'$ is executed by simulating $\mathcal{M}$ together with a random choice if action stay is taken. Consequently, a simulation starts from s_{init} and ends at one of the terminal states ($\{s_+, s_-, s_?\}$). During simulation, we enhance our estimate of $\mathcal{M}'$ by visiting new states, exploring new actions and improving our estimate of $\mathbb{T}'$ with more samples. When states are visited for the first time, actions are chosen at random, and subsequently, actions with a higher potential reward are chosen. If a simulation is stuck in a loop, we check for the presence of an MEC with δ_{TP} confidence. If a δ_{TP}-sure MEC is found, we add a stay action with $l, u = 0, 1$, otherwise we keep simulating until the required confidence is achieved. After that, we take the action with the highest upper bound that is leaving the MEC to continue the simulation. We do several such simulations to build a large enough model before doing value iteration in the next steps.

Estimating Transition Probabilities. [3] gives an analysis to estimate bounds on transition probabilities for reachability objective in MDPs. For completeness, we briefly restate it here. Given an MP-inconfidence δ_{MP}, we distribute the inconfidence over all individual transitions as

$$\delta_{TP} := \frac{\delta_{MP} \cdot p_{min}}{|\{a \mid s \in S' \wedge a \in Av'(s)\}|},$$

where $\frac{1}{p_{min}}$ gives an upper bound on the maximum number of possible successors for an available action from a state[7]. The Hoeffding's inequality gives us a bound on the number of times an action a needs to be sampled from state s, denoted $\#(s, a)$, to achieve a TP-imprecision $\varepsilon_{TP} \geqslant \sqrt{\dfrac{\ln \delta_{TP}}{-2\#(s, a)}}$ on $\mathbb{T}(s, a, t)$, such that

$$\widehat{\mathbb{T}}(s, a, t) := \max(0, \frac{\#(s, a, t)}{\#(s, a)} - \varepsilon_{TP})$$

---

[7] Knowing additionally $\max_{s \in S, a \in Av(s)} |Post(s, a)|$ gives slightly smaller TP-imprecision. See Appendix G.4 in [1].

Algorithm 1. Mean-payoff learning for black-box MDP

Input: MDP $\mathcal{M}$, imprecision $\varepsilon_{MP} > 0$, MP-inconfidence $\delta_{MP} > 0$, lower bound $p_{\min}$ on transition probabilities in $\mathcal{M}$

Parameters: revisit threshold $k \geq 2$, episode length $n \geq 1$

Output: upon termination ε_{MP}-precise estimate of the maximum mean payoff for $\mathcal{M}$ with confidence $1 - \delta_{MP}$, i.e. $(\varepsilon_{MP}, 1 - \delta_{MP})$-PAC estimate

1: **procedure** ON_DEMAND_BVI
    //*Initialization*
2:    Set $\mathsf{L}(s_+) = \mathsf{U}(s_+) = \mathsf{U}(s_?) = 1$, $\mathsf{L}(s_-) = \mathsf{U}(s_-) = \mathsf{L}(s_?) = 0$ ▷ Augmentation
3:    $S' = \emptyset$ ▷ States of learnt model
4:    **repeat**
        //*Get n simulation runs and update MP of MECs where they end up*
5:        **for** n times **do**
6:            $w \leftarrow$ SIMULATE(k) ▷ Path taken by the simulation
7:            $S' \leftarrow S' \cup w$ ▷ Add states to the model
8:            $\delta_{TP} \leftarrow \frac{\delta_{MP} \cdot p_{\min}}{|\{a \mid s \in S' \wedge a \in Av'(s)\}|}$ ▷ Split inconfidence among all transitions
9:            **if** last state of w is s_+ or $s_?$ **then** ▷ Probably entered a good MEC M
10:                $M \leftarrow$ MEC from which we entered the last state of w
11:                UPDATE_MEC_VALUE(M) ▷ Increase precision using more VI
12:                Update $\mathbb{T}'(s, \mathsf{stay})$ according to Definition 4 for all $s \in M$
        //*Identify δ_{TP}-sure MECs and propagate their MP by VI for reachability*
13:        $ProbableMECs \leftarrow$ FIND_MECS ▷ δ_{TP}-sure MECs
14:        INITIALIZE_VI_BOUNDS ▷ Reinitialize L, U for all states
15:        **repeat**
16:            UPDATE(S') ▷ One Bellman update per state
17:            **for** $T \in ProbableMECs$ **do**
18:                DEFLATE(T) ▷ Ensure safe but converging U
19:        **until** L and U close to their respective fixpoints
20:    **until** $\mathsf{U}(s_{\mathsf{init}})$ - $\mathsf{L}(s_{\mathsf{init}}) < \frac{2\varepsilon_{MP}}{r_{\max}}$ ▷ ε_{MP} is the absolute error; we use "$< \frac{2\varepsilon_{MP}}{r_{\max}}$"
    for relative difference between upper and lower values, where $r_{\max} = \max\limits_{s \in S'} r(s)$.

where, $\#(s, a, t)$ is the number of times t is sampled when action a is chosen in s.

Updating mean-payoff values Using $\widehat{\mathbb{T}}(s, a, t)$, we compute estimates of the upper and lower bounds of the values corresponding to every action from a state visited in the partial model that is constructed so far. We use the following *modified* Bellman Eq. [3]:

$$\widehat{\mathsf{L}}(s, a) := \sum_{t: \#(s,a,t) > 0} \widehat{\mathbb{T}}(s, a, t) \cdot \mathsf{L}(t)$$

$$\widehat{\mathsf{U}}(s, a) := \sum_{t: \#(s,a,t) > 0} \widehat{\mathbb{T}}(s, a, t) \cdot \mathsf{U}(t) + \left(1 - \sum_{t: \#(s,a,t) > 0} \widehat{\mathbb{T}}(s, a, t)\right),$$

where $\mathsf{L}(t) = \max\limits_{a \in Av(t)} \widehat{\mathsf{L}}(t, a)$ and $\mathsf{U}(t) = \max\limits_{a \in Av(t)} \widehat{\mathsf{U}}(t, a)$ are bounds on the value of from a state, $v(s)$. When a state is discovered for the first time during the simulation, and is added to the partial model, we initialize $L(s)$, and $U(s)$ to 0, and 1, respectively. Note that $\sum_{t:\#(s,a,t)>0} \widehat{\mathbb{T}}(s,a,t) < 1$. We attribute the remaining probability to unseen successors and assume their value to be 0 (1) to safely under-(over-)approximate the lower (upper) bounds. We call these *blackbox Bellman update* equations, since it assumes that all the successors of a state-action pair may not have been visited.

Estimating Values of End-Components. End-components are identified with an inconfidence of δ_{TP}. As observed in [13], assuming an action has been sampled n times, the probability of missing a transition for that action is at most $(1 - p_{\min})^n$. Thus, for identifying (T, A) as a δ_{TP}-*sure* MEC, every action in A that is available from a state $s \in T$ needs to be sampled at least $\frac{\ln \delta_{TP}}{\ln(1-p_{\min})}$ times.

Once a δ_{TP}-*sure* MEC M is identified, we estimate its upper (v_M^u) and lower (v_M^l) bounds using value iteration.[8] While running value iteration, we assume, with a small inconfidence, that there are no unseen outgoing transitions. So we use the following modified Bellman update equations inside the MEC where we under-(over-)approximate the lower(upper) bound to a much lesser degree.

$$\widehat{L}(s,a) := \sum_{t:\#(s,a,t)>0} \widehat{\mathbb{T}}(s,a,t) \cdot L(t) + \min_{t:\#(s,a,t)>0} L(t) \cdot \left(1 - \sum_{t:\#(s,a,t)>0} \widehat{\mathbb{T}}(s,a,t)\right)$$

$$\widehat{U}(s,a) := \sum_{t:\#(s,a,t)>0} \widehat{\mathbb{T}}(s,a,t) \cdot U(t) + \max_{t:\#(s,a,t)>0} U(t) \cdot \left(1 - \sum_{t:\#(s,a,t)>0} \widehat{\mathbb{T}}(s,a,t)\right)$$

Following the assumption, we call these *greybox* (See Definition 3) Bellman update equations. The value iteration algorithm further gives us bounds on v_M^u and v_M^l. We say that the upper estimate of v_M^u $(\widehat{v}_M^u)$ and the lower estimate of v_M^l $(\widehat{v}_M^l)$ are the overall upper and lower bounds of the mean-payoff value of M, respectively. To converge the overall bounds, we need value iteration to return more precise estimates of v_M^l and v_M^u, and we need to sample the actions inside M many times to reduce the difference between v_M^l and v_M^u. We call this procedure, UPDATE_MEC_VALUE.

Now, some MECs may have very low values or may not be reachable from s_{init} with high probability. In such cases, no optimal strategy may visit these MECs, and it might not be efficient to obtain very precise mean-payoff values for every MEC that is identified in an MDP. We follow the on-demand heuristic [2] where we progressively increase the precision on mean-payoff values as an MEC seems more likely to be a part of an optimal strategy. The stay action on MECs helps in guiding simulation towards those MECs that have a higher lower bound of the mean-payoff value. In particular, whenever the simulation ends up in s_+ or $s_?$, we run UPDATE_MEC_VALUE with higher precision on the MEC that led to these states. If the simulation ends up in these states through a particular MEC more often, it indicates that the MEC is likely to be a part of an optimal strategy, and it would be worth increasing the precision on its mean-payoff value.

---

[8] Note that one requires the ECs to be aperiodic for the VI to converge. [30] suggests a way that deals with this.

Deflate Operation. Unlike in the case of computation of mean payoff for whitebox models [3] where a MEC is collapsed following the computation of its value, for blackbox learning, once a set of states is identified as a δ_{TP}-*sure* MEC, we cannot collapse them. This is because collapsing would prevent a proper future analysis of those states, which is undesirable in a blackbox setting. However, this leads to other problems. To illustrate this, we consider an MDP that only has a single MEC M and one outgoing action from every individual state. Recall from Eq. 2 that we compute the mean-payoff by reducing it to a reachability problem. Once the mean-payoff for the MEC, and the probabilities corresponding to stay action in Line 12 are computed, to compute the reachability probability, the upper and lower bounds of all states in the MECs are initialized to 1 and 0 respectively. Now suppose that the sum of probabilities to s_+ and $s_?$ be p denoting the upper bound on the value of the mean-payoff to be $p \cdot r_{\max}$. Clearly, the upper bound on the reachability value of this MDP is p. Now, when we do BVI to calculate this value, from every state in M, there would be *at least* two action choices, one that stays inside the MEC, and one that corresponds to the stay action. Initially, all states, except the terminal states, would have upper and lower values set to 0 and 1, respectively. Thus, among the two action choices, one would have upper value p, while the other would have upper value 1, and hence, the Bellman update assigns the upper value of the state to 1. As one can see, this would go on, and convergence wouldn't happen, and hence the true mean-payoff value will not be propagated to the initial state of the MDP. To avoid this, we need the deflate operation which lowers the upper reachability value to the best outgoing action, i.e. in this case, the stay action with value p.

Statistical Guarantees. The following theorem shows that the mean-payoff value learnt by Algorithm 1 is PAC on an input blackbox MDP.

Theorem 1. *Algorithm 1 has the property that when it stops, it returns an interval for the mean-payoff value of the MDP that is PAC for the given MP-inconfidence δ_{MP} and the MP-imprecision ε_{MP}.*

Anytime Algorithm. As a direct consequence, we obtain an anytime algorithm from Algorithm 1 by (1) dropping the termination test on Line 20, i.e. replacing it with **until false**, and (2) upon query (or termination) by the user, we output $(\mathsf{U}(s_{\mathsf{init}}) + \mathsf{L}(s_{\mathsf{init}}))/2$ as the estimate and, additionally, we output $(\mathsf{U}(s_{\mathsf{init}}) - \mathsf{L}(s_{\mathsf{init}}))/2$ as the current imprecision.

Using Greybox Update Equations During Blackbox Learning. We also consider the variant where we use greybox update equations to estimate the mean-payoff values. However, assuming we keep the TP-imprecision unchanged, the overall TP-inconfidence now has to include the probability of missing some successor of a state s for an action a[9]. Given a number of samples $\#(s, a)$, the probability that we miss a particular successor is at most $(1 - p_{\mathsf{min}})^{\#(s,a)}$, and hence the

---

[9] Assuming $\#(s, a)$ to be as small as 200, and $p_{\mathsf{min}} = 0.05$, the probability of missing a transition is $3.5 \cdot 10^{-5}$.

overall TP-inconfidence corresponding to using greybox equations for blackbox learning increases to $\delta_{TP} + (1 - p_{\mathsf{min}})^{\#(s,a)}$.

We also note that the use of greybox update equations on estimating the transition probabilities also gives us a PAC guarantee but with an increased MP-Inconfidence resulting from an increased TP-inconfidence.

5   Algorithm for Continuous-Time MDP

In this section, we describe an algorithm to learn blackbox CTMDP models for mean-payoff objective while respecting the PAC guarantees. As in the case of MDPs, we reduce the mean-payoff problem to a reachability problem. We follow the same overall framework as in MDPs, where we compute the probability to reach the end-components under an optimal strategy, and we compute their respective mean-payoff values. Computing reachability probabilities in a CTMDP is the same as computing reachability probabilities in the underlying embedded MDP. Similar to estimating $\mathbb{T}(s, a, t)$ in Sect. 4 for MDPs, we estimate $\Delta(s, a, t)^{10}$ for CTMDPs, and follow the simulation-based procedure in Algorithm 1 to compute reachability probabilities. However, unlike MECs in MDPs, where the mean-payoff value depends solely on the transition probabilities, the mean-payoff value in a CTMDP also depends on the rates $\lambda(s, a)$ for $s \in T$ and $a \in A(s)$ for an MEC $M = (T, A)$. Thus to compute the value of an MEC, we also estimate the rates of the state-action pairs. Once we get the estimates of the rates, we uniformize the CTMDP to obtain a uniform CTMDP that can be treated as an MDP by disregarding the rates while preserving the mean-payoff value [30]. Detailed pseudocode of the algorithms for this section are provided in Appendix F of [1].

Estimating Rates. Recall that for an action a, the time spent in s is exponentially distributed with a parameter $\lambda(s, a)$, and $\frac{1}{\lambda(s,a)}$ is the mean of this distribution. During the simulation of a CTMDP, for every state s reached and action a chosen from s, we construct a sequence $\tau_{s,a}$ of the time difference between the entry and the corresponding exit from s when action a is chosen. Then, the average over the sequence $\tau_{s,a}$ gives us an estimate $\frac{1}{\lambda(s,a)}$ of $\frac{1}{\lambda(s,a)}$ (Abbreviated to $\frac{1}{\lambda}$ from now on when (s, a) is clear from the context.).

Assuming a multiplicative error α_R on our estimates of $\frac{1}{\lambda}$, the lemma below uses Chernoff bounds[11] to give the number of samples that need to be collected from an exponential distribution so that the estimated mean $\frac{1}{\lambda}$ is at most α_R-fraction away from the actual mean $\frac{1}{\lambda}$ with probability at least $1 - \delta_R$, where $\alpha_R, \delta_R \in (0, 1)$. Further by Cramer's theorem [15], it follows that this is the tightest possible bound for the number of samples collected.

---

[10] Recall that an estimate of $\Delta(s, a, t)$ is the ratio between $\#(s, a, t)$ and $\#(s, a)$, and is the probability with which we go to state t from s when action a is chosen from s.

[11] Since λ is not bounded, we cannot use Hoeffding's inequality as in the case of estimating the transition probabilities.

Lemma 1. *Let $X_1, \ldots, X_n$ be exponentially distributed i.i.d. random variables with mean $\frac{1}{\lambda}$. Then we have that*

$$\mathbb{P}\left[\left|\frac{1}{\widehat{\lambda}} - \frac{1}{\lambda}\right| \geq \frac{1}{\lambda} \cdot \alpha_R)\right] \leq \inf_{-\lambda < t < 0}\left(\frac{\lambda}{\lambda + t}\right)^n \cdot e^{\frac{tn}{\lambda}(1+\alpha_R)} + \inf_{t > 0}\left(\frac{\lambda}{\lambda + t}\right)^n \cdot e^{\frac{tn}{\lambda}(1-\alpha_R)},$$

where $\frac{1}{n}\sum_{i=1}^{n} X_i = \frac{1}{\widehat{\lambda}}$.

Assuming the right-side of the inequality is at most δ_R, we have that $\lambda \in [\widehat{\lambda}(1 - \alpha_R), \widehat{\lambda}(1 + \alpha_R)]$, or $\widehat{\lambda} \in [\frac{\lambda}{1+\alpha_R}, \frac{\lambda}{1-\alpha_R}]$ with probability at least $1 - \delta_R$. Table 1 shows the number of samples required for various values of α_R and δ_R[12].

Table 1. Lookup table for number of samples based on α_R and δ_R

$\alpha_R \setminus \delta_R$	10%	5%	0.01%	0.00001%
3%	7000	9000	23000	60000
5%	2500	3100	8000	13400

Given a maximum multiplicative error α_R on the mean of the exponential distributions of the state-action pairs in a CTMDP, we say that the rate λ is known α_R-*precisely* if $\widehat{\lambda} \in [\frac{\lambda}{1+\alpha_R}, \frac{\lambda}{1-\alpha_R}]$. We now quantify the bounds on the estimated mean-payoff value. Let $\mathcal{M}$ be a CTMDP, $v_{\mathcal{M}}$ be its actual mean-payoff value, and let $\widehat{v}_{\mathcal{M}}$ denote its mean-payoff when the rates of the state-action pairs are known α_R-precisely. Then we have the following.

Lemma 2. *Given a CTMDP $\mathcal{M}$ with rates known α_R-precisely, with transition probabilities known precisely, and with maximum reward per unit time over all states r_{max}, we have $v_{\mathcal{M}}(\frac{1-\alpha_R}{1+\alpha_R}) \leq \widehat{v}_{\mathcal{M}} \leq v_{\mathcal{M}}(\frac{1+\alpha_R}{1-\alpha_R})$ and $|\widehat{v}_{\mathcal{M}} - v_{\mathcal{M}}| \leq r_{max}\frac{2\alpha_R}{1-\alpha_R}$.*

Estimating Mean-Payoff Values of MECs. Using our bounds on the rates of the transitions, we now compute bounds on the mean-payoff values of MECs in CTMDPs. We first show that the mean payoff is maximized or minimized at the boundaries of the estimates of the rates. Intuitively, to maximise the mean-payoff value, for a state s_i with a high reward, we would like to maximise the time spent in s_i or equivalently, minimise the rate $\lambda(s_i, a)$ for every outgoing action a from s_i. We do the opposite when we want to find a lower bound on the mean-payoff value in the MEC. Consider an MEC M having states $T = \{s_1, \ldots, s_m\}$. Assume that λ_i is the rate of an action a from state s_i, such that a positional mean-payoff maximizing strategy σ chooses a from s_i. Then, the expected mean-payoff value of M is given by,

---

[12] In Appendix E of [1], we show the computation of the number of samples for one of the entries.

$$v_M = \frac{\sum\limits_{s_i \in T} \frac{r(s_i)\pi_i}{\lambda_i}}{\sum\limits_{s_i \in T} \frac{\pi_i}{\lambda_i}}, \tag{3}$$

where π_i denotes the expected fraction of total time spent in s_i under σ.

Now, we have estimates $\frac{1}{\widehat{\lambda_i}}$ of $\frac{1}{\lambda}$, such that, $\lambda_i \in \left[\widehat{\lambda}_i \left(1 - \alpha_R\right), \widehat{\lambda}_i \left(1 + \alpha_R\right)\right]$ with high probability. Let $\lambda_i^l = \widehat{\lambda}_i \left(1 - \alpha_R\right)$ and $\lambda_i^u = \widehat{\lambda}_i \left(1 + \alpha_R\right)$.

Proposition 1. *In Eq. 3, the maximum and the minimum values of v_M occur at the boundaries of the estimates of λ_i for each $1 \leqslant i \leqslant m$.*

In particular, v_M is maximized when,

$$\lambda_i = \begin{cases} \lambda_i^l, & \text{if } r(s_i) \geq v_M \\ \lambda_i^u, & \text{otherwise} \end{cases} \tag{4}$$

Once we fix the rates for each of the states in M, we uniformize M to obtain a uniform CTMDP M_C which is an MEC and can be treated as an MDP for computing its mean-payoff value [30]. Let for a state-action pair, the rate be $\lambda(s, a)$, and the uniformization constant be C. For a successor t from s under action a such that $t \neq s$, we have $\Delta(s, a, t) = \frac{\#(s,a,t)}{\#(s,a)} \cdot \frac{\lambda(s,a)}{C}$, and $\Delta(s, a, s) = 1 - \sum\limits_{t \neq s} \Delta(s, a, t)$. Finally, value iteration on M_C with appropriate confidence width gives us the lower and the upper estimates of the mean-payoff value of the MEC M.

We now describe an iterative procedure to identify those states of the MEC for which the upper bound on the estimates of the rates are assigned, and those states for which the lower bound on the estimates of the rates are assigned in order to maximize or minimize the mean-payoff value of the MEC. Assume w.l.o.g. that the states $s_1, \ldots, s_m$ are sorted in decreasing order of their rewards $r(s_i)$. In iteration j, we set $\lambda_i = \lambda_i^l$ for $1 \leqslant i \leqslant j$, and we set $\lambda_i = \lambda_i^u$ for the remaining states and recompute v_M. The maximum value of v_M across all iterations gives the upper bound on v_M. Similarly we can find the lower bound on v_M. Overall, value iteration is done $2|T|$ times[13].

Overall Algorithm. As stated in the beginning of this section, an algorithm for computing the mean payoff in blackbox CTMDP models largely follows the same overall framework as stated in Sect. 4. By sampling the actions, we obtain estimates of the rates and the transition probabilities. The reachability probabilities

---

[13] In our experiments, we use a heuristic to estimate v_M that provides good approximate bounds and is more efficient. We first compute an initial estimate of $\widehat{v}_M$ using our current estimates, $\widehat{\lambda}$. We then compute the upper bound by assigning the rates as in Eq. 4 where v_M is replaced with $\widehat{v}_M$. Similarly, the lower bound can also be found. A detailed pseudocode of this algorithm is described in Algorithm 18 of [1].

to the MECs of the CTMDP are estimated using the estimates of the transition probabilities while the mean-payoff values of MECs are estimated using uniformization as decribed above. The confidence widths on the transition probabilities in a uniformized MEC are assigned based on the number of samples $\#(s,a)$ for a state-action pair (s,a).

Statistical Guarantees. Let δ_{TP} and δ_R be the TP-inconfidence and the inconfidence on individual transition rates, respectively. Further, let δ_{MP1} and δ_{MP2} be the overall inconfidence on the transition probabilities and transition rates, respectively. Then, $\delta_{TP} := \dfrac{\delta_{MP1} \cdot p_{min}}{|\{a \mid s \in \widehat{S} \wedge a \in \mathsf{Av}(s)\}|}$, and $\delta_R := \dfrac{\delta_{MP2}}{|\{a \mid s \in \widehat{S} \wedge a \in \mathsf{Av}(s)\}|}$. Thus, we have that the overall inconfidence on the mean-payoff value, $\delta_{MP} = \delta_{MP1} + \delta_{MP2}$. Thus, to achieve a given inconfidence on the mean-payoff value, we fix δ_{TP} and δ_R, and adjust the imprecisions ε_{TP} and α_R accordingly.[14]

As in the case of MDPs, our learning algorithm for blackbox CTMDP models is an anytime algorithm that is PAC for the given MP-inconfidence δ_{MP}.

6   Experimental Results

We implemented our algorithms as an extension of PRISM [27] and tested it on 15 MDP benchmarks and 10 CTMDP benchmarks. Several of these benchmarks were selected from the Quantitative Verification Benchmark Set [21][15]. The results for MDP and CTMDP blackbox learning are shown in Table 2 and Table 3 respectively. Here, we scale the upper and lower bounds to 1 and 0, and show the average values taken over 10 experiments. The experiments were run on a desktop machine with an Intel $i5$ 3.2 GHz quad core processor and 16 GB RAM. The MP-imprecision ε_{MP} is set to 10^{-2}, revisitThreshold k is set to 6, MP-inconfidence δ_{MP} is set to 0.1 and n is set to 10000. We further use a timeout of 30 minutes. In the case of a timeout, the reported upper and lower bounds on the mean payoff still correspond to the input MP-inconfidence δ_{MP}, although the MP-imprecision may not be the desired one.

Blackbox Learning for MDPs. We see that in Table 2 for blackbox learning, 9 out of 15 benchmarks converge well, such that the precision is within 0.1. In fact, for many of these 9 benchmarks, a precision of 0.1 is achieved much before the timeout (TO). In Fig. 1a and Fig. 1b, we show this for zeroconf and pacman. zeroconf has a large transient part and a lot of easily reachable single state

---

[14] See Appendix G of [1] for a more detailed calculation of the number of samples required to make transition probabilities and the rates precise.

[15] The CTMDP benchmarks are available as Markov automata models that were converted to CTMDP models using a tool developed in the thesis [11].

Table 2. Results on MDP benchmarks.

Benchmarks	Number of states[a]	Value	Blackbox				Blackbox with greybox update equations			
			States explored	Lower bound	Upper bound	Time (s)	States explored	Lower bound	Upper bound	Time (s)
virus	809	0	809	0.0	0.5319	TO	809	0.0	0.008	273.01
cs_nfail	184	0.333	184	0.3275	0.3618	TO	184	0.332	0.337	126.77
investor	6688	0.95	6284	0.8458	0.9559	TO	5835	0.945	0.954	620.23
zeroconf	3001911	TO	487	0.923	1.0	TO	360	0.990	1.0	116.04
sensors	189	0.333	189	0.3299	0.3513	TO	189	0.332	0.336	64.64
consensus	272	0.1083	272	0.093	0.1605	TO	272	0.103	0.113	190.32
ij10	1023	1	1023	0.3626	1.0	TO	1023	0.999	1.0	26.822
ij3	7	1	7	0.990	1.0	15.92	7	0.999	1.0	0.7127
pacman	498	0.5511	496	0.5356	0.5754	TO	496	0.5477	0.5577	215.36
wlan	2954	1	2954	0.6577	1.0	TO	2935	1.0	1.0	16.924
blackjack	3829	0	3829	0.0	0.3014	TO	3829	0.0	0.006	91.503
counter	8	0.5	8	0.4998	0.5	30.37	8	0.4999	0.5	15.215
recycling	5	0.727	5	0.726	0.727	1.309	5	0.726	0.727	0.927
busyRing	1912	1	1733	0.706	1.0	TO	1542	0.999	1.0	34.86
busyRingMC	2592	1	2574	0.969	1.0	TO	2507	0.999	1.0	114.50

[a] The number of states and the values are computed using the probabilistic model-checker STORM [14]

The number of states and the true mean-payoff values are computed by first uniformizing the CTMDP, and then using STORM on the underlying MDP.

MECs. Since it has a true value of 1, the upper and the lower values converge after exploring only a few MECs. Our algorithm only needed to explore a very small percentage of the states to attain the input precision. cs_nfail has many significant MECs, and the learning algorithm needs to explore each of these MECs, while in sensor there is a relatively large MEC of around 30 states, and the simulation inside this MEC takes considerable amount of time.

virus consists of a single large MEC of more than 800 states, and its true value is 0. As we simulate the MEC more and more, the TP-imprecision on the transition probabilities decreases and the upper bound on the mean-payoff reduces over time. ij10 contains one MEC with 10 states in it. The value converges faster and reaches a value of 1, during blackbox learning. This model has relatively high number of actions, more than 5, for many of its states outside the MEC. This leads to a higher TP-imprecision. Further, due to the conservative nature of the blackbox update equations, the upper and the lower values converge very slowly.

consensus, ij10, ij3, pacman, wlan were used in [3] for learning policies for reachability objectives. The target states in these benchmarks are sink states with self loops, and we add a reward of 1 on these target states so that the rechability probability becomes the same as the mean payoff. The mean-payoff

Table 3. Results on CTMDP benchmarks

Benchmarks	Number of states	Value	Blackbox				Blackbox with greybox update equations			
			States explored	lower bound	upper bound	Time (s)	States explored	lower bound	upper bound	Time (s)
DynamicPM	816	1.0	816	0.436	1.0	TO	816	0.998	1.0	37.68
ErlangStages	508	1.0	508	0.962	1.0	TO	508	0.999	1.0	8.118
PollingSystem1	16	0.922	16	0.811	0.937	TO	16	0.816	0.937	TO
PollingSystem2	348	0.999	348	0.637	0.999	TO	348	0.998	0.999	21.893
PollingSystem3	1002	0.999	1002	0.232	1.0	TO	1002	0.99	1.0	864.05
QueuingSystem	266	0.8783	266	0.703	0.906	TO	266	0.865	0.886	TO
SJS1	17	1.0	17	0.999	1.0	133.96	17	0.997	1.0	1.05
SJS2	7393	0.999	7341	0.02	1.0	TO	7268	0.936	1.0	TO
SJS3	433	1.0	433	0.919	1.0	TO	432	0.999	0.999	5.3814
toy	12	1.0	12	0.99	1.0	5.6	12	0.999	1.0	1.112

results we observe are similar to the bounds reported for reachability probability in [3], and our experiments also take similar time as reported in [3].

The blackjack model [35] is similar to zeroconf model. It has 3829 states and 2116 MECs. It has a large transient part and a lot of single state MECs. However, unlike zeroconf all of the MECs have a value of 0. Thus, simulation takes more time as the TP-imprecision reduces slowly.

Blackbox Learning with Greybox Update Equations. We show the results of these experiments in the right side of Table 2. As observed, convergence is much faster here for all the benchmarks. All our benchmarks converged correctly within a few seconds to a few minutes. Hence for a small degradation in MP-inconfidence use of greybox update equations works well in practice. We show the effect on MP-inconfidence in more detail in Table 8 in Appendix G of [1].

Blackbox Learning for CTMDPs. In Table 3 we show the results for CTMDP benchmarks. The number of states in these benchmarks vary from as low as 12 to more than 7000. All the models used here have a lot of small end-components. We observe that the upper and the lower values take more time to converge as the size of the model grows. Figure 1c and Fig. 1d show the convergence of lower and upper bounds for QueuingSystem and SJS3. As in the case of MDPs, using *greybox update equations* speeds up the learning process significantly.

Greybox Learning. Recall from Definition 3 that in greybox learning, for every state-action pair, we know the number of successors of the state for the given action. As expected, their convergence is much faster than that for blackbox learning, but the convergence is comparable to the case where we do blackbox learning with greybox update equations. The details of the greybox learning experiments can be found in Appendix G of [1].

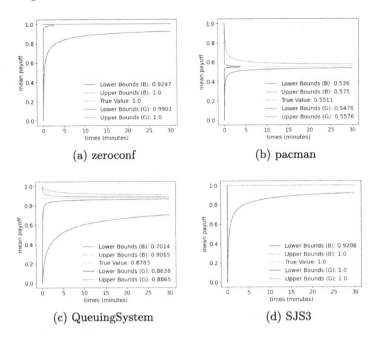

Fig. 1. Convergence of lower and upper bounds for blackbox update equations and greybox update equations.

7   Conclusion

We presented the first PAC SMC algorithm for computing mean payoff in unknown MDPs and CTMDPs, where the only information needed is a lower bound on minimum transition probability, as advocated in [13]. In contrast to a naive algorithm, which follows in a quite straightforward way from the literature, our algorithm is practically applicable, overcoming the astronomic number of simulation steps required. To this end, in particular, the inconfidence had to be distributed in non-uniformly over the transitions and then imprecision propagated by value iteration with precision guarantees. In future, we would like to thoroughly analyse how well weakening the PAC bounds can be traded for a yet faster convergence. On the practical side, applying importance sampling and importance splitting could further improve the efficiency.

Acknowledgements. The second author would like to thank Subhajit Goswami for insightful discussions on learning transition rate matrix in a CTMDP and for pointing to useful references.

References

1. Agarwal, C., Guha, S., Pazhamalai, M., Křetínský, J.: Pac statistical model checking of mean payoff in discrete- and continuous-time mdp (2022). CoRR, abs/2206.01465

2. Ashok, P., Chatterjee, K., Daca, P., Křetínský, J., Meggendorfer, T.: Value iteration for long-run average reward in markov decision processes. In: Majumdar, R., Kunčak, V. (eds.) CAV 2017. LNCS, vol. 10426, pp. 201–221. Springer, Cham (2017). https://doi.org/10.1007/978-3-319-63387-9_10

3. Ashok, P., Křetínský, J., Weininger, M.: PAC statistical model checking for markov decision processes and stochastic games. In: Dillig, I., Tasiran, S. (eds.) CAV 2019. LNCS, vol. 11561, pp. 497–519. Springer, Cham (2019). https://doi.org/10.1007/978-3-030-25540-4_29

4. Auer, P., Ortner, R.: Logarithmic online regret bounds for undiscounted reinforcement learning. In: NIPS, pp. 49–56. MIT Press (2006)

5. Baier, C., Haverkort, B.R., Hermanns, H., Katoen, J.-P.: Performance evaluation and model checking join forces. Commun. ACM **53**(9), 76–85 (2010)

6. Baier, C., Katoen, J-P.: Principles of Model Checking. MIT Press (2008)

7. Bertsekas, D.P.: Dynamic Programming and Optimal Control, vol. II. Athena Scientific (1995)

8. Brázdil, T., Brožek, V., Chatterjee, K., Forejt, V., Kučera, A.: Two views on multiple mean-payoff objectives in Markov decision processes. LMCS **10**(1), 1–29 (2014)

9. Brázdil, T., et al.: Verification of markov decision processes using learning algorithms. In: Cassez, F., Raskin, J.-F. (eds.) ATVA 2014. LNCS, vol. 8837, pp. 98–114. Springer, Cham (2014). https://doi.org/10.1007/978-3-319-11936-6_8

10. Bruno, J.L., Downey, P.J., Frederickson, G.N.: Sequencing tasks with exponential service times to minimize the expected flow time or makespan. J. ACM **28**(1), 100–113 (1981)

11. Butkova, Y.: Towards efficient analysis of Markov automata. PhD thesis, Saarland University, Saarbrücken, Germany (2020)

12. Chatterjee, K.: Robustness of structurally equivalent concurrent parity games. In: FOSSACS, pp. 270–285 (2012)

13. Daca, P., Henzinger, T.A., Křetínský, J., Petrov, T.: Faster statistical model checking for unbounded temporal properties. In: Chechik, M., Raskin, J.-F. (eds.) TACAS 2016. LNCS, vol. 9636, pp. 112–129. Springer, Heidelberg (2016). https://doi.org/10.1007/978-3-662-49674-9_7

14. Dehnert, C., Junges, S., Katoen, J.-P., Volk, M.: A storm is coming: a modern probabilistic model checker. In: Majumdar, R., Kunčak, V. (eds.) CAV 2017. LNCS, vol. 10427, pp. 592–600. Springer, Cham (2017). https://doi.org/10.1007/978-3-319-63390-9_31

15. Dembo, A., Zeitouni, O.: Large deviations techniques and applications. Springer, Cham (2010). https://doi.org/10.1007/978-3-642-03311-7

16. Feinberg, E.A.: Continuous time discounted jump markov decision processes: a discrete-event approach. Math. Oper. Res. **29**(3), 492–524 (2004)

17. Feinberg, E.A., Shwartz, A.: Handbook of Markov decision processes: methods and applications, volume 40. Springer Science & Business Media, New York (2012). https://doi.org/10.1007/978-1-4615-0805-2

18. Fu, J., Topcu, U.: Probably approximately correct MDP learning and control with temporal logic constraints. Science and Systems, In Robotics (2014)

19. Ghemawat, S., Gobioff, H., Leung, S.: The google file system. In: SOSP (2003)

20. Hahn, E.M., Perez, M., Schewe, S., Somenzi, F., Trivedi, A., Wojtczak, D.: Omega-regular objectives in model-free reinforcement learning. In: Vojnar, T., Zhang, L. (eds.) TACAS 2019. LNCS, vol. 11427, pp. 395–412. Springer, Cham (2019). https://doi.org/10.1007/978-3-030-17462-0_27

21. Hartmanns, A., Klauck, M., Parker, D., Quatmann, T., Ruijters, E.: The quantitative verification benchmark set. In: Vojnar, T., Zhang, L. (eds.) TACAS 2019. LNCS, vol. 11427, pp. 344–350. Springer, Cham (2019). https://doi.org/10.1007/978-3-030-17462-0_20

22. Haverkort, B.R., Hermanns, H., Katoen, J-P.: On the use of model checking techniques for dependability evaluation. In: SRDS 2000 (2000)

23. Henriques, D., Martins, J.G., Zuliani, P., Platzer, A., Clarke, E.M.: Statistical model checking for markov decision processes. In: QEST, pp. 84–93. IEEE Computer Society (2012)

24. Kelmendi, E., Krämer, J., Křetínský, J., Weininger, M.: Value iteration for simple stochastic games: stopping criterion and learning algorithm. In: Chockler, H., Weissenbacher, G. (eds.) CAV 2018. LNCS, vol. 10981, pp. 623–642. Springer, Cham (2018). https://doi.org/10.1007/978-3-319-96145-3_36

25. J. Kretínský, Michel, F., Michel, L., Pérez, G.A.: Finite-memory near-optimal learning for markov decision processes with long-run average reward. In: UAI of Proceedings of Machine Learning Research, vol. 124, pp. 1149–1158. AUAI Press (2020)

26. Křetínský, J., Pérez, G.A., Raskin, J.-F.: Learning-based mean-payoff optimization in an unknown MDP under omega-regular constraints. In: CONCUR, Dagstuhl, pp. 8:1–8:18 (2018)

27. Kwiatkowska, M., Norman, G., Parker, D.: PRISM: probabilistic symbolic model checker. In: Field, T., Harrison, P.G., Bradley, J., Harder, U. (eds.) TOOLS 2002. LNCS, vol. 2324, pp. 200–204. Springer, Heidelberg (2002). https://doi.org/10.1007/3-540-46029-2_13

28. Kwiatkowska, M.Z., Norman, G., Parker, D.: The PRISM benchmark suite. In: QEST, pp. 203–204. IEEE Computer Society (2012)

29. Lassaigne, R., Peyronnet, S.: Approximate planning and verification for large Markov decision processes. In: SAC, pp. 1314–1319. ACM (2012)

30. Puterman, M.L.: Markov decision processes: Discrete stochastic dynamic programming. John Wiley and Sons (1994)

31. Qiu, Q., Qu, Q., Pedram, M.: Stochastic modeling of a power-managed system-construction and optimization. IEEE Trans. CAD Integrated Circuits Syst. **20**(10), 1200–1217 (2001)

32. Sennott, L.I.: Stochastic Dynamic Programming and the Control of Queueing Systems. Wiley-Interscience, New York (1999)

33. Solan, E.: Continuity of the value of competitive markov decision processes. J. Theor. Probab. **16**, 831–845 (2003)

34. Strehl, A.L., Li, L., Wiewiora, E., Langford, J., Littman, M.L.: PAC model-free reinforcement learning. In: ICML, pp. 881–888. ACM (2006)

35. Sutton, R.S., Barto, A.G.: Reinforcement learning - an introduction. Adaptive computation and machine learning. MIT Press (1998)

36. Ortner, R., Jaksch, T., Auer, P.: Near-optimal regret bounds for reinforcement learning. J. Mach. Learn. Res. **11**, 1563–1600 (2010)

37. Younes, H.L.S., Simmons, R.G.: Probabilistic verification of discrete event systems using acceptance sampling. In: Brinksma, E., Larsen, K.G. (eds.) CAV 2002. LNCS, vol. 2404, pp. 223–235. Springer, Heidelberg (2002). https://doi.org/10.1007/3-540-45657-0_17

Sampling-Based Verification of CTMCs
with Uncertain Rates

Thom S. Badings[1(✉)], Nils Jansen[1], Sebastian Junges[1],
Marielle Stoelinga[1,2], and Matthias Volk[2]

[1] Radboud University, Nijmegen, The Netherlands
thom.badings@ru.nl
[2] University of Twente, Enschede, The Netherlands

Abstract. We employ uncertain parametric CTMCs with parametric transition rates and a prior on the parameter values. The prior encodes uncertainty about the actual transition rates, while the parameters allow dependencies between transition rates. Sampling the parameter values from the prior distribution then yields a standard CTMC, for which we may compute relevant reachability probabilities. We provide a principled solution, based on a technique called scenario-optimization, to the following problem: From a finite set of parameter samples and a user-specified confidence level, compute prediction regions on the reachability probabilities. The prediction regions should (with high probability) contain the reachability probabilities of a CTMC induced by any additional sample. To boost the scalability of the approach, we employ standard abstraction techniques and adapt our methodology to support approximate reachability probabilities. Experiments with various well-known benchmarks show the applicability of the approach.

1 Introduction

Continuous-time Markov chains (CTMCs) are widely used to model complex probabilistic systems in reliability engineering [51], network processes [36,38], systems biology [11,23] and epidemic modeling [2]. A key verification task is to compute aspects of system behavior from these models, expressed as, e.g., continuous stochastic logic (CSL) formulae [4,7]. Typically, we compute reachability probabilities for a set of horizons, such as: *what is the probability that a target state is reached before time $t_1, \ldots, t_n$?* Standard algorithms [7] implemented in mature model checking tools such as Storm [37] or Prism [42] provide efficient means to compute these *reachability probabilities*. However, these methods typically require that transition rates and probabilities are precisely known. This assumption is often unrealistic [34] and led to some related work, which we discuss in Sect. 7.

Illustrative Example. An epidemic can abstractly be modeled as a finite-state CTMC, e.g., the SIR (susceptible-infected-recovered) model [3], which is shown

This work has been partially funded by NWO under the grant PrimaVera, number NWA.1160.18.238, and by EU Horizon 2020 project MISSION, number 101008233.

S. Shoham and Y. Vizel (Eds.): CAV 2022, LNCS 13372, pp. 26–47, 2022.
https://doi.org/10.1007/978-3-031-13188-2_2

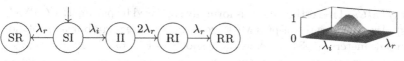

(a) pCTMC $\mathcal{M}$ with parameters λ_i, λ_r.   (b) Distribution $\mathbb{P}$ over values for (λ_i, λ_r).

Fig. 1. An upCTMC $(\mathcal{M}, \mathbb{P})$ for the SIR (pop=2) model.

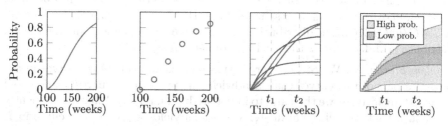

(a) Curve for a single CTMC with precise transition rates.   (b) Point abstraction of a curve for a single CTMC.   (c) Curves for five CTMCs with different rates.   (d) Two prediction regions with different probabilities.

Fig. 2. The probability of extinction in the SIR (140) model for horizons $[100, t]$. (Color figure online)

in Fig. 1a for a population of two. Such a CTMC assumes a *fixed set of transition rates*, in this case an infection rate λ_i, and a recovery rate λ_r. The outcome of analyzing this CTMC for fixed values of λ_i and λ_r may yield a *probability curve* like in Fig. 2a[1], where we plot the probability (y-axis) of reaching a target state that corresponds to the epidemic becoming extinct against varying time horizons (x-axis). In fact, the plot is obtained via a smooth interpolation of the results at finitely many horizons, cf. Fig. 2b. To acknowledge that λ_i, λ_r are in fact unknown, we may analyze the model for different values of λ_i, λ_r, resulting in a set of curves as in Fig. 2c. These individual curves, however, provide no guarantees about the shape of the curve obtained from another infection and recovery rate. Instead, we assume a *probability distribution* over the transition rates and aim to compute *prediction regions* as those in shown Fig. 2d, in such a way that with a certain (high) probability, any rates λ_i and λ_r yield a curve within this region.

Overall Goal. From the illustrative example, we state the following goal. Each fixed set of transition rates induces a *probability curve*, i.e., a mapping from horizons to the corresponding reachability probabilities. We aim to construct *prediction regions* around a set of probability curves, such that with high probability and high confidence, sampling a set of transition rates induces a probability curve within this region. Our key contribution is an efficient *probably approximately correct*, or PAC-style method that computes these prediction regions. The remainder of the introduction explores the technical steps toward this goal.

---

[1] For visual clarity, we plot the reachability probability *between* time 100 and $t_1, \ldots, t_n$.

Uncertain CTMCs. The setting above is formally captured by parametric CTMCs (pCTMCs). Transition rates of pCTMCs are not given precisely but as (polynomials over) parameters [15, 34], such as those shown in Fig. 1a. We assume a *prior* on each parameter valuation, i.e., assignment of values to parameters, similar to settings in [11, 44] and in contrast to, e.g., [23, 34]. These priors may result from asking different experts which value they would assume for, e.g., the infection rate. The prior may also be the result of Bayesian reasoning [56]. Formally, we capture the uncertainty in the rates by an arbitrary and potentially unknown *probability distribution* over the parameter space, see Fig. 1b. We call this model an *uncertain pCTMC (upCTMC)*. The distribution allows drawing independent and identically distributed (i.i.d.) *samples* that yield (parameter-free) CTMCs.

Problem Statement. We consider prediction regions on probability curves in the form of a pair of two curves that 'sandwich' the probability curves, as depicted in Fig. 2d. Intuitively, we then aim to find a prediction region R that is sufficiently large, such that sampling parameter valuations yields a probability curve in R with high probability p. We aim to compute a lower bound on this *containment probability p*. Naturally, we also aim to compute a meaningful, i.e. small (tight), prediction region R. As such, we aim to solve the following problem:

Problem Statement. Given a upCTMC with a target state, compute
1. a (tight) *prediction region R* on the probability curves, and
2. a (tight) *lower bound on the containment probability* that a sampled parameter valuation induces a probability curve that will lie in R.

We solve this problem with a user-specified confidence level β.

The Problem Solved. In this paper, we present a method that samples probability curves as in Fig. 2c, but now for, say 100 curves. From these curves, we compute prediction regions (e.g., both tubes in Fig. 2d) and compute a lower bound (one for both tubes) on the containment probability that the curve associated with any sampled parameter value will lie in the specific prediction region (tube). Specifically, for a confidence level of 99% and considering 100 curves, we conclude that this lower bound is 79.4% for the red region and 7.5% for the blue region. For a higher confidence level of 99.9%, the lower bounds are slightly more conservative.

A Change in Perspective. Toward the algorithm, we make a change in perspective. For two horizons t_1 and t_2, reachability probabilities for fixed CTMCs are two-dimensional points in $[0, 1]^2$ that we call *solution vectors*, as shown in Fig. 3a. Here, these solution vectors represent pairs of the probabilities that the disease becomes extinct before time t_1 and before t_2. The prediction regions as in Fig. 2d are shown as the shaded boxes in Fig. 3a.

Solving the problem algorithmically. We solve the problem using a sampling-based approach. Starting with a set of solution vectors, we use techniques from *scenario optimization*, a data-driven methodology for solving stochastic optimization problems [18, 21]. As such, we construct the prediction region from the solution to an optimization problem. Our method can balance the size of the prediction region with the containment probability, as illustrated by the two boxes in Fig. 3a.

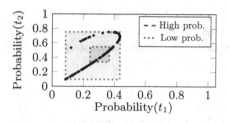

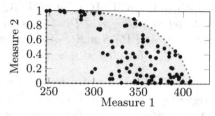

(a) Reachability at time points t_1 and t_2.   (b) Pareto front for two measures.

Fig. 3. Prediction regions on the solutions vectors for two different upCTMCs.

Extensions. Our approach offers more than prediction regions on probability curves from precise samples. The change in perspective mentioned above allows for solution vectors that represent *multiple objectives*, such as the reachability with respect to different goal states, expected rewards or even the probability mass of paths satisfying more complex temporal properties. In our experiments, we show that this multi-objective approach —also on probability curves— yields much tighter bounds on the containment probability than an approach that analyzes each objective independently. We can also produce prediction regions as other shapes than boxes, as, for example, shown in Fig. 3b. To accelerate our approach, we significantly extend the methodology for dealing with *imprecise verification results*, given as an interval on each entry of the solution vector.

Contributions. Our key contribution is the approach that provides prediction regions and lower bounds on probability curves for upCTMCs. The approach requires only about 100 samples and scales to upCTMCs with tens of parameters. Furthermore: (1) We extend our approach such that we can also handle the case where only imprecise intervals on the verification results are available. (2) We develop a tailored batch verification method in the model checker Storm [37] to accelerate the required batches of verification tasks. We accompany our contributions by a thorough empirical evaluation and remark that our batch verification method can be used beyond scenario optimization. Our scenario optimization results are independent of the model checking and are, thus, applicable to any model where solution vectors are obtained in the same way as for upCTMCs.

Data Availability. All source code, benchmarks, and logfiles used to produce the data are archived: https://doi.org/10.5281/zenodo.6523863.

2   Problem Statement

In this section, we introduce pCTMCs and upCTMCs, and we define the formal problem statement. We use probability distributions over finite and infinite sets; see [9] for details. The set of all distributions over a set X is denoted by $Dist(X)$. The set of polynomials over parameters V, with rational coefficients, is denoted by $\mathbb{Q}[V]$. An *instantiation* $u: V \to \mathbb{Q}$ maps parameters to concrete values. We often fix a parameter ordering and denote instantiations as vectors, $u \in \mathbb{Q}^{|V|}$.

Definition 1 (pCTMC). *A pCTMC is a tuple* $\mathcal{M} = (S, s_I, V, \mathbf{R})$, *where S is a finite set of states, $s_I \in Dist(S)$ is the initial distribution, V are the (ordered) parameters, and* $\mathbf{R} \colon S \times S \to \mathbb{Q}[V]$ *is a parametric transition rate function. If* $\mathbf{R}(s, s) \in \mathbb{Q}_{\geq 0}$ *for all $s, s' \in S$, then $\mathcal{M}$ is a (parameter-free) CTMC.*

For any pair of states $s, s' \in S$ with a non-zero rate $\mathbf{R}(s, s') > 0$, the probability of triggering a transition from s to s' within t time units is $1 - e^{-\mathbf{R}(s, s') \cdot t}$ [41].

Applying an *instantiation* u to a pCTMC $\mathcal{M}$ yields an *instantiated* CTMC $\mathcal{M}[u] = (S, s_I, V, \mathbf{R}[u])$ where $\mathbf{R}[u](s, s') = \mathbf{R}(s, s')[u]$ for all $s, s' \in S$. In the remainder, we only consider instantiations u for a pCTMC $\mathcal{M}$ which are *well-defined*. The set of such instantiations is the parameter space $\mathcal{V}_\mathcal{M}$.

A central *measure* on CTMCs is the *(time-bounded) reachability* $\Pr(\lozenge^{\leq \tau} E)$, which describes the probability that one of the error states E[2] is reached within the horizon $\tau \in \mathbb{Q}$. Other measures include the expected time to reach a particular state, or the average time spent in particular states. We refer to [41] for details.

Given a concrete (instantiated) CTMC $\mathcal{M}[u]$, the *solution* for measure φ is denoted by $\mathsf{sol}^\varphi_{\mathcal{M}[u]} \in \mathbb{R}$; the *solution vector* $\mathsf{sol}^\Phi_{\mathcal{M}[u]} \in \mathbb{R}^m$ generalizes this concept to an (ordered) set of m measures $\Phi = \varphi_1, \ldots, \varphi_m$. We abuse notation and introduce the *solution function* to express solution vectors on a pCTMC:

Definition 2 (Solution function). *A solution function* $\mathsf{sol}^\Phi_\mathcal{M} \colon \mathcal{V}_\mathcal{M} \to \mathbb{R}^{|\Phi|}$ *is a mapping from a parameter instantiation $u \in \mathcal{V}_\mathcal{M}$ to the solution vector* $\mathsf{sol}^\Phi_{\mathcal{M}[u]}$.

We often omit the scripts in $\mathsf{sol}^\Phi_\mathcal{M}(u)$ and write $\mathsf{sol}(u)$ instead. We also refer to $\mathsf{sol}(u)$ as the solution vector of u. For n parameter samples $\mathcal{U}_n = \{u_1, \ldots, u_n\}$ with $u_i \in \mathcal{V}_\mathcal{M}$, we denote the solution vectors by $\mathsf{sol}(\mathcal{U}_n) \in \mathbb{R}^{m \times n}$.

Using solution vectors, we can define the probability curves shown in Fig. 2c.

Definition 3 (Probability curve). *The* probability curve *for reachability probability* $\phi_\tau = \Pr(\lozenge^{\leq \tau} E)$ *and CTMC $\mathcal{M}[u]$ is given by* $\mathsf{probC} \colon \tau \mapsto \mathsf{sol}^{\varphi_\tau}_{\mathcal{M}[u]}$.

We can approximate the function probC for a concrete CTMC by computing $\mathsf{probC}(t_1), \ldots, \mathsf{probC}(t_m)$ for a finite set of time horizons. As such, we compute the solution vector w.r.t. m different reachability measures $\Phi = \{\varphi_{t_1}, \ldots, \varphi_{t_m}\}$. By exploiting the monotonicity[3] of the reachability over time, we obtain an upper and lower bound on $\mathsf{probC}(\tau)$ as two step functions, see Fig. 2d. We can smoothen the approximation, by taking an upper and lower bound on these step functions.

We study pCTMCs where the parameters follow a probability distribution. This probability distribution can be highly complex or even unknown; we merely assume that we can sample from this distribution.

Definition 4 (upCTMC). *A upCTMC is a tuple* $(\mathcal{M}, \mathbb{P})$ *with $\mathcal{M}$ a pCTMC and $\mathbb{P}$ a probability distribution over the parameter space $\mathcal{V}_\mathcal{M}$ of $\mathcal{M}$.*

---

[2] Formally, states are labeled and E describes the label, see [8].

[3] In Definition 3, only the upper limit on the timebound is varied, so measures are monotonic.

A upCTMC defines a probability space $(\mathcal{V}_\mathcal{M}, \mathbb{P})$ over the parameter values, whose domain is defined by the parameter space $\mathcal{V}_\mathcal{M}$. In the remainder, we denote a *sample* from $\mathcal{V}_\mathcal{M}$ drawn according to $\mathbb{P}$ by $u \in \mathcal{V}_\mathcal{M}$.

To quantify the performance of a upCTMC, we may construct a *prediction region* on the solution vector space, such as those shown in Fig. 3a. In this paper, we consider only prediction regions which are compact subsets $R \subseteq \mathbb{R}^{|\Phi|}$. We define the so-called *containment probability* of a prediction region, which is the probability that the solution vector $\mathsf{sol}(u)$ for a randomly sampled parameter $u \in \mathcal{V}_\mathcal{M}$ is contained in R, as follows:

Definition 5 (Containment probability). *For a prediction region R, the containment probability $\mathsf{contain}_\mathcal{V}(R)$ is the probability that the solution vector $\mathsf{sol}(u)$ for any parameter sample $u \in \mathcal{V}_\mathcal{M}$ is contained in R:*

$$\mathsf{contain}_\mathcal{V}(R) = \mathrm{Pr}\{u \in \mathcal{V}_\mathcal{M} : \mathsf{sol}(u) \in R\}. \tag{1}$$

Recall that we solve the problem in Sect. 1 with a user-specified confidence level, denoted by $\beta \in (0, 1)$. Formally, we solve the following problem:

Formal Problem. Given a upCTMC $(\mathcal{M}, \mathbb{P})$, a set Φ of measures, and a confidence level $\beta \in (0, 1)$, compute a (tight) prediction region R and a (tight) lower bound $\mu \in (0, 1)$ on the containment probability, such that $\mathsf{contain}(R) \geq \mu$ holds with a confidence level of at least β.

The problem in Sect. 1 is a special case of the formal problem, with Φ the reachability probability over a set of horizons. In that case, we can overapproximate a prediction region as a rectangle, yielding an interval $[\underline{c}, \bar{c}]$ for every horizon t that defines where the two step functions (see below Definition 3) change. We smoothen these step functions (similar to probability curves) to obtain the following definition:

Definition 6 (Prediction region for a probability curve). *A prediction region R over a probability curve probC is given by two curves $\underline{c}, \bar{c} : \mathbb{Q}_{\geq 0} \to \mathbb{R}$ as the area in-between: $R = \{(t, y) \in \mathbb{Q} \times \mathbb{R} \mid \underline{c}(t) \leq y \leq \bar{c}(t)\}$.*

We solve the problem by sampling a finite set $\mathcal{U}_n$ of parameter values of the upCTMC and computing the corresponding solution vectors $\mathsf{sol}(\mathcal{U}_n)$. In Sect. 3, we solve the problem assuming that we can compute solution vectors exactly. In Sect. 4, we consider a less restricted setting in which every solution is imprecise, i.e. only known to lie in a certain interval.

3   Precise Sampling-Based Prediction Regions

In this section, we use scenario optimization [16,18] to compute a high-confidence lower bound on the containment probability. First, in Sect. 3.1, we describe how to compute a prediction region using the solution vectors $\mathsf{sol}(\mathcal{U}_n)$ for the parameter samples $\mathcal{U}_n$. In Sect. 3.2, we clarify how to compute a lower bound on the containment probability with respect to this prediction region. In Sect. 3.3, we construct an algorithm based on those results that solves the formal problem.

3.1   Constructing Prediction Regions

We assume that we are given a set of solution vectors $\mathsf{sol}(\mathcal{U}_n)$ obtained from n parameter samples. We construct a prediction region R based on these vectors such that we can annotate these regions with a lower bound on the containment probability, as in the problem statement. For conciseness, we restrict ourselves to the setting where R is a hyperrectangle in $\mathbb{R}^m$, with $m = |\Phi|$ the number of measures, cf. Remark 1 below. In the following, we represent R using two vectors (points) $\underline{x}, \bar{x} \in \mathbb{R}^m$ such that, using pointwise inequalities, $R = \{x \mid \underline{x} \le x \le \bar{x}\}$. For an example of such a rectangular prediction region, see Fig. 3a.

As also shown in Fig. 3a, we do *not* require R to contain all solutions in $\mathsf{sol}(\mathcal{U}_n)$. Instead, we have two orthogonal goals: we aim to minimize the size of R, while also minimizing the (Manhattan) distance of samples to R, measured in their 1-norm. Solutions contained in R are assumed to have a distance of zero, while solutions not contained in R are called *relaxed*. These goals define a *multi-objective problem*, which we solve by weighting the two objectives using a fixed parameter $\rho > 0$, called the *cost of relaxation*, that is used to scale the distance to R. Then, $\rho \to \infty$ enforces $\mathsf{sol}(\mathcal{U}_n) \subseteq R$, as in the outer box in Fig. 3a, while for $\rho \to 0$, R is reduced to a point. Thus, the cost of relaxation ρ is a tuning parameter that determines the size of the prediction region R and hence the fraction of the solution vectors that is contained in R (see [19, 21] for details).

We capture the problem described above in the following convex optimization problem $\mathcal{L}_{\mathcal{U}}^{\rho}$. We define the decision variables $\underline{x}, \bar{x} \in \mathbb{R}^m$ to represent the prediction region. In addition, we define a decision variable $\xi_i \in \mathbb{R}_{\ge 0}^m$ for every sample $i = 1, \ldots, n$ that acts as a slack variable representing the distance to R.

$$\mathcal{L}_{\mathcal{U}}^{\rho} : \text{minimize} \quad \|\bar{x} - \underline{x}\|_1 + \rho \sum_{i=1}^{n} \|\xi_i\|_1 \tag{2a}$$

$$\text{subject to} \quad \underline{x} - \xi_i \le \mathsf{sol}(u_i) \le \bar{x} + \xi_i \quad \forall i = 1, \ldots, n. \tag{2b}$$

The objective function in Eq. (2a) minimizes the size of R —by minimizing the sum of the width of the prediction region in all dimensions— plus ρ times the distances of the samples to R. We denote the optimal solution to problem $\mathcal{L}_{\mathcal{U}}^{\rho}$ for a given ρ by R_{ρ}^*, ξ_{ρ}^*, where $R_{\rho}^* = [\underline{x}_{\rho}^*, \bar{x}_{\rho}^*]$ for the rectangular case.

Assumption 1. *The optimal solution R_{ρ}^*, ξ_{ρ}^* to $\mathcal{L}_{\mathcal{U}}^{\rho}$ exists and is unique.*

Note that Definition 2 ensures finite-valued solution vectors, thus guaranteeing the existence of a solution to Eq. (2). If the solution is not unique, we apply a suitable tie-break rule that selects one solution of the optimal set (e.g., the solution with a minimum Euclidean norm, see [16]). The following example shows that values of ρ exist for which such a tie-break rule is necessary to obtain a unique solution.

Example 1. Figure 4 shows a set of solution vectors in one dimension, labeled A–F. Consider prediction region $R_1 = [A, F]$. The corresponding objective value Eq. (2a) is $\|\bar{x} - \underline{x}\| + \rho \cdot \sum \xi_i = \|\bar{x} - \underline{x}\| = \delta_1 + \cdots + \delta_5$, as all $\xi_i = 0$. For prediction region $R_2 = [B, E]$, the objective value is $\delta_2 + \delta_3 + \delta_4 + \rho \cdot \delta_1 + \rho \cdot \delta_5$. Thus, for $\rho > 1$,

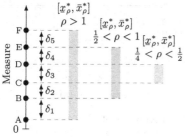

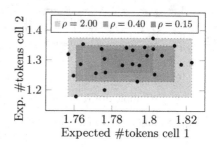

Fig. 4. The prediction region changes with the cost of relaxation ρ.

Fig. 5. Prediction regions as boxes, for different costs of relaxations ρ.

solving $\mathfrak{L}_{\mathcal{U}}^{\rho}$ yields R_1 whereas for $\rho < 1$, relaxing solutions A and F is cheaper than not doing so, so R_2 is optimal. When $\rho = 1$, however, relaxing solutions A and F yields the same cost as not relaxing these samples, so a tie-break rule is needed (see above). For $\rho < \frac{1}{2}$, relaxing samples A, B, E, and F is cost-optimal, resulting in the prediction region containing exactly $\{C, D\}$. □

Similarly, we can consider cases with more samples and multiple measures, as shown in Fig. 5 (see [6, Appendix A] for more details). The three prediction regions in Fig. 5 are obtained for different costs of relaxation ρ. For $\rho = 2$, the region contains all vectors, while for a lower ρ, more vectors are left outside.

Remark 1. While problem $\mathfrak{L}_{\mathcal{U}}^{\rho}$ in Eq. (2) yields a rectangular prediction region, we can also produce other shapes. We may, e.g., construct a Pareto front as in Fig. 3b, by adding additional affine constraints [12]. In fact, our only requirement is that the objective function is convex, and the constraints are convex in the decision variables (the dependence of the constraints on u may be arbitrary) [21]. □

3.2 Bounding the Containment Probability

The previous section shows how we compute a prediction region based on convex optimization. We now characterize a valid high-confidence lower bound on the containment probability w.r.t. the prediction region given by the optimal solution to this optimization problem. Toward that result, we introduce the so-called *complexity* of a solution to problem $\mathfrak{L}_{\mathcal{U}}^{\rho}$ in Eq. (2), a concept used in [21] that is related to the compressibility of the solution vectors $\mathsf{sol}(\mathcal{U}_n)$:

Definition 7 (Complexity). *For $\mathfrak{L}_{\mathcal{U}}^{\rho}$ with optimal solution R_ρ^*, ξ_ρ^*, consider a set $\mathcal{W} \subseteq \mathcal{U}_n$ and the associated problem $\mathfrak{L}_{\mathcal{W}}^{\rho}$ with optimal solution $\tilde{R}_\rho, \tilde{\xi}_\rho$. The set $\mathcal{W}$ is critical, if*

$$\tilde{R}_\rho = R_\rho^* \quad and \quad \{u_i \mid \xi_{\rho,i}^* > 0\} \subseteq \mathcal{W}.$$

The complexity c_ρ^* of R_ρ^*, ξ_ρ^* is the cardinality of the smallest critical set. We also call c_ρ^* the complexity of $\mathfrak{L}_{\mathcal{U}}^{\rho}$.

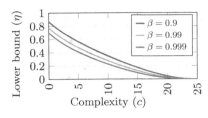
(a) Number of samples $n = 25$.

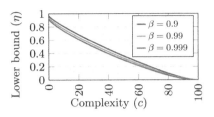
(b) Number of samples $n = 100$.

Fig. 6. Lower bounds η on the containment probability as a function of the complexity c, obtained from Theorem 1 for different confidence levels β.

If a sample u_i has a value $\xi^*_{\rho,i} > 0$, its solution vector has a positive distance to the prediction region, R^*_ρ (i.e., $[\underline{x}^*_\rho, \bar{x}^*_\rho]$ for the rectangular case). Thus, the complexity c^*_ρ is the number of samples for which $\mathsf{sol}(u_i) \notin R^*_\rho$, plus the minimum number of samples needed on the boundary of the region to keep the solution unchanged. We describe in Sect. 3.3 how we algorithmically determine the complexity.

Example 2. In Fig. 5, the prediction region for $\rho = 2$ contains all solution vectors, so $\xi^*_{2,i} = 0 \, \forall i$. Moreover, if we remove *all but four* solutions (the ones on the boundary of the region), the optimal solution to problem $\mathcal{L}^\rho_\mathcal{U}$ remains unchanged, so the complexity is $c^*_{1.12} = 0 + 4$. Similarly, the complexity for $\rho = 0.4$ is $c^*_{0.4} = 8 + 2 = 10$ (8 solutions outside the region, and 2 on the boundary). $\square$

Recall that Definition 5 defines the containment probability of a generic prediction region R, so $\mathsf{contain}(R^*_\rho)$ is the containment probability w.r.t. the optimal solution to $\mathcal{L}^\rho_\mathcal{U}$. We adapt the following theorem from [21], which gives a lower bound on the containment probability $\mathsf{contain}(R^*_\rho)$ of an optimal solution to $\mathcal{L}^\rho_\mathcal{U}$ for a predefined value of ρ. This lower bound is correct with a user-defined confidence level of $\beta \in (0,1)$, which we typically choose close to one (e.g., $\beta = 0.99$).

Theorem 1. *Let $\mathcal{U}_n$ be a set of n samples, and let c^* be the complexity of problem $\mathcal{L}^\rho_\mathcal{U}$. For any confidence level $\beta \in (0,1)$ and any upper bound $d^* \geq c^*$, it holds that*

$$\mathbb{P}^n \left\{ \mathsf{contain}(R^*_\rho) \geq \eta(d^*) \right\} \geq \beta, \qquad (3)$$

where R^*_ρ is the prediction region for $\mathcal{L}^\rho_\mathcal{U}$. Moreover, η is a function defined as $\eta(n) = 0$, and otherwise, $\eta(c)$ is the smallest positive real-valued solution to the following polynomial equality in the t variable for a complexity of c:

$$\binom{n}{c} t^{n-c} - \frac{1-\beta}{2n} \sum_{i=c}^{n-1} \binom{i}{c} t^{i-c} - \frac{1-\beta}{6n} \sum_{i=n+1}^{4n} \binom{i}{c} t^{i-c} = 0. \qquad (4)$$

We provide the proof of Theorem 1 in [6, Appendix B.1]. With a probability of at least β, Theorem 1 yields a correct lower bound. That is, if we solve $\mathcal{L}^\rho_\mathcal{U}$

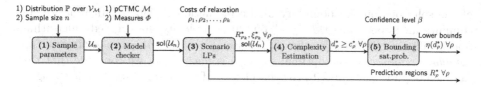

Fig. 7. Overview of our approach for solving the problem statement.

for many more sets of n parameter samples (note that, as the samples are i.i.d., these sets are drawn according to the product probability $\mathbb{P}^n$), the inequality in Eq. (3) is incorrect for *at most* a $1 - \beta$ fraction of the cases. We plot the lower bound $\eta(c)$ as a function of the complexity $c = 0, \ldots, n$ in Fig. 6, for different samples sizes n and confidence levels β. These figures show that an increased complexity leads to a lower η, while increasing the sample size leads to a tighter bound.

Example 3. We continue Example 2. Recall that the complexity for the outer region in Fig. 5 is $c^*_{1.12} = 4$. With Theorem 1, we compute that, for a confidence level of $\beta = 0.9$, the containment probability for this prediction region is at least $\eta = 0.615$ (cf. Figure 6a). For a stronger confidence level of $\beta = 0.999$, we obtain a more conservative lower bound of $\eta = 0.455$. □

3.3 An Algorithm for Computing Prediction Regions

We combine the previous results in our algorithm, which is outlined in Fig. 7. The goal is to obtain a set of prediction regions as in Fig. 5 and their associated lower bounds. To strictly solve the problem statement, assume $k = 1$ in the exposition below. We first outline the complete procedure before detailing Steps 4 and 5.

As preprocessing steps, given a upCTMC $(\mathcal{M}, \mathbb{P})$, we first (1) sample a set $\mathcal{U}_n$ of n parameter values. Using $\mathcal{M}$ and Φ, a (2) model checking algorithm then computes the solution vector $\mathrm{sol}^{\Phi}_{\mathcal{M}}(u)$ for each $u \in \mathcal{U}_n$, yielding the set of solutions $\mathrm{sol}(\mathcal{U}_n)$. We then use $\mathrm{sol}(\mathcal{U}_n)$ as basis for (3) the scenario problem $\mathfrak{L}^{\rho}_{\mathcal{U}}$ in Eq. (2), which we solve for k predefined values $\rho_1, \ldots, \rho_k$, yielding k prediction regions $R^*_{\rho_1}, \ldots R^*_{\rho_k}$. We (4) compute an upper bound d^*_ρ on the complexity $c^*_\rho \, \forall \rho$. Finally, we (5) use the result in Theorem 1, for a given confidence β, to compute the lower bound on the containment probability $\eta(d^*_\rho)$ of R^*_ρ. Using Definition 6, we can postprocess this region to a prediction region over the probability curves.

Step (3): Choosing values for ρ. Example 1 shows that relaxation of additional solution vectors (and thus a change in the prediction region) only occurs at *critical* values of $\rho = \frac{1}{n}$, for $n \in \mathbb{N}$. In practice, we will use $\rho = \frac{1}{n+0.5}$ for ± 10 values of $n \in \mathbb{N}$ to obtain gradients of prediction regions as in Sect. 6.

Step (4): Computing complexity. Computing the complexity c^*_ρ is a combinatorial problem in general [30], because we must consider the removal of all combinations of the solutions on the boundary of the prediction region R_ρ^*. In practice, we compute an upper bound $d_\rho^* \geq c_\rho^*$ on the complexity via a greedy algorithm. Specifically, we iteratively solve $\mathfrak{L}_\mathcal{U}^\rho$ in Eq. (2) with *one more sample on the boundary removed*. If the optimal solution is unchanged, we conclude that this sample does not contribute to the complexity. If the optimal solution is changed, we put the sample back and proceed by removing a different sample. This greedy algorithm terminates when we have tried removing all solutions on the boundary.

Step (5): Computing lower bounds. Theorem 1 characterizes a computable function $B(d^*, n, \beta)$ that returns zero for $d^* = n$ (i.e., all samples are critical), and otherwise uses the polynomial Eq. (4) to obtain η, which we solve with an approximate root finding method in practice (see [31] for details on how to ensure that we find the smallest root). For every upper bound on the complexity d^* and any requested confidence, we obtain the lower bound $\eta = B(d^*, n, \beta)$ for the containment probability w.r.t. the prediction region R_ρ^*.

4   Imprecise Sampling-Based Prediction Regions

Thus far, we have solved our problem statement under the assumption that we compute the solution vectors precisely (up to numerics). For some models, however, computing precise solutions is expensive. In such a case, we may choose to compute an approximation, given as an *interval* on each entry of the solution function. In this section, we deal with such *imprecise solutions*.

Setting. Formally, imprecise solutions are described by the bounds $\mathsf{sol}^-(u), \mathsf{sol}^+(u) \in \mathbb{R}^m$ such that $\mathsf{sol}^-(u) \leq \mathsf{sol}(u) \leq \mathsf{sol}^+(u)$ holds with pointwise inequalities. Our goal is to compute a prediction region R and a (high-confidence) lower bound μ such that $\mathsf{contain}(R) \geq \mu$, i.e., a lower bound on the probability that any *precise solution* $\mathsf{sol}(u)$ is contained in R. However, we must now compute R and $\mathsf{contain}(R)$ from the imprecise solutions $\mathsf{sol}^-, \mathsf{sol}^+$. Thus, we aim to provide a guarantee with respect to the *precise* solution $\mathsf{sol}(u)$, based on *imprecise* solutions.

Challenge. Intuitively, if we increase the (unknown) prediction region R^* from problem $\mathfrak{L}_\mathcal{U}^\rho$ (for the unknown precise solutions) while also overapproximating the complexity of $\mathfrak{L}_\mathcal{U}^\rho$, we obtain sound bounds. We formalize this idea as follows.

Lemma 1. *Let R_ρ^* be the prediction region and c_ρ^* the complexity that result from solving $\mathfrak{L}_\mathcal{U}^\rho$ for the precise (unknown) solutions $\mathsf{sol}(\mathcal{U}_n)$. Given a set $R \in \mathbb{R}^n$ and $d \in \mathbb{N}$, for any confidence level $\beta \in (0, 1)$, the following implication holds:*

$$R_\rho^* \subseteq R \text{ and } c_\rho^* \leq d \quad \Longrightarrow \quad \mathbb{P}^n \Big\{ \mathsf{contain}(R) \geq \eta(d) \Big\} \geq \beta, \qquad (5)$$

where $\eta(n) = 0$, and otherwise, $\eta(d)$ is the smallest positive real-valued solution to the polynomial equality in Eq. (4).

The proof is in [6, Appendix B.2]. In what follows, we clarify how we compute the appropriate R and d in Lemma 1. As we will see, in contrast to Sect. 3, these results do *not* carry over to other definitions $\mathfrak{L}_\mathcal{U}^\rho$ (for non-rectangular regions R).

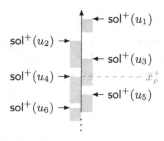

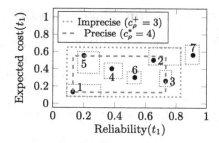

Fig. 8. Imprecise solutions and the upper bound $\bar{x}'_\rho$ of the prediction region.

Fig. 9. Complexity of the imprecise solution vs. that of the precise solution.

4.1   Prediction Regions on Imprecise Solutions

In this section, we show how to compute $R \supseteq R^*_\rho$, satisfying the first term in the premise of Lemma 1. We construct a *conservative box* around the imprecise solutions as in Fig. 9, containing both $\mathsf{sol}^-(u)$ and $\mathsf{sol}^+(u)$. We compute this box by solving the following problem $\mathfrak{G}^\rho_{\mathcal{U}}$ as a modified version of $\mathcal{L}^\rho_{\mathcal{U}}$ in Eq. (2):

$$\mathfrak{G}^\rho_{\mathcal{U}} : \text{minimize} \ \|\bar{x} - x\|_1 + \rho \sum_{i=1}^{n} \|\xi_i\|_1 \tag{6a}$$

$$\text{subject to} \quad x - \xi_i \leq \mathsf{sol}^-(u_i), \ \mathsf{sol}^+(u_i) \leq \bar{x} + \xi_i \ \ \forall i = 1,\ldots,n. \tag{6b}$$

We denote the optimal solution of $\mathfrak{G}^\rho_{\mathcal{U}}$ by $[x'_\rho, \bar{x}'_\rho], \xi'$ (recall that the optimum to $\mathcal{L}^\rho_{\mathcal{U}}$ is written as $[x^*_\rho, \bar{x}^*_\rho], \xi^*_\rho$).[4] If a sample $u_i \in \mathcal{V}_{\mathcal{M}}$ in problem $\mathfrak{G}^\rho_{\mathcal{U}}$ is relaxed (i.e., has a non-zero ξ_i), part of the interval $[\mathsf{sol}^-(u_i), \mathsf{sol}^+(u_i)]$ is not contained in the prediction region. The following result (for which the proof is in [6, Appendix B.3]. relates $\mathcal{L}^\rho_{\mathcal{U}}$ and $\mathfrak{G}^\rho_{\mathcal{U}}$, showing that we can use $[x'_\rho, \bar{x}'_\rho]$ as R in Lemma 1.

Theorem 2. *Given ρ, sample set $\mathcal{U}_n$, and prediction region $[x'_\rho, \bar{x}'_\rho]$ to problem $\mathfrak{G}^\rho_{\mathcal{U}}$, it holds that $[x^*_\rho, \bar{x}^*_\rho] \subseteq [x'_\rho, \bar{x}'_\rho]$, with $[x^*_\rho, \bar{x}^*_\rho]$ the optimal solution to $\mathcal{L}^\rho_{\mathcal{U}}$.*

We note that this result is not trivial. In particular, the entries ξ_i from both LPs are incomparable, as are their objective functions. Instead, Theorem 2 relies on two observations. First, due to the use of the 1-norm, the LP $\mathfrak{G}^\rho_{\mathcal{U}}$ can be decomposed into n individual LPs, whose results combine into a solution to the original LP. This allows us to consider individual dimensions. Second, the solution vectors that are relaxed depend on the value of ρ and on their *relative order*, but not on the *precise position* within that order, which is also illustrated by Example 1. In combination with the observation from Example 1 that the *outermost* samples are relaxed at the (relatively) highest ρ, we can provide conservative guarantees on which samples are (or are surely not) relaxed. We formalize these observations and provide a proof of Theorem 2 in [6, Appendix B.3].

---

[4] We write $[x^*_\rho, \bar{x}^*_\rho]$ and $[x'_\rho, \bar{x}'_\rho]$, as results in Sect. 4 apply only to rectangular regions.

4.2   Computing the Complexity

To satisfy the second term of the premise in Lemma 1, we compute an upper bound on the complexity. We first present a negative result. Let the complexity c'_ρ of problem $\mathfrak{G}^\rho_\mathcal{U}$ be defined analogous to Definition 7, but with $[\underline{x}'_\rho, \bar{x}'_\rho]$ as the region.

Lemma 2. *In general, $c^*_\rho \le c'_\rho$ does not hold.*

Proof. In Fig. 9, the smallest critical set for the imprecise solutions are those labeled $\{1, 2, 7\}$, while this set is $\{1, 3, 5, 7\}$ under precise solutions, so $c^*_\rho > c'_\rho$. $\square$

Thus, we cannot upper bound the complexity directly from the result to $\mathfrak{G}^\rho_\mathcal{U}$. We can, however, determine the samples that are certainly *not* in any critical set (recall Definition 7). Intuitively, a sample is *surely noncritical* if its (imprecise) solution is strictly within the prediction region and does not overlap with any solution on the region's boundary. In Fig. 8, sample u_6 is surely noncritical, but sample u_5 is not (whether u_5 is critical depends on its precise solution). Formally, let δR be the boundary[5] of region $[\underline{x}'_\rho, \bar{x}'_\rho]$, and let $\mathcal{B}$ be the set of samples whose solutions overlap with δR, which is $\mathcal{B} = \{u \in \mathcal{U}_n : [\text{sol}^-(u), \text{sol}^+(u)] \cap \delta R \ne \varnothing\}$.

Definition 8. *For a region $[\underline{x}'_\rho, \bar{x}'_\rho]$, let $\mathcal{I} \subset [\underline{x}'_\rho, \bar{x}'_\rho]$ be the rectangle of largest volume, such that $\mathcal{I} \cap [\text{sol}^-(u), \text{sol}^+(u)] = \varnothing$ for any $u \in \mathcal{B}$. A sample $u_i \in \mathcal{V}_\mathcal{M}$ is surely noncritical if $[\text{sol}^-(u_i), \text{sol}^+(u_i)] \subseteq \mathcal{I}$. The set of all surely noncritical samples w.r.t. the (unknown) prediction region $[\underline{x}^*_\rho, \bar{x}^*_\rho]$ is denoted by $\mathcal{X} \subset \mathcal{U}_n$.*

As a worst case, any sample not surely noncritical can be in the smallest critical set, leading to the following bound on the complexity as required by Lemma 1.

Theorem 3. *Let $\mathcal{X}$ be the set of surely noncritical samples. Then $c^*_\rho \le |\mathcal{U}_n \setminus \mathcal{X}|$.*

The proof is in [6, Appendix B.4]. For imprecise solutions, the bound in Theorem 3 is conservative but can potentially be improved, as discussed in the following.

4.3   Solution Refinement Scheme

Often, we can *refine* imprecise solutions arbitrarily (at the cost of an increased computation time). Doing so, we can improve the prediction regions and upper bound on the complexity, which in turn improves the computed bound on the containment probability. Specifically, we propose the following rule for refining solutions. After solving $\mathfrak{G}^\rho_\mathcal{U}$ for a given set of imprecise solutions, we refine the solutions on the boundary of the obtained prediction region. We then resolve problem $\mathfrak{G}^\rho_\mathcal{U}$, thus adding a loop back from (4) to (2) in our algorithm shown in Fig. 7. In our experiments, we demonstrate that with this refinement scheme, we iteratively improve our upper bound $d \ge c^*_\rho$ and the smallest superset $R \supseteq R^*_\rho$.

---

[5] The boundary of a compact set is defined as its closure minus its interior [45].

5   Batch Verification for CTMCs

One bottleneck in our method is to obtain the necessary number of solution vectors $\mathsf{sol}(\mathcal{U}_n)$ by model checking. The following improvements, while mild, are essential in our implementation and therefore deserve a brief discussion.

In general, computing $\mathsf{sol}(u)$ via model checking consists of two parts. First, the high-level representation of the upCTMC —given in Prism [42], JANI [13], or a dynamic fault tree[6]— is translated into a concrete CTMC $\mathcal{M}[u]$. Then, from $\mathcal{M}[u]$ we construct $\mathsf{sol}(u)$ using off-the-shelf algorithms [7]. We adapt the pipeline by tailoring the translation and the approximate analysis as outlined below.

Our implementation supports two methods for building the concrete CTMC for a parameter sample: (1) by first instantiating the valuation in the specification and then building the resulting concrete CTMC, or (2) by first building the pCTMC $\mathcal{M}$ (only once) and then instantiating it for each parameter sample to obtain the concrete CTMC $\mathcal{M}[u]$. Which method is faster depends on the specific model (we only report results for the fastest method in Sect. 6 for brevity).

Partial models. To accelerate the time-consuming computation of solution vectors by model-checking on large models, it is natural to abstract the models into smaller models amenable to faster computations. Similar to ideas used for dynamic fault trees [55] and infinite CTMCs [48], we employ an abstraction which only keeps the most relevant parts of a model, i.e., states with a sufficiently large probability to be reached from the initial state(s). Analysis on this partial model then yields best- and worst-case results for each measure by assuming that all removed states are either target states (best case) or are not (worst case), respectively. This method returns imprecise solution vectors as used in Sect. 4, which can be refined up to an arbitrary precision by retaining more states of the original model.

Similar to building the complete models, two approaches are possible to create the partial models: (1) fixing the valuation and directly abstracting the concrete CTMC, or (2) first building the complete pCTMC and then abstracting the concrete CTMC. We reuse partial models for similar valuations to avoid costly computations. We cluster parameter valuations which are close to each other (in Euclidean distance). For parameter valuations within one cluster, we reuse the same partial model (in terms of the states), albeit instantiating it according to the precise valuation.

6   Experiments

We answer three questions about (a prototype implementation of) our approach:

Q1. Can we verify CTMCs taking into account the uncertainty about the rates?
Q2. How well does our approach scale w.r.t. the number of measures and samples?
Q3. How does our approach compare to naïve baselines (to be defined below)?

Setup. We implement our approach using the explicit engine of Storm [37] and the improvements of Sect. 5 to sample from upCTMCs in Python. Our current

---

[6] Fault trees are a common formalism in reliability engineering [51].

Table 1. Excerpt of the benchmark statistics (sampling time is per 100 CTMCs).

Benchmark	$|\Phi|$	#pars	#states	#trans	Init.	Sample (×100)	$N = 100$	$N = 200$
			Model size			Storm run time [s]	Scen.opt. time [s]	
SIR (140)	26	2	9 996	19 716	0.29	2947.29	18.26	63.27
SIR (140)[a]	26	2	9 996	19 716	0.29	544.27	25.11	129.66
Kanban (3)	4	13	58 400	446 400	4.42	46.95	2.28	6.69
Kanban (5)	4	13	2 546 432	24 460 016	253.39	4363.63	2.03	5.94
Polling (9)	2	2	6 912	36 864	0.64	22.92	2.13	6.66
buffer	2	6	5 632	21 968	0.48	20.70	1.21	4.15
Tandem (31)	2	5	2 016	6 819	0.11	862.41	5.19	24.30
rbc	40	6	2 269	12 930	0.01	1.40	5.27	16.88
rc (1,1)	25	21	8 401	49 446	27.20	74.90	5.75	20.34
rc (1,1)[a]	25	21	n/a[b]	n/a[b]	0.02	2.35	29.23	150.61
rc (2,2)[a]	25	29	n/a[b]	n/a[b]	0.03	27.77	24.86	132.63
hecs (2,1)[a]	25	5	n/a[b]	n/a[b]	0.02	9.83	26.78	145.77
hecs (2,2)[a]	25	24	n/a[b]	n/a[b]	0.02	194.25	33.06	184.32

[a] Computed using approximate model checking up to a relative gap between upper bound $\mathsf{sol}^+(u)$ and lower bound $\mathsf{sol}^-(u)$ below 1% for every sample $u \in \mathcal{V}_\mathcal{M}$.
[b] Model size is unknown, as the approximation does not build the full state-space.

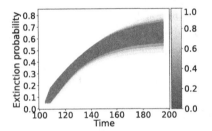

Fig. 10. Prediction regions for the SIR (60) benchmark with $n = 400$.

Fig. 11. Pareto front for the buffer benchmark with $n = 200$ samples.

implementation is limited to pCTMC instantiations that are *graph-preserving*, i.e. for any pair $s, s' \in S$ either $\mathbf{R}(s, s')[u] = 0$ or $\mathbf{R}(s, s')[u] > 0$ for all u. We solve optimization problems using the ECOS solver [29]. All experiments ran single-threaded on a computer with 32 3.7 GHz cores and 64 GB RAM. We show the effectiveness of our method on a large number of publicly available pCTMC [35] and fault tree benchmarks [50] across domains (details in [6, Appendix C]).

Q1. Applicability

An excerpt of the benchmark statistics is shown in Table 1 (see [6, Appendix C] for the full table). For all but the smallest benchmarks, sampling and computing the solution vectors by model checking is more expensive than solving the scenario problems. In the following, we illustrate that 100 samples are sufficient to provide qualitatively good prediction regions and associated lower bounds.

Table 2. Lower bounds $\bar{\mu}$ and standard deviation (SD), vs. the observed number of 1 000 additional solutions that indeed lie within the obtained regions.

(a) Kanban (3).

	$\beta = 0.9$		$\beta = 0.999$		Frequentist
n	$\bar{\mu}$	SD	$\bar{\mu}$	SD	Observed
100	0.862	0.000	0.798	0.000	959 ± 22.7
200	0.930	0.000	0.895	0.000	967 ± 17.4
400	0.965	0.001	0.947	0.001	984 ± 8.6
800	0.982	0.000	0.973	0.000	994 ± 3.2

(b) Railway crossing (1,1,hc).

	$\beta = 0.9$		$\beta = 0.999$		Frequentist
n	$\bar{\mu}$	SD	$\bar{\mu}$	SD	Observed
100	0.895	0.018	0.835	0.020	954 ± 26.8
200	0.945	0.007	0.912	0.008	980 ± 12.8
400	0.975	0.004	0.958	0.005	990 ± 8.3
800	0.986	0.002	0.977	0.003	995 ± 4.3

Plotting prediction regions. Figure 10 presents prediction regions on the extinction probability of the disease in the SIR model and is analogous to the tubes in Fig. 2d (see [6, Appendix C.1] for plots for various other benchmarks). These regions are obtained by applying our algorithm with varying values for the cost of relaxation ρ. For a confidence level of $\beta = 99\%$, the widest (smallest) tube in Fig. 10 corresponds to a lower bound probability of $\mu = 91.1\%$ ($\mu = 23.9\%$). Thus, we conclude that, with a confidence of at least 99%, the curve created by the CTMC for any sampled parameter value will lie within the outermost region in Fig. 10 with a probability of at least 91.1%. We highlight that our approach supports more general prediction regions. We show $n = 200$ solution vectors for the buffer benchmark with two measures in Fig. 11 and produce regions that approach the Pareto front. For a confidence level of $\beta = 99\%$, the outer prediction region is associated with a lower bound probability of $\mu = 91.1\%$, while the inner region has a lower value of $\mu = 66.2\%$. We present more plots in [6, Appendix C.1].

Tightness of the solution. In Table 2 we investigate the tightness of our results. For the experiment, we set $\rho = 1.1$ and solve $\mathcal{L}_{\mathcal{U}}^{\rho}$ for different values of n, repeating every experiment 10 times, resulting in the average bounds $\bar{\mu}$. Then, we sample 1 000 solutions and count the *observed* number of solutions contained in every prediction regions, resulting in an empirical approximation of the containment probability. Recall that for $\rho > 1$, we obtain a prediction region that contains all solutions, so this observed count grows toward n. The lower bounds grow toward the empirical count for an increased n, with the smallest difference (RC, $n = 800$, $\beta = 0.9$) being as small as 0.9%. Similar observations hold for other values of ρ.

Handling imprecise solutions. The approximate model checker is significantly faster (see Table 1 for SIR (140) and RC), at the cost of obtaining imprecise solution vectors.[7] For SIR (140), the sampling time is reduced from 49 to 9 min, while the scenario optimization time is slightly higher at 129 s. This difference only grows larger with the size of the CTMC. For the larger instances of RC and HECS, computing exact solutions is infeasible at all (one HECS (2,2) sample alone takes 15 min). While the bounds on the containment probability under imprecise solu-

---

[7] We terminate at a relative gap between upper/lower bound of the solution below 1%.

Table 3. Run times in [s] for solving the scenario problems for SIR and RC with $\rho = 0.1$ (timeout (TO) of 1 hour) for different sample sizes n and measures m.

<table>
<tr><td colspan="6" align="center">(a) SIR (population 20).</td><td colspan="5" align="center">(b) Railway crossing (1,1,hc).</td></tr>
<tr><td>n / m</td><td>50</td><td>100</td><td>200</td><td>400</td><td>800</td><td>n / m</td><td>50</td><td>100</td><td>200</td><td>400</td></tr>
<tr><td>100</td><td>0.97</td><td>1.59</td><td>3.36</td><td>9.17</td><td>25.41</td><td>100</td><td>1.84</td><td>3.40</td><td>8.18</td><td>24.14</td></tr>
<tr><td>200</td><td>3.69</td><td>7.30</td><td>22.91</td><td>59.45</td><td>131.78</td><td>200</td><td>6.35</td><td>14.56</td><td>45.09</td><td>113.09</td></tr>
<tr><td>400</td><td>29.43</td><td>76.13</td><td>153.03</td><td>310.67</td><td>640.70</td><td>400</td><td>34.74</td><td>96.68</td><td>203.77</td><td>427.80</td></tr>
<tr><td>800</td><td>261.97</td><td>491.73</td><td>955.77</td><td>1924.15</td><td>TO</td><td>800</td><td>292.32</td><td>579.09</td><td>1215.67</td><td>2553.98</td></tr>
</table>

tions may initially be poor (see Fig. 12a, which results in $\mu = 2.1\%$), we can improve the results significantly using the refinement scheme proposed in Sect. 4.3. For example, Fig. 12c shows the prediction region after refining 31 of the 100 solutions, which yields $\mu = 74.7\%$. Thus, *by iteratively refining only the imprecise solutions on the boundary of the resulting prediction regions, we significantly tighten the obtained bounds on the containment probability.*

Q2. Scalability

In Table 3, we report the run times for steps (3)–(5) of our algorithm shown in Fig. 7 (i.e., for solving the scenario problems, but not for computing the solution vectors in Storm). Here, we solve problem $\mathcal{L}_{\mathcal{U}}^{\rho}$ for $\rho = 0.1$, with different numbers of samples and measures. Our approach scales well to realistic numbers of samples (up to 800) and measures (up to 400). The computational complexity of the scenario problems is largely *independent of the size of the CTMC*, and hence, similar run times are observed across the benchmarks (cf. Table 1).

Q3. Comparison to baselines

We compare against two baselines: (1) Scenario optimization to analyze each measure independently, yielding a separate probabilistic guarantee on each measure. (2) A frequentist (Monte Carlo) baseline, which samples a large number of parameter values and counts the number of associated solutions within a region.

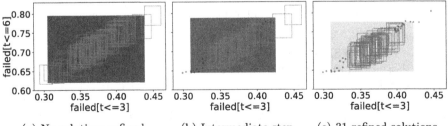

(a) No solutions refined.   (b) Intermediate step.   (c) 31 refined solutions.

Fig. 12. Refining imprecise solution vectors (red boxes) for RC (2,2), $n = 100$. (Color figure online)

Analyzing measures independently. To show that analyzing a full *set of measures* at once, e.g., the complete probability curve, is essential, we compare our method to the baseline that analyzes *each measure independently* and combines the obtained bounds on each measure afterward. We consider the PCS benchmark with precise samples and solve $\mathcal{L}_{\mathcal{U}}^{\rho}$ for $\rho = 2$ (see [6, Table 5] for details). For $n = 100$ samples and $\beta = 99\%$, our approach returns a lower bound probability of $\mu = 84.8\%$. By contrast, the naïve baseline yields a lower bound of only 4.5%, and similar results are observed for different values of n (cf. [6, Table 5 in Appendix C]). There are two reasons for this large difference. First, the baseline applies Theorem 3 once for each of the 25 measures, so it must use a more conservative confidence level of $\tilde{\beta} = 1 - \frac{1-\beta}{25} = 0.9996$. Second, the baseline takes the conjunction over the 25 independent lower bounds, which drastically reduces the obtained bound.

Frequentist baseline. The comparison to the frequentist baseline on the Kanban and RC benchmarks yields the previously discussed results in Table 2. The results in Tables 1 and 3 show that *the time spent for sampling is (for most benchmarks) significantly higher than for scenario optimization.* Thus, our scenario-based approach has a relatively low cost, while resulting in valuable guarantees which the baseline does not give. To still obtain a high confidence in the result, a much larger sample size is needed for the frequentist baseline than for our approach.

7   Related Work

Several verification approaches exist to handle uncertain Markov models.

For (discrete-time) *interval* Markov chains (DTMCs) or Markov decision processes (MDPs), a number of approaches verify against all probabilities within the intervals [32, 39, 46, 53, 54]. Lumpability of interval CTMCs is considered in [22]. In contrast to upCTMCs, interval Markov chains have no dependencies between transition uncertainties and no distributions are attached to the intervals.

Parametric Markov models generally define probabilities or rates via functions over the parameters. The standard parameter synthesis problem for discrete-time models is to find all valuations of parameters that satisfies a specification. Techniques range from computing a solution function over the parameters, to directly solving the underlying optimization problems [24, 28, 33, 40]. Parametric CTMCs are investigated in [23, 34], but are generally restricted to a few parameters. The work [15] aims to find a robust parameter valuation in pCTMCs.

For all approaches listed so far, the results may be rather conservative, as no prior information on the uncertainties (the intervals) is used. That is, the uncertainty is not quantified and all probabilities or rates are treated equally as likely. In our approach, we do not compute solution functions, as the underlying methods are computationally expensive and usually restricted to a few parameters.

Quantified uncertainty is studied in [44]. Similarly to our work, the approach draws parameter values from a probability distribution over the model parameters and analyzes the instantiated model via model checking. However, [44] studies DTMCs and performs a frequentist (Monte Carlo) approach, cf. Sect. 6, to compute estimates for a single measure, without prediction regions. Moreover, our approach requires significantly fewer samples, cf. the comparison in Sect. 6.

The work in [10,11] takes a sampling-driven Bayesian approach for pCTMCs. In particular, they take a prior on the solution function over a single measure and update it based on samples (potentially obtained via statistical model checking). We assume no prior on the solution function, and, as mentioned before, do not compute the solution function due to the expensive underlying computations.

Statistical model checking (SMC) [1,43] samples path in stochastic models to perform model checking. This technique has been applied to numerous models [25–27,47], including CTMCs [52,57]. SMC analyzes a *concrete* CTMC by sampling from the known transition rates, whereas for upCTMC these rates are parametric.

Finally, scenario optimization [16,21] is widely used in control theory [14] and recently in machine learning [20] and reliability engineering [49]. Within a verification context, closest to our work is [5], which considers the verification of single measures for uncertain MDPs. [5] relies on the so-called sampling-and-discarding approach [17], while we use the risk-and-complexity perspective [31], yielding better results for problems with many decision variables like we have.

8   Conclusion

This paper presents a novel approach to the analysis of parametric Markov models with respect to a set of performance characteristics. In particular, we provide a method that yields statistical guarantees on the typical performance characteristics from a finite set of samples of those parameters. Our experiments show that high-confidence results can be given based on a few hundred of samples. Future work includes supporting models with nondeterminism, exploiting aspects of parametric models such as monotonicity, and integrating methods to infer the distributions on the parameter space from observations.

References

1. Agha, G., Palmskog, K.: A survey of statistical model checking. ACM Trans. Model. Comput. Simul. **28**(1), 6:1–6:39 (2018)
2. Allen, L.J.: A primer on stochastic epidemic models: Formulation, numerical simulation, and analysis. Infect. Dis. Model. **2**(2), 128–142 (2017)
3. Andersson, H., Britton, T.: Stochastic Epidemic Models and Their Statistical Analysis, vol. 151. Springer Science & Business Media, New York (2012). https://doi.org/10.1007/978-1-4612-1158-7
4. Aziz, A., Sanwal, K., Singhal, V., Brayton, R.: Model-checking continuous-time Markov chains. ACM Trans. Comput. Logic **1**(1), 162–170 (2000)
5. Badings, T.S., Cubuktepe, M., Jansen, N., Junges, S., Katoen, J.P., Topcu, U.: Scenario-based verification of uncertain parametric MDPs. CoRR **abs/2112. 13020** (2021)
6. Badings, T.S., Jansen, N., Junges, S., Stoelinga, M., Volk, M.: Sampling-based verification of CTMCs with uncertain rates. Technical report, CoRR, abs/2205.08300 (2022)

7. Baier, C., Haverkort, B.R., Hermanns, H., Katoen, J.P.: Model-checking algorithms for continuous-time Markov chains. IEEE Trans. Softw. Eng. **29**(6), 524–541 (2003)
8. Baier, C., Katoen, J.P.: Principles of Model Checking. MIT Press, Cambridge (2008)
9. Bertsekas, D.P., Tsitsiklis, J.N.: Introduction to Probability. Athena Scientinis (2000)
10. Bortolussi, L., Milios, D., Sanguinetti, G.: Smoothed model checking for uncertain continuous-time Markov chains. Inf. Comput. **247**, 235–253 (2016)
11. Bortolussi, L., Silvetti, S.: Bayesian statistical parameter synthesis for linear temporal properties of stochastic models. In: Beyer, D., Huisman, M. (eds.) TACAS 2018. LNCS, vol. 10806, pp. 396–413. Springer, Cham (2018). https://doi.org/10.1007/978-3-319-89963-3_23
12. Boyd, S., Vandenberghe, L.: Convex Optimization. Cambridge University Press, New York (2004)
13. Budde, C.E., Dehnert, C., Hahn, E.M., Hartmanns, A., Junges, S., Turrini, A.: JANI: quantitative model and tool interaction. In: Legay, A., Margaria, T. (eds.) TACAS 2017. LNCS, vol. 10206, pp. 151–168. Springer, Heidelberg (2017). https://doi.org/10.1007/978-3-662-54580-5_9
14. Calafiore, G.C., Campi, M.C.: The scenario approach to robust control design. IEEE Trans. Autom. Control. **51**(5), 742–753 (2006)
15. Calinescu, R., Ceska, M., Gerasimou, S., Kwiatkowska, M., Paoletti, N.: Efficient synthesis of robust models for stochastic systems. J. Syst. Softw. **143**, 140–158 (2018)
16. Campi, M.C., Garatti, S.: The exact feasibility of randomized solutions of uncertain convex programs. SIAM J. Optim. **19**(3), 1211–1230 (2008)
17. Campi, M.C., Garatti, S.: A sampling-and-discarding approach to chance-constrained optimization: feasibility and optimality. J. Optim. Theory App. **148**(2), 257–280 (2011)
18. Campi, M.C., Garatti, S.: Introduction to the scenario approach. SIAM (2018)
19. Campi, M.C., Garatti, S.: Wait-and-judge scenario optimization. Math. Program. **167**(1), 155–189 (2018)
20. Campi, M.C., Garatti, S.: Scenario optimization with relaxation: a new tool for design and application to machine learning problems. In: CDC, pp. 2463–2468. IEEE (2020)
21. Campi, M., Carè, A., Garatti, S.: The scenario approach: a tool at the service of data-driven decision making. Ann. Rev. Control **52**, 1–17 (2021)
22. Cardelli, L., Grosu, R., Larsen, K.G., Tribastone, M., Tschaikowski, M., Vandin, A.: Lumpability for uncertain continuous-time Markov chains. In: Abate, A., Marin, A. (eds.) QEST 2021. LNCS, vol. 12846, pp. 391–409. Springer, Cham (2021). https://doi.org/10.1007/978-3-030-85172-9_21
23. Ceska, M., Dannenberg, F., Paoletti, N., Kwiatkowska, M., Brim, L.: Precise parameter synthesis for stochastic biochemical systems. Acta Inform. **54**(6), 589–623 (2017)
24. Cubuktepe, M., Jansen, N., Junges, S., Katoen, J.P., Topcu, U.: Convex optimization for parameter synthesis in MDPs. IEEE Trans Autom Control pp. 1–1 (2022)
25. D'Argenio, P.R., Hartmanns, A., Sedwards, S.: Lightweight statistical model checking in nondeterministic continuous time. In: Margaria, T., Steffen, B. (eds.) ISoLA 2018. LNCS, vol. 11245, pp. 336–353. Springer, Cham (2018). https://doi.org/10.1007/978-3-030-03421-4_22
26. David, A., Larsen, K.G., Legay, A., Mikucionis, M., Poulsen, D.B.: UPPAAL SMC tutorial. Int. J. Softw. Tools Technol. Transf. **17**(4), 397–415 (2015)

27. David, A., Larsen, K.G., Legay, A., Mikučionis, M., Wang, Z.: Time for statistical model checking of real-time systems. In: Gopalakrishnan, G., Qadeer, S. (eds.) CAV 2011. LNCS, vol. 6806, pp. 349–355. Springer, Heidelberg (2011). https://doi.org/10.1007/978-3-642-22110-1_27

28. Daws, C.: Symbolic and parametric model checking of discrete-time Markov chains. In: Liu, Z., Araki, K. (eds.) ICTAC 2004. LNCS, vol. 3407, pp. 280–294. Springer, Heidelberg (2005). https://doi.org/10.1007/978-3-540-31862-0_21

29. Domahidi, A., Chu, E., Boyd, S.P.: ECOS: an SOCP solver for embedded systems. In: ECC, pp. 3071–3076. IEEE (2013)

30. Garatti, S., Campi, M.C.: The risk of making decisions from data through the lens of the scenario approach. IFAC-PapersOnLine **54**(7), 607–612 (2021)

31. Garatti, S., Campi, M.: Risk and complexity in scenario optimization. Math. Program. **191**, 1–37 (2019)

32. Givan, R., Leach, S.M., Dean, T.L.: Bounded-parameter Markov decision processes. Artif. Intell. **122**(1–2), 71–109 (2000)

33. Hahn, E.M., Hermanns, H., Zhang, L.: Probabilistic reachability for parametric Markov models. Int. J. Softw. Tools Technol. Transf. **13**(1), 3–19 (2011)

34. Han, T., Katoen, J.P., Mereacre, A.: Approximate parameter synthesis for probabilistic time-bounded reachability. In: RTSS, pp. 173–182. IEEE CS (2008)

35. Hartmanns, A., Klauck, M., Parker, D., Quatmann, T., Ruijters, E.: The quantitative verification benchmark set. In: Vojnar, T., Zhang, L. (eds.) TACAS 2019. LNCS, vol. 11427, pp. 344–350. Springer, Cham (2019). https://doi.org/10.1007/978-3-030-17462-0_20

36. Haverkort, B.R., Hermanns, H., Katoen, J.P.: On the use of model checking techniques for dependability evaluation. In: SRDS, pp. 228–237. IEEE CS (2000)

37. Hensel, C., Junges, S., Katoen, J.P., Quatmann, T., Volk, M.: The probabilistic model checker Storm. Softw. Tools Technol. Transf. (2021)

38. Hermanns, H., Meyer-Kayser, J., Siegle, M.: Multi terminal binary decision diagrams to represent and analyse continuous time Markov chains. In: 3rd International Workshop on the Numerical Solution of Markov Chains, pp. 188–207. Citeseer (1999)

39. Jonsson, B., Larsen, K.G.: Specification and refinement of probabilistic processes. In: LICS, pp. 266–277. IEEE CS (1991)

40. Junges, S., et al.: Parameter synthesis for Markov models. CoRR **abs/1903.07993** (2019)

41. Katoen, J.P.: The probabilistic model checking landscape. In: LICS, pp. 31–45. ACM (2016)

42. Kwiatkowska, M., Norman, G., Parker, D.: PRISM 4.0: verification of probabilistic real-time systems. In: Gopalakrishnan, G., Qadeer, S. (eds.) CAV 2011. LNCS, vol. 6806, pp. 585–591. Springer, Heidelberg (2011). https://doi.org/10.1007/978-3-642-22110-1_47

43. Legay, A., Lukina, A., Traonouez, L.M., Yang, J., Smolka, S.A., Grosu, R.: Statistical Model Checking. In: Steffen, B., Woeginger, G. (eds.) Computing and Software Science. LNCS, vol. 10000, pp. 478–504. Springer, Cham (2019). https://doi.org/10.1007/978-3-319-91908-9_23

44. Meedeniya, I., Moser, I., Aleti, A., Grunske, L.: Evaluating probabilistic models with uncertain model parameters. Softw. Syst. Model. **13**(4), 1395–1415 (2014)

45. Mendelson, B.: Introduction to topology. Courier Corporation (1990)

46. Puggelli, A., Li, W., Sangiovanni-Vincentelli, A.L., Seshia, S.A.: Polynomial-time verification of PCTL properties of MDPs with convex uncertainties. In: CAV. LNCS, vol. 8044, pp. 527–542. Springer (2013)

47. Rao, K.D., Gopika, V., Rao, V.V.S.S., Kushwaha, H.S., Verma, A.K., Srividya, A.: Dynamic fault tree analysis using Monte Carlo simulation in probabilistic safety assessment. Reliab. Eng. Syst. Saf. **94**(4), 872–883 (2009)

48. Roberts, R., Neupane, T., Buecherl, L., Myers, C.J., Zhang, Z.: STAMINA 2.0: improving scalability of infinite-state stochastic model checking. In: Finkbeiner, B., Wies, T. (eds.) VMCAI 2022. LNCS, vol. 13182, pp. 319–331. Springer, Cham (2022). https://doi.org/10.1007/978-3-030-94583-1_16

49. Rocchetta, R., Crespo, L.G.: A scenario optimization approach to reliability-based and risk-based design: soft-constrained modulation of failure probability bounds. Reliab. Eng. Syst. Saf. **216**, 107900 (2021)

50. Ruijters, E., et al.: FFORT: a benchmark suite for fault tree analysis. In: ESREL (2019)

51. Ruijters, E., Stoelinga, M.I.A.: Fault tree analysis: a survey of the state-of-the-art in modeling, analysis and tools. Comput. Sci. Rev. **15**, 29–62 (2015)

52. Sen, K., Viswanathan, M., Agha, G.: On statistical model checking of stochastic systems. In: Etessami, K., Rajamani, S.K. (eds.) CAV 2005. LNCS, vol. 3576, pp. 266–280. Springer, Heidelberg (2005). https://doi.org/10.1007/11513988_26

53. Sen, K., Viswanathan, M., Agha, G.: Model-checking Markov chains in the presence of uncertainties. In: Hermanns, H., Palsberg, J. (eds.) TACAS 2006. LNCS, vol. 3920, pp. 394–410. Springer, Heidelberg (2006). https://doi.org/10.1007/11691372_26

54. Skulj, D.: Discrete time Markov chains with interval probabilities. Int. J. Approx. Reason. **50**(8), 1314–1329 (2009)

55. Volk, M., Junges, S., Katoen, J.P.: Fast dynamic fault tree analysis by model checking techniques. IEEE Trans. Ind. Inform. **14**(1), 370–379 (2018)

56. Wijesuriya, V.B., Abate, A.: Bayes-adaptive planning for data-efficient verification of uncertain Markov decision processes. In: Parker, D., Wolf, V. (eds.) QEST 2019. LNCS, vol. 11785, pp. 91–108. Springer, Cham (2019). https://doi.org/10.1007/978-3-030-30281-8_6

57. Younes, H.L.S., Simmons, R.G.: Statistical probabilistic model checking with a focus on time-bounded properties. Inf. Comput. **204**(9), 1368–1409 (2006)

Playing Against Fair Adversaries
in Stochastic Games with Total Rewards

Pablo F. Castro[1,3]([✉]) [iD], Pedro R. D'Argenio[2,3,4] [iD], Ramiro Demasi[2,3] [iD],
and Luciano Putruele[1,3] [iD]

[1] Departamento de Computación, FCEFQyN, Universidad Nacional de Río Cuarto,
Río Cuarto, Argentina
[2] FAMAF, Universidad Nacional de Córdoba, Córdoba, Argentina
[3] Consejo Nacional de Investigaciones Científicas y Técnicas (CONICET),
Buenos Aires, Argentina
pcastro@dc.exa.unrc.edu.ar
[4] Saarland University, Saarland Informatics Campus, Saarbrücken, Germany

Abstract. We investigate zero-sum turn-based two-player stochastic
games in which the objective of one player is to maximize the amount of
rewards obtained during a play, while the other aims at minimizing it. We
focus on games in which the minimizer plays in a fair way. We believe that
these kinds of games enjoy interesting applications in software verification, where the maximizer plays the role of a system intending to maximize the number of "milestones" achieved, and the minimizer represents
the behavior of some uncooperative but yet fair environment. Normally,
to study total reward properties, games are requested to be stopping (i.e.,
they reach a terminal state with probability 1). We relax the property to
request that the game is stopping only under a fair minimizing player. We
prove that these games are determined, i.e., each state of the game has a
value defined. Furthermore, we show that both players have memoryless
and deterministic optimal strategies, and the game value can be computed
by approximating the greatest-fixed point of a set of functional equations.
We implemented our approach in a prototype tool, and evaluated it on an
illustrating example and an Unmanned Aerial Vehicle case study.

1 Introduction

Game theory [25] admits an elegant and profound mathematical theory. In
the last decades, it has received widespread attention from computer scientists
because it has important applications to software synthesis and verification. The
analogy is appealing, the operation of a system under an uncooperative environment (faulty hardware, malicious agents, unreliable communication channels,
etc.) can be modeled as a game between two players (the system and the environment), in which the system tries to fulfill certain goals, whereas the environment tries to prevent this from happening. This view is particularly useful for

This work was supported by ANPCyT PICT-2017-3894 (RAFTSys), ANPCyT PICT
2019-03134, SeCyT-UNC 33620180100354CB (ARES), and EU Grant agreement ID:
101008233 (MISSION).

S. Shoham and Y. Vizel (Eds.): CAV 2022, LNCS 13372, pp. 48–69, 2022.
https://doi.org/10.1007/978-3-031-13188-2_3

controller synthesis, i.e., to automatically generate decision-making policies from high-level specifications. Thus, synthesizing a controller consists of computing optimal strategies for a given game.

In this paper we focus on zero-sum, perfect-information, two-player, turn-based stochastic games with (non-negative) rewards [18]. Intuitively, these games are played in a graph by two players who move a token in turns. Some vertices are probabilistic, in the sense that, if a token is in a probabilistic vertex, then the next vertex is randomly selected. Furthermore, the players select their moves using strategies. Associated with each vertex there is a reward (which, in this paper, is taken to be non-negative). The goal of Player 1 is to maximize the expected amount of collected rewards during the game, whereas Player 2 aims at minimizing this value. This is what [28] calls *total reward objective*. These kinds of games have been shown useful to reason about several classes of systems such as autonomous vehicles, fault-tolerant systems, communication protocols, energy production plants, etc. Particularly, in this paper we consider those games in which one of the players employs fair strategies.

Fairness restrictions, understood as fair resolutions of non-determinism of actions, play an important role in software verification and controller synthesis. Especially, fairness assumptions over environments make possible the verification of liveness properties on open systems. Several authors have indicated the need for fairness assumptions over the environment in the controller synthesis approach, e.g., [2,16]. As a simple example consider an autonomous vehicle that needs to traverse a field where moving objects may interfere in its path. Though the precise behavior of the objects may be unknown, it is reasonable to assume that they will not continuously obstruct the vehicle attempts to avoid them. In this sense, while stochastic behavior may be a consequence of the vehicle faults, we can only assume a fair behavior of the surrounding moving objects. In this work, we consider stochastic games in which one of the players (the one playing the environment) is assumed to play only with strong fair strategies.

In order to guarantee that the expected value of accumulated rewards is well defined in (perhaps infinite) plays, some kind of stopping criteria is needed. A common way to do this is to force the strategies to decide to stop with some positive probability in every decision. This corresponds to the so-called discounted stochastic games [18,27], and has the implications that the collected rewards become less important as the game progresses (the "importance reduction" is given by the discount factor). Alternatively, one may be interested in knowing the expected *total* reward, that is, the expected accumulated reward *without* any loss of it as time progresses. For this value to be well defined, the game itself needs to be stopping. That is, no matter the strategies played by the players, the probability of reaching a terminal state needs to be 1 [13,18]. We focus on this last type of game. However, we study here games that may not be stopping in general (i.e., for every strategy), but instead, require that they become stopping only when the minimizer plays in a fair way. We use a notion of (almost-sure) strong fairness, mostly following the ideas introduced in [7] for Markov decision processes. We show that these kinds of games are determined, i.e., each state of the game has a value defined. Furthermore, we show that memoryless and deterministic optimal strategies exist for both players. Moreover, the value of the game can be calculated via the greatest fixed point of the corresponding functionals. It is important to remark that most of the properties discussed in this paper hold when the fairness assumptions are made over the minimizer. Similar properties may not hold if the role of players is changed. However, these conditions encompass a large class of scenarios, where the system intends to maximize the total collected reward and the environment has the opposite objective.

In summary, the contributions of this paper are the following: (1) we introduce the notion of stopping under fairness stochastic game, a generalization of stopping game that takes into account fair environments; (2) we prove that it can be decided in polynomial time whether a game is stopping under fairness; (3) we show that these kinds of games are determined and both players possess optimal stationary strategies, which can be computed using Bellman equations; and (4) we implemented these ideas in a prototype tool embedded in the PRISM-games toolset [22], which we used to evaluate the viability of our approach through illustrative case studies.

The paper is structured as follows. Section 2 introduces an illustrating example to motivate the use of having fairness restrictions over the minimizer. Section 3 fixes terminology and introduces background concepts. In Sect. 4 we describe a polynomial procedure to check whether a game stops under fairness assumptions, we also prove that determinacy is preserved in these games as well as the existence of (memoryless and deterministic) optimal strategies. Experimental results are described in Sect. 5. Finally, Sects. 6 and 7 discuss related work and draw some conclusions, respectively.

2   Roborta vs. the Fair Light (A Motivating Example)

Consider the following scenario. Roborta the robot is navigating a grid of 4×4 cells. Roborta's moves respond to a traffic light: if the light is yellow, she must move sideways (at a border cell, Roborta is allowed to wrap around to the other side); if the light is green she ought to move forward; if the light is red, she cannot perform any movement; finally, if the light is off, Roborta is free to move either sideways or forward. The light and Roborta change their states in turns. In addition, a (non-negative) reward is associated with each cell of the grid. Also, some cells restrict the sideway movement to only one direction. Moreover, we consider possible failures on the behavior of the robot and the light. If Roborta fails, she loses her turn to move. If the light fails, it turns itself off. The failures occur with a given probability and are not permanent (they only affect the current play). The goal of Roborta is to collect as many rewards as possible. In opposition, the light aims at minimizing this value.

The specification of this game is captured in Fig. 1 (using PRISM-like notation [23]). In this model, WIDTH and LENGTH are constants defining the dimension of the grid. MOVES is a two-dimensional array modeling the possible sideways movements in the grid (0 allows the robot to move only to the left, 1, to either side, and 2, only to the right). The light plays when it is red (light=0) and it

```
module Roborta _vs_the_light
col : [0..WIDTH] init 0;
row : [0..LENGTH] init 0;
light : [0..3] init 0; // current light color
                        // 0: red (light's turn)
                        // 1: yellow (Roborta moves sideways)
                        // 2: green (Roborta moves foreward)
                        // 3: off (light fails, any move)
// light moves
[l_y] (light=0) -> (1-Q) : (light'=1) + Q : (light'=3);
[l_g] (light=0) -> (1-Q) : (light'=2) + Q : (light'=3);
// Roborta moves
[r_l] ((light=1) | (light=3)) & (MOVES[col,row] <= 1)
         -> (1-P) : (light'=0) & (col'=(col-1)%WIDTH) +
            P : (light'=0) ;
[r_r] ((light=1) | (light=3)) & (MOVES[col,row] >= 1)
         -> (1-P) : (light'=0) & (col'=(col+1)%WIDTH) +
            P : (light'= 0);
[r_f] ((light=2) | (light=3)) & (row < LENGTH)
         -> (1-P) : (light'=0) & (row'=row+1) +
            P : (light'= 0);
endmodule
```

Fig. 1. Model for the Game

can choose whether to turn on the yellow light (transition labelled with `l_y`) or green (transition labelled `l_g`). Notice that with any choice, the light may fail with probability Q, in which case it turns itself off (`light'=3`). If the light is not red, then it is Roborta's turn to play. If the light is yellow (`light=1`) or off (`light=3`), Roborta can chose whether to move left (`r_l`) or right

(`r_r`), provided the grid allows the movements. If the light is green (`light=2`) or off (`light=3`), she can choose to move forward (notice that if `light=2` this is the only possible move). Like the light, each of Roborta's choices has a failure probability of P, in which case, she does not move and only passes the turn to the light (by setting `light'=0`). For completeness, we mention that the rewards are stored in a secondary matrix which is not shown in Fig. 1.

Figure 2 shows the assignment of rewards to each cell of the 4 × 4 grid as well as the sideway movement restrictions (shown on the bottom-right of each cell with white arrows). The game starts at the cell (0,0) and it stops when Roborta escapes through the end of the grid (i.e., `row = LENGTH`).

A possible scenario in this game is as follows. Roborta starts in cell (0,0) and, in an attempt to minimize the rewards accumulated by the robot, the environment switches the yellow light on. For the sake of simplicity, we assume no failures on the light, i.e., Q = 0. Notice that, if the environment plays always in this way (signaling a yellow light), then Roborta does not collect rewards (since all rewards in the first row are 0) but also she will never reach the goal and

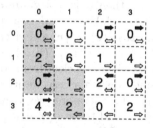

Fig. 2. A robot on a 4 × 4 grid

the game never stops. This scenario occurs when the light plays in an unfair way, i.e., an action (the one that turns the green light on) is enabled infinitely often, but it is not executed infinitely often. Assuming fairness over the environment, we can ensure that a green light will be eventually switched on, allowing the robot to move forward.

For the case in which Q = 0, the best strategy for Roborta when the light is yellow is shown in black arrows on the top-right of each cells with no movement restrictions (restricting cells provide only one choice). As a result, when both players play their optimal strategies, the path taken by Roborta to achieve the goal can be observed in the yellow-highlighted portion of the grid in Fig. 2. In Sect. 5, we evaluate this problem experimentally with different configurations of the game.

3 Preliminaries

We introduce some basic definitions and results on stochastic games that will be necessary across the paper.

A (discrete) *probability distribution* μ over a denumerable set S is a function $\mu : S \to [0,1]$ such that $\mu(S) = \sum_{s \in S} \mu(s) = 1$. Let $\mathcal{D}(S)$ denote the set of all probability distributions on S. $\Delta_s \in \mathcal{D}(S)$ denotes the Dirac distribution for $s \in S$, i.e., $\Delta_s(s) = 1$ and $\Delta_s(s') = 0$ for all $s' \in S$ such that $s' \neq s$. The *support* set of μ is defined by $Supp(\mu) = \{s \mid \mu(s) > 0\}$.

Given a set V, V^* (resp. V^∞) denotes the set of all finite sequences (resp. infinite sequences) of elements of V. Concatenation is represented using juxtaposition. We use variables $\omega, \omega', \cdots \in V^\infty$ as ranging over infinite sequences, and variables $\hat{\omega}, \hat{\omega}', \cdots \in V^*$ as ranging over finite sequences. The i-th element of a finite (resp. infinite) sequence $\hat{\omega}$ (resp. ω) is denoted $\hat{\omega}_i$ (resp. ω_i). Furthermore, for any finite sequence $\hat{\omega}$, $|\hat{\omega}|$ denotes its length. For $\omega \in V^\infty$, $\inf(\omega)$ denotes the set of items appearing infinitely often in ω. Given $S \subseteq V^*$, S^k is the set obtained by concatenating k times the sequences in S.

A *stochastic game* [11,28] is a tuple $\mathcal{G} = (V, (V_1, V_2, V_\mathsf{P}), \delta)$, where V is a finite set of vertices (or states) with $V_1, V_2, V_\mathsf{P} \subseteq V$ being a partition of V, and $\delta : V \times V \to [0,1]$ is a probabilistic transition function, such that for every $v \in V_1 \cup V_2$, $\delta(v, v') \in \{0,1\}$, for any $v' \in V$; and $\delta(v, \cdot) \in \mathcal{D}(V)$ for $v \in V_\mathsf{P}$. If $V_\mathsf{P} = \emptyset$, then $\mathcal{G}$ is called a two-player game graph. Moreover, if $V_1 = \emptyset$ or $V_2 = \emptyset$, then $\mathcal{G}$ is a *Markov decision process* (or MDP). Finally, in case that $V_1 = \emptyset$ and $V_2 = \emptyset$, $\mathcal{G}$ is a *Markov chain* (or MC). For all states $v \in V$ we define $post^\delta(v) = \{v' \in V \mid \delta(v, v') > 0\}$, the set of successors of v. Similarly, $pre^\delta(v') = \{v \in V \mid \delta(v, v') > 0\}$ as the set of predecessors of v', we omit the index δ when it is clear from context. Also, when useful, we fix an initial state for a game, in such a case we use the notation $\mathcal{G}_v$ to indicate that the game starts from v. Furthermore, we assume that $post(v) \neq \emptyset$ for every $v \in V$. A vertex $v \in V$ is said to be *terminal* if $\delta(v, v) = 1$, and $\delta(v, v') = 0$ for all $v \neq v'$. Most results on MDPs rely on the notion of *end component* [5], we straightforwardly extend this notion to two-player games: an end component of $\mathcal{G}$ is a pair (V', δ') such that (a) $V' \subseteq V$; (b) $\delta'(v) = \delta(v)$ for $v \in V_\mathsf{P}$; (c) $\emptyset \neq post^{\delta'}(v) \subseteq post^\delta(v)$ for $v \in V_1 \cup V_2$; (d) $post^{\delta'}(v) \subseteq V'$ for all $v \in V'$; (e) the underlying graph of (V', δ') is strongly connected. Note that an end component can also be considered as being a game. The set of end components of $\mathcal{G}$ is denoted $EC(\mathcal{G})$.

A *path* in the game $\mathcal{G}$ is an infinite sequence of vertices $v_0 v_1 \ldots$ such that $\delta(v_k, v_{k+1}) > 0$ for every $k \in \mathbb{N}$. $Paths_\mathcal{G}$ denotes the set of all paths, and $FPaths_\mathcal{G}$ denotes the set of finite prefixes of paths. Similarly, $Paths_{\mathcal{G},v}$ and $FPaths_{\mathcal{G},v}$ denote the set of paths and the set of finite paths starting at vertex v.

A *strategy* for Player i (for $i \in \{1,2\}$) in a game $\mathcal{G}$ is a function $\pi_i : V^*V_i \to \mathcal{D}(V)$ that assigns a probabilistic distribution to each finite sequence of states such that $\pi_i(\hat{\omega}v)(v') > 0$ only if $v' \in post(v)$. The set of all the strategies for Player i is named Π_i. A strategy π_i is said to be *pure* or *deterministic* if, for every $\hat{\omega}v \in V^*V_i$, $\pi_i(\hat{\omega}v)$ is a Dirac distribution, and it is called *memoryless* if $\pi_i(\hat{\omega}v) = \pi_i(v)$, for every $\hat{\omega} \in V^*$. Let Π_i^M and Π_i^D be respectively the set of all memoryless strategies and the set of all deterministic strategies for Player i. $\Pi_i^{MD} = \Pi_i^M \cap \Pi_i^D$ is the set of all its deterministic and memoryless strategies.

Given two strategies $\pi_1 \in \Pi_1$, $\pi_2 \in \Pi_2$ and an initial vertex v, the *result* of the game is a Markov chain [11], denoted $\mathcal{G}_v^{\pi_1,\pi_2}$. An event $\mathcal{A}$ is a measurable set in the Borel σ-algebra generated by the cones of $Paths_\mathcal{G}$. The *cone* or *cylinder* spanned by the finite path $\hat{\omega} \in FPaths_\mathcal{G}$ is the set $cyl(\hat{\omega}) = \{\omega \in Paths_\mathcal{G} \mid \forall 0 \leq i < |\hat{\omega}| : \omega_i = \hat{\omega}_i\}$. $Prob_{\mathcal{G},v}^{\pi_1,\pi_2}$ is the associated probability measure obtained when fixing strategies π_1, π_2, and an initial vertex v [11]. Intuitively, $Prob_{\mathcal{G},v}^{\pi_1,\pi_2}(\mathcal{A})$ is the probability that strategies π_1 and π_2 generates a path belonging to the set $\mathcal{A}$ when the game $\mathcal{G}$ starts in v. When no confusion is possible, we just write $Prob_{\mathcal{G},v}^{\pi_1,\pi_2}(\hat{\omega})$ instead of $Prob_{\mathcal{G},v}^{\pi_1,\pi_2}(cyl(\hat{\omega}))$. Similar notations are used for MDPs and MCs. A stochastic game (defined as above) is said to be *stopping* [14] if for all pair of strategies π_1, π_2 the probability of reaching a terminal state is 1. We use LTL notation to represent specific set of paths, e.g., $\lozenge T = \{\omega \in Paths_\mathcal{G} \mid \exists i \geq 0 : \omega_i \in T\}$ is the set of all the plays in the game that reach vertices in T.

A *quantitative objective* or *payoff function* is a measurable function $f : V^\infty \to \mathbb{R}$. Let $\mathbb{E}_{\mathcal{G},v}^{\pi_1,\pi_2}[f]$ be the expectation of measurable function f under probability $Prob_{\mathcal{G},v}^{\pi_1,\pi_2}$. The goal of Player 1 is to maximize this value whereas the goal of Player 2 is to minimize it. Sometimes quantitative objective functions can be defined via *rewards*. These are assigned by a *reward function* $r : V \to \mathbb{R}^+$. We usually consider stochastic games augmented with a reward function. Moreover, we assume that for every terminal vertex v, $r(v) = 0$.

The value of the game for Player 1 at vertex v under strategy π_1 is defined as the infimum over all the values resulting from Player 2 strategies in that vertex, i.e., $\inf_{\pi_2 \in \Pi_2} \mathbb{E}_{\mathcal{G},v}^{\pi_1,\pi_2}[f]$. The *value of the game* for Player 1 is defined as the supremum of the values of all Player 1 strategies, i.e., $\sup_{\pi_1 \in \Pi_1} \inf_{\pi_2 \in \Pi_2} \mathbb{E}_{\mathcal{G},v}^{\pi_1,\pi_2}[f]$. Similarly, the value of the game for a Player 2 under strategy π_2 and the value of the game for Player 2 are defined as $\sup_{\pi_1 \in \Pi_1} \mathbb{E}_{\mathcal{G},v}^{\pi_1,\pi_2}[f]$ and $\inf_{\pi_2 \in \Pi_2} \sup_{\pi_1 \in \Pi_1} \mathbb{E}_{\mathcal{G},v}^{\pi_1,\pi_2}[f]$, respectively. We say that a game is *determined* if both values are the same, that is, $\sup_{\pi_1 \in \Pi_1} \inf_{\pi_2 \in \Pi_2} \mathbb{E}_{\mathcal{G},v}^{\pi_1,\pi_2}[f] = \inf_{\pi_2 \in \Pi_2} \sup_{\pi_1 \in \Pi_1} \mathbb{E}_{\mathcal{G},v}^{\pi_1,\pi_2}[f]$. Martin [24] proved the determinacy of stochastic games for Borel and bounded objective functions.

In this paper we focus on the *total accumulated reward payoff* function, i.e., $rew(\omega) = \sum_{i=0}^\infty r(\omega_i)$. Since rew is unbounded, the results of Martin [24] do not apply to this function. In this paper we restrict ourselves to non-negative rewards, as shown in the next sections, non-negative rewards are enough to deal with interesting case studies, we briefly discuss in Sect. 7 the possible extension of the results presented here to games having negative rewards.

4   Stopping Games and Fair Strategies

We begin this section by introducing the notions of *(almost sure) fair strategy* and *stopping games under fairness*. From now on, we assume that Player 2 represents the environment, which tries to minimize the amount of rewards obtained by the system, thus fairness restrictions will be applied to this player.

Definition 1. *Given a stochastic game* $\mathcal{G} = (V, (V_1, V_2, V_{\mathsf{P}}), \delta)$. *The set of fair plays for Player 2 (denoted FP^2) is defined as follows:*

$$FP^2 = \{\omega \in Paths_{\mathcal{G}} \mid \forall v' \in V_2 : v' \in \inf(\omega) \Rightarrow post(v') \subseteq \inf(\omega)\}$$

Alternatively, if we consider each vertex as a proposition, FP^2 can be written using LTL notation as: $\bigwedge_{v \in V_2} \bigwedge_{v' \in post(v)} (\square\Diamond v \Rightarrow \square\Diamond v')$. This property is ω-regular, thus it is measurable in the σ-algebra generated by the cones of $Paths_{\mathcal{G}}$ (see e.g., [5, p.804]). This is a state-based notion of fairness, but it can be straightforwardly extended to settings where transitions are considered. For the sake of simplicity we do not do so in this paper.

Next, we introduce the notion of (almost-sure) *fair strategies* for Player 2.

Definition 2. *Given a stochastic game* $\mathcal{G} = (V, (V_1, V_2, V_{\mathsf{P}}), \delta)$, *a strategy* $\pi_2 \in \Pi_2$ *is said to be* almost-sure fair *(or simply fair) iff it holds that:* $Prob_{\mathcal{G},v}^{\pi_1,\pi_2}(FP^2) = 1$, *for every* $\pi_1 \in \Pi_1$ *and* $v \in V$.

The set of all the fair strategies for Player 2 is denoted by $\Pi_2^{\mathcal{F}}$. We combine this notation with the notation introduced in Sect. 3, e.g., $\Pi_2^{M\mathcal{F}}$ refers to the set of all memoryless and fair strategies for Player 2. The previous definition is based on the notion of fair scheduler as introduced for Markov decision processes [5,7].

Note that for stopping games, every strategy is fair, because the probability of visiting a vertex infinitely often is 0. Also notice that there are games which are not stopping, but they become stopping if Player 2 uses only fair strategies. This is the main idea behind the notion of *stopping under fairness* as introduced in the following definition.

Definition 3. *A stochastic game* $\mathcal{G} = (V, (V_1, V_2, V_{\mathsf{P}}), \delta)$ *is said to be* stopping under fairness *iff for all strategies* $\pi_1 \in \Pi_1, \pi_2 \in \Pi_2^{\mathcal{F}}$ *and vertex* $v \in V$, *it holds that* $Prob_{\mathcal{G},v}^{\pi_1,\pi_2}(\Diamond T) = 1$, *where T is the set of terminal vertices of $\mathcal{G}$.*

Checking stopping criteria. This section is devoted to the effective characterization of games that are stopping under fairness. The following lemma states that, for every game that is not stopping under fairness, there is a *memoryless deterministic* strategy for Player 1 and a fair strategy for Player 2 that witnesses it.

Lemma 1. *Let* $\mathcal{G} = (V, (V_1, V_2, V_{\mathsf{P}}), \delta)$ *be a stochastic game,* $v \in V$, *and T the set of terminal states of $\mathcal{G}$. If $Prob_{\mathcal{G},v}^{\pi_1,\pi_2}(\Diamond T) < 1$ for some $\pi_1 \in \Pi_1$ and $\pi_2 \in \Pi_2^{\mathcal{F}}$, then, for some memoryless and deterministic strategy $\pi_1' \in \Pi_1^{MD}$ and fair strategy $\pi_2' \in \Pi_2^{\mathcal{F}}$, $Prob_{\mathcal{G},v}^{\pi_1',\pi_2'}(\Diamond T) < 1$.*

The proof of this lemma follows by noticing that, if $Prob_{\mathcal{G},v}^{\pi_1,\pi_2}(\Diamond T) < 1$, there must be a finite path that leads with some probability to an end component not containing a terminal state and which is a trap for the fair strategy π_2. This part of the game enables the construction of a memoryless deterministic strategy for Player 1 by ensuring that it follows the same finite path (but skipping loops) and that it traps Player 2 in the same end component.

The next theorem states that checking stopping under fairness in a stochastic game $\mathcal{G}$ can be reduced to check the stopping criteria in a MDP, which is obtained from $\mathcal{G}$ by fixing a strategy in Player 2 that selects among the output transitions according to a uniform distribution. Thus, this theorem enables a graph solution to determine stopping under fairness.

Theorem 1. *Let $\mathcal{G} = (V, (V_1, V_2, V_\mathsf{P}), \delta)$ be a stochastic game and T its set of terminal states. Consider the Player 2 (memoryless) strategy $\pi_2^\mathsf{u} : V_2 \to \mathcal{D}(V)$ defined by $\pi_2^\mathsf{u}(v)(v') = \frac{1}{\#post(v)}$, for all $v \in V_2$ and $v' \in post(v)$. Then, $\mathcal{G}$ is stopping under fairness iff $Prob_{\mathcal{G},v}^{\pi_1,\pi_2^\mathsf{u}}(\Diamond T) = 1$ for every $v \in V$ and $\pi_1 \in \Pi_1$.*

While the "only if" part of the theorem is direct, the "if" part is proved by contraposition using Lemma 1.

Theorem 1 introduces an algorithm to check if the stochastic game $\mathcal{G}$ is stopping under fairness: transform $\mathcal{G}$ into the MDP $\mathcal{G}^{\pi_2^\mathsf{u}}$ by fixing π_2^u in $\mathcal{G}$ and check whether $Prob_{\mathcal{G}^{\pi_2^\mathsf{u}},v}^{\pi_1}(\Diamond T) = 1$ for all $v \in V$. As a consequence, we have the following theorem.

Theorem 2. *Checking whether the stochastic game $\mathcal{G}$ is stopping under fairness or not is in $O(poly(size(\mathcal{G})))$.*

Alternatively, we can use Theorem 1 to provide a direct algorithm on $\mathcal{G}$ and avoiding the construction of the intermediate MDP. The main idea is to use a modification of the standard *pre* operator, as shown in the following definition:

$$\exists Pre_f(C) = \{v \in V \mid \delta(v, C) > 0\}$$
$$\forall Pre_f(C) = \{v \in V_2 \cup V_\mathsf{P} \mid \delta(v, C) > 0\} \cup \{v \in V_1 \mid \forall v' \in V : \delta(v, v') > 0 \Rightarrow v' \in C\}$$

As usual we consider the transitive closures of these operators denoted $\exists Pre_f^*$ and $\forall Pre_f^*$, respectively.

Theorem 3. *Let $\mathcal{G} = (V, (V_1, V_2, V_\mathsf{P}), \delta)$, be a stochastic game and let T be the set of its terminal states. Then, (1) $Prob_{\mathcal{G},v}^{\pi_1,\pi_2}(\Diamond T) = 1$ for every $\pi_1 \in \Pi_1$ and $\pi_2 \in \Pi_2^\mathcal{F}$ iff $v \in V \setminus \exists Pre_f^*(V \setminus \forall Pre_f^*(T))$, and (2) $\mathcal{G}$ is stopping under fairness iff $\exists Pre_f^*(V \setminus \forall Pre_f^*(T)) = \emptyset$.*

Determinacy of Stopping Games under Fairness. The determinacy of stochastic games with Borel and bounded payoff functions follows from Martin's results [24]. The function *rew* is unbounded, so Martin's theorems do not apply to it. In [18], the determinacy of a general class of stopping stochastic games (called *transient*) with total rewards is proven. However, note that we restrict Player 2 to only play with fair strategies and hence, the last result does not apply either. In [26] the authors classify Player 2's strategies into proper (those ensuring termination) and improper (those prolonging the game indefinitely). For proving determinacy, the authors assume that the value of the game for Player 2's improper strategies is ∞. It is worth noting that, for proving the results below, we do not make any assumption about unfair strategies. In the following we prove that the restriction to fair plays does not affect the determinacy of the games.

Figure 3 shows the dependencies of the lemmas that eventually lead to our main results, namely, Theorem 4, which states that the general problem can be limited to only memoryless and deterministic strategies, and Theorem 5, which establishes determinacy and the correctness of the algorithmic solution through the Bellman equations. To prove Theorem 4 we use the intermidiate notion of *semi-Markov* strategies [18] and a first step to this reduction is presented in Lemma 2. Lemmas 3 and 4 ensure the transient carachteristics of stopping under fairness problems. They are essential to prove that every possible total reward play yields a solution (Lemma 5). Already approaching Theorem 4, Lemma 6 states that there is always a minimizing fair strategy that is memoryless and deterministic, and Lemma 7 helps to reduce the problem from the domain of semi-Markov strategies to the domain of memoryless deterministic strategies. Using Theorem 4 and Proposition 1, which states that the Bellman equations are well behaved in the lattice of solutions, Theorem 5 is finally proved.

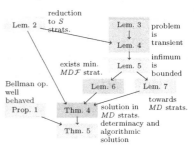

Fig. 3. A roadmap to proving Theorems 4 and 5

Intuitively, a semi-Markov strategy only takes into account the length of a play, the initial state, and the current state to select the next step in the play.

Definition 4. *Let* $\mathcal{G} = (V, (V_1, V_2, V_P), \delta)$ *be a stochastic game. A strategy* $\pi_i \in \Pi_i$ *is called semi-Markov if:* $\pi_i(v\hat{\omega}v') = \pi_i(v\hat{\omega}'v')$, *for every* $v \in V$ *and* $\hat{\omega}, \hat{\omega}' \in V^*$ *such that* $|\hat{\omega}| = |\hat{\omega}'|$.

Notice that, by fixing an initial state v, a semi-Markov strategy π_i can be thought of as a sequence of memoryless strategies $\pi_i^{0,v}\pi_i^{1,v}\pi_i^{2,v}\ldots$ where $\pi_i(v) = \pi_i^{0,v}(v)$ and $\pi_i(v\hat{\omega}v') = \pi_i^{|\hat{\omega}|+1,v}(v')$. The set of all semi-Markov (resp. semi-Markov fair) strategies for player i is denoted Π_i^S (resp. Π_i^{SF}).

The importance of semi-Markov strategies lies in the fact that, when Player 2 plays a semi-Markov strategy, any Player 1's strategy can be mimicked by a semi-Markov strategy as stated in the following lemma.

Lemma 2. *Let* $\mathcal{G}$ *be a stopping under fairness stochastic game, and let* $\pi_2 \in \Pi_2^{SF}$ *be a fair and semi-Markov strategy. Then, for any* $\pi_1 \in \Pi_1$, *there is a semi-Markov strategy* $\pi_1^* \in \Pi_1^S$ *such that* $\mathbb{E}_{\mathcal{G},v}^{\pi_1,\pi_2}[rew] = \mathbb{E}_{\mathcal{G},v}^{\pi_1^*,\pi_2}[rew]$.

Proof (Sketch). The proof follows the arguments of Theorem 4.2.7 in [18] adapted to our setting.

Consider the event $\Diamond^k v' = \{\omega \in Paths_{\mathcal{G}} \mid \omega_k = v'\}$, for $k \geq 0$. That is, the set of runs in which v' is reached after exactly k steps. We define π_1^* as follows. For v' with $Prob_{\mathcal{G},v}^{\pi_1,\pi_2}(\Diamond^k v') > 0$ and $|\hat{\omega}v'| = k$,

$$\pi_1^*(\hat{\omega}v')(v'') = Prob_{\mathcal{G},v}^{\pi_1,\pi_2}(\Diamond^{k+1}v'' \mid \Diamond^k v').$$

For v' with $Prob_{\mathcal{G},v}^{\pi_1,\pi_2}(\Diamond^k v') = 0$ and $|\hat{\omega}v'| = k$ we define $\pi_1^*(\hat{\omega}v')$ to be the uniform distribution on $post(v')$. Notice that π_1^* is a semi-Markov strategy. We prove that π_1^* is the strategy that satisfies the conclusion of the lemma. For this, we first show that $Prob_{\mathcal{G},v}^{\pi_1,\pi_2}(\Diamond^k v') = Prob_{\mathcal{G},v}^{\pi_1^*,\pi_2}(\Diamond^k v')$ by induction on k, and use it to conclude the following.

$$\mathbb{E}_{\mathcal{G},v}^{\pi_1,\pi_2}[rew] = \sum_{N=0}^{\infty} \sum_{\hat{\omega} \in V^{N+1}} Prob_{\mathcal{G},v}^{\pi_1,\pi_2}(\hat{\omega})r(\hat{\omega}_N) = \sum_{N=0}^{\infty} \sum_{v' \in V} Prob_{\mathcal{G},v}^{\pi_1,\pi_2}(\Diamond^N v')r(v')$$

$$= \sum_{N=1}^{\infty} \sum_{v' \in V} Prob_{\mathcal{G},v}^{\pi_1^*,\pi_2}(\Diamond^N v')r(v') = \mathbb{E}_{\mathcal{G},v}^{\pi_1^*,\pi_2}[rew] \qquad \square$$

In a stopping game, all non-terminal states are transient (a state is transient if the expected time that both players spend in it is finite). In fact, [18] defines a stopping game with terminal states in T as a *transient game*, i.e., a game in which $\sum_{N=1}^{\infty} \sum_{\hat{\omega} \in (V \backslash T)^N} Prob_{\mathcal{G},v}^{\pi_1,\pi_2}(\hat{\omega}) < \infty$ for all strategies $\pi_1 \in \Pi_1$ and $\pi_2 \in \Pi_2$. Obviously, this generality does not hold in our case since unfair strategies make the game dwell infinitely on a set of non-terminal states. Therefore, we prove a weaker property in our setting. Roughly speaking, the next lemma states that, in games that stop under fairness, non-terminal states are transient, provided that the two players play memoryless strategies, and in particular, that Player 2 plays only fair.

Lemma 3. *Let* $\mathcal{G} = (V, (V_1, V_2, V_P), \delta)$ *be a stochastic game that is stopping under fairness with* T *being the set of terminal states. Let* $\pi_1 \in \Pi_1^M$ *be a memoryless strategy for Player 1 and* $\pi_2 \in \Pi_2^{MF}$ *a memoryless fair strategy for Player 2. Then* $\sum_{N=1}^{\infty} \sum_{\hat{\omega} \in (V \backslash T)^N} Prob_{\mathcal{G},v}^{\pi_1,\pi_2}(\hat{\omega}) < \infty$.

This result can be extended to all the strategies of Player 1. The main idea behind the proof is to fix a stationary fair strategy for Player 2 (e.g., a uniform distributed strategy). This yields an MDP that stops for every strategy of Player 1, and furthermore, it can be seen as a one-player *transient game* (as defined in [18]). Hence, the result follows from Lemma 3 and Theorem 4.2.12 in [18].

Lemma 4. *Let* $\mathcal{G}$ *be a stochastic game that is stopping under fairness and let* T *be the set of terminal states. In addition, let* $\pi_1 \in \Pi_1$ *be a strategy for Player 1 and* $\pi_2 \in \Pi_2^{MF}$ *be a fair and memoryless strategy for Player 2. Then* $\sum_{N=0}^{\infty} \sum_{\hat{\omega} \in v(V \backslash T)^N} Prob_{\mathcal{G},v}^{\pi_1,\pi_2}(\hat{\omega}) < \infty$.

Using the previous lemma, some fairly simple calculations lead to the fact that the value of the total accumulated reward payoff game is well-defined for any strategy of the players. As a consequence, the value of the game is bounded from above for any Player 1's strategy. This is stated in the next lemma.

Lemma 5. *Let* $\mathcal{G} = (V, (V_1, V_2, V_P), \delta, r)$ *be a stochastic game that is stopping under fairness,* $\pi_1 \in \Pi_1$ *a strategy for Player 1. Then, for all memoryless fair strategy* $\pi_2 \in \Pi_2^{M\mathcal{F}}$ *for Player 2 and all* $v \in V$, $\mathbb{E}_{\mathcal{G},v}^{\pi_1,\pi_2}[rew] < \infty$. *Moreover, for every vertex* $v \in V$, $\inf_{\pi_2 \in \Pi_2^{\mathcal{F}}} \mathbb{E}_{\mathcal{G},v}^{\pi_1,\pi_2}[rew] < \infty$.

The following lemma is crucial and plays an important role in the rest of the paper. Intuitively, it states that, when Player 1 plays with a memoryless strategy, Player 2 has an optimal deterministic memoryless fair strategy. This lemma is the guarantee of the eventual existence of a minimizing memoryless deterministic fair strategy for Player 2 in general.

Lemma 6. *Let* $\mathcal{G} = (V, (V_1, V_2, V_P), \delta, r)$ *be a stochastic game that is stopping under fairness and let* $\pi_1 \in \Pi_1^M$ *be a memoryless strategy for Player 1. There exists a deterministic memoryless fair strategy* $\pi_2^* \in \Pi_2^{MD\mathcal{F}}$ *such that* $\inf_{\pi_2 \in \Pi_2^{\mathcal{F}}} \mathbb{E}_{\mathcal{G},v}^{\pi_1,\pi_2}[rew] = \mathbb{E}_{\mathcal{G},v}^{\pi_1,\pi_2^*}[rew]$, *for every* $v \in V$.

Proof (Sketch). Though it differs in the details, the proof strategy is inspired by the proof of Lemma 10.102 in [5]. We first construct a reduced MDP $\mathcal{G}_{\min}^{\pi_1}$ which preserves exactly the optimizing part of the MDP $\mathcal{G}^{\pi_1}$. Thus $\delta_{\min}^{\pi_1}(v,v') = \delta^{\pi_1}(v,v')$ if $v \in V_1 \cup V_P$, or $v \in V_2$ and $x_v = r(v) + x_{v'}$, where, for every $v \in V$, $x_v = \inf_{\pi_2 \in \Pi_2^{\mathcal{F}}} \mathbb{E}_{\mathcal{G},v}^{\pi_1,\pi_2}[rew]$ (which exists due to Lemma 5). Otherwise, $\delta_{\min}^{\pi_1}(v,v') = 0$. $\mathcal{G}_{\min}^{\pi_1}$ can be proved to be stopping under fairness.

Then, the strategy π_2^* for $\mathcal{G}_{\min}^{\pi_1}$ is constructed as follows. For every $v \in V$, let $\|v\|$ be the length of the shortest path fragment to some terminal vertex in T in the MDP $\mathcal{G}_{\min}^{\pi_1}$. Define $\pi_2^*(v)(v') = 1$ for some v' such that $\delta_{\min}^{\pi_1}(v,v') = 1$ and $\|v\| = \|v'\| + 1$. By definition, π_2^* is memoryless. We prove first that π_2^* yields the optimal solution of $\mathcal{G}^{\pi_1}$ by showing that the vector $(x_v)_{v \in V}$ (i.e., the optimal values of $\mathcal{G}^{\pi_1}$) is a solution to the set of equations for expected rewards of the Markov chain $\mathcal{G}^{\pi_1,\pi_2^*}$. Being the solution unique, we have that $x_v = \mathbb{E}_{\mathcal{G}^{\pi_1,\pi_2^*},v}[rew]$ for all $v \in V$ and hence the optimality of π_2^*. To conclude the proof we show by contradiction that π_2^* is fair.   □

As already noted, semi-Markov strategies can be thought of as sequences of memoryless strategies. The next lemma uses this fact to show that, when Player 2 plays a memoryless and fair strategy, semi-Markov strategies do not improve the value that Player 1 can obtain via memoryless deterministic strategies. The proof of the following lemma adapts the ideas of Theorem 4.2.9 in [18] to our games.

Lemma 7. *For any stochastic game* $\mathcal{G}$ *that is stopping under fairness, and vertex* v, *it holds that:*

$$\sup_{\pi_1 \in \Pi_1^S} \inf_{\pi_2 \in \Pi_2^{MD\mathcal{F}}} \mathbb{E}_{\mathcal{G},v}^{\pi_1,\pi_2}[rew] = \sup_{\pi_1 \in \Pi_1^{MD}} \inf_{\pi_2 \in \Pi_2^{MD\mathcal{F}}} \mathbb{E}_{\mathcal{G},v}^{\pi_1,\pi_2}[rew]$$

Using the previous lemma, we can conclude that the problem of finding $\sup_{\pi_1 \in \Pi_1} \inf_{\pi_2 \in \Pi_2^{\mathcal{F}}} \mathbb{E}^{\pi_1,\pi_2}[rew]$, for any vertex v, can be solve by only focusing on deterministic memoryless strategies as stated and proved in the following theorem.

Theorem 4. *For any stochastic game $\mathcal{G}$ that is stopping under fairness we have:*

$$\sup_{\pi_1 \in \Pi_1} \inf_{\pi_2 \in \Pi_2^{\mathcal{F}}} \mathbb{E}_{\mathcal{G},v}^{\pi_1,\pi_2}[rew] = \sup_{\pi_1 \in \Pi_1^{MD}} \inf_{\pi_2 \in \Pi_2^{MD\mathcal{F}}} \mathbb{E}_{\mathcal{G},v}^{\pi_1,\pi_2}[rew]$$

Proof. First, we prove that the left-hand term is less than or equal to the right-hand one:

$$\sup_{\pi_1 \in \Pi_1} \inf_{\pi_2 \in \Pi_2^{\mathcal{F}}} \mathbb{E}_{\mathcal{G},v}^{\pi_1,\pi_2}[rew] \leq \sup_{\pi_1 \in \Pi_1} \inf_{\pi_2 \in \Pi_2^{MD\mathcal{F}}} \mathbb{E}_{\mathcal{G},v}^{\pi_1,\pi_2}[rew]$$

$$\leq \sup_{\pi_1 \in \Pi_1^{S}} \inf_{\pi_2 \in \Pi_2^{MD\mathcal{F}}} \mathbb{E}_{\mathcal{G},v}^{\pi_1,\pi_2}[rew]$$

$$\leq \sup_{\pi_1 \in \Pi_1^{MD}} \inf_{\pi_2 \in \Pi_2^{MD\mathcal{F}}} \mathbb{E}_{\mathcal{G},v}^{\pi_1,\pi_2}[rew].$$

The first inequality follows from $\Pi_2^{MD\mathcal{F}} \subseteq \Pi_2^{\mathcal{F}}$, the second inequality is due to Lemma 2 and the fact that memoryless strategies are semi-Markov, and the last inequality is obtained by applying Lemma 7.

To prove the other inequality, we calculate:

$$\sup_{\pi_1 \in \Pi_1^{MD}} \inf_{\pi_2 \in \Pi_2^{MD\mathcal{F}}} \mathbb{E}_{\mathcal{G},v}^{\pi_1,\pi_2}[rew] = \sup_{\pi_1 \in \Pi_1^{MD}} \inf_{\pi_2 \in \Pi_2^{\mathcal{F}}} \mathbb{E}_{\mathcal{G},v}^{\pi_1,\pi_2}[rew]$$

$$\leq \sup_{\pi_1 \in \Pi_1} \inf_{\pi_2 \in \Pi_2^{\mathcal{F}}} \mathbb{E}_{\mathcal{G},v}^{\pi_1,\pi_2}[rew].$$

The first equality is a consequence of Lemma 6 and the second inequality is due to properties of suprema. $\square$

The standard technique to prove the determinacy of stopping games is by showing that the Bellman operator

$$\Gamma(f)(v) = \begin{cases} r(v) + \sum_{v' \in post(v)} \delta(v,v')f(v') & \text{if } v \in V_{\mathsf{P}} \setminus T \\ \max\{r(v) + f(v') \mid v' \in post(v)\} & \text{if } v \in V_1 \setminus T, \\ \min\{r(v) + f(v') \mid v' \in post(v)\} & \text{if } v \in V_2 \setminus T, \\ 0 & \text{if } v \in T. \end{cases}$$

has a unique fixpoint. However, in the case of games stopping under fairness, Γ has several fixpoints as shown by the next example.

Example 1. Consider the (one-player) game in Fig. 4, where Player 1's vertices are drawn as boxes, Player 2's vertices are drawn as diamonds, and probabilistic vertices are depicted as circles. Note that, in that game, the greatest fixpoint is $(1,1,1,0)$. Yet, $(0.5,0.5,1,0)$ is also a

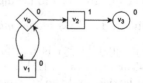

Fig. 4. A game with infinite fixpoints

fixpoint as $\Gamma(0.5, 0.5, 1, 0) = (0.5, 0.5, 1, 0)$. In fact, the Bellman operator for this game has infinite fixpoints: any f of the form $(x, x, 1, 0)$ with $x \in [0, 1]$.

Thus, the standard approach cannot be used here. Instead, we use the greatest fixpoint for proving determinacy, but this cannot be done directly on Γ. A main difficulty is that the Knaster-Tarski theorem does not apply for Γ since $(\mathbb{R}^V, \leq)$ is not a complete lattice. Using instead the extended reals $((\mathbb{R} \cup \{\infty\})^V)$ is not a solution, as in some cases the greatest fixpoint will assign ∞ to some vertices (e.g., $(\infty, \infty, 0)$ would be the greatest fixpoint in the Markov chain of Fig. 5). One possible approach is to approximate the greatest fixpoint from an estimated upper bound via value iteration. Unfortunately, there may not be an order relation between f and $\Gamma(f)$ and it may turn out that for some vertex v, $\Gamma(f)(v) > f(v)$ before converging to the fixpoint. This is shown in the next example.

Example 2. Consider the game depicted in Fig. 5. The (unique) fixpoint in this case is $(100, 90, 0)$. Observe that, we have that $\Gamma(120, 100, 0) = (110, 108, 0)$, thus the value at v_1 increases after one iteration. Several iterations are needed then to reach the greatest fixpoint. Thus, in general, starting value iteration from an estimated upper bound does not guarantee a monotone convergence to the greatest fixpoint.

We overcome the aforementioned issues by using a modified version of Γ. Roughly speaking, we modify the Bellman operator in such a way that it operates over a complete lattice.

Fig. 5. A game where value iteration may go up

Notice that, by Lemma 5, the value $\mathbb{E}_{\mathcal{G}, v}^{\pi_1, \pi_2}[rew]$ is finite for every stopping game under fairness $\mathcal{G}$ and strategies $\pi_1 \in \Pi_1^{MD}$, $\pi_2 \in \Pi_2^{MD\mathcal{F}}$. Furthermore, because the number of deterministic memoryless strategies is finite, we also have that the number $\max\{\inf_{\pi_2 \in \Pi_2^{MD}} \sup_{\pi_1 \in \Pi_1^{MD}} \mathbb{E}_{\mathcal{G}, v}^{\pi_1, \pi_2}[rew] \mid v \in V\}$ is well defined. From now on, fix a number $\mathbf{U} \geq \max\{\inf_{\pi_2 \in \Pi_2^{MD\mathcal{F}}} \sup_{\pi_1 \in \Pi_1^{MD}} \mathbb{E}_{\mathcal{G}, v}^{\pi_1, \pi_2}[rew] \mid v \in V\}$. We define a modified Bellman operator $\Gamma^* : [0, \mathbf{U}]^V \to [0, \mathbf{U}]^V$ as follows.

$$
\Gamma^*(f)(v) = \begin{cases}
\min\left(r(v) + \sum_{v' \in post(v)} \delta(v, v') f(v'), \ \mathbf{U}\right) & \text{if } v \in V_\mathsf{P} \setminus T \\
\min\left(\max\{r(v) + f(v') \mid v' \in post(v)\}, \ \mathbf{U}\right) & \text{if } v \in V_1 \setminus T, \\
\min\left(\min\{r(v) + f(v') \mid v' \in post(v)\}, \ \mathbf{U}\right) & \text{if } v \in V_2 \setminus T, \\
0 & \text{if } v \in T.
\end{cases}
$$

Note that Γ^* is monotone, which can be proven by observing that maxima, minima and convex combinations are all monotone operators. Furthermore, Γ^* is also Scott continuous (it preserves suprema of directed sets), this can be proven similarly as in [10]. The following proposition formalizes these properties.

Proposition 1. Γ^* *is monotone and Scott-continuous.*

Note that $([0, \mathbf{U}]^V, \leq)$ is a complete lattice. Thus by Proposition 1 and the Knaster-Tarski theorem [15], the (non-empty) set of fixed points of Γ^* forms a complete lattice, and the greatest fixpoint of the operator can be approximated by successive applications of Γ^* to the top element (i.e., $\mathbf{U}$) [15]. In the following we denote by $\nu\Gamma^*$ the greatest fixed point of Γ^*.

The following theorem states that games restricted to fair strategies on Player 2 are determinate. Furthermore, the value of the game is given by the greatest fixpoint of Γ^*.

Theorem 5. *Let $\mathcal{G}$ be a stochastic game that is stopping under fairness. It holds that:*

$$\inf_{\pi_2 \in \Pi_2^{\mathcal{F}}} \sup_{\pi_1 \in \Pi_1} \mathbb{E}_{\mathcal{G},v}^{\pi_1,\pi_2}[rew] = \sup_{\pi_1 \in \Pi_1} \inf_{\pi_2 \in \Pi_2^{\mathcal{F}}} \mathbb{E}_{\mathcal{G},v}^{\pi_1,\pi_2}[rew] = \nu\Gamma^*(v)$$

Proof. First, note that $\inf_{\pi_2 \in \Pi_2^{MD\mathcal{F}}} \sup_{\pi_1 \in \Pi_1^{MD}} \mathbb{E}_{\mathcal{G},v}^{\pi_1,\pi_2}[rew]$ is a fixed point of Γ^*. Thus we have:

$$\sup_{\pi_1 \in \Pi_1} \inf_{\pi_2 \in \Pi_2^{\mathcal{F}}} \mathbb{E}_{\mathcal{G},v}^{\pi_1,\pi_2}[rew] \leq \inf_{\pi_2 \in \Pi_2^{\mathcal{F}}} \sup_{\pi_1 \in \Pi_1} \mathbb{E}_{\mathcal{G},v}^{\pi_1,\pi_2}[rew]$$

$$\leq \inf_{\pi_2 \in \Pi_2^{MD\mathcal{F}}} \sup_{\pi_1 \in \Pi_1^{MD}} \mathbb{E}_{\mathcal{G},v}^{\pi_1,\pi_2}[rew] \leq \nu\Gamma^*(v)$$

for any v. The first inequality is a standard property of suprema and infima [21], the second inequality holds because $\Pi_2^{MD\mathcal{F}} \subseteq \Pi_2^{\mathcal{F}}$ and standard properties of MDPs: by fixing a deterministic memoryless fair strategy for Player 2 we obtain a transient MDP, the optimal strategy for Player 1 in this MDP is obtained via a deterministic memoryless strategy [20]. The last inequality holds because $\inf_{\pi_2 \in \Pi_2^{MD\mathcal{F}}} \sup_{\pi_1 \in \Pi_1^{MD}} \mathbb{E}_{\mathcal{G},v}^{\pi_1,\pi_2}[rew]$ is a fixpoint of Γ^*.

Rest to prove that $\sup_{\pi_1 \in \Pi_1} \inf_{\pi_2 \in \Pi_2^{\mathcal{F}}} \mathbb{E}_{\mathcal{G},v}^{\pi_1,\pi_2}[rew] \geq \nu\Gamma^*(v)$. Note that, if there is $\pi_1 \in \Pi_1$ such that $\inf_{\pi_2 \in \Pi_2^{\mathcal{F}}} \mathbb{E}_{\mathcal{G},v}^{\pi_1,\pi_2}[rew] \geq \nu\Gamma^*(v)$ the property above follows by properties of supremum. Consider the strategy π_1^* defined as follows: $\pi_1^*(v) \in \text{argmax}\{\nu\Gamma^*(v') + r(v) \mid v' \in post(v)\}$. Note that π_1^* is a memoryless and deterministic strategy. For any memoryless, deterministic and fair strategy $\pi_2 \in \Pi_2^{MD\mathcal{F}}$ we have $\nu\Gamma^*(v) \leq \mathbb{E}_{\mathcal{G},v}^{\pi_1^*,\pi_2}[rew]$ (by definition of Γ^*). Thus, $\nu\Gamma^*(v) \leq \inf_{\pi_2 \in \Pi_2^{MD\mathcal{F}}} \mathbb{E}_{\mathcal{G},v}^{\pi_1^*,\pi_2}[rew]$ and then: $\nu\Gamma^*(v) \leq \sup_{\pi_1 \in \Pi_1^{MD}} \inf_{\pi_2 \in \Pi_2^{MD\mathcal{F}}} \mathbb{E}_{\mathcal{G},v}^{\pi_1,\pi_2}[rew]$. Finally, by Theorem 4 we get: $\nu\Gamma^*(v) \leq \sup_{\pi_1 \in \Pi_1} \inf_{\pi_2 \in \Pi_2^{\mathcal{F}}} \mathbb{E}_{\mathcal{G},v}^{\pi_1,\pi_2}[rew]$. □

Considerations for an algorithmic solution. Value iteration [9] has been used to compute maximum/minimum expected accumulated reward in MDPs, e.g., in the PRISM model checker. Usually, the value is computed by approximating the least fixpoint from below using the Bellman equations [9]. In [6], the authors propose to approach these values from both a lower and an upper bound (known as interval iteration [19]). To do so, [6] shows a technique for computing upper bounds for the expected total rewards for MDPs. This approach is based on the fact that, given a stopping MDP $\mathcal{G}$, $\mathbb{E}_{\mathcal{G},v}^{\pi_1}[rew] = \sum_{v' \in R(v)} \zeta_v^{\pi_1}(v') * r(v')$, where $R(v)$ denotes the set of reachable states from v, and $\zeta_v^{\pi_1}(v')$ denotes the expected number of times to visit v' in the Markov chain induced by π_1 when starting at v. [6] describes how to compute a value $\zeta_v^*(v')$, such that $\zeta_v^*(v') \geq \sup_{\pi_1 \in \Pi_1} \zeta_v^{\pi_1}(v')$. Thus, $\sum_{v' \in R(v)} \zeta_v^*(v') * r(v')$ gives an upper bound for $\sup_{\pi_1} \mathbb{E}_{\mathcal{G},v}^{\pi_1}[rew]$. Our algorithm uses these ideas to provide an upper bound for two-player games. Roughly speaking, the above defined functional Γ^* presents a form of Bellman equations that enables a value iteration algorithm to solve these games. We need to start with some value vector larger than such a fixpoint. Given a stopping under fairness game, we fix a (memoryless) fair strategy for the environment, thus obtaining an MDP. We then use the techniques described above to find an upper bound for this MDP, which in turn is an upper bound in the original game. The obvious fair strategy to use is the one based on the uniform distribution (as in Theorem 1). This idea is described in Algorithm 1. It is worth noting that, instead of using a unique upper bound for every vertex (as in the definition of Γ^*), the algorithm may use a different upper bound for each component of the value vector, this improves the number of iterations performed by the algorithm. We have implemented Algorithm 1 as a prototype embedded in the PRISM-games toolset [22], as described in the next section.

Algorithm 1 Algorithm for computing GFP

Require: $\mathcal{G}$ is a stopping under fairness game

$\delta' \leftarrow \lambda(v, v').(v \in V_1 \cup V_{\mathsf{P}}) ? \delta(v, v') : \frac{1}{|post^{\mathcal{G}}(v)|}$

$\mathcal{G}' \leftarrow (V, (V_1, \emptyset, V_2 \cup V_{\mathsf{P}})), \delta')$

$x' \leftarrow \lambda v : \sum_{v' \in R(v)} : \zeta_v^*(v') * r(v')$

repeat

    $x \leftarrow x'$

    $x' \leftarrow \Gamma^*(x)$

until $||x - x'|| \leq \varepsilon$

return x'

---

5   Experimental Validation

In order to evaluate the viability of our approach we have extended the model checker PRISM [22,23] with an operator to compute the expected rewards for stochastic games that stop under fairness. The prototype also allows one to check whether a game is stopping under fairness. The tool takes as input a model describing the game in PRISM notation and returns as output the optimal expected total reward for a given initial state as well as the synthesized optimal controller strategy (under fairness assumptions). The experimental evaluation shows that our approach can cope with non-trivial case studies. For computing these values we set a relative error of at most $\varepsilon = 10^{-6}$.

Roborta vs. the Fair Light. Table 1 shows the results of the example introduced in Sect. 2 for multiple configurations. We considered three variants of the case study: version A (the light does not fail), version B (the light can only fail when trying to signal a green light), and version C (the light can fail when trying to signal any kind of light). We assumed that, when Roborta fails, she cannot move (this is beneficial to Roborta since she can re-collect the reward); when the light fails, the robot can freely move into any allowed direction. The grid configuration (movement restrictions and rewards) are randomly generated. For each setting, Table 1 describes the results for three different scenarios generated starting at different seeds. For the grid configuration shown in Sect. 2 with parameters $P = 0.1$ and $Q = 0$, the tool derived the optimal strategy depicted in Fig. 2 and reports an expected total reward of 5.55.

Autonomous UAV vs. Human Operator. We adapted the case study analyzed in [17]. A remotely controlled Unmanned Aerial Vehicle (UAV) is used to perform intelligence, surveillance, and reconnaissance (ISR) missions over a road network. The UAV performs piloting functions autonomously (selecting a path to fly between *waypoints*). The human operator (environment) controls the onboard sensor to capture imagery at a waypoint as well as the piloting functions on certain waypoints (called checkpoints). Note that an operator can continuously try to get a better image by making the UAV loiter around a certain waypoint, this may lead to an unfair behavior. Each successful capture from an unvisited waypoint grants a reward. Figure 6 shows an example of road network consisting of six surveillance waypoints labeled $w_0, w_2, ..., w_5$, the edges represent connecting paths, a red-dashed line means that the path is dangerous enough to make the

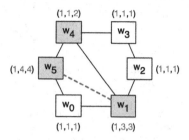

Fig. 6. UAV Network for ISR missions adapted from [17]

UAV stop working with probability 1, while on any other path, this probability is S. Checkpoints are depicted as pink nodes, therein the operator can still delegate the piloting task to the UAV with probability D. Each node is annotated with three possible rewards. For instance, for $S = 0.3$ and $D = 0.5$ and the leftmost reward values in each triple, the synthesized strategy for the UAV tries to follow the optimal circuit $w_0, w_1, w_2, w_3, w_4, w_5$. While for the middle and rightmost reward values, the optimal circuits to follow are $w_0, w_5, w_0, w_1, w_2, w_3, w_4$ and $w_0, w_5, w_4, w_1, w_2, w_3$, respectively. Table 2 shows the results obtained for this game for several randomly generated road networks.

Tables 1 and 2 do not report the time taken to compute the results, but in all cases the output was computed in less than 400 s. All the experiments were run on a MacBook Air with Intel Core i5 at 1.3 GHz and 4 Gb of RAM.

6   Related Work

Stochastic games with payoff functions have been extensively investigated in the literature. In [18], several results are presented about *transient games*, a generalized version of stopping stochastic games with total reward payoff. In transient games, both players possess optimal (memoryless and deterministic) strategies. Most importantly, the games are determined and their value can be computed as the least fixed point of a set of equations. Most of these results are based on the fact that the Γ functional (see Sect. 4) for transient games has a unique fixed point. Notice that in this paper we have dealt with games that are stopping only under fairness assumptions. Thus, the corresponding functional may have several fixed points. Hence, the main results presented in [18] do not apply to our setting.

[12] and [28] present logical frameworks for the verification and synthesis of systems. While [12] provides a solution for a probabilistic branching temporal

Table 1. Results for Roborta vs. Light Game. First column describes the grid size. Second column indicates the fault probability for the robot (P) and light (Q). The other columns describe the size of the model, the expected total reward for the optimal strategy, and the number of iterations performed, respectively, for three different randomly generated grid configurations.

Version	Fault prob.		Size (States/Transitions)			Opt. Expect. Total Rew.			Iterations		
	P	Q	s. 1	s. 2	s. 3	s. 1	s. 2	s. 3	s. 1	s. 2	s. 3
A	0.1	–	st. 1448	st. 1418	st. 1421	26.66	31.11	27.77	711	681	252
60×8	0.5	–	tr. 3220	tr. 3112	tr. 3132	48	56	50	2253	2225	475
A	0.1	–	st. 5686	st. 5716	st. 5716	62.22	55.55	48.88	687	700	685
120×16	0.5	–	tr. 12586	tr. 12658	tr. 12722	112	100	88	2231	2265	2229
	0.1	0.1				42.6	44.59	42.23	479	335	388
B		0.5	st. 1928	st. 1888	st. 1892	130.14	127.7	136.22	772	689	824
60×8	0.5	0.1	tr. 5952	tr. 5746	tr. 5785	76.68	80.26	76.02	873	764	909
		0.5				234.26	229.87	245.21	1263	1139	1341
	0.1	0.1				91.19	87.27	80.07	538	544	616
B		0.5	st. 7576	st. 7616	st. 7616	281.83	281.48	265.33	1076	1118	1252
120×16	0.5	0.1	tr. 23266	tr. 23400	tr. 23528	164.15	157.1	144.13	1147	1223	1373
		0.5				507.30	506.67	477.6	1850	1865	2088
	0.1	0.1				46.32	47.07	44.87	379	336	390
C		0.5	st. 1928	st. 1888	st. 1892	143.35	146.41	153.98	742	658	774
60×8	0.5	0.1	tr. 6432	tr. 6216	tr. 6256	83.37	84.73	80.77	879	769	914
		0.5				258.04	263.53	277.17	1202	1076	1246
	0.1	0.1				98.25	93.74	88.33	533	544	606
C		0.5	st. 7576	st. 7616	st. 7616	321.18	317.61	311.62	1002	1068	1188
120×16	0.5	0.1	tr. 25156	tr. 25300	tr. 25428	176.85	168.73	158.99	1147	1227	1365
		0.5				578.13	571.71	560.92	1700	1760	1956

Table 2. Results for the UAV vs. Operator Game. First column describes the number of waypoints used. Second column indicates probability of delegation (D), and the probability that the UAV stops working (S). The other columns show the size of the model, the expected total reward for the optimal strategy, and the number of iterations performed, respectively, for three different randomly generated roadmap configurations.

Version	Prob.		Size(States/Transitions)			Opt. Expect. Total Rew.			Iterations		
	D	S	s. 1	s. 2	s. 3	s. 1	s. 2	s. 3	s. 1	s. 2	s. 3
	0.1	0.05				16.72	12.47	13.14	142	248	22
UAV		0.1	st. 213	st. 508	st. 136	15.73	11.15	12.63	73	188	22
6w.	0.5	0.05	tr. 504	tr. 1368	tr. 312	20.49	12.77	17.05	103	133	22
		0.1				18.87	11.67	15.95	55	70	22
	0.1	0.05				17.88	40.59	24.6	407	332	779
UAV		0.1	st. 2177	st. 3591	st. 1426	17.11	34.3	21.48	280	233	437
8w.	0.5	0.05	tr. 5959	tr. 9991	tr. 3604	26	42.21	30.87	128	214	257
		0.1				23.44	36.08	24.72	116	113	194
	0.1	0.05				39.76	28.7	19.76	256	377	356
UAV		0.1	st. 6631	st. 5072	st. 8272	35.43	23.36	16.2	136	260	154
10w.	0.5	0.05	tr. 17306	tr. 13052	tr. 24376	42.13	30.77	24.56	250	247	292
		0.1				37.11	26.08	19.27	130	134	151

logic extended with expected total, discounted, and average reward objective functions, [28] does the same in a similar extension of a probabilistic linear temporal logic. Both frameworks were implemented in the tool PRISM [22,23]. Although a vast class of properties can be expressed in these frameworks, none of them are presented under fair environments. In fact, these works are on stochastic multiplayer games in which each player is treated equally.

However, of all the operators in [12,22,28], $\langle\langle p_1\rangle\rangle$ $R_{\max=?}[F^\infty T]$ is the closest to our proposal and it deserves a deeper comparison. $\langle\langle p_1\rangle\rangle$ $R_{\max=?}[F^\infty T]$ returns the expected accumulated reward until reaching T in which infinite plays receive an infinite value [12,22]. PRISM approximates this value by computing a greatest fixpoint. It uses a two-phase algorithm to do so: (i) it first replaces zero rewards with a small positive value and applies value iteration on this modification to get an estimated upper bound, and (ii) this upper bound is used to start another value iteration process aimed to compute the greatest fixpoint.

This heuristic could return erroneous approximations of the greatest fixpoint. We illustrate this with a simple example. Consider the game depicted in Fig. 7, For any p, the value of the greatest fixpoint in vertex v_0 is 2. However, by taking p = 0.99 and tolerance $\epsilon = 10^{-6}$, PRISM returns a value close to 39608. This occurs because PRISM changes 0 to

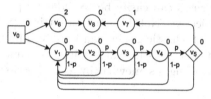

Fig. 7. A simple two-player game: only probability less than 1 are shown

the value 0.02, which results in an extremely large upper bound. Obviously, it also returns an incorrect strategy for vertex v_0. We have checked this example with our tool, and it returned the correct value for vertex v_0 in 2 iterations, regardless of the value of p. We have chosen a large value for p to make the difference noticeable. Small values also may produce different values in, e.g., v_1 only that it could be blamed on approximation errors. We have also run this operator on our case studies and observed small differences in many of them (particularly on Roborta) that get larger when the fault probabilities get larger as well.

Stochastic shortest path games [26] are two-player stochastic games with (negative or positive) rewards in which the minimizer's strategies are classified into *proper* and *improper*, proper strategies are those ensuring termination. As proven in [26], these games are determined, and both players posses memoryless optimal strategies. To prove these results, the authors assume that the expected game value for improper strategies is ∞, this ensures that the corresponding functional is a contraction and thus it has a unique fixpoint. In contrast, we restrict ourselves to non-negative rewards but we do not make any assumptions over unfair strategies, as mentioned above the corresponding functional for our games may have several fixpoints. Furthermore, we proved that the value of the game is given by the greatest fixpoint of Γ. In recent years, several authors have investigated stochastic shortest path problems for MDPs (i.e., one-player games), where the assumption over improper strategies is relaxed (e.g., [3]); to the best of our knowledge, these results have not be extended to two-player games.

In [4] the authors tackle the problem of synthesizing a controller that maximizes the probability of satisfying an LTL property. Fairness strategies are used to reduce this problem to the synthesis of a controller maximizing a PCTL property over a product game. However, this article does not address expected rewards and game determinacy under fairness assumptions.

Interestingly, in [2] the authors consider the problem of winning a (non-stochastic) two-player games with fairness assumptions over the environment. The objective of the system is to guarantee an ω-regular property. The authors show that winning in these games is equivalent to almost-sure winning in a Markov decision process. It must be noted that this work only considers non-stochastic games. Furthermore, payoff functions are not considered therein.

Finally, we remark that in *qualitative* ω-regular stochastic games [1] strong fairness can easily be consider by properly transforming the original ω-regular objective. Notably, in this setting, [8] shows that qualitative Rabin conditions on stochastic games can be solved by translating this problem into a two-player (non-stochastic) game with the same Rabin condition under extreme fairness following a somewhat inverse direction to that we used to prove Theorem 2.

7   Concluding Remarks

In this paper, we have investigated the properties of stochastic games with total reward payoff under the assumption that the minimizer (i.e., the environment) plays only with fair strategies. We have shown that, in this scenario, determinacy is preserved and both players have optimal memoryless and deterministic strategies; furthermore, the value of the game can be calculated by approximating a greatest fixed point of a Bellman operator. We have only considered non-negative rewards in this paper. A possible way of extending the results presented here to games with negative rewards is to adapt the techniques presented in [3] for MDPs with negative costs, we leave this as a further work.

In order to show the applicability of our technique, we have presented two examples of applications and an experimental validation over diverse instances of these case studies using our prototype tool. We believe that fairness assumptions allow one to consider more realistic behavior of the environment.

We have not investigated other common payoff functions such as discounted payoff or limiting-average payoff. A benefit of these classes of functions is that the value of games are well-defined even when the games are not stopping. At first sight, the notion of fairness is little relevant for games with discounted payoff, since these kinds of payoff functions take most of their value from the initial parts of runs. For limiting-average the situation is different, and fairness assumptions may be relevant as they could change the value of games, we leave this as further work.

References

1. de Alfaro, L., Henzinger, T.A.: Concurrent omega-regular games. In: 15th Annual IEEE Symposium on Logic in Computer Science, pp. 141–154. IEEE Computer Society (2000). https://doi.org/10.1109/LICS.2000.855763
2. Asarin, E., Chane-Yack-Fa, R., Varacca, D.: Fair adversaries and randomization in two-player games. In: Ong, L. (ed.) FoSSaCS 2010. LNCS, vol. 6014, pp. 64–78. Springer, Heidelberg (2010). https://doi.org/10.1007/978-3-642-12032-9_6
3. Baier, C., Bertrand, N., Dubslaff, C., Gburek, D., Sankur, O.: Stochastic shortest paths and weight-bounded properties in Markov decision processes. In: Dawar, A., Grädel, E. (eds.) Proceedings of the 33rd Annual ACM/IEEE Symposium on Logic in Computer Science, LICS 2018, pp. 86–94. ACM (2018). https://doi.org/10.1145/3209108.3209184
4. Baier, C., Größer, M., Leucker, M., Bollig, B., Ciesinski, F.: Controller synthesis for probabilistic systems. In: Lévy, J., Mayr, E.W., Mitchell, J.C. (eds.) Exploring New Frontiers of Theoretical Informatics, IFIP 18th World Computer Congress, TC1 3rd International Conference on Theoretical Computer Science (TCS2004). IFIP, vol. 155, pp. 493–506. Kluwer/Springer (2004). https://doi.org/10.1007/1-4020-8141-3_38
5. Baier, C., Katoen, J.P.: Principles of Model Checking. The MIT Press (2008)
6. Baier, C., Klein, J., Leuschner, L., Parker, D., Wunderlich, S.: Ensuring the reliability of your model checker: interval iteration for Markov decision processes. In: Majumdar, R., Kunčak, V. (eds.) CAV 2017. LNCS, vol. 10426, pp. 160–180. Springer, Cham (2017). https://doi.org/10.1007/978-3-319-63387-9_8
7. Baier, C., Kwiatkowska, M.Z.: Model checking for a probabilistic branching time logic with fairness. Distrib. Comput. **11**(3), 125–155 (1998). https://doi.org/10.1007/s004460050046
8. Banerjee, T., Majumdar, R., Mallik, K., Schmuck, A., Soudjani, S.: A direct symbolic algorithm for solving stochastic Rabin games. In: Fisman, D., Rosu, G. (eds.) Tools and Algorithms for the Construction and Analysis of Systems - 28th International Conference, TACAS 2022, Proceedings, Part II. LNCS, vol. 13244, pp. 81–98. Springer, Cham (2022). https://doi.org/10.1007/978-3-030-99527-0_5
9. Bellman, R.: Dynamic Programming, 1st edn. Princeton University Press, Princeton (1957)
10. Brázdil, T., Kučera, A., Novotný, P.: Determinacy in stochastic games with unbounded payoff functions. In: Kučera, A., Henzinger, T.A., Nešetřil, J., Vojnar, T., Antoš, D. (eds.) MEMICS 2012. LNCS, vol. 7721, pp. 94–105. Springer, Heidelberg (2013). https://doi.org/10.1007/978-3-642-36046-6_10
11. Chatterjee, K., Henzinger, T.A.: A survey of stochastic ω-regular games. J. Comput. Syst. Sci. **78**(2), 394–413 (2012). https://doi.org/10.1016/j.jcss.2011.05.002
12. Chen, T., Forejt, V., Kwiatkowska, M.Z., Parker, D., Simaitis, A.: Automatic verification of competitive stochastic systems. Formal Methods Syst. Des. **43**(1), 61–92 (2013). https://doi.org/10.1007/s10703-013-0183-7
13. Condon, A.: On algorithms for simple stochastic games. In: Cai, J. (ed.) Advances in Computational Complexity Theory, Proceedings of a DIMACS Workshop. DIMACS Series in Discrete Mathematics and Theoretical Computer Science, vol. 13, pp. 51–71. DIMACS/AMS (1990)
14. Condon, A.: The complexity of stochastic games. Inf. Comput. **96**(2), 203–224 (1992). https://doi.org/10.1016/0890-5401(92)90048-K

15. Davey, B.A., Priestley, H.A.: Introduction to Lattices and Order. Cambridge University Press, Cambridge (1990)
16. D'Ippolito, N., Braberman, V.A., Piterman, N., Uchitel, S.: Synthesis of live behaviour models for fallible domains. In: Taylor, R.N., Gall, H.C., Medvidovic, N. (eds.) Proceedings of the 33rd International Conference on Software Engineering, ICSE 2011. pp. 211–220. ACM (2011). https://doi.org/10.1145/1985793.1985823
17. Feng, L., Wiltsche, C., Humphrey, L.R., Topcu, U.: Controller synthesis for autonomous systems interacting with human operators. In: Bayen, A.M., Branicky, M.S. (eds.) Proceedings of the ACM/IEEE Sixth International Conference on Cyber-Physical Systems, ICCPS 2015, pp. 70–79. ACM (2015). https://doi.org/10.1145/2735960.2735973
18. Filar, J., Vrieze, K.: Competitive Markov Decision Processes. Springer, Heidelberg (1996). https://doi.org/10.1007/978-1-4612-4054-9
19. Haddad, S., Monmege, B.: Interval iteration algorithm for MDPs and IMDPs. Theor. Comput. Sci. **735**, 111–131 (2018). https://doi.org/10.1016/j.tcs.2016.12.003
20. Kallenberg, L.: Linear Programming and Finite Markovian Control Problems. Mathematisch Centrum, Amsterdam (1983)
21. Kučera, A.: Turn-based stochastic games. In: Apt, K.R., Grädel, E. (eds.) Lectures in Game Theory for Computer Scientists, pp. 146–184. Cambridge University Press (2011). https://doi.org/10.1017/CBO9780511973468.006
22. Kwiatkowska, M., Norman, G., Parker, D., Santos, G.: PRISM-games 3.0: stochastic game verification with concurrency, equilibria and time. In: Lahiri, S.K., Wang, C. (eds.) CAV 2020. LNCS, vol. 12225, pp. 475–487. Springer, Cham (2020). https://doi.org/10.1007/978-3-030-53291-8_25
23. Kwiatkowska, M., Norman, G., Parker, D.: PRISM 4.0: verification of probabilistic real-time systems. In: Gopalakrishnan, G., Qadeer, S. (eds.) CAV 2011. LNCS, vol. 6806, pp. 585–591. Springer, Heidelberg (2011). https://doi.org/10.1007/978-3-642-22110-1_47
24. Martin, D.A.: The determinacy of Blackwell games. J. Symb. Log. **63**(4), 1565–1581 (1998). https://doi.org/10.2307/2586667
25. Morgenstern, O., von Neumann, J.: Theory of Games and Economic Behavior, 1st edn. Princeton University Press (1942)
26. Patek, S.D., Bertsekas, D.P.: Stochastic shortest path games. SIAM J. Control Optimiz. **37**, 804–824 (1999)
27. Shapley, L.: Stochastic games. Proc. Natl. Acad. Sci. **39**(10), 1095–1100 (1953). https://doi.org/10.1073/pnas.39.10.1095
28. Svorenová, M., Kwiatkowska, M.: Quantitative verification and strategy synthesis for stochastic games. Eur. J. Control **30**, 15–30 (2016). https://doi.org/10.1016/j.ejcon.2016.04.009

Automated Expected Amortised Cost Analysis of Probabilistic Data Structures

Lorenz Leutgeb[1]($\boxtimes$) , Georg Moser[2] , and Florian Zuleger[3]

[1] Max Planck Institute for Informatics
and Graduate School of Computer Science,
Saarland Informatics Campus,
Saarbrücken, Germany
lorenz@mpi-inf.mpg.de
[2] Department of Computer Science,
Universität Innsbruck, Innsbruck, Austria
[3] Institute of Logic and Computation 192/4,
Technische Universität Wien, Vienna, Austria

Abstract. In this paper, we present the first fully-automated *expected amortised cost analysis* of self-adjusting data structures, that is, of *randomised splay trees*, *randomised splay heaps* and *randomised meldable heaps*, which so far have only (semi-)manually been analysed in the literature. Our analysis is stated as a type-and-effect system for a first-order functional programming language with support for sampling over discrete distributions, non-deterministic choice and a ticking operator. The latter allows for the specification of fine-grained cost models. We state two soundness theorems based on two different—but strongly related—typing rules of ticking, which account differently for the cost of non-terminating computations. Finally we provide a prototype implementation able to fully automatically analyse the aforementioned case studies.

Keywords: amortised cost analysis · functional programming · probabilistic data structures · automation · constraint solving

1 Introduction

Probabilistic variants of well-known computational models such as automata, Turing machines or the λ-calculus have been studied since the early days of computer science (see [16,17,25] for early references). One of the main reasons for considering probabilistic models is that they often allow for the design of more efficient algorithms than their deterministic counterparts (see e.g. [6,23,25]). Another avenue for the design of efficient algorithms has been opened up by Sleator and Tarjan [34,36] with their introduction of the notion of *amortised complexity*. Here, the cost of a single data structure operation is not analysed in isolation but as part of a sequence of data structure operations. This allows for the design of algorithms where the cost of an expensive operation is averaged out over multiple operations and results in a good overall *worst-case cost*. Both methodologies—*probabilistic programming* and *amortised complexity*—can

© The Author(s) 2022
S. Shoham and Y. Vizel (Eds.): CAV 2022, LNCS 13372, pp. 70–91, 2022.
https://doi.org/10.1007/978-3-031-13188-2_4

be combined for the design of even more efficient algorithms, as for example in *randomized splay trees* [1], where a rotation in the splaying operation is only performed with some probability (which improves the overall performance by skipping some rotations while still guaranteeing that enough rotations are performed).

In this paper, we present the first fully-automated *expected amortised cost analysis* of probabilistic data structures, that is, of *randomised splay trees, randomised splay heaps, randomised meldable heaps* and a *randomised analysis* of a *binary search tree*. These data structures have so far only (semi-)manually been analysed in the literature. Our analysis is based on a novel type-and-effect system, which constitutes a generalisation of the type system studied in [14, 18] to the non-deterministic and probabilistic setting, as well as an extension of the type system introduced in [37] to sublinear bounds and non-determinism. We provide a prototype implementation that is able to fully automatically analyse the case studies mentioned above. We summarise here the main contributions of our article: (i) We consider a first-order functional programming language with support for *sampling over discrete distributions, non-deterministic choice* and a *ticking* operator, which allows for the specification of fine-grained cost models. (ii) We introduce compact *small-step* as well as *big-step* semantics for our programming language. These semantics are equivalent wrt. the obtained normal forms (i.e., the resulting probability distributions) but differ wrt. the cost assigned to non-terminating computations. (iii) Based on [14,18], we develop a novel type-and-effect system that strictly generalises the prior approaches from the literature. (iv) We state two soundness theorems (see Sect. 5.3) based on two different—but strongly related—typing rules of ticking. The two soundness theorems are stated wrt. the small-step resp. big-step semantics because these semantics precisely correspond to the respective ticking rule. The more restrictive ticking rule can be used to establish (positive) almost sure termination (AST), while the more permissive ticking rule supports the analysis of a larger set of programs (which can be very useful in case termination is not required or can be established by other means); in fact, the more permissive ticking rule is essential for the precise cost analysis of randomised splay trees. We note that the two ticking rules and corresponding soundness theorems do not depend on the details of the type-and-effect system, and we believe that they will be of independent interest (e.g., when adapting the framework of this paper to other benchmarks and cost functions). (v) Our prototype implementation ATLAS strictly extends the earlier version reported on in [18], and all our earlier evaluation results can be replicated (and sometimes improved).

With our implementation and the obtained experimental results we make two contributions to the complexity analysis of data structures:

1. *We automatically infer bounds on the expected amortised cost, which could previously only be obtained by sophisticated pen-and-paper proofs. In particular, we verify that the amortised costs of randomised variants of self-adjusting data structures improve upon their non-randomised variants.* In Table 1 we state the expected cost of the randomised data structures considered and their deterministic counterparts; the benchmarks are detailed in Sect. 2.

Table 1. Expected Amortised Cost of Randomised Data Structures. We also state the deterministic counterparts considered in [18] for comparison.

	probabilistic	deterministic [18]
Splay Tree		
`insert`	$3/4 \log_2(|t|) + 3/4 \log_2(|t|+1)$	$2 \log_2(|t|) + 3/2$
`delete`	$9/8 \log_2(|t|)$	$5/2 \log_2(|t|) + 3$
`splay`	$9/8 \log_2(|t|)$	$3/2 \log_2(|t|)$
Splay Heap		
`insert`	$3/4 \log_2(|h|) + 3/4 \log_2(|h|+1)$	$1/2 \log_2(|h|) + \log_2(|h|+1) + 3/2$
`delete_min`	$3/4 \log_2(|h|)$	$\log_2(|h|)$
Meldable Heap		
`insert`	$\log_2(|h|) + 1$	
`delete_min`	$2 \log_2(|h|)$	*not applicable*
`meld`	$\log_2(|h_1|) + \log_2(|h_2|)$	
Coin Search Tree		
`insert`	$3/2 \log_2(|t|) + 1/2$	
`delete`	$3/2 \log_2(|t|) + 1$	*not applicable*
`delete_max`	$3/2 \log_2(|t|)$	

2. *We establish a novel approach to the expected cost analysis of data structures.* Our research has been greatly motivated by the detailed study of Albers et al. in [1] of the expected amortised costs of *randomised splaying*. While [1] requires a sophisticated pen-and-paper analysis, our approach allows us to fully-automatically compare the effect of different rotation probabilities on the expected cost (see Table 2 of Sect. 6).

Related Work. The generalisation of the model of computation and the study of the expected resource usage of *probabilistic* programs has recently received increased attention (see e.g. [2,4,5,7,10,11,15,21,22,24,27,37,38]). We focus on related work concerned with automations of expected cost analysis of deterministic or non-deterministic, probabilistic programs—imperative or functional. (A probabilistic program is called *non-deterministic*, if it additionally makes use of non-deterministic choice.)

In recent years the *automation* of expected cost analysis of probabilistic data structures or programs has gained momentum, cf. [2–5,22,24,27,37,38]. Notably, the Absynth prototype by [27], implement Kaminski's ert-calculus, cf. [15] for reasoning about expected costs. Avanzini et al. [5] generalise the ert-calculus to an expected cost transformer and introduce the tool eco-imp, which provides a modular and thus a more efficient and scalable alternative for non-deterministic, probabilistic programs. In comparison to these works, we base our analysis on a dedicated type system finetuned to express sublinear bounds; further our prototype implementation ATLAS derives bounds on the expected amortised costs. Neither is supported by Absynth or eco-imp.

Martingale based techniques have been implemented, e.g., by Peixin Wang et al. [38]. Related results have been reported by Moosbrugger et al. [24]. Meyer et al. [22] provide an extension of the KoAT tool, generalising the concept of alternating size and runtime analysis to probabilistic programs. Again, these innovative tools are not suited to the benchmarks considered in our work. With respect to probabilistic *functional* programs, Di Wang et al. [37] provided the only prior expected cost analysis of (deterministic) probabilistic programs; this work is most closely related to our contributions. Indeed, our typing rule (ite : coin) stems from [37] and the soundness proof wrt. the big-step semantics is conceptually similar. Nevertheless, our contributions strictly generalise their results. First, our core language is based on a simpler semantics, giving rise to cleaner formulations of our soundness theorems. Second, our type-and-effect provides two different typing rules for ticking, a fact we can capitalise on in additional strength of our prototype implementation. Finally, our amortised analysis allows for logarithmic potential functions.

A bulk of research concentrates on specific forms of *martingales* or *Lyapunov ranking functions*. All these works, however, are somewhat orthogonal to our contributions, as foremostly *termination* (i.e. AST or PAST) is studied, rather than computational complexity. Still these approaches can be partially suited to a variety of quantitative program properties, see [35] for an overview, but are incomparable in strength to the results established here.

Structure. In the next section, we provide a bird's eye view on our approach. Sections 3 and 4 detail the core probabilistic language employed, as well as its small- and big-step semantics. In Sect. 5 we introduce the novel type-and-effect system formally and state soundness of the system wrt. the respective semantics. In Sect. 6 we present evaluation results of our prototype implementation ATLAS. Finally, we conclude in Sect. 7. All proofs, part of the benchmarks and the source codes are given in [19].

2   Overview of Our Approach and Results

In this section, we first sketch our approach on an introductory example and then detail the benchmarks and results depicted in Table 1 in the Introduction.

2.1   Introductory Example

Consider the definition of the function descend, depicted in Fig. 1. The *expected* amortised complexity of descend is $\log_2(|t|)$, where $|t|$ denotes the size of a tree t (defined as the number of leaves of the tree).[1] Our analysis is set up in terms of template potential functions with unknown coefficients, which will be instantiated by our analysis. Following [14,18], our potential functions are composed of two types of resource functions, which can express *logarithmic* amortised cost: For a sequence of n trees $t_1, \ldots, t_n$ and coefficients $a_i \in \mathbb{N}, b \in \mathbb{Z}$, with $\sum_{i=1}^{n} a_i + b \geqslant$

---

[1] An amortised analysis may always default to a wort-case analysis. In particular the analysis of descend in this section can be considered as a worst-case analysis. However, we use the example to illustrate the general setup of our amortised analysis.

```
1  descend t = match t with
2  | leaf        → leaf
3  | node l a r → if coin 1/2    Denotes p = 1/2, the default which could be omitted.
4     then let xl = (descend l)✓ in node xl a r   The symbol ✓ denotes a tick.
5     else let xr = (descend r)✓ in node l a xr
```

Fig. 1. descend function

0, the resource function $p_{(a_1,\ldots,a_n,b)}(t_1,\ldots,t_n) \log_2(a_1 \cdot |t_1| + \cdots + a_n \cdot |t_n| + b)$ denotes the logarithm of a linear combination of the sizes of the trees. The resource function $\mathsf{rk}(t)$, which is a variant of Schoenmakers' potential, cf. [28,31,32], is inductively defined as (i) $\mathsf{rk}(\mathtt{leaf}) := 1$; (ii) $\mathsf{rk}(\mathtt{node}\ l\ d\ r) := \mathsf{rk}(l) + \log_2(|l|) + \log_2(|r|) + \mathsf{rk}(r)$, where l, r are the left resp. right child of the tree $\mathtt{node}\ l\ d\ r$, and d is some data element that is ignored by the resource function. (We note that $\mathsf{rk}(t)$ is not needed for the analysis of descend but is needed for more involved benchmarks, e.g. randomised splay trees.) With these resource functions at hand, our analysis introduces the coefficients q_*, $q_{(1,0)}$, $q_{(0,2)}$, q'_*, $q'_{(1,0)}$, $q'_{(0,2)}$ and employs the following *Ansatz*:[2]

$$q_* \cdot \mathsf{rk}(t) + q_{(1,0)} \cdot p_{(1,0)}(t) + q_{(0,2)} \cdot p_{(0,2)}(t) \geqslant c_{\mathsf{descend}}(t)$$
$$+ q'_* \, \mathsf{rk}(\mathsf{descend}\ t) + q'_{(1,0)} \cdot p_{(1,0)}(\mathsf{descend}\ t) + q'_{(0,2)} \cdot p_{(0,2)}(\mathsf{descend}\ t)\,.$$

Here, $c_{\mathsf{descend}}(t)$ denotes the expected cost of executing descend on tree t, where the cost is given by the ticks as indicated in the source code (each tick accounts for a recursive call). The result of our analysis will be an instantiation of the coefficients, returning $q_{(1,0)} = 1$ and zero for all other coefficients, which allows to directly read off the logarithmic bound $\log_2(|t|)$ of descend.

Our analysis is formulated as a *type-and-effect system*, introducing the above *template potential functions* for every subexpression of the program under analysis. The typing rules of our system give rise to a constraint system over the unknown coefficients that capture the relationship between the potential functions of the subexpressions of the program. Solving the constraint system then gives a valid instantiation of the potential function coefficients. Our type-and-effect system constitutes a generalisation of the type system studied in [14,18] to the non-deterministic and probabilistic setting, as well as an extension of the type system introduced in [37] to sublinear bounds and non-determinism.

In the following, we survey our type-and-effect system by means of example descend. A partial type derivation is given in Fig. 2. For brevity, type judgements and the type rules are presented in a simplified form. In particular, we restrict our attention to tree types, denoted as T. This omission is inessential to the actual complexity analysis. For the full set of rules see [19]. We now discuss this type derivation step by step.

Let e denote the body of the function definition of descend, cf. Fig. 1. Our automated analysis infers an *annotated type* by verifying that the type

---

[2] For ease of presentation, we elide the underlying semantics for now and simply write "descend t" for the resulting tree t', obtained after evaluating descend t.

$$\frac{\dfrac{\text{descend}:\mathsf{T}|Q \to \mathsf{T}|Q'}{l:\mathsf{T}|Q_5 \vdash \text{descend } 1:\mathsf{T}|Q_6}\ (\text{app})}{l:\mathsf{T}|Q_4 \vdash (\text{descend } 1)^{\checkmark}:\mathsf{T}|Q_6}\ (\text{tick}:\text{now})$$

$$\frac{\dfrac{l:\mathsf{T}|Q_4 \vdash (\text{descend } 1)^{\checkmark}:\mathsf{T}|Q_6 \qquad x_l:\mathsf{T},r:\mathsf{T}|Q_7 \vdash \text{node } x_l\ a\ r:\mathsf{T}|Q'}{l:\mathsf{T},r:\mathsf{T}|Q_3 \vdash \text{let } x_l = (\text{descend } 1)^{\checkmark} \text{ in node } x_l\ a\ r:\mathsf{T}|Q'}\ (\text{let})}{\dfrac{l:\mathsf{T},r:\mathsf{T}|Q_2 \vdash \text{if coin } 1/2 \text{ then } e_2 \text{ else } e_3:\mathsf{T}|Q'}{\dfrac{l:\mathsf{T},r:\mathsf{T}|Q_1 \vdash \text{if coin } 1/2 \text{ then } e_2 \text{ else } e_3:\mathsf{T}|Q'}{t:\mathsf{T}|Q \vdash \text{match } t \text{ with}|\text{leaf} \to \text{leaf }|\text{node } l\ a\ r \to e_1:\mathsf{T}|Q'}\ (\text{w})}\ (\text{ite}:\text{coin})}\ (\text{match})$$

Fig. 2. Partial Type Derivation for Function descend

judgement $t:\mathsf{T}|Q \vdash e:\mathsf{T}|Q'$ is derivable. Types are decorated with *annotations* $Q := [q_*, q_{(1,0)}, q_{(0,2)}]$ and $Q' := [q'_*, q'_{(1,0)}, q'_{(0,2)}]$—employed to express the potential carried by the arguments to descend and its results. Annotations fix the coefficients of the resource functions in the corresponding potential functions, e.g., (i) $\Phi(t:\mathsf{T}|Q) := q_* \cdot \text{rk}(t) + q_{(1,0)} \cdot p_{(1,0)}(t) + q_{(0,2)} \cdot p_{(0,2)}(t)$ and (ii) $\Phi(e:\mathsf{T}|Q') := q'_* \cdot \text{rk}(e) + q'_{(1,0)} \cdot p_{(1,0)}(e) + q'_{(0,2)} \cdot p_{(0,2)}(e)$.

By our soundness theorems (see Sect. 5.3), such a typing guarantees that the *expected* amortised cost of descend is bounded by the expectation (wrt. the value distribution in the limit) of the difference between $\Phi(t:\mathsf{T}|Q)$ and $\Phi(\text{descend } t:\mathsf{T}|Q')$. Because e is a match expression, the following rule is applied (we only state a restricted rule here, the general rule can be found in [19]):

$$\frac{\varepsilon|\varnothing \vdash \text{leaf}:\mathsf{T}|Q' \qquad l:\mathsf{T},r:\mathsf{T}|Q_1 \vdash e_1:\mathsf{T}|Q'}{t:\mathsf{T}|Q \vdash \text{match } t \text{ with}|\text{leaf} \to \text{leaf }|\text{node } l\ a\ r \to e_1:\mathsf{T}|Q'}\ (\text{match})$$

Here e_1 denotes the subexpression of e that corresponds to the node case of match. Apart from the annotations Q, Q_1 and Q', the rule (match) constitutes a standard type rule for pattern matching. With regard to the annotations Q and Q_1, (match) ensures the correct distribution of potential by inducing the constraints

$$q_1^1 = q_2^1 = q_* \qquad q_{(1,1,0)}^1 = q_{(1,0)} \qquad q_{(1,0,0)}^1 = q_{(0,1,0)}^1 = q_* \qquad q_{(0,0,2)}^1 = q_{(0,2)}\ ,$$

where the constraints are immediately justified by recalling the definitions of the resource functions $p_{(a_1,\ldots,a_n,b)}(t_1,\ldots,t_n) := \log_2(a_1 \cdot |t_1| + \cdots + a_n \cdot |t_n| + b)$ and $\text{rk}(t) = \text{rk}(l) + \log_2(|l|) + \log_2(|r|) + \text{rk}(r)$.

The next rule is a structural rule, representing a *weakening* step that rewrites the annotations of the variable context. The rule (w) allows a suitable adaptation of the coefficients based on the following inequality, which holds for any substitution σ of variables by values, $\Phi(\sigma; l:\mathsf{T}, r:\mathsf{T}|Q_1) \geqslant \Phi(\sigma; l:\mathsf{T}, r:\mathsf{T}|Q_2)$.

$$\frac{l:\mathsf{T},r:\mathsf{T}|Q_2 \vdash e_1:\mathsf{T}|Q'}{l:\mathsf{T},r:\mathsf{T}|Q_1 \vdash e_1:\mathsf{T}|Q'}\ (\text{w})$$

In our prototype implementation this comparison is performed *symbolically*. We use a variant of Farkas' Lemma [19,33] in conjunction with simple

```
1  meld h1 h2 = match h1 with
2  | leaf                    → h2
3  | node h1l h1x h1r → match h2 with
4    | node h2l h2x h2r → if h1x > h2x
5      then if coin
6        then (node (meld h2l (node h1l h1x h1r))ˇ h2x h2r)
7        else (node h2l h2x (meld h2r (node h1l h1x h1r))ˇ)
8      else   Omitted for brevity,  symmetric to the the depicted case.
```

Fig. 3. Partial `meld` function of Randomised Meldable Heaps

mathematical facts about the logarithm to linearise this symbolic comparison, namely the monotonicity of the logarithm and the fact that $2+\log_2(x)+\log_2(y) \leqslant 2\log_2(x+y)$ for all $x, y \geqslant 1$. For example, Farkas' Lemma in conjunction with the latter fact gives rise to

$$q^1_{(0,0,2)} + 2f \geqslant q^2_{(0,0,2)} \qquad\qquad q^1_{(1,1,0)} - 2f \geqslant q^2_{(1,1,0)}$$
$$q^1_{(1,0,0)} + f \geqslant q^2_{(1,0,0)} \qquad\qquad q^1_{(0,1,0)} + f \geqslant q^2_{(0,1,0)} \,,$$

for some fresh rational coefficient $f \geqslant 0$ introduced by Farkas' Lemma. After having generated the constraint system for `descend`, the solver is free to instantiate f as needed. In fact in order to discover the bound $\log_2(|t|)$ for `descend`, the solver will need to instantiate $f = 1/2$, corresponding to the inequality $\log_2(|l| + |r|) \geqslant 1/2\log_2(|l|) + 1/2\log_2(|r|) + 1$.

So far, the rules did not refer to sampling and are unchanged from their (non-probabilistic) counterpart introduced in [14,18]. The next rule, however, formalises a coin toss, biased with probability p. Our general rule (ite : coin) is depicted in Fig. 12 and is inspired by a similar rule for coin tosses that has been recently been proposed in the literature, cf. [37]. This rule specialises as follows to our introductory example:

$$\frac{l : \mathsf{T}, r : \mathsf{T}|Q_4 \vdash e_3 : \mathsf{T}|Q' \qquad l : \mathsf{T}, r : \mathsf{T}|Q_3 \vdash \text{let } x_l = (\textbf{descend } l)^{\vee} \text{ in node } x_l \ a \ r : \mathsf{T}|Q'}{l : \mathsf{T}, r : \mathsf{T}|Q_2 \vdash \text{ if coin } 1/2 \text{ then } e_2 \text{ else } e_3 : \mathsf{T}|Q'} \ \text{(ite : coin)}$$

Here e_2 and e_3 respectively, denote the subexpressions of the conditional and in addition the crucial condition $Q_2 = 1/2 \cdot Q_3 + 1/2 \cdot Q_4$ holds. This condition, expressing that the corresponding annotations are subject to the probability of the coin toss, gives rise to the following constraints (among others)

$$q^2_{(0,0,2)} = 1/2 \cdot q^3_{(0,0,2)} + 1/2 \cdot q^4_{(0,0,2)} \qquad q^2_{(0,1,0)} = 1/2 \cdot q^3_{(0,1,0)} + 1/2 \cdot q^4_{(0,1,0)}$$
$$q^2_{(1,0,0)} = 1/2 \cdot q^3_{(1,0,0)} + 1/2 \cdot q^4_{(1,0,0)} \,.$$

In the following, we will only consider one alternative of the coin toss and proceed as in the partial type derivation depicted in Fig. 1 (ie. we state the then-branch and omit the symmetric else-branch). Thus next, we apply the rule for the `let` expression. This rule is the most involved typing rule in the system proposed in [14,18]. However, for our leading example it suffices to consider the following simplified variant:

```
1 splay a t = match t with
2  | node cl c cr → match cl with
3    | node bl b br → match (splay a bl)✓¹ᐟ² with Recursive call costs ¹/₂.
4    | node al a1 ar → if coin
5      then (node al a1 (node ar b (node br c cr)))✓¹ᐟ² Rotation costs ¹/₂.
6      else          node (node (node al a1 ar) b br) c cr  No rotation.
```

Fig. 4. Partial **splay** function of Randomised Splay Trees (zigzig-case)

$$\frac{l:\mathsf{T}|Q_4 \vdash (\textbf{descend } l)^\checkmark : \mathsf{T}|Q_6 \quad l:\mathsf{T}|Q_7 \vdash \texttt{node } x_l \ a \ r : \mathsf{T}|Q'}{l:\mathsf{T}, r:\mathsf{T}|Q_3 \vdash \texttt{let } x_l = (\textbf{descend } l)^\checkmark \text{ in } \texttt{node } x_l \ a \ r : \mathsf{T}|Q'} \text{ (let)}$$

Focusing on the annotations, the rule (let : tree) suitably distributes potential assigned to the variable context, embodied in the annotation Q_3, to the recursive call within the let expression (via annotation Q_4) and the construction of the resulting tree (via annotation Q_7). The distribution of potential is facilitated by generating constraints that can roughly be stated as two "equalities", that is, (i) "$Q_3 = Q_4 + D$", and (ii) "$Q_7 = D + Q_6$". Equality (i) states that the input potential is split into some potential Q_4 used for typing (**descend** l)$^\checkmark$ and some remainder potential D (which however is not constructed explicitly and only serves as a placeholder for potential that will be passed on). Equality (ii) states that the potential Q_7 used for typing node x_l a r equals the remainder potential D plus the leftover potential Q_6 from the typing of (**descend** l)$^\checkmark$. The (tick : now) rule then ensures that costs are properly accounted for by generating constraints for $Q_4 = Q_5 + 1$ (see Fig. 2). Finally, the type derivation ends by the application rule, denoted as (app), that verifies that the recursive call is well-typed wrt. the (annotated) signature of the function descend: $\mathsf{T}|Q \to \mathsf{T}|Q'$, ie. the rule enforces that $Q_5 = Q$ and $Q_6 = Q'$. We illustrate (a subset of) the constraints induced by (let), (tick : now) and (app):

$$\begin{array}{llll}
q^3_{(1,0,0)} = q^4_{(1,0)} & q^3_{(0,1,0)} = q^7_{(0,1,0)} & q'_1 = q^6_1 & q^4_{(0,2)} = q^5_{(0,2)} + 1 \\
q^3_{(0,0,2)} = q^4_{(0,2)} & q^3_2 = q^7_2 & q'_{(1,0)} = q^6_{(1,0)} & q^4_{(1,0)} = q^5_{(1,0)} \\
q^3_1 = q^4_1 & q'_{(0,2)} = q^6_{(0,2)} & q^6_1 = q^7_1 & q^5_{(1,0)} = q_{(1,0)} \, ,
\end{array}$$

where (i) the constraints in the first three columns—involving the annotations Q_3, Q_4, Q_6 and Q_7—stem from the constraints of the rule (let : tree); (ii) the constraints in the last column—involving Q_4, Q_5, Q and Q'—stem from the constraints of the rule (tick : now) and (app). For example, $q^3_{(1,0,0)} = q^4_{(1,0)}$ and $q^3_{(0,1,0)} = q^7_{(0,1,0)}$ distributes the part of the logarithmic potential represented by Q_3 to Q_4 and Q_7; $q^6_1 = q^7_1$ expresses that the rank of the result of evaluating the recursive call can be employed in the construction of the resulting tree node x_l a r; $q^4_{(1,0)} = q^5_{(1,0)}$ and $q^4_{(0,2)} = q^5_{(0,2)} + 1$ relate the logarithmic resp. constant potential according to the tick rule, where the addition of one accounts for the cost embodied by the tick rule; $q^5_{(1,0)} = q_{(1,0)}$ stipulates that the potential at the recursive call site must match the function type.

Our prototype implementation ATLAS collects all these constraints and solves them fully automatically. Following [14,18], our implementation in fact searches

```
1  insert d t = match t with
2  | leaf          → node leaf d leaf
3  | node l a r → if coin 1/2          Assuming probability 1/2 for a < d.
4      then node (insert d l)✓ a r
5      else node l a (insert d r)✓
```

Fig. 5. insert function of a Binary Search Tree with randomized comparison

for a solution that minimises the resulting complexity bound. For the descend function, our implementation finds a solution that sets $q_{(1,0)}$ to 1, and all other coefficients to zero. Thus, the logarithmic bound $\log_2(|t|)$ follows.

2.2   Overview of Benchmarks and Results

Randomised Meldable Heaps. Gambin et al. [13] proposed meldable heaps as a simple priority-queue data structure that is guaranteed to have expected logarithmic cost for all operations. All operations can be implemented in terms of the meld function, which takes two heaps and returns a single heap as a result. The partial source code of meld is given in Fig. 3 (the full source code of all examples can be found in [19]). Our tool ATLAS fully-automatically infers the bound $\log_2(|h_1|) + \log_2(|h_2|)$ on the expected cost of meld.

Randomised Splay Trees. Albers et al. in [1] propose these splay trees as a variation of deterministic splay trees [34], which have better expected runtime complexity (the same computational complexity in the O-notation but with smaller constants). Related results have been obtained by Fürer [12]. The proposal is based on the observation that it is not necessary to rotate the tree in every (recursive) splaying operation but that it suffices to perform rotations with some fixed positive probability in order to reap the asymptotic benefits of self-adjusting search trees. The theoretical analysis of randomised splay trees [1] starts by refining the cost model of [34], which simply counts the number of rotations, into one that accounts for recursive calls with a cost of c and for rotations with a cost of d.

We present a snippet of a functional implementation of randomised splay trees in Fig. 4. We note that in this code snippet we have set $c = d = 1/2$; this choice is arbitrary; we have chosen these costs in order to be able to compare the resulting amortised costs to the deterministic setting of [18], where the combined cost of the recursive call and rotation is set to 1; we note that our analysis requires fixed costs c and d but these constants can be chosen by the user; for example one can set $c = 1$ and $d = 2.75$ corresponding to the costs observed during the experiments in [1]. Likewise the probability of the coin toss has been arbitrarily set to $p = 1/2$ but could be set differently by the user. (We remark that to the best of our knowledge no theoretical analysis has been conducted on how to chose the best value of p for given costs c and d.) Our prototype implementation is able to fully automatically infer an amortised complexity bound of $9/8 \log_2(|t|)$ for splay (with c, d and p fixed as above), which improves on the complexity

```
1  pre—condition: t is not a leaf
2  delete_max t = match t with
3    | node l b r → match r with
4      | leaf      → (l,b)
5      | node rl c rr → match rr with
6        | leaf → ((node l b rl),c)
7        | rr   → let (t',max) = (delete_max rr)⌄ in match t' with
8          | node rrll x xa → (node (node (node l b rl) c rrll) x xa,max)
```

Fig. 6. `delete_max` function of a Coin Search Tree with one rotation

bound of $3/2 \log_2(|t|)$ for the deterministic version of `splay` as reported in [18], confirming that randomisation indeed improves the expected runtime.

We remark on how the amortised complexity bound of $9/8 \log_2(|t|)$ for `splay` is computed by our analysis. Our tool ATLAS computes an annotated type for `splay` that corresponds to the inequality

$$3/4 \, \mathrm{rk}(t) + 9/8 \log_2(|t|) + 3/4 \geqslant c_{\mathtt{splay}}(t) + 3/4 \, \mathrm{rk}(\mathtt{splay}\ t) + 3/4 \ .$$

By setting $\phi(t) := 3/4 \, \mathrm{rk}(t) + 3/4$ as potential function in the sense of Tarjan and Sleator [34, 36], the above inequality allows us to directly read out an upper bound on the amortised complexity $a_{\mathtt{splay}}(t)$ of `splay` (we recall that the amortised complexity in the sense of Tarjan and Sleator is defined as the sum of the actual costs plus the output potential minus the input potential):

$$a_{\mathtt{splay}}(t) = c_{\mathtt{splay}}(t) + \phi(\mathtt{splay}\ t) - \phi(t) \leqslant 9/8 \cdot \log_2(|t|) \ .$$

Probabilistic Analysis of Binary Search Trees. We present a probabilistic analysis of a deterministic binary search tree, which offers the usual `contains`, `insert`, and `delete` operations, where `delete` uses `delete_max` given in Fig. 6, as a subroutine (the source code of the missing operations is given in [19]). We assume that the elements inserted, deleted and searched for are equally distributed; hence, we conduct a probabilistic analysis by replacing every comparison with a coin toss of probability one half. We will refer to the resulting data structure as Coin Search Tree in our benchmarks. The source code of `insert` is given in Fig. 5.

Our tool ATLAS infers an logarithmic expected amortised cost for all operations, ie., for `insert` and `delete_max` we obtain (i) $1/2 \, \mathrm{rk}(t) + 3/2 \log_2(|t|) + 3/2 \geqslant c_{\mathtt{insert}}(t) + 1/2 \mathrm{rk}(\mathtt{insert}\ t) + 1$; and (ii) $1/2 \mathrm{rk}(t) + 3/2 \log_2(|t|) + 1 \geqslant c_{\mathtt{delete\_max}}(t) + 1/2 \mathrm{rk}(\mathtt{delete\_max}\ t) + 1$, from which we obtain an expected amortised cost of $3/2 \log_2(|t|) + 1/2$ and $3/2 \log_2(|t|)$ respectively.

3   Probabilistic Functional Language

Preliminaries. Let $\mathbb{R}_0^+$ denote the non-negative reals and $\mathbb{R}_0^{+\infty}$ their extension by ∞. We are only concerned with *discrete distributions* and drop "discrete" in the following. Let A be a countable set and let $\mathsf{D}(A)$ denote the set of *(sub)distributions* d over A, whose support $\mathsf{supp}(\mu) := \{a \in A \mid \mu(a) \neq 0\}$ is countable. Distributions are denoted by Greek letters. For $\mu \in \mathsf{D}(A)$, we may

```
o ::= < | > | =

e ::= f x₁ ... xₙ                    | e^√a/b
    | false | true | e₁ o e₂         | if x then e₁ else e₂
                                     | if nondet then e₁ else e₂
                                     | if coin a/b then e₁ else e₂
    | leaf | node x₁ x₂ x₃           | match x with | leaf → e₁ | node x₁ x₂ x₃ → e₂
    | ( x₁ , x₂ )                    | match x with | ( x₁ , x₂ ) → e
    | let x = e₁ in e₂               | x
```

Fig. 7. A Core Probabilistic (First-Order) Programming Language

write $\mu = \{a_i^{p_i}\}_{i \in I}$, assigning probabilities p_i to $a_i \in A$ for every $i \in I$, where I is a suitable chosen index set. We set $|\mu| := \sum_{i \in I} p_i$. If the support is finite, we simply write $\mu = \{a_1^{p_1}, \ldots, a_n^{p_n}\}$ The *expected value* of a function $f \colon A \to \mathbb{R}_0^+$ on $\mu \in \mathsf{D}(A)$ is defined as $\mathbb{E}_\mu(f) := \sum_{a \in \mathsf{supp}(\mu)} \mu(a) \cdot f(a)$. Further, we denote by $\sum_{i \in I} p_i \cdot \mu_i$ the *convex combination of distributions* μ_i, where $\sum_{i \in I} p_i \leqslant 1$. As by assumption $\sum_{i \in I} p_i \leqslant 1$, $\sum_{i \in I} p_i \cdot \mu_i$ is always a (sub-)distribution.

In the following, we also employ a slight extension of (discrete) distributions, dubbed *multidistributions* [4]. Multidistributions are countable *multisets* $\{a_i^{p_i}\}_{i \in I}$ over pairs $p_i \colon a_i$ of *probabilities* $0 < p_i \leqslant 1$ and *objects* $a_i \in A$ with $\sum_{i \in I} p_i \leqslant 1$. (For ease of presentation, we do not distinguish notationally between sets and multisets.) Multidistributions over objects A are denoted by $\mathsf{M}(A)$. For a multidistribution $\mu \in \mathsf{M}(A)$ the induced distribution $\overline{\mu} \in \mathsf{D}(A)$ is defined in the obvious way by summing up the probabilities of equal objects.

Syntax. In Fig. 7, we detail the syntax of our core probabilistic (first-order) programming language. With the exception of ticks, expressions are given in let-normal form to simplify the presentation of the operational semantics and the typing rules. In order to ease the readability, we make use of mild syntactic sugaring in the presentation of actual code (as we already did above).

To make the presentation more succinct, we assume only the following types: a set of *base types* $\mathcal{B}$ such as Booleans $\mathsf{Bool} = \{\mathtt{true}, \mathtt{false}\}$, integers Int, or rationals Rat, product types, and binary trees T, whose internal nodes are labelled with elements $b \colon \mathsf{B}$, where B denotes an arbitrary base type. *Values* are either of base types, trees or pairs of values. We use lower-case Greek letters (from the beginning of the alphabet) for the denotation of types. Elements $t \colon \mathsf{T}$ are defined by the following grammar which fixes notation. $t ::= \mathtt{leaf} \mid \mathtt{node}\ t_1\ b\ t_2$. The size of a tree is the number of leaves: $|\mathtt{leaf}| := 1$, $|\mathtt{node}\ t\ a\ u| := |t| + |u|$.

We skip the standard definition of integer constants $n \in \mathbb{Z}$ as well as variable declarations, cf. [29]. Furthermore, we omit binary operators with the exception of essential comparisons. As mentioned, to represent sampling we make use of a dedicated if-then-else expression, whose guard evaluates to true depending on a coin toss with fixed probability. Further, non-deterministic choice is similarly rendered via an if-then-else expression. Moreover, we make use of *ticking*, denoted by an operator $\cdot^{\surd a/b}$ to annotate costs, where a, b are optional

$$f \; x_1\sigma \; \ldots \; x_k\sigma \mapsto e\sigma \qquad\qquad\qquad \text{if true then } e_1 \text{ else } e_2 \mapsto e_1$$

$$\text{let } x = w \text{ in } e_2 \mapsto e_2[x \mapsto w] \qquad\qquad \text{if false then } e_1 \text{ else } e_2 \mapsto e_2$$

$$\text{match leaf with} | \text{leaf->} e_1 | \text{node } x_0 \; x_1 \; x_2 \text{->} e_2 \mapsto e_1$$

$$\text{match node } t \; a \; u \text{ with} | \text{leaf->} e_1 | \text{node } x_0 \; x_1 \; x_2 \text{->} e_2 \mapsto e_2$$

$$\text{match } (t,u) \text{ with } | (t,u) \text{->} e \mapsto e$$

$$\text{if coin } a/b \text{ then } e_1 \text{ else } e_2 \mapsto \{e_1^{a/b}, e_2^{1-a/b}\} \quad \text{if nondet then } e_1 \text{ else } e_2 \mapsto e_1$$

$$e^{\checkmark \, a/b} \overset{a/b}{\mapsto} e \qquad\qquad\qquad\qquad\qquad \text{if nondet then } e_1 \text{ else } e_2 \mapsto e_2$$

Assuming $f \; x_1 \; \ldots \; x_k = e \in \mathsf{P}$, σ respects the signature of f, and w is a value.

Fig. 8. One-Step Reduction Rules

and default to one. Following Avanzini et al. [2], we represent ticking $\cdot^{\checkmark}$ as an operation, rather than in let-normal form, as in Wang et al. [37]. (This allows us to suit a big-step semantics that only accumulates the cost of terminating expressions.) The set of all expressions is denoted $\mathcal{E}$.

A *typing context* is a mapping from variables $\mathcal{V}$ to types. Type contexts are denoted by upper-case Greek letters, and the empty context is denoted ε. A program P consists of a signature $\mathcal{F}$ together with a set of function definitions of the form $f \; x_1 \; \ldots \; x_n = e_f$, where the x_i are variables and e_f an expression. When considering some expression e that includes function calls we will always assume that these function calls are defined by some program P. A *substitution* or *(environment)* σ is a mapping from variables to values that respects types. Substitutions are denoted as sets of assignments: $\sigma = \{x_1 \mapsto t_1, \ldots, x_n \mapsto t_n\}$. We write $\mathsf{dom}(\sigma)$ to denote the domain of σ.

4 Operational Semantics

Small-Step Semantics. The small-step semantics is formalised as a (weighted) non-deterministic, probabilistic abstract reduction system [4,9] over $\mathsf{M}(\mathcal{E})$. In this way (expected) cost, non-determinism and probabilistic sampling are taken care of. Informally, a probabilistic abstract reduction system is a transition systems where reducts are chosen from a probability distribution. A reduction wrt. such a system is then given by a stochastic process [9], or equivalently, as a reduction relation over *multidistributions* [4], which arise naturally in the context of non-determinism (we refer the reader to [4] for an example that illustrates the advantage of multidistributions in the presence of non-determinism).

Following [5], we equip transitions with (positive) weights, amounting to the cost of the transition. Formally, a *(weighted) Probabilistic Abstract Reduction System* (PARS) on a countable set A is a ternary relation $\cdot \mapsto \cdot \; \subseteq A \times \mathbb{R}_0^+ \times \mathsf{D}(A)$. For $a \in A$, a rule $a \overset{c}{\mapsto} \{b^{\mu(b)}\}_{b \in A}$ indicates that a reduces to b with probability $\mu(b)$ and cost $c \in \mathbb{R}_0^+$. Note that any right-hand-side of a PARS is supposed to be a *full* distribution, ie. the probabilities in μ sum up to 1. Given two objects a and b, $a \overset{c}{\mapsto} \{b^1\}$ will be written $a \overset{c}{\mapsto} b$ for brevity. An object $a \in A$ is called *terminal* if there is no rule $a \overset{c}{\mapsto} \mu$, denoted $a \not\mapsto$. We suit the one-step reduction relation $\mapsto$ given in Fig. 8 as a (non-deterministic) PARS over multidistributions.

$$\frac{e \xmapsto{c} \{e_i^{p_i}\}_{i \in I}}{\{\mathbb{C}[e^1]\} \xrightarrow{c} \{\mathbb{C}[e_i]^{p_i}\}_{i \in I}} \text{ (Step)} \qquad \frac{\mu_i \xrightarrow{c_i} \nu_i \quad \sum_i p_i \leqslant 1}{\biguplus_i p_i \cdot \mu_i \xrightarrow{\sum_i p_i c_i} \biguplus_i p_i \cdot \nu_i} \text{ (Conv)}$$

$$\frac{v \not\mapsto}{\{v^1\} \xrightarrow{0} \{v^1\}} \text{ (NF)}$$

Fig. 9. Probabilistic Reduction Rules of Distributions of Expressions

As above, we sometimes identify Dirac distributions $\{e^1\}$ with e. *Evaluation contexts* are formed by `let` expressions, as in the following grammar: $\mathbb{C} ::= \square \mid \text{let } x = \mathbb{C} \text{ in } e$. We denote with $\mathbb{C}[e]$ the result of substitution the empty context $\square$ with expression e. Contexts are exploited to lift the one-step reduction to a ternary weighted reduction relation $\xrightarrow{\cdot} \subseteq \mathsf{M}(\mathcal{E}) \times \mathbb{R}_0^{+\infty} \times \mathsf{M}(\mathcal{E})$, cf. Fig. 9. (In (Conv), $\biguplus$ refers to the usual notion of multiset union.)

The relation $\xrightarrow{\cdot}$ constitutes the operational (small-step) semantics of our simple probabilistic function language. Thus $\mu \xrightarrow{c} \nu$ states that the submultidistribution of objects μ evolves to a submultidistribution of reducts ν in one step, with an expected cost of c. Note that since $\mapsto$ is non-deterministic, so is the reduction relation $\xrightarrow{}$. We now define the evaluation of an expression $e \in \mathcal{E}$ wrt. to the small-step relation $\xrightarrow{}$: We set $e \xrightarrow{c}_\infty \mu$, if there is a (possibly infinite) sequence $\{e^1\} \xrightarrow{c_1} \mu_1 \xrightarrow{c_2} \mu_2 \xrightarrow{c_3} \ldots$ with $c = \sum_{n \geqslant} c_n$ and $\mu = \lim_{n \to \infty} \overline{\mu_n}|_V$, where $\overline{\mu_n}|_V$ denotes the restriction of the distribution $\overline{\mu_n}$ (induced by the multidistribution μ_n) to a (sub-)distribution over values. Note that the $\overline{\mu_n}|_V$ form a CPO wrt. the pointwise ordering, cf. [39]. Hence, the fixed point $\mu = \lim_{n \to \infty} \overline{\mu_n}|_V$ exists. We also write $e \xrightarrow{}_\infty \mu$ in case the cost of the evaluation is not important.

(Positive) Almost Sure Termination. A program P is *almost surely terminating* (*AST*) if for any substitution σ, and any evaluation $e\sigma \xrightarrow{}_\infty \mu$, we have that μ forms a full distribution. For the definition of positive almost sure termination we assume that every statement of P is enclosed in an ticking operation with cost one; we note that such a cost models the length of the computation. We say P is *positively almost surely terminating* (*PAST*), if for any substitution σ, and any evaluation $e\sigma \xrightarrow{c}_\infty \mu$, we have $c < \infty$. It is well known that PAST implies AST, cf. [9].

Big-Step Semantics. We now define the aforementioned big-step semantics. We first define approximate judgments $\sigma \vdash_n^c e \Rightarrow \mu$, see Fig. 10, which say that in derivation trees with depth up to n the expression e evaluates to a subdistribution μ over values with cost c. We now consider the cost c_n and subdistribution μ_n in $\sigma \vdash_n^{c_n} e \Rightarrow \mu_n$ for $n \to \infty$. Note that the subdistributions μ_n in $\sigma \vdash_n^{c_n} e \Rightarrow \mu_n$ form a CPO wrt. the pointwise ordering, cf. [39]. Hence, there exists a fixed point $\mu = \lim_{n \to \infty} \mu_n$. Moreover, we set $c = \lim_{n \to \infty} c_n$ (note that either c_n converges to some real $c \in \mathbb{R}_0^{+\infty}$ or we have $c = \infty$). We now define the big-step judgments $\sigma \vdash e \Rightarrow \mu$ by setting $\mu = \lim_{n \to \infty} \mu_n$ and $c = \lim_{n \to \infty} c_n$ for $\sigma \vdash_n^{c_n} e \Rightarrow \mu_n$.

$$\frac{e \text{ is not a value}}{\sigma \vdash_0^0 e \Rightarrow \{\}} \qquad \sigma \vdash_0^0 \text{leaf} \Rightarrow \{\text{leaf}^1\} \qquad \frac{x_1\sigma = t \quad x_2\sigma = b \quad x_3\sigma = u}{\sigma \vdash_0^0 \text{node } x_1\ x_2\ x_3 \Rightarrow \{(\text{node } t\ b\ u)^1\}}$$

$$\frac{x\sigma = v}{\sigma \vdash_0^0 x \Rightarrow \{v^1\}} \qquad \frac{x_1\sigma = t \quad x_2\sigma = u}{\sigma \vdash_0^0 (x_1,x_2) \Rightarrow \{(t,u)^1\}} \qquad \frac{f\ y_1\ \cdots\ y_k = e \in \mathsf{P} \quad \sigma' \vdash_n^c e \Rightarrow \mu}{\sigma \vdash_{n+1}^c f\ x_1\ \cdots\ x_k \Rightarrow \mu}$$

$$\frac{\sigma \vdash_n^{c_1} e_1 \Rightarrow \nu \quad \text{for all } w \in \mathsf{supp}(\nu): \sigma[x \mapsto w] \vdash_n^{c_w} e_2 \Rightarrow \mu_w}{\sigma \vdash_{n+1}^{\,c_1+\sum_{w\in\mathsf{supp}(\nu)}\nu(w)\cdot c_w} \text{let } x = e_1 \text{ in } e_2 \Rightarrow \sum_{w\in\mathsf{supp}(\nu)} \nu(w)\cdot \mu_w}$$

$$\frac{x\sigma = \text{leaf} \quad \sigma \vdash_n^c e_1 \Rightarrow \mu}{\sigma \vdash_{n+1}^c \text{match } x \text{ with} \mid \text{leaf} \to e_1 \qquad\qquad \Rightarrow \mu \atop \qquad\qquad\quad\ \mid \text{node } x_0\ x_1\ x_2 \to e_2}$$

$$\frac{x\sigma = \text{node } t\ a\ u \quad \sigma'' \vdash_n^c e_2 \Rightarrow \mu}{\sigma \vdash_{n+1}^c \text{match } x \text{ with} \mid \text{leaf} \to e_1 \qquad\qquad \Rightarrow \mu \atop \qquad\qquad\quad\ \mid \text{node } x_0\ x_1\ x_2 \to e_2}$$

$$\frac{x\sigma = \text{true} \quad \sigma \vdash_n^c e_1 \Rightarrow \mu}{\sigma \vdash_{n+1}^c \text{if } x \text{ then } e_1 \text{ else } e_2 \Rightarrow \mu} \qquad\qquad \frac{\sigma \vdash_n^c e_1 \Rightarrow \mu}{\sigma \vdash_{n+1}^c \text{if nondet then } e_1 \text{ else } e_2 \Rightarrow \mu}$$

$$\frac{x\sigma = \text{false} \quad \sigma \vdash_n^c e_2 \Rightarrow \mu}{\sigma \vdash_{n+1}^c \text{if } x \text{ then } e_1 \text{ else } e_2 \Rightarrow \mu} \qquad\qquad \frac{\sigma \vdash_n^c e_2 \Rightarrow \mu}{\sigma \vdash_{n+1}^c \text{if nondet then } e_1 \text{ else } e_2 \Rightarrow \mu}$$

$$\frac{x\sigma = (t,u) \quad \sigma''' \vdash_n^c e \Rightarrow \mu}{\sigma \vdash_{n+1}^c \text{match } x \text{ with} \mid (x_1,x_2) \to e \Rightarrow \mu} \qquad\qquad \frac{\sigma \vdash_n^c e \Rightarrow \mu}{\sigma \vdash_{n+1}^{c+|\mu|\cdot a/b} e^{\checkmark a/b} \Rightarrow \mu}$$

$$\frac{\sigma \vdash_n^{c_1} e_1 \Rightarrow \mu_1 \quad \sigma \vdash_n^{c_2} e_2 \Rightarrow \mu_2 \quad p = a/b}{\sigma \vdash_{n+1}^{\,pc_1+(1-p)c_2} \text{if coin } a/b \text{ then } e_1 \text{ else } e_2 \Rightarrow p\mu_1 + (1-p)\mu_2}$$

Here $\sigma[x \mapsto w]$ denotes the update of the environment σ such that $\sigma[x \mapsto w](x) = w$ and the value of all other variables remains unchanged. For function application we set $\sigma' := \{y_1 \mapsto x_1\sigma, \ldots, y_k \mapsto x_k\sigma\}$. In the rules covering match we set $\sigma'' := \sigma \uplus \{x_0 \mapsto t, x_1 \mapsto a, x_2 \mapsto u\}$ and $\sigma''' := \sigma \uplus \{x_0 \mapsto t, x_2 \mapsto u\}$ for trees and tuples respectively.

Fig. 10. Big-Step Semantics.

We want to emphasise that the cost c in $\sigma \vdash^c e \Rightarrow \mu$ only counts the ticks on terminating computations.

Theorem 1 (Equivalence). *Let* P *be a program and* σ *a substitution. Then,* *(i)* $\sigma \vdash^c e \Rightarrow \mu$ *implies that* $e\sigma \xrightarrow{c'}_\infty \mu$ *for some* $c' \geq c$, *and (ii)* $e\sigma \xrightarrow{c}_\infty \mu$ *implies that* $\sigma \vdash^{c'} e \Rightarrow \mu$ *for some* $c' \leqslant c$. *Moreover, if* $e\sigma$ *almost-surely terminates, we can choose* $c = c'$ *in both cases.*

The provided operational big-step semantics generalises the (big-step) semantics given in [18]. Further, while partly motivated by big-step semantics introduced in [37], our big-step semantics is technically incomparable—due to a different representation of ticking—while providing additional expressivity.

$$\frac{\Gamma|Q \vdash e : \alpha|Q'}{\Gamma|Q + {}^a\!/_b \vdash e^{\checkmark\, a/b} : \alpha|Q'} \quad \text{(tick : now)}$$

$$\frac{\Gamma|Q \vdash e : \alpha|Q'}{\Gamma|Q \vdash e^{\checkmark\, a/b} : \alpha|Q' - {}^a\!/_b} \quad \text{(tick : defer)}$$

Fig. 11. Ticking Operator. Note that a, b are not variables but literal numbers.

5   Type-and-Effect System for Expected Cost Analysis

5.1   Resource Functions

In Sect. 2, we introduced a variant of Schoenmakers' potential function, denoted as $\mathsf{rk}(t)$, and the additional potential functions $p_{(a_1,\ldots,a_n,b)}(t_1,\ldots,t_n) = \log_2(a_1 \cdot |t_1| + \cdots + a_n \cdot |t_n| + b)$, denoting the $\log_2$ of a linear combination of tree sizes. We demand $\sum_{i=1}^{n} a_i + b \geqslant 0$ ($a_i \in \mathbb{N}, b \in \mathbb{Z}$) for well-definedness of the latter; $\log_2$ denotes the logarithm to the base 2. Throughout the paper we stipulate $\log_2(0) := 0$ in order to avoid case distinctions. Note that the constant function 1 is representable: $1 = \lambda t.\, \log_2(0 \cdot |t| + 2) = p_{(0,2)}$. We are now ready to state the resource annotation of a sequence of trees.

Definition 1. *A* resource annotation *or simply* annotation *of length m is a sequence $Q = [q_1,\ldots,q_m] \cup \big[(q_{(a_1,\ldots,a_m,b)})\, a_i, b \in \mathbb{N}\big]$, vanishing almost everywhere. The length of Q is denoted $|Q|$. The empty annotation, that is, the annotation where all coefficients are set to zero, is denoted as $\varnothing$. Let $t_1,\ldots,t_m$ be a sequence of trees. Then, the potential of $t_m,\ldots,t_n$ wrt. Q is given by*

$$\Phi(t_1,\ldots,t_m \mid Q) := \sum_{i=1}^{m} q_i \cdot \mathsf{rk}(t_i) + \sum_{a_1,\ldots,a_m \in \mathbb{N}, b \in \mathbb{Z}} q_{(a_1,\ldots,a_m,b)} \cdot p_{(a_1,\ldots,a_m,b)}(t_1,\ldots,t_m).$$

In case of an annotation of length 1, we sometimes write q_* instead of q_1. We may also write $\Phi(v : \alpha|Q)$ for the potential of a value of type α annotated with Q. Both notations were already used above. Note that only values of tree type are assigned a potential. We use the convention that the sequence elements of resource annotations are denoted by the lower-case letter of the annotation, potentially with corresponding sub- or superscripts.

Example 1. Let t be a tree. To model its potential as $\log_2(|t|)$ in according to Definition 1, we simply set $q_{(1,0)} := 1$ and thus obtain $\Phi(t|Q) = \log_2(|t|)$, which describes the potential associated to the input tree t of our leading example `descend` above. □

Let σ be a substitution, let Γ denote a typing context and let $x_1 : \top, \ldots, x_n : \top$ denote all tree types in Γ. A *resource annotation for Γ* or simply *annotation* is an annotation for the sequence of trees $x_1\sigma, \ldots, x_n\sigma$. We define the *potential* of the annotated context $\Gamma|Q$ wrt. a substitution σ as $\Phi(\sigma; \Gamma \mid Q) := \Phi(x_1\sigma, \ldots, x_n\sigma \mid Q)$.

$$\frac{\Gamma|Q_1 \vdash e_1 : \alpha|Q' \quad \Gamma|Q_2 \vdash e_2 : \alpha|Q' \quad p = {}^a/_b \quad Q = p \cdot Q_1 + (1-p) \cdot Q_2}{\Gamma|Q \vdash \text{if coin } a/b \text{ then } e_1 \text{ else } e_2 : \alpha|Q'} \text{ (ite : coin)}$$

Fig. 12. Conditional expression that models tossing a coin.

Definition 2. *An annotated signature $\mathcal{F}$ maps functions f to sets of pairs of annotated types for the arguments and the annotated type of the result:*

$$\mathcal{F}(f) := \{\alpha_1 \times \cdots \times \alpha_n \,|Q \to \beta_1 \times \cdots \times \beta_k| \, Q'|m = |Q|, 1 = |Q'|\}.$$

We suppose f takes n arguments of which m are trees; $m \leqslant n$ by definition. Similarly, the return type may be the product $\beta_1 \times \cdots \times \beta_i$. In this case, we demand that at most one β_i is a tree type.[3]

Instead of $\alpha_1 \times \cdots \times \alpha_n \,|Q \to \beta_1 \times \cdots \times \beta_k| \, Q' \in \mathcal{F}(f)$, we sometimes succinctly write $f : \alpha|Q \to \beta|Q'$ where α, β denote the product types $\alpha_1 \times \cdots \times \alpha_n$, $\beta_1 \times \cdots \times \beta_k$, respectively. It is tacitly understood that the above syntactic restrictions on the length of the annotations Q, Q' are fulfilled. For every function f, we also consider its *cost-free* variant from which all ticks have been removed. We collect the cost-free signatures of all functions in the set $\mathcal{F}^{cf}$.

Example 2. Consider the function `descend` depicted in Fig. 2. Its signature is formally represented as $\mathsf{T}|Q \to \mathsf{T}|Q'$, where $Q := [q_*] \cup [(q_{(a,b)})_{a,b \in \mathbb{Z}}]$ and $Q' := [q'_*] \cup [(q'_{(a,b)})_{a,b \in \mathbb{Z}}]$. We leave it to the reader to specify the coefficients in Q, Q' so that the rule (app) as depicted in Sect. 2 can indeed be employed to type the recursive call of `descend`.

Let $Q = [q_*] \cup [(q_{(a,b)})_{a,b \in \mathbb{N}}]$ be an annotation and let K be a rational such that $q_{(0,2)} + K \geqslant 0$. Then, $Q' := Q + K$ is defined as follows: $Q' = [q_*] \cup [(q'_{(a,b)})_{a,b \in \mathbb{N}}]$, where $q'_{(0,2)} := q_{(0,2)} + K$ and for all $(a,b) \neq (0,2)$ $q'_{(a,b)} := q_{(a,b)}$. Recall that $q_{(0,2)}$ is the coefficient of function $p_{(0,2)}(t) = \log_2(0|t|+2) = 1$, so the annotation $Q+K$ increments or decrements cost from the potential induced by Q by $|K|$, respectively. Further, we define the multiplication of an annotation Q by a constant K, denoted as $K \cdot Q$ pointwise. Moreover, let $P = [p_*] \cup [(p_{(a,b)})_{a,b \in \mathbb{N}}]$ be another annotation. Then the addition $P+Q$ of annotations P, Q is similarly defined pointwise.

5.2 Typing Rules

The non-probabilistic part of the type system is given in [19]. In contrast to the type system employed in [14,18], the cost model is not fixed but controlled by the ticking operator. Hence, the corresponding application rule (app) has been adapted. Costing of evaluation is now handled by a dedicated *ticking* operator, cf. Fig. 11. In Fig. 12, we give the rule (ite : coin) responsible for typing probabilistic conditionals.

---

[3] The restriction to at most one tree type in the resulting type is non-essential and could be lifted. However, as our benchmark functions do not require this extension, we have elided it for ease of presentation.

```
1 foo t = match t with
2   | leaf          → leaf
3   | node l a r → let l' = (foo l)ˇ in let r' = (foo r)ˇ in
4       if nondet then l' else r'
```

Fig. 13. Function `foo` illustrates the difference between (tick : now) and (tick : defer).

We remark that the core type system, that is, the type system given by Fig. 12 together with the remaining rules [19], ignoring annotations, enjoys subject reduction and progress in the following sense, which is straightforward to verify.

Lemma 1. *Let e be such that $e : \alpha$ holds. Then: (i) If $e \xmapsto{c} \{e_i^{p_i}\}_{i \in I}$, then $e_i : \alpha$ holds for all $i \in I$. (ii) The expression e is in normal form wrt. $\xmapsto{c}$ iff e is a value.*

5.3 Soundness Theorems

A program P is called *well-typed* if for any definition $f(x_1, \ldots, x_n) = e \in \mathsf{P}$ and any annotated signature $f : \alpha_1 \times \cdots \times \alpha_n | Q \to \beta | Q'$, we have a corresponding typing $x_1 : \alpha_1, \ldots, x_k : \alpha_k | Q \vdash e : \beta | Q'$. A program P is called *cost-free* well-typed, if the cost-free typing relation is used (which employs the cost-free signatures of all functions).

Theorem 2 (Soundness Theorem for (tick : now)). *Let P be well-typed. Suppose $\Gamma | Q \vdash e : \alpha | Q'$ and $e\sigma \xrightarrow{c}_\infty \mu$. Then $\Phi(\sigma; \Gamma | Q) \geqslant c + \mathbb{E}_\mu(\lambda v. \Phi(v | Q'))$. Further, if $\Gamma | Q \vdash^{cf} e : \alpha | Q'$, then $\Phi(\sigma; \Gamma | Q) \geqslant \mathbb{E}_\mu(\lambda v. \Phi(v | Q'))$.*

Corollary 1. *Let P be a well-typed program such that ticking accounts for all evaluation steps. Suppose $\Gamma | Q \vdash e : \alpha | Q'$. Then e is positive almost surely terminating (and thus in particular almost surely terminating).*

Theorem 3 (Soundness Theorem for (tick : defer)). *Let P be well-typed. Suppose $\Gamma | Q \vdash e : \alpha | Q'$ and $\sigma \xmapsto{c} e \Rightarrow \mu$. Then, we have $\Phi(\sigma; \Gamma | Q) \geqslant c + \mathbb{E}_\mu(\lambda v. \Phi(v | Q'))$. Further, if $\Gamma | Q \vdash^{cf} e : \alpha | Q'$, then $\Phi(\sigma; \Gamma | Q) \geqslant \mathbb{E}_\mu(\lambda v. \Phi(v | Q'))$.*

We comment on the trade-offs between Theorems 2 and 3. As stated in Corollary 1 the benefit of Theorem 2 is that when every recursive call is accounted for by a tick, then a type derivation implies the termination of the program under analysis. The same does not hold for Theorem 3. However, Theorem 3 allows to type more programs than Theorem 2, which is due to the fact that (tick : defer) rule is more permissive than (tick : now). This proves very useful, in case termination is not required (or can be established by other means).

We exemplify this difference on the `foo` function, see Fig. 13. Theorem 3 supports the derivation of the type $\mathsf{rk}(t) + \log_2(|t|) + 1 \geqslant \mathsf{rk}(\mathtt{foo}\ t) + 1$, while Theorem 2 does not. This is due to the fact that potential can be "borrowed" with Theorem 3. To wit, from the potential $\mathsf{rk}(t) + \log_2(|t|) + 1$ for `foo` one can derive the potential $\mathsf{rk}(l') + \mathsf{rk}(r')$ for the intermediate context after both let-expression (note there is no +1 in this context, because the +1 has been used to

Table 2. Coefficients q such $q \cdot \log_2(|t|)$ is a bound on the expected amortized complexity of splay depending on the probability p of a rotation and the cost c of a recursive call, where the cost of a rotation is $1 - c$. Coefficients are additionally presented in decimal representation to ease comparison.

c p	$1/2$		$1/3$		$2/3$	
$1/2$	$9/8$	1.125	1	1	$5/4$	1.25
$1/3$	1	1	$5/6$	$0.8\dot{3}$	$7/6$	$1.\dot{6}$
$2/3$	$55/36$	$1.52\dot{7}$	$77/54$	$1.4\overline{259}$	$44/27$	$1.\overline{629}$

pay for the ticks around the recursive calls). Afterwards one can restore the $+1$ by weakening $\mathsf{rk}(l') + \mathsf{rk}(r')$ to $\mathsf{rk}(\mathtt{foo}\ t) + 1$ (using in addition that $\mathsf{rk}(t) \geqslant 1$ for all trees t). On the other hand, we cannot "borrow" with Theorem 2 because the rule (tick : now) forces to pay the $+1$ for the recursive call immediately (but there is not enough potential to pay for this). In the same way, the application of rule (tick : defer) and Theorem 3 is essential to establish the logarithmic amortised costs of randomised splay trees. (We note that the termination of foo as well as of splay is easy to establish by other means: it suffices to observe that recursive calls are on sub-trees of the input tree).

6   Implementation and Evaluation

Implementation. Our prototype ATLAS is an extension of the tool described in [18]. In particular, we rely on the preprocessing steps and the implementation of the weakening rule as reported in [18] (which makes use of Farkas' Lemma in conjunction with selected mathematical facts about the logarithm as mentioned above). We only use the fully-automated mode reported in [18]. We have adapted the generation of the constraint system to the rules presented in this paper. We rely on Z3 [26] for solving the generated constraints. We use the optimisation heuristics of [18] for steering the solver towards solutions that minimize the resulting expected amortised complexity of the function under analysis.

Evaluation. We present results for the benchmarks described in Sect. 2 (plus a randomised version of splay heaps, the source code can be found in [19]) in Table 1. Table 3 details the computation time for type checking our results. Note that type inference takes considerably longer (tens of hours). To the best of our knowledge this is the first time that an expected amortised cost could be inferred for these data structures.

By comparing the costs of the operations of randomised splay trees and heaps to the costs of their deterministic versions (see Table 1), one can see the randomised variants have equal or lower complexity in all cases (as noted in Table 2 we have set the costs of the recursive call and the rotation to $1/2$, such that in the deterministic case, which corresponds to a coin toss with $p = 1$, these

Table 3. Number of assertions, solving time for type checking, and maximum memory usage (in mebibytes) for the combined analysis of functions per-module. The number of functions and lines of code is given for comparison.

Module	Functions	Lines	Assertions	Time	Memory
RandSplayTree	4	129	195 339	33M27S	19424.44
RandSplayHeap	2	34	77 680	6M15S	14914.51
RandMeldableHeap	3	15	25 526	20S	4290.67
CoinSearchTree	3	24	14 045	4S	1798.59
Tree	1	5	151	<1S	45.23

costs will always add up to one). Clearly, setting the costs of the recursion to the same value as the cost of the rotation does not need to reflect the relation of the actual costs. A more accurate estimation of the relation of these two costs will likely require careful experimentation with data structure implementations, which we consider orthogonal to our work. Instead, we report that our analysis is readily adapted to different costs and different coin toss probabilities. We present an evaluation for different values of p, recursion cost c and rotation cost $1 - c$ in Table 2. In preparing Table 2 the template $q^* \cdot \mathsf{rk}(t) + q_{(1,0)} \cdot \log_2(|t|) + q_{(0,2)}$ was used for performance reasons. The memory usage according to Z3's "max memory" statistic was 7129MiB per instance. The total runtime was 1H45M, with an average of 11M39S and a median of 2M33S. Two instances took longer time (36M and 49M).

Deterministic Benchmarks. For comparison we have also evaluated our tool ATLAS on the benchmarks of [18]. All results could be reproduced by our implementation. In fact, for the function SplayHeap.insert it yields an improvement of $1/4 \log_2(|h|)$, ie. $1/2 \log_2(|h|) + \log_2(|h| + 1) + 3/2$ compared to $3/4 \log_2(|h|) + \log_2(|h|+1) + 3/2$. We note that we are able to report better results because we have generalised the resource functions $p_{(a_1......a_m,b)} (t_1, \ldots, t_m) := \log_2(a_1 \cdot |t_1| + \cdots + a_m \cdot |t_m| + b)$ to also allow negative values for b (under the condition that $\sum_i a_i + b \geq 1$) and our generalised (let : tree) rule can take advantage of these generalized resource functions (see [19] for a statement of the rule and the proof of its soundness as part of the proof of Theorem 3).

7   Conclusion

In this paper, we present the first fully-automated *expected amortised cost analysis* of self-adjusting data structures, that is, of *randomised splay trees*, *randomised splay heaps* and *randomised meldable heaps*, which so far have only (semi-)manually been analysed in the literature.

In future work, we envision to extend our analysis to related probabilistic settings such as skip lists [30], randomised binary search trees [20] and *randomised treaps* [8]. We note that adaptation of the framework developed in this paper to new benchmarks will likely require to identify new potential functions and the extension of the type-effect-system with typing rules for these potential functions. Further, on more theoretical grounds we want to clarify the connection of the here proposed expected amortised cost analysis with Kaminski's ert-calculus, cf. [15], and study whether the expected cost transformer is conceivable as a potential function.

References

1. Albers, S., Karpinski, M.: Randomized splay trees: theoretical and experimental results. IPL **81**(4), 213–221 (2002). https://doi.org/10.1016/S0020-0190(01)00230-7

2. Avanzini, M., Barthe, G., Lago, U.D.: On continuation-passing transformations and expected cost analysis. PACMPL **5**(ICFP), 1–30 (2021). https://doi.org/10.1145/3473592

3. Avanzini, M., Lago, U.D., Ghyselen, A.: Type-based complexity analysis of probabilistic functional programs. In: Proceedings of 34th LICS, pp. 1–13. IEEE (2019). https://doi.org/10.1109/LICS.2019.8785725

4. Avanzini, M., Lago, U.D., Yamada, A.: On probabilistic term rewriting. Sci. Comput. Program. **185**, 102338 (2020). https://doi.org/10.1016/j.scico.2019.102338

5. Avanzini, M., Moser, G., Schaper, M.: A modular cost analysis for probabilistic programs. PACMPL **4**(OOPSLA), 172:1–172:30 (2020). https://doi.org/10.1145/3428240

6. Barthe, G., Katoen, J.P., Silva, A. (eds.): Foundations of Probabilistic Programming. Cambridge University Press, Cambridge (2020). https://doi.org/10.1017/9781108770750

7. Batz, K., Kaminski, B.L., Katoen, J., Matheja, C., Noll, T.: Quantitative separation logic: a logic for reasoning about probabilistic pointer programs. PACMPL **3**(POPL), 34:1–34:29 (2019). https://doi.org/10.1145/3290347

8. Blelloch, G.E., Reid-Miller, M.: Fast set operations using treaps. In: Proceedings of 10th SPAA, pp. 16–26 (1998). https://doi.org/10.1145/277651.277660

9. Bournez, O., Garnier, F.: Proving positive almost-sure termination. In: Giesl, J. (ed.) RTA 2005. LNCS, vol. 3467, pp. 323–337. Springer, Heidelberg (2005). https://doi.org/10.1007/978-3-540-32033-3_24

10. Chatterjee, K., Fu, H., Murhekar, A.: Automated recurrence analysis for almost-linear expected-runtime bounds. In: Majumdar, R., Kunčak, V. (eds.) CAV 2017. LNCS, vol. 10426, pp. 118–139. Springer, Cham (2017). https://doi.org/10.1007/978-3-319-63387-9_6

11. Eberl, M., Haslbeck, M.W., Nipkow, T.: Verified analysis of random binary tree structures. J. Autom. Reason. **64**(5), 879–910 (2020). https://doi.org/10.1007/s10817-020-09545-0

12. Fürer, M.: Randomized splay trees. In: Proceedings of 10th SODA, pp. 903–904 (1999). http://dl.acm.org/citation.cfm?id=314500.315079

13. Gambin, A., Malinowski, A.: Randomized meldable priority queues. In: Rovan, B. (ed.) SOFSEM 1998. LNCS, vol. 1521, pp. 344–349. Springer, Heidelberg (1998). https://doi.org/10.1007/3-540-49477-4_26

14. Hofmann, M., Leutgeb, L., Moser, G., Obwaller, D., Zuleger, F.: Type-based analysis of logarithmic amortised complexity. MSCS (2021). https://doi.org/10.1017/S0960129521000232
15. Kaminski, B.L., Katoen, J., Matheja, C., Olmedo, F.: Weakest precondition reasoning for expected runtimes of randomized algorithms. JACM **65**(5), 30:1–30:68 (2018). https://doi.org/10.1145/3208102
16. Kozen, D.: Semantics of probabilistic programs. J. Comput. Syst. Sci. **22**(3), 328–350 (1981)
17. Kozen, D.: A probabilistic PDL. JCSC **30**(2), 162–178 (1985). https://doi.org/10.1016/0022-0000(85)90012-1
18. Leutgeb, L., Moser, G., Zuleger, F.: ATLAS: automated amortised complexity analysis of self-adjusting data structures. In: Silva, A., Leino, K.R.M. (eds.) CAV 2021. LNCS, vol. 12760, pp. 99–122. Springer, Cham (2021). https://doi.org/10.1007/978-3-030-81688-9_5
19. Leutgeb, L., Moser, G., Zuleger, F.: Automated expected amortised cost analysis of probabilistic data structures. arXiv:2206.03537 (2022)
20. Martínez, C., Roura, S.: Randomized binary search trees. JACM **45**(2), 288–323 (1998). https://doi.org/10.1145/274787.274812
21. McIver, A., Morgan, C., Kaminski, B.L., Katoen, J.: A new proof rule for almost-sure termination. PACMPL **2**(POPL), 33:1–33:28 (2018). https://doi.org/10.1145/3158121
22. Meyer, F., Hark, M., Giesl, J.: Inferring expected runtimes of probabilistic integer programs using expected sizes. In: TACAS 2021. LNCS, vol. 12651, pp. 250–269. Springer, Cham (2021). https://doi.org/10.1007/978-3-030-72016-2_14
23. Mitzenmacher, M., Upfal, E.: Probability and Computing: Randomized Algorithms and Probabilistic Analysis. Cambridge University Press, Cambridge (2005). https://doi.org/10.1017/CBO9780511813603
24. Moosbrugger, M., Bartocci, E., Katoen, J.-P., Kovács, L.: Automated termination analysis of polynomial probabilistic programs. In: ESOP 2021. LNCS, vol. 12648, pp. 491–518. Springer, Cham (2021). https://doi.org/10.1007/978-3-030-72019-3_18
25. Motwani, R., Raghavan, P.: Randomized algorithms. In: Algorithms and Theory of Computation Handbook. Cambridge University Press (1999). https://doi.org/10.1201/9781420049503-c16
26. de Moura, L., Björner, N.: Z3: an efficient SMT solver. In: Ramakrishnan, C.R., Rehof, J. (eds.) TACAS 2008. LNCS, vol. 4963, pp. 337–340. Springer, Heidelberg (2008). https://doi.org/10.1007/978-3-540-78800-3_24
27. Ngo, V.C., Carbonneaux, Q., Hoffmann, J.: Bounded expectations: resource analysis for probabilistic programs. In: Proceedings of 39th PLDI, pp. 496–512 (2018). https://doi.org/10.1145/3192366.3192394
28. Nipkow, T., Brinkop, H.: Amortized complexity verified. JAR **62**(3), 367–391 (2019)
29. Pierce, B.: Types and Programming Languages. MIT Press, Cambridge (2002)
30. Pugh, W.: Skip lists: a probabilistic alternative to balanced trees. CACM **33**(6), 668–676 (1990). https://doi.org/10.1145/78973.78977
31. Schoenmakers, B.: A systematic analysis of splaying. IPL **45**(1), 41–50 (1993)
32. Schoenmakers, B.: Data structures and amortized complexity in a functional setting. Ph.D. thesis, Eindhoven University of Technology (1992)
33. Schrijver, A.: Theory of Linear and Integer Programming. Wiley, Hoboken (1999)
34. Sleator, D., Tarjan, R.: Self-adjusting binary search trees. JACM **32**(3), 652–686 (1985)

35. Takisaka, T., Oyabu, Y., Urabe, N., Hasuo, I.: Ranking and repulsing supermartingales for reachability in probabilistic programs. In: Lahiri, S.K., Wang, C. (eds.) ATVA 2018. LNCS, vol. 11138, pp. 476–493. Springer, Cham (2018). https://doi.org/10.1007/978-3-030-01090-4_28

36. Tarjan, R.: Amortized computational complexity. SIAM J. Alg. Disc. Meth $6(2)$, 306–318 (1985)

37. Wang, D., Kahn, D.M., Hoffmann, J.: Raising expectations: automating expected cost analysis with types. PACMPL 4(ICFP), 110:1–110:31 (2020). https://doi.org/10.1145/3408992

38. Wang, P., Fu, H., Goharshady, A.K., Chatterjee, K., Qin, X., Shi, W.: Cost analysis of nondeterministic probabilistic programs. In: Proceedings of 40th PLDI, pp. 204–220. ACM (2019)

39. Winskel, G.: The Formal Semantics of Programming Languages. FCS, MIT Press (1993). https://doi.org/10.7551/mitpress/3054.003.0004

Murxla: A Modular and Highly Extensible API Fuzzer for SMT Solvers

Aina Niemetz$^{(\boxtimes)}$ ⓘ, Mathias Preiner ⓘ,
and Clark Barrett ⓘ

Stanford University, Stanford, USA
{niemetz,preiner,barrett}@cs.stanford.edu

Abstract. SMT solvers are highly complex pieces of software with performance, robustness, and correctness as key requirements. Complementing traditional testing techniques for these solvers with randomized stress testing has been shown to be quite effective. Recent work has showcased the value of input fuzzing for finding issues, but this approach typically does not comprehensively test a solver's API. Previous work on model-based API fuzzing was tailored to a single solver and a small subset of SMT-LIB. We present Murxla, a comprehensive, modular, and highly extensible model-based API fuzzer for SMT solvers. Murxla randomly generates valid sequences of solver API calls based on a customizable API model, with full support for the semantics and features of SMT-LIB. It is solver-agnostic but extensible to allow for solver-specific testing and supports option fuzzing, cross-checking with other solvers, translation to SMT-LIBv2, and SMT-LIBv2 input fuzzing. Our evaluation confirms its efficacy in finding issues in multiple state-of-the-art SMT solvers.

1 Introduction

Satisfiability Modulo Theories (SMT) solvers determine the satisfiability of formulas over first-order theories and their combinations. They serve as back-end reasoning engines for a wide range of applications in academia and industry [18, 27], including hardware and software verification [14,29,31,35,38,40], model checking [23,24,46], security [12,33], automated test-case generation [22,50], and synthesis [10,34]. Notable SMT solvers include Bitwuzla [42], Boolector [46], cvc5 [13], MathSAT [26], OpenSMT2 [36], SMTInterpol [25], SMT-RAT [28], STP [32], veriT [20], Yices2 [30], and Z3 [41]. State-of-the-art SMT solvers are complex pieces of software with up to hundreds of thousands lines of code. Because of their frequent use as back-ends in higher-level tool chains, strong requirements include performance, robustness, and a high level of trust. Due to their complex nature, full verification of SMT solvers has so far remained out of reach. Furthermore, most SMT solvers are under active development, meaning that there is a constant risk of introducing new issues. While traditional testing techniques

This work was supported in part by DARPA (award no. FA8650-18-2-7861), ONR (award no. N68335-17-C-0558), and by an Amazon Research Award.

S. Shoham and Y. Vizel (Eds.): CAV 2022, LNCS 13372, pp. 92–106, 2022.
https://doi.org/10.1007/978-3-031-13188-2_5

such as unit testing and a regression test suite are important, these techniques alone are insufficient for achieving high levels of robustness.

SMT solvers usually provide two user-facing interfaces: (i) a textual interface (expecting input in either SMT-LIBv2 [15] or some solver-specific format); and (ii) the application programming interface (API), which allows users to directly integrate the solver into a tool chain. Randomized stress testing (fuzz testing) can be used as a complement to traditional testing to attack these interfaces and has been shown to be very effective at finding issues and thereby helping to improve the correctness and robustness of SMT solvers. In 2009, Brummayer et al. [21] presented a grammar-based generative black-box input fuzzer for the SMT-LIBv1 language [48] called FuzzSMT, and in 2017, Niemetz et al. [45] presented a model-based API fuzz testing framework called BtorMBT for the SMT solver Boolector. More recently, fuzz testing of SMT solvers via their textual interface has gained even more traction with a series of papers on the subject in top venues [19,39,47,49,51,52]. Note that these approaches (and this paper) assume full knowledge of the input structure, i.e., they only generate valid textual input or sequences of API calls. Fuzz testing approaches that are unaware of the input structure can also be useful for testing whether invalid inputs or API calls are handled correctly. This is, however, not a direction we address in this paper.

As mentioned, recent work has focused on fuzzing the textual interface. This is not surprising, as it typically requires significantly less effort than API fuzzing. Input fuzzers generate a new input file or mutate an existing (so-called) seed input file and pass it to a solver binary. Fuzz testing of the solver API is more involved since it requires interaction with the solver—API fuzzers generate sequences of calls to the solver API and typically link against the solver library.

There are, however unique advantages that API fuzzers have. For example, API call sequences generated by API fuzzers may include features and extensions that are not supported by or cannot be expressed via the textual interface. Moreover, even if restricted to standard features, API fuzzers may be able to generate sequences of calls that are not possible using the textual interface, even if the textual interface is built on top of the user-facing API, and especially if it is not. On the other hand, API fuzzing cannot find bugs in parser code. Thus, both fuzzing strategies have unique benefits.

API fuzzing has been an integral part of the development workflow of the SMT solver Boolector [46] since 2013. Boolector supports quantified bit-vector formulas and quantifier-free formulas in the theories of fixed-size bit-vectors, arrays and uninterpreted functions. It ships with BtorMBT [45], an API fuzzer tailored to Boolector, which covers all features of Boolector except quantifiers. BtorMBT has been regularly and rigorously applied during active development of Boolector (locally, prior to major commits to master, and in a cluster setting on 30 nodes prior to every release), with great success. Notably, recent SMT fuzzing campaigns did not report any issues in code covered by BtorMBT [39]; in particular, the few that have been reported [2] all made use of quantified formulas, which are unsupported by BtorMBT. To the best of our knowledge,[1]

---

[1] The first two authors of this paper are the main developers of the SMT solvers Bitwuzla [42] and Boolector [46], and all three authors are part of the development team of the SMT solver CVC4 [16] and its successor cvc5 [13].

Boolector is the only SMT solver for which API fuzzing has been integrated as a core component of the development workflow.

One of BtorMBT's major weaknesses, however, is that it cannot (easily be extended to) be used with other SMT solvers—it is monolithic, tailored towards the supported theories, and directly calls Boolector's API. Further, it lacks support for quantified formulas, only supports a subset of the theories standardized in SMT-LIB, and even for those, not the full feature set since Boolector only supports a subset. For recording API call sequences, it relies on the API tracing feature of Boolector, the system under test. And for replaying and minimizing such recorded sequences, it requires additional tools.

Contributions. In this paper, we present Murxla, a modular and highly extensible model-based API fuzzer for SMT solvers. Murxla is a comprehensive fuzzing tool that generates valid sequences of solver API calls, records these sequences in a simple text-based trace format, and provides support for minimizing and replaying these traces while preserving the original behavior of the solver. Murxla builds on top of a generic solver interface that can be used with any SMT solver and provides full SMT-LIB support in terms of semantics, features, and standard theories. It further has experimental support for some non-standard theories (sequences, sets, bags) and is fully compatible with and configurable for solver-specific features, extensions, and restrictions. Murxla provides support for option fuzzing (randomly configuring solver options based on the options model of the solver) and can be run in cross-checking mode, where the answers of two different solvers are compared with each other. It additionally implements correctness checks for retrieved model values, unsat assumptions, and unsat cores. Finally, it can optionally translate generated API traces to SMT-LIBv2 (provided that the traces do not contain solver-specific extensions), and can thus be used as a textual interface fuzzer for any solver that supports SMT-LIBv2.

Murxla currently supports the SMT solvers Bitwuzla [42], Boolector [46], cvc5 [13], and Yices2 [30]. Our goal so far has been to fully cover solvers we are actively developing (the first three). We additionally added support for Yices2 as a proof of concept for showing that the tool is sufficiently general and modular to be used with solvers other than our own.

Related Work. The first application of model-based API fuzzing in the context of verification back-ends was proposed by Artho et al. [11] for the SAT solver Lingeling [17]. In the context of SMT solvers, the first and only integration of model-based API fuzzing as a core component of the development workflow was for the solver Boolector [45], as described above. In both instances, the authors showed the effectiveness of the approach for testing solvers, in particular in combination with option fuzzing and delta debugging.

The first input fuzzer for the SMT-LIB language was FuzzSMT [21], a generative grammar-based fuzzer supporting most of SMT-LIBv1 [48]. In 2018, Blotsky et al. [19] presented an SMT-LIBv2 input fuzzer specifically for strings, which generates and mutates SMT-LIBv2 input and mainly targets performance issues. In 2020, Winterer et al. [51,52] proposed two mutational approaches, one based on merging two inputs and the other based on mutating operators. The former supports only integers, reals, and strings, whereas the latter supports all benchmarks in SMT-LIB but only mutations for the most basic operators. In the same year, Mansur et al. [39] presented Storm, an SMT-LIBv2 fuzzer based on mutating the Boolean structure of an input. Most recently, Park et al. [47] presented TypeFuzz, a hybrid approach for integers, reals, and strings which mutates SMT-LIBv2 by replacing expressions with newly generated expressions. Finally, Scott et al. [49] recently proposed a mutational fuzzer for all of SMT-LIB which leverages reinforcement learning and targets performance issues.

2   Model-Based API Fuzzing for SMT Solvers

Generally speaking, model-based API fuzzing can be seen as lifting grammar-based input fuzzing to the API level: it requires a "model" of the solver that defines what sequences of API calls are valid. For convenience, we consider this model to be made up of three distinct parts: (i) the *semantic (or data) model*, which defines constructs (such as theories, sorts, operators, and commands) and their semantics (usually based on the SMT-LIBv2 [15] standard); (ii) the *API model*, which defines the usage of the API itself; and (iii) the *options model*, which defines configuration options and how they may or may not be combined.

The main requirements for SMT solvers, especially when used as back-ends of higher-level tool chains, are correctness, performance, and robustness. Within the SMT community, the notion of "issue" is thus commonly defined as one of the following: (i) *soundness* issues—either refutation unsoundness (the solver answers *unsat* when the input is *sat*) or model unsoundness (the solver answers *sat* when the input is *unsat*); (ii) *incorrect witnesses*—models (values), proofs, unsat cores, or unsat assumptions; (iii) *crashes*—assertion failures, segmentation faults; and (iv) *performance regressions*. The most critical issues are soundness issues. Refutation unsoundness is especially problematic, as most solvers provide limited or no means for checking the correctness of an *unsat* result. Model unsoundness is less problematic, since state-of-the-art SMT solvers usually provide models for satisfiable formulas, which are easier to check for correctness. The easiest way to identify soundness issues is to check one solver against a second solver, unless the satisfiability of the input formula is known or can be determined by construction. Witnesses are very often checked inside the solver when in debug mode, and their correctness can be determined outside the solver with relatively little effort for all but proofs, which require more involved checking.

As SMT solver developers, we are interested in catching issues as close to the source as possible. For that purpose, in the context of model-based API fuzzing, we configure solvers under test in debug mode with assertions enabled.

3   Murxla

Murxla is a modular model-based API fuzzing tool for SMT solvers which generates valid solver API call sequences and supports the recording, replaying, and minimizing of these sequences for debugging purposes. Murxla is written in C++ and available under the GPLv3 at [43]. Extensive documentation is

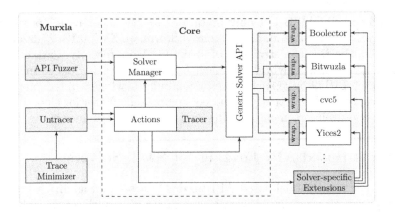

Fig. 1. Murxla architecture. (Color figure online)

available at [44]. A high-level view of its architecture is given as a call graph in Fig. 1. Murxla can integrate any SMT solver (provided that it exposes an API in a programming language that can be integrated). Murxla provides a solver API abstraction, the *Generic Solver API*, which is then specialized via a solver wrapper for a specific solver. Solver-specific components are indicated in blue in Fig. 1 and consist of the solver wrappers and solver-specific extensions of the general API model and options model implemented by Murxla. The four main components of Murxla (green) are the *API Fuzzer*, the *Tracer*, the *Untracer*, and the *Trace Minimizer*.

The API Fuzzer is responsible for generating random but valid API call sequences to the solver under test. The Tracer records these sequences in an *API trace*, which stores all the information required to replay the trace with the Untracer. Replaying a trace with the Untracer executes the exact same API call sequence that was executed when recording the trace. This is particularly useful for replicating interesting behavior that was uncovered while fuzzing the API of the solver under test. The Trace Minimizer takes an API trace as input and tries to minimize it while preserving its behavior with respect to the solver under test. Murxla's core connects all of these components. It is also responsible for interfacing with the SMT solvers and maintaining all sorts and terms created by a solver. In the following, we will describe these components in more detail.

3.1   The Core

Murxla's Core manages communication and the sorts and terms created by a solver. It consists of three modules: the *Actions*, the *Solver Manager*, and the *Generic Solver API*.

Actions. An action is an abstraction defining a particular interaction with the solver under test. These interactions are represented internally as a set of calls to the Generic Solver API. Actions are responsible for three tasks: (1) randomly *generating* API call arguments; (2) *executing* API calls with a given set of arguments; and (3) *replaying* a traced copy of the action.

Murxla currently implements a base set of 25 actions which wrap the methods of the Generic Solver API and include creating and deleting a solver instance, configuring solver options, creating sorts and terms, asserting formulas, altering the context levels via push and pop, checking satisfiability of asserted formulas (with assumptions), and many more. When executing API calls, actions may perform sanity checks on results retrieved from solver API calls. For this, Murxla provides a macro MURXLA_TEST which allows C-style assertion checks. These remain in the code even if the tool is compiled without assertions. If a solver supports more functionality than that covered by the Generic Solver API, the solver wrapper can extend the base set with *solver-specific actions* which directly interact with the solver API.

Solver Manager. The Solver Manager is the central manager for sorts, operators, and terms created by the solver. It exposes an interface for actions to (i) randomly pick enabled sorts and operators based on certain criteria, and (ii) notify the manager of new terms and sorts. The Solver Manager further maintains *solver-specific configurations* of supported theories, sorts, and operators. It configures solver-specific behavior by querying the solver wrapper to obtain solver-specific configuration information (e.g., solver-specific operators) and restrictions (e.g., unsupported sorts and operators).

Generic Solver API. The Generic Solver API provides a common solver interface for interacting with a solver under test. It covers the majority of the features defined in SMT-LIB, and defines abstract base classes for sort, term and solver implementations. It further provides an interface for configuring the Solver Manager as mentioned above. Integrating a new SMT solver into Murxla amounts to implementing these three classes, and optionally, solver-specific configurations, in a solver wrapper.

The Generic Solver API aims at being as general as possible while supporting all semantic features of the SMT-LIB data model. The Generic Solver API further supports "meta" solvers for different purposes. Murxla implements meta solvers for: (i) performing checks of witnesses that require additional solver instances (model value, unsat core, and unsat assumptions checks); (ii) checking the results of one solver instance against another to identify soundness issues; (iii) translating API call sequences to the SMT-LIBv2 format; and (iv) SMT-LIBv2 input fuzzing of SMT solver binaries in interactive SMT-LIB mode.

3.2 API Fuzzer

The *API Fuzzer* is responsible for generating random but valid API call sequences and is the central component of Murxla. Valid API call sequences are generated based on an API model which is implemented as a weighted finite-state machine (FSM), where states correspond to the current state of the SMT solver, and transitions have a weight, a pre-condition, and an associated action. Each state of the FSM may provide a pre-condition that defines when it is legal to transition into that state. Taking a transition also executes its action. The associated action of a transition may be empty, in which case it leads to the next state without calling the solver. The pre-condition of a transition and the pre-condition of its next state define the conditions under which the transition can be selected, whereas its weight determines the probability of it being taken in cases where multiple transitions are enabled at the same time.

By default, the FSM implements an API model that captures the functionality and constraints defined in the SMT-LIB standard. And as described above, its associated actions call the Generic Solver API. Murxla supports arbitrary solver-specific modifications to this FSM by providing a configuration interface for solver wrappers (which we discuss in Sect. 3.3 below).

Configuration of the API Fuzzer and execution of its FSM to generate API call sequences for a single run is performed using the following steps.

1. The solver wrapper makes solver-specific modifications to the FSM.
2. The API Fuzzer picks a set of enabled theories, with or without quantifiers.
3. The Solver Manager queries the solver wrapper via the Generic Solver API to configure solver-specific extensions and restrictions.
4. The FSM and Murxla's core components are finalized, and the FSM is set to its initial state; this also creates and initializes the actual solver instance.
5. Next, a set of compatible solver options is selected and configured.
6. After that, the API fuzzer chooses an execution of the FSM and executes the actions associated with that execution, thereby generating a sequence of calls to the solver. This continues until either the solver crashes, the final state is reached, or a configured time limit is exceeded.

In contrast to some recent mutation-based SMT-LIBv2 input fuzzing approaches [39,49,51,52], the API Fuzzer is *generation-based*: it generates expressions that, importantly, respect the semantic and API models of the solver under test. Non-leaf terms are generated by combining leaf terms (variables or theory-specific constants) and previously generated terms via any of the enabled operators. To bias the generated terms towards more variety and structure, each term maintains a reference count, and terms with lower reference counts are selected with a higher probability when constructing new terms. For indexed operator kinds (e.g., the `extract` operator in the theory of fixed-size bit-vectors), random integer values up to a configured maximum value (if not otherwise restricted by the semantics of the operator) are selected. Similarly, arguments to sort constructors (e.g., `Array`) are sampled from previously generated sorts, and sorts with numeric parameters (e.g., bit-vector and floating-point sorts) are constructed from randomly selected integer values up to a configured maximum value.

The API fuzzer utilizes a random number generator (RNG) for random decisions, which is deterministic in the sense that it is guaranteed to produce the same sequence of values when given the same starting seed. The API fuzzer supports two usage modes: (i) single run, starting with a specific seed; and (ii) continuous, consisting of repeated single runs with seeds selected by a dedicated Seed Generator, which uses the current time and process ID to generate seeds.

Each mode can be restricted to a given set of theories (with or without quantifiers) via the command line (in this case, step two of the fuzzer configuration detailed above is skipped). When in *single run mode*, Murxla by default sends a trace of the run to stdout (and optionally to a file). In *continuous mode*, each run is first executed without tracing. If a run uncovers an issue, it is replayed with the same seed and recorded to a trace file. In this mode, Murxla maintains a statistics summary with the current number of issues, timeouts, and *sat*, *unsat*, and *unknown* results. When an issue is discovered, it reports the corresponding seed and solver output. On termination, it provides an overview of all issues, *deduplicated* based on fuzzy matching on the solver output.

Murxla only reports false positives in rare cases where false positives may only be avoided with unreasonable effort, e.g., implementing well-formedness checks for algebraic datatypes.

3.3   Solver Wrappers

As mentioned above, a solver wrapper is used to connect Murxla to a solver. Solver wrappers are typically 2k–4k LOC in size and implement the Generic Solver API. If a solver provides features that are different from those covered by the Generic Solver API, a solver wrapper can accommodate these differences by reconfiguring the FSM of the API Fuzzer to add or remove states, transitions, and actions (added actions can be configured to call the API of the solver under test directly). Solver wrappers are further responsible for configuring the semantic model of the API Fuzzer by (i) adding or removing supported theories and their corresponding sorts and operators; and (ii) extending or restricting the set of operators for supported theories. Solver wrappers may also implement sanity checks of arbitrary complexity by utilizing the MURXLA_TEST macro.

The option model of a solver is implemented as part of the Generic Solver API. For Bitwuzla, Boolector, and cvc5, this amounts to 15–55 LOC since all three can be queried for available options and valid configuration values via the API. This allows an automated registration of options with the Solver Manager. Yices2 does not provide this feature which requires that options are registered explicitly. Note that its option model is currently not implemented.

Each solver wrapper maintains its own RNG which is used to make choices when there are multiple alternative solver API calls for one specific task. This RNG is independent from the main RNG of the API Fuzzer and is seeded with a value generated by the main RNG for each action execution. These seeds are recorded by the Tracer to ensure that random choices can be deterministically replicated when replaying a traced run of the API Fuzzer.

3.4   Tracer, Untracer, Trace Minimizer

The **Tracer** records all action executions with their corresponding arguments and return values in a text-based format. Each action line in the trace follows the pattern `<seed> <action> [<args...>]`, optionally followed by a return statement of the form `return <values...>` for actions that create sorts or terms. The `<seed>`

```
74761  new
65471  set-logic QF_BV
33949  mk-sort SORT_BOOL
       return s1
64345  mk-sort SORT_BV 8
       return s2
49391  mk-const s2 "a"
       return t1
89712  mk-const s2 "b"
       return t2
 6548  mk-term OP_EQUAL SORT_BOOL 2 t1 t2
       return t3 s1
20351  assert-formula t3
47017  check-sat
74496  delete
```

Fig. 2. Murxla trace for checking $a = b$ for bit-vectors a and b of size 8.

in an action is the seed of the solver wrapper's RNG when executing the action. It is recorded to ensure that random choices made by the solver wrapper can be deterministically replicated. This is especially important when minimizing a trace, since modifying trace lines may change the way the main RNG behaves when replaying the trace. Sorts are recorded as s<id> and terms as t<id>, and the <args...> of an action line determine all sort, term and numerical arguments required to replay the execution of the given action. Similarly, the <values..> of a return statement record all of its sort and term return values. Figure 2 shows an example of a trace generated by Murxla. It records the action sequence for checking the satisfiability of $a = b$, where a and b are bit-vectors of size 8. Note that when creating terms via mk-term, we trace argument lists while also providing the number of arguments, e.g., 2 t1 t2. The same applies for indices of indexed operators. Further, for any action that creates terms that are added to the term database (e.g., mk-term), we also need to trace the sort of the created term, e.g., return t3 s1. This is due to the fact that some operators create terms of new sorts that may not have been encountered in the trace yet.

The **Untracer** takes a trace as input and replays each recorded action, thereby replicating the behavior of the original execution. This is especially useful for debugging erroneous behavior of the solver under test. Additionally, if a trace does not contain any solver-specific extensions, the Untracer can replay it using a different solver or translate it to the SMT-LIBv2 format. Tracing actions instead of calls to the Generic Solver API has the advantage that both the API Fuzzer and the Untracer can use the same infrastructure for communicating with the solver under test. Furthermore, supporting solver-specific actions does not require changes to any component other than the solver wrapper.

The **Trace Minimizer** is built on top of the Untracer and minimizes a given trace while preserving the behavior of the original execution. It implements simple ddmin-style [53] minimization techniques in three phases: (i) line-based minimization to reduce the number of trace lines; (ii) minimization of action lines to reduce the number of arguments; and (iii) term substitution, where terms are replaced with simpler terms of the same sort. Even though all of these minimization techniques are rather basic, the Trace Minimizer typically reduces the size of a trace to less than 10% of the original trace. If the minimized trace can be translated to SMT-LIB, then it can often be further reduced using a delta-debugging tool such as ddSMT [37]. Even if a minimized trace cannot be expressed in SMT-LIB due to solver-specific extensions, we have found that in practice, the reduction due to the Trace Minimizer is typically good enough to allow efficient debugging.

4   Evaluation

We evaluate the efficacy of Murxla in three experiments, comparing: (1) Murxla and BtorMBT, testing Boolector; (2) Murxla and the current state-of-the-art input fuzzers STORM [39] and TypeFuzz [47]; and (3) Murxla with and without option fuzzing. For this evaluation, we target soundness issues and crashes, and do not consider performance regressions. In the following, we use *issues* to mean crashes unless explicitly otherwise noted. We use Bitwuzla commit eea0973 [5], Boolector commit b157b10 [6], cvc5 commit 0f5ee6b [7], and Yices2 commit 09f1621 [8]. For each experiment we compare the number of issues uncovered by each tool, and the code coverage of the solver under test. Code coverage was measured with gcov, which is part of the GNU Compiler Collection [9]. We performed all experiments in an Ubuntu 21.04 Docker container on a machine with an AMD Threadripper 3970X CPU and 128GB of memory and used a one hour wall-clock time limit for each experiment and tool.

Murxla vs. BtorMBT. We compare the effectiveness of fuzzing Boolector with Murxla against that of its own custom API fuzzer BtorMBT. We ran both tools in continuous mode with a one second time limit per single run. Murxla achieves a line (function) coverage of 81% (88%) and finds 18 issues (including 3 known reported issues). BtorMBT achieves 72% (81%) coverage, but does not find any issues. BtorMBT does not support quantifiers, and three of the issues found by Murxla are located in Boolector's quantifiers module. The other issues, however, occur in code that is covered by BtorMBT.

Murxla vs. STORM, TypeFuzz. We test cvc5 with Murxla, STORM, and TypeFuzz on QF_SLIA problems. We use all QF_SLIA benchmarks in the SMT-LIB benchmark library as seed files for STORM and TypeFuzz. Both Storm and TypeFuzz mainly target soundness issues. TypeFuzz requires using at least two SMT solvers as it relies on comparing their results, whereas Storm creates satisfiable formulas by construction and does not require cross-checking. Hence, we additionally use a cross-checking configuration of Murxla (*Murxla-cc*), which compares Z3 version 4.8.14 and cvc5. Since Murxla does not yet integrate Z3, we use it via Murxla's SMT-LIBv2 interface in interactive SMT-LIB mode (the input fuzzing mode). Note that this requires disabling solver-specific extensions

Table 1. Number of issues (I), and line (L) and function (F) coverage for experiments two (top) and three (bottom). Option fuzzing for Yices2 is not yet implemented (-).

	Murxla			STORM			Murxla-cc			TypeFuzz		
	L [%]	F [%]	I	L [%]	F [%]	I	L [%]	F [%]	I	L [%]	F [%]	I
	37.8	52.5	7	20.2	34.3	0	21.5	36.3	1	17.4	30.8	0

Option	Bitwuzla			Boolector			cvc5			Yices2		
Fuzzing	L [%]	F [%]	I	L [%]	F [%]	I	L [%]	F [%]	I	L [%]	F [%]	I
no	47.4	63.9	7	68.5	79.2	6	38.9	56.8	11	37.0	42.4	1
yes	62.9	75.8	23	81.1	87.7	13	49.1	66.8	21	-	-	

of cvc5, since they are unsupported by Z3. The results are shown in Table 1. Murxla and Murxla-cc have consistently higher coverage than the other tools and find 8 issues, whereas the other tools find none. Most notably Murxla-cc was able to find a model unsoundness issue in cvc5, where cvc5 incorrectly reports *satisfiable* due to an incorrect rewrite rule for the re.loop operator [1].

Option Fuzzing. We evaluate the effectiveness of Murxla with and without option fuzzing on all supported solvers. We use the default configuration of Murxla, which tests all supported features for each solver. The results are shown in Table 1 and showcase the efficacy of option fuzzing both for improving coverage and for finding issues. In its best configuration, Murxla achieves an API function coverage of 85% for Bitwuzla, 94% for Boolector, 68% for cvc5, and 46% for Yices2. cvc5 provides the richest API, supporting not only all of SMT-LIB but also non-standard theories and non-SMT features like SyGuS and high-order reasoning, which are not yet supported in Murxla. Bitwuzla and Boolector export parsing via the API, which is currently only supported in Murxla for Boolector. Coverage for Yices2 is low in comparison as it was integrated as a proof of concept, and its wrapper does not yet implement all of its features nor its option model.

The artifact containing the experimental data of this evaluation is available at https://zenodo.org/record/6494381.

5   Conclusion

Our experimental evaluation shows that Murxla quickly and effectively finds issues in multiple state-of-the-art SMT solvers—even for logics like QF_SLIA which have been the subject of month-long fuzzing campaigns [39,47,51,52] over the last two years. Furthermore, during the past few months, while finalizing and testing Murxla, we found many more issues in these solvers—more than 100 for cvc5 alone, and some of them critical [3,4]. Based on this success, we believe that Murxla will be a valuable tool for stress-testing SMT solvers and thereby improving their correctness and robustness. We are currently in the process of integrating it into the development workflow of Bitwuzla, Boolector and cvc5.

References

1. cvc5 model unsoundness issue found by Murxla-cc. https://github.com/cvc5/cvc5-projects/issues/409
2. Boolector issue tracker (2022). https://github.com/boolector/boolector/issues
3. cvc5 issues found by Murxla, reported on internal issue tracker (2022). https://github.com/cvc5/cvc5-projects/issues?q=is:issue+is:open+label:murxla
4. cvc5 issues found by Murxla, reported on official issue tracker (2022). https://github.com/cvc5/cvc5/issues?q=is:open+is:issue+label:murxla
5. Bitwuzla GitHub repository (2022). https://github.com/bitwuzla/bitwuzla
6. Boolector GitHub repository (2022). https://github.com/boolector/boolector
7. cvc5 GitHub repository (2022). https://github.com/cvc5/cvc5
8. Yices2 GitHub repository (2022). https://github.com/SRI-CSL/yices2
9. GNU Compiler Collection (2022). https://gcc.gnu.org/
10. Alur, R., et al.: Syntax-guided synthesis. In: FMCAD, pp. 1–8. IEEE (2013)
11. Artho, C., Biere, A., Seidl, M.: Model-based testing for verification back-ends. In: Veanes, M., Viganò, L. (eds.) TAP 2013. LNCS, vol. 7942, pp. 39–55. Springer, Heidelberg (2013). https://doi.org/10.1007/978-3-642-38916-0_3
12. Backes, J., et al.: Stratified Abstraction of Access Control Policies. In: Lahiri, S.K., Wang, C. (eds.) CAV 2020. LNCS, vol. 12224, pp. 165–176. Springer, Cham (2020). https://doi.org/10.1007/978-3-030-53288-8_9
13. Barbosa, H., et al.: cvc5: a versatile and industrial-strength SMT solver. In: TACAS (1). LNCS, vol. 13243, pp. 415–442. Springer, Cham (2022). https://doi.org/10.1007/978-3-030-99524-9_24
14. Barnett, M., Chang, B.-Y.E., DeLine, R., Jacobs, B., Leino, K.R.M.: Boogie: a modular reusable verifier for object-oriented programs. In: de Boer, F.S., Bonsangue, M.M., Graf, S., de Roever, W.-P. (eds.) FMCO 2005. LNCS, vol. 4111, pp. 364–387. Springer, Heidelberg (2006). https://doi.org/10.1007/11804192_17
15. Barrett, C., Stump, A., Tinelli, C.: The SMT-LIB Standard: Version 2.0. In: Gupta, A., Kroening, D. (eds.) Proceedings of the 8th International Workshop on Satisfiability Modulo Theories (Edinburgh, UK) (2010)
16. Barrett, C., et al.: CVC4. In: Gopalakrishnan, G., Qadeer, S. (eds.) CAV 2011. LNCS, vol. 6806, pp. 171–177. Springer, Heidelberg (2011). https://doi.org/10.1007/978-3-642-22110-1_14
17. Biere, A.: CaDiCaL, Lingeling, Plingeling, Treengeling, YalSAT entering the sat competition 2017. In: Balyo, T., Heule, M., Järvisalo, M. (eds.) SAT Competition 2017 - Solver and Benchmark Descriptions. Department of Computer Science Series of Publications B, vol. B-2017-1, pp. 14–15. University of Helsinki (2017)
18. Bjørner, N.: SMT in verification, modeling, and testing at microsoft. In: Biere, A., Nahir, A., Vos, T. (eds.) HVC 2012. LNCS, vol. 7857, pp. 3–3. Springer, Heidelberg (2013). https://doi.org/10.1007/978-3-642-39611-3_3
19. Blotsky, D., Mora, F., Berzish, M., Zheng, Y., Kabir, I., Ganesh, V.: StringFuzz: a fuzzer for string solvers. In: Chockler, H., Weissenbacher, G. (eds.) CAV 2018. LNCS, vol. 10982, pp. 45–51. Springer, Cham (2018). https://doi.org/10.1007/978-3-319-96142-2_6
20. Bouton, T., Caminha B. de Oliveira, D., Déharbe, D., Fontaine, P.: veriT: an open, trustable and efficient smt-solver. In: Schmidt, R.A. (ed.) CADE 2009. LNCS (LNAI), vol. 5663, pp. 151–156. Springer, Heidelberg (2009). https://doi.org/10.1007/978-3-642-02959-2_12

21. Brummayer, R., Biere, A.: Fuzzing and delta-debugging SMT solvers. In: SMT, pp. 1–5 (2009)

22. Cadar, C., Dunbar, D., Engler, D.R.: KLEE: unassisted and automatic generation of high-coverage tests for complex systems programs. In: OSDI, pp. 209–224. USENIX Association (2008)

23. Cavada, R., et al.: The NUXMV symbolic model checker. In: Biere, A., Bloem, R. (eds.) CAV 2014. LNCS, vol. 8559, pp. 334–342. Springer, Cham (2014). https://doi.org/10.1007/978-3-319-08867-9_22

24. Champion, A., Mebsout, A., Sticksel, C., Tinelli, C.: The KIND 2 model checker. In: Chaudhuri, S., Farzan, A. (eds.) CAV 2016. LNCS, vol. 9780, pp. 510–517. Springer, Cham (2016). https://doi.org/10.1007/978-3-319-41540-6_29

25. Christ, J., Hoenicke, J., Nutz, A.: SMTInterpol: an interpolating smt solver. In: Donaldson, A., Parker, D. (eds.) SPIN 2012. LNCS, vol. 7385, pp. 248–254. Springer, Heidelberg (2012). https://doi.org/10.1007/978-3-642-31759-0_19

26. Cimatti, A., Griggio, A., Schaafsma, B.J., Sebastiani, R.: The MathSAT5 SMT solver. In: Piterman, N., Smolka, S.A. (eds.) TACAS 2013. LNCS, vol. 7795, pp. 93–107. Springer, Heidelberg (2013). https://doi.org/10.1007/978-3-642-36742-7_7

27. Cook, B.: Formal reasoning about the security of amazon web services. In: Chockler, H., Weissenbacher, G. (eds.) CAV 2018. LNCS, vol. 10981, pp. 38–47. Springer, Cham (2018). https://doi.org/10.1007/978-3-319-96145-3_3

28. Corzilius, F., Kremer, G., Junges, S., Schupp, S., Ábrahám, E.: SMT-RAT: an open source C++ toolbox for strategic and parallel smt solving. In: Heule, M., Weaver, S. (eds.) SAT 2015. LNCS, vol. 9340, pp. 360–368. Springer, Cham (2015). https://doi.org/10.1007/978-3-319-24318-4_26

29. Cuoq, P., Kirchner, F., Kosmatov, N., Prevosto, V., Signoles, J., Yakobowski, B.: Frama-C. In: Eleftherakis, G., Hinchey, M., Holcombe, M. (eds.) SEFM 2012. LNCS, vol. 7504, pp. 233–247. Springer, Heidelberg (2012). https://doi.org/10.1007/978-3-642-33826-7_16

30. Dutertre, B.: Yices 2.2. In: Biere, A., Bloem, R. (eds.) CAV 2014. LNCS, vol. 8559, pp. 737–744. Springer, Cham (2014). https://doi.org/10.1007/978-3-319-08867-9_49

31. Filliâtre, J.-C., Paskevich, A.: Why3 — where programs meet provers. In: Felleisen, M., Gardner, P. (eds.) ESOP 2013. LNCS, vol. 7792, pp. 125–128. Springer, Heidelberg (2013). https://doi.org/10.1007/978-3-642-37036-6_8

32. Ganesh, V., Dill, D.L.: A decision procedure for bit-vectors and arrays. In: Damm, W., Hermanns, H. (eds.) CAV 2007. LNCS, vol. 4590, pp. 519–531. Springer, Heidelberg (2007). https://doi.org/10.1007/978-3-540-73368-3_52

33. Godefroid, P., Levin, M.Y., Molnar, D.A.: SAGE: whitebox fuzzing for security testing. Commun. ACM 55(3), 40–44 (2012)

34. Gulwani, S., Jha, S., Tiwari, A., Venkatesan, R.: Synthesis of loop-free programs. In: PLDI, pp. 62–73. ACM (2011)

35. Hajdu, Á., Jovanović, D.: SOLC-VERIFY: a modular verifier for solidity smart contracts. In: Chakraborty, S., Navas, J.A. (eds.) VSTTE 2019. LNCS, vol. 12031, pp. 161–179. Springer, Cham (2020). https://doi.org/10.1007/978-3-030-41600-3_11

36. Hyvärinen, A.E.J., Marescotti, M., Alt, L., Sharygina, N.: OpenSMT2: an smt solver for multi-core and cloud computing. In: Creignou, N., Le Berre, D. (eds.) SAT 2016. LNCS, vol. 9710, pp. 547–553. Springer, Cham (2016). https://doi.org/10.1007/978-3-319-40970-2_35

37. Kremer, G., Niemetz, A., Preiner, M.: ddSMT 2.0: better delta debugging for the smt-libv2 language and friends. In: Silva, A., Leino, K.R.M. (eds.) CAV 2021. LNCS, vol. 12760, pp. 231–242. Springer, Cham (2021). https://doi.org/10.1007/978-3-030-81688-9_11

38. Leino, K.R.M.: Dafny: an automatic program verifier for functional correctness. In: Clarke, E.M., Voronkov, A. (eds.) LPAR 2010. LNCS (LNAI), vol. 6355, pp. 348–370. Springer, Heidelberg (2010). https://doi.org/10.1007/978-3-642-17511-4_20

39. Mansur, M.N., Christakis, M., Wüstholz, V., Zhang, F.: Detecting critical bugs in SMT solvers using blackbox mutational fuzzing. In: ESEC/SIGSOFT FSE, pp. 701–712. ACM (2020)

40. Mattarei, C., Mann, M., Barrett, C.W., Daly, R.G., Huff, D., Hanrahan, P.: Cosa: Integrated verification for agile hardware design. In: FMCAD, pp. 1–5. IEEE (2018)

41. de Moura, L., Bjørner, N.: Z3: an efficient SMT solver. In: Ramakrishnan, C.R., Rehof, J. (eds.) TACAS 2008. LNCS, vol. 4963, pp. 337–340. Springer, Heidelberg (2008). https://doi.org/10.1007/978-3-540-78800-3_24

42. Niemetz, A., Preiner, M.: Bitwuzla at the SMT-COMP 2020 (2020). CoRR abs/2006.01621

43. Niemetz, A., Preiner, M.: Murxla (2022). https://github.com/murxla/murxla

44. Niemetz, A., Preiner, M.: Murxla Documentation (2022). https://murxla.github.io

45. Niemetz, A., Preiner, M., Biere, A.: Model-based API testing for SMT solvers. In: SMT. CEUR Workshop Proceedings, vol. 1889, pp. 3–14. CEUR-WS.org (2017)

46. Niemetz, A., Preiner, M., Wolf, C., Biere, A.: BTOR2, BtorMC and Boolector 3.0. In: Chockler, H., Weissenbacher, G. (eds.) CAV 2018. LNCS, vol. 10981, pp. 587–595. Springer, Cham (2018). https://doi.org/10.1007/978-3-319-96145-3_32

47. Park, J., Winterer, D., Zhang, C., Su, Z.: Generative type-aware mutation for testing SMT solvers. In: Proc. ACM Program. Lang. (OOPSLA), vol. 5, pp. 1–19 (2021)

48. Ranise, S., Tinelli, C.: The SMT-LIB Standard: Version 1.2. Tech. rep., Department of Computer Science, The University of Iowa (2006)

49. Scott, J., Sudula, T., Rehman, H., Mora, F., Ganesh, V.: BanditFuzz: fuzzing SMT solvers with multi-agent reinforcement learning. In: Huisman, M., Păsăreanu, C., Zhan, N. (eds.) FM 2021. LNCS, vol. 13047, pp. 103–121. Springer, Cham (2021). https://doi.org/10.1007/978-3-030-90870-6_6

50. Tillmann, N., de Halleux, J.: Pex–white box test generation for .NET. In: Beckert, B., Hähnle, R. (eds.) TAP 2008. LNCS, vol. 4966, pp. 134–153. Springer, Heidelberg (2008). https://doi.org/10.1007/978-3-540-79124-9_10

51. Winterer, D., Zhang, C., Su, Z.: On the unusual effectiveness of type-aware operator mutations for testing SMT solvers. Proc. ACM Program. Lang. (OOPSLA), vol. 1, pp. 193:1–193:25 (2020)

52. Winterer, D., Zhang, C., Su, Z.: Validating SMT solvers via semantic fusion. In: PLDI, pp. 718–730. ACM (2020)

53. Zeller, A., Hildebrandt, R.: Simplifying and isolating failure-inducing input. IEEE Trans. Software Eng. 28(2), 183–200 (2002)

Automata and Logic

FORQ-Based Language Inclusion Formal Testing

Kyveli Doveri[1,2], Pierre Ganty[1(✉)], and Nicolas Mazzocchi[1,3]

[1] IMDEA Software Institute,
Madrid, Spain
{kyveli.doveri,pierre.ganty,
nicolas.mazzocchi}@imdea.org
[2] Universidad Politécnica de Madrid,
Madrid, Spain
[3] Institute of Science and Technology Austria, Klosterneuburg, Austria

Abstract. We propose a novel algorithm to decide the language inclusion between (nondeterministic) Büchi automata, a PSPACE-complete problem. Our approach, like others before, leverage a notion of quasiorder to prune the search for a counterexample by discarding candidates which are subsumed by others for the quasiorder. Discarded candidates are guaranteed to not compromise the completeness of the algorithm. The novelty of our work lies in the quasiorder used to discard candidates. We introduce FORQs (family of right quasiorders) that we obtain by adapting the notion of family of right congruences put forward by Maler and Staiger in 1993. We define a FORQ-based inclusion algorithm which we prove correct and instantiate it for a specific FORQ, called the structural FORQ, induced by the Büchi automaton to the right of the inclusion sign. The resulting implementation, called FORKLIFT, scales up better than the state-of-the-art on a variety of benchmarks including benchmarks from program verification and theorem proving for word combinatorics. **Artifact:** https://doi.org/10.5281/zenodo.6552870

Keywords: Language inclusion · Büchi automata · Well-quasiorders

1 Introduction

In verification [19,20] and theorem proving [31], Büchi automata have been used as the underlying formal model. In these settings, Büchi automata respectively encode 1) the behaviors of a system as well as properties about it; and 2) the set of valuations satisfying a predicate. Questions like asking whether a system complies with a specification naturally reduce to a language inclusion problem and so does proving a theorem of the form $\forall x \, \exists y, \, P(x) \Rightarrow Q(y)$.

This work was partially funded by the ESF Investing in your future, the Madrid regional project S2018/TCS-4339 BLOQUES, the Spanish project PGC2018-102210-B-I00 BOSCO, the Ramón y Cajal fellowship RYC-2016-20281, and the ERC grant PR1001ERC02.

S. Shoham and Y. Vizel (Eds.): CAV 2022, LNCS 13372, pp. 109–129, 2022.
https://doi.org/10.1007/978-3-031-13188-2_6

In this paper we propose a new algorithm for the inclusion problem between ω-regular languages given by Büchi automata. The problem is PSPACE-complete [23] and significant effort has been devoted to the discovery of algorithms for inclusion that behave well in practice [8,10,14,18,22,25]. Each proposed algorithm is characterized by a set of techniques (e.g. Ramsey-based, rank-based) and heuristics (e.g. antichains, simulation relations). The algorithm we propose falls into the category of Ramsey-based algorithms and uses the antichain [11] heuristics: the search for counterexamples is pruned using quasiorders. Intuitively when two candidate counterexamples are comparable with respect to some considered quasiorder, the "higher" of the two can be discarded without compromising completeness of the search. In our setting, counterexamples to inclusion are ultimately periodic words, i.e., words of the form uv^ω, where u and v are called a *stem* and a *period*, respectively. Therefore pruning is done by comparing stems and periods of candidate counterexamples during the search.

In the work of Abdulla et al. [7,8] which was further refined by Clemente et al. [10] they use a single quasiorder to compare both stems and periods. Their effort has been focused on refining that single quasiorder by enhancing it with simulation relations. Others including some authors of this paper, followed an orthogonal line [13,22] that investigates the use of two quasiorders: one for the stems and another one, independent, for the periods. The flexibility of using different quasiorders yields more pruning when searching for a counterexample. In this paper, we push the envelope further by using an unbounded number of quasiorders: one for the stems and a family of quasiorders for the periods each of them depending on a distinct stem. We use the acronym FORQ, which stands for *family of right quasiorders*, to refer to these quasiorders. Using FORQs leads to significant algorithmic differences compared to the two quasiorders approaches. More precisely, the algorithms with two quasiorders [13,22] compute exactly two fixpoints (one for the stems and one for the periods) independently whereas the FORQ-based algorithm that we present computes two fixpoints for the stems and unboundedly many fixpoints for the periods (depending on the number of stems that belong to the first two fixpoints). Even though we lose the stem/period independence and we compute more fixpoints, in practice, the use of FORQs scales up better than the approaches based on one or two quasiorders.

We formalize the notion of FORQ by relaxing and generalizing the notion of *family of right congruences* introduced by Maler and Staiger [30] to advance the theory of recognizability of ω-regular languages and, in particular, questions related to minimal-state automata. Recently, families of right congruences have been used in other contexts like the learning of ω-regular languages (see [9] and references therein) and Büchi automata complementation [26].

Below, we describe how our contributions are organized:

- We define the notion of FORQs and leverage them to identify key finite sets of stems and periods that are sound and complete to decide the inclusion problem (Sect. 3).
- We introduce a FORQ called the structural FORQ which relies on the structure of a given Büchi automaton (Sect. 4).

- We formulate a FORQ-based inclusion algorithm that computes such key sets as fixpoints, and then use these key stems and periods to search for a counterexample to inclusion via membership queries (Sect. 5).
- We study the algorithmic complexity of the FORQ-based inclusion algorithm instantiated with structural FORQs (Sect. 6).
- We implement the inclusion algorithm with structural FORQs in a prototype called FORKLIFT and we conduct an empirical evaluation on a set of 674 benchmarks (Sect. 7).

2 Preliminaries

Languages. Let Σ be a finite and non-empty *alphabet*. We write Σ^* to refer to the set of finite words over Σ and we write ε to denote the empty word. Given $u \in \Sigma^*$, we denote by $|u|$ the length of u. In particular $|\varepsilon| = 0$. We also define $\Sigma^+ \triangleq \Sigma^* \setminus \{\varepsilon\}$, and $\Sigma^{\nabla n} \triangleq \{u \in \Sigma^* \mid |u| \nabla n\}$ with $\nabla \in \{\leq, \geq\}$, hence $\Sigma^* = \Sigma^{\geq 0}, \Sigma^+ = \Sigma^{\geq 1}$. We write Σ^ω to refer to the set of infinite words over Σ. An infinite word $\mu \in \Sigma^\omega$ is said to be *ultimately periodic* if it admits a decomposition $\mu = uv^\omega$ with $u \in \Sigma^*$ (called a *stem*) and $v \in \Sigma^+$ (called a *period*). We fix an alphabet Σ throughout the paper.

Order Theory. Let E be a set of elements and $\bowtie$ be a binary relation over E. The relation $\bowtie$ is said to be a *quasiorder* when it is *reflexive* and *transitive*. Given a subset X of E, we define its *upward closure* with respect to the quasiorder $\bowtie$ by $_\bowtie\!\uparrow\! X \triangleq \{e \in E \mid \exists x \in X, x \bowtie e\}$. Given two subsets $X, Y \subseteq E$ the set Y is said to be a *basis* for X with respect to $\bowtie$, denoted $\mathfrak{B}_\bowtie(Y, X)$, whenever $Y \subseteq X$ and $_\bowtie\!\uparrow\! X = {}_\bowtie\!\uparrow\! Y$. The quasiorder $\bowtie$ is a *well-quasiorder* iff for each set $X \subseteq E$ there exists a finite set $Y \subseteq E$ such that $\mathfrak{B}_\bowtie(Y, X)$. This property on bases is also known as the *finite basis property*. Other equivalent definitions of well-quasiorders can be found in the literature [27], we will use the followings:

1. For every $\{e_i\}_{i\in\mathbb{N}} \in E^\mathbb{N}$ there exists $i, j \in \mathbb{N}$ with $i < j$ such that $e_i \bowtie e_j$.
2. No sequence $\{X_i\}_{i\in\mathbb{N}} \in \wp(E)^\mathbb{N}$ is such that $_\bowtie\!\uparrow\! X_1 \subsetneq {}_\bowtie\!\uparrow\! X_2 \subsetneq \ldots$ holds.[1]

Automata. A (nondeterministic) *Büchi automaton* $\mathcal{B}$ (BA for short) is a tuple (Q, q_I, Δ, F) where Q is a finite set of states including q_I, the initial state, $\Delta \subseteq Q \times \Sigma \times Q$ is the transition relation, and, $F \subseteq Q$ is the set of accepting states. We lift Δ to finite words as expected. We prefer to write $\mathcal{B}: q_1 \xrightarrow{u} q_2$ instead of $(q_1, u, q_2) \in \Delta$. In addition, we write $\mathcal{B}: q_1 \xrightarrow{u}_F q_2$ when there exists a state $q_F \in F$ and two words u_1, u_2 such that $\mathcal{B}: q_1 \xrightarrow{u_1} q_F \xrightarrow{u_2} q_2$, and $u = u_1 u_2$.

A run π of $\mathcal{B}$ over $\mu = a_0 a_1 \cdots \in \Sigma^\omega$ is a function $\pi\colon \mathbb{N} \to Q$ such that $\pi(0) = q_I$ and for all position $i \in \mathbb{N}$, we have that $\mathcal{B}: \pi(i) \xrightarrow{a_i} \pi(i+1)$. A run is said to be *accepting* if $\pi(i) \in F$ for infinitely many values of $i \in \mathbb{N}$. The language $L(\mathcal{B})$ of words *recognized* by $\mathcal{B}$ is the set of ω-words for which $\mathcal{B}$ admits an accepting run. A language L is ω-*regular* if it is recognized by some BA.

---

[1] The notation $\wp(E)$ denotes the set of all subsets of E.

3   Foundations of Our Approach

Let $\mathcal{A} \triangleq (P, p_I, \Delta_\mathcal{A}, F_\mathcal{A})$ be a Büchi automaton and M be an ω-regular language. The main idea behind our approach is to compute a finite subset $T_\mathcal{A}$ of ultimately periodic words of $L(\mathcal{A})$ such that:

$$T_\mathcal{A} \subseteq M \iff L(\mathcal{A}) \subseteq M . \tag{†}$$

Then $L(\mathcal{A}) \subseteq M$ holds iff each of the finitely many words of $T_\mathcal{A}$ belongs to M which is tested via membership queries.

First we observe that such a subset always exists: if the inclusion holds take $T_\mathcal{A}$ to be any finite subset of $L(\mathcal{A})$ (empty set included); else take $T_\mathcal{A}$ to contain some ultimately periodic word that is a counterexample to inclusion. In what follows, we will show that a finite subset $T_\mathcal{A}$ satisfying (†) can be computed by using an ordering to prune the ultimately periodic words of $L(\mathcal{A})$. We will obtain such an ordering using a family of right quasiorders, a notion introduced below.

Definition 1 (FORQ). *A family of right quasiorders is a pair* $\langle \lesssim, \{\lessdot_u\}_{u \in \Sigma^*} \rangle$ *where* $\lesssim \, \subseteq \Sigma^* \times \Sigma^*$ *is a right-monotonic[2] quasiorder as well as every* $\lessdot_u \subseteq \Sigma^* \times \Sigma^*$ *where* $u \in \Sigma^*$. *Additionally, for all* $u, u' \in \Sigma^*$, *we require* $u \lesssim u' \Rightarrow \lessdot_{u'} \subseteq \lessdot_u$ *called the* FORQ *constraint.*

First, we observe that the above definition uses separate orderings for stems and periods. The definition goes even further, the ordering used for periods is depending on stems so that a period may or may not be discarded depending on the stem under consideration. The FORQ constraint tells us that if the periods v and w compare for a stem u', that is $v \lessdot_{u'} w$, then they also compare for every stem u subsuming u', that is $v \lessdot_u w$ if $u \lesssim u'$.

Expectedly, a FORQ needs to satisfy certain properties for $T_\mathcal{A}$ to be finite, computable and for (†) to hold (in particular the left to right direction). The property of right-monotonicity of FORQs is needed so that we can iteratively compute $T_\mathcal{A}$ via a fixpoint computation (see Sect. 5).

Definition 2 (Suitable FORQ). *A FORQ* $\mathcal{F} \triangleq \langle \lesssim, \{\lessdot_u\}_{u \in \Sigma^*} \rangle$ *is said to be finite (resp. decidable) when* $\lesssim$, *its converse* $\lesssim^{-1}$, *and* $\{\lessdot_u\}$ *for all* $u \in \Sigma^*$ *are all well-quasiorders (resp. computable). Given* $L \subseteq \Sigma^\omega$, $\mathcal{F}$ *is said to* preserve L *when for all* $u, \hat{u} \in \Sigma^*$ *and all* $v, \hat{v} \in \Sigma^+$ *if* $uv^\omega \in L$, $u \lesssim \hat{u}$, $v \lessdot_{\hat{u}} \hat{v}$ *and* $\hat{u}\hat{v} \lesssim \hat{u}$ *then* $\hat{u}\hat{v}^\omega \in L$. *Finally,* $\mathcal{F}$ *is said to be* L-suitable *(for inclusion) if it is finite, decidable and preserves* L.

Intuitively, the "well" property on the quasiorders ensures finiteness of $T_\mathcal{A}$. The preservation property ensures completeness: a counterexample to $L(\mathcal{A}) \subseteq M$ can only be discarded (that is, not included in $T_\mathcal{A}$) if it is subsumed by another ultimately periodic word in $T_\mathcal{A}$ that is also a counterexample to inclusion.

Before defining $T_\mathcal{A}$ we introduce for each state $p \in P$ the sets of words

$$\text{Stem}_p \triangleq \{u \in \Sigma^* \mid \mathcal{A} \colon p_I \xrightarrow{u} p\} \quad \text{and} \quad \text{Per}_p \triangleq \{v \in \Sigma^+ \mid \mathcal{A} \colon p \xrightarrow{v} p\} .$$

---

[2] A quasiorder $\ltimes$ on Σ^* is *right-monotonic* when $u \ltimes v$ implies $u\,w \ltimes v\,w$ for all $w \in \Sigma^*$.

The set $\mathtt{Stem}_p$ is the set of stems of $L(\mathcal{A})$ that reach state p in $\mathcal{A}$ while the set $\mathtt{Per}_p$ is the set of periods read by a cycle of $\mathcal{A}$ on state p.

Given a M-suitable FORQ $\mathcal{F} \triangleq \langle \lesssim, \{\lesssim_u\}_{u \in \Sigma^*}\rangle$, we let

$$T_{\mathcal{A}} \triangleq \{uv^\omega \mid \exists s \in F_{\mathcal{A}} : u \in U_s, v \in V_s^w \text{ for some } w \in W_s \text{ with } u \lesssim w\} \quad (\ddagger)$$

where for all $p \in P$, the set U_p is a basis of $\mathtt{Stem}_p$ with respect to $\lesssim$, that is $\mathfrak{B}_{\lesssim}(U_p, \mathtt{Stem}_p)$ holds. Moreover $\mathfrak{B}_{\lesssim^{-1}}(W_p, \mathtt{Stem}_p)$ holds and $\mathfrak{B}_{\lesssim_w}(V_p^w, \mathtt{Per}_p)$ holds for all $w \in W_p$. Note that the quasiorder $\lesssim_w$ used to prune the periods of $\mathtt{Per}_p$ depends on a maximal w.r.t. $\lesssim$ stem w of $\mathtt{Stem}_p$ since w belongs to the basis W_p for $\lesssim^{-1}$. The correctness argument for choosing $\lesssim_w$ essentially relies on the FORQ constraint as the proof of (†) given below shows. In Sect. 8 we will show, that when w is not "maximal" the quasiorder $\lesssim_w$ yields a set $T_{\mathcal{A}}$ for which (†) does not hold.

Furthermore, we conclude from the finite basis property of the quasiorders of $\mathcal{F}$ that U_p, W_p and $\{V_p^w\}_{w \in \Sigma^*}$ are finite for all $p \in P$, hence $T_{\mathcal{A}}$ is a finite subset of ultimately periodic words of $L(\mathcal{A})$. Next we prove the equivalence (†). The proof crucially relies on the preservation property of $\mathcal{F}$ which allows discarding candidate counterexamples without loosing completeness, that is, if inclusion does not hold a counterexample will be returned.

Proof (of (†)). Consider $\mathtt{Ultim}_{\mathcal{A}} \triangleq \{uv^\omega \mid \exists s \in F_{\mathcal{A}} : u \in \mathtt{Stem}_s, v \in \mathtt{Per}_s, uv \lesssim u\}$. It is easy to show that $\mathtt{Ultim}_{\mathcal{A}} = \{uv^\omega \mid \exists s \in F_{\mathcal{A}} : u \in \mathtt{Stem}_s, v \in \mathtt{Per}_s\}$ (same definition as $\mathtt{Ultim}_{\mathcal{A}}$ but without the constraint $uv \lesssim u$) by reasoning on properties of well-quasi orders.[3] It is well-known that ω-regular language inclusion holds if and only if it holds for ultimately periodic words. Formally $L(\mathcal{A}) \subseteq M$ holds if and only if $\mathtt{Ultim}_{\mathcal{A}} \subseteq M$ holds. Therefore, to prove (†), we show that $T_{\mathcal{A}} \subseteq M \Leftrightarrow \mathtt{Ultim}_{\mathcal{A}} \subseteq M$.

To prove the implication $\mathtt{Ultim}_{\mathcal{A}} \subseteq M \Rightarrow T_{\mathcal{A}} \subseteq M$ we start by taking a word $uv^\omega \in T_{\mathcal{A}}$ such that, by definition ($\ddagger$), $u \in U_s$ and $v \in V_s^w$ for some $s \in F_{\mathcal{A}}$ and $w \in W_s$. We conclude from $\mathfrak{B}_{\lesssim}(U_s, \mathtt{Stem}_s)$ and $\mathfrak{B}_{\lesssim_w}(V_s^w, \mathtt{Per}_s)$ that $u \in U_s \subseteq \mathtt{Stem}_s$ and $v \in V_s^w \subseteq \mathtt{Per}_s$. Thus, we find that $uv^\omega \in \mathtt{Ultim}_{\mathcal{A}}$ hence the assumption $\mathtt{Ultim}_{\mathcal{A}} \subseteq M$ shows that $uv^\omega \in M$ which proves the implication.

Next, we prove that $T_{\mathcal{A}} \subseteq M \Rightarrow \mathtt{Ultim}_{\mathcal{A}} \subseteq M$ holds as well. Let $uv^\omega \in \mathtt{Ultim}_{\mathcal{A}}$, i.e., such that there exists $s \in F_{\mathcal{A}}$ for which $u \in \mathtt{Stem}_s$ and $v \in \mathtt{Per}_s$, satisfying $uv \lesssim u$. Since $u \in \mathtt{Stem}_s$ and $v \in \mathtt{Per}_s$, there exist $u_0 \in U_s$, $w_0 \in W_s$ and $v_0 \in V_s^{w_0}$ such that $u_0 \lesssim u \lesssim w_0$ and $v_0 \lesssim_{w_0} v$ thanks to the finite basis property. By definition we have $u_0 v_0^\omega \in T_{\mathcal{A}}$ and thus we find that $u_0 v_0^\omega \in M$ since $T_{\mathcal{A}} \subseteq M$. Next since $u \lesssim w_0$, the FORQ constraint shows that $\lesssim_{w_0} \subseteq \lesssim_u$ which, in turn, implies that $v_0 \lesssim_u v$ holds. Finally, we deduce from $u_0 v_0^\omega \in M$, $u_0 \lesssim u$, $v_0 \lesssim_u v$, $uv \lesssim u$ and the preservation of M by the FORQ $\mathcal{F}$ that $uv^\omega \in M$. We thus obtain that $\mathtt{Ultim}_{\mathcal{A}} \subseteq M$ and we are done. $\square$

---

[3] The case $\subseteq$ is trivial. For the case $\supseteq$, let uv^ω with $u \in \mathtt{Stem}_s$ and $v \in \mathtt{Per}_s$. If $uv \lesssim u$ then we are done for otherwise consider the sequence $\{uv^i\}_{i \in \mathbb{N}}$. Since $\lesssim^{-1}$ is a well-quasiorder, there exists $x, y \in \mathbb{N}$ such that $x < y$ and $uv^x \lesssim^{-1} uv^y$ (viz. $uv^y \lesssim uv^x$). Therefore we have $(uv^x)(v^{y-x})^\omega = uv^\omega$, $(uv^x) \in \mathtt{Stem}_s$, $(v^{y-x}) \in \mathtt{Per}_s$, and $(uv^x)(v^{y-x}) \lesssim (uv^x)$, hence $uv^\omega \in \mathtt{Ultim}_{\mathcal{A}}$.

Example 3. To gain more insights about our approach consider the BAs of Fig. 1 for which we want to check whether $L(\mathcal{A}) \subseteq L(\mathcal{B})$ holds. From the description of $\mathcal{A}$ it is routine to check that $\mathtt{Stem}_{p_I} = \Sigma^*$ and $\mathtt{Per}_{p_I} = \Sigma^+$. Let us assume the existence[4] of $\lesssim$ (hence $\lesssim^{-1}$), $\ll_\varepsilon$ and $\ll_{aa}$ such that $a \lesssim aa$ holds and so does $\mathfrak{B}_\lesssim(\{\varepsilon, a\}, \Sigma^*)$, $\mathfrak{B}_{\lesssim^{-1}}(\{\varepsilon, aa\}, \Sigma^*)$, $\mathfrak{B}_{\ll_\varepsilon}(\{b\}, \Sigma^+)$ and $\mathfrak{B}_{\ll_{aa}}(\{a\}, \Sigma^+)$. In addition, we set $U_{p_I} = \{\varepsilon, a\}$ since $\mathfrak{B}_\lesssim(\{\varepsilon, a\}, \Sigma^*)$ and $W_{p_I} = \{\varepsilon, aa\}$ since $\mathfrak{B}_{\lesssim^{-1}}(\{\varepsilon, aa\}, \Sigma^*)$. Moreover $V_{p_I}^\varepsilon = \{b\}$ since $\mathfrak{B}_{\ll_\varepsilon}(\{b\}, \Sigma^+)$, and $V_{p_I}^{aa} = \{a\}$ since $\mathfrak{B}_{\ll_{aa}}(\{a\}, \Sigma^+)$. Next by definition ($\ddagger$) of $T_\mathcal{A}$ and from $a \lesssim aa$ we deduce that $T_\mathcal{A} = \{\varepsilon(b)^\omega, a(a)^\omega\}$. Finally, we conclude from ($\dagger$) and $a^\omega \in T_\mathcal{A}$ that $a^\omega \in L(\mathcal{A})$ (since $T_\mathcal{A} \subseteq L(\mathcal{A})$) hence that $L(\mathcal{A}) \not\subseteq L(\mathcal{B})$ because $a^\omega \notin L(\mathcal{B})$. By checking membership of the two ultimately periodic words of $T_\mathcal{A}$ into $L(\mathcal{B})$ we thus have shown that $L(\mathcal{A}) \subseteq L(\mathcal{B})$ does not hold.

In the example above we did not detail how the FORQ was obtained let alone how to compute the finite bases. We fill that gap in the next two sections: we define FORQs based on the underlying structure of a given BA in Sect. 4 and show they are suitable; and we give an effective computation of the bases hence our FORQ-based inclusion algorithm in Sect. 5.

4   Defining **FORQs** from the Structure of an Automaton

In this section we introduce a type of FORQs called structural FORQs such that given a BA $\mathcal{B}$ the structural FORQ induced by $\mathcal{B}$ is $L(\mathcal{B})$-suitable.

Definition 4. *Let $\mathcal{B} \triangleq (Q, q_I, \Delta_\mathcal{B}, F_\mathcal{B})$ be a BA. The structural FORQ of $\mathcal{B}$ is the pair $\langle \lesssim^\mathcal{B}, \{\ll_u^\mathcal{B}\}_{u \in \Sigma^*} \rangle$ where the quasiorders are defined by:*

$$u_1 \lesssim^\mathcal{B} u_2 \overset{\triangle}{\Longleftrightarrow} \mathtt{Tgt}_\mathcal{B}(u_1) \subseteq \mathtt{Tgt}_\mathcal{B}(u_2)$$

$$v_1 \ll_u^\mathcal{B} v_2 \overset{\triangle}{\Longleftrightarrow} \mathtt{Cxt}_\mathcal{B}(\mathtt{Tgt}_\mathcal{B}(u), v_1) \subseteq \mathtt{Cxt}_\mathcal{B}(\mathtt{Tgt}_\mathcal{B}(u), v_2)$$

with $\mathtt{Tgt}_\mathcal{B} \colon \wp(Q) \times \Sigma^* \to \wp(Q)$ and $\mathtt{Cxt}_\mathcal{B} \colon \wp(Q) \times \Sigma^* \to \wp(Q^2 \times \{\bot, \top\})$

$$\mathtt{Tgt}_\mathcal{B}(u) \triangleq \{q' \in Q \mid \mathcal{B} \colon q_I \overset{u}{\longrightarrow} q'\}$$

$$\mathtt{Cxt}_\mathcal{B}(X, v) \triangleq \{(q, q', k) \mid q \in X, \mathcal{B} \colon q \overset{v}{\longrightarrow} q', (k = \top \Rightarrow \mathcal{B} \colon q \overset{v}{\longrightarrow}_F q')\}$$

Given $u \in \Sigma^*$, the set $\mathtt{Tgt}_\mathcal{B}(u)$ contains states that u can "target" from the initial state q_I. A "context" (q, q', k) returned by $\mathtt{Cxt}_\mathcal{B}$, consists in a source state $q \in Q$, a sink state $q' \in Q$ and a boolean $k \in \{\top, \bot\}$ that keeps track whether an accepting state is visited. Note that, having $\bot$ as last component of a context does *not* mean that no accepting state is visited. When it is clear from the context, we often omit the subscript $\mathcal{B}$ from $\mathtt{Tgt}_\mathcal{B}$ and $\mathtt{Cxt}_\mathcal{B}$. Analogously, we omit the BA from the structural FORQ quasiorders when there is no ambiguity.

Lemma 5. *Given a BA $\mathcal{B}$, the pair $\langle \lesssim^\mathcal{B}, \{\ll_u^\mathcal{B}\}_{u \in \Sigma^*} \rangle$ of Definition 4 is a FORQ.*

---

[4] The definition of the orderings, needed to compute the bases, are given in Example 6.

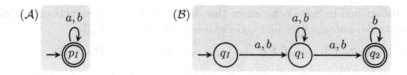

Fig. 1. Büchi automata $\mathcal{A}$ and $\mathcal{B}$ over the alphabet $\Sigma = \{a, b\}$.

Proof. Let $\mathcal{B} \triangleq (Q, q_I, \Delta_\mathcal{B}, F_\mathcal{B})$ be a BA, we start by proving that the FORQ constraint holds: $u \lesssim^\mathcal{B} u' \implies \lessapprox^\mathcal{B}_{u'} \subseteq \lessapprox^\mathcal{B}_u$. First, we observe that, for all $Y \subseteq X \subseteq Q$ and all $v, v' \in \Sigma^*$, we have that $\mathtt{Cxt}(X, v) \subseteq \mathtt{Cxt}(X, v') \Rightarrow \mathtt{Cxt}(Y, v) \subseteq \mathtt{Cxt}(Y, v')$. Consider $u, u' \in \Sigma^*$ such that $u \lesssim^\mathcal{B} u'$ and $v, v' \in \Sigma^*$ such that $v \lessapprox^\mathcal{B}_{u'} v'$. Let $X \triangleq \mathtt{Tgt}(u)$ and $X' \triangleq \mathtt{Tgt}(u')$, we have that $X \subseteq X'$ following $u \lesssim^\mathcal{B} u'$. Next, we conclude from $v \lessapprox^\mathcal{B}_{u'} v'$ that $\mathtt{Cxt}(X', v) \subseteq \mathtt{Cxt}(X', v')$, hence that $\mathtt{Cxt}(X, v) \subseteq \mathtt{Cxt}(X, v')$ by the above reasoning using $X \subseteq X'$, and finally that $v \lessapprox^\mathcal{B}_u v'$.

For the right monotonicity, Definition 4 shows that if $\mathtt{Tgt}(u) \subseteq \mathtt{Tgt}(v)$ then $\mathtt{Tgt}(ua) \subseteq \mathtt{Tgt}(va)$, hence we have $u \lesssim v$ implies $ua \lesssim va$ for all $a \in \Sigma$. The reasoning with the other quasiorders and $\mathtt{Cxt}$ proceeds analogously.   □

Example 6. Consider the BA $\mathcal{B}$ of Fig. 1 and let $\langle \lesssim, \{\lessapprox_u\}_{u \in \Sigma^*} \rangle$ be its structural FORQ. More precisely, we have $\mathtt{Tgt}(\varepsilon) = \{q_I\}$; $\mathtt{Tgt}(a) = \mathtt{Tgt}(b) = \{q_1\}$; and $\mathtt{Tgt}(u) = \{q_1, q_2\}$ for all $u \in \Sigma^{\geq 2}$. In particular we conclude from $u_1 \lesssim u_2 \overset{\triangle}{\iff} \mathtt{Tgt}(u_1) \subseteq \mathtt{Tgt}(u_2)$ that $a \lesssim aa$, $a \lesssim b$ and $b \lesssim a$; ε and a are incomparable; and so are ε and aa. Since $\mathtt{Tgt}$ has only three distinct outputs, the set $\{\lessapprox_u\}_{u \in \Sigma^*}$ contains three distinct quasiorders.

1. $v_1 \lessapprox_\varepsilon v_2 \overset{\triangle}{\iff} \mathtt{Cxt}(\{q_I\}, v_1) \subseteq \mathtt{Cxt}(\{q_I\}, v_2)$ where
   - $\mathtt{Cxt}(\{q_I\}, \varepsilon) = \{(q_I, q_I, \bot)\}$
   - $\mathtt{Cxt}(\{q_I\}, a) = \mathtt{Cxt}(\{q_I\}, b) = \{(q_I, q_1, \bot)\}$
   - $\mathtt{Cxt}(\{q_I\}, v) = \{(q_I, q_1, \bot), (q_I, q_2, \bot), (q_I, q_2, \top)\}$ for all $v \in \Sigma^{\geq 2}$
2. $v_1 \lessapprox_a v_2 \iff v_1 \lessapprox_b v_2 \overset{\triangle}{\iff} \mathtt{Cxt}(\{q_1\}, v_1) \subseteq \mathtt{Cxt}(\{q_1\}, v_2)$ where
   - $\mathtt{Cxt}(\{q_1\}, \varepsilon) = \{(q_1, q_1, \bot)\}$
   - $\mathtt{Cxt}(\{q_1\}, v) = \{(q_1, q_1, \bot), (q_1, q_2, \bot), (q_1, q_2, \top)\}$ for all $v \in \Sigma^+$
3. $v_1 \lessapprox_{u_1} v_2 \iff v_1 \lessapprox_{u_2} v_2 \overset{\triangle}{\iff} \mathtt{Cxt}(\{q_1, q_2\}, v_1) \subseteq \mathtt{Cxt}(\{q_1, q_2\}, v_2)$ for all $u_1, u_2 \in \Sigma^{\geq 2}$ where
   - $\mathtt{Cxt}(\{q_1, q_2\}, \varepsilon) = \{(q_1, q_1, \bot), (q_2, q_2, \bot), (q_2, q_2, \top)\}$
   - $\mathtt{Cxt}(\{q_1, q_2\}, v) = \{(q_1, q_1, \bot), (q_1, q_2, \bot), (q_1, q_2, \top)\}$ for all $v \in \Sigma^+ \setminus \{b\}^+$
   - $\mathtt{Cxt}(\{q_1, q_2\}, v) = \{(q_1, q_1, \bot), (q_1, q_2, \bot), (q_1, q_2, \top), (q_2, q_2, \bot), (q_2, q_2, \top)\}$ for all $v \in \{b\}^+$

With the above definitions the reader is invited to check the following predicates $\mathfrak{B}_\lesssim(\{\varepsilon, a\}, \Sigma^*)$, $\mathfrak{B}_\lesssim(\{\varepsilon, b\}, \Sigma^*)$, $\mathfrak{B}_{\lesssim^{-1}}(\{\varepsilon, aa\}, \Sigma^*)$, $\mathfrak{B}_{\lessapprox_\varepsilon}(\{b\}, \Sigma^+)$, $\mathfrak{B}_{\lessapprox_a}(\{b\}, \Sigma^+)$ and $\mathfrak{B}_{\lessapprox_{aa}}(\{a\}, \Sigma^+)$. Also observe that none of the above finite bases contains comparable words for the ordering thereof. We also encourage the reader to revisit Example 3.

As prescribed in Sect. 3, we show that for every BA $\mathcal{B}$ its structural FORQ is $L(\mathcal{B})$-suitable, namely it is finite, decidable and preserves $L(\mathcal{B})$.

Proposition 7. *Given a BA $\mathcal{B}$, its structural FORQ is $L(\mathcal{B})$-suitable.*

Proof. Let $\mathcal{B} \triangleq (Q, q_I, \Delta_\mathcal{B}, F_\mathcal{B})$ be a BA and $\mathcal{F} \triangleq \langle \lesssim, \{\lesssim_u\}_{u \in \Sigma^*} \rangle$ be its structural FORQ. The finiteness proof of $\mathcal{F}$ is trivial since Q is finite and so is the proof of decidability by Definition 4. For the preservation, given $u_0 v_0^\omega \in L(\mathcal{B})$, we show that for all $u \in \Sigma^*$ and all $v \in \Sigma^+$ such that $uv \lesssim u$ and $u_0 \lesssim u$ and $v_0 \lesssim_u v$ then $uv^\omega \in L(\mathcal{B})$ holds. Let a run $\pi_0 \triangleq q_I \xrightarrow{u_0} q_0 \xrightarrow{v_0} q_1 \xrightarrow{v_0} q_2 \ldots$ of $\mathcal{B}$ over $u_0 v_0^\omega$ which is accepting. Stated equivalently, we have $q_0 \in \mathrm{Tgt}(u_0)$ and $(q_i, q_{i+1}, x_i) \in \mathrm{Cxt}(\mathrm{Tgt}(u_0 v_0^i), v_0)$ for every $i \in \mathbb{N}$ with the additional constraint that $x_i = \top$ holds infinitely often.

We will show that $\mathcal{B}$ has an accepting run over uv^ω by showing that $q_0 \in \mathrm{Tgt}(u)$ holds; $(q_i, q_{i+1}, x_i) \in \mathrm{Cxt}(\mathrm{Tgt}(uv^i), v)$ holds for every $i \in \mathbb{N}$; and $x_i = \top$ holds infinitely often. Since $u_0 \lesssim u$ and $q_0 \in \mathrm{Tgt}(u_0)$ we find that $q_0 \in \mathrm{Tgt}(u)$ by definition of $\lesssim$. Next we show the remaining constraints by induction. The induction hypothesis states that for all $0 \leq n$ we have $(q_n, q_{n+1}, x_n) \in \mathrm{Cxt}(\mathrm{Tgt}(uv^n), v)$. For the base case ($n = 0$) we have to show that $(q_0, q_1, x_0) \in \mathrm{Cxt}(\mathrm{Tgt}(u), v)$. We conclude from $(q_0, q_1, x_0) \in \mathrm{Cxt}(\mathrm{Tgt}(u), v_0)$, $v_0 \lesssim_u v$ and the definition of $\lesssim_u$ that $\mathrm{Cxt}(\mathrm{Tgt}(u), v_0) \subseteq \mathrm{Cxt}(\mathrm{Tgt}(u), v)$ and finally that $(q_0, q_1, x_0) \in \mathrm{Cxt}(\mathrm{Tgt}(u), v)$. For the inductive case, assume $(q_n, q_{n+1}, x_n) \in \mathrm{Cxt}(\mathrm{Tgt}(uv^n), v)$. The definition of context shows that $q_{n+1} \in \mathrm{Tgt}(uv^{n+1})$. It takes an easy an induction to show that $uv^n \lesssim u$ for all n using $uv \lesssim u$ and right-monotonicity of $\lesssim$. We conclude from $uv^{n+1} \lesssim u$, the definition of $\lesssim$ and $q_{n+1} \in \mathrm{Tgt}(uv^{n+1})$ that $q_{n+1} \in \mathrm{Tgt}(u)$ also holds, hence that $(q_{n+1}, q_{n+2}, x_{n+1}) \in \mathrm{Cxt}(\mathrm{Tgt}(u), v_0)$ following the definition of contexts and that of π_0. Next, we find that $(q_{n+1}, q_{n+2}, x_{n+1}) \in \mathrm{Cxt}(\mathrm{Tgt}(u), v)$ following a reasoning analogous to the base case, this time starting with $(q_{n+1}, q_{n+2}, x_{n+1}) \in \mathrm{Cxt}(\mathrm{Tgt}(u), v_0))$. Finally, $q_{n+1} \in \mathrm{Tgt}(uv^{n+1})$ implies that $(q_{n+1}, q_{n+2}, x_{n+1}) \in \mathrm{Cxt}(\mathrm{Tgt}(uv^{n+1}), v)$. We have thus shown that $q_0 \in \mathrm{Tgt}(u)$ and $(q_i, q_{i+1}, x_i) \in \mathrm{Cxt}(\mathrm{Tgt}(uv^i), v)$ for every $i \in \mathbb{N}$ with the additional constraint that $x_i = \top$ holds infinitely often and we are done. $\qquad\square$

5   A **FORQ**-Based Inclusion Algorithm

As announced at the end of Sect. 3 it remains, in order to formulate our FORQ-based algorithm deciding whether $L(\mathcal{A}) \subseteq M$ holds, to give an effective computation for the bases defining $T_\mathcal{A}$. We start with a fixpoint characterization of the stems and periods of BAs using the function $\mathrm{Rcat}_\mathcal{A} \colon \wp(\Sigma^*)^{|P|} \to \wp(\Sigma^*)^{|P|}$:

$$\mathrm{Rcat}_\mathcal{A}(\vec{X}).p \triangleq \vec{X}.p \cup \{wa \in \Sigma^* \mid w \in \vec{X}.p', a \in \Sigma, \mathcal{A} \colon p' \xrightarrow{a} p\}$$

where $\vec{S}.p$ denotes the p-th element of the vector $\vec{S} \in \wp(\Sigma^*)^{|P|}$. In Fig. 2, the repeat/until loops at lines 4 and 5 compute iteratively subsets of the stems of $\mathcal{A}$, while the loop at line 10 computes iteratively subsets of the periods of $\mathcal{A}$. The following lemma formalizes the above intuition.

Input: Büchi automaton $\mathcal{A} \triangleq (P, p_I, \Delta_{\mathcal{A}}, F_{\mathcal{A}})$
Input: ω-regular language M with procedure deciding $uv^\omega \in M$ given u, v
Input: M-suitable FORQ $\mathcal{F} \triangleq \langle \lesssim, \{\lessapprox_u\}_{u \in \Sigma^*} \rangle$
Output: Returns ok if $L(\mathcal{A}) \subseteq M$ and ko otherwise

1 **Function:**
2   let $\vec{U}_0 \in \wp(\Sigma^*)^{|P|}$ as $\vec{U}_0.p \triangleq \varnothing$ with $p \neq p_I$ and $\vec{U}_0.p_I \triangleq \{\varepsilon\}$
3      $\vec{W} := \vec{U} := \vec{U}_0$
4   **repeat** $\vec{W} := \text{Rcat}_{\mathcal{A}}(\vec{W})$ **until** $\mathfrak{B}_{\lesssim^{-1}}(\vec{W}.p, \text{Rcat}_{\mathcal{A}}(\vec{W}).p)$ *for all* $p \in P$
5   **repeat** $\vec{U} := \text{Rcat}_{\mathcal{A}}(\vec{U})$ **until** $\mathfrak{B}_{\lesssim}(\vec{U}.p, \text{Rcat}_{\mathcal{A}}(\vec{U}).p)$ *for all* $p \in P$
6   **for each** $s \in F_{\mathcal{A}}$ **do**
7   let $\vec{V}_1^s \in \wp(\Sigma^*)^{|P|}$ as $\vec{V}_1^s.p \triangleq \{a \in \Sigma \mid \mathcal{A}: s \xrightarrow{a} p\}$ with $p \in P$
8   **for each** $w \in \vec{W}.s$ **do**
9            $\vec{V}^s := \vec{V}_1^s$
10   **repeat** $\vec{V}^s := \text{Rcat}_{\mathcal{A}}(\vec{V}^s)$ **until** $\mathfrak{B}_{\lessapprox_w}(\vec{V}^s.p, \text{Rcat}_{\mathcal{A}}(\vec{V}^s).p)$ *for all* $p \in P$
11   **for each** $v \in \vec{V}^s.s$ **do**
12   **for each** $u \in \vec{U}.s$ such that $u \lesssim w$ **do**
13   **if** $uv^\omega \notin M$ **then return** ko
14   **return** ok

Fig. 2. FORQ-based algorithm

Lemma 8. *Consider $\vec{U}_0$ and $\vec{V}_1^s$ (with $s \in F_{\mathcal{A}}$) in the FORQ-based algorithm. The following holds for all $n \in \mathbb{N}$:*

$$\text{Rcat}_{\mathcal{A}}^n(\vec{U}_0).p = \text{Stem}_p \cap \Sigma^{\leq n} \text{ for all } p \in P, \text{ and } \text{Rcat}_{\mathcal{A}}^n(\vec{V}_1^s).s = \text{Per}_s \cap \Sigma^{\leq n+1} \ .$$

Prior to proving the correctness of the algorithm of Fig. 2 we need the following result which is key for establishing the correctness of the repeat/until loop conditions of lines 4, 5, and 10.

Lemma 9. *Let $\ltimes$ be a right-monotonic quasiorder over Σ^*. Given $\mathcal{A} \triangleq (P, p_I, \Delta_{\mathcal{A}}, F_{\mathcal{A}})$ and $\vec{S}, \vec{S}' \in \wp(\Sigma^*)^{|P|}$, if $\mathfrak{B}_{\ltimes}(\vec{S}'.p, \vec{S}.p)$ holds for all $p \in P$ then $\mathfrak{B}_{\ltimes}(\text{Rcat}_{\mathcal{A}}(\vec{S}').p, \text{Rcat}_{\mathcal{A}}(\vec{S}).p)$ holds for all $p \in P$.*

Proof. Consider $w \in \text{Rcat}_{\mathcal{A}}(\vec{S}).p$ where $p \in P$, we show that there exists $w' \in \text{Rcat}_{\mathcal{A}}(\vec{S}').p$ such that $w' \ltimes w$. Assume that $\mathfrak{B}_{\ltimes}(\vec{S}'.p, \vec{S}.p)$ holds for all $p \in P$. In particular, for all $w_1 \in \vec{S}.p$, there exists $w_1' \in \vec{S}'.p$ such that $w_1' \ltimes w_1$. In the case where $w_1 \in \text{Rcat}_{\mathcal{A}}(\vec{S}).p \setminus \vec{S}.p$, by definition of $\text{Rcat}_{\mathcal{A}}$ w_1 is of the form $w_2 a$ for some $a \in \Sigma$ and some $w_2 \in \vec{S}.\hat{p}$ such that $\mathcal{A}: \hat{p} \xrightarrow{a} p$. Since $\mathfrak{B}_{\ltimes}(\vec{S}'.\hat{p}, \vec{S}.\hat{p})$ and $w_2 \in \vec{S}.\hat{p}$, there exists $w_3 \in \vec{S}'.\hat{p}$ such that $w_3 \ltimes w_2$. We deduce that $w_3 a \ltimes w_2 a$ holds, hence $w_3 a \ltimes w_1$ holds as well from the right-monotonicity of $\ltimes$. Furthermore $w_3 a \in \text{Rcat}_{\mathcal{A}}(\vec{S}').p$ by definition of $\text{Rcat}_{\mathcal{A}}$ and since $\mathcal{A}: \hat{p} \xrightarrow{a} p$. Finally, we conclude that $\mathfrak{B}_{\ltimes}(\text{Rcat}_{\mathcal{A}}(\vec{S}'), \text{Rcat}_{\mathcal{A}}(\vec{S}))$ holds. $\square$

Theorem 10. *The FORQ-based algorithm decides the inclusion of BAs.*

Proof. We first show that every loop of the algorithm eventually terminates. First, we conclude from the definition of $\mathrm{Rcat}_{\mathcal{A}}$ and the initializations (lines 3 and 9) of each repeat/until loop (lines 4, 5, and 10) that each component of each vector holds a finite set of words. Observe that the halting conditions of the repeat/until loops are effectively computable since every quasiorder of $\mathcal{F}$ is decidable and because, in order to decide $\mathfrak{B}_{\ltimes}(Y, X)$ where X, Y are finite sets and $\ltimes$ is decidable, it suffices to check that $Y \subseteq X$ and that for every $x \in X$ there exists $y \in Y$ such that $y \ltimes x$. Next, we conclude from the fact that all the quasiorders of $\mathcal{F}$ used in the repeat/until loops are all well-quasiorders that there is no infinite sequence $\{X_i\}_{i \in \mathbb{N}}$ such that $_{\ltimes}\!\!\uparrow\!X_1 \subsetneq {}_{\ltimes}\!\!\uparrow\!X_2 \subsetneq \ldots$ Since $\mathfrak{B}_{\ltimes}(Y, X)$ is equivalent to $Y \subseteq X \wedge {}_{\ltimes}\!\!\uparrow\!X \subseteq {}_{\ltimes}\!\!\uparrow\!Y$ and since each time $\mathrm{Rcat}_{\mathcal{A}}$ updates a component its upward closure after the update includes the one before, we find that every repeat/until loop must terminate after finitely many iterations.

Next, we show that when the repeat/until loop of line 5 halts, $\mathfrak{B}_{\leq}(\vec{U}.p, \mathrm{Stem}_p)$ holds for all $p \in P$. It takes an easy induction on n together with Lemma 9 to show that if $\mathfrak{B}_{\leq}(\mathrm{Rcat}_{\mathcal{A}}^{n+1}(\vec{U}_0).p, \mathrm{Rcat}_{\mathcal{A}}^{n}(\vec{U}_0).p)$ holds for all $p \in P$ then $\mathfrak{B}_{\leq}(\mathrm{Rcat}_{\mathcal{A}}^{n}(\vec{U}_0).p, \mathrm{Rcat}_{\mathcal{A}}^{m}(\vec{U}_0).p)$ holds for all $m > n$. Hence Lemma 8 shows that $\mathfrak{B}_{\leq}(\mathrm{Rcat}_{\mathcal{A}}^{k}(\vec{U}_0).p, \mathrm{Stem}_p)$ holds for all $p \in P$ where k is the number of iterations of the repeat/until loop implying $\mathfrak{B}_{\leq}(\vec{U}.p, \mathrm{Stem}_p)$ holds when the loop of line 5 halts.

An analogue reasoning shows that $\mathfrak{B}_{\leq^{-1}}(\vec{W}.p, \mathrm{Stem}_p)$ holds for all $p \in P$, as well as $\mathfrak{B}_{\ll_w}(\vec{V}^s.s, \mathrm{Per}_s)$ holds for all $w \in \vec{W}.s$ and all $s \in F_{\mathcal{A}}$ upon termination of the loops of lines 4 and 10.

To conclude, we observe that each time a membership query is performed at line 13, the ultimately periodic word uv^ω belongs to $T_{\mathcal{A}}$ defined by ($\ddagger$). This is ensured since $u \in \mathfrak{B}_{\leq}(\vec{U}.s, \mathrm{Stem}_s)$, $w \in \mathfrak{B}_{\leq^{-1}}(\vec{W}.s, \mathrm{Stem}_s)$, $v \in \mathfrak{B}_{\ll_w}(\vec{V}^s.s, \mathrm{Per}_s)$ for some $s \in F_{\mathcal{A}}$ and, thanks to the test at line 12, the comparison $u \lesssim w$ holds. □

Remark 11. The correctness of the FORQ-based algorithm still holds when, after every ":=" assignment (at lines 3, 4, 5, 9 and 10), we remove from the variable content zero or more subsumed words for the corresponding ordering. The effect of removing zero or more subsumed words from a variable can be achieved by replacing assignments like, for instance, $\vec{U} := \mathrm{Rcat}_{\mathcal{A}}(\vec{U})$ at line 5 with $\vec{U} := \mathrm{Rcat}_{\mathcal{A}}(\vec{U}); \vec{U} := \vec{U}_r$ where $\vec{U}_r$ satisfies $\mathfrak{B}_{\leq}(\vec{U}_r.p, \vec{U}.p)$ for all $p \in P$. The correctness of the previous modification follows from Lemma 9. Therefore, the sets obtained by discarding subsumed words during computations still satisfy the basis predicates of $T_{\mathcal{A}}$ given at ($\ddagger$).

It is worth pointing out that the correctness arguments developed above, do not depend on the specifics of the structural FORQs. The FORQ-based algorithm is sound as long as we provide a suitable FORQ. Next we study the algorithmic complexity of the algorithm of Fig. 2.

6 Complexity of the Structural **FORQ**-Based Algorithm

In this Section, we establish an upper bound on the runtime of the algorithm of Fig. 2 when the input FORQ is the structural FORQ induced by a BA $\mathcal{B}$. Let $n_{\mathcal{A}}$ and $n_{\mathcal{B}}$ be respectively the number of states in the BA $\mathcal{A}$ and $\mathcal{B}$. We start by bounding the number of iterations in the repeat/until loops. In each repeat/until loop, each component of the vector holds a finite set of words the upward closure of which grows (for $\subseteq$) over time and when all the upward closures stabilize the loop terminates. In the worst case, an iteration of the repeat/until loop adds exactly one word to some component of the vector which keeps the halting condition falsified (the upward closure strictly increases). Therefore a component of the vector cannot be updated more than $2^{n_{\mathcal{B}}}$ times for otherwise its upward closure has stabilized. We thus find that the total number of iterations is bounded from above by $n_{\mathcal{A}} \cdot 2^{n_{\mathcal{B}}}$ for the loops computing $\vec{U}$ and $\vec{W}$. Using an analogous reasoning we conclude that each component of the $\vec{V}$ vector has no more than $2^{(2n_{\mathcal{B}}^2)}$ elements and the total number of iterations is upper-bounded by $n_{\mathcal{A}} \cdot 2^{(2n_{\mathcal{B}}^2)}$. To infer an upper bound on the runtime of each repeat/until loop we also need to multiply the above expressions by a factor $|\Sigma|$ since the number of concatenations in Rcat depends on the size of the alphabet.

Next, we derive an upper bound on the number of membership queries performed at line 13. The number of iterations of the loops of lines 6, 8, 10, 11 and 12 is $n_{\mathcal{A}}$, $2^{n_{\mathcal{B}}}$, $n_{\mathcal{A}} \cdot 2^{(2n_{\mathcal{B}}^2)}$, $2^{(2n_{\mathcal{B}}^2)}$ and $2^{n_{\mathcal{B}}}$, respectively. Since all loops are nested, we multiply these bounds to end up with $n_{\mathcal{A}}^2 \cdot 2^{\mathcal{O}(n_{\mathcal{B}}^2)}$ as an upper bound on the number of membership queries. The runtime for each ultimately periodic word membership query (with a stem, a period and $\mathcal{B}$ as input) is upper bounded by an expression polynomial in the size $n_{\mathcal{B}}$ of $\mathcal{B}$, $2^{n_{\mathcal{B}}}$ for the length of the stem and $2^{(2n_{\mathcal{B}}^2)}$ for the length of the period.

We conclude from the above that the runtime of the algorithm of Fig. 2 is at most $|\Sigma| \cdot n_{\mathcal{A}}^2 \cdot 2^{\mathcal{O}(n_{\mathcal{B}}^2)}$.

7 Implementation and Experiments

We implemented the FORQ-based algorithm of Fig. 2 instantiated by the structural FORQ in a tool called FORKLIFT [2]. In this section, we provide algorithmic details about FORKLIFT and then analyze how it behaves in practice (Sect. 7.1). **Data Structures.** Comparing two words given a structural FORQ requires to compute the corresponding sets of target for stems (Tgt), and sets of context for periods (Cxt). A naïve implementation would be to compute Tgt and Cxt every time a comparison is needed. We avoid to compute this information over and over again by storing each stem together with its Tgt set and each period together with its Cxt set.

Moreover, the function Rcat inserts new words in the input vector by concatenating a letter on the right to some words already in the vector. In our implementation, we do not recompute the associated set of targets nor context for the newly computed word from scratch. For all stem $u \in \Sigma^*$ and all letter $a \in \Sigma$, the set of states $\text{Tgt}(ua)$ can be computed from $\text{Tgt}(u)$ thanks to the following equality essentially stating that $\text{Tgt}()$ can be computed inductively:

$$\text{Tgt}(ua) = \left\{ q \in Q \mid q' \in \text{Tgt}(u),\, \mathcal{B} \colon q' \xrightarrow{a} q \right\} .$$

Analogously, for all period $v \in \Sigma^+$, all $X \subseteq Q$ and all $a \in \Sigma$, the set of contexts $\text{Cxt}(X, va)$ can be computed from $\text{Cxt}(X, v)$ thanks to the following equality:

$$\text{Cxt}(X, va) = \left\{ (q_0, q, k) \in Q^2 \times \{\bot, \top\} \;\middle|\; \begin{array}{l} (q_0, q', k') \in \text{Cxt}(X, v),\, \mathcal{B} \colon q' \xrightarrow{a} q \\ (k = \bot \vee k' = \top \vee \mathcal{B} \colon q' \xrightarrow{a}_F q) \end{array} \right\} .$$

Intuitively Cxt can be computed inductively as we did for Tgt. The first part of the condition defines how new context are obtained by appending a transition to the right of an existing context while the second part defines the bit of information keeping record of whether an accepting state was visited.

Bases, Frontier and Membership Test. We stated in Remark 11 that the correctness of the FORQ-based algorithm is preserved when removing, from the computed sets, zero or more subsumed words for the corresponding ordering. In FORKLIFT, we remove all the subsumed words from all the sets we compute which, intuitively, means each computed set is a basis that contains as few words as possible. To remove subsumed words we leverage the target or context sets kept along with the words. It is worth pointing out that the least fixpoint computations at lines 4, 5, and 10 are implemented using a frontier. Finally, the ultimately periodic word membership procedure is implemented as a classical depth-first search as described in textbooks [17, Chapter 13.1.1].

Technical Details. FORKLIFT, a naïve prototype implemented by a single person over several weeks, implements the algorithm of Fig. 2 with the structural FORQ in less than 1 000 lines of Java code. One of the design goals of our tool was to have simple code that could be easily integrated in other tools. Therefore, our implementation relies solely on a few standard packages from the Java SE Platform (notably collections such as HashSet or HashMap).

7.1   Experimental Evaluation

Benchmarks. Our evaluation uses benchmarks stemming from various application domains including benchmarks from theorem proving, software verification, and from previous work on the ω-regular language inclusion problem. In this section, a *benchmark* means an ordered pair of BAs such that the "left"/"right" BAs refer, resp., to the automata on the left/right of the inclusion sign. The BAs of the Pecan [31] benchmarks encode sets of solutions of predicates, hence a logical implication between predicates reduces to a language inclusion problem between BAs. The benchmarks correspond to theorems of type $\forall x, \exists y,\, P(x) \implies Q(y)$ about Sturmian words [21]. We collected 60 benchmarks from Pecan for which inclusion holds, where the BAs have alphabets of up to 256 symbols and have up to 21 395 states.

The second collection of benchmarks stems from software verification. The Ultimate Automizer (UA) [19,20] benchmarks encode termination problems for programs where the left BA models a program and the right BA its termination proof. Overall, we collected 600 benchmarks from UA for which inclusion holds for all but one benchmark. The BAs have alphabets of up to 13 173 symbols and are as large as 6 972 states.

The RABIT benchmarks are BAs modeling mutual exclusion algorithms [8], where in each benchmark one BA is the result of translating a set of guarded commands defining the protocol while the other BA translates a modified set of guarded commands, typically obtained by randomly weakening or strengthening one guard. The resulting BAs are on a binary alphabet and are as large as 7 963 states. Inclusion holds for 9 out of the 14 benchmarks.

All the benchmarks are publicly available on GitHub [12]. We used all the benchmarks we collected, that is, we discarded no benchmarks.

Tools. We compared FORKLIFT with the following tools: SPOT 2.10.3, GOAL (20200822), RABIT 2.5.0, ROLL 1.0, and BAIT 0.1.

SPOT [15,16] decides inclusion problems by complementing the "right" BA via determinization to parity automata with some additional optimizations including simulation-based optimizations. It is invoked through the command line tool `autfilt` with the option `--included-in`. It is worth pointing out that SPOT works with symbolic alphabets where symbols are encoded using Boolean propositions, and sets of symbols are represented and processed using OBDDs. SPOT is written in C++ and its code is publicly available [6].

GOAL [34] contains several language inclusion checkers available with multiple options. We used the Piterman algorithm using the options `containment -m piterman` with and without the additional options `-sim -pre`. In our plots GOAL is the invocation with the additional options `-sim -pre` which compute and use simulation relations to further improve performance while GOAL⁻ is the one without the additional options. Inclusion is checked by constructing on-the-fly the intersection of the "left" BA and the complement of the "right" BA which is itself built on-the-fly by the Piterman construction [32]. The Piterman check was deemed the "best effort" (cf. [10, Section 9.1] and [33]) among the inclusion checkers provided in GOAL. GOAL is written in Java and the source code of the release we used is not publicly available [3].

RABIT [10] performs the following operations to check inclusion: (1) Removing dead states and minimizing the automata with simulation-based techniques, thus yielding a smaller instance; (2) Witnessing inclusion by simulation already during the minimization phase; (3) Using a Ramsey-based method with antichain heuristics to witness inclusion or non-inclusion. The antichain heuristics of Step (3) uses a unique quasiorder leveraging simulation relations to discard candidate counterexamples. In our experiments we ran RABIT with options `-fast -jf` which RABIT states as providing the "best performance". RABIT is written in Java and is publicly available [4].

ROLL [24,25] contains an inclusion checker that does a preprocessing analogous to that of RABIT and then relies on automata learning and word sampling techniques to decide inclusion. ROLL is written in Java and is publicly available [5].

BAIT [13] which shares authors with the authors of the present paper, implements a Ramsey-based algorithm with the antichain heuristics where two quasiorders (one for the stems and the other for the periods) are used to discard candidate counterexamples as described in Sect. 1. BAIT is written in Java and is publicly available [1].

As far as we can tell all the above implementations, including FORKLIFT, are sequential except for RABIT which, using the -jf option, performs some computations in a separate thread.

Experimental Setup. We ran our experiments on a server with 24 GB of RAM, 2 Xeon E5640 2.6 GHz CPUs and Debian Stretch 64-bit. We used openJDK 11.0.12 2021-07-20 when compiling Java code and ran the JVM with default options. For RABIT, BAIT and FORKLIFT the execution time is computed using timers internal to their implementations. For ROLL, GOAL and SPOT the execution time is given by the "real" value of the time(1) command. We preprocessed the benchmarks passed to FORKLIFT and BAIT with a reduction of the set of final states of the "left" BA that does not alter the language it recognizes. This preprocessing aims to minimize the number of iterations of the loop at line 6 of Fig. 2 over the set of final states. It is carried out by GOAL using the acc -min command. Internally, GOAL uses a polynomial time algorithm that relies on computing strongly connected components. The time taken by this preprocessing is negligible.

Plots. We use survival plots for displaying our experimental results in Fig. 3. Let us recall how to obtain them for a family of benchmarks $\{p_i\}_{i=1}^n$: (1) run the tool on each benchmark p_i and store its runtime t_i; (2) sort the t_i's in increasing order and discard pairs corresponding to abnormal program termination like time out or memory out; (3) plot the points $(t_1, 1), (t_1 + t_2, 2), \dots$, and in general $(\sum_{i=1}^k t_i, k)$; (4) repeat for each tool under evaluation.

Survival plots are effective at comparing how tools scale up on benchmarks: the further right and the flatter a plot goes, the better the tool thereof scales up. Also the closer to the x-axis a plot is, the less time the tool needs to solve the benchmarks.

Analysis. It is clear from Fig. 3a and 3b that FORKLIFT scales up best on both the Pecan and UA benchmarks. FORKLIFT's scalability is particularly evident on the PECAN benchmarks of Fig. 3a where its curve is the flattest and no other tool finishes on all benchmarks. Note that, in Fig. 3b, the plot for SPOT is missing because we did not succeed into translating the UA benchmarks in the input format of SPOT. On the UA benchmarks, FORKLIFT, BAIT and GOAL scale up well and we expect SPOT to scale up at least equally well. On the other hand, RABIT and ROLL scaled up poorly on these benchmarks.

On the RABIT benchmarks at Fig. 3c both FORKLIFT and SPOT terminate 13 out of 14 times; BAIT terminates 9 out of 14 times; and GOAL, ROLL and

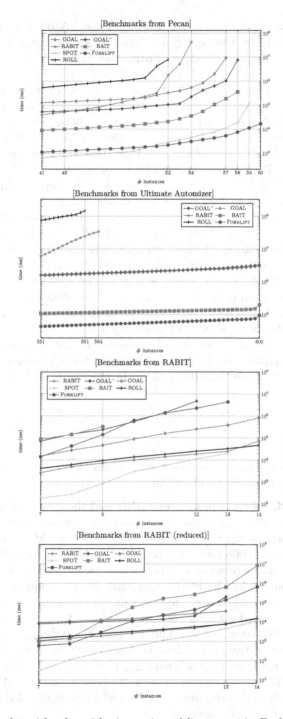

Fig. 3. Survival plot with a logarithmic y axis and linear x axis. Each benchmark has a timeout value of 12 h. Parts of the plots left out for clarity. A point is plotted for abscissa value x and tool r iff r returns with an answer for x benchmarks. All the failures of BAIT and the one of FORKLIFT are memory out.

RABIT terminate all the times. We claim that the RABIT benchmarks can all be solved efficiently by leveraging simulation relations which FORKLIFT does not use let alone compute. Next, we justify this claim. First observe at Fig. 3c how GOAL is doing noticeably better than GOAL⁻ while we have the opposite situation for the Pecan benchmarks Fig. 3a and no noticeable difference for the UA benchmarks Fig. 3b. Furthermore observe how ROLL and RABIT, which both leverage simulation relations in one way or another, scale up well on the RABIT benchmarks but scale up poorly on the PECAN and UA benchmarks.

The reduced RABIT benchmarks at Fig. 3d are obtained by pre-processing every BA of every RABIT benchmark with the simulation-based reduction operation of SPOT given by `autfilt --high --ba`. This preprocessing reduces the state space of the BAs by more than 90% in some cases. The reduction significantly improves how FORKLIFT scales up (it now terminates on all benchmarks) while it has less impact on RABIT, ROLL and SPOT which, as we said above, already leverage simulation relation internally. It is also worth noting that GOAL has a regression (from 14/14 before the reduction to 13/14).

Overall FORKLIFT, even though it is a prototype implementation, is the tool that returns most often (673/674). Its unique failure disappears after a preprocessing using simulation relations of the two BAs. The FORKLIFT curve for the Pecan benchmarks shows FORKLIFT scales up best.

Our conclusion from the empirical evaluation is that, in practice FORKLIFT is competitive compared to the state-of-the-art in terms of scalability. Moreover the behavior of the FORQ-based algorithm in practice is far from its worst case exponential runtime.

8   Discussions

This section provides information that we consider of interest although not essential for the correctness of our algorithm or its evaluation.

Origin of FORQs. Our definition of FORQ and their suitability property (in particular the language preservation) are directly inspired from the definitions related to families of right congruences introduced by Maler and Staiger in 1993 [28] (revised in 2008 [30]). We now explain how our definition of FORQs generalizes and relaxes previous definitions [30, Definitions 5 and 6].

First we explain why the FORQ constraint does not appear in the setting of families of right congruences. In the context of congruences, relations are symmetric and thus, the FORQ constraint reduces to $u \lesssim u' \Rightarrow \lesssim_{u'} = \lesssim_u$. Therefore the FORQ constraint trivially holds if the set $\{\lesssim_u\}_{u \in \Sigma^*}$ is quotiented by the congruence relation $\lesssim$, which is the case in the definition [29, Definition 5].

Second, we point that the condition $v \lesssim_u v' \Rightarrow uv \lesssim uv'$ which appears in the definition for right families of congruences [30, Definition 5] is not needed in our setting. Nevertheless, this condition enables an improvement of the FORQ-based algorithm that we describe next.

Less Membership Queries. We put forward a property of structural FORQs allowing us to reduce the number of membership queries performed by FORK-LIFT. Hereafter, we refer to the *picky constraint* as the property of a FORQ stating $v \lesssim_u v' \Rightarrow uv \lesssim uv'$ where $u, v, v' \in \Sigma^*$. We first show how thanks to the picky constraint we can reduce the number of candidate counterexamples in the FORQ-based algorithm and then, we show that every structural FORQ satisfies the picky constraint.

In the algorithm of Fig. 2, periods are taken in a basis for the ordering $\lesssim_w$ where $w \in \Sigma^*$ belongs to a finite basis for the ordering $\lesssim^{-1}$. The only restriction on w is that of being comparable to the stem u, as ensured by the test at line 12. The following lemma formalizes the fact that we could consider a stronger restriction.

Lemma 12. *Let $\lesssim$ be a quasiorder over Σ^* such that $\lesssim^{-1}$ is a right-monotonic well-quasiorder. Let $S, S' \subseteq \Sigma^*$ be such that $\mathfrak{B}_{\lesssim^{-1}}(S', S)$ and S' contains no two distinct comparable words. For all $u \in \Sigma^*$ and $v \in \Sigma^+$ such that $u \in S$ and $\{wv \mid w \in S\} \subseteq S$, there exists $\mathring{w} \in S'$ such that $uv^i \lesssim \mathring{w}$ and $\mathring{w}v^j \lesssim \mathring{w}$ for some $i, j \in \mathbb{N} \setminus \{0\}$.*

As in Sect. 3, we show that the equivalence (†) holds but this time for an alternative definition of $T_{\mathcal{A}}$ we provide next. Given a M-suitable FORQ $\mathcal{F} \triangleq \langle \lesssim, \{\lesssim_u\}_{u \in \Sigma^*} \rangle$, let

$$\hat{T}_{\mathcal{A}} \triangleq \{uv^\omega \mid \exists s \in F_{\mathcal{A}} : u \in U_s, v \in V_s^w \text{ for some } w \in W_s \text{ with } u \lesssim w, uv \lesssim w\}$$

where for all $p \in P$ the sets U_p, W_p and $\{V_p^w\}_{w \in \Sigma^*}$ such that $\mathfrak{B}_{\lesssim}(U_p, \text{Stem}_p)$, $\mathfrak{B}_{\lesssim^{-1}}(W_p, \text{Stem}_p)$ and $\mathfrak{B}_{\lesssim_w}(V_p^w, \text{Per}_p)$ for all $w \in \Sigma^*$. Since $\hat{T}_{\mathcal{A}} \subseteq T_{\mathcal{A}}$ by definition, it suffices to prove the implication $\hat{T}_{\mathcal{A}} \subseteq M \Rightarrow \text{Ultim}_{\mathcal{A}} \subseteq M$. Let $uv^\omega \in \text{Ultim}_{\mathcal{A}}$, i.e., such that there exists $s \in F_{\mathcal{A}}$ for which $u \in \text{Stem}_s$ and $v \in \text{Per}_s$, satisfying $uv \lesssim u$. In the context of Lemma 12, taking $S \triangleq \text{Stem}_s$ and $S' \triangleq W_s$ fulfills the requirements $u \in S$ and $\{wv \mid w \in S\} \subseteq S$. We can thus apply the lemma and ensure the existence of some $w_0 \in W_s$ satisfying $uv^i \lesssim w_0$ and $w_0 v^j \lesssim w_0$ for some $i, j \in \mathbb{N} \setminus \{0\}$. Since $uv^i \in \text{Stem}_s$ and $v^j \in \text{Per}_s$ we find that there exist $u_0 \in U_s$ and $v_0 \in V_s^{w_0}$ such that $u_0 \lesssim uv^i$ and $v_0 \lesssim_{w_0} v^j$ thanks to the finite basis property. We conclude from above that $v_0 \lesssim_{w_0} v^j$, hence that $w_0 v_0 \lesssim w_0 v^j$ by the picky condition, and finally that $w_0 v_0 \lesssim w_0$ by Lemma 12 and transitivity. By definition $u_0 v_0^\omega \in \hat{T}_{\mathcal{A}}$ and the proof continues as the one in Sect. 3 for $T_{\mathcal{A}}$.

To summarize, if the considered FORQ fulfills the picky constraint then the algorithm of Fig. 2 remains correct when discarding the periods v at line 11 such that $wv \not\lesssim w$. Observe that discarding one period v possibly means skipping several membership queries $(u_1 v^\omega, u_2 v^\omega, \ldots)$. As proved below, the picky constraint holds for all structural FORQs.

Lemma 13. *Let $\mathcal{B} \triangleq (Q, q_I, \Delta_{\mathcal{B}}, F_{\mathcal{B}})$ be a BA and $\mathcal{F} \triangleq \langle \lesssim^{\mathcal{B}}, \{\lesssim_u^{\mathcal{B}}\}_{u \in \Sigma^*} \rangle$ its structural FORQ. For all $u \in \Sigma^*$ and all $v, v' \in \Sigma^+$ if $v \lesssim_u^{\mathcal{B}} v'$ then $uv \lesssim^{\mathcal{B}} uv'$.*

Proof. For all $q' \in \text{Tgt}(uv)$, there exists $q \in Q$ such that $\mathcal{B}\colon q_I \xrightarrow{u} q \xrightarrow{v} q'$. Hence $(q, q', \bot) \in \text{Cxt}(\text{Tgt}(u), v)$. In fact $(q, q', \bot) \in \text{Cxt}(\text{Tgt}(u), v')$ holds as well since $v \leqslant_u^{\mathcal{B}} v'$. We deduce from the definition of Cxt that $\mathcal{B}\colon q_I \xrightarrow{u} q \xrightarrow{v'} q'$ which implies $q' \in \text{Tgt}(uv')$. Thus $\text{Tgt}(uv) \subseteq \text{Tgt}(uv')$, i.e., $uv \leq^{\mathcal{B}} uv'$. □

We emphasize that this reduction of the number of membership queries was not included in our experimental evaluation since (1) the proof of correctness is simpler and (2) FORKLIFT already scales up well without this optimization. We leave for future work the precise effect of such optimization.

Why a Basis for $\leq^{-1}$ is Computed? Taking periods in a basis for the ordering $\leqslant_w$ where $w \in \Sigma^*$ is picked in a basis for the ordering $\leq^{-1}$ may seem unnatural. In fact, the language preservation property of FORQs even suggests that an algorithm without computing a basis for $\leq^{-1}$ may exist. Here, we show that taking periods in a basis for the ordering $\leqslant_u$ where $u \in \Sigma^*$ is picked in a basis for the ordering $\leq$ is not correct. More precisely, redefining $T_\mathcal{A}$ as

$$\tilde{T}_\mathcal{A} \triangleq \{uv^\omega \mid \exists s \in F_\mathcal{A}\colon u \in U_s, v \in V_s^u\}$$

where for all $p \in P$ we have that $\mathfrak{B}_{\leq}(U_p, \text{Stem}_p)$ and $\mathfrak{B}_{\leqslant_w}(V_p^w, \text{Per}_p)$ for all $w \in \Sigma^*$, leads to an *incorrect* algorithm because the equivalence (†) given by $\tilde{T}_\mathcal{A} \subseteq M \iff L(\mathcal{A}) \subseteq M$ no longer holds as shown below in Example 14.

Example 14. Consider the BAs given by Fig. 1. We have that $L(\mathcal{A}) \nsubseteq L(\mathcal{B})$ and, in Example 3, we have argued that $T_\mathcal{A} = \{\varepsilon(b)^\omega, a(a)^\omega\}$ contains the ultimately periodic a^ω which is a counterexample to inclusion. Recall from Example 3 and 6 that we can set $U_{p_I} = \{\varepsilon, a\}$ since $\mathfrak{B}_{\leq}(\{\varepsilon, a\}, \Sigma^*)$, and $V_{p_I}^a = V_{p_I}^\varepsilon = \{b\}$ since $\mathfrak{B}_{\leqslant_a}(\{b\}, \Sigma^+)$ and $\mathfrak{B}_{\leqslant_\varepsilon}(\{b\}, \Sigma^+)$. We conclude from the above definition that $\tilde{T}_\mathcal{A} = \{\varepsilon(b)^\omega, a(b)^\omega\}$, hence that $\tilde{T}_\mathcal{A} \subseteq L(\mathcal{B})$ which contradicts (†) since $L(\mathcal{A}) \nsubseteq L(\mathcal{B})$.

9   Conclusion and Future Work

We presented a novel approach to tackle in practice the language inclusion problem between Büchi automata. Our antichain heuristics is driven by the notion of FORQs that extends the notion of family of right congruences introduced in the nineties by Maler and Staiger [29]. We expect the notion of FORQs to have impact beyond the inclusion problem, e.g. in learning [9] and complementation [26]. A significant difference of our inclusion algorithm compared to other algorithms which rely on antichain heuristics, is the increased number of fixpoint computations that, counterintuitively, yield better scalability. Indeed our prototype FORKLIFT, which implements the FORQ-based algorithm, scales up well on benchmarks taken from real applications in verification and theorem proving.

In the future we want to increase further the search pruning capabilities of FORQs by enhancing them with simulation relations. We also plan to study whether FORQs can be extended to other settings like ω-visibly pushdown languages.

References

1. BAIT: an ω-regular language inclusion checker. https://github.com/parof/bait. Accessed 17 Jan 2022
2. FORKLIFT: FORQ-based language inclusion formal testing. https://github.com/Mazzocchi/FORKLIFT. Accessed 7 Jun 2022
3. GOAL: graphical tool for omega-automata and logics. http://goal.im.ntu.edu.tw/wiki/doku.php. Accessed 17 Jan 2022
4. RABIT/Reduce: tools for language inclusion testing and reduction of nondeterministic Büchi automata and NFA. http://www.languageinclusion.org/doku.php?id=tools. Accessed 17 Jan 2022
5. ROLL library: Regular Omega Language Learning library. https://github.com/ISCAS-PMC/roll-library. Accessed 17 Jan 2022
6. Spot: a platform for LTL and ω-automata manipulation. https://spot.lrde.epita.fr/. Accessed 17 Jan 2022
7. Abdulla, P.A.: Simulation subsumption in Ramsey-based Büchi automata universality and inclusion testing. In: Touili, T., Cook, B., Jackson, P. (eds.) CAV 2010. LNCS, vol. 6174, pp. 132–147. Springer, Heidelberg (2010). https://doi.org/10.1007/978-3-642-14295-6_14
8. Abdulla, P.A.: Advanced Ramsey-based Büchi automata inclusion testing. In: Katoen, J.-P., König, B. (eds.) CONCUR 2011. LNCS, vol. 6901, pp. 187–202. Springer, Heidelberg (2011). https://doi.org/10.1007/978-3-642-23217-6_13
9. Angluin, D., Boker, U., Fisman, D.: Families of DFAs as acceptors of ω-regular languages. Log. Meth. Comput. Sci. **14** (2018). https://doi.org/10.23638/LMCS-14(1:15)2018
10. Clemente, L., Mayr, R.: Efficient reduction of nondeterministic automata with application to language inclusion testing. Log. Meth. Comput. Sci. **15**(1) (2019). https://doi.org/10.23638/LMCS-15(1:12)2019
11. De Wulf, M., Doyen, L., Henzinger, T.A., Raskin, J.-F.: Antichains: a new algorithm for checking universality of finite automata. In: Ball, T., Jones, R.B. (eds.) CAV 2006. LNCS, vol. 4144, pp. 17–30. Springer, Heidelberg (2006). https://doi.org/10.1007/11817963_5
12. Doveri, K., Ganty, P., Parolini, F., Ranzato, F.: Büchi automata benchmarks for language inclusion (2021). https://github.com/parof/buchi-automata-benchmark
13. Doveri, K., Ganty, P., Parolini, F., Ranzato, F.: Inclusion testing of Büchi automata based on well-quasiorders. In: 32nd International Conference on Concurrency Theory (CONCUR). LIPIcs (2021). https://doi.org/10.4230/LIPIcs.CONCUR.2021.3
14. Doyen, L., Raskin, J.F.: Antichains for the automata-based approach to model-checking. Log. Meth. Comput. Sci. **5**(1) (2009). https://doi.org/10.2168/lmcs-5(1:5)2009

15. Duret-Lutz, A., Lewkowicz, A., Fauchille, A., Michaud, T., Renault, É., Xu, L.: Spot 2.0—a framework for LTL and ω-automata manipulation. In: Artho, C., Legay, A., Peled, D. (eds.) ATVA 2016. LNCS, vol. 9938, pp. 122–129. Springer, Cham (2016). https://doi.org/10.1007/978-3-319-46520-3_8

16. Duret-Lutz, A., et al.: From spot 2.0 to spot 2.10: what's new? In: Shoham, S., Vizel, Y. (eds.) CAV 2022. LNCS, vol. 13372, pp. xx–yy (2022). https://doi.org/10.1007/978-3-031-13188-2_18

17. Esparza, J.: Automata Theory - An Algorithmic Approach. Lecture Notes (2017). https://www7.in.tum.de/~esparza/autoskript.pdf

18. Fogarty, S., Vardi, M.Y.: Efficient Büchi universality checking. In: Esparza, J., Majumdar, R. (eds.) TACAS 2010. LNCS, vol. 6015, pp. 205–220. Springer, Heidelberg (2010). https://doi.org/10.1007/978-3-642-12002-2_17

19. Heizmann, M.: Ultimate automizer and the search for perfect interpolants. In: Beyer, D., Huisman, M. (eds.) TACAS 2018. LNCS, vol. 10806, pp. 447–451. Springer, Cham (2018). https://doi.org/10.1007/978-3-319-89963-3_30

20. Heizmann, M., Hoenicke, J., Podelski, A.: Software model checking for people who love automata. In: Sharygina, N., Veith, H. (eds.) CAV 2013. LNCS, vol. 8044, pp. 36–52. Springer, Heidelberg (2013). https://doi.org/10.1007/978-3-642-39799-8_2

21. Hieronymi, P., Ma, D., Oei, R., Schaeffer, L., Schulz, C., Shallit, J.: Decidability for Sturmian words. In: 30th EACSL Annual Conference on Computer Science Logic (CSL). LIPIcs (2022). https://doi.org/10.4230/LIPIcs.CSL.2022.24

22. Kuperberg, D., Pinault, L., Pous, D.: Coinductive algorithms for Büchi automata. Fundam. Informaticae **180**(4) (2021). https://doi.org/10.3233/FI-2021-2046

23. Kupferman, O., Vardi, M.Y.: Verification of fair transition systems. In: Alur, R., Henzinger, T.A. (eds.) CAV 1996. LNCS, vol. 1102, pp. 372–382. Springer, Heidelberg (1996). https://doi.org/10.1007/3-540-61474-5_84

24. Li, Y., Chen, Y.F., Zhang, L., Liu, D.: A novel learning algorithm for Büchi automata based on family of DFAs and classification trees. Inf. Comput. **281**, 104678 (2020). https://doi.org/10.1016/j.ic.2020.104678

25. Li, Y., Sun, X., Turrini, A., Chen, Y.-F., Xu, J.: ROLL 1.0: ω-regular language learning library. In: Vojnar, T., Zhang, L. (eds.) TACAS 2019. LNCS, vol. 11427, pp. 365–371. Springer, Cham (2019). https://doi.org/10.1007/978-3-030-17462-0_23

26. Li, Y., Tsay, Y.-K., Turrini, A., Vardi, M.Y., Zhang, L.: Congruence relations for büchi automata. In: Huisman, M., Păsăreanu, C., Zhan, N. (eds.) FM 2021. LNCS, vol. 13047, pp. 465–482. Springer, Cham (2021). https://doi.org/10.1007/978-3-030-90870-6_25

27. de Luca, A., Varricchio, S.: Well quasi-orders and regular languages. Acta Informatica **31**(6) (1994). https://doi.org/10.1007/BF01213206

28. Maler, O., Staiger, L.: On syntactic congruences for ω—languages. In: Enjalbert, P., Finkel, A., Wagner, K.W. (eds.) STACS 1993. LNCS, vol. 665, pp. 586–594. Springer, Heidelberg (1993). https://doi.org/10.1007/3-540-56503-5_58

29. Maler, O., Staiger, L.: On syntactic congruences for ω-languages. Theor. Comput. Sci. **183**(1) (1997). https://doi.org/10.1016/S0304-3975(96)00312-X

30. Maler, O., Staiger, L.: On syntactic congruences for ω-languages. Technical report, Verimag, France (2008). http://www-verimag.imag.fr/~maler/Papers/congr.pdf

31. Oei, R., Ma, D., Schulz, C., Hieronymi, P.: Pecan: an automated theorem prover for automatic sequences using Büchi automata. CoRR abs/2102.01727 (2021). https://arxiv.org/abs/2102.01727

32. Piterman, N.: From nondeterministic Büchi and Streett automata to deterministic parity automata. Log. Meth. Comput. Sci. **3**(3) (2007). https://doi.org/10.2168/lmcs-3(3:5)2007

33. Tsai, M., Fogarty, S., Vardi, M.Y., Tsay, Y.: State of Büchi complementation. Log. Meth. Comput. Sci. **10**(4) (2014). https://doi.org/10.2168/LMCS-10(4:13)2014

34. Tsai, M.-H., Tsay, Y.-K., Hwang, Y.-S.: GOAL for games, omega-automata, and logics. In: Sharygina, N., Veith, H. (eds.) CAV 2013. LNCS, vol. 8044, pp. 883–889. Springer, Heidelberg (2013). https://doi.org/10.1007/978-3-642-39799-8_62

Sound Automation of Magic Wands

Thibault Dardinier[1]([✉]) , Gaurav Parthasarathy[1], Noé Weeks[2],
Peter Müller[1] , and Alexander J. Summers[3]

[1] Department of Computer Science, ETH Zurich, Zurich, Switzerland
{thibault.dardinier,gaurav.parthasarathy,peter.mueller}@inf.ethz.ch
[2] École Normale Supérieure, Paris, France
noe.weeks@ens.psl.eu
[3] University of British Columbia, Vancouver, Canada
alex.summers@ubc.ca

Abstract. The magic wand $-\!\!*$ (also called separating implication) is a separation logic connective commonly used to specify properties of partial data structures, for instance during iterative traversals. A *footprint* of a magic wand formula $A -\!\!* B$ is a state that, combined with any state in which A holds, yields a state in which B holds. The key challenge of proving a magic wand (also called *packaging* a wand) is to find such a footprint. Existing package algorithms either have a high annotation overhead or, as we show in this paper, are unsound.

We present a formal framework that precisely characterises a wide design space of possible package algorithms applicable to a large class of separation logics. We prove in Isabelle/HOL that our formal framework is sound and complete, and use it to develop a novel package algorithm that offers competitive automation and is sound. Moreover, we present a novel, restricted definition of wands and prove in Isabelle/HOL that it is possible to soundly combine fractions of such wands, which is not the case for arbitrary wands. We have implemented our techniques for the Viper language, and demonstrate that they are effective in practice.

1 Introduction

Separation logic [38] (SL hereafter) is a program logic that has been widely used to prove complex properties of heap-manipulating programs. The two main logical connectives that enable such reasoning are the *separating conjunction* $*$ and the *separating implication* (more commonly known as the *magic wand*) $-\!\!*$, in combination with *resource assertions* which represent e.g. exclusive ownership of (and permission to access) particular heap locations. The separating conjunction expresses that two assertions prescribe ownership of disjoint parts of the heap, useful, for instance, to reason about aliasing or race conditions. More precisely, the assertion $A * B$ holds in a program state σ if and only if σ can be split into two *compatible* program states σ_A and σ_B such that A and B hold in σ_A and σ_B, respectively. In SL, heaps of program states are *partial* maps from locations to values; their domains represent heap locations exclusively owned. Two program states are compatible if (the domains of) their heaps are disjoint.

© The Author(s) 2022
S. Shoham and Y. Vizel (Eds.): CAV 2022, LNCS 13372, pp. 130–151, 2022.
https://doi.org/10.1007/978-3-031-13188-2_7

Intuitively, a magic wand $A \mathbin{-\!\!*} B$ can be used to express the difference between the heap locations that B and A provide permission to access. The magic wand is useful, for instance, to specify partial data structures, where B specifies the entire data structure and A specifies a part that is missing [33, 41]. $A \mathbin{-\!\!*} B$ holds in a state σ_w, if and only if for *any* program state σ_A in which A holds and that is compatible with σ_w, B holds in the state obtained by combining the heaps of σ_A and σ_w. Thus, if $A * (A \mathbin{-\!\!*} B)$ holds in a state, then so does B, analogously to the *modus ponens* inference rule in propositional logic.

The magic wand has been shown to enable or greatly simplify proofs in many different cases [1, 9, 20, 21, 28, 33, 41, 42]. For instance, Yang [42] uses the magic wand to prove the Schorr-Waite graph marking algorithm. Dodds *et al.* [20] employ the wand to specify synchronisation barriers for deterministic parallelism. Examples using magic wands to specify partial data structures include tracking ongoing traversals of a data structure [33, 41], where the left-hand side of the wand specifies the part of the data structure yet to be traversed, or for specifying protocols that enforce orderly modification of data structures [21, 25, 28] (e.g. the protocol governing Java iterators). More recently, wands have been used for formal reasoning about borrowed references in the Rust programming language, which employs an ownership type system to ensure memory safety [1]. Magic wands concisely represent the *remainder* of a data structure from which a borrowed reference was taken, as well as reflecting back modifications to the part accessible via the reference. For example, consider a struct Point (represented by a SL predicate Point) with two fields x and y of type i32 (represented by the SL predicate i32). A Rust method that takes as input a Point p and returns a borrow of its field x is specified with the postcondition int32(x) * (int32(x) $\mathbin{-\!\!*}$ Point(p)), thus enabling the caller to regain ownership of the entire data structure Point(p).

The complexity of SL proofs has given rise to a variety of automatic SL verifiers that reduce the required proof effort. Given the usefulness of magic wands, it is important that such verifiers also provide automatic support for wands. However, reasoning about a magic wand requires reasoning about *all* states in which the left-hand side holds, which is challenging. It has been shown that a separation logic even without the separating conjunction (but with the magic wand) is as expressive as a variant of second-order logic and, thus, undecidable [6].

Two different approaches [3, 39] that provide partially-automated support are implemented in the verifiers Viper [34] and VerCors [2]. However, the approach implemented in VerCors [3] incurs significant annotation overhead, and the approach in Viper [39] suffers from a fundamental, previously undiscovered flaw that renders the approach unsound. Both approaches require user-provided *package operations* to direct the verifier's proof search. *Packaging* a wand $A \mathbin{-\!\!*} B$ expresses that the verifier should prove and subsequently record $A \mathbin{-\!\!*} B$. To package $A \mathbin{-\!\!*} B$ the verifier must split the current state into two compatible states σ' and σ_w such that $A \mathbin{-\!\!*} B$ holds in σ_w. We call σ_w a *footprint* of the wand. After successfully packaging a wand, the verifier must disallow changes to σ_w to preserve the wand's validity: the verifier *packages the footprint into the wand*.

The key challenge for supporting magic wands in automatic verifiers is to define a *package algorithm* that packages a wand. In VerCors's package algorithm [3], a user must manually specify a footprint for the wand and the algorithm checks whether the wand holds in the specified footprint. This leads to a lot of annotation overhead. Viper's current package algorithm [39] reduces this overhead significantly by automatically inferring a suitable footprint. Unfortunately, as we show in this paper, Viper's current algorithm has a fundamental flaw that causes the algorithm to infer an *incorrect* footprint in certain cases, which may lead to unsound reasoning. We will explain the fundamental flaw in Sect. 2; it illustrates the subtlety of supporting this important connective.

Approach and Contributions. In this paper, we present a formal foundation for sound package algorithms, and we implement a novel such algorithm based on these foundations. Our algorithm requires the same annotation overhead as the prior, flawed Viper algorithm, which is (to our knowledge) the most automatic existing approach. We introduce a formal framework expressed via a novel *package logic* that defines the design space for package algorithms. The soundness of a package algorithm can be justified by showing that the algorithm finds a proof in our package logic. The design space for package algorithms is large since there are various aspects that affect how one expresses the algorithm including (1) which footprint an algorithm infers or checks (there are often multiple options, see Sect. 3), (2) the state model (which differs between different SL verifiers), and (3) restricted definitions of wands (for instance, to ensure each wand has a unique minimal footprint). Our package logic deals with (1) by capturing all sound derivations for the same wand. To deal with (2) and (3), our logic is parametric along multiple dimensions. For instance, the state model can be any separation algebra to support different SL extensions (e.g. fractional permissions [4]).

Our logic also supports parameters to restrict the allowed footprints for wands in systematic ways. Such restrictions are useful, for instance, in a logic supporting *fractional permissions*. Fractional permissions permit splitting ownership/resources into shared fragments which typically permit read access to the underlying data. However, as we show in Sect. 4, fractional parts of general magic wands cannot always be soundly recombined. Existing solutions for other connectives impose side conditions to enable sound recombinations [29], which are often hard to check automatically. We instead introduce a novel restriction of magic wands to avoid such side conditions and develop a corresponding second package algorithm again based on the formal framework provided by our package logic. We make the following contributions:

- We formalise a *package logic* that can be used as a basis for a wide range of package algorithms (Sect. 3). The logic has multiple parameters including: a separation algebra to model the states and a parameter to restrict the definition of a wand in a systematic way. We formally prove the logic sound and complete for any instantiation of the parameters in Isabelle/HOL [13].
- We develop a novel, restricted definition of a wand (Sect. 4) and prove in Isabelle/HOL that this wand can always be recombined [14].

- We implement sound package algorithms for both the standard and the restricted wand in the Viper verifier and justify their soundness directly via our package logic (Sect. 5). We evaluate both algorithms on the Viper test suite. Our evaluation shows that (1) our algorithms perform similarly well to prior work and correctly reject examples where prior work is unsound, and (2) our restricted wand definition is expressive enough for most examples.

Our Isabelle formalisation and the implementation of our new package algorithm are publicly available [13–15]. Further details are available in our accompanying technical report (TR hereafter) [16].

2   Background and Motivation

In this section, we present the necessary background for this paper. We use *implicit dynamic frames* [40] to represent SL assertions, since both existing automatic verifiers that support wands (VerCors and Viper) are based on it. There is a known strong correspondence between SL and implicit dynamic frames [36].

2.1   Implicit Dynamic Frames

Just like SL assertions, implicit dynamic frames (IDF hereafter) assertions specify not only value information, but also *permissions* to heap locations that are allowed to be accessed. To justify dereferencing a heap location, the corresponding permission is required, ensuring memory safety. IDF assertions specify permissions to locations and value information separately. An assertion acc(x.val) (an *accessibility predicate*) denotes permission to the heap *location* x.val, while x.val $= v$ expresses that x.val contains *value* v. The separating conjunction in IDF enforces disjointness (formally: acts multiplicatively) with respect to resource assertions such as accessibility predicates; in particular, if acc(x.val) * acc(y.val) holds in a state, then x and y must be different (analogously to SL).

The main difference between IDF and SL is that SL does not allow general heap-dependent expressions such as x.val = v or x.left.right [40] to be specified separately from the permissions to the heap locations they depend on. The IDF assertion acc(x.val)*x.val = v must be expressed in SL via the *points-to assertion* x.val $\mapsto$ v, which also conveys exclusive permission to the location x.val. IDF supports heap dependent expressions within *self-framing* assertions: those which require permissions to all the heap locations on whose values they depend (e.g. acc(x.val) * x.val = v is self-framing but x.val = v is not) [40].

2.2   A Typical Example Using Magic Wands

Figure 1 shows a variation of an example from the VerifyThis competition [22]. The method leftLeaf iteratively computes the leftmost leaf of a binary tree (package and apply operations, shown in blue, should be ignored for now). The

```
1   method leftLeaf(x: Ref) : (y: Ref)          Tree(x: Ref) ≜
2     requires Tree(x)                             acc(x.val) *
3     ensures Tree(x) {                            acc(x.left) * acc(x.right)
4     y := x                                       (x.left != null ⇒
5     package Tree(x) —* Tree(x)                           Tree(x.left)) *
6                                                  (x.right != null ⇒
7     while(y.left != null)                                Tree(x.right))
8       inv Tree(y) * (Tree(y) —* Tree(x)) {
9       y := y.left
10      package Tree(y) —* Tree(x)
11        // { hints for package}
12    }
13    apply Tree(y) —* Tree(x)
14  }
```

Fig. 1. The code on the left finds the leftmost leaf of a binary tree and includes speci-fications to prove memory safety. The predicate describing the permissions of a tree is defined on the right. The loop invariant uses a wand to summarise the permissions of the input tree excluding the tree not yet traversed. The blue operations are ghost oper-ations to guide the verifier; we omit those specific to predicates. The package requires further hints in existing approaches, see App. J of the TR [16]. (Color figure online)

pre- and postconditions of leftLeaf are both Tree(x), which is a *predicate instance* used to specify all permissions to the fields of the tree rooted at x (the recursive definition of this predicate is on the right of Fig. 1). Proving this specification amounts to proving that leftLeaf is memory-safe and that the permissions to the input tree are preserved, enabling further calls on the same tree.

The key challenge when verifying leftLeaf is specifying an appropriate loop invariant. The loop invariant must track the permissions to the subtree rooted at y that still needs to be traversed, since otherwise dereferencing y.left in the loop body is not allowed. Additionally, the invariant must track all of the remaining permissions in the input tree rooted at x (the permissions to the nodes already traversed and others unreachable from y), since otherwise the postcondition can-not be satisfied. The former can be easily expressed with Tree(y). The latter can be elegantly achieved with a magic wand Tree(y) —* Tree(x). This wand promises Tree(x) if one combines the wand with Tree(y). That is, the wand represents (at least) the difference between the permissions making up the two trees. Using SL's modus-ponens-like inference rule (directed by the apply operation on line 13, explained next), one can show that the loop invariant entails the postcondition.

2.3   Wand Ghost Operations

Automatic SL verifiers such as GRASShopper [37], VeriFast [24], VerCors, and Viper generally represent permissions owned by a program state in two ways: by recording predicate instances (such as Tree(x) in Fig. 1) and *direct* permissions to heap locations. Magic wand instances provide a third way to represent per-missions and are recorded analogously. Verifiers that support them require two wand-specific *ghost operations*, which instruct the verifiers when to prove a wand and when to apply a recorded wand instance using SL's modus-ponens-like rule.

A `package` ghost operation expresses that a verifier should prove a new wand instance in the current state and report an error if the proof attempt fails. To prove a new wand instance, the verifier must split the current state into two states σ' and σ_w such that the wand holds in the *footprint* state σ_w; on success, permissions in the footprint are effectively exchanged for the resulting magic wand instance. We call a procedure that selects a footprint by splitting the current state a *package algorithm*. On lines 5 and 10 of Fig. 1, new wands are packaged to establish and preserve the invariant, respectively.

The `apply` operation *applies* a wand $A \twoheadrightarrow B$ using SL's modus-ponens-like rule if the verifier records a wand instance of $A \twoheadrightarrow B$ and A holds in the current state (and otherwise fails), exchanging these for the assertion B. The `apply` operation is directly justified by the wand's semantics: Combining a wand's footprint with *any* state in which A holds is guaranteed to yield a state in which B holds. For the `apply` operation on line 13 of Fig. 1, the verifier removes the applied wand instance and `Tree(y)`, in exchange for the predicate instance `Tree(x)`.

2.4   The Footprint Inference Attempt (FIA)

Package algorithms differ in how a footprint for the specified magic wand is selected. In VerCors [3], the user must manually provide the footprint and the algorithm checks whether the specified footprint is correct. In Viper's current approach [39], a footprint is inferred. We explain and compare to the latter approach since it is the more automatic of the two; hereafter, we refer to its package algorithm as *the Footprint Inference Attempt (FIA)*. Inferring a correct footprint is challenging due the complexity of the wand connective. In particular, we have discovered that, in certain cases, the FIA infers *incorrect* footprints, leading to unsound reasoning[1]. The goal of this subsection is to understand the FIA's key ideas, which our solution will build on, and why it is unsound.

In general, there may be multiple valid footprints for a magic wand $A \twoheadrightarrow B$. The FIA attempts to infer a footprint which is as close as possible to the *difference* between the permissions required by B and A, taking as few permissions as possible while aiming for a footprint compatible with A (so that the resulting wand can be later applied) [39]. That is, the FIA includes only permissions in the footprint it infers that are specified by B *and not* guaranteed by A.

For a wand $A \twoheadrightarrow B$, the FIA constructs an arbitrary state σ_A that satisfies A (representing σ_A symbolically). Then, the FIA tries to construct a state σ_B in which B holds by taking permissions (and copying corresponding heap values) from σ_A if possible and the current state otherwise. If this algorithm succeeds, the (implicit) inferred footprint consists of the permissions that were taken from the current state. The FIA constructs σ_B by iterating over the permissions and logical constraints in B. For each permission, the FIA checks whether σ_A owns the permission. If so,

---

[1] This unsoundness might not be observable in restricted logics, but it is in Viper (see App. B of the TR [16]) and the rich logics supported by existing verification tools.

the FIA adds the permission to σ_B and removes the permission from σ_A. Otherwise, the FIA removes the permission from the current state or fails if the current state does not have the permission. For each logical constraint, the FIA checks that the constraint holds in σ_B as constructed so far. We show an example of the FIA correctly packaging a wand in App. A of the TR [16].

Unsoundness of the FIA. We have discovered that for some wands $A \twoheadrightarrow B$, the FIA determines an *incorrect* footprint for the magic wand. This unsoundness can arise when the FIA performs a case split on the content of the arbitrary state σ_A satisfying A. In such situations, the FIA infers a footprint for each case *separately*, making use of properties that hold in that case. For certain wands, this leads to different footprints being selected for each case, while *none* of the inferred footprints can be used to justify B in *all* cases, i.e. for *all* states σ_A that satisfy A. As a result, the packaged wand does *not* hold in any of the inferred footprints, which can make verification unsound, as we illustrate below.

The wand $w := \mathsf{acc(x.f)} * (\mathsf{x.f} = \mathsf{y} \vee \mathsf{x.f} = \mathsf{z}) \twoheadrightarrow \mathsf{acc(x.f)} * \mathsf{acc(x.f.g)}$ illustrates the problem. For this wand, every state σ_A satisfying the left-hand side must have permission to $\mathsf{x.f}$. However $\mathsf{x.f}$ may either point to y or z. If $\mathsf{x.f}$ points to y in σ_A, then to justify the right-hand side's second conjunct, the footprint must contain permission to $\mathsf{y.g}$. Analogously, if $\mathsf{x.f}$ points to z in σ_A, then the footprint must contain permission to $\mathsf{z.g}$. The wand's semantics requires a footprint to justify the wand's right-hand side for all states in which the left-hand side holds, and thus, a correct footprint must be able to justify *both* cases. Hence, the footprint must have permission to *both* $\mathsf{y.g}$ and $\mathsf{z.g}$. However, the FIA's inferred footprint is in effect the disjunction of these two permissions.

Packaging the above wand w using the FIA leads to unsound reasoning. After the incorrect package described above in a state with permission to $\mathsf{x.f}$, $\mathsf{y.g}$, and $\mathsf{z.g}$, the assertion $\mathsf{acc(x.f)} * (\mathsf{acc(y.g)} \vee \mathsf{acc(z.g)}) * w$ can be proved since the FIA removes permission to either $\mathsf{y.g}$ or $\mathsf{z.g}$ from the current state, but not both. However, this assertion does not actually hold! According to the semantics of wands, w's footprint must include permission to $\mathsf{x.f}$ or permission to both $\mathsf{y.g}$ and $\mathsf{z.g}$, which implies that the assertion $\mathsf{acc(x.f)} * (\mathsf{acc(y.g)} \vee \mathsf{acc(z.g)}) * w$ is equivalent to false.

The unsoundness of the FIA shows the subtlety and challenge of developing sound package algorithms. Algorithms that soundly infer a single footprint for all states in which the wand's left-hand side holds must be more involved than the FIA. Ensuring their soundness requires a *formal* framework to construct them and justify their correctness. We introduce such a framework in the next section.

3   A Logical Framework for Packaging Wands

In this section, we present a new logical framework that defines the design space for (sound) package algorithms. The core of this framework is our *package logic*, which defines the space of potential algorithmic choices of a footprint for a particular magic wand. Successfully packaging a wand in a given state is (as we will show) equivalent to finding a derivation in our package logic, and any actual package algorithm must correspond to a proof search in our logic (if it is sound). In particular, we provide soundness (Theorem 1) and completeness (Theorem 2) results for our logic. We define a specific package algorithm with this logic at its foundation, inspired by the FIA package algorithm [39] (described in Sect. 2.4) but amending its unsoundness, resulting in (to the best of our knowledge) the first sound and relatively automatic package algorithm.

All definitions and results in this section have been fully mechanised [13] in Isabelle/HOL. Our mechanised definitions are parametric with the underlying verification logic in various senses: the underlying separation algebra is a parameter, the syntax of assertions is defined in a way which allows simple extension with different base cases and connectives, and the semantics of magic wands itself can be restricted if only particular kinds of footprint are desired in practice. As a specific example of the latter parameter, in Sect. 4 we define a novel restriction of magic wand footprints which guarantees better properties in combination with certain usages of fractional permissions; this is seamlessly supported by the general package logic presented here. Nonetheless, to simplify the exposition of this section, we will assume that any magic wand footprint satisfying the connective's standard semantics is an acceptable result.

3.1   Footprint Selection Strategies

As we explained in Sect. 1, there is a wide design space for package algorithms; in particular, many potential strategies for finding a magic wand's footprint exist and none is clearly optimal. Recall that a footprint is a state, and thus consists of permissions to certain heap locations as well as storing their corresponding values; for simplicity we identify a footprint by the permissions it contains.

For example, consider the following magic wand (using fractional permissions) acc(x.b, 1/2) —∗ acc(x.b, 1/2) ∗ (x.b ⇒ acc(x.f)). Suppose this magic wand is to be packaged in a state where full permissions to both x.b and x.f are held, and the value of x.b is currently false. Two valid potential footprints are:

1. Full permission to x.f. This is sufficient to guarantee the right-hand side will hold regardless of the value that x.b has by the time the wand is applied.
2. Half permission to x.b. By including this permission, the fact that x.b is currently false is also included, and thus permission to x.f is not needed.

There is no clear reason to prefer one choice over the other: different package algorithms (or manual choices) might choose either. Our package logic allows either choice along with any of many less optimal choices, such as taking both permissions. On the other hand, as motivated earlier in Sect. 3.1, our package logic must (and does) enforce that a single valid footprint is chosen for a wand that works for each and every potential state satisfying its left-hand side.

3.2   Package Logic: Preliminaries

To capture different state models and flavours of separation logic, our package logic is parameterised by a separation algebra. For space reasons, we present here a simplified overview of this algebra, but all definitions (including our assertion semantics) are given in App. D of the TR [16] and have been mechanised. We consider a separation algebra [8,19] where Σ is the set of states, $\oplus : \Sigma \times \Sigma \to \Sigma$ is a partial operation that is commutative and associative, and $e \in \Sigma$, which corresponds to the empty state, is a neutral element for $\oplus$. We write $\succeq$ for the induced partial order of the resulting partial commutative monoid, and $\sigma_1 \# \sigma_2$ iff $\sigma_1 \oplus \sigma_2$ is defined (i.e. σ_1 and σ_2 are compatible). Finally, if $\sigma_2 \succeq \sigma_1$, we define the subtraction $\sigma_2 \ominus \sigma_1$ to be the $\succeq$-largest state σ_r such that $\sigma_2 = \sigma_1 \oplus \sigma_r$.

We define our package logic for an assertion language with the following grammar: $A = A*A \mid B{\Rightarrow}A \mid B$, where A ranges over assertions and B over *semantic assertions*. To allow our package logic to be applied to a variety of underlying assertion logics, we distinguish only the two most-relevant connectives: the separating conjunction and an implication (for expressing conditional assertions). To support additional constructs of the assertion logic, the third type of assertion we consider is a *semantic assertion*, i.e. a function from Σ to Booleans. This third type can be instantiated to represent logical assertions that do not match the first two cases. In particular, assertions such as x.f = 5, acc(x.f), abstract predicates (such as Tree(x)) or magic wands can be represented as semantic assertions. This core assertion language can also be easily extended with native support for e.g. the logical conjunction and disjunction connectives; we explain in App. E of the TR [16] how to extend the rules of the logic accordingly.

3.3   The Package Logic

We define our package logic to prescribe the design space of algorithms for deciding how, in an initial state σ_0, to select a valid footprint (or fail) for a magic wand $A \mathbin{-\!\!*} B$. The aim is to infer states σ_w and σ_1 that partition σ_0 (i.e. $\sigma_0 = \sigma_1 \oplus \sigma_w$) such that σ_w is a valid footprint for $A \mathbin{-\!\!*} B$ (when combined with any compatible state satisfying A, the resulting state satisfies B). In particular, all permissions (and logical facts) required by the assertion B must either come from the footprint or be guaranteed to be provided by any compatible state satisfying A.

Recall from Sect. 2.4 that the mistake underlying the FIA approach ultimately resulted from allowing multiple different footprints to be selected conditionally on a state satisfying A, rather than a single footprint which works for all such states. Our package logic addresses this concern by defining judgements in terms of the *set* of all states satisfying A; whenever *any* of these tracked states is insufficient to provide a permission required by B, our logic will force this permission to be added *in general* to the wand's footprint (taken from the current state).

A *witness set* S is a set of pairs of states (σ_A, σ_B); conceptually, the first represents the state available for trying to prove B *in addition* to the current state; this is initially a state satisfying the wand's left-hand side A. The second represents the state assembled (so-far) to attempt to satisfy the right-hand side B. We write S^1 for the set of first elements of all pairs in a witness set S. A *context* Δ is a pair (σ, S) of a state and a witness set; here, σ represents the (as-yet unused remainder of the) current state in which the wand is being packaged.

The basic idea behind a derivation in our logic is to show how to assemble a witness set in which *all* second elements are states satisfying B, via some combinations of: (1) moving a part of the first element of a pair in the witness set into the second, and (2) moving a part of the outer state σ into *all* first elements of the pairs (this becomes a part of the wand's footprint). The actual judgements of the logic are a little more complex, to correctly record any hypotheses (called *path-conditions*) that result from deconstructing conditional assertions in B.

Configurations and Reductions. A *configuration* represents a current objective in our package logic: the part of the wand's right-hand side still to be satisfied as well as the current state of a footprint computation. A configuration is a triple $\langle B, pc, (\sigma, S) \rangle$, where B is an assertion, pc is a *path condition* (a function from Σ to Booleans), and (σ, S) is a context. Conceptually, B is the assertion still to be satisfied, pc represents hypotheses we are currently working under, and the context (σ, S) tracks the current state and witness set, as described above.

A *reduction* is a judgement $\langle B, pc, (\sigma_0, S_0) \rangle \rightsquigarrow (\sigma_1, S_1)$, representing the achievement of the objective described via the configuration on the left, resulting in the final context on the right; σ_1 is the new version of the outer state (and becomes the new current state after the package operation); whatever was removed from the initial outer state is implicitly the selected footprint state σ_w. If a reduction is derivable in our package logic, this footprint σ_w guarantees that for all $(\sigma_A, \sigma_B) \in S_0$, if $(\sigma_A \oplus \sigma_B)\#\sigma_w$, then $\sigma_A \oplus \sigma_w$ satisfies $pc \Rightarrow B$. The condition $(\sigma_A \oplus \sigma_B)\#\sigma_w$ ensures that the pair (σ_A, σ_B) actually corresponds to a state in which the wand can be applied given the chosen footprint σ_w, as we explain later. The package logic defines the steps an algorithm may take to achieve this goal.

We represent packaging a wand $A \mathbin{-\!\!*} B$ in state σ_0 by the derivation of a reduction $\langle B, \lambda\sigma.\ \top, (\sigma_0, \{(\sigma_A, e) \mid \sigma_A \models A\}) \rangle \rightsquigarrow (\sigma_1, S_1)$, for some state σ_1 and witness set S_1. The path condition is initially true (we are not yet under any hypotheses). The initial witness set contains all pairs of a state σ_A that satisfies A and the empty state e, to which a successful reduction will add permissions in order to satisfy B[2]. An actual algorithm need not explicitly compute this (possibly infinite) set, but can instead track it symbolically. If the algorithm finds a derivation of this reduction, it has proven that the difference between σ_0 and σ_1 is a valid footprint of the wand $A \mathbin{-\!\!*} B$, since the logic is sound (Theorem 1 below).

Rules. Figure 2 presents the four rules of our logic, defining (via derivable reductions) how a configuration can be reduced to a context. There is a rule for each type of assertion B: *Implication* for an implication, *Star* for a separating conjunction, and *Atom* for a semantic assertion. The logic also includes the rule *Extract*, which represents a choice to extract permissions from the outer state and adds

---

[2] If B is intuitionistic, this can be simplified to only the $\succeq$-*minimal* states that satisfy A. B is intuitionistic [38] iff, if B holds in a state σ, then B holds in any state σ' such that $\sigma' \succeq \sigma$. In intuitionistic SL or in IDF, all assertions are intuitionistic.

$$\frac{\langle A, \lambda\sigma.\, pc(\sigma) \wedge b(\sigma), \Delta \rangle \rightsquigarrow \Delta'}{\langle b \Rightarrow A, pc, \Delta \rangle \rightsquigarrow \Delta'} \; Implication \qquad \frac{\langle A_1, pc, \Delta_0 \rangle \rightsquigarrow \Delta_1 \quad \langle A_2, pc, \Delta_1 \rangle \rightsquigarrow \Delta_2}{\langle A_1 * A_2, pc, \Delta_0 \rangle \rightsquigarrow \Delta_2} \; Star$$

$$\frac{\begin{array}{c} \forall(\sigma_A, \sigma_B) \in S.\, pc(\sigma_A) \Longrightarrow \sigma_A \succeq choice(\sigma_A, \sigma_B) \wedge \mathcal{B}(choice(\sigma_A, \sigma_B)) \\ S_\top = \{(\sigma_A \ominus choice(\sigma_A, \sigma_B), \sigma_B \oplus choice(\sigma_A, \sigma_B)) | (\sigma_A, \sigma_B) \in S \wedge pc(\sigma_A)\} \\ S_\perp = \{(\sigma_A, \sigma_B) | (\sigma_A, \sigma_B) \in S \wedge \neg pc(\sigma_A)\} \end{array}}{\langle \mathcal{B}, pc, (\sigma, S) \rangle \rightsquigarrow (\sigma, S_\top \cup S_\perp)} \; Atom$$

$$\frac{\begin{array}{c} \sigma_0 = \sigma_1 \oplus \sigma_w \quad \mathsf{stable}(\sigma_w) \quad \langle A, pc, (\sigma_1, S_1) \rangle \rightsquigarrow \Delta \\ S_1 = \{(\sigma_A \oplus \sigma_w, \sigma_B) | (\sigma_A, \sigma_B) \in S_0 \wedge (\sigma_A \oplus \sigma_B) \# \sigma_w\} \end{array}}{\langle A, pc, (\sigma_0, S_0) \rangle \rightsquigarrow \Delta} \; Extract$$

Fig. 2. Rules of the package logic.

them to all pairs of states in the witness set. In the following, we informally write *reducing an assertion* to refer to the process of deriving (in the logic) that the relevant configuration containing this assertion reduces to some context.

To reduce an implication $\mathcal{B} \Rightarrow A$, the rule *Implication* conjoins the hypothesis $\mathcal{B}$ with the previous path condition, leaving A to be reduced. Informally, this expresses that satisfying $pc \Rightarrow (b \Rightarrow A)$ is equivalent to satisfying $(pc \wedge b) \Rightarrow A$.

For a separating conjunction $A_1 * A_2$, the *Star* rule expresses that both A_1 and A_2 must be reduced, in order to reduce $A_1 * A_2$; permissions used in the reduction of the first conjunct must not be used again, which is reflected by the threading-through of the intermediate context Δ_1.[3]

The *Atom* rule specifies how to prove that all states in S^1 (where S is the witness set) satisfy the assertion $pc \Rightarrow \mathcal{B}$. To understand the premises, consider a pair $(\sigma_A, \sigma_B) \in S$. If σ_A does not satisfy the path condition, i.e. $\neg pc(\sigma_A)$, then σ_A *does not* have to justify $\mathcal{B}$, and thus the pair (σ_A, σ_B) is left unchanged; this case corresponds to the set $S_\perp$. Conversely, if σ_A satisfies the path condition, i.e. $pc(\sigma_A)$, then σ_A must satisfy $\mathcal{B}$, and the corresponding permissions must be transferred from σ_A to σ_B. Since some assertions may be satisfied in different ways, such as disjunctions, the algorithm has a choice in how to satisfy $\mathcal{B}$, which might be different for each pair (σ_A, σ_B). This choice is represented by $choice(\sigma_A, \sigma_B)$, which must satisfy $\mathcal{B}$ and be smaller or equal to σ_A. We update the witness set by transferring $choice(\sigma_A, \sigma_B)$ from σ_A to σ_B. This second case corresponds to the set $S_\top$. Note that the *Atom* rule can be applied only if σ_A satisfies $\mathcal{B}$, for all pairs $(\sigma_A, \sigma_B) \in S$ such that $pc(\sigma_A)$. If not, a package algorithm must either first extract more permissions from the outer state with the *Extract* rule, or fail.

The *Extract* rule (applicable at any step of a derivation), expresses that we can extract permissions (the state[4] σ_w) from the outer state σ_0, and combine

---

[3] The order in the premises is unimportant since $A_1 * A_2$ and $A_2 * A_1$ are equivalent.
[4] We explain formally in App. D of the TR [16] the notion of a stable state, which is a technicality of our general state model; in standard SL, all states are stable.

them with the first element of each pair of states in the witness set. Note that (σ_A, σ_B) is removed from the witness set if $\sigma_A \oplus \sigma_B$ is not compatible with σ_w. In such cases, adding σ_w to σ_A would create a pair in the witness set representing a state in which the wand cannot be applied. Consequently, there is no need to establish the right-hand side of the wand for this pair and our logic correspondingly removes it. Finally, the rule requires that we reduce the assertion A in the new context.

A package algorithm's strategy is mostly reflected by how it uses the *Extract* rule. To package `acc(x.b, 1/2)` $\twoheadrightarrow$ `acc(x.b, 1/2)` $*$ `(x.b` $\Rightarrow$ `acc(x.f))` from Sect. 3.1 one algorithm might use this rule to extract permission to `x.f`; another might use it to extract permission to `x.b` (if `x.b` had value false in the original state).

Example of a Derivation. Let us now illustrate how these rules can be used to package the wand from Sect. 3.1, $w :=$ `acc(x.f)`$*$`(x.f` `=` `y`$\vee$`x.f` `=` `z)`$\twoheadrightarrow$`*acc(x.f)`$*$ `acc(x.f.g)`. We omit the path condition since it is always the trivial condition $(\lambda\sigma. \top)$. Assume that the outer state σ_0 is the addition of σ_{yz}, a state that contains permission to `y.g` and `z.g`, and σ_1. $S_0 := \{(\sigma_A, e) \mid \sigma_A \in \Sigma \wedge \sigma_A \models$ `acc(x.f)` $*$ `(x.f` `=` `y` $\vee$ `x.f` `=` `z)`$\}$ is the initial witness set. We show below a part of a proof that $\langle$`acc(x.f)` $*$ `acc(x.f.g)`$, (\sigma_0, S_0)\rangle \rightsquigarrow (\sigma_1, S_3)$ is correct, and thus that σ_{yz} is a correct footprint of the wand w (since $\sigma_0 = \sigma_1 \oplus \sigma_{yz}$):

$$
\cfrac{
  \cfrac{\cdots}{\langle\texttt{acc(x.f)}, (\sigma_0, S_0)\rangle \rightsquigarrow (\sigma_0, S_1)}\; Atom
  \quad
  \cfrac{
    \cfrac{
      \cfrac{\cdots}{\langle\texttt{acc(x.f.g)}, (\sigma_1, S_2)\rangle \rightsquigarrow (\sigma_1, S_3)}\; Atom \quad \dagger
    }{\langle\texttt{acc(x.f.g)}, (\sigma_0, S_1)\rangle \rightsquigarrow (\sigma_1, S_3)}\; Extract
  }{}
}{\langle\texttt{acc(x.f)} * \texttt{acc(x.f.g)}, (\sigma_0, S_0)\rangle \rightsquigarrow (\sigma_1, S_3)}\; Star
$$

This derivation, which reflects the package algorithm that we will describe in Sect. 3.5, can be read from bottom to top and from left to right. Using the rule *Star*, we split the assertion into its two conjuncts, `acc(x.f)` (on the left) and `acc(x.f.g)` (on the right). We then handle `acc(x.f)` using the rule *Atom*. `acc(x.f)` holds in the first element of each pair of S_0, since any state that satisfies the wand's left-hand side owns `x.f`. Therefore, we use the rule *Atom* with a *choice* function that always chooses the relevant state with exactly full permission to `x.f`. S_1 is the updated witness set where this permission to `x.f` has been transferred from the first to the second element of each pair of states. Next, we handle `acc(x.f.g)`. We cannot do this directly using the rule *Atom* from S_1. We know that, for each $(\sigma_A, \sigma_B) \in S_1$, `x.f.g` evaluated in σ_A is either `y` or `z`, but σ_A owns neither `y.g` nor `z.g`. So, we transfer the permissions to both `y.g` and `z.g` from the outer state σ_0 to all states of S_1^1, using the rule *Extract*, which results in the context (σ_1, S_2); $\dagger$ represents the three other premises of the rule, namely $\sigma_0 = \sigma_{yz} \oplus \sigma_1$, $\mathsf{stable}(\sigma_{yz})$, and S_2's definition. Finally, we apply the rule *Atom* to prove $\langle$`acc(x.f.g)`$, (\sigma_1, S_2)\rangle \rightsquigarrow (\sigma_1, S_3)$, where the *choice* function chooses for each pair the corresponding state that contains full permission to `x.f.g`.

3.4 Soundness and Completeness

We write $\vdash \langle B, pc, \Delta \rangle \rightsquigarrow \Delta'$ to express that a reduction can be derived in the logic. As explained above, the goal of a package algorithm is to find a derivation of $\langle B, \lambda\_ . \top, (\sigma, \{(\sigma_A, e) \mid \sigma_A \in S_A\}) \rangle \rightsquigarrow (\sigma', S')$. If it succeeds, then the difference between σ' and σ is a valid footprint of $A \mathbin{-\!\ast} B$, since our package logic is sound. In particular, we have proven the following soundness result in Isabelle/HOL:

Theorem 1 *Soundness*. *Let B be a well-formed[5] assertion. If*

1. *the set S_A contains all states that satisfy A. i.e. $\forall \sigma_A . \sigma_A \models A \Rightarrow \sigma_A \in S_A$,*
2. $\vdash \langle B, \lambda\_ . \top, (\sigma, \{(\sigma_A, e) \mid \sigma_A \in S_A\}) \rangle \rightsquigarrow (\sigma', S')$*, and*
3. *at least one of the following conditions holds:*
   (a) B is intuitionistic
   (b) For all $(\sigma_A, \sigma_B) \in S'$, σ_A contains no permission (i.e. $\sigma_A \oplus \sigma_A = \sigma_A$)

then there exists a stable state σ_w s.t. $\sigma = \sigma' \oplus \sigma_w$ and σ_w is a footprint of $A \mathbin{-\!\ast} B$.

The third premise shows that, in an intuitionistic SL or in IDF, the correspondence between a derivation in the logic and a valid footprint of a wand is straightforward (case (a)). However, in classical SL, one must additionally check that all permissions in the witness set have been consumed (case (b)).

We have also proved in Isabelle/HOL that our package logic is complete, i.e. *any* valid footprint can be computed via a derivation in our package logic:

Theorem 2 *Completeness*. *Let B be a well-formed (see footnote 5) assertion. If σ_w is a stable footprint of $A \mathbin{-\!\ast} B$, and $\sigma = \sigma' \oplus \sigma_w$, then there exists a witness set S' such that $\vdash \langle B, \lambda\_ . \top, (\sigma, \{(\sigma_A, e) \mid \sigma_A \in S_A\}) \rangle \rightsquigarrow (\sigma', S')$.*

3.5 A Sound Package Algorithm

We now describe an automatic package algorithm that corresponds to a proof search strategy in our package logic, and which is thus sound. To convey the main ideas, consider packaging a wand of the shape $A \mathbin{-\!\ast} B_1 \ast \ldots \ast B_n$.[6] Our algorithm traverses the assertion $B_1 \ast \ldots \ast B_n$ from left to right, similarly to the FIA approach; this traversal is justified by repeated applications of the rule *Star*. Assume at some point during this traversal that the current context is (σ_0, S). When we encounter the assertion B_i, we have two possible cases:

1. All states $\sigma_A \in S^1$ satisfy B_i, which means that the permissions (or values) required by B_i are provided by the left-hand side of the wand. In this case, for each pair $(\sigma_A, \sigma_B) \in S$, we transfer permissions (and the corresponding values) to satisfy B_i from σ_A to σ_B, using the rule *Atom*. Note that the transferred permissions might be different for each pair (σ_A, σ_B). This gives us a new witness set S', while the outer state σ_0 is left unchanged. We must then handle the next assertion B_{i+1} in the context (σ_0, S').

---

[5] We formally define well-formedness in App. D of the TR [16]. Intuitively, a well-formed assertion roughly corresponds to a self-framing assertion as defined in Sect. 2.1.

[6] In App. I of the TR [16], we also show how our package algorithm handles implications.

2. There is at least one pair $(\sigma_A, \sigma_B) \in S$ such that B_i does not hold in σ_A. In this case, the algorithm fails if combining the permissions (and values) contained in the outer state with each $\sigma_A \in S^1$ is not sufficient to satisfy B_i. Otherwise, we apply the rule *Extract* to transfer permissions from the outer state σ_0 to each state σ_A in S^1 such that B_i holds in σ_A. This gives us a new context (σ_0', S'). We can now apply the first case with the context (σ_0', S').

4   Using the Logic with Combinable Wands

Extending SL with fractional permissions [4] is well-known to be useful for reasoning about heap-manipulating concurrent programs with shared state. In this setting, permission amounts are generalised to fractions $0 \le p \le 1$. Reading a heap location is permitted if $p > 0$, and writing if $p = 1$, which permits concurrent reads and ensures exclusive writes. The assertion acc(x.f, p) holds in a state that has *at least* p permission to x.f. A permission amount $p + q$ to a heap location x.f can be split into a permission amount p and a permission amount q, i.e. acc(x.f, p + q) $\models$ acc(x.f, p) * acc(x.f, q), and these two permissions can be recombined, i.e. acc(x.f, p) * acc(x.f, q) $\models$ acc(x.f, p + q).

This concept has been generalised [5,7,17,23,29] to *fractional assertions* A^p, representing a fraction p of A. A^p holds in a state σ iff there exists a state σ_A in which A holds and σ is obtained from σ_A by multiplying all permission amounts held by p [7,29]; in this case, we write $\sigma = p \cdot \sigma_A$. For example, acc(x.f)$^p \equiv$ acc(x.f, p), and Tree(x)^p (where Tree is the predicate defined in Fig. 1) expresses p permission to all nodes of the tree rooted in x.

Using fractional assertions, one might specify a function find, which searches a binary tree and yields a subtree whose root contains key key, as follows [7]: { Tree(x)^p } find(x, key) { λret. (Tree(ret) * (Tree(ret) $-\!*$ Tree(x)))^p }, in which ret corresponds to the return value of find. This postcondition is similar to the loop invariant in Fig. 1, except that it needs only a fraction p of Tree(x). A number of automatic SL verifiers, such as Caper [18], Chalice [31], VerCors [2], VeriFast [24], and Viper [34], support fractional assertions in some form.

Combinable Assertions. While it is always possible to split an assertion A^{p+q} into $A^p * A^q$, recombining $A^p * A^q$ into A^{p+q} is sound only under some conditions, for example [29] if A is *precise* (in the usual SL sense [38]). We say that A is *combinable* iff the entailment $A^p * A^q \models A^{p+q}$ holds for any two positive fractions p and q such that $p + q \le 1$. As an example, acc(x.f) is combinable, but acc(x.f) $\vee$ acc(x.g) is not because a state containing half permission to both x.f and x.g satisfies (acc(x.f) $\vee$ acc(x.g))$^{0.5}$ * (acc(x.f) $\vee$ acc(x.g))$^{0.5}$, but not acc(x.f) $\vee$ acc(x.g). Combinable assertions are particularly useful to reason about concurrent programs, for instance, to combine the postconditions of parallel branches when they terminate [7].

However, a magic wand is in general *not* combinable, as we show below. This is problematic for SL verifiers; they cannot soundly combine wands, nor predicates that could possibly contain wands in their bodies. One way to prevent the latter is to forbid magic wands in predicate bodies entirely, but this limits the common usage of predicates to abstract over general assertions in specifications [35]. Another solution is to disallow combining fractional instances of a predicate if its body contains a wand, which means requiring additional annotations to "taint" such predicates transitively. This is overly restrictive for wands which are actually combinable and complicates reasoning about abstract predicate families [35].

To address this issue, we propose a novel restriction of the wand, called *combinable wand* (we use *standard wand* to refer to the usual, unrestricted connective). Unlike standard wands in general, a combinable wand is always combinable if its right-hand side is combinable. Thus, by only using combinable wands instead of standard wands, all assertions in logics such as those employed by VerCors and Viper can be made combinable without any of the other aforementioned restrictions regarding predicates. Section 5 shows that the restriction combinable wands impose is sufficiently weak for practical purposes. Finally, footprints of combinable wands can be automatically inferred by package algorithms built on our package logic. All results in this section have been proven in Isabelle/HOL.

Standard Wands are Not Combinable in General. Even if B is combinable, the standard wand $A \mathbin{-\!\!*} B$ is, in general, not. As an example, the wand $w := \mathtt{acc(x.f,\ 1/2)} \mathbin{-\!\!*} \mathtt{acc(x.g)}$ is not combinable, because $w^{0.5} * w^{0.5} \not\models w$. To see this, consider two states σ_f and σ_g, containing full permissions to only $\mathtt{x.f}$ and $\mathtt{x.g}$, respectively. Both states are valid footprints of w, i.e. $\sigma_f \models w$ (because σ_f is incompatible with all states that satisfy the left-hand side) and $\sigma_g \models w$ (because σ_g entails the right-hand side). Thus, by definition, $0.5 \cdot \sigma_f \models w^{0.5}$ and $0.5 \cdot \sigma_g \models w^{0.5}$. However, $0.5 \cdot \sigma_f \oplus 0.5 \cdot \sigma_g$, i.e. a state with half permission to both $\mathtt{x.f}$ and $\mathtt{x.g}$, is *not* a valid footprint of w, and thus $w^{0.5} * w^{0.5} \not\models w$.

Intuitively, w is not combinable because one of its footprints, σ_f, is incompatible with the left-hand side of the wand, but becomes compatible when the footprint is scaled down to a fraction. After scaling, the wand no longer holds trivially, and the footprint does not necessarily establish the right-hand side.

To make this intuition more precise, we introduce the notion of *scalable footprints*. For a state σ, we define $scaled(\sigma)$ to be the set of copies of σ multiplied by any fraction $0 < \alpha \le 1$, i.e. $scaled(\sigma) := \{\alpha \cdot \sigma \mid 0 < \alpha \le 1\}$. A footprint σ_w is *scalable w.r.t. a state* σ_A iff either (1) σ_A is compatible with *all* states from $scaled(\sigma_w)$, or (2) σ_A is compatible with *no* state in $scaled(\sigma_w)$. A footprint is *scalable for a wand* $A \mathbin{-\!\!*} B$ iff it is scalable w.r.t. all states that satisfy A. Intuitively, this means that the footprint does not "jump" between satisfying the wand trivially and having to satisfy the right-hand side. In the above example, σ_g is a scalable footprint for w, but σ_f is not.

Making Wands Combinable. The previous paragraphs show that, even if B is combinable, the standard wand $A \mathbin{-\!\!*} B$ is in general not combinable because it can be satisfied by non-scalable footprints. Therefore, we define a novel restricted interpretation for wands that *forces* footprints to be scalable, in the following sense. The restricted interpretation of a wand accepts all scalable footprints, and transforms non-scalable footprints before checking whether they actually satisfy the wand. We call a wand with this restricted interpretation a *combinable wand*, and write $A \twoheadrightarrow_c B$ to differentiate it from the standard wand $A \twoheadrightarrow B$.

For standard wands, *any* state σ_w is a footprint of $A \twoheadrightarrow B$ iff, for all states σ_A that satisfy A, $\sigma_A \# \sigma_w \Rightarrow \sigma_A \oplus \sigma_w \models B$. We obtain the definition of combinable wands by replacing σ_w with a (possibly smaller) state $\mathcal{R}(\sigma_A, \sigma_w)$ that is scalable w.r.t. σ_A. $\mathcal{R}(\sigma_A, \sigma_w)$ is defined as σ_w if *no* state in $scaled(\sigma_w)$ is compatible with any σ_A; in that case, condition (2) of scalable footprints holds for $\mathcal{R}(\sigma_A, \sigma_w)$ w.r.t. σ_A. Otherwise, $\mathcal{R}(\sigma_A, \sigma_w)$ is obtained by removing just enough permissions from σ_w to ensure that *all* states in $scaled(\mathcal{R}(\sigma_A, \sigma_w))$ are compatible with σ_A, which ensures that condition (1) holds for $\mathcal{R}(\sigma_A, \sigma_w)$ w.r.t. σ_A.

To formally define $\mathcal{R}(\sigma_A, \sigma_w)$, we fix a concrete separation algebra (formally defined in App. G of the TR [16]), whose states are pairs (π, h) of a *permission mask* π, which maps heap locations to fractional permissions, and a partial heap h, which maps heap locations to values.

Definition 1. *Let (π_A, h_A) and (π_w, h_w) be two states, and let π'_w be the permission mask such that $\forall l. \pi'_w(l) = \min(\pi_w(l), 1 - \pi_A(l))$. Then*

$$\mathcal{R}((\pi_A, h_A), (\pi_w, h_w)) = \begin{cases} (\pi_w, h_w) & \text{if } \forall \sigma \in scaled((\pi_w, h_w)). \neg(\pi_A, h_A)\#\sigma \\ (\pi'_w, h_w) & \text{otherwise} \end{cases}$$

The combinable wand $A \twoheadrightarrow_c B$ *is then interpreted as follows:*

$$\sigma_w \models A \twoheadrightarrow_c B \iff (\forall \sigma_A. \sigma_A \models A \land \sigma_A \# \mathcal{R}(\sigma_A, \sigma_w) \implies \sigma_A \oplus \mathcal{R}(\sigma_A, \sigma_w) \models B)$$

The following theorem (proved in Isabelle/HOL) shows some key properties of combinable wands.

Theorem 3. *Let B be an intuitionistic assertion.*

1. *If B is combinable, then $A \twoheadrightarrow_c B$ is combinable.*
2. $A \twoheadrightarrow_c B \models A \twoheadrightarrow B$.
3. *If A is a binary assertion, then $A \twoheadrightarrow_c B$ and $A \twoheadrightarrow B$ are equivalent.*

Property 1 expresses that combinable wands constructed from combinable assertions are combinable, which enables verification methodologies underlying tools such as VerCors and Viper to support flexible combinations of wands and predicates (as motivated at the start of this section). Property 2 implies that $A * (A \twoheadrightarrow_c B) \models B$, that is, combinable wands can be applied like standard wands. Property 3 states that combinable wands pose no restrictions if the left-hand side is binary, that is, if it can be expressed without fractional permissions (formally defined in App. G of the TR [16]). For example, the predicate Tree(x) from Fig. 1 is binary, which implies that the wands Tree(y) $\twoheadrightarrow_c$ Tree(x) and Tree(y) $\twoheadrightarrow$ Tree(x) are equivalent. This property is an important reason for why combinable wands are expressive enough for practical purposes, as we further evidence in Sect. 5.

Table 1. Verification results on our 56 benchmarks with the FIA, our algorithm for standard wands (S-Alg), and for combinable wands (C-Alg). For each algorithm, we report the number of correct verification results, false negatives, and false positives.

Algorithm	Expected result	Incorrectly verified	Spurious errors
FIA	55	1	0
S-Alg	51	0	5
C-Alg	48	0	8

Footprints of combinable wands can be automatically inferred by algorithms built on our package logic. We explain (along with examples) in App. H of the TR [16] how to lift the package logic presented in Sect. 3 to handle alternative definitions of allowable footprints such as the restrictions imposed by Definition 1.

5 Evaluation

We have implemented package algorithms for the standard wands and combinable wands in a custom branch of Viper's [34] verification condition generator (VCG). Both are based on the package logic described in Sect. 3, adapted to the fractional permission setting. Both algorithms automate the proof search strategy outlined in Sect. 3.5. Viper's VCG translates Viper programs to Boogie [32] programs. It uses a total-heap semantics of IDF [36], where Viper states include a heap and a permission mask (tracking fractional permission amounts). The heap and mask are represented in Boogie as maps; we also represent witness sets as Boogie maps.

We evaluate our implementations of the package algorithms on Viper's test suite and compare them to Viper's implementation of the FIA as presented in Sect. 2.4. Our key findings are that our algorithms (1) enable the verification of almost all correct package operations. (2) correctly report package operations that are supposed to fail (in contrast to the FIA), and (3) have an acceptable performance overhead compared to the FIA. Moreover, interpreting wands as combinable wands as explained in Sect. 4 has only a minor effect on the results, but correctly rejects attempts to package a non-combinable wand. This finding suggests that verifiers could improve their expressiveness by allowing flexible combinations of wands and predicates with only a minor completeness penalty.

For our evaluation, we considered all 85 files in the test suite for Viper's VCG with at least one package operation. From these 85 files, we removed 29 files containing features that our implementation does not yet support. 28 of these 29 files require proof scripts to guide the footprint inference, which are orthogonal to the concerns of this paper (see App. J of the TR [16] for details).

Table 1 gives an overview of our results. These confirm that our algorithms for standard and combinable wands (S-Alg and C-Alg) do not produce false negatives, that is, are sound. In contrast, the FIA does verify an incorrect program (which is similar to the example in Sect. 2.4). While this is only a single unsound example, it is worth emphasing that (a) it comes from the pre-existing test suite of the tool itself, (b) the unsoundness was not known of until our work, and (c) soundness issues in a program verifier are critical to address; we show how to achieve this.

Compared with the FIA, our implementation reports a handful of false positives (spurious errors). For S-Alg, 3 out of 5 false positives are caused by missing features of our implementation (such as remembering a subset of the permissions that are inside predicate instances when manipulating predicates); these features could be straightforwardly added in the future. The other 2 false positives are caused by S-Alg's strategy. In one, the only potential footprint prevents the wand from ever being applied; although technically a false positive, it seems useful to reject the wand and alert the user. The other case is due to a coarse-grained heuristic applied by S-Alg that can be improved.

C-Alg reports the expected result in 48 benchmarks. Importantly, it correctly rejects one wand that indeed does not hold as a combinable wand. 5 of the 8 false positives are identical to those for S-Alg. In the other three benchmarks, the wands still do hold as combinable wands, but further extensions to C-Alg are required to handle them due to technical challenges regarding predicate instances. Once these extensions have been implemented, C-Alg will be as precise as S-Alg, indicating that comparable program verifiers could switch to combinable wands to simply enable sound, flexible combinations with predicates.

To evaluate performance, we ran each of the three implementations 5 times on each of the 56 benchmarks on a Lenovo T480 with 32 GB of RAM and a i7-8550U 1.8 GhZ CPU, running on Windows 10. We removed the slowest and fastest time, and then took the mean of the remaining 3 runs. The FIA takes between 1 and 11 seconds per benchmark. On average, S-Alg is 21% slower than the FIA. For 46 of the 56 examples, the increase is less than 30%, and for 3 examples S-Alg is between a factor 2 and 3.4 slower. The overhead is most likely due to the increased complexity of our algorithms, which track more states explicitly and require more quantified axioms in the Boogie encoding. C-Alg is on average 10% slower than S-Alg. We consider the performance overhead of our algorithms to be acceptable, especially since wands occur much more frequently in our benchmarks than in average Viper projects, as judged by existing tests and examples. More representative projects will, thus, incur a much smaller slow-down.

6   Related Work

VerCors [2] and Viper [34] are to the best of our knowledge the only automatic SL verifiers that support magic wands. Both employ package and apply ghost operations. VerCors' package algorithm requires a user to manually specify a footprint whereas Viper infers footprints using the FIA, which is unsound as we show in Sect. 2.4. Our package algorithm is as automatic as the FIA but is sound.

Lee and Park [30] develop a sound and complete proof system for SL including the magic wand. Moreover, they derive a decision procedure from their completeness proof for propositional SL. However, more expressive versions of SL (that include e.g. predicates and quantifiers) are undecidable [6] and so this decision procedure cannot be directly applied in the logics employed by program verifiers.

Chang *et al.* [11] define a shape analysis that derives magic wands $A \rightarrow\!\!\!\ast B$ of a restricted form (A and B cannot contain general imprecise assertions); our package logic does not impose such restrictions, which rule out some useful kinds of wands. For example, A may be a data structure with a read-only part expressed via existentially-quantified fractional permissions or A may contain the necessary permission to invoke a method, which may be an arbitrary assertion. In follow-up work, Chang and Rival [10] present a restricted "inductive" magic wand. Footprints of inductive wands are expressed via a finite unrolling of an inductive predicate defining B until the permissions in A are revealed. Such wands are useful to reason about data structures with back-pointers such as doubly-linked lists.

Iris [26] provides a custom proof mode [27] for interactive SL proofs in Coq [12]. Separation logics expressed in Iris support wands and are more expressive than those of automatic SL verifiers at the cost of requiring more user guidance. Packaging a wand in the proof mode requires manually specifying a footprint and proving that the footprint is correct. While tactics can be used in principle to automate parts of this process, there are no specific tactics to infer footprints.

Fractional assertions have been used in various forms [5,7,17,23,29]. Le and Hobor [29] allow combining two fractional assertions A^p and A^q only if A is *precise* in the SL sense (i.e. A describes the contents of the heaps in which it holds precisely). To avoid requiring A to be precise, Brotherston *et al.* [7] introduce *nominal labels* for assertions. If an assertion is split into two fractional assertions, then the same fresh label can be associated with both parts to indicate that they were split from the same assertion.

Two fractional assertions with the same label can be combined. However, this solution has not been implemented and does not deal with packaging wands. Our solution also avoids requiring that an assertion is precise and allows combining assertions even if they were not split from the same assertion. Instead of introducing labels, we introduce a light restriction that ensures that wands are always combinable. As a result, assertions containing combinable wands but no other potentially imprecise connectives (such as disjunction) are combinable. In particular, all assertions employed in verifiers such as VerCors and Viper can be made combinable thanks to our work.

7 Conclusion

We presented a package logic that precisely characterises sound package algorithms for automated reasoning about magic wands. Based on this logic, we developed a novel package algorithm that is inspired by an existing approach, but is sound. Moreover, we identified a sufficient criterion for wands to be combinable, such that they can be used flexibly in logics with fractional permissions, and presented a package algorithm for combinable wands. We implemented our solutions in Viper and demonstrated their practical usefulness. The soundness and completeness of our package logic, as well as key properties of combinable wands are all proved in Isabelle/HOL. As future work, we plan to extend the implementation of the two package algorithms described in Sect. 5 by porting various features of the pre-existing FIA implementation. Moreover, we will use our package logic to develop another algorithm for Viper's symbolic-execution verifier.

Acknowledgement. This work was partially funded by the Swiss National Science Foundation (SNSF) under Grant No. 197065.

References

1. Astrauskas, V., Müller, P., Poli, F., Summers, A.J.: Leveraging Rust types for modular specification and verification. In: OOPSLA (2019)
2. Blom, S., Darabi, S., Huisman, M., Oortwijn, W.: The VerCors tool set: verification of parallel and concurrent software. In: Polikarpova, N., Schneider, S. (eds.) IFM 2017. LNCS, vol. 10510, pp. 102–110. Springer, Cham (2017). https://doi.org/10.1007/978-3-319-66845-1_7
3. Blom, S., Huisman, M.: Witnessing the elimination of magic wands. Int. J. Softw. Tools Technol. Transfer **17**(6), 757–781 (2015). https://doi.org/10.1007/s10009-015-0372-3
4. Boyland, J.: Checking interference with fractional permissions. In: Cousot, R. (ed.) SAS 2003. LNCS, vol. 2694, pp. 55–72. Springer, Heidelberg (2003). https://doi.org/10.1007/3-540-44898-5_4
5. Boyland, J.T.: Semantics of fractional permissions with nesting. TOPLAS **32**(6), 1–33 (2010)
6. Brochenin, R., Demri, S., Lozes, E.: On the almighty wand. Inf. Comput. **211**, 106–137 (2012)
7. Brotherston, J., Costa, D., Hobor, A., Wickerson, J.: Reasoning over permissions regions in concurrent separation logic. In: Lahiri, S.K., Wang, C. (eds.) CAV 2020. LNCS, vol. 12225, pp. 203–224. Springer, Cham (2020). https://doi.org/10.1007/978-3-030-53291-8_13
8. Calcagno, C., O'Hearn, P.W., Yang, H.: Local action and abstract separation logic. In: LICS (2007)
9. Cao, Q., Wang, S., Hobor, A., Appel, A.W.: Proof pearl: magic wand as frame (2019). https://arxiv.org/abs/1909.08789
10. Chang, B.E., Rival, X.: Relational inductive shape analysis. In: POPL (2008)
11. Chang, B.-Y.E., Rival, X., Necula, G.C.: Shape analysis with structural invariant checkers. In: Nielson, H.R., Filé, G. (eds.) SAS 2007. LNCS, vol. 4634, pp. 384–401. Springer, Heidelberg (2007). https://doi.org/10.1007/978-3-540-74061-2_24
12. Coq Development Team, T.: The Coq Reference Manual, version 8.10 (2019). Available electronically at http://coq.inria.fr/documentation
13. Dardinier, T.: Formalization of a framework for the sound automation of magic wands. AFP, May 2022. https://isa-afp.org/entries/Package_logic.html

14. Dardinier, T.: A restricted definition of the magic wand to soundly combine fractions of a wand. AFP, May 2022. https://isa-afp.org/entries/Combinable_Wands.html
15. Dardinier, T., Parthasarathy, G., Weeks, N., Müller, P., Summers, A.J.: Sound automation of magic wands (artifact) (2022). https://doi.org/10.5281/zenodo.6526611
16. Dardinier, T., Parthasarathy, G., Weeks, N., Summers, A.J., Müller, P.: Sound automation of magic wands (extended version) (2022). https://arxiv.org/abs/2205.11325
17. Dinsdale-Young, T., Dodds, M., Gardner, P., Parkinson, M.J., Vafeiadis, V.: Concurrent abstract predicates. In: D'Hondt, T. (ed.) ECOOP 2010. LNCS, vol. 6183, pp. 504–528. Springer, Heidelberg (2010). https://doi.org/10.1007/978-3-642-14107-2_24
18. Dinsdale-Young, T., da Rocha Pinto, P., Andersen, K.J., Birkedal, L.: CAPER. In: Yang, H. (ed.) ESOP 2017. LNCS, vol. 10201, pp. 420–447. Springer, Heidelberg (2017). https://doi.org/10.1007/978-3-662-54434-1_16
19. Dockins, R., Hobor, A., Appel, A.W.: A fresh look at separation algebras and share accounting. In: Hu, Z. (ed.) APLAS 2009. LNCS, vol. 5904, pp. 161–177. Springer, Heidelberg (2009). https://doi.org/10.1007/978-3-642-10672-9_13
20. Dodds, M., Jagannathan, S., Parkinson, M.J.: Modular reasoning for deterministic parallelism. In: POPL (2011)
21. Haack, C., Hurlin, C.: Resource usage protocols for iterators. JOT 8(4), 55–83 (2009)
22. Huisman, M., Klebanov, V., Monahan, R.: VerifyThis 2012 - a program verification competition. STTT 17(6), 647–657 (2015)
23. Jacobs, B., Piessens, F.: Expressive modular fine-grained concurrency specification. In: POPL (2011)
24. Jacobs, B., Smans, J., Philippaerts, P., Vogels, F., Penninckx, W., Piessens, F.: VeriFast: a powerful, sound, predictable, fast verifier for C and Java. In: NFM (2011)
25. Jensen, J., Birkedal, L., Sestoft, P.: Modular verification of linked lists with views via separation logic. JOT 10, 1–20 (2011)
26. Jung, R., Krebbers, R., Jourdan, J., Bizjak, A., Birkedal, L., Dreyer, D.: Iris from the ground up: a modular foundation for higher-order concurrent separation logic. JFP 28, e20 (2018)
27. Krebbers, R., et al.: MoSeL: a general, extensible modal framework for interactive proofs in separation logic. In: ICFP (2018)
28. Krishnaswami, N.R.: Reasoning about iterators with separation logic. In: SAVCBS (2006)
29. Le, X.-B., Hobor, A.: Logical reasoning for disjoint permissions. In: Ahmed, A. (ed.) ESOP 2018. LNCS, vol. 10801, pp. 385–414. Springer, Cham (2018). https://doi.org/10.1007/978-3-319-89884-1_14
30. Lee, W., Park, S.: A proof system for separation logic with magic wand. In: POPL (2014)
31. Leino, K.R.M., Müller, P., Smans, J.: Verification of concurrent programs with Chalice. In: Aldini, A., Barthe, G., Gorrieri, R. (eds.) FOSAD 2007-2009. LNCS, vol. 5705, pp. 195–222. Springer, Heidelberg (2009). https://doi.org/10.1007/978-3-642-03829-7_7
32. Leino, K.R.M.: This is Boogie 2, June 2008. https://www.microsoft.com/en-us/research/publication/this-is-boogie-2-2/

33. Maeda, T., Sato, H., Yonezawa, A.: Extended alias type system using separating implication. In: TLDI (2011)
34. Müller, P., Schwerhoff, M., Summers, A.J.: Viper: a verification infrastructure for permission-based reasoning. In: Jobstmann, B., Leino, K.R.M. (eds.) VMCAI 2016. LNCS, vol. 9583, pp. 41–62. Springer, Heidelberg (2016). https://doi.org/10.1007/978-3-662-49122-5_2
35. Parkinson, M., Bierman, G.: Separation logic and abstraction. In: POPL (2005)
36. Parkinson, M.J., Summers, A.J.: The relationship between separation logic and implicit dynamic frames. Log. Methods Comput. Sci. **8**(3:01), 1–54 (2012). https://doi.org/10.1007/978-3-642-35182-2_8
37. Piskac, R., Wies, T., Zufferey, D.: GRASShopper–complete heap verification with mixed specifications. In: Ábrahám, E., Havelund, K. (eds.) TACAS 2014. LNCS, vol. 8413, pp. 124–139. Springer, Heidelberg (2014). https://doi.org/10.1007/978-3-642-54862-8_9
38. Reynolds, J.C.: Separation logic: a logic for shared mutable data structures. In: LICS (2002)
39. Schwerhoff, M., Summers, A.J.: Lightweight support for magic wands in an automatic verifier. In: ECOOP (2015)
40. Smans, J., Jacobs, B., Piessens, F.: Implicit dynamic frames: combining dynamic frames and separation logic. In: ECOOP (2009)
41. Tuerk, T.: Local reasoning about while-loops. In: VS-Theory (2010)
42. Yang, H.: An example of local reasoning in bi pointer logic: the Schorr-Waite graph marking algorithm. In: SPACE (2001)

Divide-and-Conquer Determinization of Büchi Automata Based on SCC Decomposition

Yong Li[1] , Andrea Turrini[1,2] , Weizhi Feng[1,3] , Moshe Y. Vardi[4] ,
and Lijun Zhang[1,2,3(✉)]

[1] State Key Laboratory of Computer Science, Institute of Software,
Chinese Academy of Sciences, Beijing, China
zhanglj@ios.ac.cn
[2] Institute of Intelligent Software, Guangzhou, China
[3] University of Chinese Academy of Sciences, Beijing, China
[4] Rice University, Houston, USA

Abstract. The determinization of a nondeterministic Büchi automaton (NBA) is a fundamental construction of automata theory, with applications to probabilistic verification and reactive synthesis. The standard determinization constructions, such as the ones based on the Safra-Piterman's approach, work on the whole NBA. In this work we propose a divide-and-conquer determinization approach. To this end, we first classify the strongly connected components (SCCs) of the given NBA as inherently weak, deterministic accepting, and nondeterministic accepting. We then present how to determinize each type of SCC *independently* from the others; this results in an easier handling of the determinization algorithm that takes advantage of the structure of that SCC. Once all SCCs have been determinized, we show how to compose them so to obtain the final equivalent deterministic Emerson-Lei automaton, which can be converted into a deterministic Rabin automaton without blow-up of states and transitions. We implement our algorithm in our tool COLA and empirically evaluate COLA with the state-of-the-art tools SPOT and OWL on a large set of benchmarks from the literature. The experimental results show that our prototype COLA outperforms SPOT and OWL regarding the number of states and transitions.

1 Introduction

Nondeterministic Büchi automata (NBAs) [6] are finite automata accepting infinite words; they are a simple and popular formalism used in model checking to represent reactive and non-terminating systems and their specifications, characterized by ω-regular languages [2]. Due to their nondeterminism, however, there are situations in which NBAs are not suitable, so deterministic automata are required, as it happens in probabilistic verification [2] and reactive synthesis from logical specifications [34]. Consequently, translating NBAs into equivalent deterministic ω-automata (that is, deterministic automata accepting the same

S. Shoham and Y. Vizel (Eds.): CAV 2022, LNCS 13372, pp. 152–173, 2022.
https://doi.org/10.1007/978-3-031-13188-2_8

ω-regular language) is a necessary operation for solving these problems. While there exists a direct translation from linear temporal logic (LTL) to deterministic ω-automata [15], not all problems of interests can be formalized by LTL formulas, since LTL cannot express the full class of ω-regular properties [42]. For instance, we have to use Linear Dynamic Logic (LDL) [11,41] instead of LTL to express the ω-regular property "the train will arrive in every odd minute". To the best of our knowledge, we still need to go through the determinization of NBAs for LDL to obtain deterministic ω-automata. Therefore, NBA determinization is very important in verifying the whole class of ω-regular properties.

The determinization of NBAs is a fundamental problem in automata theory that has been actively studied for decades. For the determinization of nondeterministic automata accepting finite words, it suffices to use a subset construction [20]. Determinization constructions for NBAs are, however, much more involved since the simple subset construction is not sufficient [36]. Safra [36] gave the first determinization construction for NBAs with the optimal complexity $2^{O(n \log n)}$, here n is the number of states of the input NBA; Michel [30] then gave a lower bound $n!$ for determinizing NBAs. Safra's construction has been further optimized by Piterman [33] to $O((n!)^2)$ [38], resulting in the widely known Safra-Piterman's construction. The Safra-Piterman's construction is rather challenging, while still being the most practical way for Büchi complementation [40]. Research on determinization since then either aims at developing alternative Safraless constructions [18,21,28] or further tightening the upper and lower bounds of the NBA determinization [9,26,39,43].

In this paper, we focus on the *practical* aspects of Büchi determinization. All works on determinization mentioned above focus on translating NBAs to either deterministic Rabin or deterministic parity automata. According to [37], the more relaxed an acceptance condition is, the more succinct a finite automaton can be, regarding the number of states. In view of this, we consider the translation of NBAs to deterministic *Emerson-Lei* automata (DELAs) [13,37] whose acceptance condition is an arbitrary Boolean combination of sets of transitions to be seen finitely or infinitely often, the most generic acceptance condition for a deterministic automaton. We consider here transition-based automata rather than the usual state-based automata since the former can be more succinct [12].

The Büchi determinization algorithms available in literature operate on the *whole* NBA structure at once, which does not scale well in practice due to the complex structure and the big size of the input NBA. In this work we apply a *divide-and-conquer* methodology to Büchi determinization. We propose a determinization algorithm for NBAs to DELAs based on their strongly connected components (SCCs) decomposition. We first classify the SCCs of the given NBA into three types: *inherently weak*, in which either all cycles do not visit accepting transitions or all must visit accepting transitions; *deterministic accepting* and *nondeterministic accepting*, which contain an accepting transition and are deterministic or nondeterministic, respectively. We show how to divide the whole Büchi determinization problem into the determinization for each type of SCCs *independently*, in which the determinization for an SCC takes advantage of the structure of that SCC. Then we show how to compose the results of the local determinization for each type of SCCs, leading to the final equivalent DELA. An extensive experimental evaluation confirms that the divide-and-conquer approach pays off also for the determinization of the whole NBA.

Contributions. First, we propose a *divide-and-conquer* determinization algorithm for NBAs, which takes advantage of the structure of different types of SCCs and determinizes SCCs independently. Our construction builds an equivalent DELA that can be converted into a deterministic Rabin automaton without blowing up states and transitions (cf. Theorem 2). To the best of our knowledge, we propose the *first* determinization algorithm that constructs a DELA from an NBA. Second, we show that there exists a family of NBAs for which our algorithm gives a DELA of size 2^{n+2} while classical works construct a DPA of size at least $n!$ (cf. Theorem 3). Third, we implement our algorithm in our tool COLA and evaluate it with the state-of-the-art tools SPOT [12] and OWL [23] on a large set of benchmarks from the literature. The experiments show that COLA outperforms SPOT and OWL regarding the number of states and transitions. Finally, we remark that the determinization complexity for some classes of NBAs can be exponentially better than the known ones (cf. Corollary 1).

2   Preliminaries

Let Σ be a given alphabet, i.e., a finite set of letters. A transition-based Emerson-Lei automaton can be seen as a generalization of other types of ω-automata, like Büchi, Rabin or parity. Formally, it is defined in the HOA format [1] as follows:

Definition 1. *A nondeterministic Emerson-Lei automaton (NELA) is a tuple* $\mathcal{A} = (Q, \iota, \delta, \Gamma_k, \mathsf{p}, \mathsf{Acc})$, *where Q is a finite set of* states; *$\iota \in Q$ is the* initial state; *$\delta \subseteq Q \times \Sigma \times Q$ is a* transition relation; *$\Gamma_k = \{0, 1, \cdots, k\}$, where $k \in \mathbb{N}$, is a set of* colors; *$\mathsf{p} \colon \delta \to 2^{\Gamma_k}$ is a* coloring function *for transitions; and Acc is an* acceptance formula *over Γ_k given by the following grammar, where $x \in \Gamma_k$:*

$$\alpha := \mathsf{tt} \mid \mathsf{ff} \mid \mathsf{Fin}(x) \mid \mathsf{Inf}(x) \mid \alpha \vee \alpha \mid \alpha \wedge \alpha.$$

We remark that the colors in Γ_k are not required to be all used in Acc. We call a NELA a *deterministic* Emerson-Lei automaton (DELA) if for each $q \in Q$ and $a \in \Sigma$, there is at most one $q' \in Q$ such that $(q, a, q') \in \delta$.

In the remainder of the paper, we consider δ also as a function $\delta \colon Q \times \Sigma \to 2^Q$ such that $q' \in \delta(q, a)$ whenever $(q, a, q') \in \delta$; we also write $q \xrightarrow{a} q'$ for $(q, a, q') \in \delta$ and we extend it to words $u = u_0 u_1 \cdots u_n \in \Sigma^*$ in the natural way, i.e., $q \xrightarrow{u} q' = q \xrightarrow{u[0]} q_1 \xrightarrow{u[1]} \cdots \xrightarrow{u[n]} q'$, where $\sigma[i]$ denotes the element s_i of the sequence of elements $\sigma = s_0 s_1 s_2 \cdots$ at position i. We assume without loss of generality that each automaton is *complete*, i.e., for each state $q \in Q$ and letter $a \in \Sigma$, we have $\delta(q, a) \neq \emptyset$. If it is not complete, we make it complete by adding a fresh state $q_\bot \notin Q$ and redirecting all missing transitions to it.

A *run* of $\mathcal{A}$ over an ω-word $w \in \Sigma^\omega$ is an infinite sequence of states ρ such that $\rho[0] = \iota$, and for each $i \in \mathbb{N}$, $(\rho[i], w[i], \rho[i+1]) \in \delta$.

The *language* $L(\mathcal{A})$ of $\mathcal{A}$ is the set of words accepted by $\mathcal{A}$, i.e., the set of words $w \in \Sigma^\omega$ such that there exists a run ρ of $\mathcal{A}$ over w such that $p(inf(\rho)) \models \mathsf{Acc}$, where $inf(\rho) = \{(q, a, q') \in \delta \mid \forall i \in \mathbb{N}.\exists j > i.(\rho[j], w[j], \rho[j+1]) = (q, a, q')\}$ and the satisfaction relation $\models$ is defined recursively as follows: given $M \subseteq \Gamma_k$,

$$M \models \mathsf{tt}, \quad M \models \mathsf{Fin}(x) \text{ iff } x \notin M, \quad M \models \alpha_1 \vee \alpha_2 \text{ iff } M \models \alpha_1 \text{ or } M \models \alpha_2,$$
$$M \not\models \mathsf{ff}, \quad M \models \mathsf{Inf}(x) \text{ iff } x \in M, \quad M \models \alpha_1 \wedge \alpha_2 \text{ iff } M \models \alpha_1 \text{ and } M \models \alpha_2.$$

Intuitively, a run ρ over w is accepting if the set of colors (induced by p) that occur infinitely often in ρ satisfies the acceptance formula Acc. Here $\mathsf{Fin}(x)$ specifies that the color x only appears for finitely many times while $\mathsf{Inf}(x)$ requires the color x to be seen infinitely often.

The more common types of ω-automata, such as Büchi, parity and Rabin can be treated as Emerson-Lei automata with the following acceptance formulas.

Definition 2. *A NELA* $\mathcal{A} = (Q, \iota, \delta, \Gamma_k, p, \mathsf{Acc})$ *is said to be*

- *a Büchi automaton (BA) if $k = 0$ and $\mathsf{Acc} = \mathsf{Inf}(0)$. Transition with color 0 are usually called* accepting *transitions. Thus, a run ρ is accepting if $p(inf(\rho)) \cap \{0\} \neq \emptyset$, i.e., ρ takes accepting transitions infinitely often;*
- *a parity automaton (PA) if k is even and $\mathsf{Acc} = \bigvee_{c=0}^{k/2}(\bigwedge_{i=1}^{c} \mathsf{Fin}(2i-1) \wedge \mathsf{Inf}(2c))$. A run ρ is accepting if the minimum color in $p(inf(\rho))$ is even;*
- *a Rabin automaton (RA) if k is an odd number and $\mathsf{Acc} = (\mathsf{Fin}(0) \wedge \mathsf{Inf}(1)) \vee \cdots \vee (\mathsf{Fin}(k-1) \wedge \mathsf{Inf}(k))$. Intuitively, a run ρ is accepting if there exists an odd integer $0 < j \leq k$ such that $j - 1 \notin p(inf(\rho))$ and $j \in p(inf(\rho))$.*

When the NELA $\mathcal{A} = (Q, \iota, \delta, \Gamma_k, p, \mathsf{Acc})$ is a nondeterministic BA (NBA), we just write $\mathcal{A}$ as (Q, ι, δ, F) where F is the set of accepting transitions. We call a set $C \subseteq Q$ a *strongly connected component* (SCC) of $\mathcal{A}$ if for every pair of states $q, q' \in C$, we have that $q \xrightarrow{u} q'$ for some $u \in \Sigma^*$ and $q' \xrightarrow{v} q$ for some $v \in \Sigma^*$, i.e., q and q' can be reached by each other; by default, each state $q \in Q$ reaches itself. C is a *maximal* SCC if it is *not* a proper subset of another SCC. All SCCs considered in the work are maximal. We call an SCC C *accepting* if there is a transition $(q, a, q') \in (C \times \Sigma \times C) \cap F$ and *nonaccepting* otherwise. We say that an SCC C' is *reachable* from an SCC C if there exist $q \in C$ and $q' \in C'$ such that $q \xrightarrow{u} q'$ for some $u \in \Sigma^*$. An SCC C is *inherently weak* if either every cycle going through the C-states visits at least one accepting transition or none of the cycles visits an accepting transition. We say that an SCC C is *deterministic* if for every state $q \in C$ and $a \in \Sigma$, we have $|\delta(q, a) \cap C| \leq 1$. Note that a state q in a deterministic SCC C can have multiple successors for a letter a, but at most one successor remains in C.

Figure 1 shows an example of NBA we will use for our examples in the remainder of the paper; we depict the accepting transitions with a double arrow. Clearly, inside each SCC, depicted as a box, each state can be reached by any other state, and the SCCs are maximal. The SCC $\{q_2, q_3\}$ is inherently weak and accepting, since every cycle takes an accepting transition; the SCC $\{q_6\}$ is also inherently weak, but nonaccepting, since every cycle never takes an accepting transition.

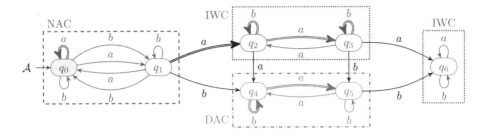

Fig. 1. An example of NBA.

The remaining two SCCs, i.e., $\{q_0, q_1\}$ and $\{q_4, q_5\}$, are not inherently weak, since some cycle takes accepting transitions (like the cycle $q_0 \xrightarrow{a} q_0$) while others do not (like the cycle $q_0 \xrightarrow{b} q_0$). Both SCCs contain an accepting transition, so they are accepting; the SCC $\{q_0, q_1\}$ is clearly nondeterministic, while the SCC $\{q_4, q_5\}$ is deterministic. Note that from q_5 we have two transitions labelled by b, but only the transition $q_5 \xrightarrow{b} q_4$ remains inside the SCC, while the other transition $q_5 \xrightarrow{b} q_6$ leaves the SCC, so the SCC is still deterministic.

The following proposition is well known and is often used in prior works.

Proposition 1. *Let $\mathcal{A}$ be an NBA and $w \in \Sigma^\omega$. A run of $\mathcal{A}$ over w will eventually stay in an SCC. Moreover, if $w \in \mathsf{L}(\mathcal{A})$, every accepting run of $\mathcal{A}$ over w will eventually stay in an accepting SCC.*

Proposition 1 is the key ingredient of our algorithm: it allows us to determinize the SCCs independently as $\mathsf{L}(\mathcal{A})$ is the union of the words whose runs stay in each accepting SCCs. In the remainder of the paper, we first present a translation from an NBA $\mathcal{A}$ to a DELA $\mathcal{A}^{\mathsf{E}}$ based on the SCC decomposition of $\mathcal{A}$. The obtained DELA $\mathcal{A}^{\mathsf{E}}$ in fact can be converted to a *deterministic* Rabin automaton (DRA) $\mathcal{A}^{\mathsf{R}}$ without blowing up states and transitions, i.e., we can just convert the coloring function and the acceptance formula of $\mathcal{A}^{\mathsf{E}}$ to DRAs.

3   Determinization Algorithms of SCCs

Determinizing each SCC of $\mathcal{A}$ independently is not straightforward since it may be reached from the initial state only after reading a nonempty finite word; moreover, there can be words of different length leading to the SCC, entering through different states. To keep track of the different arrivals in an SCC at different times, we make use of run DAGs [24], that are a means to organize the runs of $\mathcal{A}$ over a word w. In this section, we first recall the concept of run DAGs and then describe how to determinize SCCs with their help.

Definition 3. *Let $\mathcal{A} = (Q, \iota, \delta, F)$ be an NBA and $w \in \Sigma^\omega$ be a word. The run DAG $\mathcal{G}_{\mathcal{A},w} = \langle V, E \rangle$ of $\mathcal{A}$ over w is defined as follows: the set of vertices $V \subseteq Q \times \mathbb{N}$ is defined as $V = \bigcup_{l \geq 0}(V_l \times \{l\})$ where $V_0 = \{\iota\}$ and $V_{l+1} = \delta(V_l, w[l])$ for every $l \in \mathbb{N}$; there is an edge $(\langle q, l\rangle, \langle q', l'\rangle) \in E$ if $l' = l+1$ and $q' \in \delta(q, w[l])$.*

Intuitively, a state q at a level ℓ may occur in several runs and only one vertex is needed to represent it, i.e., the vertex $\langle q, \ell \rangle$ who is said to be on level ℓ. Note that by definition, there are at most $|Q|$ vertices on each level. An edge $(\langle q, l \rangle, \langle q', l+1 \rangle)$ is an F-edge if $(q, w[l], q') \in F$. An infinite sequence of vertices $\gamma = \langle q_0, 0 \rangle \langle q_1, 1 \rangle \cdots$ is called an ω-branch of $\mathcal{G}_{\mathcal{A},w}$ if $q_0 = \iota$ and for each $\ell \in \mathbb{N}$, we have $(\langle q_\ell, \ell \rangle, \langle q_{\ell+1}, \ell+1 \rangle) \in E$. We can observe that there is a bijection between the set of runs of $\mathcal{A}$ on w and the set of ω-branches in $\mathcal{G}_{\mathcal{A},w}$. In fact, to a run $\rho = q_0 q_1 \cdots$ of $\mathcal{A}$ over w corresponds the ω-branch $\hat{\rho} = \langle q_0, 0 \rangle \langle q_1, 1 \rangle \cdots$ and, symmetrically, to an ω-branch $\gamma = \langle q_0, 0 \rangle \langle q_1, 1 \rangle \cdots$ corresponds the run $\hat{\gamma} = q_0 q_1 \cdots$. Thus w is accepted by $\mathcal{A}$ if and only if there exists an ω-branch in $\mathcal{G}_{\mathcal{A},w}$ that takes F-edges infinitely often.

In the remainder of this section, we will introduce the algorithms for computing the successors of the current states inside different types of SCCs, with the help of run DAGs. We fix an NBA $\mathcal{A} = (Q, \iota, \delta, F)$ and a word $w \in \Sigma^\omega$. We let $Q = \{q_1, \ldots, q_n\}$ and apply a total order $\preccurlyeq$ on Q such that $q_i \preccurlyeq q_j$ if $i < j$. Let $S_\ell \subseteq Q$, $\ell \in \mathbb{N}$, be the set of states reached at the level ℓ in the run DAG $\mathcal{G}_{\mathcal{A},w}$; we assume that this sequence $S_0, \cdots, S_\ell, \cdots$ is available as a *global* variable during the computations of every SCC where $S_0 = \{\iota\}$ and $S_{\ell+1} = \delta(S_\ell, w[\ell])$.

When determinizing the given NBA $\mathcal{A}$, we classify its SCCs into three types, namely inherently weak SCCs (IWCs), deterministic-accepting SCCs (DACs) and nondeterministic-accepting SCCs (NACs). We assume that all DACs and NACs are *not* inherently weak, otherwise they will be classified as IWCs.

In our determinization construction, every level in $\mathcal{G}_{\mathcal{A},w}$ corresponds to a state in our constructed DELA $\mathcal{A}^\mathsf{E}$ while reading the ω-word w. Let m_ℓ be the state of $\mathcal{A}^\mathsf{E}$ at level ℓ. The computation of the successor $m_{\ell+1}$ of m_ℓ for the letter $w[\ell]$ will be divided into the successor computation for states in IWCs, DACs and NACs independently. Then the successor $m_{\ell+1}$ is just the Cartesian product of these successors. In the remainder of this section, we present how to compute the successors for the states in each type of SCCs.

3.1 Successor Computation Inside IWCs

As we have seen, $\mathcal{G}_{\mathcal{A},w}$ contains all runs of $\mathcal{A}$ over w, including those within DACs and NACs. Since we want to compute the successor only for IWCs, we focus on the states inside the IWCs and ignore other states in DACs and NACs. Let W be the set of states in all IWCs and $\mathsf{WA} \subseteq \mathsf{W}$ be the set of states in all accepting IWCs.

For the run DAG $\mathcal{G}_{\mathcal{A},w}$, we use a pair of sets of states $(P_\ell, O_\ell) \in 2^\mathsf{W} \times 2^\mathsf{WA}$ to represent the set of IWC states reached in $\mathcal{G}_{\mathcal{A},w}$ at level ℓ. The set P_ℓ is used to keep track of the states in W reached at level ℓ, while O_ℓ, inspired by the breakpoint construction used in [31], keeps only the states reached in WA, that is, it is used to track the runs that stay in accepting IWCs. Since by definition each cycle inside an accepting IWC must visit an accepting transition, for each run tracked by O_ℓ we do not need to remember whether we have taken an accepting transition: it suffices to know whether the run is still inside some accepting IWC or whether the run has left them.

We now show how to compute the sets (P_ℓ, O_ℓ) along w. For level 0, we simply set $P_0 = \{\iota\} \cap W$ and $O_0 = \emptyset$. For the other levels, given (P_ℓ, O_ℓ) at level $\ell \in \mathbb{N}$, the encoding $(P_{\ell+1}, O_{\ell+1})$ for the next level $\ell + 1$ is defined as follows:

- $P_{\ell+1} = S_{\ell+1} \cap W$, i.e., $P_{\ell+1}$ keeps track of the W-states reached at level $\ell + 1$;
- if $O_\ell \neq \emptyset$, then $O_{\ell+1} = \delta(O_\ell, w[\ell]) \cap WA$, otherwise $O_{\ell+1} = P_{\ell+1} \cap WA$.

Intuitively, the O-set keeps track of the runs that stay in the accepting IWCs. So if $O_\ell \neq \emptyset$, then $O_{\ell+1}$ maintains the runs remaining in some accepting IWC; otherwise, $O_\ell = \emptyset$ means that at level ℓ all runs seen so far in the accepting IWCs have left them, so we can just start to track the new runs that entered the accepting IWCs but were not tracked yet.

On the right we show the fragment of the run DAG $\mathcal{G}_{\mathcal{A}, a^\omega}$ for the NBA $\mathcal{A}$ shown in Fig. 1 and its IWCs; we have $W = \{q_2, q_3, q_6\}$ and $WA = \{q_2, q_3\}$. The set P_ℓ contains all states q at level ℓ; the set O_ℓ contains the underlined ones. As a concrete application of the construction given above, from $P_3 = \{q_2, q_3\}$ and $O_3 = \delta(O_2, a) \cap WA = \{q_3\}$, at level 4 we get $P_4 = \{q_2, q_3, q_6\}$ and $O_4 = \delta(O_3, a) \cap WA = \{q_2\}$.

It is not difficult to see that checking whether w is accepted reduces to check whether the number of empty O-sets is finite. We assign color 1 to the transition from (P_ℓ, O_ℓ) to $(P_{\ell+1}, O_{\ell+1})$ via $w[\ell]$ if $O_\ell = \emptyset$, otherwise we assign color 2. Lemma 1 formalizes the relation between accepting runs staying in accepting IWCs and the colors we get from our construction.

Lemma 1. *(1) There exists an accepting run of $\mathcal{A}$ over w eventually staying in an accepting IWC if and only if we receive color 1 finitely many times when constructing the sequence $(P_0, O_0) \cdots (P_\ell, O_\ell) \cdots$ while reading w. (2) The number of possible (P, O) pairs is at most $3^{|W|}$.*

The proof idea is trivial: an accepting run ρ that stays in an accepting IWC will make the O-set contain ρ forever and we always get color 2 from some point on. A possible pair (P, O) can be seen as choosing a state from W, which can be from $W \setminus P$, $P \cap O$ and $P \setminus O$, respectively. It thus gives at most $3^{|W|}$ possibilities.

To ease the construction for the whole NBA $\mathcal{A}$, we make the above computation of successors available as a function weakSucc, which takes as input a pair of sets (P, O) and a letter a, and returns the successor (P', O') and the corresponding color $c \in \{1, 2\}$ for the transition $((P, O), a, (P', O'))$.

The construction we gave above works on all IWCs at the same time; considering IWCs separately does not improve the resulting complexity. If there are two accepting IWCs with n_1 and n_2 states, respectively, then the number of possible (P, O) pairs for the two IWCs is 3^{n_1} and 3^{n_2}, respectively. When combining the pairs for each IWC together, the resulting number of pairs in the Cartesian product is $3^{n_1} \times 3^{n_2} = 3^{n_1 + n_2}$, which is the same as considering them together. On the other hand, for each accepting IWC, we need to use two colors, so we need $2 \cdot i$ colors in total for i accepting IWCs, instead of just two colors by operating on all IWCs together. Hence, we prefer to work on all IWCs at once.

3.2   Successor Computation Inside DACs

In contrast to IWCs, we do not work on all DACs at once but we process each DAC separately. This is because there may be nondeterminism between DACs: a run in a DAC may branch into multiple runs that jump to different DACs, which requires us to resort to a Safra-Piterman's construction [33, 36] when considering all DACs at once. Working on each DAC separately, instead, allows us to take advantage of the internal determinism: for a given DAC D, the transition relation δ inside D, denoted as $\delta_D = (D \times \Sigma \times D) \cap \delta$, is now deterministic.

Although every run ρ entering D can have only one successor in D, ρ may just leave D while new runs can enter D, which makes it difficult to check whether there exists an accepting run that remains trapped into D. In order to identify accepting runs staying in D, we identify the following two rules for distinguishing runs that come to D by means of *unique* labelling numbers: **(1)** the runs already in D have precedence over newly entering runs, thus the latter get assigned a higher number. In practice, the labelling keeps track of the relative order of entering D, thus the lower the labelling value is, the earlier the run came to D; **(2)** when two runs in D merge, we only keep the run that came to D earlier, i.e., the run with lower number. If two runs enter D at the same time, we let them enter according to the total state order $\preccurlyeq$ for their respective entry states.

We use a level-labelling function $\mathfrak{g}_\ell \colon D \to \{1, \cdots, 2 \cdot |D|\} \cup \{\infty\}$ to encode the set of D-states reached at level ℓ of the run DAG $\mathcal{G}_{A,w}$. Here we use $\mathfrak{g}_\ell(q) = \infty$ to indicate that the state $q \in D$ is not reached by $\mathcal{A}$ at level ℓ.

At level 0, we set $\mathfrak{g}_0(q) = \infty$ for every state $q \in D \setminus \{\iota\}$, and $\mathfrak{g}_0(\iota) = 1$ if $\iota \in D$. Note that the SCC that ι resides in can be an IWC, a DAC or a NAC.

For a given level-labelling function $\mathfrak{g}_\ell$, we will make $\{ q \in D \mid \mathfrak{g}_\ell(q) \neq \infty \} = S_\ell \cap D$ hold, i.e., tracing correctly the set of D-states reached by $\mathcal{A}$ at level ℓ; we denote the set $\mathfrak{g}_\ell(D) \setminus \{\infty\}$ by $\beta(\mathfrak{g}_\ell)$, so $\beta(\mathfrak{g}_\ell)$ is the set of unique labelling numbers at level ℓ. By the construction given below about how to generate $\mathfrak{g}_{\ell+1}$ from $\mathfrak{g}_\ell$ on reading $w[\ell]$, we ensure that $\beta(\mathfrak{g}_\ell) \subseteq \{1, \cdots, 2 \cdot |D|\}$ for all $\ell \in \mathbb{N}$.

We now present how to compute the successor level-labelling function $\mathfrak{g}_{\ell+1}$ of $\mathfrak{g}_\ell$ on letter $w[\ell]$. The states reached by $\mathcal{A}$ at level $\ell+1$, i.e., $S_{\ell+1} \cap D$, may come from two sources: some state may come from states not in D via transitions in $\delta \setminus \delta_D$; some other via δ_D from states in $S_\ell \cap D$. In order to generate $\mathfrak{g}_{\ell+1}$, we first compute an intermediate level-labelling function $\mathfrak{g}'_{\ell+1}$ as follows.

1. To obey Rule **(2)**, for every state $q' \in \delta_D(S_\ell \cap D, w[\ell])$, we set

$$\mathfrak{g}'_{\ell+1}(q') = \min\{ \mathfrak{g}_\ell(q) \mid q \in S_\ell \cap D \wedge \delta_D(q, w[\ell]) = q' \}.$$

   That is, when two runs merge, we only keep the run with the lower labelling number, i.e., the run entered in D earlier.

2. To respect Rule **(1)**, we set $\mathfrak{g}'_{\ell+1}(q') = |D| + i$ for the i-th newly entered state $q' \in (S_{\ell+1} \cap D) \setminus \delta_D(S_\ell \cap D, w[\ell])$ and the states q' are ordered by the total order $\preccurlyeq$ of the states. Since every state in $\delta_D(S_\ell \cap D, w[\ell])$ is on a run that already entered D, its labelling has already been determined by the case 1.

It is easy to observe that in order to compute the transition relation between two consecutive levels, we only need to know the labelling at the previous level. More precisely, we do not have to know the exact labelling numbers, since it suffices to know their relative order. Therefore, we can compress the level-labelling $\mathfrak{g}'_{\ell+1}$ to $\mathfrak{g}_{\ell+1}$ as follows. Let $\text{ord} \colon \beta(\mathfrak{g}'_{\ell+1}) \to \{1, \cdots, |\beta(\mathfrak{g}'_{\ell+1})|\}$ be the function that maps each labelling value in $\beta(\mathfrak{g}'_{\ell+1})$ to its relative position once the values in $\beta(\mathfrak{g}'_{\ell+1})$ have been sorted in ascending order. For instance, if $\beta(\mathfrak{g}'_{\ell+1}) = \{2, 4, 7\}$, then $\text{ord} = \{2 \mapsto 1, 4 \mapsto 2, 7 \mapsto 3\}$. Then we set $\mathfrak{g}_{\ell+1}(q) = \text{ord}(\mathfrak{g}'_{\ell+1}(q))$ for each $q \in S_{\ell+1} \cap \mathsf{D}$, and $\mathfrak{g}_{\ell+1}(q') = \infty$ for each $q' \in \mathsf{D} \setminus S_{\ell+1}$. In this way, all level-labelling functions $\mathfrak{g}_\ell$ we use are such that $\beta(\mathfrak{g}_\ell) \subseteq \{1, \cdots, |\mathsf{D}|\}$.

The intuition behind the use of these level-labelling functions is that, if we always see a labelling number h in the intermediate level-labelling $\mathfrak{g}'_\ell$ for all $\ell \geq k$ after some level k, we know that there is a run that eventually stays in D and is eventually always labelled with h. To check whether this run also visits infinitely many accepting transitions, we will color every transition $e = (\mathfrak{g}_\ell, w[\ell], \mathfrak{g}_{\ell+1})$. To decide what color to assign to e, we first identify which runs have merged with others or got out of D (corresponding to *bad* events and *odd* colors) and which runs still continue to stay in D and take an accepting transition (corresponding to *good* events and *even* colors).

The bad events correspond to the discontinuation of labelling values between $\mathfrak{g}_\ell$ and $\mathfrak{g}'_{\ell+1}$, defined as $\mathsf{B}(e) = \beta(\mathfrak{g}_\ell) \setminus \beta(\mathfrak{g}'_{\ell+1})$. Intuitively, if a labelling value k exists in the set $\mathsf{B}(e)$, then the run ρ associated with labelling k merged with a run with lower labelling value $k' < k$, or ρ left the DAC D. The good events correspond to the occurrence of accepting transitions in some runs, whose labelling we collect into $\mathsf{G}(e) = \{ k \in \beta(\mathfrak{g}_\ell) \mid \exists (q, w[\ell], q') \in F.\mathfrak{g}_\ell(q) = \mathfrak{g}'_{\ell+1}(q') = k \neq \infty \}$. In practice, a labelling value k in $\mathsf{G}(e)$ indicates that we have seen a run with labelling k that visits an accepting transition. We then let $\mathsf{B}(e) = \mathsf{B}(e) \cup \{|\mathsf{D}| + 1\}$ and $\mathsf{G}(e) = \mathsf{G}(e) \cup \{|\mathsf{D}| + 1\}$ where the value $|\mathsf{D}| + 1$ is used to indicate that no bad (i.e., no run merged or left the DAC) or no good (i.e., no run took an accepting transition) events happened, respectively.

In order to declare a sequence of labelling functions as accepting, we want the good events to happen infinitely often and bad events to happen only finitely often, when the runs with bad events have a labelling number lower than that of the runs with good events. So we assign the color $c = \min\{2 \cdot \min \mathsf{B}(e) - 1, 2 \cdot \min \mathsf{G}(e)\}$ to the transition e. Since the labelling numbers are in $\{1, \cdots, |\mathsf{D}|\}$, we have that $c \in \{1, \cdots, 2 \cdot |\mathsf{D}| + 1\}$. The intuition why we assign colors in this way is given as the proof idea of the following lemma.

Lemma 2. *(1) An accepting run of $\mathcal{A}$ over w eventually stays in the DAC D if and only if the minimal color c we receive infinitely often is even. (2) The number of possible labelling functions $\mathfrak{g}$ is at most $3 \cdot |\mathsf{D}|!$.*

The proof idea is as follows: an accepting run ρ on the word w that stays in D will have stable labelling number, say $k \geq 1$, after some level since the labelling value cannot increase by construction and is finite. So all runs on w that have labelling values lower than k will not leave D: if they would leave or just merge with other runs, their labelling value vanishes, so ord would decrease the value for ρ. This implies that the color we receive afterwards infinitely often is either 1) an odd color larger than $2k$, due to vanishing runs with value at least $k+1$ or simply because no bad or good events occur, or 2) an even color at most $2k$, depending on whether there is some run with value smaller than ρ also taking accepting transitions. Thus the minimum color occurring infinitely often is even. The number of labelling functions $\mathfrak{g}$ is bounded by $\sum_{i=0}^{|D|} \binom{|D|}{i} \cdot i! \leq 3 \cdot |D|!$.

The fragment of the DAG $\mathcal{G}_{\mathcal{A},a^\omega}$ shown on the right is relative to the only DAC $D = \{q_4, q_5\}$. The value of $\mathfrak{g}'_\ell(q)$, $\mathfrak{g}_\ell(q)$ and the corresponding ord is given by the mapping near each state q; as a concrete application of the construction given above, consider how to get $\mathfrak{g}_4$ from $\mathfrak{g}_3$, defined as $\mathfrak{g}_3(q_4) = 1$ and $\mathfrak{g}_3(q_5) = \infty$: since $q_5 \in \delta_D(S_3 \cap D, a)$, according to case 1 we define $\mathfrak{g}'_4(q_5) = 1$ because $q_5 = \delta_D(q_4, a)$ and $\mathfrak{g}_3(q_4) = 1$; since $q_4 \in (S_4 \cap D) \setminus \delta_D(S_3 \cap D, a)$, then case 2 applies, so $\mathfrak{g}'_4(q_4) = 3$. The function ord is $\mathrm{ord} = [1 \mapsto 1, 3 \mapsto 2]$, thus we get $\mathfrak{g}_4(q_4) = 2$ and $\mathfrak{g}_4(q_5) = 1$. As bad/good sets for the transition $e = \mathfrak{g}_3 \xrightarrow{a} \mathfrak{g}_4$, we have $\mathsf{B}(e) = \emptyset \cup \{3\}$ while $\mathsf{G}(e) = \{1\} \cup \{3\}$, so the resulting color is 2.

Again, we make the above computation of successors available as a function detSucc, which takes as input the DAC D, a labelling $\mathfrak{g}$ and a letter a, and returns the successor labelling $\mathfrak{g}'$ and the color $c \in \{1, \cdots, 2 \cdot |D| + 1\}$.

The diagram on the right:

ℓ		
3	$q_4, 3 \mapsto 1$	
4	$q_5, 1 \mapsto 1$	$q_4, 3 \mapsto 2$
5	$q_4, 1 \mapsto 1$	$q_5, 2 \mapsto 2$

3.3 Successor Computation Inside NACs

The computation of the successor inside a NAC is more involved since runs can branch, so it is more difficult to check whether there exists an accepting run. To identify accepting runs, researchers usually follow the Safra-Piterman's idea [33,36] to give the runs that take more accepting transitions the precedence over other runs that join them. We now present how to compute labelling functions encoding this idea for NACs, instead of the whole NBA. Differently to the previous case about DACs, the labelling functions we use here use lists of numbers, instead of single numbers, to keep track of the branching, merging and new incoming runs. This can be seen as a generalization of the numbered brackets used in [35] to represent ordinary Safra-Piterman's trees. Differently from this construction, in our setting the main challenge we have to consider is how to manage correctly the newly entering runs, which are simply not occurring in [35] since there the whole NBA is considered. The fact that runs can merge, instead, is a common aspect, while the fact that a run ρ leaves the current NAC can be treated similarly to dying out runs in [35]. Below we assume that N is a given NAC; we denote by $\delta_N = (N \times \Sigma \times N) \cap \delta$ the transition function δ inside N.

To manage the branching and merging of runs of $\mathcal{A}$ over w inside a NAC, and to keep track of the accepting transitions taken so far, we use level-labelling functions as for the DAC case. For a given NAC N, the functions we use have lists of natural numbers as codomain; more precisely, let $\mathcal{L}_N$ be the set of lists taking value in the set $\{1, \cdots, 2 \cdot |N|\}$, where a list is a finite sequence of values in ascending order. Given two lists $[v_1, \cdots, v_k]$ and $[v'_1, \cdots, v'_{k'}]$, we say that

$[v_1, \cdots, v_k]$ is a prefix of $[v'_1, \cdots, v'_{k'}]$ if $1 \le k \le k'$ and for each $1 \le j \le k$, we have $v_j = v'_j$. Note that the empty list *is not* a prefix of any list. Given two lists $[v_1, \cdots, v_k]$ and $[v'_1, \cdots, v'_{k'}]$, we denote by $[v_1, \cdots, v_k] \frown [v'_1, \cdots, v'_{k'}]$ their concatenation, that is the list $[v_1, \cdots, v_k, v'_1, \cdots, v'_{k'}]$. Moreover, we define a total order on lists as follows: given two lists $[v_1, \cdots, v_k]$ and $[v'_1, \cdots, v'_{k'}]$, we order them by padding the shorter of the two with ∞ in the rear, so to make them of the same length, and then by comparing them by the usual lexicographic order. This means, for instance, that the empty list $[]$ is the largest list and that $[1, 3, 5]$ is smaller than $[1, 3]$ but larger than $[1, 2]$. The lists help to keep track of the branching history from their prefixes, such as $[1, 2]$ is branched from $[1]$.

As done for DACs, we use a level-labelling function $t_\ell \colon \mathsf{N} \to \mathcal{L}_\mathsf{N}$ to encode the set of N-states reached in the run DAG $\mathcal{G}_{\mathcal{A}, w}$ at level ℓ. We denote by $\beta(t_\ell)$ the set of non-empty lists in the image of t_ℓ, that is, $\beta(t_\ell) = \{\, t_\ell(q) \mid q \in \mathsf{N} \wedge t_\ell(q) \ne [] \,\}$. We use the empty list $[]$ for the states in N that do not occur in the vertexes of $\mathcal{G}_{\mathcal{A}, w}$ at level ℓ, so $\beta(t_\ell)$ contains only lists associated with states that $\mathcal{A}$ is currently located at. Similarly to the other types of SCCs, at level 0, we set $t_0(\iota) = [1]$ if $\iota \in \mathsf{N}$, and $t_0(q) = []$ for each state $q \in \mathsf{N} \setminus \{\iota\}$.

To define the transition from t_ℓ to $t_{\ell+1}$ through the letter $w[\ell]$, we use again an intermediate level-labelling function $t'_{\ell+1}$ that we construct step by step as follows. We start with $t'_{\ell+1}(q) = []$ for each $q \in \mathsf{N}$ and with the set of unused numbers $U = \{\, u \ge 1 \mid u \notin \beta(t_\ell) \,\}$, i.e., the numbers not used in $\beta(t_\ell)$.

1. For every state $q' \in \delta_\mathsf{N}(S_\ell \cap \mathsf{N}, w[\ell])$, let $P_{q'} = \{\, q \in S_\ell \cap \mathsf{N} \mid (q, w[\ell], q') \in \delta_\mathsf{N} \,\}$ be the set of currently reached predecessors of q', and $C_{q'} = \emptyset$. For each $q \in P_{q'}$, if $(q, w[\ell], q') \in F$, then we add $t_\ell(q) \frown [u]$ to $C_{q'}$, where $u = \min U$, and we remove u from U, so that each number in U is used only once; otherwise, for $(q, w[\ell], q') \in \delta_\mathsf{N} \setminus F$, we add $t_\ell(q)$ to $C_{q'}$. Lastly, we set $t'_{\ell+1}(q') = \min C_{q'}$, where the minimum is taken according to the list order.

   Intuitively, if a run ρ can branch into two kinds of runs, some via accepting transitions and some others via nonaccepting transitions at level $\ell + 1$, then we let those from nonaccepting transitions inherit the labelling from ρ, i.e., $t_\ell(\rho[\ell])$; for the runs taking accepting transitions we create a new labelling $t_\ell(\rho[\ell]) \frown [u]$. In this way, the latter get precedence over the former. Moreover, if a run ρ has received multiple labelling values, collected in $C_{\rho[\ell+1]}$, then it will keep the smallest one, by $t'_{\ell+1}(\rho[\ell+1]) = \min C_{\rho[\ell+1]}$.

2. For each state $q' \in (S_{\ell+1} \cap \mathsf{N}) \setminus \delta_\mathsf{N}(S_\ell \cap \mathsf{N}, w[\ell])$ taken according to the state order $\preccurlyeq$, we first set $t'_{\ell+1}(q') = [u]$, where $u = \min U$, and then we remove u from U, so we do not reuse the same values. That is, we give the newly entered runs lower precedence than those already in N, by means of the larger list $[u]$.

We now need to prune the lists in $\beta(t'_{\ell+1})$ and recognize good and bad events. Similarly to DACs, a bad event means that a run has left N or has been merged with runs with smaller labelling, which is indicated by a discontinuation of a labelling between $\beta(t_\ell)$ and $\beta(t'_{\ell+1})$. For the transition $e = (t_\ell, w[\ell], t_{\ell+1})$ we are constructing, to recognize bad events, we put into the set $B(e)$ the number $|N| + 1$ and all numbers in $\beta(t_\ell)$ that have disappeared in $\beta(t'_{\ell+1})$, that is, $B(e) = \{|N| + 1\} \cup \{ v \in \mathbb{N} \mid v \text{ occurs in } \beta(t_\ell) \text{ but not in } \beta(t'_{\ell+1}) \}$.

Differently from the good events for DACs, which require to visit an accepting transition, we need all runs branched from a run to visit an accepting transition, which is indicated by the fact that there are no states labelled by $t'_{\ell+1}$ with some list $l \in \beta(t_\ell)$ but there are extensions of l associated with some state. To recognize good events, let $G(e) = \{|N| + 1\}$ and $t''_{\ell+1}$ be another intermediate labelling function. For each $q' \in S_{\ell+1} \cap N$, consider the list $t'_{\ell+1}(q')$: if for each prefix $[v_1, \cdots v_k]$ of $t'_{\ell+1}(q')$ we have $[v_1, \cdots v_k] \in \beta(t'_{\ell+1})$, then we set $t''_{\ell+1}(q') = t'_{\ell+1}(q')$. Otherwise, let $[v_1, \cdots v_{\bar{k}}] \notin \beta(t'_{\ell+1})$ be the shortest prefix of $t'_{\ell+1}(q')$ not in $\beta(t'_{\ell+1})$; we set $t''_{\ell+1}(q') = [v_1, \cdots v_{\bar{k}}]$ and add $v_{\bar{k}}$ to $G(e)$. Setting $t''_{\ell+1}(q') = [v_1, \cdots v_{\bar{k}}]$ in fact corresponds, in the Safra's construction [36], to the removal of all children of a node $\mathfrak{N}$ for which the union of the states in the children is equal to the states in $\mathfrak{N}$. Lastly, similarly to the DAC case, we set $t_{\ell+1}(q) = \mathrm{ord}(t''_{\ell+1}(q))$ for each $q \in S_{\ell+1} \cap N$ and $t_{\ell+1}(q') = []$ for each $q' \in N \setminus S_{\ell+1}$, where $\mathrm{ord}([v_1, \cdots, v_k]) = [\mathrm{ord}(v_1), \cdots, \mathrm{ord}(v_k)]$. Regarding the color to assign to the transition e, we just assign the color $c = \min\{2 \cdot \min G(e), 2 \cdot \min B(e) - 1\}$.

Lemma 3. *(1) An accepting run of $\mathcal{A}$ over w eventually stays in the NAC N if and only if the minimal color c we receive infinitely often is even. (2) The number of possible labelling functions t is at most $2 \cdot (|N|!)^2$.*

Similarly to DACs, also for NACs we have handled each NAC independently. The reason for this is that this potentially reduces the complexity of the single cases: assume that we have two NACs N_1 and N_2. If we apply the Safra-Piterman's construction directly to $N_1 \cup N_2$, we might incur in the worst-case complexity $2 \cdot ((|N_1| + |N_2|)!)^2$, as mentioned in the introduction. However, if we determinize them separately, then the worst complexity for each NAC N_i is $2 \cdot (N_i!)^2$, for an overall $4 \cdot (|N_1|! \cdot |N_2|!)^2$, much smaller than $2 \cdot ((|N_1| + |N_2|)!)^2$.

As usual, we make the above construction available as a function nondetSucc, which takes as input the NAC N, a labelling t and a letter a, and returns the successor labelling t' and the corresponding color $c \in \{1, \cdots, 2 \cdot |N| + 1\}$.

Similarly to the constructions for other SCCs, we show on the right the fragment of run DAG $\mathcal{G}_{\mathcal{A},a^\omega}$ for the NAC $N = \{q_0, q_1\}$, with $q_0 \preccurlyeq q_1$. The construction of t_1 is easy, so consider its a-successor t_2: we start with $U = \{3, 4, \cdots\}$; for q_0, we have $P_{q_0} = \{q_0, q_1\}$ and $C_{q_0} = \{[1, 2, 3], [1]\}$, hence $t'_2(q_0) = [1, 2, 3]$. For q_1, we get $P_{q_1} = \{q_0\}$ and $C_{q_1} = \{[1, 2]\}$, so $t'_2(q_1) = [1, 2]$. Thus, for $e = (t_1, w[1], t_2)$, we have $B(e) = \{3\}$ while $G(e) = \{1, 3\}$, since both lists in $\beta(t'_2) = \{[1, 2], [1, 2, 3]\}$ are missing the prefix $[1]$, so we get $t_2(q_0) = t_2(q_1) = [1]$ and color $c = 2$.

$$
\begin{array}{cc}
\ell & \downarrow \\
0 & q_0, [1] \\
& \downarrow \searrow \\
1 & q_0, [1, 2] \quad q_1, [1] \\
& \downarrow \times \\
2 & q_0, [1] \quad q_1, [1] \\
\end{array}
$$

4 Determinization of NBAs to DELAs

In this section, we fix an NBA $\mathcal{A} = (Q, \iota, \delta, F)$ with $n = |Q|$ states and we show how to construct an equivalent DELA $\mathcal{A}^E = (Q^E, \iota^E, \delta^E, \Gamma^E, p^E, \mathrm{Acc}^E)$, by using the algorithms developed in the previous section. We assume that $\mathcal{A}$ has $\{D^1, \cdots, D^d\}$ as set of DACs and $\{N^1, \cdots, N^k\}$ as set of NACs.

When computing the successor for each type of SCCs while reading a word w, we just need to know the set S_ℓ of states reached at the current level ℓ and the letter $a \in \Sigma$ to read. We can ignore the actual level ℓ, since if $S_\ell = S_{\ell'}$, then their successors under the same letter will be the same. As mentioned before, every state of $\mathcal{A}^E$ corresponds to a level of $\mathcal{G}_{\mathcal{A},w}$. We call a state of $\mathcal{A}^E$ a *macrostate* and a run of $\mathcal{A}^E$ a *macrorun*, to distinguish them from those of $\mathcal{A}$.

Macrostates Q^E. Each macrostate consists of the pair (P, O) for encoding the states in IWCs, a labelling function $\mathfrak{g}^i \colon D^i \to \{1, \cdots, |D^i|\} \cup \{\infty\}$ for the states of each DAC D^i and a labelling function $\mathfrak{t}^j \colon N^j \to \mathcal{L}_{N^j}$ for each NAC N^j, without the explicit level number. The initial macrostate ι^E of $\mathcal{A}^E$ is the encoding of level 0, defined as the set $\{(P_0, O_0)\} \cup \{\mathfrak{g}_0^i \mid D^i \text{is a DAC}\} \cup \{\mathfrak{t}_0^j \mid N^j \text{is a NAC}\}$, where each encoding for the different types of SCCs is the one for level 0.

We note that ι must be present in one type of SCCs. In particular, if ι is a transient state, then $\{\iota\}$ is classified as an IWC.

Transition Function δ^E. Let m be the current macrostate in Q^E and $a \in \Sigma$ be the letter to read. Then we define $m' = \delta^E(m, a)$ as follows.

(i) For $(P_m, O_m) \in m$, we set $(P_{m'}, O_{m'}) = \mathsf{weakSucc}((P_m, O_m), a)$ in m'.
(ii) For $\mathfrak{g}_m^i \in m$ relative to the DAC D^i, we set $\mathfrak{g}_{m'}^i = \mathsf{detSucc}(D^i, \mathfrak{g}_m^i, a)$ in m'.
(iii) For $\mathfrak{t}_m^j \in m$ from the NAC N^j, we set $\mathfrak{t}_{m'}^j = \mathsf{nondetSucc}(N^j, \mathfrak{t}_m^j, a)$ in m'.

Note that the set S of the current states of $\mathcal{A}$ used by the different successor functions is implicitly given by the sets P, $\{q \in D^i \mid \mathfrak{g}^i(q) \neq \infty\}$ for each DAC D^i and $\{q \in N^j \mid \mathfrak{t}^j(q) \neq []\}$ for each NAC N^j in the current macrostate m.

Color Set Γ^E and Coloring Function p^E. From the constructions given in Sect. 3, we have two colors from the IWCs, $2 \cdot |D^i| + 1$ colors for each DAC D^i, and $2 \cdot |N^j| + 1$ colors for each NAC N^j, yielding a total of at most $3 \cdot |Q|$ colors. Thus we set $\Gamma^E = \{0, 1, \cdots, 3 \cdot |Q|\}$ with color 0 not being actually used.

Regarding the color to assign to each transition, we need to ensure that the colors returned by the single SCCs are treated separately, so we transpose them. For a transition $e = (m, a, m') \in \delta^E$, we define the coloring function p^E as follows.

- If we receive color 1 for the transition $((P_m, O_m), a, (P_{m'}, O_{m'}))$, then we put $1 \in \mathsf{p}^E(e)$. Intuitively, every time we see an empty O-set along reading an ω-word w in the IWCs, we put the color 1 on the transition (m, a, m').
- For each DAC D^i, we transpose its colors after the colors for the IWCs and the other DACs with smaller index. So we set the base number for the colors of the DAC D^i to be $b_i = 2 + \sum_{1 \leq h < i}(2 \cdot |D^h| + 1)$, i.e., the number of colors already being used. Then, if we receive the color c for the transition $(\mathfrak{g}_m^i, a, \mathfrak{g}_{m'}^i)$ from $\mathsf{detSucc}$, we put $c + b_i \in \mathsf{p}^E(e)$.
- We follow the same approach for the NAC N^j: we set its base number to be $b_j = 2 + \sum_{1 \leq h \leq d}(2 \cdot |D^h| + 1) + \sum_{1 \leq h < j}(2 \cdot |N^h| + 1)$. Then, if we receive the color c for the transition $(\mathfrak{t}_m^j, a, \mathfrak{t}_{m'}^j)$ from $\mathsf{nondetSucc}$, we put $c + b_j \in \mathsf{p}^E(e)$.

Intuitively, we make the colors returned for each SCC not overlap with those of other SCCs without changing their relative order. In this way, we can still independently check whether there exists an accepting run staying in an SCC.

Acceptance Formula Acc^E. We now define the acceptance Acc^E, which is basically the *disjunction* of the acceptance formula for each different types of SCCs, after transposing them. Regarding the IWCs, we trivially define $\mathsf{Acc}^E_W = \mathsf{Fin}(1)$, since this is the acceptance formula for IWCs; as said before, color 0 is not used.

For DACs and NACs, the definition is more involved. For instance, regarding the DAC D^i, we know that all returned colors are inside $\{1, \cdots, 2 \cdot |D^i| + 1\}$. According to Lemma 2, an accepting run eventually stays in D^i if and only if the minimum color that we receive infinitely often is even. Thus, the acceptance formula for the above lemma is $\mathsf{parity}(|D^i|) = \bigvee_{c=1}^{|D^i|}(\bigwedge_{j=1}^{c} \mathsf{Fin}(2j-1) \wedge \mathsf{Inf}(2c))$. Let $b_i = 2 + \sum_{h<i}(2 \cdot |D_h| + 1)$ be the base number for the colors of D^i, which is also the number of colors already used by IWCs and the DACs D^h with $h < i$. Since we have added the base number b^i to every color of D^i, we then have the acceptance formula $\mathsf{Acc}^E_{D^i} = \bigvee_{c=1}^{|D^i|}(\bigwedge_{j=1}^{c} \mathsf{Fin}(2j-1+b_i) \wedge \mathsf{Inf}(2c+b_i))$.

For each NAC N^j, the colors we receive are in $\{1, \cdots, 2 \cdot |N^j| + 1\}$. Let $b_j = 2 + \sum_{1 \leq h \leq d}(2 \cdot |D^h| + 1) + \sum_{h<j}(2 \cdot |N^j| + 1)$ be the base number for N^j. Similarly to the DAC case, for each NAC N^j, we let $\mathsf{Acc}^E_{N^j} = \bigvee_{c=1}^{|N^j|}(\bigwedge_{i=1}^{c} \mathsf{Fin}(2i-1+b_j) \wedge \mathsf{Inf}(2c+b_j))$.

The acceptance formula for $\mathcal{A}^E$ is $\mathsf{Acc}^E = \mathsf{Acc}^E_W \vee \bigvee_{i=1}^{d} \mathsf{Acc}^E_{D^i} \vee \bigvee_{j=1}^{k} \mathsf{Acc}^E_{N^j}$.

Consider again the NBA $\mathcal{A}$ given in Fig. 1 and its various SCCs. As acceptance formula for the constructed DELA, it is the disjunction of the formulas $\mathsf{Acc}^E_W = \mathsf{Fin}(1)$; $\mathsf{Acc}^E_D = \bigvee_{c=1}^{2}(\bigwedge_{j=1}^{c} \mathsf{Fin}(2j-1+2) \wedge \mathsf{Inf}(2c+2))$, since the base number for D is 2; and $\mathsf{Acc}^E_N = \bigvee_{c=1}^{2}(\bigwedge_{i=1}^{c} \mathsf{Fin}(2i-1+7) \wedge \mathsf{Inf}(2c+7))$, since 7 is the base number for N.

The construction given in this section is correct, as stated by Theorem 1.

Theorem 1. *Given an NBA $\mathcal{A}$ with $n = |Q|$ states, let $\mathcal{A}^E$ be the DELA constructed by our method. Then (1) $\mathsf{L}(\mathcal{A}^E) = \mathsf{L}(\mathcal{A})$ and (2) $\mathcal{A}^E$ has at most $3^{|W|} \cdot \left(\prod_{i=1}^{d} 3 \cdot |D^i|!\right) \cdot \left(\prod_{j=1}^{k} 2 \cdot (|N^i|!)^2\right)$ macrostates and $3n+1$ colors.*

Obviously, if $d = k = 0$, $\mathcal{A}$ is a weak BA [32]. If $k = 0$, $\mathcal{A}$ is an elevator BA, a new class of BAs recently introduced in [19] which have only IWCs and DACs, a strict superset of semi-deterministic BAs (SDBAs) [10]. SDBAs will behave *deterministically* after seeing acceptance transitions. An elevator BA that is not an SDBA can be obtained from the NBA $\mathcal{A}$ shown in Fig. 1 by setting q_2 as initial state and by removing all states and transitions relative to the NAC.

It is known that the lower bound for determinizing SDBAs is $n!$ [14,27]. Then the determinization complexity of weak BAs and elevator BAs can be easily improved exponentially as follows.

Corollary 1. *(1) Given a weak Büchi automaton $\mathcal{A}$ with $n = |Q|$ states, the DELA constructed by our algorithm has at most 3^n macrostates. (2) Given an* *elevator Büchi automaton $\mathcal{A}$ with $n = |Q|$ states, our algorithm constructs a DELA with $\Theta(n!)$ macrostates; it is asymptotically optimal.*

The upper bound for determinizing weak BAs is already known [5]. Elevator BAs are, to the best of our knowledge, the *largest* subclass of NBAs known so far to have determinization complexity $\Theta(n!)$.

The acceptance formula for an SCC can be seen as a parity acceptance formula with colors being shifted to different ranges. A parity automaton can be converted into a Rabin one without blow-up of states and transitions [16]. Since Acc^E is a disjunction of parity acceptance formulas, Theorem 2 then follows.

Theorem 2. *Let $\mathcal{A}^\mathsf{E}$ be the constructed DELA for the given NBA $\mathcal{A}$. Then $\mathcal{A}^\mathsf{E}$ can be converted into a DRA $\mathcal{A}^\mathsf{R}$ without blow-up of states and transitions.*

Translation to Deterministic Parity Automata (DPAs). We note that there is an *optimal* translation from a DRA to a DPA described in [7], implemented in Spot via the function acd_transform [8].

5   Empirical Evaluation

To analyze the effectiveness of our Divide-and-Conquer determinization construction proposed in Sect. 3, we implemented it in our tool COLA, which is built on top of Spot [12]. The source code of COLA is publicly available from https://github.com/liyong31/COLA. We compared COLA with the official versions of Spot [12] (2.10.2) and Owl [23] (21.0). Spot implements the algorithm described in [35], a variant of [33] for transition-based NBAs, while Owl implements the algorithms described in [28,29], both constructing DPAs as result. To make the comparison fair, we let all tools generate DPAs, so we used the command autfilt --deterministic --parity=min\ even -F file.hoa to call Spot and owl nbadet -i file.hoa to call Owl. Recall that we use the function acd_transform [8] from Spot for obtaining DPAs from our DRAs. The tools above also implement optimizations for reducing the size of the output DPA, like simulation and state merging [29], or stutter invariance [22] (except for Owl); we use the default settings for all tools. We performed our experiments on a desktop machine equipped with 16GB of RAM and a 3.6 GHz Intel Core i7-4790 CPU. We used BenchExec[1] [3] to trace and constrain the tools' executions: we allowed each execution to use a single core and 12 GB of memory, and imposed a timeout of 10 min. We used Spot to verify the results generated by three tools and found only outputs equivalent to the inputs.

As benchmarks, we considered all NBAs in the HOA format [1] available in the AUTOMATA-BENCHMARKS repository.[2] We have pre-filtered them with autfilt to exclude all deterministic cases and to have nondeterministic BAs, obtaining in total 15,913 automata coming from different sources in literature.

The artifact with tools, benchmarks, and scripts to run the experiments and generate the plots is available at [25].

---

[1] https://github.com/sosy-lab/benchexec/.
[2] https://github.com/ondrik/automata-benchmarks/.

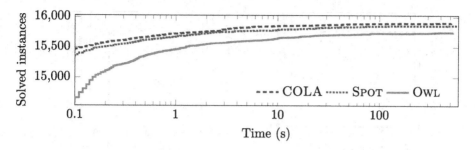

Fig. 2. The cactus plot for the determinization of NBAs from AUTOMATA-BENCHMARKS.

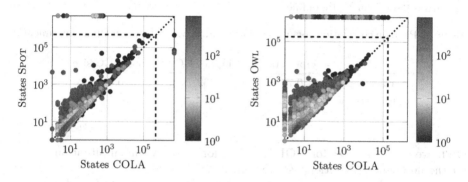

Fig. 3. States comparison for the determinization of NBAs from AUTOMATA-BENCHMARKS. (Color figure online)

In Fig. 2 we show a cactus plot reporting how many input automata have been determinized by each tool, over time. As we can see, COLA works better than SPOT, with COLA solving in total 15,903 cases and SPOT 15,862 cases, with OWL solving in total 15,749 cases and taking more time to solve as many instances as COLA and SPOT. From the plot given in Fig. 2 we see that COLA is already very competitive with respect to its performance.

In Fig. 3 we show the number of states of the generated DPAs. In the plot we indicate with the bold dashed line the maximum number of states of the automata produced by either of the two tools, and we place a mark on the upper or right border of the plot to indicate that one tool has generated an automaton with that size while the other tool just failed. The color of each mark represents how many instances have been mapped to the corresponding point. As the plots show, SPOT and COLA generate automata with similar size, with COLA being more likely to generate smaller automata, in particular for larger outputs. OWL, instead, very frequently generates automata larger than COLA. In fact, on the 15,710 cases solved by all tools, on average COLA generated 44 states, SPOT 65, and OWL 87. If we compare COLA with just one tool at a time, on the 15,854 cases solved by both COLA and SPOT, we have 125 states for COLA and 246 for SPOT; on the 15,749 cases solved by both COLA and

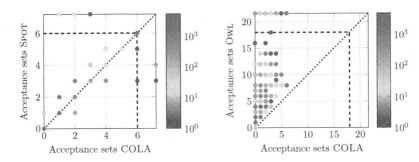

Fig. 4. Acceptance sets comparison for the determinization of NBAs from AUTOMATA-BENCHMARKS. (Color figure online)

Table 1. Pearson correlation coefficients for the AUTOMATA-BENCHMARKS experiments.

	# input states	# input SCCs	average SCC size
runtime	0.77	0.62	−0.01
output states	0.41	0.17	0.05

OWL, we have 45 states for COLA and 88 for OWL. A similar situation occurs for the number of transitions, so we omit it.

Lastly, in Fig. 4 we compare the number of acceptance sets (i.e., the colors in Definition 1) of the generated DPAs; more precisely, we consider the integer value occurring in the mandatory `Acceptance: INT acceptance-cond` header item of the HOA format [1], which can be 0 for the automata with all or none accepting transitions. From the plots we can see that COLA generates more frequently DPAs with a number of colors that is no more than the number used by SPOT, as indicated by the yellow/red marks on (10,394 cases) or above (5,495 cases) the diagonal. Only in very few cases COLA generates DPAs with more colors than SPOT (22 cases), as indicated by the few blue/greenish marks below the diagonal. Regarding OWL, however, from the plot we can clearly see that COLA uses almost always (15,840 cases) fewer colors than OWL; the only exception is for the mark at $(0, 0)$ representing 63 cases.

The number and sizes of SCCs influence the performance of COLA, so we provide some statistics about the correlation between these and the runtime and size of the generated DPA. By combining the execution statistics with the input SCCs and states, we get the Pearson correlation coefficients shown in Table 1. Here the larger the number in a cell is, the stronger the positive correlation between the element that the row and the column represent. From these coefficients we can say that there is a quite strong positive correlation between the number of states and of SCCs and the running time, but not for the average SCC size; regarding the output states, the situation is similar but much weaker.

We also considered a second set of benchmarks – 644 NBAs generated by SPOT's `ltl2tgba` on the LTL formulas considered in [23], as available in the

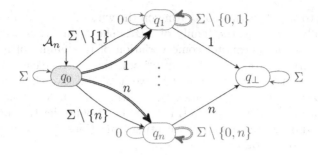

Fig. 5. The family of NBAs $\mathcal{A}_n$ with $\Sigma = \{0, 1, \cdots, n\}$.

OWL's repository at https://gitlab.lrz.de/i7/owl. The outcomes for these benchmarks are similar, but a bit better for COLA, to the ones for AUTOMATA-BENCHMARKS, so we do not present them in detail.

6   Related Work

To the best of our knowledge, our determinization construction is the *first* algorithm that determinizes SCCs *independently* while taking advantage of different structures of SCCs, which is the main difference between our algorithm and existing works. We illustrate other minor differences below.

Different types of SCCs, like DACs and IWCs, are also taken with special care in [29] as in our work, modulo the handling details. However, the work [29] does not treat them independently as the labelling numbers in those SCCs still have relative order with those in other SCCs. Thus their algorithm can be exponentially worse than ours (cf. Theorem 3) and performs not as well as ours in practice; see the comparison with OWL in Sect. 5. The determinization algorithm given in [14] for SDBAs is a special case of the one presented in [35] for NBAs, which gives precedence to the deterministic runs seeing accepting transitions earlier, while we give precedence to runs that enter DACs earlier. More importantly, the algorithm from [14] does not work when there is nondeterminism between DACs, while our algorithm overcomes this by considering DACs separately and by ignoring runs going to other SCCs.

Current works for determinization of general NBAs, such as [18, 21, 28, 35, 36, 38] can all be interpreted as different flavours of the Safra-Piterman based algorithm. Our determinization of NACs is also based on Safra-trees and inspired by SPOT, except that we may have newly arriving states from other SCCs while other works only need to consider the successors from the current states in the Safra-tree. The modular approach for determinizing Büchi automata given in [17] builds on reduced split trees [21] and can construct the deterministic automaton with a given tree-width. The algorithm constructs the final deterministic automaton by running in parallel the NBA for all possible tree-widths, rather than working on SCCs independently as we do in this work.

Compared to the algorithms operating on the whole NBA, our algorithm can be exponentially better on the family of NBAs shown in Fig. 5, as formalized in Theorem 3; we can encounter some variation of this family of NBAs when working with fairness properties. The intuition is that we take care of the DACs $\{q_i\}_{i=1}^n$ independently, so for each of them we have only two choices: either the run is in the DAC, or it is not in the DAC; resulting in a single exponential number of combinations. Existing works [14,21,28,33,35,36] order the runs entering the DACs based on when they visit accepting transitions, in which every order corresponds to a permutation of $\{q_1, \cdots, q_n\}$.

Theorem 3. *There exists a family of NBAs $\mathcal{A}_n$ with $n + 2$ states for which the algorithms in [14, 21, 28, 33, 35, 36] give a DPA with at least $n!$ macrostates while ours gives a DELA with at most 2^{n+2} macrostates.*

In practice, for each NBA $\mathcal{A}_n$, $n \geq 3$, COLA produces a DELA/DPA with n macrostates, while both SPOT and OWL give a DPA with $n! + 1$ macrostates.

7   Conclusion and Future Work

We proposed a divide-and-conquer determinization construction for NBAs that takes advantage of the structure of different types of SCCs and determinizes them independently. In particular, our construction can be exponentially better than classical works on a family of NBAs. Experiments showed that our algorithm outperforms the state-of-the-art implementations regarding the number of states and transitions on a large set of benchmarks. To summarize, our divide-and-conquer determinization construction is very *practical*, being a good complement to existing theoretical approaches.

Our divide-and-conquer approach for NBAs can also be applied to the complementation problems of NBAs. By Proposition 1, w is not accepted by $\mathcal{A}$ if and only if there are no accepting runs staying in an SCC. Thus we can construct a *generalized* Büchi automaton with a conjunction of $\mathsf{Inf}(i)$ as the acceptance formula to accept the complement language $\Sigma^\omega \setminus \mathsf{L}(\mathcal{A})$ of $\mathcal{A}$; the generalized Büchi automaton in fact takes the *intersection* of the complement language of each type of SCCs. For complementing IWCs, we use the same construction as determinization except that the acceptance formula will be $\mathsf{Inf}(1)$. For complementing DACs, we can borrow the idea of NCSB complementation construction [4] which complements SDBAs in time 4^n. For complementing NACs, we just adapt the *slice-based* complementation [21] of general NBAs. We leave the details of this divide-and-conquer complementation construction for NBAs as future work.

Acknowledgement. We thank the anonymous reviewers for their valuable suggestions to this paper. This work is supported in part by the National Natural Science Foundation of China (Grant Nos. 62102407 and 61836005), NSF grants IIS-1527668, CCF-1704883, IIS-1830549, CNS-2016656, DoD MURI grant N00014-20-1-2787, and an award from the Maryland Procurement Office.
■ This project has received funding from the European Union's Horizon 2020 research and innovation programme under the Marie Skłodowska-Curie grant agreement No 101008233.

References

1. Babiak, T., et al.: The Hanoi omega-automata format. In: Kroening, D., Păsăreanu, C.S. (eds.) CAV 2015. LNCS, vol. 9206, pp. 479–486. Springer, Cham (2015). https://doi.org/10.1007/978-3-319-21690-4_31
2. Baier, C., Katoen, J.P.: Principles of Model Checking. MIT Press, Cambridge (2008)
3. Beyer, D., Löwe, S., Wendler, P.: Reliable benchmarking: requirements and solutions. Int. J. Softw. Tools Technol. Transfer 21(1), 1–29 (2017). https://doi.org/10.1007/s10009-017-0469-y
4. Blahoudek, F., Heizmann, M., Schewe, S., Strejček, J., Tsai, M.-H.: Complementing semi-deterministic Büchi automata. In: Chechik, M., Raskin, J.-F. (eds.) TACAS 2016. LNCS, vol. 9636, pp. 770–787. Springer, Heidelberg (2016). https://doi.org/10.1007/978-3-662-49674-9_49
5. Boigelot, B., Jodogne, S., Wolper, P.: On the use of weak automata for deciding linear arithmetic with integer and real variables. In: Goré, R., Leitsch, A., Nipkow, T. (eds.) IJCAR 2001. LNCS, vol. 2083, pp. 611–625. Springer, Heidelberg (2001). https://doi.org/10.1007/3-540-45744-5_50
6. Büchi, J.R.: On a decision method in restricted second order arithmetic. In: The Collected Works of J. Richard Büchi, pp. 425–435. Springer, Cham (1990). https://doi.org/10.1007/978-1-4613-8928-6_23
7. Casares, A., Colcombet, T., Fijalkow, N.: Optimal transformations of games and automata using Muller conditions. In: ICALP. LIPIcs, vol. 198, pp. 123:1–123:14 (2021)
8. Casares, A., Duret-Lutz, A., Meyer, K.J., Renkin, F., Sickert, S.: Practical applications of the alternating cycle decomposition. In: TACAS. LNCS, vol. 13244, pp. 99–117. Springer, Cham (2022). https://doi.org/10.1007/978-3-030-99527-0_6
9. Colcombet, T., Zdanowski, K.: A tight lower bound for determinization of transition labeled Büchi automata. In: Albers, S., Marchetti-Spaccamela, A., Matias, Y., Nikoletseas, S., Thomas, W. (eds.) ICALP 2009. LNCS, vol. 5556, pp. 151–162. Springer, Heidelberg (2009). https://doi.org/10.1007/978-3-642-02930-1_13
10. Courcoubetis, C., Yannakakis, M.: The complexity of probabilistic verification. J. ACM 42(4), 857–907 (1995)
11. De Giacomo, G., Vardi, M.Y.: Linear temporal logic and linear dynamic logic on finite traces. In: IJCAI, pp. 854–860 (2013)
12. Duret-Lutz, A., Lewkowicz, A., Fauchille, A., Michaud, T., Renault, É., Xu, L.: Spot 2.0 — a framework for LTL and ω-automata manipulation. In: Artho, C., Legay, A., Peled, D. (eds.) ATVA 2016. LNCS, vol. 9938, pp. 122–129. Springer, Cham (2016). https://doi.org/10.1007/978-3-319-46520-3_8
13. Emerson, E.A., Lei, C.: Modalities for model checking: branching time logic strikes back. Sci. Comput. Program. 8(3), 275–306 (1987)
14. Esparza, J., Křetínský, J., Raskin, J.-F., Sickert, S.: From LTL and limit-deterministic Büchi automata to deterministic parity automata. In: Legay, A., Margaria, T. (eds.) TACAS 2017. LNCS, vol. 10205, pp. 426–442. Springer, Heidelberg (2017). https://doi.org/10.1007/978-3-662-54577-5_25
15. Esparza, J., Křetínský, J., Sickert, S.: A unified translation of linear temporal logic to ω-automata. J. ACM 67(6), 1–61 (2020)
16. Farwer, B.: Omega-automata. In: Automata, Logics, and Infinite Games: A Guide to Current Research. LNCS, vol. 2500, pp. 3–20 (2001)

17. Fisman, D., Lustig, Y.: A modular approach for Büchi determinization. In: CONCUR. LIPIcs, vol. 42, pp. 368–382 (2015)
18. Fogarty, S., Kupferman, O., Vardi, M.Y., Wilke, T.: Profile trees for Büchi word automata, with application to determinization. Inf. Comput. **245**, 136–151 (2015)
19. Havlena, V., Lengál, O., Smahlíková, B.: Sky is not the limit. In: Fisman, D., Rosu, G. (eds.) TACAS 2022. LNCS, vol. 13244, pp. 118–136. Springer, Cham (2022). https://doi.org/10.1007/978-3-030-99527-0_7
20. Hopcroft, J.E., Motwani, R., Ullman, J.D.: Introduction to Automata Theory, Languages, and Computation. Addison-Wesley Longman Publishing Co., Inc., Boston (2006)
21. Kähler, D., Wilke, T.: Complementation, disambiguation, and determinization of Büchi automata unified. In: Aceto, L., Damgård, I., Goldberg, L.A., Halldórsson, M.M., Ingólfsdóttir, A., Walukiewicz, I. (eds.) ICALP 2008. LNCS, vol. 5125, pp. 724–735. Springer, Heidelberg (2008). https://doi.org/10.1007/978-3-540-70575-8_59
22. Klein, J., Baier, C.: On-the-fly stuttering in the construction of deterministic ω-automata. In: Holub, J., Žďárek, J. (eds.) CIAA 2007. LNCS, vol. 4783, pp. 51–61. Springer, Heidelberg (2007). https://doi.org/10.1007/978-3-540-76336-9_7
23. Křetínský, J., Meggendorfer, T., Sickert, S.: Owl: a library for ω-words, automata, and LTL. In: Lahiri, S.K., Wang, C. (eds.) ATVA 2018. LNCS, vol. 11138, pp. 543–550. Springer, Cham (2018). https://doi.org/10.1007/978-3-030-01090-4_34
24. Kupferman, O., Vardi, M.Y.: Weak alternating automata are not that weak. ACM Trans. Comput. Log. **2**(3), 408–429 (2001)
25. Li, Y., Turrini, A., Feng, W., Vardi, M.V., Zhang, L.: Artifact for "Divide-and-conquer determinization of Büchi automata based on SCC decomposition" (2022). https://doi.org/10.5281/zenodo.6558928
26. Liu, W., Wang, J.: A tighter analysis of Piterman's Büchi determinization. Inf. Process. Lett. **109**(16), 941–945 (2009)
27. Löding, C.: Optimal bounds for transformations of ω-automata. In: Rangan, C.P., Raman, V., Ramanujam, R. (eds.) FSTTCS 1999. LNCS, vol. 1738, pp. 97–109. Springer, Heidelberg (1999). https://doi.org/10.1007/3-540-46691-6_8
28. Löding, C., Pirogov, A.: Determinization of Büchi automata: unifying the approaches of Safra and Muller-Schupp. In: ICALP. LIPIcs, vol. 132, pp. 120:1–120:13 (2019)
29. Löding, C., Pirogov, A.: New optimizations and heuristics for determinization of Büchi automata. In: Chen, Y.-F., Cheng, C.-H., Esparza, J. (eds.) ATVA 2019. LNCS, vol. 11781, pp. 317–333. Springer, Cham (2019). https://doi.org/10.1007/978-3-030-31784-3_18
30. Michel, M.: Complementation is more difficult with automata on infinite words. Technical report, CNET, Paris (Manuscript) (1988)
31. Miyano, S., Hayashi, T.: Alternating finite automata on ω-words. Theor. Comput. Sci. **32**(3), 321–330 (1984)
32. Muller, D.E., Saoudi, A., Schupp, P.E.: Alternating automata, the weak monadic theory of trees and its complexity. Theor. Comput. Sci. **97**(2), 233–244 (1992)
33. Piterman, N.: From nondeterministic Büchi and Streett automata to deterministic parity automata. Log. Methods Comput. Sci. **3**(3), 1–21 (2007)
34. Pnueli, A., Rosner, R.: On the synthesis of a reactive module. In: POPL, pp. 179–190 (1989)
35. Redziejowski, R.R.: An improved construction of deterministic omega-automaton using derivatives. Fundam. Informaticae **119**(3–4), 393–406 (2012)

36. Safra, S.: On the complexity of ω-automata. In: FOCS, pp. 319–327 (1988)
37. Safra, S., Vardi, M.Y.: On omega-automata and temporal logic (preliminary report). In: STOC, pp. 127–137 (1989)
38. Schewe, S.: Büchi complementation made tight. In: STACS. LIPIcs, vol. 3, pp. 661–672 (2009)
39. Schewe, S.: Tighter bounds for the determinisation of Büchi automata. In: de Alfaro, L. (ed.) FoSSaCS 2009. LNCS, vol. 5504, pp. 167–181. Springer, Heidelberg (2009). https://doi.org/10.1007/978-3-642-00596-1_13
40. Tsai, M., Fogarty, S., Vardi, M., Tsay, Y.: State of Büchi complementation. Log. Methods Comput. Sci. **10**(4), 1–27 (2014)
41. Vardi, M.Y.: The rise and fall of linear temporal logic. In: GandALF (2011). Invited talk
42. Vardi, M.Y., Wolper, P.: Reasoning about infinite computations. Inf. Comput. **115**(1), 1–37 (1994)
43. Yan, Q.: Lower bounds for complementation of ω-automata via the full automata technique. Log. Methods Comput. Sci. **4**(1:5), 1–20 (2008)

From Spot 2.0 to Spot 2.10: What's New?

Alexandre Duret-Lutz[1]([✉]), Etienne Renault[1], Maximilien Colange[2],
Florian Renkin[1], Alexandre Gbaguidi Aisse[2], Philipp Schlehuber-Caissier[1],
Thomas Medioni[2], Antoine Martin[1], Jérôme Dubois[1], Clément Gillard[2],
and Henrich Lauko[2]

LRDE, EPITA, Le Kremlin-Bicêtre, France
{adl,renault,frenkin,philipp,
amartin,jdubois}@lrde.epita.fr
[2] Bicêtre, France

Abstract. Spot is a C++17 library for LTL and ω-automata manipulation, with command-line utilities, and Python bindings. This paper summarizes its evolution over the past six years, since the release of Spot 2.0, which was the first version to support ω-automata with arbitrary acceptance conditions, and the last version presented at a conference. Since then, Spot has been extended with several features such as acceptance transformations, alternating automata, games, LTL synthesis, and more. We also shed some lights on the data-structure used to store automata. **Artifact:** https://zenodo.org/record/6521395.

1 Availability, Purpose, and Evolution

Spot is a library for LTL and ω-automata manipulation, distributed under a GPLv3 license. Its source code is available from https://spot.lrde.epita.fr/. We provide packages for some Linux distributions like Debian and Fedora, but other packages can also be found for Conda-Forge [17] (for Linux & Darwin), Arch Linux, FreeBSD...

Spot can be used via three interfaces: a C++17 library, a set of command-line tools that give easy access to many features of the library, and Python bindings, that makes prototyping and interactive work very attractive. Our web site now contains many examples of how to perform some tasks using these three interfaces, and we have a public mailing list for questions.

In our last tool paper [21], Spot 2.0 had just converted from being a library for working on Transition-based Generalized Büchi Automata and had become a library supporting ω-automata with arbitrary Emerson-Lei [22,41] acceptance conditions, as enabled by the development of the HOA format [5].

In the HOA format, transitions can carry multiple colors, and acceptance conditions are expressed as a positive Boolean formulas over atoms like $\mathsf{Fin}(i)$ or $\mathsf{Inf}(i)$ that tell if a color should be seen finitely or infinitely often for a run to be accepting. Table 1 gives some examples.

M. Colange, A. Gbaguidi Aisse, T. Medioni, C. Gillard and H. Lauko—Previously at LRDE.

© The Author(s) 2022
S. Shoham and Y. Vizel (Eds.): CAV 2022, LNCS 13372, pp. 174–187, 2022.
https://doi.org/10.1007/978-3-031-13188-2_9

Table 1. Acceptance formulas corresponding to classical names.

Büchi	$\mathsf{Inf}(0)$
generalized Büchi	$\bigwedge_i \mathsf{Inf}(i)$
Fin-less [9]	any positive formula of $\mathsf{Inf}(...)$
co-Büchi	$\mathsf{Fin}(0)$
generalized co-Büchi	$\bigvee_i \mathsf{Fin}(i)$
Rabin	$\bigvee_i (\mathsf{Fin}(2i) \wedge \mathsf{Inf}(2i+1))$
generalized Rabin [29]	$\bigvee_i (\mathsf{Fin}(i) \wedge \bigwedge_{j \in J_i} \mathsf{Inf}(j))$
Streett	$\bigwedge_i (\mathsf{Inf}(2i) \vee \mathsf{Fin}(2i+1))$
parity min even	$\mathsf{Inf}(0) \vee (\mathsf{Fin}(1) \wedge (\mathsf{Inf}(2) \vee (\mathsf{Fin}(3) \wedge \ldots)))$
parity min odd	$\mathsf{Fin}(0) \wedge (\mathsf{Inf}(1) \vee (\mathsf{Fin}(2) \wedge (\mathsf{Inf}(3) \vee \ldots)))$
parity max even	$(((\mathsf{Inf}(0) \wedge \mathsf{Fin}(1)) \vee \mathsf{Inf}(2)) \wedge \mathsf{Fin}(3)) \vee \ldots$
parity max odd	$(((\mathsf{Fin}(0) \vee \mathsf{Inf}(1)) \wedge \mathsf{Fin}(2)) \vee \mathsf{Inf}(3)) \wedge \ldots$

While Spot 2.0 was able to read automata with arbitrary acceptance conditions, not all of its algorithms were able to support such a generality. For instance testing an automaton for emptiness or finding an accepting word, would only work on automata with "Fin-less" acceptance conditions. For other conditions, Spot 2.0 would rely on a procedure called `remove_fin()` to convert automata with arbitrary acceptance conditions into "Fin-less" acceptance conditions [9]. This was ultimately fixed by developing a generic emptiness check [6]. Additionally the support for arbitrary acceptance conditions has allowed us to implement many useful algorithms; the most recent being the Alternating Cycle Decomposition [15,16] a powerful data structure with many applications (conversion to parity acceptance, degeneralization, typeness checks...)[1].

There have been 56 releases of Spot since version 2.0, but only 10 of these are major releases. Releases are numbered $2.x.y$ where y is updated for minor upgrades that mostly fix bugs, and x is updated for major release that add new features. (The leading 2 would be incremented in case of a serious redesign of the API.) Table 2 summarizes the highlights of the various releases in chronological order. Not appearing in this list are many micro-optimizations and usability improvements that Spot has accumulated over the years.

2 Use-cases of Spot, and Related Tools

As it is a library, there are many ways to use Spot. We are mostly aware of such uses via citations[2]. Historical and frequent uses-cases are to use Spot for translating LTL formulas to automata (Winners of the sequential LTL and parallel LTL tracks of RERS'19 challenge [26] both used Spot to translate the properties into automata, many competitors on the Model Checking Contest [28] also use

---

[1] https://spot.lrde.epita.fr/ipynb/zlktree.html.
[2] Our previous tool paper [21] has over 250 citations according to Google scholar.

Table 2. Milestones in the history of Spot.

2004	0.x	C++03	Prehistory of the project. [20]
2012	0.9		Support for some PSL operators.
2013	1.0		Command-line tools, mostly focused on LTL/PSL input [19]. Includes ltlcross, a clone of LBTT [42]. Python bindings.
	1.1		Automatic detection of stutter-invariant formulas. [36]
	1.2		SAT-based minimization [3,4]. ltlcross and the new dstar2tgba can read Rabin and Streett automata produced by ltl2dstar [27].
2016	2.0	C++11	Rewrite of the LTL formulas representation. Rewrite of the automaton class to allow arbitrary acceptance. Support for the HOA format. More command-line tools, now that automata can be exchanged with other tools. [21] New determinization procedure.
	2.1		Conversion to generalized Streett or Rabin. Small usability improvements all around (like better support for CSV files).
	2.2		LTLf→LTL conversion [24]. Faster simulation-based reduction of deterministic automata.
2017	2.3		Initial support for alternating automata and alternation removal. 400% faster emptiness check. Incremental SAT-based minimization. Classification in the temporal hierarchy of Manna & Pnueli [34].
	2.4	C++14	New command-line tools: autcross to check and compare automata transformations, genaut to generate families of automata. Dualization of automata. Conversion from Rabin to Büchi [31] updated to support transition-based input. Relabeling of LTL formulas with large Boolean subformulas to speedup their translation.
2018	2.5		New command-line tool ltlsynt for synthesis of AIGER circuits from LTL specifications. [35] Conversions to co-Büchi [10]. Utilities for converting between parity acceptance conditions. Detection of stutter-invariant *states*. Determinization optimized.
	2.6		Compile-time option to support more than 32 colors. Specialized translation for formulas of the type $\mathsf{GF}(\varphi)$ if φ is a guarantee. New translation mode to output automata with unconstrained acceptance condition. Semi-deterministic complementation [8]. Faster detection of obligation properties. Online LTL translator replaced by a new web application (see Fig. 4).
	2.7		LAR-based paritization in ltlsynt. Generic emptiness check [6]. Detection of liveness properties [2].
2019	2.8		Accepting run extraction for arbitrary acceptance. Introduction of an "output_aborter" to abort constructions that are too large. Support for SVA's delay syntax, and first_match operator [1]. Minimization of parity acceptance [14].
2020	2.9		Better paritization, partial degeneralization, and acceptance simplifications [39]. Weak and strong variants of X. Xor product of automata, used while translating formulas to automata with unconstrained acceptance.
2021	2.10	C++17	ltlsynt overhauled [40]. Support for games and Mealy machines. Mealy machines simplifications. Multiple encodings from Mealy machine to AIGER. Experimental twacube class for parallel algorithms. Support for transition-based Büchi. Zielonka Trees and Alternating Cycle Decomposition [15,16]

Spot this way), or to use it as a research/development toolbox, since it provides helper tools for generation of random formulas/automata, verification of LTL-to-automata translation, simplifications, syntax conversions, etc. Nowadays, the algorithms for ω-automata implemented in Spot are often used as baseline for studying better algorithms [e.g., 18,25,32,33], but we also see some new applications built on top of ω-automata algorithms from Spot [e.g., 12,13].

The projects that have the largest intersections of features with Spot seem to be GOAL [43] and Owl [30]. These are two Java-based frameworks that deal with similar objects and provide a range of algorithms. Owl and Spot share a similar and traditional Unix view of the command-line experience, where multiple commands are expected to be chained with pipes, and they both communicate smoothly via the HOA format [5]. GOAL is centered on a graphical interface in which the user can edit automata, and apply algorithms listed in menu entries. Using GOAL from the command-line is possible by writing short scripts in a custom language.

As far as interfacing goes, the most important feature of Spot is probably that it exposes its algorithms and data structures in Python. Beside being usable as a glue language between various tools, this allows us (1) to leverage Python's ecosystem and (2) to quickly prototype new algorithms in Python.

3   Automata Representation

In this section and the next three, we focuses on how the storage of automata evolved to support alternation, games, and Mealy machines.

The main automaton class of Spot is called twa_graph and inherits from the twa class. The letters twa stand for *Transition-based* ω-Automaton.

The class twa implements an abstract interface that allows on-the-fly exploration of an automaton similar to what had been present in Spot from the start: essentially, one can query the initial state, and query the transitions leaving any known state. In particular, before exploring the state-space of a twa, it is unknown how many states are reachable. Various subclasses of twa are provided in Spot, for instance to represent the state-space of Promela or Divine models [21]. Users may create subclasses, for instance to create a Kripke structure on-the-fly.[3]

The class twa_graph, introduced in Spot 2.0, implements an explicit, graph-based, representation of an automaton, in which states and edges are designated by integers. This makes for a much simpler interface[4] and usually simplifies the data structures used in algorithms (since states and edges can be used as indices in arrays). The data structure is best illustrated by using the show_storage() method of the Python bindings, as shown by Fig. 1. A twa_graph is stored as two C++ vectors: a vector of states, and a vector of edges. For each state, the first vector stores two edge numbers: succ is the first outgoing edge, and succ_tail is the last one. These number are indices into the edge vector, which stores five pieces of information per edge. Four of them are related to the identity of the

---

[3] As demonstrated by https://spot.lrde.epita.fr/tut51.html.

[4] Contrast on-the-fly and explicit APIs at https://spot.lrde.epita.fr/tut50.html.

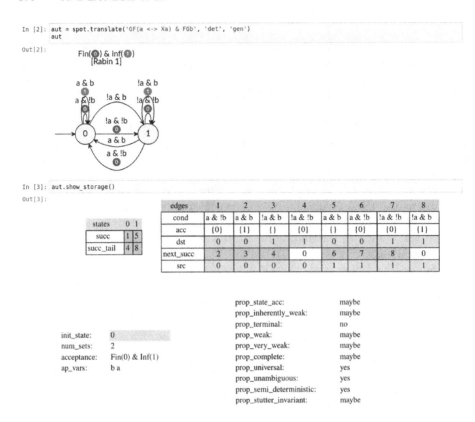

```
In [2]: aut = spot.translate('GF(a <-> Xa) & FGb', 'det', 'gen')
        aut
```

Out[2]:

```
In [3]: aut.show_storage()
```

Out[3]:

Fig. 1. Internal representation of a `twa_graph` as two vectors.

edge: `src`, `dst`, `cond`, `acc` are respectively the source, destination, guard, and color sets of the edge. The remaining field, `next_succ` gives the next outgoing edge, effectively creating a linked list of all edges leaving a given state. There is no edge 0: this value is used as terminator for such lists. Outgoing edges of the same state are not necessarily adjacent in that structure. When a new edge is added to the automaton, it is simply appended to the edge vector, and the `succ_tail` field of the state is used to update the previous end of the list.

To iterate over successors of state 1 in C++ or Python, one can ignore the above linked list implementation and write one of the following loops:

```
for (auto& e: aut->out(1))        for e in aut.out(1):
  // use e.cond, e.acc, e.dst       # use e.cond, e.acc, e.dst
```

The `twa_graph::out` methods simply returns a lightweight temporary object which can be iterated upon using iterators that will follow the linked list. Then the object `e` is effectively a reference to a column of the edge vector.

As seen on Fig. 1, the automaton additionally stores an initial state (Spot only supports a single initial state), a number of colors (`num_sets`), an acceptance condition, a list of atomic propositions (Spot only supports alphabets of the form 2^{AP}), and 10 fields storing structural properties of the automaton.

These property fields have only three possible values: they default to *maybe*, but can be set to *no* or *yes* by algorithms that work on the automaton. They can also be read and written in the HOA format. For instance if `prop_universal` is set to *yes*, it means that automaton does not have any existential choice (a.k.a. non-determinism). Spot's *is_deterministic()* algorithm can return in constant time if `prop_universal` is known, otherwise it will inspect the automaton and set that property before returning, so that the next call to *is_deterministic()* will be instantaneous. Some algorithms know how to take advantage of any hint they get from those properties: for instance the `product()` of two automata is optimized to use fewer colors when one of the arguments is known to be weak (i.e., in an SCC all transitions have the same colors).

Note that algorithms that modify an automaton in place have to remember to update those properties. This has caused a couple of bugs over the years.

4   Introduction of Alternating Automata

Support for alternating ω-automata, as defined in the HOA format, was added to Spot in version 2.3 without introducing a new class. Rather, the `twa_graph` class was extended to support alternation in such a way that existing algorithms would not require any modification to continue working on automata without universal branching. This was done by reserving the sign bit of the destination state number of each transition to signal universal branching.

Figure 2 shows an example of Alternating automaton (top-left) with co-Büchi acceptance. In many works on alternating automata, it is conventional to not represent accepting sinks, and instead have transition without destination. The top-right picture shows that Spot has a rendering option to hide accepting sinks.

The bottom of the figure shows that the automaton has `prop_state_acc` set, which means that the automaton is meant to be interpreted as using state-based acceptance. Colors are still stored on edges internally, but all edges leaving a state have the same colors. Seeing that the condition is co-Büchi (Fin(0)), the display code automatically switched to the convention of using double-circles for rejecting states.

Destinations with the sign bit set are called *universal destination groups* and appear as pink in the figure. There are two groups here: ~0 and ~3. The complement of these numbers can be used as indices in the `dests` vector, that actually store the destination groups. At the given index, one can read the size n of the destination group, followed by the state number of the n destinations.

Algorithms that work on alternating automata need to be able to iterate over all destinations of an edge. The process of checking the sign bit of the destination to decide if its a group, and to iterate on that group is hidden by the `univ_dests()` method:

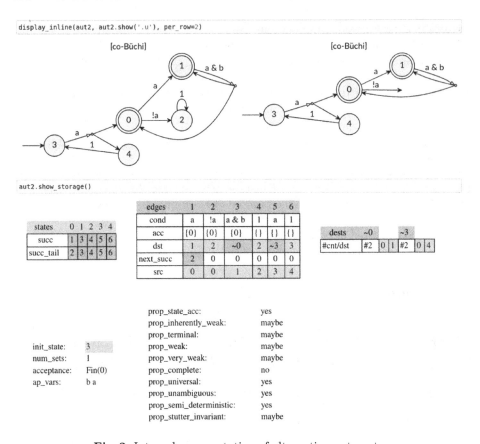

Fig. 2. Internal representation of alternating automata.

```
for(auto& e: aut->out(1)) {              for e in aut.out(1):
  // use e.cond, e.acc, e.src              # use e.cond, e.acc, e.src
  for(unsigned d:aut->univ_dests(e))       for d in aut.univ_dests(e):
    // use d                                 # use d
}
```

Note that this code works on non-universal branches as well: if e.dst is unsigned, univ_dests(e) will simply iterate on that unique value.

Spot has two alternation removal procedures. One is an on-the-fly implementation of the Breakpoint construction [37] which transforms an n-state alternating Büchi automaton into a non-alternating Büchi automaton with at most 3^n states. For very weak alternating automata, it is known that a powerset-based procedure can produce a transition-based generalized Büchi automaton with 2^n states [23]; in fact that algorithm even works on *ordered* automata [11], i.e., alternating automata where the only rejecting cycles are self-loops. The second alternation removal procedure of Spot is a mix between these two procedures but does not work on the fly: it takes a *weak* automaton as input, and uses the break-point construction on rejectings SCCs that have more than one state, and uses the powerset construction for other SCCs.

5   Extending Automata via Named Properties

Spot's automata have a mechanism to attach arbitrary data to automata, called *named properties*. (This is similar to the notion of attributes in the R language.) An object can be attached to the automaton with:

```
aut->set_named_prop("property-name", new mytype(...));
```

and later retrieved with:

```
mytype* data = aut->get_named_prop<mytype>("property-name");
```

Ensuring that `mytype` is the correct type for the retrieved property is the programmer's responsibility.

Spot has grown a list of many such properties over time.[5] For instance `automaton-name` stores a string that would be displayed as the name of the automaton. The `highlight-edges` and `highlight-states` properties can be used to color edges and states. The `state-names` is a vector of strings that gives a name to each state, etc. While those examples are mostly related to the graphical rendering of the automata, some algorithms store useful byproducts as properties. For instance the `product()` algorithm will define a `product-states` named property that store a vector of pairs of the original states.

These named properties are sometimes used to provide additional semantics to the automaton, for instance to obtain a game or a Mealy machine.

6   Games, Mealy Machines, and LTL Synthesis

The application of Spot to LTL synthesis was introduced in Spot 2.5 in the form of the `ltlsynt` tool [35], but the inner workings of this tool were progressively redesigned and publicly exposed until version 2.10.

An automaton can now be turned into a game by attaching the `state-player` property to it.[6] Only two-player games are supported, so `state-player` should be a `std::vector<bool>`. Currently, Spot has solvers for safety games and for games with *parity max odd* acceptance, but we plan to at least generalize the latter to any kind of parity condition. Once a game has been solved, it contains two new named properties: `state-winner` (a `std::vector<bool>` indexed by state numbers indicating the player winning in each state), and `strategy` (a `std::vector<unsigned>` that gives for each state the edge that its owner should follow to win).

---

[5] https://spot.lrde.epita.fr/concepts.html#named-properties.

[6] https://spot.lrde.epita.fr/tut40.html illustrates how a game can be used to decide if a state simulates another one.

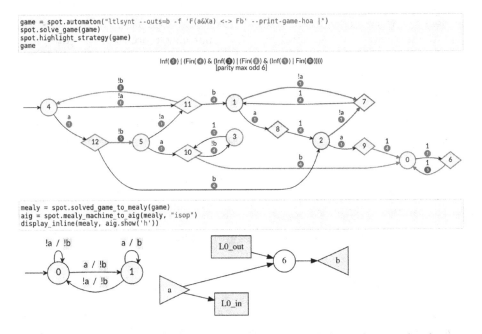

Fig. 3. (top) Solving a game to display the strategy. States with green borders are winning for player 1, who wants to satisfy the acceptance condition, by following the green arrows. States with red color are winning for player 0, who wants to fail the acceptance condition, by following the red arrows. (bottom) Conversion of the winning strategy to a Mealy machine and then an AIGER circuit. (Color figure online)

Figure 3 shows an example of game generated by `ltlsynt`, and how we can display the winning strategy once the game is solved. The winning strategy can be extracted and converted into a Mealy machine, which is just an automaton that uses the `synthesis-output` property to specify which atomic propositions belong to the output. Such a Mealy machine can then be encoded into an AND-inverter graph, and saved into the AIGER format [7]. Here L0 represents a latch, i.e., one bit of memory, that stores the previous value of a so that the circuit can output b if and only if a is true in the present and in the previous step.

7   Online Application for LTL Formulas

The Python ecosystem makes it easy to develop web interfaces for convenient access to a subset of features of Spot. For instance Fig. 4 shows screenshots of a web application built using a React frontend, and running Spot on the server. It can transform LTL formulas into automata, can display many properties of a formula (membership to the Manna & Pnueli hierarchy [34], Safety/Liveness classification [2], Rabin and Streett indices [14], stutter-invariance [36]), or simply compare two formulas using a Venn diagram.

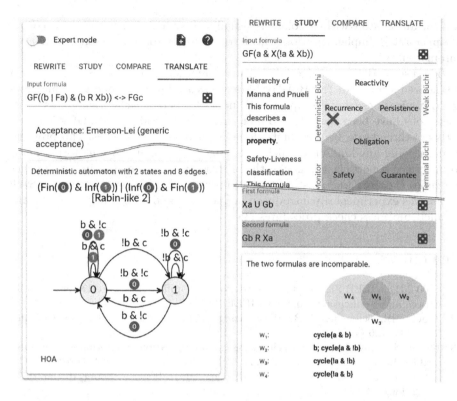

Fig. 4. A web application, built on top of Spot. https://spot.lrde.epita.fr/app/

This application has been found to be useful for teaching about LTL and its relation with automata, but is also a helpful research tool.

8   Shortcomings and One Future Direction

While Spot has been used for many applications, there are two recurrent issues: they are related to the types used for some fields of the edge vector (see Figs. 1–2). By default, the set of colors that labels an edge (the `acc` field) is stored as a 32-bit bit-vector, the transition label (`cond`, a formula over 2^{AP}), is stored as a BDD identified by a unique 32-bit integer, and the other three fields (`src`, `dst`, `next_succ`) are all 32-bit integers. One edge therefore takes 20 bytes.

While limiting the number of states to 32-bit integers has never been a problem so far, the limit of 32 colors can be hit easily. Spot 2.6 added a compile-time option to enlarge the number of supported colors to any multiple of 32; this evidently has a memory cost (and therefore also a runtime cost) as the `acc` field will be larger for each edge. However this constraint generally means that all the algorithms we implement try to be "color-efficient", i.e., to not introduce useless colors. For instance while the product of an automaton with x colors and an automaton with y colors is usually an automaton with $x + y$ colors, the `product()` implementation will output fewer colors in presence of a *weak* automaton.

The use of BDDs as edge labels causes another type of issues. Spot uses a customized version of the BuDDy library, with additional functions, and several optimizations (more compact BDD nodes for better cache friendliness, most operations have been rewritten to be recursion-free). However BuDDy is inherently not thread safe, because of its global unicity table and caches. This prevents us from doing any kind of parallel processing on automata. A long term plan is to introduce a new class `twacube` that represent an automaton in which edges are cubes (i.e., conjunctions of literals) represented using two bit-vectors. Such a class was experimentally introduced in Spot 2.10 and is currently used in some parallel emptiness check procedures [38].

References

1. 1800-2017 - IEEE Standard for SystemVerilog-Unified Hardware Design, Specification, and Verification Language. IEEE (2018)
2. Alpern, B., Schneider, F.B.: Recognizing safety and liveness. Distrib. Comput. **2**(3), 117–126 (1987)
3. Baarir, S., Duret-Lutz, A.: Mechanizing the minimization of deterministic generalized Büchi automata. In: Ábrahám, E., Palamidessi, C. (eds.) FORTE 2014. LNCS, vol. 8461, pp. 266–283. Springer, Heidelberg (2014). https://doi.org/10.1007/978-3-662-43613-4_17
4. Baarir, S., Duret-Lutz, A.: SAT-based minimization of deterministic ω-automata. In: Davis, M., Fehnker, A., McIver, A., Voronkov, A. (eds.) LPAR 2015. LNCS, vol. 9450, pp. 79–87. Springer, Heidelberg (2015). https://doi.org/10.1007/978-3-662-48899-7_6
5. Babiak, T., et al.: The Hanoi omega-automata format. In: Kroening, D., Păsăreanu, C.S. (eds.) CAV 2015. LNCS, vol. 9206, pp. 479–486. Springer, Cham (2015). https://doi.org/10.1007/978-3-319-21690-4_31
6. Baier, C., Blahoudek, F., Duret-Lutz, A., Klein, J., Müller, D., Strejček, J.: Generic emptiness check for fun and profit. In: Chen, Y.-F., Cheng, C.-H., Esparza, J. (eds.) ATVA 2019. LNCS, vol. 11781, pp. 445–461. Springer, Cham (2019). https://doi.org/10.1007/978-3-030-31784-3_26
7. Biere, A., Heljanko, K., Wieringa, S.: AIGER 1.9 and beyond. Technical Report 11/2, Institute for Formal Models and Verification, Johannes Kepler University, Altenbergerstr. 69, 4040 Linz, Austria (2011)
8. Blahoudek, F., Heizmann, M., Schewe, S., Strejček, J., Tsai, M.-H.: Complementing semi-deterministic Büchi automata. In: Chechik, M., Raskin, J.-F. (eds.) TACAS 2016. LNCS, vol. 9636, pp. 770–787. Springer, Heidelberg (2016). https://doi.org/10.1007/978-3-662-49674-9_49
9. Bloemen, V., Duret-Lutz, A., van de Pol, J.: Model checking with generalized Rabin and Fin-less automata. Int. J. Soft. Tools Technol. Transfer **21**(3), 307–324 (2019). https://doi.org/10.1007/s10009-019-00508-4
10. Boker, U., Kupferman, O.: Co-Büching them all. In: Hofmann, M. (ed.) FoSSaCS 2011. LNCS, vol. 6604, pp. 184–198. Springer, Heidelberg (2011). https://doi.org/10.1007/978-3-642-19805-2_13

11. Boker, U., Kupferman, O., Rosenberg, A.: Alternation removal in Büchi automata. In: Abramsky, S., Gavoille, C., Kirchner, C., Meyer auf der Heide, F., Spirakis, P.G. (eds.) ICALP 2010. LNCS, vol. 6199, pp. 76–87. Springer, Heidelberg (2010). https://doi.org/10.1007/978-3-642-14162-1_7

12. Brotherston, J., Gorogiannis, N., Petersen, R.L.: A generic cyclic theorem prover. In: Jhala, R., Igarashi, A. (eds.) APLAS 2012. LNCS, vol. 7705, pp. 350–367. Springer, Heidelberg (2012). https://doi.org/10.1007/978-3-642-35182-2_25

13. Bruyère, V., Raskin, J.-F., Tamines, C.: Pareto-rational verification (2022). https://arxiv.org/abs/2202.13485

14. Carton, O., Maceiras, R.: Computing the Rabin index of a parity automaton. Informatique théorique et applications **33**(6), 495–505 (1999). http://www.numdam.org/item/ITA_1999__33_6_495_0/

15. Casares, A., Colcombet, T., Fijalkow, N.: Optimal transformations of games and automata using Muller conditions. In: ICALP 2021, vol. 198, pp. 1–14 (2021)

16. Casares, A., Duret-Lutz, A., Meyer, K.J., Renkin, F., Sickert, S.: Practical applications of the alternating cycle decomposition. In: Fisman, D., Rosu, G. (eds.) Tools and Algorithms for the Construction and Analysis of Systems. TACAS 2022. LNCS, vol. 13244, pp. 99–117. Springer, Cham (2022). https://doi.org/10.1007/978-3-030-99527-0_6

17. Conda-Forge Community: The conda-forge project: community-based software distribution built on the conda package format and ecosystem, July 2015. https://doi.org/10.5281/zenodo.4774216

18. Doveri, K., Ganty, P., Mazzocchi, N.: FORQ-based language inclusion formal testing. In: Shoham, S., Vizel, Y. (eds.) CAV 2022, LNAI, vol. 13372, pp. yy–zz (2022). https://doi.org/10.1007/978-3-031-13188-2_9

19. Duret-Lutz, A.: Manipulating LTL formulas using spot 1.0. In: Van Hung, D., Ogawa, M. (eds.) ATVA 2013. LNCS, vol. 8172, pp. 442–445. Springer, Cham (2013). https://doi.org/10.1007/978-3-319-02444-8_31

20. Duret-Lutz, A., Poitrenaud, D.: SPOT: an extensible model checking library using transition-based generalized Büchi automata. In: MASCOTS 2004, pp. 76–83. IEEE Computer Society Press (2004)

21. Duret-Lutz, A., Lewkowicz, A., Fauchille, A., Michaud, T., Renault, É., Xu, L.: Spot 2.0—a framework for LTL and ω-automata manipulation. In: Artho, C., Legay, A., Peled, D. (eds.) ATVA 2016. LNCS, vol. 9938, pp. 122–129. Springer, Cham (2016). https://doi.org/10.1007/978-3-319-46520-3_8

22. Emerson, E.A., Lei, C.-L.: Modalities for model checking: branching time logic strikes back. Sci. Comput. Program. **8**(3), 275–306 (1987)

23. Gastin, P., Oddoux, D.: Fast LTL to Büchi automata translation. In: Berry, G., Comon, H., Finkel, A. (eds.) CAV 2001. LNCS, vol. 2102, pp. 53–65. Springer, Heidelberg (2001). https://doi.org/10.1007/3-540-44585-4_6

24. Giacomo, G.D., Vardi, M.Y.: Linear temporal logic and linear dynamic logic on finite traces. In: IJCAI 2013, pp. 854–860 (2013)

25. Havlena, V., Lengál, O., Šmahlíková, B.: Complementing Büchi automata with Ranker. In: Shoham, S., Vizel, Y. (eds.) CAV 2022, LNAI, vol. 13372, pp. yy–zz (2022). https://doi.org/10.1007/978-3-031-13188-2_9

26. Jasper, M., et al.: RERS 2019: combining synthesis with real-world models. In: Beyer, D., Huisman, M., Kordon, F., Steffen, B. (eds.) TACAS 2019. LNCS, vol. 11429, pp. 101–115. Springer, Cham (2019). https://doi.org/10.1007/978-3-030-17502-3_7

27. Klein, J., Baier, C.: On-the-fly stuttering in the construction of deterministic ω-automata. In: Holub, J., Žd'árek, J. (eds.) CIAA 2007. LNCS, vol. 4783, pp. 51–61. Springer, Heidelberg (2007). https://doi.org/10.1007/978-3-540-76336-9_7

28. Kordon, F., et al.: Complete results for the 2021 edition of the model checking contest, June 2021. http://mcc.lip6.fr/2021/results.php

29. Křetínský, J., Esparza, J.: Deterministic automata for the (F, G)-fragment of LTL. In: Madhusudan, P., Seshia, S.A. (eds.) CAV 2012. LNCS, vol. 7358, pp. 7–22. Springer, Heidelberg (2012). https://doi.org/10.1007/978-3-642-31424-7_7

30. Křetínský, J., Meggendorfer, T., Sickert, S.: Owl: a Library for ω-words, automata, and LTL. In: Lahiri, S.K., Wang, C. (eds.) ATVA 2018. LNCS, vol. 11138, pp. 543–550. Springer, Cham (2018). https://doi.org/10.1007/978-3-030-01090-4_34

31. Krishnan, S.C., Puri, A., Brayton, R.K.: Deterministic ω automata vis-a-vis deterministic Buchi automata. In: Du, D.-Z., Zhang, X.-S. (eds.) ISAAC 1994. LNCS, vol. 834, pp. 378–386. Springer, Heidelberg (1994). https://doi.org/10.1007/3-540-58325-4_202

32. Křetínský, J., Meggendorfer, T., Waldmann, C., Weininger, M.: Index appearance record with preorders. Acta Informatica, 1–34 (2021). https://doi.org/10.1007/s00236-021-00412-y

33. Löding, C., Pirogov, A.: New optimizations and heuristics for determinization of Büchi automata. In: Chen, Y.-F., Cheng, C.-H., Esparza, J. (eds.) ATVA 2019. LNCS, vol. 11781, pp. 317–333. Springer, Cham (2019). https://doi.org/10.1007/978-3-030-31784-3_18

34. Manna, Z., Pnueli, A.: A hierarchy of temporal properties. In: PODC 1990, pp. 377–410. ACM (1990)

35. Michaud, T., Colange, M.: Reactive synthesis from LTL specification with spot. In: SYNT 2018 (2018). http://www.lrde.epita.fr/dload/papers/michaud.18.synt.pdf

36. Michaud, T., Duret-Lutz, A.: Practical stutter-invariance checks for ω-regular languages. In: Fischer, B., Geldenhuys, J. (eds.) SPIN 2015. LNCS, vol. 9232, pp. 84–101. Springer, Cham (2015). https://doi.org/10.1007/978-3-319-23404-5_7

37. Miyano, S., Hayashi, T.: Alternating finite automata on ω-words. Theoret. Comput. Sci. **32**, 321–330 (1984)

38. Renault, E., Duret-Lutz, A., Kordon, F., Poitrenaud, D.: Variations on parallel explicit model checking for generalized Büchi automata. Int. J. Softw. Tools Technol. Transfer (STTT) **19**(6), 653–673 (2017)

39. Renkin, F., Duret-Lutz, A., Pommellet, A.: Practical "paritizing" of emerson-Lei automata. In: Hung, D.V., Sokolsky, O. (eds.) ATVA 2020. LNCS, vol. 12302, pp. 127–143. Springer, Cham (2020). https://doi.org/10.1007/978-3-030-59152-6_7

40. Renkin, F., Schlehuber, P., Duret-Lutz, A., Pommellet, A.: Improvements to ltlsynt. Presented at the SYNT 2021 Workshop, Without Proceedings, July 2021. https://www.lrde.epita.fr/~adl/dl/adl/renkin.21.synt.pdf

41. Safra, S., Vardi, M.Y.: On ω-automata and temporal logic. In: STOC 1989, pp. 127–137. ACM (1989)

42. Tauriainen, H.: A randomized testbench for algorithms translating linear temporal logic formulæ into Büchi automata. In: CS&P 1999, pp. 251–262 (1999)

43. Tsai, M.-H., Tsay, Y.-K., Hwang, Y.-S.: GOAL for games, omega-automata, and logics. In: Sharygina, N., Veith, H. (eds.) CAV 2013. LNCS, vol. 8044, pp. 883–889. Springer, Heidelberg (2013). https://doi.org/10.1007/978-3-642-39799-8_62

Complementing Büchi Automata
with Ranker

Vojtěch Havlena⬤, Ondřej Lengál$^{(\boxtimes)}$⬤, and Barbora Šmahlíková⬤

Faculty of Information Technology,
Brno University of Technology, Brno, Czech Republic
ihavlena@fit.vut.cz, {lengal,xsmahl00}@vut.cz

Abstract. We present the tool RANKER for complementing Büchi automata (BAs). RANKER builds on our previous optimizations of rank-based BA complementation and pushes them even further using numerous heuristics to produce even smaller automata. Moreover, it contains novel optimizations of specialized constructions for complementing (i) inherently weak automata and (ii) semi-deterministic automata, all delivered in a robust tool. The optimizations significantly improve the usability of RANKER, as shown in an extensive experimental evaluation with real-world benchmarks, where RANKER produced in the majority of cases a strictly smaller complement than other state-of-the-art tools.

1 Introduction

Büchi automata (BA) complementation is an essential operation in the toolbox of automata theory, logic, and formal methods. It has many applications, e.g., implementing negation in decision procedures of some logics (such as the monadic second-order logic S1S [1,2], the temporal logics EPTL and QPTL [3], or the first-order logic over Sturmian words [4]), proving termination of programs [5–7], or model checking of temporal properties [8]. BA complementation also serves as the foundation stone of algorithms for checking inclusion and equivalence of ω-regular languages. In all applications of BAs, the number of states of a BA affects the overall performance. The many uses of BA complementation, as well as the challenging theoretical nature of the problem, has incited researchers to develop a number of different approaches, e.g., *determinization-based* [9–11], *rank-based* [12–14], or *Ramsey-based* [1,15], some of them [14,16] producing BAs with the number of states asymptotically matching the lower bound $(0.76n)^n$ of Yan [17]. Despite their theoretical optimality, for many real-world cases the constructions create BAs with a lot of unnecessary states, so optimizations making the algorithms efficient in practice are needed.

We present RANKER, a robust tool for complementing (transition-based) BAs. RANKER uses several complementation approaches based on properties of the input BA: it combines an optimization of the rank-based procedure developed in [18–20] with specialized (and further optimized) procedures for complementing semi-deterministic BAs [21], inherently weak BAs [22,23],

© The Author(s) 2022
S. Shoham and Y. Vizel (Eds.): CAV 2022, LNCS 13372, pp. 188–201, 2022.
https://doi.org/10.1007/978-3-031-13188-2_10

and elevator BAs [19]. An extensive experimental evaluation on a wide range of automata occurring in practice shows that RANKER can obtain a smaller complement in the majority of cases compared to the other state-of-the-art tools.

Contribution. We describe a major improvement of RANKER [18,19], turning it from a prototype into a robust tool. We list the particular optimizations below.

- We extended the original BA complementation procedure with improved deelevation (cf. [19]) and advanced automata reductions.
- We also equipped RANKER with specialized constructions tailored for widely-used semi-deterministic and inherently weak automata.
- On top of that, we propose novel optimizations of the original NCSB construction for semi-deterministic BAs and a simulation-based optimization of the Miyano-Hayashi algorithm for complementing inherently weak automata.

All of these improvements are pushing the capabilities of RANKER, and also of practical BA complementation itself, much further.

2   Büchi Automata

Words, Functions. We fix a finite nonempty alphabet Σ and the first infinite ordinal $\omega = \{0, 1, \ldots\}$. An (infinite) word α is a function $\alpha\colon \omega \to \Sigma$ where the i-th symbol is denoted as α_i. We abuse notation and sometimes represent α as an infinite sequence $\alpha = \alpha_0\alpha_1 \ldots$ Σ^ω denotes the set of all infinite words over Σ.

Büchi Automata. A (nondeterministic transition/state-based) *Büchi automaton* (BA) over Σ is a quintuple $\mathcal{A} = (Q, \delta, I, Q_F, \delta_F)$ where Q is a finite set of *states*, $\delta\colon Q \times \Sigma \to 2^Q$ is a *transition function*, $I \subseteq Q$ is the sets of *initial* states, and $Q_F \subseteq Q$ and $\delta_F \subseteq \delta$ are the sets of *accepting states* and *accepting transitions* respectively. $\mathcal{A}$ is called *deterministic* if $|I| \leq 1$ and $|\delta(q, a)| \leq 1$ for each $q \in Q$ and $a \in \Sigma$. We sometimes treat δ as a set of transitions $p \xrightarrow{a} q$, for instance, we use $p \xrightarrow{a} q \in \delta$ to denote that $q \in \delta(p, a)$. Moreover, we extend δ to sets of states $P \subseteq Q$ as $\delta(P, a) = \bigcup_{p \in P} \delta(p, a)$. The notation $\delta|_S$ for $S \subseteq Q$ is used to denote the restriction of the transition function $\delta \cap (S \times \Sigma \times S)$. Moreover, for $q \in Q$, we use $\mathcal{A}[q]$ to denote the automaton $(Q, \delta, \{q\}, Q_F, \delta_F)$.

A *run* of $\mathcal{A}$ from $q \in Q$ on an input word α is an infinite sequence $\rho\colon \omega \to Q$ that starts in q and respects δ, i.e., $\rho_0 = q$ and $\forall i \geq 0\colon \rho_i \xrightarrow{\alpha_i} \rho_{i+1} \in \delta$. Let $\inf_{Q,\delta}(\rho) \subseteq Q \cup \delta$ denote the set of states and transitions occurring in ρ infinitely often. The run ρ is called *accepting* iff $\inf_{Q,\delta}(\rho) \cap (Q_F \cup \delta_F) \neq \emptyset$. A word α is *accepted by* $\mathcal{A}$ *from* a state $q \in Q$ if $\mathcal{A}$ has an accepting run ρ on α from q, i.e., $\rho_0 = q$. The set $\mathcal{L}_\mathcal{A}(q) = \{\alpha \in \Sigma^\omega \mid \mathcal{A} \text{ accepts } \alpha \text{ from } q\}$ is called the *language* of q (in $\mathcal{A}$). Given a set of states $R \subseteq Q$, we define the language of R as $\mathcal{L}_\mathcal{A}(R) = \bigcup_{q \in R} \mathcal{L}_\mathcal{A}(q)$ and the language of $\mathcal{A}$ as $\mathcal{L}(\mathcal{A}) = \mathcal{L}_\mathcal{A}(I)$. If $\delta_F = \emptyset$, we call $\mathcal{A}$ *state-based* and if $Q_F = \emptyset$, we call $\mathcal{A}$ *transition-based*.

A *co-Büchi automaton* (co-BA) $\mathcal{C}$ is the same as a BA except the definition of when a run is accepting: a run ρ of $\mathcal{C}$ is *accepting* iff $\inf_{Q,\delta}(\rho) \cap (Q_F \cup \delta_F) = \emptyset$.

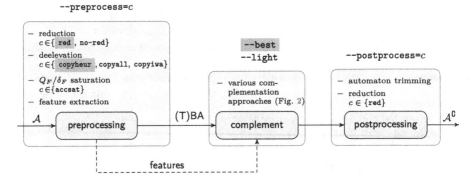

Fig. 1. Overview of the architecture of RANKER with the most important command-line options. Default settings are highlighted in blue. (Color figure online)

Automata Types. Let $\mathcal{A} = (Q, \delta, I, Q_F, \delta_F)$ be a BA. $C \subseteq Q$ is a *strongly connected component* (SCC) of $\mathcal{A}$ if for any pair of states $q, q' \in C$ it holds that q is reachable from q' and q' is reachable from q. C is *maximal* (MSCC) if it is not a proper subset of another SCC. An MSCC is *non-accepting* if it contains no accepting state and no accepting transition. We say that an SCC C is *inherently weak accepting* (IWA) iff *every cycle* in the transition diagram of $\mathcal{A}$ restricted to C contains an accepting state or an accepting transition. We say that an SCC C is *deterministic* iff $(C, \delta|_C, \emptyset, \emptyset, \emptyset)$ is deterministic. $\mathcal{A}$ is *inherently weak* (IW) if all its MSCCs are inherently weak accepting or non-accepting, and *weak* if for states q, q' that belong to the same SCC, $q \in Q_F$ iff $q' \in Q_F$. $\mathcal{A}$ is *semi-deterministic* (SDBA) if $\mathcal{A}[q]$ is deterministic for every $q \in Q_F \cup \{p \in Q \mid s \xrightarrow{a} p \in \delta_F, s \in Q, a \in \Sigma\}$. Finally, $\mathcal{A}$ is called *elevator* if all its MSCCs are inherently weak accepting, deterministic, or non-accepting.

3   Architecture

RANKER [24] is a publicly available command line tool, written in C++, implementing several approaches for complementation of (transition/state-based) Büchi automata. As an input, RANKER accepts BAs in the HOA [25] or the simpler ba [26] format. The architecture overview is shown in Fig. 1. An input automaton is first adjusted by various structural preprocessing steps to an intermediate equivalent automaton with a form suitable for a complementation procedure. Based on the intermediate automaton type, a concrete complementation procedure is used. The result of the complementation is subsequently polished by postprocessing steps, yielding an automaton on the output. In the following text, we provide details about the internal blocks of RANKER's architecture.

3.1   Preprocessing and Postprocessing

Before an input BA is sent to the complementation block itself, it is first transformed into a form most suitable for a concrete complementation technique.

On top of that as a part of preprocessing, we identify structural features that are further used to enabling/disabling certain optimizations during the complementation. After the complementation, the resulting automaton is optionally reduced in a postprocessing step. RANKER provides several options of preprocessing/postprocessing that are discussed below.

Preprocessing. The following are the most important settings for preprocessing:

- *Reduction*: In order to obtain a smaller automaton, reduction using *direct simulation* [27] can be applied (`--preprocess=red`). Moreover, if the input automaton is IW or SDBA, we transform it into a transition-based BA, which might be smaller (we only do local modifications and merge two states if they have the same successors while moving the acceptance condition from states to transitions entering accepting states). We, however, do not use this strategy for other BAs, because despite their possibly more compact representation, this reduction limits the effect of some optimizations used in the rank-based complementation procedure (the presence of accepting states allows to decrease the rank bound, cf. [19]).
- *Deelevation* [19]: For elevator automata, RANKER supports a couple of deelevation strategies (extending a basic version introduced in [19]). Roughly speaking, deelevation makes a copy of MSCCs such that each copied MSCC becomes a terminal component (i.e., no run can leave it) and accepting states/transitions are removed from the original component (we call this the *deelevation* of the component). Deelevation increases the number of states but decreases the rank bounds for rank-based complementation. RANKER offers several strategies that differ on which components are deelevated:
  - `--preprocess=copyall`: Every component is deelevated.
  - `--preprocess=copyiwa`: Only IWA components are deelevated.
  - `--preprocess=copyheur`: This option combines two modifications applied in sequence: (i) If the input BA is not IW and the rank bound estimation [19] of the BA is at least 5, then all MSCCs with an accepting state/transition are deelevated (the higher rank bound indicates a longer sequence of components, for which deelevation is likely to be benefical). (ii) If on all paths from all initial states of the intermediate BA, the first non-trivial MSCC is non-accepting, then we partially determinize the initial part of the BA (up to the first non-trivial MSCCs); this reduces sizes of macrostates obtained in rank-based complementation.
- *Saturation of accepting states/transitions*: Since a higher number of accepting states and transitions can help the rank-based complementation procedure, RANKER can (using `--preprocess=accsat`) saturate accepting states/transitions in the input BA (while preserving the language). This is, however, not always beneficial; for instance, saturation can break the structure for elevator rank estimation (cf. [19]).
- *Feature extraction*: During preprocessing, we extract features of the BA that can help the complementation procedure in the second step. The features are, e.g., the type of the BA, rank bounds for individual states [19], or settings of particular optimizations from [18] (e.g., for deterministic automata with

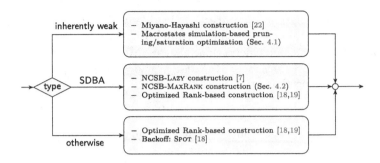

Fig. 2. Overview of complementation approaches used in RANKER.

a smaller rank bound, it is counter-productive to use techniques reducing the rank bound based on reasoning about the waiting part).

Postprocessing. After the complementation procedure finishes, RANKER removes useless states and optionally applies simulation reduction (`--postprocess=red`).

3.2 Complementation Approaches

Based on the automaton type, RANKER uses several approaches for complementation (cf. Fig. 2). These are, ordered by decreasing priority, the following:

- *Inherently weak BAs*: For the complementation of inherently weak automata, both the Miyano-Hayashi construction [22] and its optimization of adjusting macrostates (described in Sect. 4.1), are implemented. The construction converts an input automaton into an intermediate equivalent co-Büchi automaton, which is then complemented. The implemented optimizations adjust macrostates of the Miyano-Hayashi construction according to a direct simulation relation. By default (`--best`), the Miyano-Hayashi construction and the optimization of pruning simulation-smaller states from macrostates are used and the smaller result is output. For the option `--light`, only the optimized construction is used.
- *Semi-deterministic BA*: For SDBAs, RANKER by default (`--best`) uses both an NCSB-based [21] procedure and an optimized rank-based construction with advanced rank estimation [18,19]; the smaller result is picked. The particular NCSB-based procedure used is NCSB-MAXRANK from Sect. 4.2 (RANKER also contains an implementation of NCSB-LAZY from [7], which can be turned on using `--ncsb-lazy`, but usually gives worse results). For the option `--light`, only NCSB-MAXRANK is used.
- *Otherwise*: For BAs with no special structure, RANKER uses the optimized rank-based complementation algorithm from [18,19] with SPOT as the backoff [18] (i.e., RANKER can determine when the input has a structure that is bad for the rank-based procedure and use another approach). Particular optimizations are selected according to the features of the input BA (e.g., the number of states or the structure of the automaton).

4   Optimizations of the Constructions

In this section, we provide details about new optimizations of complementation of inherently weak and semi-deterministic automata implemented in RANKER. Proofs of their correctness can be found in the technical report [28].

4.1   Macrostates Adjustment for Inherently Weak Automata

For complementing IW automata, RANKER uses a method based on the Miyano-Hayashi construction (denoted as MIHAY) [22]: In the first step, accepting states of an input IW BA $\mathcal{A}$ are saturated to obtain a language-equivalent weak automaton $\mathcal{W} = (Q, \delta, I, Q_F, \emptyset)$ (we remove accepting transitions because they do not provide any advantage for IW automata). In the second step, $\mathcal{W}$ is converted to the equivalent co-Büchi automaton $\mathcal{C} = (Q, \delta, I, Q_F' = Q \setminus Q_F, \emptyset)$ by swapping accepting and non-accepting states. Finally, the Miyano-Hayashi construction is used to obtain the complement (state-based) BA.

Our optimizations of the MIHAY procedure are inspired by optimizations of the determinization algorithm for automata over finite words [29] and by saturation of macrostates in rank-based BA complementation procedure [20], where simulation relations are used to adjust macrostates in order to obtain a smaller automaton. We modify the original construction by introducing an *adjustment function* that modifies obtained macrostates, either to obtain *smaller* macrostates (for *pruning* strategy) or *larger* macrostates (for *saturating* strategy; the hope is that *more* original macrostates map to *the same* saturated macrostate). Formally, given a co-BA $\mathcal{C}$ and an *adjustment function* $\theta \colon 2^Q \to 2^Q$, the construction MIHAY$_\theta$ gives the (deterministic, state-based) BA MIHAY$_\theta(\mathcal{C}) = (Q', \delta', I', Q_F', \emptyset)$, whose components are defined as follows:

- $Q' = 2^Q \times 2^Q$,
- $I' = \{(\theta(I), \theta(I) \setminus Q_F')\}$,
- $\delta'((S, B), a) = (S', B')$ where
  - $S' = \theta(\delta(S, a))$,
  - and
    * $B' = S' \setminus Q_F'$ if $B = \emptyset$ or
    * $B' = (\delta(B, a) \cap S') \setminus Q_F'$ if $B \neq \emptyset$, and
- $F' = 2^Q \times \{\emptyset\}$.

Intuitively, the construction tracks in the S-component all runs over a word and uses the B-component to check that each of the runs sees infinitely many accepting states from Q_F' (by a cut-point construction). The original MIHAY procedure can be obtained by using identity for the adjustment function, $\theta = \text{id}$.

In the following, we use $\preceq_{di}^{\mathcal{W}}$ and $\preceq_f^{\mathcal{C}}$ to denote a *direct simulation* on $\mathcal{W}$ and a *fair simulation* on $\mathcal{C}$ respectively (see, e.g., [30] for more details; in particular, $p \preceq_f^{\mathcal{C}} q$ iff for every trace of $\mathcal{C}$ from state p over α with finitely many accepting states, there exists a trace from q with finitely many accepting states over α).

Let $\sqsubseteq \subseteq Q \times Q$ be a relation on the states of $\mathcal{C}$ defined as follows: $p \sqsubseteq q$ iff (i) $p \preceq_f^{\mathcal{C}} q$, (ii) q is reachable from p in $\mathcal{C}$, and (iii) either p is not reachable from q

in $\mathcal{C}$ or $p = q$. The two adjustment functions $pr, sat : 2^Q \to 2^Q$ are then defined for each $S \subseteq Q$ as follows:

- *pruning*: $pr(S) = S'$ where $S' \subseteq S$ is the lexicographically smallest set (given a fixed ordering on Q) such that $\forall q \in S \exists q' \in S' : q \sqsubseteq q'$ and
- *saturating*: $sat(S) = \{p \in Q \mid \exists q \in Q : p \preceq_f^{\mathcal{C}} q\}$.

Informally, *pr* removes simulation-smaller states and *sat* saturates a macrostate with all simulation-smaller states.[1] The correctness of the constructions is summarized by the following theorem:

Theorem 1. *For a co-BA $\mathcal{C}$, $\mathcal{L}(\text{MIHAY}_{sat}(\mathcal{C})) = \mathcal{L}(\text{MIHAY}_{pr}(\mathcal{C})) = \Sigma^\omega \setminus \mathcal{L}(\mathcal{C})$.*

In RANKER, we approximate a fair simulation $\preceq_f^{\mathcal{C}}$ by a direct simulation $\preceq_{di}^{\mathcal{W}}$ (which is easier to compute); the correctness holds due to the following lemma:

Lemma 2. *Let $\mathcal{W} = (Q, \delta, I, Q_F, \emptyset)$ be a weak BA and $\mathcal{C} = (Q, \delta, I, Q_F' = Q \setminus Q_F, \emptyset)$ be a co-BA. Then $\preceq_{di}^{\mathcal{W}} \subseteq \preceq_f^{\mathcal{C}}$.*

4.2 NCSB-MaxRank Construction

The structure of semi-deterministic BAs allows to use more efficient complementation techniques. From the point of view of rank-based complementation, the maximum rank of semi-deterministic automata can be bounded by 3. If a rank-based complementation procedure based on *tight rankings* (such as [18,19]) is used to complement an SDBA, it can suffer from having too many states due to the presence of the *waiting* part (intuitively, runs wait in the waiting part of the complement until they can see only tight rankings, then they jump to the *tight* part where they can accept, cf. [13,14,18] for more details). Furthermore, the information about ranks of individual runs may sometimes be more precise than necessary, which disables merging some runs. The NCSB construction [21] overcomes these issues by not considering the waiting part and keeping only rough information about the ranks. As a matter of fact, NCSB and the rank-based approach are not comparable due to tight-rankings and additional techniques restricting the ranking functions [18,19], taking into account structural properties of the automaton, which is why RANKER in the default setting tries both rank-based and NCSB-based procedures for complementing SDBAs.

An issue of the NCSB algorithm is a high degree of nondeterminism of the constructed BA (and therefore also a higher number of states). The NCSB-LAZY construction [7] improves the original algorithm with postponing the nondeterministic choices, which usually produces smaller results. Even the NCSB-LAZY construction may, however, suffer in some cases from generating too many successors. We propose an improvement of the original NCSB algorithm, inspired by the MAXRANK construction in rank-based complementation from [18] (which

---

[1] It has been brought to our attention by Alexandre Duret-Lutz that a strategy similar to *pruning* with direct simulation has been implemented in SPOT's [31] determinization and, moreover, generalized in [32] to also work in some cases *within* SCCs.

is inspired by [14, Section 4]), hence called the NCSB-MAXRANK construction, reducing the number of successors of any macrostate and symbol to at most two.

Formally, for a given SDBA $\mathcal{A} = (Q_1 \uplus Q_2, \delta = \delta_1 \uplus \delta_2 \uplus \delta_t, I, Q_F, \delta_F)$ where Q_2 are the states reachable from an accepting state or transition and Q_1 is the rest, $\delta_1 = \delta_{|Q_1}$, $\delta_2 = \delta_{|Q_2}$, and δ_t is the transition function between Q_1 and Q_2, we define NCSB-MAXRANK$(\mathcal{A}) = (Q', I', \delta', Q'_F, \emptyset)$ to be the (state-based) BA whose components are the following:

- $Q' = \{(N, C, S, B) \in 2^{Q_1} \times 2^{Q_2} \times 2^{Q_2 \setminus Q_F} \times 2^{Q_2} \mid B \subseteq C\}$,
- $I' = \{(Q_1 \cap I, Q_2 \cap I, \emptyset, Q_2 \cap I)\}$,
- $\delta' = \gamma_1 \cup \gamma_2$ where the successors of a macrostate (N, C, S, B) over $a \in \Sigma$ are defined such that if $\delta_F(S, a) \neq \emptyset$ then $\delta'((N, C, S, B), a) = \emptyset$, else
  - $\gamma_1((N, C, S, B), a) = \{(N', C', S', B')\}$ where
    * $N' = \delta_1(N, a)$,
    * $S' = \delta_2(S, a)$,
    * $C' = (\delta_t(N, a) \cup \delta_2(C, a)) \setminus S'$, and
    * $B' = C'$ if $B = \emptyset$, otherwise $B' = \delta_2(B, a) \cap C'$.
  - If $B' \cap Q_F = \emptyset$, we also set $\gamma_2((N, C, S, B), a) = \{(N', C^{\bullet}, S^{\bullet}, B^{\bullet})\}$ with
    * $B^{\bullet} = \emptyset$,
    * $S^{\bullet} = S' \cup B'$, and
    * $C^{\bullet} = C' \setminus S^{\bullet}$,
    else $\gamma_2((N, C, S, B), a) = \emptyset$.
- $Q'_F = \{(N, C, S, B) \in Q' \mid B = \emptyset\}$.

Intuitively, NCSB-MAXRANK provides at most two choices for each macrostate: either keep all states in B or move all states from B to S (if B contains no accepting state). If a word is not accepted by $\mathcal{A}$, it will be safe to put all states from B to S at some point. The construction is in fact incomparable to the original NCSB algorithm [21] (in particular due to the condition $C' \subseteq \delta_2(C \setminus Q_F, a)$, which need not hold in NCSB-MAXRANK). Correctness of the construction is given by the following theorem.

Theorem 3. *Let $\mathcal{A}$ be an SDBA. Then $\mathcal{L}(NCSB\text{-}MAXRANK(\mathcal{A})) = \Sigma^{\omega} \setminus \mathcal{L}(\mathcal{A})$.*

5 Experimental Evaluation

We compared the improved version of RANKER presented in this paper with other state-of-the-art tools, namely, GOAL [33] (implementing PITERMAN [10], SAFRA [9], and FRIBOURG [16]), SPOT 2.9.3 [31] (implementing Redziejowski's algorithm [11]), SEMINATOR 2 [34], LTL2DSTAR 0.5.4 [35], ROLL [36], and the previous version of RANKER from [19], denoted as RANKER$_{OLD}$. All tools were set to the mode where they output a state-based BA. The correctness of our implementation was tested using SPOT's autcross on all of BAs from our benchmarks. The experimental evaluation was performed on a 64-bit GNU/LINUX DEBIAN workstation with an Intel(R) Xeon(R) CPU E5-2620 running at 2.40 GHz with 32 GiB of RAM, using a 5-minute timeout. Axes in plots are logarithmic. An artifact that allows reproduction of the results is available as [37].

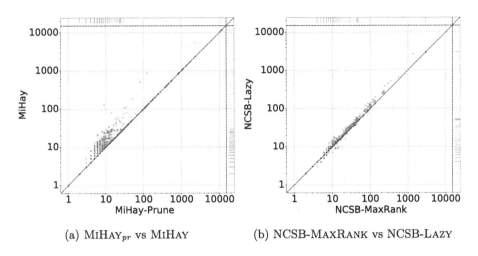

(a) MiHay$_{pr}$ vs MiHay   (b) NCSB-MaxRank vs NCSB-Lazy

Fig. 3. Evaluation of the effect of our optimizations for IW and SDBA automata.

Datasets. We use automata from the following three datasets: (i) <u>random</u> containing 11,000 BAs over a two letter alphabet used in [38], which were randomly generated via the Tabakov-Vardi approach [39], starting from 15 states and with various parameter settings; (ii) <u>LTL</u> with 1,721 BAs over larger alphabets (up to 128 symbols) used in [34], obtained from LTL formulae from literature (221) or randomly generated (1,500), (iii) <u>Automizer</u> containing 906 BAs over larger alphabets (up to 2^{35} symbols) used in [7], which were obtained from the ULTIMATE AUTOMIZER tool (all benchmarks are available at [40]). Note that we included <u>random</u> in order to simulate applications that cannot easily generate BAs of one of the easier fragments (unlike, e.g., ULTIMATE AUTOMIZER, which generates in most cases SDBAs) and have thus, so far, not been seriously considered by the community due to the lack of practically efficient BA complementation approaches (e.g., the automata-based S1S decision procedure [1]). All automata were preprocessed using SPOT's `autfilt` (using the `{-}{-}high` simplification level), and converted to the HOA format [25]. We also removed trivial one-state BAs. In the end, we were left with 4,533 (<u>random</u>, **blue** data points), 1,716 (<u>LTL</u>, red data points), and 906 (<u>Automizer</u>, green data points) automata. We use <u>all</u> to denote their union (7,155 BAs).

5.1   Effect of the Proposed Optimizations

In the first part of the experimental evaluation, we measured the effect of the proposed optimizations from Sect. 4 on the size of the generated state space, i.e., sizes of output automata without any postprocessing. This use case is motivated by language inclusion and equivalence checking, where the size of the generated state space directly affects the performance of the algorithm. We carried out the evaluation on <u>LTL</u> and <u>Automizer</u> benchmarks (we use <u>both</u> to denote their union) since most of the automata there are either IW or SDBAs.

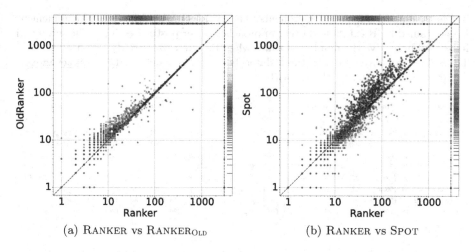

(a) RANKER vs RANKER$_{OLD}$ (b) RANKER vs SPOT

Fig. 4. Comparison of the complement size obtained by RANKER, RANKER$_{OLD}$, and SPOT (horizontal and vertical dashed lines represent timeouts).

The first experiment compares the number of states generated by the original MIHAY and by the macrostates-pruning optimization MIHAY$_{pr}$ from Sect. 4.1 on inherently weak BAs (948 BAs from LTL and 360 BAs from Automizer = 1,308 BAs). Note that we omit MIHAY$_{sat}$ as it is overall worse than MIHAY$_{pr}$. The scatter plot is shown in Fig. 3a and statistics are in the top part of Table 1. We can clearly see

Table 1. Effects of our optimizations for IW and SDBA automata. Sizes of output BAs are given as "both (LTL : Automizer)".

method	mean	median
MIHAY$_{pr}$	43.4 (7.3:140.7)	7 (5:21)
MIHAY	46.1 (10.9:141.3)	7 (6:23)
NCSB-MAXRANK	30 (20.3:38.3)	12 (8:28)
NCSB-LAZY	35.7 (25.1:44.8)	13 (9:32)

that the optimization works well, substantially decreasing both the mean and the median size of the output BAs.

The second experiment compares the size of the state space generated by NCSB-LAZY [7] and NCSB-MAXRANK from Sect. 4.2 on 735 SDBAs (that are not IW) from LTL (328 BAs) and Automizer (407 BAs). We omit a comparison with the original NCSB [21] procedure, since NCSB-LAZY behaves overall better [7]. The results are in Fig. 3b and the bottom part of Table 1. Again, both the mean and the median are lower for NCSB-MAXRANK. The scatter plot shows that the effect of the optimization is stronger when the generated state space is larger (for BAs where the output had ≥ 150 states, our optimization was never worse).

5.2 Comparison with Other Tools

In the second part of the experimental evaluation, we compared RANKER with other state-of-the-art tools for BA complementation. We measured how small output BAs we can obtain, therefore, we compared the number of states after

Table 2. Statistics for our experiments. The table compares the sizes of complement BAs obtained by RANKER and other approaches (after postprocessing). The **wins** and **losses** columns give the number of times when RANKER was strictly better and worse. The values are given for the three datasets as "<u>all</u> (<u>random</u> : <u>LTL</u> : <u>Automizer</u>)". Approaches in GOAL are labelled with ☺.

method	mean	median	wins	losses	timeouts
RANKER	38 (44 : 9 : 67)	11 (18 : 5 : 22)			158 (53 : 0 : 105)
RANKER_{OLD}	30 (38 : 10 : 32)	12 (18 : 6 : 22)	1554 (356 : 650 : 548)	264 (142 : 69 : 53)	458 (259 : 7 : 192)
PITERMAN ☺	43 (56 : 12 : 38)	14 (19 : 8 : 24)	2881 (1279 : 966 : 636)	392 (263 : 68 : 61)	309 (12 : 4 : 293)
SAFRA ☺	49 (60 : 17 : 56)	15 (18 : 10 : 24)	3109 (1348 : 1117 : 644)	274 (229 : 31 : 14)	599 (160 : 30 : 409)
SPOT	46 (57 : 8 : 66)	11 (18 : 5 : 18)	1347 (935 : 339 : 73)	1057 (327 : 343 : 387)	73 (13 : 0 : 60)
FRIBOURG ☺	49 (68 : 8 : 27)	11 (18 : 6 : 19)	2223 (1177 : 503 : 543)	586 (245 : 207 : 134)	399 (93 : 2 : 304)
LTL2DSTAR	44 (56 : 12 : 47)	14 (19 : 7 : 24)	2794 (1297 : 924 : 573)	448 (283 : 88 : 77)	288 (130 : 13 : 145)
SEMINATOR 2	46 (58 : 8 : 64)	11 (17 : 5 : 21)	1626 (1297 : 291 : 38)	1113 (286 : 398 : 429)	419 (368 : 1 : 50)
ROLL	18 (15 : 11 : 54)	9 (8 : 8 : 28)	6050 (3824 : 1551 : 675)	620 (369 : 125 : 126)	1893 (1595 : 8 : 290)

reduction using `autfilt` (with the simplification level `--high`). The scatter plots in Fig. 4 compare the numbers of states of automata generated by RANKER, RANKER_{OLD}, and SPOT. Summarizing statistics are given in Table 2. The backoff strategy in RANKER was applied in 278 (264:1:13) cases.

First, observe that RANKER significantly outperforms RANKER_{OLD}, especially in the much lower number of timeouts, which decreased by 65 % (moreover, 66 of the 158 timeouts were due to the timeout of `autfilt` in postprocessing). The higher mean of RANKER compared to RANKER_{OLD} is also caused by less timeouts). From Table 2, we can also see that RANKER has the

Table 3. Run times of the tools [s] given as "<u>all</u> (<u>random</u> : <u>LTL</u> : <u>Automizer</u>)"

method	mean	median
RANKER	3.72 (4.34:0.45:7.30)	0.05 (0.10:0.04:0.08)
RANKER_{OLD}	4.62 (5.33:0.72:9.69)	0.07 (0.19:0.03:0.15)
PITERMAN ☺	8.06 (6.07:5.95:28.38)	5.12 (4.96:5.08:8.68)
SAFRA ☺	11.58 (10.41:6.51:38.65)	5.41 (5.32:5.26:9.02)
SPOT	0.64 (0.57:0.02:2.28)	0.02 (0.02:0.01:0.02)
FRIBOURG ☺	13.13 (14.14:6.06:23.88)	5.69 (6.82:4.92:6.57)
LTL2DSTAR	2.1 (2.25:0.34:5.15)	0.02 (0.02:0.01:0.05)
SEMINATOR 2	4.16 (6.33:0.03:1.88)	0.03 (0.08:0.01:0.03)
ROLL	23.65 (29.82:3.88:49.02)	3.34 (6.19:1.71:17.14)

smallest mean and median (except ROLL and RANKER_{OLD}, but they have a much higher number of timeouts). RANKER has also the second lowest number of timeouts (SPOT has the lowest). If we look at the number of **wins** and **loses**, we can see that RANKER in majority of cases produces a strictly smaller automaton compared to other tools. In Table 3, see that the run time of RANKER is comparable to the run times of other tools (much better than GOAL and ROLL, comparable with SEMINATOR 2, and a bit worse than SPOT and LTL2DSTAR).

Acknowledgements. We thank the anonymous reviewers for their useful remarks that helped us improve the quality of the paper, the artifact evaluation committee for their thorough testing of the artifact, and Alexandre Duret-Lutz for useful feedback on an earlier version of the paper. This work was supported by the Czech Ministry of Education, Youth and Sports project LL1908 of the ERC.CZ programme, the Czech Science Foundation project 20-07487S, and the FIT BUT internal project FIT-S-20-6427.

References

1. Büchi, J.R.: On a decision method in restricted second order arithmetic. In: Proceedings of the International Congress on Logic, Method, and Philosophy of Science 1960. Stanford University Press, Stanford (1962)
2. Havlena, V., Lengál, O., Šmahlíková, B.: Deciding S1S: down the rabbit hole and through the looking glass. In: Echihabi, K., Meyer, R. (eds.) NETYS 2021. LNCS, vol. 12754, pp. 215–222. Springer, Cham (2021). https://doi.org/10.1007/978-3-030-91014-3_15
3. Sistla, A.P., Vardi, M.Y., Wolper, P.: The complementation problem for Büchi automata with applications to temporal logic. Theor. Comput. Sci. **49**(2–3), 217–237 (1987)
4. Oei, R., Ma, D., Schulz, C., Hieronymi, P.: Pecan: an automated theorem prover for automatic sequences using Büchi automata. arXiv preprint arXiv:2102.01727 (2021)
5. Fogarty, S., Vardi, M.Y.: Büchi complementation and size-change termination. In: Kowalewski, S., Philippou, A. (eds.) TACAS 2009. LNCS, vol. 5505, pp. 16–30. Springer, Heidelberg (2009). https://doi.org/10.1007/978-3-642-00768-2_2
6. Heizmann, M., Hoenicke, J., Podelski, A.: Termination analysis by learning terminating programs. In: Biere, A., Bloem, R. (eds.) CAV 2014. LNCS, vol. 8559, pp. 797–813. Springer, Cham (2014). https://doi.org/10.1007/978-3-319-08867-9_53
7. Chen, Y., et al.: Advanced automata-based algorithms for program termination checking. In: Proceedings of PLDI'18, pp. 135–150. ACM (2018)
8. Vardi, M.Y., Wolper, P.: An automata-theoretic approach to automatic program verification (preliminary report). In: Proceedings of LICS'86, pp. 332–344. IEEE (1986)
9. Safra, S.: On the complexity of ω-automata. In: Proceedings of FOCS'88, pp. 319–327. IEEE (1988)
10. Piterman, N.: From nondeterministic Büchi and Streett automata to deterministic parity automata. In: Proceedings of LICS'06, pp. 255–264. IEEE (2006)
11. Redziejowski, R.R.: An improved construction of deterministic omega-automaton using derivatives. Fundam. Informat. **119**(3–4), 393–406 (2012)
12. Kupferman, O., Vardi, M.Y.: Weak alternating automata are not that weak. ACM Trans. Comput. Log. **2**(3), 408–429 (2001)
13. Friedgut, E., Kupferman, O., Vardi, M.: Büchi complementation made tighter. Int. J. Found. Comput. Sci. **17**, 851–868 (2006)
14. Schewe, S.: Büchi complementation made tight. In: Albers, S., Marion, J., (eds.) Proceedings of STACS'09. Volume 3 of LIPIcs, Schloss Dagstuhl - Leibniz-Zentrum fuer Informatik, Germany, pp. 661–672 (2009)
15. Breuers, S., Löding, C., Olschewski, J.: Improved Ramsey-based Büchi complementation. In: Birkedal, L. (ed.) FoSSaCS 2012. LNCS, vol. 7213, pp. 150–164. Springer, Heidelberg (2012). https://doi.org/10.1007/978-3-642-28729-9_10
16. Allred, J.D., Ultes-Nitsche, U.: A simple and optimal complementation algorithm for Büchi automata. In: Proceedings of LICS'18, pp. 46–55. IEEE (2018)
17. Yan, Q.: Lower bounds for complementation of ω-automata via the full automata technique. In: Proceedings of ICALP'06, pp. 589–600. Springer, Heidelberg (2006)
18. Havlena, V., Lengál, O.: Reducing (to) the ranks: efficient rank-based Büchi automata complementation. In: Proceedings of CONCUR'21. Volume 203 of LIPIcs, pp. 2:1–2:19. Schloss Dagstuhl - Leibniz-Zentrum für Informatik (2021)

19. Havlena, V., Lengál, O., Šmahlíková, B.: Sky is not the limit: tighter rank bounds for elevator automata in Büchi automata complementation. In: Proceedings of TACAS'22, vol. 13244, LNCS, pp. 118–136. Springer, Cham (2022). https://doi.org/10.1007/978-3-030-99527-0_7

20. Chen, Y.-F., Havlena, V., Lengál, O.: Simulations in Rank-Based Büchi Automata Complementation. In: Lin, A.W. (ed.) APLAS 2019. LNCS, vol. 11893, pp. 447–467. Springer, Cham (2019). https://doi.org/10.1007/978-3-030-34175-6_23

21. Blahoudek, F., Heizmann, M., Schewe, S., Strejček, J., Tsai, M.-H.: Complementing Semi-deterministic Büchi Automata. In: Chechik, M., Raskin, J.-F. (eds.) TACAS 2016. LNCS, vol. 9636, pp. 770–787. Springer, Heidelberg (2016). https://doi.org/10.1007/978-3-662-49674-9_49

22. Miyano, S., Hayashi, T.: Alternating finite automata on ω-words. Theor. Comput. Sci. **32**(3), 321–330 (1984)

23. Boigelot, B., Jodogne, S., Wolper, P.: On the use of weak automata for deciding linear arithmetic with integer and real variables. In: Goré, R., Leitsch, A., Nipkow, T. (eds.) IJCAR 2001. LNCS, vol. 2083, pp. 611–625. Springer, Heidelberg (2001). https://doi.org/10.1007/3-540-45744-5_50

24. Havlena, V., Lengál, O., Šmahlíková, B.: RANKER (2022). https://github.com/vhavlena/ranker

25. Babiak, T., et al.: The Hanoi omega-automata format. In: Kroening, D., Păsăreanu, C.S. (eds.) CAV 2015. LNCS, vol. 9206, pp. 479–486. Springer, Cham (2015). https://doi.org/10.1007/978-3-319-21690-4_31

26. Abdulla, P.A., et al.: Simulation subsumption in Ramsey-based Büchi automata Universality and inclusion testing. In: Touili, T., Cook, B., Jackson, P. (eds.) CAV 2010. LNCS, vol. 6174, pp. 132–147. Springer, Heidelberg (2010). https://doi.org/10.1007/978-3-642-14295-6_14

27. Mayr, R., Clemente, L.: Advanced automata minimization. In: Proceedings of POPL'13, pp. 63–74 (2013)

28. Havlena, V., Lengál, O., Šmahlíková, B.: Complementing Büchi automata with Ranker (technical report). arXiv preprint arXiv:2206.01946 (2021)

29. van Glabbeek, R., Ploeger, B.: Five determinisation algorithms. In: Ibarra, O.H., Ravikumar, B. (eds.) CIAA 2008. LNCS, vol. 5148, pp. 161–170. Springer, Heidelberg (2008). https://doi.org/10.1007/978-3-540-70844-5_17

30. Etessami, K.: A hierarchy of polynomial-time computable simulations for automata. In: Brim, L., Křetínský, M., Kučera, A., Jančar, P. (eds.) CONCUR 2002. LNCS, vol. 2421, pp. 131–144. Springer, Heidelberg (2002). https://doi.org/10.1007/3-540-45694-5_10

31. Duret-Lutz, A., Lewkowicz, A., Fauchille, A., Michaud, T., Renault, É., Xu, L.: Spot 2.0 — A framework for LTL and ω-automata manipulation. In: Artho, C., Legay, A., Peled, D. (eds.) ATVA 2016. LNCS, vol. 9938, pp. 122–129. Springer, Cham (2016). https://doi.org/10.1007/978-3-319-46520-3_8

32. Löding, C., Pirogov, A.: New optimizations and heuristics for determinization of Büchi automata. In: Chen, Y.-F., Cheng, C.-H., Esparza, J. (eds.) ATVA 2019. LNCS, vol. 11781, pp. 317–333. Springer, Cham (2019). https://doi.org/10.1007/978-3-030-31784-3_18

33. Tsai, M.-H., Tsay, Y.-K., Hwang, Y.-S.: GOAL for games, omega-automata, and logics. In: Sharygina, N., Veith, H. (eds.) CAV 2013. LNCS, vol. 8044, pp. 883–889. Springer, Heidelberg (2013). https://doi.org/10.1007/978-3-642-39799-8_62

34. Blahoudek, F., Duret-Lutz, A., Strejček, J.: Seminator 2 can complement generalized Büchi automata via improved semi-determinization. In: Lahiri, S.K., Wang, C. (eds.) CAV 2020. LNCS, vol. 12225, pp. 15–27. Springer, Cham (2020). https://doi.org/10.1007/978-3-030-53291-8_2

35. Klein, J., Baier, C.: On-the-fly stuttering in the construction of deterministic ω-automata. In: Proceedings of CIAA'07, vol. 4783, LNCS, pp. 51–61. Springer, Heidelberg (2007). https://doi.org/10.1007/978-3-540-76336-9_7

36. Li, Y., Sun, X., Turrini, A., Chen, Y.-F., Xu, J.: ROLL 1.0: ω-regular language learning library. In: Vojnar, T., Zhang, L. (eds.) TACAS 2019. LNCS, vol. 11427, pp. 365–371. Springer, Cham (2019). https://doi.org/10.1007/978-3-030-17462-0_23

37. Havlena, V., Lengál, O., Šmahlíková, B.: Artifact for the CAV'22 submission "Complementing Büchi Automata with Ranker" (2022). https://doi.org/10.5281/zenodo.6558229

38. Tsai, M.-H., Fogarty, S., Vardi, M.Y., Tsay, Y.-K.: State of Büchi complementation. In: Domaratzki, M., Salomaa, K. (eds.) CIAA 2010. LNCS, vol. 6482, pp. 261–271. Springer, Heidelberg (2011). https://doi.org/10.1007/978-3-642-18098-9_28

39. Tabakov, D., Vardi, M.Y.: Experimental evaluation of classical automata constructions. In: Sutcliffe, G., Voronkov, A. (eds.) LPAR 2005. LNCS (LNAI), vol. 3835, pp. 396–411. Springer, Heidelberg (2005). https://doi.org/10.1007/11591191_28

40. Lengál, O.: Automata Benchmarks Repository (2022). https://github.com/ondrik/automata-benchmarks/tree/master/omega

Deductive Verification and Decision Procedures

Even Faster Conflicts and Lazier Reductions for String Solvers

Andres Nötzli[1]($\boxtimes$) , Andrew Reynolds[2],
Haniel Barbosa[3], Clark Barrett[1], and Cesare Tinelli[2]

[1] Department of Computer Science, Stanford University, Stanford, USA
noetzli@cs.standford.edu
[2] Department of Computer Science, The University of Iowa, Iowa City, USA
[3] Universidade Federal de Minas Gerais, Belo Horizonte, Brasil

Abstract. In the past decade, satisfiability modulo theories (SMT) solvers have been extended to support the theory of strings and regular expressions. This theory has proven to be useful in a wide range of applications in academia and industry. To accommodate the expressive nature of string constraints used in those applications, string solvers use a multi-layered architecture where extended operators are reduced to a set of core operators. These reductions, however, are often costly to reason about. In this work, we propose new techniques for eagerly discovering conflicts based on equality reasoning and lazily avoiding reductions for certain extended functions based on lightweight reasoning. We present a strategy for integrating and scheduling these techniques in a CDCL(T)-based theory solver for strings and regular expressions. We implement the techniques and the strategy in cvc5, a state-of-the-art SMT solver, and show that they lead to a significant performance improvement.

1 Introduction

Most software processes strings and, as a result, modern programming languages integrate rich functionality to represent and manipulate strings. The semantics of string-manipulating functions are often complex, which makes reasoning about them challenging. In recent years, researchers have proposed various approaches to tackle this challenge with dedicated solvers for string constraints [3,5,11,19,21], often as extensions of satisfiability modulo theories (SMT) solvers [10]. Dedicated solvers have been successfully used in a wide range of applications, including: finding or proving the absence of SQL injections and XSS vulnerabilities in web applications [30,32,35]; reasoning about access policies in cloud infrastructure [6,7,13]; and generating database tables from SQL queries for unit testing [34].

SMT solvers are frequently used as back ends for formal tools that reason about software or hardware. These tools typically produce a mix of easy and hard proof obligations that must be discharged by the solver. For many applications,

This work was supported by a gift from Amazon Web Services.

S. Shoham and Y. Vizel (Eds.): CAV 2022, LNCS 13372, pp. 205–226, 2022.
https://doi.org/10.1007/978-3-031-13188-2_11

it is crucial that the SMT solver responds quickly, and modern solvers are finely tuned to deliver the required performance. String solvers often stratify reasoning about constraints by combining different reasoning techniques rather than relying on a single, monolithic procedure. Specifically, it is common for a string solver to have a core procedure that processes only a basic language of string constraints with a minimal set of string operators. *Extended constraints*, containing additional operators, are supported by applying transformations that reduce them to combinations of basic constraints. Optimizations to this design have been explored in previous work, e.g., by simplifying extended string constraints based on the current *context* (i.e., the current set of asserted constraints) [29]. However, existing techniques still sometimes fall short for industrial applications, which continue to require richer languages of constraints while expecting the underlying solvers to remain efficient. To meet these needs, string solvers must have an even greater understanding of extended constraints and be equipped with fast procedures that leverage this knowledge.

In this work, we focus on CDCL(T)-based SMT solvers [26], where solving is done through the cooperation of a SAT solver and one or more theory solvers. The SAT solver is responsible for finding truth assignments M that satisfy the Boolean abstraction of the input formula, and the theory solvers are responsible for returning *conflict clauses* (disjunctions of literals that are valid in the theory T but are falsified by M) and, optionally, *lemmas* (selected clauses that are valid in T). The conflict clauses and lemmas from theory solvers are then added to the original input formula, and the process of finding a satisfying assignment M is repeated until no conflicts are detected, indicating that the input formula is satisfiable in T, or an unrecoverable conflict is derived, indicating that the input is unsatisfiable in T. Theory reasoning done while the SAT solver is constructing the assignment M is characterized as *eager*. Theory reasoning done after a full assignment has been computed is called *lazy*.

Inspired by real-world benchmarks, we propose new techniques for string solvers that make them more eager, and hence *faster*, in their discovery of conflicts and *lazier* in reducing constraints that are hard to handle such as, for instance, negated regular expression membership constraints. For the former, we extend the congruence closure [24] module at the heart of the string solver to perform selected theory-specific forms of reasoning including eager evaluation, reasoning based on inferred prefixes and suffixes, and (integer) arithmetic approximations (Sect. 3). For the latter, we introduce several new techniques for avoiding reductions involving extended string operators (Sects. 4 and 5). This set of techniques is particularly useful for satisfiable benchmarks, where it is possible to determine that a (candidate) model indeed satisfies the input formula without having to fully process extended constraints. We have designed these techniques to be compatible with most existing solving techniques for strings. In Sect. 6, we propose an extended strategy that describes the integration of the new techniques within an existing string solver.

In summary, our contributions are as follows:

- We describe new techniques for eagerly detecting conflicts based on an enriched congruence closure procedure for the theory of strings.

- We describe a strategy for *model-based reductions*, which can be used to minimize the reductions considered during string solving.
- We describe a procedure for efficiently reasoning about inclusion relationships for a common fragment of regular membership constraints. This procedure is used both for detecting conflicts and for avoiding unfoldings of regular expressions.
- We evaluate an implementation of the new techniques in CVC5 [8], an open source state-of-the-art SMT solver, on a wide range of string benchmarks and show a significant improvement in overall performance.

1.1 Related Work

As mentioned above, string solvers typically reduce the input constraints to a basic form. Common basic representations include finite automata [14,17,18,31, 33], bit-vectors [19], arrays [20], variations of word equations and length constraints [12,29,32,36], and hybrid approaches that combine word equations and bit-vector representations [23]. Our techniques for lazier reductions are primarily targeted at reductions to word equations, but our other techniques are more broadly applicable and could be used with any of the other basic representations.

In general, the theory of strings is undecidable [12], but modern solvers integrate a wide range of techniques to solve problems that appear in practice. One line of work has been exploring techniques that avoid reductions or make them more efficient. Reynolds et al. [29] describe an approach for lazily performing reductions after simplifying extended functions based on other constraints in the current context. In later work, Reynolds et al. [27] propose the use of aggressive rewriting to eliminate or simplify extended string constraints before performing reductions. In this work, we propose techniques that can be combined with that earlier work to perform reductions even more lazily. Reynolds et al. [28] also proposed a technique for improving the efficiency of reductions by introducing fewer fresh variables. Our approach is orthogonal to this work, because it further avoids reductions, but cannot avoid them entirely.

Both Reynolds et al. [28] and Backes et al. [7] reduce a fragment of regular expression constraints to extended string constraints. In contrast, our approach avoids reductions of certain regular membership constraints.

2 Preliminaries

We work in many-sorted first-order logic with equality and assume the reader is familiar with the notions of signature, term, literal, (quantified) formula, and free variable (see, e.g., [16]). We consider many-sorted signatures Σ, each containing a family of logical symbols $\approx$ for equality and interpreted as the identity relation, with input sort $\sigma \times \sigma$ for all sorts σ in Σ. A Σ-interpretation is a Σ-structure that additionally assigns a value to each variable. A *theory* is a pair $T = (\Sigma, \mathbf{I})$, in which Σ is a signature and $\mathbf{I}$ is a class of Σ-interpretations, the *models* of T. A Σ-formula φ is *satisfiable* (resp., *unsatisfiable*) *in* T if it is satisfied by

$n :$ Int for all $n \in \mathbb{N}$ $+ :$ Int $\times$ Int $\rightarrow$ Int $- :$ Int $\rightarrow$ Int $\geqslant :$ Int $\times$ Int $\rightarrow$ Bool
$l :$ Str for all $l \in \mathcal{A}^*$ $\_ \cdot \ldots \cdot \_ :$ Str $\times \cdots \times$ Str $\rightarrow$ Str $|\_| :$ Str $\rightarrow$ Int

substr : Str $\times$ Int $\times$ Int $\rightarrow$ Str   ctn :   Str $\times$ Str $\rightarrow$ Bool
indexof : Str $\times$ Str $\times$ Int $\rightarrow$ Int   replace : Str $\times$ Str $\times$ Str $\rightarrow$ Str

$\_ \in \_ :$ Str $\times$ Lan $\rightarrow$ Bool $\Sigma :$ Lan
rcon :   Lan $\times \cdots \times$ Lan $\rightarrow$ Lan   re :   Str $\rightarrow$ Lan
inter : Lan $\times \cdots \times$ Lan $\rightarrow$ Lan $\_^* :$ Lan $\rightarrow$ Lan
union : Lan $\times \cdots \times$ Lan $\rightarrow$ Lan $\text{range}_{c_1,c_2} :$ Lan

Fig. 1. Functions in signature of the theory of strings T_{S}.

some (resp., no) interpretation in **I**. By convention and unless otherwise stated, we use letters x, y, z to denote variables and s, t to denote terms.

We consider an (extended) theory T_{S} of strings whose signature Σ_{S} is given in Fig. 1. We fix a totally ordered finite alphabet $\mathcal{A}$ of characters. The signature includes the sorts Str, Lan, Int, and Bool, denoting $\mathcal{A}^*$, regular languages over $\mathcal{A}$, integers, and Booleans respectively. The *core* signature is given on the first two lines. It includes the usual symbols of linear integer arithmetic, interpreted as expected. We will write $t_1 \bowtie t_2$, with $\bowtie \in \{>, <, \leqslant\}$, as syntactic sugar for the equivalent inequality between t_1 and t_2 expressed using only $\geqslant$. The core string symbols are given on the second line, and include a constant symbol, or *string constant*, for each word of $\mathcal{A}^*$ interpreted as that word; a variadic function symbol $\_ \cdot \ldots \cdot \_ :$ Str $\times \ldots \times$ Str $\rightarrow$ Str, interpreted as word concatenation; and a function symbol $|\_| :$ Str $\rightarrow$ Int, interpreted as the word length function. In our examples, we will take a $\mathcal{A}$ to be the set of ASCII characters and denote string constants by double-quote-delimited string literals (as in "abc").

The four function symbols in the next two lines of Fig. 1 encode operations on strings that often occur in applications: a substring operator, a string containment predicate, an operation to find the position of one string in another, and one to replace a substring with another. We refer to these function symbols as *extended functions*. For details on the semantics of these operators, see for example [29].

The remainder of the signature covers regular expressions. It includes an infix binary predicate symbol $\_ \in \_ :$ Str $\times$ Lan $\rightarrow$ Bool, which denotes word membership in a given regular language. The remaining symbols are used to construct regular expressions. In particular, Σ denotes (the language of) all strings of length one; $\mathsf{re}(s)$ denotes the singleton language containing just the word denoted by s; $\mathsf{rcon}(R_1, \cdots, R_n)$ denotes all strings that are a concatenation of strings denoted by the arguments; the Kleene star operator R^* denotes all strings that are obtained as the concatenation of zero or more repetitions of the strings denoted by R; $\mathsf{inter}(R_1, \cdots, R_n)$ denotes the intersection of the languages denoted its arguments; and $\mathsf{union}(R_1, \cdots, R_n)$ denotes the union of the languages denoted by its arguments. Finally, we include the class of all indexed regular expression symbols of the form range_{c_1,c_2} where c_1 and c_2 are string constants of length one. We call this a *regular expression range* and interpret it as the language containing all strings of length one that are between c_1 and c_2 (inclusive) in the ordering associated with $\mathcal{A}$.

3 Eager Equality-Based Conflicts for Strings

We consider theory solvers for strings like those described by Liang et al. [21], which have at their core a congruence closure algorithm that determines whether a set of string constraints S is satisfiable in the empty theory (i.e., all function symbols, including string operations, are treated as uninterpreted). In this section, we describe two enhancements to such congruence closure algorithms, which can help detect theory-inconsistencies in S. We stress that our extended congruence closure is computed eagerly and *incrementally* as the SAT solver assigns truth values to string equalities. This enables the enhanced congruence closure algorithm to detect theory inconsistencies early, when the truth assignment is still only partially specified. We elaborate on how this enables eager backtracking in Sect. 6.

3.1 Enhancing Congruence Closure with Evaluation

The string solver implements a procedure to compute the congruence closure $\mathcal{C}(\mathsf{S})$ over the set S of currently asserted string equalities. Let $\mathcal{T}(\mathsf{S})$ be the set of all terms and subterms in S. Formally, $\mathcal{C}(\mathsf{S})$ is the set of all equalities between terms in $\mathcal{T}(\mathsf{S})$ that are entailed by the empty theory:

$$\mathcal{C}(\mathsf{S}) = \{s \approx t \mid s, t \in \mathcal{T}(\mathsf{S}), \mathsf{S} \models s \approx t\}$$

The output of the procedure that computes $\mathcal{C}(\mathsf{S})$ can be represented as a set of *equivalence classes*, that is, a partition of $\mathcal{T}(\mathsf{S})$ where each block of the partition is a maximal set of equivalent terms. For each equivalence class, we designate a unique term in it as the *representative* for that class; if the class contains at least one constant term, then the representative must be one of them. We will denote by $[t]$ the equivalence class of a term t induced by $\mathcal{C}(\mathsf{S})$. By a slight abuse of notation we will use $[t]$ also to denote the representative of that class.

Computing the congruence closure $\mathcal{C}(\mathsf{S})$ allows the string solver to detect theory conflicts in the current context which occur when the context contains a disequality $s \not\approx t$, where $[s] = [t]$. It also allows the string solver to propagate to the SAT solver entailed equalities that occur in the input formula but have not been explicitly asserted yet.

By default, congruence closure procedures effectively treat theory symbols as uninterpreted functions. Here, we propose a lightweight approach for injecting some theory-specific reasoning by *evaluating* string terms whenever possible. Specifically, for every term that is a function application $f(t_1, \ldots, t_n)$, where f is a string theory symbol, if the representatives $[t_1], \ldots, [t_n]$ are all constants, the enhanced congruence closure procedure adds the equality $f(t_1, \ldots, t_n) \approx f([t_1], \ldots, [t_n])\!\downarrow$ to $\mathcal{C}(\mathsf{S})$, where $f([t_1], \ldots, [t_n])\!\downarrow$ is the constant resulting from the evaluation of $f([t_1], \ldots, [t_n])$. Adding these equalities improves the ability of the congruence closure layer to detect more theory conflicts and propagations, as illustrated in the following example.

Example 1. Consider the constraints $\{y \approx$ "b"$, z \approx$ replace$(x, y,$ "d"$), x \approx z, x \approx$ "abc"$\}$, where the term replace$(x, y,$ "d"$)$ denotes the result of replacing the first occurrence of y in x by "d" if one exists. The congruence closure for this set of constraints determines the following equivalence classes, each with a constant representative:

$$\{"b", y\}, \quad \{"d"\}, \quad \{"abc", x, z, \text{replace}(x, y, "d")\} .$$

This means that the term replace$(x, y,$ "d"$)$ is equivalent to the concrete term replace$($"abc"$,$ "b"$,$ "d"$)$. Evaluating the latter results in the constant "adc". Hence, the congruence closure procedure will add the equality replace$(x, y,$ "d"$) \approx$ "adc" to its input set of equalities and recompute the congruence closure. This will cause the third equivalence class in the list above to contain the (distinct) string constants "abc" and "adc", thus resulting in a conflict.

In our implementation, we must track explanations for inferred equalities for the purposes of reporting conflict clauses. In the above example, the equality replace$(x, y,$ "d"$) \approx$ "adc" is added to the congruence with the explanation $x \approx$ "abc" $\wedge$ $y \approx$ "b", which is then used in the standard technique for constructing explanations for congruence-closure-based reasoning [25].

We remark that enhancing congruence closure with evaluation is not specific to the theory of strings, and can be leveraged by other theory solvers based on congruence closure. Further exploration of this technique and its impact on other theories is left as future work.

3.2   Tracking Properties of Equivalence Classes

In addition to the use of evaluation, we enhance our congruence closure procedure with further information that can be used to discover conflicts eagerly based on string-specific reasoning. We describe two examples of this mechanism below.

First, we maintain a mapping $\mathcal{Z}$ from integer equivalence classes e to intervals of the form $[\ell, u]$, indicating concrete lower and upper bounds on the value that the terms in e can have. Open intervals are achieved by letting ℓ and u be $-\infty$ and ∞ respectively. The interval can be inferred using string-specific reasoning over the terms in e.

Second, we maintain a mapping $\mathcal{S}$ from string equivalence classes e to a pair of string constants (l_1, l_2) denoting the maximal known prefix l_1 and suffix l_2 of the value that the terms in e can have. For example, if e contains the term "abc" $\cdot x$ then l_1 for e is, at least, "abc". When no prefix is known, l_1 is the empty string. The suffix l_2 is handled similarly.

Figure 2 shows how the maps $\mathcal{Z}$ and $\mathcal{S}$ are updated when new equivalence classes are created (newEqc) and when equivalence classes are merged newEqc(t) :

$$t : \text{Int} \quad \mathcal{Z}\,[t] := \begin{cases} [n,n] & \text{if } t = n \\ [\ell_{|s|}, u_{|s|}] & \text{if } t = |s| \\ [-\infty, \infty] & \text{otherwise} \end{cases}$$

$$t : \text{Str} \quad \mathcal{S}\,[t] := \begin{cases} (t,t) & \text{if } t \text{ is a constant} \\ (l_1, l_2) & \text{if } t \text{ reduces to } l_1 \cdot t' \cdot l_2 \text{ with } l_1, l_2 \text{ constants} \end{cases}$$

mergeEqc($[t_1]$, $[t_2]$) :

$t_1, t_2 : \text{Bool}$
$$\begin{aligned} &\text{if } (t_1, t_2) = (\top, x \in R) \text{ where } R = \text{rcon}(\text{re}(l_1), R', \text{re}(l_2)) \text{ then} \\ &\quad \text{mergeEntry}(\mathcal{Z}\,[x], [\ell_{|R|}, u_{|R|}]) \\ &\quad \text{mergeEntry}(\mathcal{S}\,[x], (l_1, l_2)) \end{aligned}$$

$t_1, t_2 : \text{Int}$ mergeEntry($\mathcal{Z}\,[t_1]$, $\mathcal{Z}\,[t_2]$)

$t_1, t_2 : \text{Str}$ mergeEntry($\mathcal{S}\,[t_1]$, $\mathcal{S}\,[t_2]$)

mergeEntry(E_1, E_2) :

$E_1, E_2 = [\ell_1, u_1], [\ell_2, u_2]$
$$\begin{aligned} &\text{if } \ell_1 > u_2 \text{ or } \ell_2 > u_1 \text{ then CONFLICT} \\ &\text{else } E_1 := [\max(\ell_1, \ell_2), \min(u_1, u_2)] \end{aligned}$$

$E_1, E_2 = (p_1, s_1), (p_2, s_2)$
$$\begin{aligned} &\text{if } p_1 \not\prec_{pre} p_2 \text{ or } s_1 \not\prec_{suf} s_2 \text{ then CONFLICT} \\ &\text{else } E_1 := (\max_{|\_|}(p_1, p_2), \max_{|\_|}(s_1, s_2)) \end{aligned}$$

Fig. 2. Methods for tracking intervals, prefixes, and suffixes for equivalence classes.

(mergeEqc), the two basic methods that are used when computing congruence closures. For the second method, a helper method (mergeEntry) is used to combine the contents of the entries in two maps. We assume without loss of generality that when mergeEqc is called on equivalence classes ($[t_1], [t_2]$), $[t_1]$ becomes the new representative for the merged class.

We now look at these methods in more detail. When a new equivalence class for term t is created, we look at the type of t. If t has integer type, there are three cases. If t is a numeral n, it is mapped to the interval $[n, n]$. If t is a length term of the form $|s|$, then we compute an interval $[\ell_{|s|}, u_{|s|}]$ where $\ell_{|s|}$ (resp., $u_{|s|}$) is a sound under-approximation (resp., over-approximation) of the length of s. We use the procedure described by Reynolds et al. [27] to compute these approximations. We use it because it is available, well-tested, and designed to be fast, but any sound approximation could be used. Otherwise, t is mapped to the open interval $[-\infty, \infty]$. If t has string type, we consider two cases. If t is a string constant, its prefix and suffix are both set to t. If t can be normalized using a simple set of rewrite rules to a concatenation term of the form $l_1 \cdot t' \cdot l_2$, where l_1 and l_2 are string constants of maximal length and t' is a non-constant term, then t is mapped to the pair (l_1, l_2). Note that the notation $l_1 \cdot t' \cdot l_2$ is meant to include the case where either l_1 or l_2 (or both) is the empty string.[1]

When two equivalence classes $[t_1]$ and $[t_2]$ are merged, first, if $[t_1]$ is $\top$ and $[t_2]$ is a regular expression membership predicate $x \in R$, then we may infer information about x, because $x \in R$ is now known to be true in the current context. We compute upper and lower bounds $[\ell_{|R|}, u_{|R|}]$ on the length of all strings that occur in R. We use fast approximate techniques for computing these bounds (e.g., sum the length of constant components of concatenations to infer lower bounds). Note that these techniques are context-independent and are solely based on the structure of R. We update the entry $\mathcal{Z}[x]$ based on this information. Similarly, we update the entry $\mathcal{S}[x]$ with information about the constant prefix and suffix of the regular expression R. On the other hand, when $[t_1]$ and $[t_2]$ are integer or string equivalence classes, we merge the entries for the appropriate mapping. We stress that the entry for $[t_1]$ is updated with the information from the entry for $[t_2]$ and not vice versa. This is because $[t_1]$ is the new representative of the merged equivalence class, and further merges may refer to it, while $[t_2]$ is subsequently unused.

When merging entries, we may determine that the constraints represented by the two entries are inconsistent, in which case we have found a conflict. For example, when merging integer equivalence classes, if the lower bound for one equivalence class is greater than the upper bound for the other, we raise a conflict. For string equivalence classes, a conflict is raised if the prefixes for the two equivalence classes are incompatible (i.e., neither is a prefix of the other) and similarly for suffixes. We write $p_1 \not\sim_{pre} p_2$ (resp., $s_1 \not\sim_{suf} s_2$) to denote that p_1 is not a prefix of p_2 or vice versa (resp., s_1 is not a suffix of s_2 or vice versa), and $\max_{|\_|}$ to denote the function returning the string constant having maximum length. If no conflict is raised, then the new entry E_1 is updated to contain the merged information: for integers, we take the maximal lower bound and minimal upper bound; and for strings, we take the prefix or suffix of maximal length.

In the context of CDCL(T), when the procedure raises a conflict, it is required to return a *conflict clause*, which in turn will cause the solver to backtrack. To make it possible to compute conflict clauses in the methods described above, each component of the entries for an equivalence class e in the two maps $\mathcal{Z}$ and $\mathcal{S}$ is additionally annotated with an explanation pair (t, φ), where t is a term in e and φ entails that t has the property represented by the component. This is maintained independently for each lower bound, upper bound, prefix and suffix. In most cases, this pair is of the form $(t, \top)$, where t is the source of the annotation. When inferring annotations from an asserted membership constraint $x \in R$ during mergeEqc above, their explanations are the pair $(x, x \in R)$. Explanations are updated when entries E_1 and E_2 are merged, where, e.g., the explanation for the lower bound is taken from E_2 when $\ell_2 > \ell_1$. When

---

[1] It is possible to produce tighter prefixes and suffixes recursively—for instance for terms $t_1 \cdot t' \cdot t_2$ where the equivalence class of t_1 (resp., t_2) is assigned a constant prefix (resp., suffix). However, in our experiments, this did not turn out to be worth the extra effort.

two entries are in conflict, the explanations are used to generate the conflict. For example, assuming two entries have explanations (t_1, φ_1) and (t_2, φ_2), we send the conflict clause $\neg(t_1 \approx t_2 \wedge \varphi_1 \wedge \varphi_2)$. The equality $t_1 \approx t_2$ may be further expanded using standard methods for explanations during congruence closure [25].

Example 2. Consider the constraints $\{x \in \mathsf{rcon}(\mathsf{re}("a"), \Sigma^*, \mathsf{re}("b")), z \approx "bcd" \cdot w, x \approx z\}$. The state of the map $\mathcal{S}$ after processing each assertion is as follows:

#	Assertion	$\mathcal{S}$	Conflict?
1	$x \in \mathsf{rcon}(\mathsf{re}("a"), \Sigma^*, \mathsf{re}("b"))$	$[x] \mapsto ("a", "b")$	
2	$z \approx "bcd" \cdot w$	$\mathcal{S}_1 \cup [z] \mapsto ("bcd", \epsilon)$	
3	$x \approx z$	$\mathcal{S}_2$	$\mathcal{S}_2([x]), \mathcal{S}_2([z]))$

When the first constraint $x \in \mathsf{rcon}(\mathsf{re}("a"), \Sigma^*, \mathsf{re}("b"))$ is asserted, we construct the (Boolean) equivalence class for this constraint and merge it with $[\top]$. Based on the $\mathsf{mergeEqc}$ method, we infer that the prefix and suffix for the string equivalence class $[x]$ are $"a"$ and $"b"$ respectively, which are added to $\mathcal{S}$ to obtain $\mathcal{S}_1$ When the second constraint is asserted, we infer the prefix $"bcd"$ for $[z]$ and add it to $\mathcal{S}_1$ to get $\mathcal{S}_2$; no suffix is inferred since we do not know the value of w. When the third constraint is asserted, the equivalence classes $[x]$ and $[z]$ merge. Since we have inferred that $"a"$ is a prefix of $[x]$ and $"bcd"$ is a prefix of $[z]$, we have a conflict, as these two strings do not have a common prefix. Our procedure will thus report a conflict containing the three constraints.

Example 3. Consider the constraints $\{|s| \not\approx 0, |"abc" \cdot w| \not\approx 0, x \approx s, x \approx "abc" \cdot w\}$, where s is the term $\mathsf{substr}(y, 0, 2)$, which takes the substring of y at position 0 of length (at most) 2. The state of the map $\mathcal{Z}$ after processing each assertion is as follows:

#	Assertion	$\mathcal{Z}$	Conflict?
1	$|s| \not\approx 0$	$[0] \mapsto [0, 0], [|s|] \mapsto [0, 2]$	
2	$|"abc" \cdot w| \not\approx 0$	$\mathcal{Z}_1 \cup [|"abc" \cdot w|] \mapsto [3, \infty]$	
3	$x \approx s$	$\mathcal{Z}_2$	
4	$x \approx "abc" \cdot w$	$\mathcal{Z}_3$	$\mathcal{Z}([|s|]), \mathcal{Z}([|"abc" \cdot w|]))$

When the first constraint $|s| \not\approx 0$ is asserted, we construct the equivalence classes $[0]$ and $[|s|]$. The former trivially has bounds $[0, 0]$. For the latter, we use the methods from [27] to infer lower and upper bounds for $|s|$. Note that every string has a lower length bound of 0. The upper bound for the length of $\mathsf{substr}(y, 0, 2)$ can easily be inferred to be 2. Similarly, when $|"abc" \cdot w| \not\approx 0$ is asserted, the equivalence class $[|"abc" \cdot w|]$ is created, whose length has a lower bound of 3 and no upper bound. After the latter two constraints are asserted, note that s becomes equal to $"abc" \cdot w$ by transitivity, and hence $|s|$ is equal to $|"abc" \cdot w|$ by congruence. When these two equivalence classes merge, we obtain a conflict from their respective entries in $\mathcal{Z}$, since the former has an upper bound of 2 and the latter has a lower bound of 3. Thus, our procedure returns the latter two constraints as a conflict.

4   Model-Based Reductions for Strings

The bottleneck for string solving often lies in reasoning about the reductions of extended string functions. Context-dependent simplification can greatly improve the scalability of string solvers for extended string constraints [29]. At a high level, this approach attempts to simplify extended terms based on information that holds in the current context, which can preempt the need for potentially expensive reasoning. In this work, we extend this strategy by additionally reasoning about candidate models.

First, we briefly review how extended string terms are reduced to more basic constructs. A *reduction formula* for term t is a formula $\varphi \wedge t \approx k$, where k is a fresh variable and φ is a formula over terms $k, t_1, \ldots, t_n$ that *characterizes* the meaning of t in the sense that a theory interpretation satisfies φ if and only if it satisfies $t \approx k$. As a result, the formula $\exists k. (\varphi \wedge t \approx k)$ is valid in the theory, and hence its Skolemized version can be given to the SAT solver as a lemma. This effectively reduces the satisfiability of constraints of the form $c[t]$ to the satisfiability of $c[k] \wedge \varphi$, where t has been replaced by k.

Example 4. Let t be the regular expression membership constraint $x \in \mathsf{re}(\texttt{"a"})^*$. The formula $(k \approx (x \approx \epsilon \vee x \in \mathsf{re}(\texttt{"a"}) \vee \psi)) \wedge t \approx k$ where ψ is

$$\exists k_1 k_2 k_3. \, x \approx k_1 \cdot k_2 \cdot k_3 \wedge k_1 \in \mathsf{re}(\texttt{"a"}) \wedge k_2 \in \mathsf{re}(\texttt{"a"})^* \wedge k_3 \in \mathsf{re}(\texttt{"a"})$$

is a reduction for t.

Reductions like the one above can be expensive to reason about, since they may introduce fresh (possibly universally) quantified variables. Context-dependent simplifications can avoid these reductions in some cases.

Given a string term t of the form $f(t_1, \ldots, t_n)$, where f is an extended function, a *context-dependent simplification* is a formula of the form $(t_1 \approx s_1 \wedge \ldots \wedge t_n \approx s_n) \Rightarrow t \approx l$ where l is the constant value obtained by evaluating or rewriting $f(s_1, \ldots, s_n)$. Whenever possible, we use context-dependent simplifications for extended string terms, where $t_1 \approx s_1, \ldots, t_n \approx s_n$ are equalities that hold in the current context. The same approach can be applied to regular expression memberships as well, where a membership constraint of the form $x \in R$ can be simplified to $\top$ or $\bot$ whenever x is inferred to be equal to a concrete string literal.

Example 5. Let t be as in the previous example. The formula $x \approx$ "b" $\Rightarrow t \approx \bot$ is a context-dependent simplification for t.[2]

While context-dependent simplification eliminates some reductions, in this paper we propose making certain reductions even lazier by taking into account *candidate* models. If a candidate model can be built that already satisfies a constraint with extended terms, it is not necessary to reduce it.

To elaborate, existing procedures for strings [21] are able to construct candidate models $\mathcal{M}$ (or, more precisely, interpretations) for satisfiable sets of string constraints before reductions are considered by treating all (sub)terms headed by an extended function as fresh variables, and by ignoring regular expression membership constraints. A strategy for *model-based* reduction only considers reductions for t if the candidate model $\mathcal{M}$ is inconsistent with the semantics of t—something that can be easily checked by evaluating t in the model and verifying that the computed value coincides with the value that $\mathcal{M}$ assigns to t as a variable. This allows us to avoid reductions for cases where a candidate model is correctly guessed in the presence of extended functions and regular expression membership constraints. A concrete instantiation of this strategy is described in Sect. 6.

Example 6. Consider the constraints $\{x \approx y \cdot$ "c"$, \neg x \in \mathsf{rcon}(\Sigma^*,$ $\mathsf{re}(\text{"j"}), \Sigma^*)\}$. A model-based reduction strategy would first construct a candidate model that satisfies the first constraint, e.g., $\mathcal{M} = \{x \mapsto$ "abc"$, y \mapsto$ "ab"$\}$. It would then check whether the membership constraint $x \in \mathsf{rcon}(\Sigma^*, \mathsf{re}(\text{"j"}), \Sigma^*)$ evaluates to false in $\mathcal{M}$. This is indeed the case, since $x^{\mathcal{M}} =$ "abc", making $\mathcal{M}$ a model for the full set of constraints. Hence, the reduction for the regular membership constraint in this example can be avoided altogether.

5   Fast Techniques for Regular Expression Inclusion

As mentioned in Sect. 4, regular expression memberships are handled by a lazy reduction, which can be seen as a single-step unfolding. While model-based reductions can avoid some reductions, the remaining ones may still be expensive. In this section, we show another technique to avoid reductions, based on the observation that most regular expressions in real programs are relatively simple. We focus on those of the form $\mathsf{rcon}(R_1, \ldots, R_n)$, where each R_i corresponds to a fixed or arbitrary number of range or constant regular expressions. Such regular expressions are frequently used to match a string that is made up of multiple segments, each with a different alphabet. For this fragment of regular expressions, our procedure allows us to detect conflicts before unfolding and may additionally tell us which regular expression memberships are entailed by others, and hence can be discarded.

We use the notation $\mathcal{L}(R_1) \subseteq \mathcal{L}(R_2)$ to denote that R_1 matches a subset of the strings matched by R_2. The derivation rules in Fig. 3 can be used to implement a

---

[2] We omit from the implication the trivial antecedent $\mathsf{re}(\text{"a"})^* \approx \mathsf{re}(\text{"a"})^*$.

$$\text{Emp}\,\frac{}{\mathcal{L}(\text{""}) \subseteq \mathcal{L}(R^*)} \qquad \text{Star}\,\frac{}{\mathcal{L}(R) \subseteq \mathcal{L}(R^*)}$$

$$\text{All}\,\frac{}{\mathcal{L}(R) \subseteq \mathcal{L}(\Sigma^*)} \qquad \text{Refl}\,\frac{}{\mathcal{L}(R) \subseteq \mathcal{L}(R)}$$

$$\text{Trans}\,\frac{\mathcal{L}(R_1) \subseteq \mathcal{L}(R_2) \quad \mathcal{L}(R_2) \subseteq \mathcal{L}(R_3)}{\mathcal{L}(R_1) \subseteq \mathcal{L}(R_3)} \qquad \text{CongStar}\,\frac{\mathcal{L}(R_1) \subseteq \mathcal{L}(R_2)}{\mathcal{L}(R_1^*) \subseteq \mathcal{L}(R_2^*)}$$

$$\text{Char}\,\frac{\text{For each } x \in \mathcal{L}(R),\ |x| = 1}{\mathcal{L}(R) \subseteq \mathcal{L}(\Sigma)} \qquad \text{Range}\,\frac{c_1 \geqslant c_3 \quad c_2 \leqslant c_4}{\mathcal{L}(\text{range}_{c_1,c_2}) \subseteq \mathcal{L}(\text{range}_{c_3,c_4})}$$

$$\text{Concat}\,\frac{\mathcal{L}(R_1) \subseteq \mathcal{L}(R_3) \quad \mathcal{L}(R_2) \subseteq \mathcal{L}(R_4)}{\mathcal{L}(\text{rcon}(R_1, R_2)) \subseteq \mathcal{L}(\text{rcon}(R_3, R_4))}$$

Fig. 3. Rules for deriving $\mathcal{L}(R_1) \subseteq \mathcal{L}(R_2)$.

fast, incomplete procedure to prove $\mathcal{L}(R_1) \subseteq \mathcal{L}(R_2)$. The procedure applies the rules bottom-up to build a derivation tree with $\mathcal{L}(R_1) \subseteq \mathcal{L}(R_2)$ as the root. The statement is proven if a derivation tree is found where all leaves have no preconditions. For any given pair of regular expressions, the number of possible rule applications is finite, and whether a rule applies can be checked in polynomial time w.r.t. the number of elements in the regular expression concatenations.

The first four rules in Fig. 3 have no preconditions. A regular expression R matches zero or more occurrences of R and the rules Emp and Star use that fact to conclude that (the language generated by) R^* includes the empty string, corresponding to zero occurrences of R, and (the language generated by) R, corresponding to a single occurrence of R. The third rule, All, concludes that every R is included in Σ^*, which matches all strings. Finally, Refl captures the reflexivity of the regular expression inclusion relation. Regular expression inclusion is transitive, which is captured by Trans. Additionally, CongStar captures that applying the Kleene star to regular expressions preserves the inclusion relation. The next two rules are related to regular expressions that match single characters: Char concludes that if a regular expression matches only single characters then it is included in Σ, which matches all characters; Range compares the bounds of two ranges to determine if one is included in the other. Finally, the rule Concat splits regular expression concatenations into two parts and ensures that the parts on the right-hand side include the parts on the left-hand side. Note that the splits themselves can be concatenations, so there is a choice regarding how those concatenations are split into two parts. In the context of this rule, we treat regular expressions that match a single word as a concatenation of the individual letters of that word. For example, for $\mathcal{L}(\text{"abc"}) \subseteq \mathcal{L}(\text{rcon}(\text{"ab"}, \Sigma))$, we could choose the subgoal $\mathcal{L}(\text{"c"}) \subseteq \mathcal{L}(\Sigma)$ after applying Concat.

Given a regular expression inclusion $\mathcal{L}(R_1) \subseteq \mathcal{L}(R_2)$, the above procedure may potentially derive conflicts or propagate regular membership constraints, avoiding reducing them. A conflict can be derived from membership constraints $x \in R_1$ and $\neg y \in R_2$ if $x \approx y$ is entailed by the current context. Similarly, from $x \approx y$ being entailed and $y \in R_1$ being asserted, we can propagate the regular membership constraint $x \in R_2$; and from $x \approx y$ and $\neg y \in R_2$ we can propagate $\neg x \in R_1$.

Example 7. Consider the following theory literals:

$$x \in \mathsf{rcon}((\mathsf{range}_{0,9})^*, \Sigma^*, \texttt{"b"}, \Sigma^*) \tag{1}$$

$$\neg x \in \mathsf{rcon}((\mathsf{range}_{0,9})^*, \Sigma^*) \tag{2}$$

We can apply Concat, Refl, and All to the two regular expressions:

$$\text{Concat} \cfrac{\text{Refl} \cfrac{}{\mathcal{L}((\mathsf{range}_{0,9})^*) \subseteq \mathcal{L}((\mathsf{range}_{0,9})^*)} \quad \text{All} \cfrac{}{\mathcal{L}(\mathsf{rcon}(\Sigma^*, \mathsf{re}(\texttt{"b"}), \Sigma^*)) \subseteq \mathcal{L}(\Sigma^*)}}{\mathcal{L}(\mathsf{rcon}((\mathsf{range}_{0,9})^*, \Sigma^*, \mathsf{re}(\texttt{"b"}), \Sigma^*)) \subseteq \mathcal{L}(\mathsf{rcon}((\mathsf{range}_{0,9})^*, \Sigma^*))}$$

This allows us to derive a conflict, since the regular expression of the negative membership constraint in Eq. (2) includes the regular expression in the positive regular membership constraint in Eq. (1).

6   An Extended Strategy for Strings in CDCL(T)

In this section, we summarize our overall strategy for solving string constraints that leverages the aforementioned techniques. This strategy integrates the techniques presented in this paper with existing techniques used in modern string solvers. In general, the techniques presented in this work are applicable to a wide range of solvers. The techniques from Sect. 3 can be combined with any string solver that computes the congruence closure of the constraints. Model-based reductions are applicable to string solvers that can compute models and have the infrastructure to selectively refine/ignore certain constraints. Regular expression inclusion can be used in all string solvers.

Recall that in a CDCL(T)-based SMT solver, the theory solvers produce conflict clauses or lemmas based on the content of the current context, the truth assignment incrementally constructed by the SAT solver. In the following, we split the discussion between checks that are performed on partial assignments and checks that are performed on full assignments from the SAT solver.

Checking Partial Assignments. Recall that M is the assignment to literals chosen by the SAT solver. In our implementation, whenever the SAT solver adds a literal $(\neg)t \approx s$ to M, that literal is immediately added to the congruence closure data structure of the appropriate theory.[3] This means that in a typical configuration,

---

[3] In our implementation, each theory locally maintains its own congruence closure data structure.

checkFull(S)
1 Let $F = $ getRefineExt(S); if $F = \varnothing$ **return SAT else return** F

getRefineExt(S)
1 $C, E, E_m := \varnothing$
2 **for all** ext. terms and r.e. memberships $t \in \mathcal{T}(S)$ where $t = f(t_1, \ldots, t_n)$ **do**
3   **if** $\exists s_1, \ldots s_n$ s.t. $S \models t_1 \approx s_1 \wedge \ldots \wedge t_n \approx s_n$ and $f(s_1, \ldots, s_n)\!\downarrow = c$ **then**
4   **if** $S \not\models t \approx c$ **then** add t to C
5   **else if** t is $x \in R$ **then**
6   Let b be the Boolean value such that $S \models t \approx b$.
7   **if** $b = \bot$ and $S \models x \approx x' \wedge (x' \in R')$ and $\mathcal{L}(R') \subseteq \mathcal{L}(R)$ **then**
8   **return** CONFLICT, $\{(x \not\approx x' \vee x \in R \vee \neg x' \in R')\}$
9   **else if** $S \models x \approx x' \wedge (x' \in R') \approx b$ and
          $((\mathcal{L}(R') \subseteq \mathcal{L}(R)$ and $b = \top)$ or $(\mathcal{L}(R) \subseteq \mathcal{L}(R')$ and $b = \bot))$ **then**
10   **continue**
11   **end if**
12   Add t to E_m if b is false, and E otherwise
13   **else**
14   Add t to E
15   **end if**
16 **end for**
17 **if** C is non-empty **then return** $\{$cd_simplify$(S, t) \mid t \in C\}$
18 $F := $ getRefine(S)
19 **if** F is non-empty **then return** F
20 **if** E is non-empty **then return** $\{$reduce$(t) \mid t \in E\}$
21 Construct model $\mathcal{M}$ for $\alpha(S)$ and **return** $\{$reduce$(t) \mid t \in E_m, S \not\models t \approx t^{\mathcal{M}}\}$

Fig. 4. Strings theory solver using context-dependent simplification, regular expression inclusion, and model-based reductions.

conflicts that are based purely on equality reasoning may be raised the moment M becomes unsatisfiable in the theory. This behavior makes the SMT solver faster, as it may backtrack without having to generate any further extension to M. The techniques in Sects. 3.1 and 3.2 increase the likelihood that such conflicts may be discovered eagerly based on evaluation, arithmetic approximations, and tracking prefixes and suffixes for string terms. Given that those techniques are executed every time the SAT solver assigns a value, it is imperative that they are inexpensive.

Checking Full Assignments. When a full assignment is generated by the SAT solver, each theory solver is called upon to do a *full effort* consistency check on the assignment M. We describe the strategy used for strings that incorporates reasoning about context-dependent simplification, regular expression inclusion, and model-based reductions.

Our approach checkFull is sketched in Fig. 4, which summarizes the behavior of our (extended) theory solver for strings to be used in the CDCL(T) loop.

The method takes as input a set of string constraints S, which is the subset of the literals assigned by the SAT solver that belongs to the theory of strings. We assume the method is called when S is satisfiable in the empty theory, and is such that the techniques from Sect. 3 did not raise a conflict. It calls the subprocedure getRefineExt, which returns a set of formulas F. This set may contain a *conflict clause*, that is, a disjunction of literals that are false in S. If F is non-empty, these formulas are returned to the SAT solver. Otherwise, if F is empty, then the method returns SAT, indicating that S is satisfiable.

In the subprocedure getRefineExt, we first classify the extended terms t from S by adding them to (at most) one of three sets: the set of terms C to simplify based on the context, the set of terms E to reduce, and the set of terms E_m to reduce if necessary based on a candidate model. This is done as follows. We first check if term t can be simplified based on the context, that is, if we can infer that its arguments are equivalent to terms $s_1, \ldots, s_n$ such that $f(s_1, \ldots, s_n)$ can be simplified to a constant c. In this case, t is added to C if it is not already entailed in S to be equal to c. Otherwise, if t is a regular expression membership $x \in R$, then we check whether t is otherwise directly in conflict with another membership or can be discarded. The former holds when it is the case that $x \in R$ holds with negative polarity, there exists a term x' that is entailed to be equal to x such that $x' \in R'$ is entailed to hold with positive polarity, and our regular expression inclusion test can prove that the language of R includes that of R'. In this case, we know that we are in conflict since x cannot be both in R' and not in R, and a conflict clause is returned. Otherwise, we may avoid reducing t if it is entailed by another membership $x' \in R'$ with the same polarity again where x' is entailed equal to x. This may occur if the language of R includes R' and the polarity of both memberships are positive, or if R' includes R and the polarity of both memberships are negative. If none of these cases hold, then we add t to E if it is a positive membership, and E_m otherwise. Here, the intuition is that *negative* memberships are both more expensive to reason about via reductions, and more likely to be satisfied by candidate models. All other extended terms are added to E, marking them to be reduced. Although not shown in the figure, if t is an application of string containment, then it is handled analogously to regular expression membership, noting that $\mathsf{ctn}(x, y)$ is equivalent to $x \in \mathsf{rcon}(\Sigma^*, \mathsf{re}(y), \Sigma^*)$.

Assuming the above classification, we run four steps in decreasing order of priority. First, if C is non-empty, we add the simplification formula for each $t \in C$, where we write $\mathsf{cd\_simplify}(S, t)$ to denote the formula corresponding to the context-dependent simplification of t in S. Second, we run the core theory solver for strings, denoted by method getRefine, which we assume runs the rule-based procedure from [21]. For our purposes, we assume this method returns a (possibly empty) set of refinement lemmas or conflict clauses, which we denote F and return this set if it is non-empty. Otherwise, if our set E of terms to reduce is non-empty, we return the set of reduction formulas $\mathsf{reduce}(t)$ for all $t \in E$. If none of these cases generated lemmas, then we construct a candidate model $\mathcal{M}$ for the abstraction of S, denoted $\alpha(S)$, which denotes a formula where all

Table 1. Number of solved problems per benchmark set for different configurations. Best results are in **bold**. All benchmarks ran with a timeout of 1200 s.

Set	cvc5	cvc5-v	cvc5-e	cvc5-m	cvc5-r	cvc5-vemr	z3
Industry (62)	**58**	57	**58**	56	57	55	31
Slog (17)	**17**	**17**	**17**	**17**	**17**	**17**	10
QGen (159)	158	158	**159**	**159**	158	153	**159**
Norn (175)	85	84	81	**98**	85	88	47
Kepler (436)	**89**	**89**	**89**	**89**	**89**	**89**	85
Kaluza (225)	**225**	**225**	**225**	**225**	**225**	**225**	65
PyEx (6,948)	6,927	6,902	**6,931**	6,767	6,926	6,716	5,949
Slent (105)	**93**	82	69	**93**	**93**	41	39
Leetcode (13)	**13**	**13**	**13**	**13**	**13**	**13**	11
FullStrInt (2,718)	**2,630**	2,608	**2,630**	2,629	2,628	2,611	2,461
SmallRw (73)	**52**	**52**	**52**	51	**52**	51	6
Total (10,931)	**10,347**	10,287	10,324	10,197	10,343	10,059	8,863

extended terms in S are replaced by fresh variables. Then, for each $t \in E_m$ we check whether the constraint for t holds in the candidate model $\mathcal{M}$. In particular, this is the case if $S \vDash t \approx t^{\mathcal{M}}$. We return reduce($t$) only for terms t for which this does not hold.

Notice that the model $\mathcal{M}$ serves only as a way of filtering our reductions. We do not apply context-dependent simplification based on the model, e.g., adding the lemma $(t_1 \approx t_1^{\mathcal{M}} \wedge \ldots \wedge t_n \approx t_n^{\mathcal{M}}) \Rightarrow t \approx f(t_1^{\mathcal{M}}, \ldots, t_n^{\mathcal{M}})\downarrow$, as this would introduce an unbounded number of new literals $t_i \approx t_i^{\mathcal{M}}$ to the search.

7   Evaluation

We have implemented the strategy from Sect. 6 by extending CVC5, a CDCL(T)-based state-of-the-art SMT solver that implements context-dependent simplifications [29], aggressive rewriting [27], and efficient reductions [28]. To evaluate our extension, we measure its performance on the 69,907 SMT-LIB benchmarks [9] that include the theory of strings[4] and on a set of 74 benchmarks which we have obtained from an industrial partner but are not allowed to make public. In this section, we present and discuss the results of that evaluation.

We test the performance impact of the four techniques presented in this paper: enhanced congruence closure (**v**), eager conflicts based on properties of equivalence classes (**e**), model-based reductions (**m**), and regular expression inclusion (**r**). We compare a configuration with all techniques enabled (**cvc5**) with configurations that disable individual techniques (prefixed with **cvc5-***). To measure the combined impact, we additionally include a configuration that disables all

---

[4] We excluded one benchmark with a quantifier in the quantifier-free logic QF_SLIA.

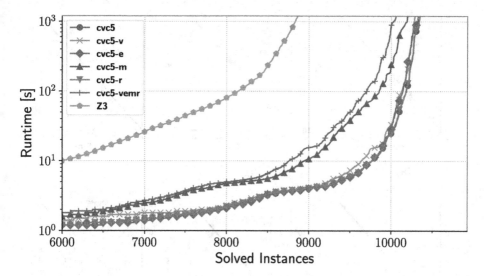

Fig. 5. Cactus plot of the number of solved benchmarks. All benchmarks ran with a timeout of 1200 s.

techniques presented in this paper, but otherwise uses all of CVC5's advanced techniques for strings (**cvc5-vmre**). Finally, as an additional reference point, we compare with another state-of-the-art solver, Z3 Version 4.8.14 [15]. In our experience, Z3 is the most stable, feature-complete competitor to CVC5's string solver. We omit a comparison with Z3STR4 [23] because it returned wrong answers at SMT-COMP 2021 [2] and there has not been a new release. Similarly, we omit a comparison with Z3-TRAU 1.1 [1] (the successor of TRAU [4]), because we found it to be unsound in earlier work [28]. Finally, OSTRICH 1.1 [14] requires inputs to be in the straight-line fragment [22], which is not the case for some of the benchmarks.

We ran all experiments on a cluster equipped with Intel Xeon E5-2620 v4 CPUs. We allocated one physical CPU core and 8 GB of RAM for each solver-benchmark pair and used a time limit of 1200 s, which is the same time limit used at SMT-COMP 2021. In the following presentation of the results, we omit the 59,050 benchmarks that are solved in less than a second by all solvers to emphasize non-trivial benchmarks. Table 1 lists the number of solved benchmarks for each benchmark family and configuration. Figure 5 shows a cactus plot of the number of solved instances for each configuration. The scatter plots in Fig. 6 compare the performance of **cvc5** with the other CVC5 configurations and Z3. Each scatter plot shows the solving times of the two solvers for each benchmark and differentiates between satisfiable and unsatisfiable inputs.

Overall, all configurations of CVC5 significantly outperform Z3, which is reflected in Fig. 5. The scatter plot Fig. 6f shows that while CVC5 outperforms Z3, they also complement each other to a certain extent, which is not surprising given the complexity of the problem and the fact that the two code bases

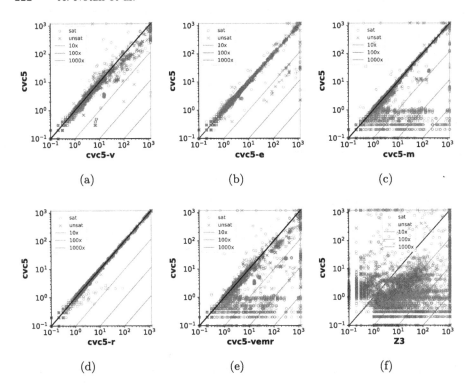

Fig. 6. Scatter plots that compare the performance of CVC5 with the other configurations. The scatter plots differentiate between satisfiable and unsatisfiable benchmarks.

differ significantly. Overall, Z3 solves 270 benchmarks that **cvc5-vmre** does not solve and 171 benchmarks that **cvc5** does not solve. Conversely, **cvc5** solves 1645 benchmarks that Z3 does not solve. Between **cvc5** and **cvc5-vmre**, **cvc5** uniquely solves 309 benchmarks and **cvc5-vmre** 15 benchmarks. This suggests that our techniques help CVC5 solve some of the benchmarks that previously only Z3 could solve, but that they also have a significant impact on benchmarks that Z3 could not solve. Thus, adapting those techniques in Z3 may be beneficial.

The PyEx benchmarks show the biggest difference in number of solved benchmarks across the techniques, with model-based reductions (**m**) solving 160 more benchmarks, significantly increasing the success rate for **cvc5**. Figure 6c indicates that primarily satisfiable benchmarks benefit from **m**. This is expected because the technique allows the solver to skip reductions if it guesses a correct model. Nevertheless, some unsatisfiable benchmarks are also solved noticeably faster due to **m**. This is possibly due to the technique resulting in a search that prioritizes reducing operators that are more likely to participate in conflicts.

Both the enhanced congruence closure (**v**) and the more eager conflicts (**e**) have a relatively low impact on the number of solved benchmarks. However, Figs. 6a and 6b show they significantly improve solving times on several benchmarks. This is expected because they allow the solver to detect conflicts more eagerly, but the same or similar conflicts would have been found (later on) with existing techniques. Since the solving procedure does not fundamentally change, roughly the same benchmarks should be solved when adding these techniques, but potentially much faster.

Finally, the regular expression inclusion technique (**r**) has a low impact overall, since it is restricted to a specific fragment, but Fig. 6d shows it significantly improves solving time for a few benchmarks. The benchmarks come from the set of industrial problems and from the QGen set of benchmarks. While the technique does not always apply, we have found it to be very important for certain industrial problems. Moreover, the scatter plot shows that having the technique available has no negative effect, which allows such a specialized procedure to be always active in a modular solver.

8 Conclusion

We have presented new techniques that make conflict detection more eager and reductions lazier in CDCL(T)-based string solvers. Our evaluation shows that both classes of techniques significantly improve performance in the state-of-the-art SMT solver CVC5 on SMT-LIB and industrial problems. As future work, we plan to generalize our eager equality-based conflict detection to leverage more sophisticated properties. We also plan to apply similar techniques to other congruence-closure-based theory solvers, such as those for the theory of finite sets and relations. The set of rules for proving regular expression inclusion was driven by empirical work on industrial benchmarks, but it could be expanded. We also plan to investigate further strategies for lazy reductions of other extended string terms that lead to bottlenecks in real-world applications.

References

1. z3-TRAU (2019). https://github.com/guluchen/z3/tree/new_trau
2. SMT-COMP 2021 (2021). https://smt-comp.github.io/2021/
3. Abdulla, P.A., et al.: Flatten and conquer: a framework for efficient analysis of string constraints. In: PLDI, pp. 602–617. ACM (2017)
4. Abdulla, P.A., et al.: TRAU: SMT solver for string constraints. In: Bjørner, N., Gurfinkel, A. (eds.) 2018 Formal Methods in Computer Aided Design, FMCAD 2018, Austin, TX, USA, 30 October–2 November, 2018, pp. 1–5. IEEE (2018)
5. Abdulla, P.A., et al.: String constraints for verification. In: Biere, A., Bloem, R. (eds.) CAV 2014. LNCS, vol. 8559, pp. 150–166. Springer, Cham (2014). https://doi.org/10.1007/978-3-319-08867-9_10
6. Backes, J., et al.: Stratified abstraction of access control policies. In: Lahiri, S.K., Wang, C. (eds.) CAV 2020. LNCS, vol. 12224, pp. 165–176. Springer, Cham (2020). https://doi.org/10.1007/978-3-030-53288-8_9
7. Backes, J., et al.: Semantic-based automated reasoning for AWS access policies using SMT. In: FMCAD, pp. 1–9. IEEE (2018)

8. Barbosa, H., et al.: cvc5: a versatile and industrial-strength SMT solver. In: Fisman, D., Rosu, G. (eds.) Tools and Algorithms for the Construction and Analysis of Systems. TACAS 2022. LNCS, vol. 13243. Springer, Cham (2022). https://doi.org/10.1007/978-3-030-99524-9_24

9. Barrett, C., Fontaine, P., Tinelli, C.: The Satisfiability Modulo Theories Library (SMT-LIB) (2016). https://www.smt-lib.org/

10. Barrett, C., Tinelli, C.: Satisfiability modulo theories. In: Handbook of Model Checking, pp. 305–343. Springer, Cham (2018). https://doi.org/10.1007/978-3-319-10575-8_11

11. Berzish, M., Ganesh, V., Zheng, Y.: Z3str3: a string solver with theory-aware heuristics. In: FMCAD, pp. 55–59. IEEE (2017)

12. Bjørner, N., Tillmann, N., Voronkov, A.: Path feasibility analysis for string-manipulating programs. In: Kowalewski, S., Philippou, A. (eds.) TACAS 2009. LNCS, vol. 5505, pp. 307–321. Springer, Heidelberg (2009). https://doi.org/10.1007/978-3-642-00768-2_27

13. Bouchet, M., et al.: Block public access: trust safety verification of access control policies. In: ESEC/SIGSOFT FSE, pp. 281–291. ACM (2020)

14. Chen, T., Hague, M., Lin, A.W., Rümmer, P., Wu, Z.: Decision procedures for path feasibility of string-manipulating programs with complex operations. PACMPL 3(POPL), 49:1–49:30 (2019)

15. de Moura, L., Bjørner, N.: Z3: an efficient SMT solver. In: Ramakrishnan, C.R., Rehof, J. (eds.) TACAS 2008. LNCS, vol. 4963, pp. 337–340. Springer, Heidelberg (2008). https://doi.org/10.1007/978-3-540-78800-3_24

16. Enderton, H.B.: A Mathematical Introduction to Logic, 2nd edn. Academic Press, Cambridge (2001)

17. Fu, X., Li, C.: A string constraint solver for detecting web application vulnerability. In: SEKE, pp. 535–542. Knowledge Systems Institute Graduate School (2010)

18. Hooimeijer, P., Veanes, M.: An evaluation of automata algorithms for string analysis. In: Jhala, R., Schmidt, D. (eds.) VMCAI 2011. LNCS, vol. 6538, pp. 248–262. Springer, Heidelberg (2011). https://doi.org/10.1007/978-3-642-18275-4_18

19. Kiezun, A., Ganesh, V., Artzi, S., Guo, P.J., Hooimeijer, P., Ernst, M.D.: HAMPI: a solver for word equations over strings, regular expressions, and context-free grammars. ACM Trans. Softw. Eng. Methodol. 21(4), 25:1–25:28 (2012)

20. Li, G., Ghosh, I.: PASS: string solving with parameterized array and interval automaton. In: Bertacco, V., Legay, A. (eds.) HVC 2013. LNCS, vol. 8244, pp. 15–31. Springer, Cham (2013). https://doi.org/10.1007/978-3-319-03077-7_2

21. Liang, T., Reynolds, A., Tinelli, C., Barrett, C., Deters, M.: A DPLL(T) theory solver for a theory of strings and regular expressions. In: Biere, A., Bloem, R. (eds.) CAV 2014. LNCS, vol. 8559, pp. 646–662. Springer, Cham (2014). https://doi.org/10.1007/978-3-319-08867-9_43

22. Lin, A.W., Barceló, P.: String solving with word equations and transducers: towards a logic for analysing mutation XSS. In: POPL, pp. 123–136. ACM (2016)

23. Mora, F., Berzish, M., Kulczynski, M., Nowotka, D., Ganesh, V.: Z3str4: a multi-armed string solver. In: Huisman, M., Păsăreanu, C., Zhan, N. (eds.) FM 2021. LNCS, vol. 13047, pp. 389–406. Springer, Cham (2021). https://doi.org/10.1007/978-3-030-90870-6_21

24. Nelson, G., Oppen, D.C.: Fast decision procedures based on congruence closure. J. ACM 27(2), 356–364 (1980)

25. Nieuwenhuis, R., Oliveras, A.: Proof-producing congruence closure. In: Giesl, J. (ed.) RTA 2005. LNCS, vol. 3467, pp. 453–468. Springer, Heidelberg (2005). https://doi.org/10.1007/978-3-540-32033-3_33

26. Nieuwenhuis, R., Oliveras, A., Tinelli, C.: Solving SAT and SAT modulo theories: from an abstract Davis-Putnam-Logemann-Loveland procedure to DPLL(T). J. ACM **53**(6), 937–977 (2006)

27. Reynolds, A., Nötzli, A., Barrett, C., Tinelli, C.: High-level abstractions for simplifying extended string constraints in SMT. In: Dillig, I., Tasiran, S. (eds.) CAV 2019. LNCS, vol. 11562, pp. 23–42. Springer, Cham (2019). https://doi.org/10.1007/978-3-030-25543-5_2

28. Reynolds, A., Nötzli, A., Barrett, C.W., Tinelli, C.: Reductions for strings and regular expressions revisited. In: FMCAD, pp. 225–235. IEEE (2020)

29. Reynolds, A., Woo, M., Barrett, C., Brumley, D., Liang, T., Tinelli, C.: Scaling up DPLL(T) string solvers using context-dependent simplification. In: Majumdar, R., Kunčak, V. (eds.) CAV 2017. LNCS, vol. 10427, pp. 453–474. Springer, Cham (2017). https://doi.org/10.1007/978-3-319-63390-9_24

30. Saxena, P., Akhawe, D., Hanna, S., Mao, F., McCamant, S., Song, D.: A symbolic execution framework for JavaScript. In: 31st IEEE Symposium on Security and Privacy, S&P 2010, Berleley/Oakland, California, USA, 16–19 May 2010, pp. 513–528. IEEE Computer Society (2010)

31. Shannon, D., Hajra, S., Lee, A., Zhan, D., Khurshid, S.: Abstracting symbolic execution with string analysis. In: Testing: Academic and Industrial Conference Practice and Research Techniques-MUTATION (TAICPART-MUTATION 2007), pp. 13–22. IEEE (2007)

32. Trinh, M., Chu, D., Jaffar, J.: S3: a symbolic string solver for vulnerability detection in web applications. In: CCS, pp. 1232–1243. ACM (2014)

33. Veanes, M., Bjørner, N., de Moura, L.: Symbolic automata constraint solving. In: Fermüller, C.G., Voronkov, A. (eds.) LPAR 2010. LNCS, vol. 6397, pp. 640–654. Springer, Heidelberg (2010). https://doi.org/10.1007/978-3-642-16242-8_45

34. Veanes, M., Tillmann, N., de Halleux, J.: Qex: symbolic SQL query explorer. In: Clarke, E.M., Voronkov, A. (eds.) LPAR 2010. LNCS (LNAI), vol. 6355, pp. 425–446. Springer, Heidelberg (2010). https://doi.org/10.1007/978-3-642-17511-4_24

35. Yu, F., Alkhalaf, M., Bultan, T.: Stranger: an automata-based string analysis tool for PHP. In: Tools and Algorithms for the Construction and Analysis of Systems, 16th International Conference, TACAS 2010, Held as Part of the Joint European Conferences on Theory and Practice of Software, ETAPS 2010, Paphos, Cyprus, 20–28 March 2010. Proceedings, pp. 154–157 (2010)

36. Zheng, Y., Zhang, X., Ganesh, V.: Z3-str: a z3-based string solver for web application analysis. In: Meyer, B., Baresi, L., Mezini, M. (eds.) Joint Meeting of the European Software Engineering Conference and the ACM SIGSOFT Symposium on the Foundations of Software Engineering, ESEC/FSE 2013, Saint Petersburg, Russian Federation, 18–26 August 2013, pp. 114–124. ACM (2013)

Local Search for SMT on Linear Integer Arithmetic

Shaowei Cai[1,2(✉)] [iD], Bohan Li[1,2] [iD], and Xindi Zhang[1,2] [iD]

[1] State Key Laboratory of Computer Science, Institute of Software,
Chinese Academy of Sciences, Beijing, China
{caisw,libh,zhangxd}@ios.ac.cn
[2] School of Computer Science and Technology,
University of Chinese Academy of Sciences, Beijing, China

Abstract. Satisfiability Modulo Linear Integer Arithmetic, SMT (LIA) for short, has significant applications in many domains. In this paper, we develop the first local search algorithm for SMT (LIA) by directly operating on variables, breaking through the traditional framework. We propose a local search framework by considering the distinctions between Boolean and integer variables. Moreover, we design a novel operator and scoring functions tailored for LIA, and propose a two-level operation selection heuristic. Putting these together, we develop a local search SMT (LIA) solver called LS-LIA. Experiments are carried out to evaluate LS-LIA on benchmarks from SMTLIB and two benchmark sets generated from job shop scheduling and data race detection. The results show that LS-LIA is competitive and complementary with state-of-the-art SMT solvers, and performs particularly well on those formulae with only integer variables. A simple sequential portfolio with Z3 improves the state-of-the-art on satisfiable benchmark sets of LIA and IDL benchmarks from SMT-LIB. LS-LIA also solves Job Shop Scheduling benchmarks substantially faster than traditional complete SMT solvers.

Keywords: SMT · Local Search · Linear Integer Arithmetic · Integer Difference Logic

1 Introduction

Satisfiability Modulo Theories (SMT) is the problem of deciding the satisfiability of a first order logic formula with respect to certain background theories. Inspired by the great success of propositional satisfiability (SAT) solving, SMT attempts to generalize the advances of satisfiability solvers from propositional logic to fragments of first order logic. Typical theories supported by SMT include the theories of integers, real numbers, lists, arrays and bit-vectors. The field of SMT

S. Cai, B. Li and X. Zhang—The authors are listed in alphabetical order, as they all contribute significantly.

S. Shoham and Y. Vizel (Eds.): CAV 2022, LNCS 13372, pp. 227–248, 2022.
https://doi.org/10.1007/978-3-031-13188-2_12

has seen significant progress in the past two decades. SMT solvers have become important formal verification engines, with applications in various domains.

In this paper, we focus on the theory of *Linear Integer Arithmetic* (LIA), consisting of arithmetic atomic formulae in the form of $\sum_i a_i x_i + c \bowtie 0$, where $\bowtie \in \{=, \leq\}$, c and a_i's are rational numbers and x_i's are integer variables. Moreover, we are also interested in a popular fragment of LIA, namely *Integer Difference Logic* (IDL), consisting of arithmetic atomic formulae to constrain the difference between pairs of integer variables in the form of $a - b \leq k$, where a, b are integer variables and k is integer constant. The SMT problem with the background theory of LIA and IDL, is to determine the satisfiability of the Boolean combination of respective arithmetic atomic formulae and propositional variables, and referred to as SMT (LIA) and SMT (IDL).

SMT (LIA) is important in software verification and automated reasoning, since most programs use integer variables and perform arithmetic operation on them [35]. Specifically, SMT (LIA) has various applications in automated termination analysis [16], sequential equivalence checking [34], and state reachability checking under weak memory models [24]. SMT (IDL) has found applications in problems with timing-related constraints [17], such as hardware models with ordered data structures [23], stable models computing [30], and job shop scheduling [40].

Much effort has been devoted to solving SMT (LIA) and SMT (IDL). The most popular approach is the *lazy* approach [3,41], also known as DPLL(T) [38], which is a central development of SMT. Many DPLL(T) solvers have been developed for SMT (LIA) [7,19] and SMT (IDL) [31,37,47]. In this approach, the formula is abstracted into a Boolean formula by replacing arithmetic atomic formulae with fresh Boolean variables. A SAT solver is used to reason about the Boolean structure and solve the Boolean formula, while a theory solver receives assignments from the SAT solver and performs decision procedure to solve the conjunctions of atomic subformulae, including consistency checking of the assignments and theory-based deduction.

The effort in this approach is mainly devoted to producing more effective theory solvers. Simplex-based linear arithmetic solvers that can be integrated efficiently in the DPLL(T) framework were studied [19]. A simplex-based decision procedure that minimizes the sum of infeasibilities of constraints was proposed [32]. A theory solver made use of layering and several heuristics to achieve good performance [26]. A theory solver called SPASS-IQ was designed to efficiently handle unbounded problems [6,8]. According to recent SMT Competitions,[1] almost all state-of-the-art SMT (LIA) and SMT (IDL) solvers are based on the lazy approach, including MathSAT5 [15], CVC5 [2], Yices2 [21], Z3 [18], SMTInterpol [14] and SPASS-SATT [7].

The other approach is the *eager* approach, where the formula is reduced to an equi-satisfiable Boolean formula and then solved by a SAT solver. This approach works well for SMT (IDL). Typically, all intrinsic dependencies between integer variables are computed and encoded as Boolean constraints. Encoding to

---

[1] https://smt-comp.github.io/.

Boolean formula is done either by deriving adequate ranges for formula variables (a.k.a. small domain encoding) [9,39,45], or by deriving all possible transitivity constraints (a.k.a per-constraint encoding) [44]. A hybrid method combining the strengths of two encoding scheme showed robust performance [43].

Local search is an incomplete method which plays an important role in many combinatorial problems [28]. Local search algorithms move from solution to solution in the space of candidate solutions by applying local changes. It has been successfully applied to Boolean Satisfiability (SAT) problem [1,4,12,13,33] and is competitive with CDCL solvers on certain types of instances. However, very limited effort has been devoted to local search for SMT. The idea of integrating local search solvers with theory solvers has been explored before, where a local search SAT solver WalkSAT is used to solve the Boolean skeleton of the SMT formula [26]. A pure local search solver [22] was proposed to solve SMT on the theory of *bit vectors* directly on the theory level, by lifting the successful techniques in local search SAT solvers to the SMT level. In [36], a precise propagation based local search for SMT on the theory of *bit vectors* is proposed, by introducing a notion of essential inputs to lift the concept of controlling inputs from the bit-level to the word-level. We are not aware of any work on local search solvers for SMT on integer arithmetic theories.

This work, for the first time, develops a local search solver for SMT (LIA), which directly operates on both Boolean and integer variables, breaking through the traditional approaches. We propose a local search framework, which switches between two modes, namely Boolean mode and Integer mode. Each mode consists of consecutive operations of the same type (either Boolean or integer). Moreover, for the Integer mode, we propose a literal-level operator named *critical move* and a fine-grained scoring function named *distance score* which takes into account the *distance to truth* of literals and *distance to satisfaction* of clauses. A two-level heuristic is proposed to pick a *critical move* operation. By putting these together, we develop a local search solver for SMT (LIA) called LS-LIA.

Experiments are conducted to evaluate LS-LIA on 4 benchmarks, including QF_LIA and QF_IDL benchmarks from SMTLIB (excluding unsatisfiable instances),[2] instances encoded from job shop scheduling (JSP) and instances generated by data race detection system on a real world benchmark [29]. We compare our solver with state of the art SMT solvers including Z3, CVC5, Yices and MathSAT5. Experimental results show that LS-LIA is competitive and complementary with state-of-the-art SMT solvers. Particularly, LS-LIA is good at solving instances without Boolean variables, noting that a large portion in SMTLIB (81.1% for LIA and 44.1% for IDL) belongs to this type. A simple sequential portfolio with Z3 improves the state-of-the-art on satisfiable QF_LIA and QF_IDL benchmarks from SMT-LIB. LS-LIA also solves Job Shop Scheduling benchmarks substantially faster than traditional complete SMT solvers.

---

[2] http://www.smt-lib.org/.

2   Preliminary

Definition 1. *Linear Integer Arithmetic (LIA): Let $P = \{p_1, p_2, ...p_n\}$ be a set of propositional (Boolean) variables and $X = \{x_1, x_2...x_m\}$ be a set of integer-valued variables. The linear integer arithmetic formulae are inductively defined.*

1) $p \in P$ is a propositional atomic LIA formula.
2) $\sum_i a_i x_i \bowtie k$ is an arithmetic atomic LIA formulae, where $\bowtie \in \{=, \leq\}$, $x_i \in X$, k, and a_i are constant coefficients (rationals or integers).
3) If ψ and φ are LIA formulae, so are $\psi \vee \varphi$, $\psi \wedge \varphi$ and $\neg\varphi$.

In the above definition, we note that with '$\leq$' and '$=$', we other inequalities can also be expressed. Specifically, we can express $\sum_i^n a_i x_i < k$ as $\sum_i^n a_i x_i \leq k - 1$, $\sum_i^n a_i x_i > k$ as $\neg(\sum_i^n (a_i x_i) \leq k)$, $\sum_i^n a_i x_i \geq k$ as $\sum_i^n (-a_i x_i) \leq (-k)$ and $(\sum_i^n a_i x_i) \neq k$ as $(\sum_i^n a_i x_i \leq (k-1) \vee \neg(\sum_i^n (a_i x_i) \leq k)$.

A popular fragment of linear integer arithmetic is call *Integer Difference Logic* (IDL), where the arithmetic atomic formulae are in the form of $x_i - x_j \bowtie k$, where $\bowtie \in \{=, \leq\}$, $x_i, x_j \in X$ and k is constant.

Example 1. A typical SMT (LIA) formula F: $(p_1 \vee (x_1 + 2x_2 \leq 2)) \wedge (p_2 \vee (3x_3 + 4x_4 + 5x_5 = 2) \vee (-x_2 - x_3 \leq 3))$, where $X = \{x_1, x_2, x_3, x_4, x_5\}$ and $P = \{p_1, p_2\}$ are the sets of integer-valued and propositional variables respectively.

A literal is an atomic formula, or the negation of an atomic formula. A *clause* is the disjunction of a set of literals, and a formula in *conjunctive normal form* (CNF) is the conjunction of a set of clauses. For an SMT (LIA) formula F, an assignment α is a mapping $X \rightarrow Z$ and $P \rightarrow \{false, true\}$, and $\alpha(x)$ denotes the value of a variable x under α. A *complete assignment* is a mapping which assigns to each variable a value. A literal is a true literal if it evaluates to true under the given assignment, and otherwise it is a false literal. A clause is *satisfied* if it has at least one true literal, and *falsified* if all literals in the clause are false. A complete assignment is a *solution* to an SMT (LIA) formula if it satisfies all the clauses.

When applying local search algorithms to solve a satisfiability problem, the search space consists of all complete assignments, each of which is a candidate solution. Typically, a local search algorithm starts from a complete assignment, and iteratively modifies the assignment by changing the value of one variable, to search for a satisfying assignment.

In local search, an *operator* defines how to modify the candidate solution. When an operator is instantiated by specifying the variable to operate, we obtain an *operation*. For example, a standard operator for SAT is *flip*, which modifies the current assignment by changing the value of a Boolean variable, and $flip(x_1)$ is an operation, where x_1 is a Boolean variable in the formula.

Given a formula F, the *cost* of an assignment α, denoted as $cost(\alpha)$, is the number of falsified clauses under α. In dynamic local search algorithms which use clause weighting techniques, however, $cost(\alpha)$ denotes the total weight of all falsified clauses under an assignment α. Given a formula and an assignment α, an operation op is said *decreasing* if $cost(\alpha') < cost(\alpha)$, where α' is the resulting assignment by applying op to α.

Algorithm 1: Local Search of Mode X

```
/* X can be Integer or Boolean                                          */
```
1 **while** $non\_impr\_steps \leq L \times P_X$ **do**
2   **if** α *satisfies* F **then** return α **if** $\exists$ *decreasing* X *operations* **then**
3          $op :=$ a decreasing X operation
4   **if** *fail to find decreasing* X *operation* **then**
5   update clause weights;
6          $op :=$ an X operation from a random falsified clause containing X literals;
7   perform op to modify α;

---

3   A Local Search Framework for SMT (LIA)

In this section, we introduce a local search framework for SMT (LIA), which switches between integer operations and Boolean operations.

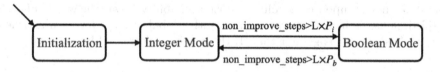

Fig. 1. An SMT Local Search Framework

In the beginning, the algorithm generates a complete assignment α. Then, it iteratively modifies α by performing operations on variables. The algorithm terminates once α becomes a solution to the formula, and outputs "SATISFIABLE" as well as the solution. If the algorithm fails to find a solution within the pre-set time limit, it is cut off and outputs "UNKNOWN".

As depicted in Fig. 1, after the initialization, the algorithm works in two modes, namely Integer mode and Boolean mode. In each mode X (X is Integer or Boolean), an X operation is picked to modify α, where an X operation refers to an operation that works on a variable of data type X. The two modes switches to each other when the number of non-improving steps (denoted as $non\_improve\_steps$) of the current mode reaches a threshold. The threshold is set to $L \times P_b$ for the Boolean mode and $L \times P_i$ for the Integer mode, where P_b and P_i denote the proportion of Boolean and integer literals to all literals in falsified clauses, and L is a parameter. Note that $non\_improve\_steps$ is set to 0 whenever entering a mode, and then in each following step, it increases by one if $cost(\alpha) \geq cost^*$ in the current step, where $cost^*$ is the cost of the best assignment visited before.

The intuitions of the two mode framework are as follows. When all variables of one type (either Boolean or integer) are fixed, the formula is reduced to a subformula that contains only variables of the other type. Thus, by consecutively performing X (X can be Boolean or Integer) operations in a certain period, the algorithm focuses on dealing with a subformula consisting of only X variables. The switching threshold is set as $L \times P_X$, as we consider that when X literals accounts for larger proportion of all literals in falsified clauses, more steps should be allocated for the corresponding mode.

Local Search in One Mode

No matter the mode in which the algorithm works, it adopts a general procedure as described in Algorithm 1. It prefers to pick a decreasing operation (according to some heuristic) if any. If the algorithm fails to find any decreasing operation, it updates clause weights by increasing the weights of falsified clauses, and then picks an X operation from a random falsified clause containing X literals. Note that we can always pick a falsified clause with X literals (line 7). This is because when the algorithm works in X mode, since $non\_impr\_steps \leq L \times P_X$, we have $P_X > 0$, and so there exists at least one falsified clause with X literals.

As for clause weighting, our algorithm employs the probabilistic version of the PAWS scheme [13,46]. When the clause weighting scheme is activated, the clause weights are updated as follows. With probability $1 - sp$, the weight of each falsified clause is increased by one, and with probability sp, for each satisfied clause whose weight is greater than 1, the weight is decreased by one.

4   The Critical Move Operator and a Two-Level Heuristic

In this section, we introduce key techniques in the Integer mode. We propose a novel operator called critical move, and also a two-level heuristic for choosing a critical move in the Integer mode.

A key and basic component of a local search algorithm is the operator. For handling Boolean variables, our algorithm adopts the typical local search operator for SAT, namely *flip*, which modifies the value of a Boolean variable to the opposite of its current value (from True to False, or from False to True). For handling integer variables, we propose a novel operator called *critical move* which works on the literal level.

4.1   Critical Move

Different from the Boolean operator, an integer operator has two parameters – besides the variable to operate, it also needs to consider the increment (may be positive or negative) on the value.

Let us first consider a simple operator, which motivates us to propose a literal-level operator. A simple integer operator is to modify the value of a variable a by a fixed increment inc, that is, $\alpha(a) := \alpha(a) \pm inc$. The parameter inc needs fine tuning. If inc is too small, it may take many iterations before making any falsified literal become true. If inc is too big, the algorithm may even become problematic that it can never make some literals true and thus essentially unable to solve some formulae.

Example 2. Given a formula $F : (b - a \geq 3) \wedge (b - a \leq 5)$ and the current assignment is $\alpha = \{a = 0, b = 0\}$. If $inc = 1$, it needs at least 3 operations to satisfy the formula. If $inc = 10$, then the formula cannot be satisfied using operations of this type, as the value of $b - a$ would be always a multiple of 10.

In fact, in order to avoid the case that some literals can never become true (when the inc is too big), the only acceptable value of inc is 1. The main reason accounting for such a drawback is that the above operator ignores the literal-level information. We propose a literal-level operator for integer variables called *critical move*, which is defined below.

Definition 2. *The critical move operator, denoted as $cm(x, \ell)$, assigns an integer variable x to the threshold value making literal ℓ true, where ℓ is a falsified literal containing x. Specifically, for each of the four basic forms of the falsified literal ℓ, let $\Delta = \sum_i a_i x_i - k$, an operation is described below:*

- $\ell : \sum_i a_i x_i \leq k$. *there exists a cm operation $cm(x_i, \ell)$ for each variable x_i: if the coefficient $a_i > 0$, then $cm(x_i, \ell_1)$ decreases $\alpha(x_i)$ by $\left\lceil \left| \frac{\Delta}{a_i} \right| \right\rceil$; if $a_i < 0$, then $cm(x_i, \ell_1)$ increases $\alpha(x_i)$ by $\left\lceil \left| \frac{\Delta}{a_i} \right| \right\rceil$.*
- $\ell : \neg(\sum_i a_i x_i \leq k)$, *that is, $\sum_i a_i x_i > k$. there exists a cm operation $cm(x_i, \ell)$ for each variable x_i: if the coefficient $a_i > 0$, then $cm(x_i, \ell_1)$ increases $\alpha(x_i)$ by $\left\lceil \left| \frac{1-\Delta}{a_i} \right| \right\rceil$; if $a_i < 0$, then $cm(x_i, \ell_1)$ decreases $\alpha(x_i)$ by $\left\lceil \left| \frac{1-\Delta}{a_i} \right| \right\rceil$.*
- $\ell : \sum_i a_i x_i = k$. *There exists an operation $cm(x_i, \ell)$ for each variable x_i with $a_i \mid \Delta$, which increases $\alpha(x_i)$ by $-\frac{\Delta}{a_i}$.*
- $\ell : \neg(\sum_i a_i x_i = k)$. *There exist 2 cm operations for each variable x_i, to +1 or -1 on x_i.*

Given the above definition of the critical move, an issue with this operator is that it may stall on equalities, when there is no such variable with $a_i \mid \Delta$ in ℓ. To address this issue, in this situation, we additionally employ a simple strategy— pick a random variable in that literal and performs +1 or −1 to decrease $|\Delta|$.

Example 3. Assume we are given two falsified literals $l_1 : (2b - a \leq -3)$ and $l_2 : (5c - d + 3a = 5)$, and the current assignment is $\alpha = \{a = 0, b = 0, c = 0, d = 0\}$. Then $cm(a, l_1)$, $cm(b, l_1)$, $cm(c, l_2)$, and $cm(d, l_2)$ refers to assigning a to 3, assigning b to −2, assigning c to 1 and assigning d to −5 respectively. Note that there does not exist $cm(a, l_2)$, since $3 \nmid -5$.

An important property of the cm operator is that after the execution of a cm operation, the corresponding literal must be true. Therefore, by picking a falsified literal and performing a cm operation on it, we can make the literal become true.

The critical move operations are analogous to update operations in other linear arithmetic model searching procedures. For example, Simplex for DPLL(T)

[20] also progresses through a sequence of candidate assignments by updating the assignment to a variable to satisfy its bound. The significant distinction of critical moves is only updating input variables and always updating by an integral amount, as we can see from Definition 2.

4.2   A Two-Level Heuristic

In this subsection, we propose a two-level heuristic for selecting a decreasing cm operation. We distinguish a special type of decreasing cm operations from others, and give a priority to such operations.

From the viewpoint of algorithm design, there is a major difference between cm and $flip$ operations. A $flip$ operation is decreasing only if the flipping variable appears in at least one falsified clause. For a $cm(x, \ell)$ operation to be decreasing, the literal ℓ does not necessarily appear in any falsified clause. This is because integer variables are multi-valued, and a $cm(x, \ell)$ operation that modifies the value of x would have impact on other literals with the same variable x.

Example 4. Given a formula $F = c_1 \wedge c_2 = (a - b \leq 0 \vee b - e \leq -2) \wedge (b - d \leq -1)$, suppose the current assignment is $\alpha = \{a = 0, b = 0, d = 0, e = 0\}$, then c_1 is satisfied and c_2 is falsified. The operation $op1 = cm(b, b - e \leq -2)$ refers to assigning b to -2, and $op2 = cm(b, b - d \leq -1)$ refers to assigning b to -1. The literal of $op1$ does not appear in any falsified clause while the literal of $op2$ appears in a falsified clause c_2. Both operations are decreasing, as either of them would make clause c_2 become satisfied without breaking any satisfied clause.

In order to find a decreasing cm operation whenever one exists, we need to scan all cm operations on false literals. That is, the candidate set of decreasing operations is $D = \{cm(x, \ell) | \ell$ is a false literal and x appears in $\ell\}$. If $D = \emptyset$, there is no decreasing cm operation. We propose to distinguish a special subset $S \subseteq D$ from the rest of D, which is $S = \{cm(x, \ell) | \ell$ appears in at least one falsified clause and x appears in $\ell\}$. Note that any cm operation in S would make at least one falsified clause become satisfied. Based on this distinction, we propose a two-level selection heuristic as follows:

- The heuristic prefers to search for a decreasing cm operation from S.
- If it fails to find any decreasing operation from S, then it searches for a decreasing cm operation from $D \backslash S$.

Besides improving the efficiency of picking a decreasing cm operation, there is an important intuition underlying this two-level heuristic. We prefer to pick a decreasing cm operation from S, because such operations are conflict driven, as any $cm \in S$ would force a falsified clause become satisfied. This idea can be seen as a LIA version of focused local search for SAT, which has been the core idea of WalkSAT-family SAT solvers [1, 4, 42].

5   Scoring Functions

Local search algorithms employ scoring functions to guide the search. We introduce two scoring functions, which are used to compare different operations and guide the local search algorithm to pick an operation to execute in each step.

A perhaps most commonly used scoring function for SAT, denoted as *score*, measures the change on the cost of the assignment by flipping a variable. This scoring function indeed can be used to evaluate all types of operations as it only concerns the clauses state (satisfied or falsified). We also employ *score* in our algorithm, for both *flip* and *cm* operations. Formally, the *score* of an operation is defined as

$$score(op) = cost(\alpha) - cost(\alpha'),$$

where α' is obtained from α by applying op. Note that, our algorithm employs a clause weighting scheme which associates a positive integer weight to each clause, and thus the *cost* of an assignment is the total weight of falsified clauses. It is easy to see that an operation op is *decreasing* if and only if $score(op) > 0$. Our algorithm prefers to choose the operation with greater *score* in the greedy mode, for both Boolean and integer operations.

For integer operations, we propose a more fine-grained scoring function, measuring the potential benefit about pushing a falsified literal towards the direction of becoming true. Firstly, we propose a property for literals to measure this merit.

Definition 3. *Given an assignment α, for an arithmetic literal $\ell : \sum_i a_i x_i \leq k$, its distance to truth is $dtt(\ell, \alpha) = max\{\sum_i a_i \alpha(x_i) - k, 0\}$. For a Boolean literal ℓ and an arithmetic literal $\ell : \sum_i a_i x_i = k$, $dtt(\ell, \alpha) = 0$ if ℓ is true under α and $dtt(\ell, \alpha) = 1$ otherwise.*

Suppose the current assignment is α, for an arithmetic literal $\ell : \sum_i a_i x_i \leq k$, if $\sum_i a_i \alpha(x_i) > k$, then the literal is falsified, and its dtt is defined to be $\sum_i a_i \alpha(x_i) - k$. In this case, if we decrease the value of x_i with $a_i > 0$, or increase the value of x_i with $a_i < 0$, the dtt of ℓ would decrease. When $\sum_i a_i \alpha(x_i) \leq k$, the literal ℓ is true, and thus its dtt is defined to be 0.

The definition of dtt for arithmetic literals somehow resembles the violation function for constraint satisfaction problems [27], and the violation operator in the simplex with sum of infeasibilities for SMT [32]. In this work, we extend it to the clause level to measure the distance of a clause away from satisfaction in a fine-grained manner. Based on the concept of *distance to truth* of literals, we define a function to measure the distance of a clause away from satisfaction.

Definition 4. *Given an assignment α, the distance to satisfaction of a clause c is $dts(c, \alpha) = min_{\ell \in c}\{dtt(\ell, \alpha)\}$.*

According to the definition, the dts is 0 for satisfied clause, since there is at least one satisfied literal with $dtt = 0$, while dts is positive for falsified clauses. It is desirable to lead the algorithm to decrease the dts of clauses. To this end, we propose a scoring function to measure the benefit of decreasing the sum of dts of all clauses. Additionally, the function takes into account the clause weights as the *score* function.

Definition 5. *Given an LIA formula F, the distance score of an operation op is defined as*

$$dscore(op) = \sum_{c \in F} (dts(c, \alpha) - dts(c, \alpha')) \cdot w(c),$$

where α and α' denotes the assignment before and after performing op.

For Boolean *flip* operations, *dscore* is equal to *score*. For integer operations, however, compared to the *score* function which only concerns the state (satisfied or falsified) transformations of clauses, *dscore* is more fine-grained, as it considers the dts of clauses, which are different among falsified clauses.

Example 5. Given a formula $F = c_1 \wedge c_3 \wedge c_3 = (a - b \leq -1) \wedge (a - c \leq -5 \vee a - d \leq -10) \wedge (b - c \leq -5 \vee b - d \leq -10)$. Suppose $w(c_1) = 1, w(c_2) = 2, w(c_3) = 3$, and the current assignment is $\alpha = \{a = 0, b = 0, c = 0, d = 0\}$, and thus all clauses are falsified. Consider two *cm* operations $op1 = cm(a, a - b \leq -1)$ and $op2 = cm(b, a - b \leq -1)$, which assign $\alpha(a) := -1$ and $\alpha(b) := 1$ respectively, leading to α' and α'' respectively. Then $score(op1) = score(op2) = 1$, as they both make c_1 satisfied. Also, $dts(c_2, \alpha) - dts(c_2, \alpha') = 1$, and $dts(c_3, \alpha) - dts(c_3, \alpha'') = -1$, so $dscore(op1) = (dts(c_1, \alpha) - dts(c_1, \alpha')) \cdot w(c_1) + (dts(c_2, \alpha) - dts(c_2, \alpha')) \cdot w(c_2) = 1 \times 1 + 1 \times 2 = 3$ and $dscore(op2) = -2$ by similar calculation. Therefore, $op1$ is a better operation.

Since the computation of *dscore* has considerable overhead, this function is only used when there is no decreasing operation, as the number of candidate operations is limited here, and it is affordable to calculate their *dscore*.

6   LS-LIA Algorithm

Based on the ideas in previous sections, we develop a local search solver for SMT (LIA) called LS-LIA. As described in Sect. 3, after the initialization, the local search works in either Boolean or Integer mode to iteratively modify α until a given time limit is reached or α satisfies the formula F. This section is dedicated to the details of the initialization and the two modes of local search, as well as other optimization techniques.

Initialization: LS-LIA generates a complete assignment α, by assigning the variables one by one until all variables are assigned. All Boolean variables are assigned with True. As for integer variables x_i, if it has upper bound ub and lower bound lb, that is, there exist unit clauses $x_i \leq ub$ and $x_i \geq lb$, it is assigned with a random value in $[lb, ub]$. If x_i only has upper(lower) bound, x_i is assigned with $ub(lb)$. Otherwise, if the variable is unbounded, it is assigned with 0.

Algorithm 2: Local Search of Boolean Mode

---

1 **while** $non\_impr\_steps \leq L \times P_b$ **do**
2 | **if** α *satisfies* F **then** return α
3 | **if** $\exists$ *decreasing flip operation* **then**
4 | | $op :=$ such an operation with the greatest *score*
5 | **else**
6 | | update clause weights according to the PAWS scheme;
7 | | $c :=$ a random falsified clause with Boolean variables;
8 | | $op :=$ a *flip* operation in c with the greatest *score*;
9 | $\alpha := \alpha$ with op performed;

Algorithm 3: Local Search of Integer Mode

---

1 **while** $non\_impr\_steps \leq L \times P_i$ **do**
2 | **if** α *satisfies* F **then** return α
3 | **if** $\exists$ *decreasing cm operation in falsified clauses* **then**
4 | | $op :=$ such an operation with the greatest *score*
5 | **else if** $\exists$ *decreasing cm operation in satisfied clauses* **then**
6 | | $op :=$ such an operation with greatest *score*
7 | **else**
8 | | update clause weights according to the PAWS scheme;
9 | | $c :=$ a random falsified clause with integer variables;
10 | | $op :=$ a *cm* operation in c with the greatest *dscore*;
11 | $\alpha := \alpha$ with op performed;

Boolean Mode (Algorithm 2): If there exist decreasing *flip* operations, the algorithm selects such an operation with highest *score*.

If the algorithm fails to find any decreasing operation, it first updates clause weights according to the weighting scheme described in Sect. 3. Then, it picks a random falsified clause with Boolean literals and chooses a *flip* operation with greatest *score*.

Integer Mode (Algorithm 3): If there exist decreasing *cm* operations, the algorithm chooses a *cm* operation using the two-level heuristic: it first traverses falsified clauses to find a decreasing *cm* operation with greatest *score* (line 9); if no such operation exists, it searches for a decreasing *cm* operation via BMS heuristic (line 10) [10]. Specifically, it samples t *cm* operations (t is a parameter) from the false literals in satisfied clauses, and selects the decreasing one with greatest *score*.

If the algorithm fails to find any decreasing operation, it first updates clause weights similarly to the Boolean mode. Then, it picks a random falsified clause with Integer literals and chooses a *cm* operation with greatest *dscore*.

Restart Mechanism: The search is restarted when the number of falsified clauses has not decreased for *MaxNoImprove* iterations, where *MaxNoImprove* is a parameter.

Forbidding Strategies. Local search methods tend to be stuck in suboptimal regions. To address the cycle phenomenon (i.e. revisiting some search regions), we employ a popular forbidding strategies, called the tabu strategy [25]. After an operation is executed, the tabu strategy forbids the reverse operations in the following tt iterations, where tt is a parameter usually called *tabu tenure*. The tabu strategy can be directly applied in LS-LIA. (1) If a *flip* operation is performed to flip a Boolean variable, then the variable is forbidden to flip in the following tt iterations. (2) If a *cm* operation that increases (decreases, resp.) the value of an integer variable x is performed, then it is forbidden to decrease (increase, resp.) the value of x in the following tt iterations.

7   Experiments

We carried out experiments to evaluate LS-LIA on 4 benchmarks, and compare it with state-of-the-art SMT solvers. Also, we combine LS-LIA with Z3 to obtain a sequential portfolio solver, which shows further improvement. Additionally, experiments are conducted to analyze the effectiveness of the proposed ideas.

7.1   Experiment Preliminaries

Implementation: LS-LIA is implemented in C++ and compiled by g++ with '−O3' option. There are 5 parameters in LS-LIA: L for switching phases, tt for the tabu scheme, $MaxNoImprove$ for restart, t (the number of samples) for the BMS heuristic and sp (the smoothing probability) for the PAWS scheme. The parameters are tuned according to suggestions from the literature and our preliminary experiments on 20% sampled instances, and are set as follows: $L = 20$, $t = 45$, $tt = 3 + rand(10)$, $MaxNoImprove = 500000$ and $sp = 0.0003$ for all benchmarks.

Competitors: We compare LS-LIA with 4 state-of-the-art SMT solvers according to SMT-COMP 2021,[3] namely MathSAT5 (version 5.6.6), CVC5 (version 0.0.4), Yices2 (version 2.6.2), and Z3 (version 4.8.14), which are the union of the top 3 solvers (excluding portfolio solvers) of QF_LIA and QF_IDL tracks. The binaries of all competitors are downloaded from their websites.

Benchmarks: Our experiments are carried out with 4 benchmarks.

- SMTLIB-LIA: This benchmark consists of SMT (LIA) instances from SMT-LIB.[4] As LS-LIA is an incomplete solver, UNSAT instances are excluded, resulting in a benchmark consisting of 2942 unknown and satisfiable instances.
- SMTLIB-IDL: This benchmark consists of SMT (IDL) instances from SMT-LIB.[5] UNSAT instances are also excluded, resulting in a benchmark consisting of 1377 unknown and satisfiable instances.

---

[3] https://smt-comp.github.io/2021.

[4] https://clc-gitlab.cs.uiowa.edu:2443/SMT-LIB-benchmarks/QF_LIA.

[5] https://clc-gitlab.cs.uiowa.edu:2443/SMT-LIB-benchmarks/QF_IDL.

- JSP: This benchmark consists of 120 instances encoded from job shop scheduling problem resembling [31]. Note that there exists a mistake in the encoding method of original instances from [31], and we fixed it in new instances.
- RVPredict: these instances are generated by a runtime predictive analysis system called RVPredict [29], which formulates data race detection in concurrent software as a constraint problem by encoding the control flow and a minimal set of feasibility constraints as a group of IDL logic formulae. The author of RVPredict kindly provides us with 15 satisfiable instances by running RVPredict on Dacapo benchmark suite [5].

Instances from SMTLIB-LIA and SMTLIB-IDL benchmarks are divided into two categories depending on whether it contains Boolean variables. From the viewpoint of algorithm design, there is a major difference between the operations on Boolean and integer variables. We observe that instances containing only integer variables takes up a large proportion, amount to 81.1% and 44.1%, in these two benchmarks.

Experiment Setup: All experiments are carried out on a server with Intel Xeon Platinum 8153 2.00 GHz and 2048G RAM under the system CentOS 7.9.2009. Each solver is executed one run with a cutoff time of 1200 s (as in the SMT-COMP) for each instance in SMTLIB-LIA, SMTLIB-IDL and JSP benchmarks, as they contain sufficient instances. For the RVPredict benchmark (15 instances), the competitors are also executed one run for each instance as they are exact solvers, while LS-LIA is performed 10 runs for each instance. "#inst" denotes the number of instances in each family. We compare the number of instances where an algorithm finds a model ("#solved"), as well as the run time. The bold value in table emphasizes the solver with greatest "#solved". For RVPredict, LS-LIA solves all instances with 100% success rate and we report the median, minimum and maximum run time among the 10 runs for each instance.

We uploaded our solver as well as JSP and RVPredict benchmarks (along with related information) in the anonymous Github repository.[6]

7.2 Results on SMTLIB-LIA and SMTLIB-IDL Benchmarks

Results on SMTLIB-LIA (Table 1 and Fig. 2). We organize the results into two categories: instances Without Boolean variables, and instances With Boolean variables. LS-LIA outperforms its competitors on the Without Boolean category, solving 2294 out of the 2385 instances. We also present the run time comparisons between LS-LIA and each competitor on the Without Boolean category of SMTLIB-LIA benchmark in Fig. 2. As for the With Boolean category,

---

[6] https://anonymous.4open.science/r/sls4lia/.

Table 1. Results on instances from SMTLIB-LIA.

Family	Type	#inst	MathSAT5	CVC5	Yices2	Z3	LS-LIA
Without Boolean	20180326-Bromberger	631	538	425	358	532	**581**
	bofill-scheduling	407	**407**	402	**407**	405	391
	CAV_2009_benchmarks	506	**506**	498	396	**506**	**506**
	check	1	1	1	1	1	1
	convert	280	273	205	186	184	**279**
	dillig	230	**230**	**230**	200	**230**	**230**
	miplib2003	16	10	9	11	8	**13**
	pb2010	41	14	5	21	**33**	28
	prime-cone	19	19	19	19	19	19
	RWS	20	11	13	11	**14**	12
	slacks	231	230	**231**	161	230	**231**
	wisa	3	3	3	3	3	3
	Total	2385	2242	2041	1774	2165	**2294**
With Boolean	2019-cmodelsdiff	144	94	**95**	**95**	**95**	51
	2019-ezsmt	108	**84**	79	81	81	54
	20210219-Dartagnan	47	22	22	**23**	**23**	2
	arctic-matrix	100	43	26	59	47	**77**
	Averest	9	**9**	**9**	**9**	**9**	7
	calypto	**24**	**24**	**24**	**24**	**24**	21
	CIRC	18	**18**	**18**	**18**	**18**	3
	fft	5	3	3	3	3	3
	mathsat	21	**21**	**21**	**21**	**21**	13
	nec-smt	1256	1244	425	**1256**	1242	581
	RTCL	2	2	2	2	2	2
	tropical-matrix	108	55	42	71	52	**98**
	Total	1842	1619	766	**1662**	1617	912

the performance of LS-LIA is overall worse than its competitors, but still comparable. A possible explanation is that as local search SAT solvers, LS-LIA is not good at exploiting the relations among Boolean variables. Nevertheless, LS-LIA has obvious advantage in "tropical-matrix" and "arctic-matrix" instances, which are industrial instances from automated program termination analysis [16], showing its complementary performance compared to CDCL(T) solvers.

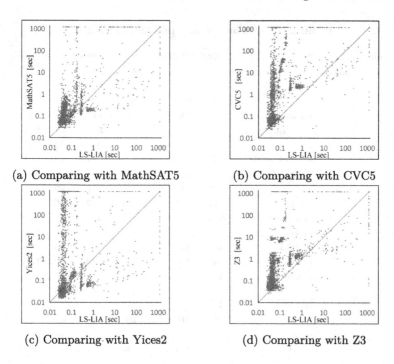

Fig. 2. Run time comparison on Without Boolean category of SMTLIB-LIA

Results on SMTLIB-IDL Benchmark (Table 2 and Fig. 3). Similar to the case for SMTLIB-LIA, our local search solver shows the best performance on IDL instances Without Boolean variables (solving 597 out of the 707 instances), which can be seen from Table 2 and Fig. 3. However, LS-LIA performs worse than its competitors on those With Boolean variables. Overall, LS-LIA cannot rival its competitors on this benchmark, but works particularly well on the instances without Boolean variables.

Combination with Z3 and Summary on SMTLIB benchmarks (Table 3). To confirm the complementarity of our local search solver with state of the art SMT solvers, we combine LS-LIA with Z3, by running Z3 with a time limit 600 s, and then LS-LIA from scratch with the remaining 600 s if Z3 fails to solve the instance. This wrapped solver can be regarded as a sequential portfolio solver, denoted as "Z3+LS".

We summarize the results of all solvers, including Z3+LS, on SMTLIB-LIA and SMTLIB-IDL benchmarks in Table 3. Among all single-engine solvers, Math-SAT5 solves the most instances of SMTLIB-LIA benchmark, while Z3 solves the most instances of SMTLIB-IDL benchmark. LS-LIA outperforms its competitors on instances Without Boolean variables, indicating that local search is an effective approach for solving SMT (LIA) instances with only integer variables.

Z3+LS solves more instances than any other solver on both benchmarks, confirming that LS-LIA and Z3 have complementary performance and their

Table 2. Results on instance from SMTLIB-IDL.

Family	Type	#inst	MathSAT	CVC5	Yices2	Z3	LS-LIA
Without Boolean	20210312-Bouvier	100	4	**44**	21	42	40
	job_shop	108	39	59	74	73	**77**
	n_queen	97	57	86	**97**	92	97
	toroidal_bench	32	11	10	12	12	**13**
	super_queen	91	57	86	**91**	91	91
	DTP	32	32	32	32	32	32
	schedulingIDL	247	100	125	**247**	247	247
	Total	707	300	442	574	589	**597**
With Boolean	asp	379	147	212	284	**291**	27
	Averest	157	**157**	**157**	**157**	**157**	120
	bcnscheduling	6	3	4	4	4	4
	fuzzy-matrix	15	0	0	0	0	1
	mathsat	16	**16**	**16**	**16**	**16**	11
	parity	136	130	**136**	**136**	**136**	**136**
	planning	2	**2**	**2**	**2**	**2**	0
	qlock	36	**36**	**36**	**36**	**36**	0
	RTCL	4	4	4	4	4	4
	sal	10	**10**	**10**	**10**	10	8
	sep	9	**9**	**9**	**9**	9	8
	Total	770	514	586	658	**665**	319

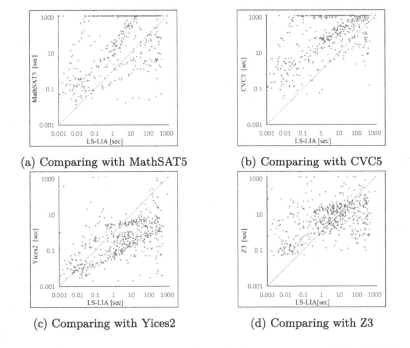

(a) Comparing with MathSAT5

(b) Comparing with CVC5

(c) Comparing with Yices2

(d) Comparing with Z3

Fig. 3. Run time comparison on Without Boolean category of SMTLIB-IDL

Table 3. Summary results on SMTLIB-LIA and SMTLIB-IDL. Instances without and with Boolean variables are denoted by "no_bool" and "with_bool" respectively.

	#inst	MathSAT5	CVC5	Yices2	Z3	LS-LIA	Z3+LS
LIA_no_bool	2385	2242	2041	1774	2165	**2294**	2316
LIA_with_bool	1842	1619	766	**1662**	1617	912	1625
Total	4227	**3861**	2807	3436	3782	3206	3941
IDL_no_bool	707	300	442	574	589	**597**	597
IDL_with_bool	770	514	586	658	**665**	319	661
Total	1477	814	1028	1232	**1254**	916	1258

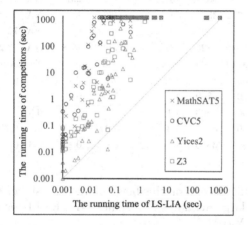

Fig. 4. Run time comparison on job shop scheduling instances.

combination pushes the state of the art in solving satisfiable instances of SMT (LIA). We also combined LS-LIA with Yices in the same manner, resulting in a wrapped solver called YicesLS [11], which won the Single-Query and Model-Validation Track on QF_IDL in SMT-COMP 2021.

7.3   Results on Job Shop Scheduling Benchmark

LS-LIA significantly outperforms the competitors on the JSP benchmark. LS-LIA solves 74 instances, while MathSAT5, CVC5, Yices2, Z3 can only solve 27, 29, 49, 44 instances respectively. The run time comparison on the JSP benchmark are presented in Fig. 4, where the instances that both the competitors and LS-LIA cannot solve are excluded. LS-LIA shows dominating advantage over it competitors on these JSP instances.

7.4   Results on RVPredict Benchmark

Table 4 presents the results on satisfiable instances generated by running RVPredict [29] on Dacapo benchmark suite [5]. LS-LIA solves all the instances

Table 4. The results on RVPredict instances, "#var" and "#clause" denotes the number of variables and clauses respectively. If a solver finds an satisfying assignment, the run time to find the assignment is reported, otherwise 'NA' is reported. For LS-LIA, we report the median (minimum, maximum) run time.

	#var	clause	MathSAT5	CVC5	Yices2	Z3	LS-LIA
RVPredict_1	19782	38262	344.8	410.2	6.3	NA	67.6(56.7,139.4)
RVPredict_2	19782	38262	427.0	429.7	3.3	NA	77.3 (54.2, 107.2)
RVPredict_3	19782	38258	329.5	378.2	9.9	NA	57.8 (56.5, 116.7)
RVPredict_4	19782	38263	333.3	403.5	3.9	NA	80.7 (58.1, 130.5)
RVPredict_5	19782	38262	346.3	412.7	5.8	NA	78.2 (52.3, 124.4)
RVPredict_6	19782	38258	457.2	332.7	2.5	NA	61.1 (43.4, 151.4)
RVPredict_7	19782	38262	541.0	382.7	11.1	NA	68.3 (44.7, 100.6)
RVPredict_8	19782	38259	357.0	405.0	6.9	NA	72.8 (54.5, 131.2)
RVPredict_9	19782	38262	431.3	443.7	12.8	NA	73.2 (41.8, 122.5)
RVPredict_10	19782	38246	460.4	280.7	4.6	NA	56.7 (43.6, 137.3)
RVPredict_11	139	174	0.1	0.1	0.1	0.1	0.1 (0.1, 0.1)
RVPredict_12	460	6309	4.7	5.6	0.1	0.3	1.3 (0.4, 4.5)
RVPredict_13	460	6503	4.1	6.1	0.1	0.3	0.1 (0.1, 0.1)
RVPredict_14	460	6313	4.3	5.8	0.1	0.3	0.7 (0.1, 1.5)
RVPredict_15	460	6313	5.5	5.8	0.1	0.3	0.8 (0.5, 1.7)

consistently, and ranks second on this benchmark, only slower than Yices2. Particularly, on the 10 large instances RVPredict_1-10, LS-LIA is much faster than competitors except Yices2.

7.5 Effectiveness of Proposed Strategies

To analyze the effectiveness of the strategies in LS-LIA, we modify LS-LIA to obtain 5 alternative versions as follows.

- To analyze the effectiveness of the *cm* operator, we modify LS-LIA by replacing the *cm* operator with the operator that directly modifies an integer variable by a fixed increment *inc*, leading to two versions v_fix_1 and v_fix_5, where *inc* is set as 1 and 5 respectively.
- To analyze the effectiveness of the two level heuristic for picking a decreasing *cm* operation, we modify LS-LIA by choosing a decreasing *cm* operation only from falsified clauses or directly from all false literals, leading to two versions, namely v_focused and v_extend.
- To analyze the effectiveness of *dscore*, we modify LS-LIA to choose a *cm* operation with the highest *score* from the selected clause at local optima, leading to the version v_score.

We compare LS-LIA with these modified version on the SMTLIB-LIA and SMTLIB-IDL benchmarks. The runtime distribution of LS-LIA and its modified versions on the two benchmarks are presented in Fig. 5, confirming the effectiveness of the strategies.

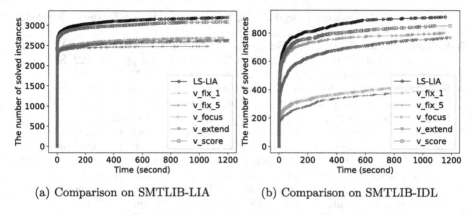

(a) Comparison on SMTLIB-LIA   (b) Comparison on SMTLIB-IDL

Fig. 5. Run time distribution comparison

8   Conclusion and Future Work

We developed the first local search solver for SMT (LIA) and SMT (IDL), open-ing the local search direction for SMT on integer theories. Main features of our solver include a framework switching between Boolean and Integer modes, the critical move operator and a scoring function based on distance to satisfaction. Experiments show that our solver is competitive and complementary to state-of-the-art SMT solvers.

We would like to enhance our solver by improving the performance on instances with Boolean variables. Also, it is interesting to explore deep coop-eration with DPLL(T) solvers.

Acknowledgements. This work is supported by NSFC Grant 62122078. We thank the reviewers of CAV 2022 for comments on improving the quality of the paper.

References

1. Balint, A., Schöning, U.: Choosing probability distributions for stochastic local search and the role of make versus break. In: Cimatti, A., Sebastiani, R. (eds.) SAT 2012. LNCS, vol. 7317, pp. 16–29. Springer, Heidelberg (2012). https://doi.org/10.1007/978-3-642-31612-8_3

2. Barrett, C., Barbosa, H., Brain, M., et al.: Cvc5 at the SMT competition 2021 (2021)

3. Barrett, C., Tinelli, C.: Satisfiability modulo theories. In: Handbook of Model Checking, pp. 305–343. Springer, Cham (2018). https://doi.org/10.1007/978-3-319-10575-8_11

4. Biere, A.: Splatz, Lingeling, Plingeling, Treengeling, YalSAT entering the SAT competition 2016. Proc. SAT Competition **2016**, 44–45 (2016)

5. Blackburn, S.M., Garner, R., Hoffmann, C., et al.: The DaCapo benchmarks: Java benchmarking development and analysis, pp. 169–190 (2006)

6. Bromberger, M.: Decision procedures for linear arithmetic. Ph.D. thesis, Saarland University, Saarbrücken, Germany (2019)
7. Bromberger, M., Fleury, M., Schwarz, S., Weidenbach, C.: SPASS-SATT. In: Fontaine, P. (ed.) CADE 2019. LNCS (LNAI), vol. 11716, pp. 111–122. Springer, Cham (2019). https://doi.org/10.1007/978-3-030-29436-6_7
8. Bromberger, M., Weidenbach, C.: Fast cube tests for LIA constraint solving. In: Olivetti, N., Tiwari, A. (eds.) IJCAR 2016. LNCS (LNAI), vol. 9706, pp. 116–132. Springer, Cham (2016). https://doi.org/10.1007/978-3-319-40229-1_9
9. Bryant, R.E., Lahiri, S.K., Seshia, S.A.: Modeling and verifying systems using a logic of counter arithmetic with lambda expressions and uninterpreted functions. In: Brinksma, E., Larsen, K.G. (eds.) CAV 2002. LNCS, vol. 2404, pp. 78–92. Springer, Heidelberg (2002). https://doi.org/10.1007/3-540-45657-0_7
10. Cai, S.: Balance between complexity and quality: local search for minimum vertex cover in massive graphs. In: Proceedings of IJCAI 2015, pp. 747–753 (2015)
11. Cai, S., Li, B., Zhang, X.: YicesLS on SMT COMP2021 (2021)
12. Cai, S., Luo, C., Su, K.: CCAnr: a configuration checking based local search solver for non-random satisfiability. In: Heule, M., Weaver, S. (eds.) SAT 2015. LNCS, vol. 9340, pp. 1–8. Springer, Cham (2015). https://doi.org/10.1007/978-3-319-24318-4_1
13. Cai, S., Su, K.: Local search for Boolean satisfiability with configuration checking and subscore. Artif. Intell. **204**, 75–98 (2013)
14. Christ, J., Hoenicke, J., Nutz, A.: SMTInterpol: an interpolating SMT solver. In: Donaldson, A., Parker, D. (eds.) SPIN 2012. LNCS, vol. 7385, pp. 248–254. Springer, Heidelberg (2012). https://doi.org/10.1007/978-3-642-31759-0_19
15. Cimatti, A., Griggio, A., Schaafsma, B.J., Sebastiani, R.: The mathSAT5 SMT solver. In: Piterman, N., Smolka, S.A. (eds.) TACAS 2013. LNCS, vol. 7795, pp. 93–107. Springer, Heidelberg (2013). https://doi.org/10.1007/978-3-642-36742-7_7
16. Codish, M., Fekete, Y., Fuhs, C., Giesl, J., Waldmann, J.: Exotic semi-ring constraints. In: SMT@ IJCAR 20, pp. 88–97 (2012)
17. Cotton, S., Podelski, A., Finkbeiner, B.: Satisfiability checking with difference constraints. IMPRS Computer Science, Saarbruceken (2005)
18. de Moura, L., Bjørner, N.: Z3: an efficient SMT solver. In: Ramakrishnan, C.R., Rehof, J. (eds.) TACAS 2008. LNCS, vol. 4963, pp. 337–340. Springer, Heidelberg (2008). https://doi.org/10.1007/978-3-540-78800-3_24
19. Dutertre, B., de Moura, L.: A fast linear-arithmetic solver for DPLL(T). In: Ball, T., Jones, R.B. (eds.) CAV 2006. LNCS, vol. 4144, pp. 81–94. Springer, Heidelberg (2006). https://doi.org/10.1007/11817963_11
20. Dutertre, B., De Moura, L.: Integrating simplex with DPLL (T). Computer Science Laboratory, SRI International, Technical Report SRI-CSL-06-01 (2006)
21. Dutertre, B., De Moura, L.: The YICES SMT solver, vol. 2, no. 2, pp. 1–2 (2006). Tool paper at http://yices.csl.sri.com/tool-paper.pdf
22. Fröhlich, A., Biere, A., Wintersteiger, C., Hamadi, Y.: Stochastic local search for satisfiability modulo theories. In: Proceedings of AAAI 2015, vol. 29 (2015)
23. Ganai, M.K., Talupur, M., Gupta, A.: *SDSAT*: tight integration of *small domain encoding* and *lazy* approaches in a separation logic solver. In: Hermanns, H., Palsberg, J. (eds.) TACAS 2006. LNCS, vol. 3920, pp. 135–150. Springer, Heidelberg (2006). https://doi.org/10.1007/11691372_9
24. Gavrilenko, N., Ponce-de-León, H., Furbach, F., Heljanko, K., Meyer, R.: BMC for weak memory models: relation analysis for compact SMT encodings. In: Dillig, I., Tasiran, S. (eds.) CAV 2019. LNCS, vol. 11561, pp. 355–365. Springer, Cham (2019). https://doi.org/10.1007/978-3-030-25540-4_19

25. Glover, F., Laguna, M.: Tabu search. In: Du, D.Z., Pardalos, P.M. (eds.) Handbook of Combinatorial Optimization. Springer, Boston (1998). https://doi.org/10.1007/978-1-4613-0303-9_33
26. Griggio, A., Phan, Q.-S., Sebastiani, R., Tomasi, S.: Stochastic local search for SMT: combining theory solvers with walkSAT. In: Tinelli, C., Sofronie-Stokkermans, V. (eds.) FroCoS 2011. LNCS (LNAI), vol. 6989, pp. 163–178. Springer, Heidelberg (2011). https://doi.org/10.1007/978-3-642-24364-6_12
27. Hentenryck, P.V., Michel, L.: Constraint-based local search (2009)
28. Hoos, H.H., Stützle, T.: Stochastic local search: foundations and applications (2004)
29. Huang, J., Meredith, P.O., Rosu, G.: Maximal sound predictive race detection with control flow abstraction. In: Proceedings of PLDI 2014, pp. 337–348 (2014)
30. Janhunen, T., Niemelä, I., Sevalnev, M.: Computing stable models via reductions to difference logic. In: Erdem, E., Lin, F., Schaub, T. (eds.) LPNMR 2009. LNCS (LNAI), vol. 5753, pp. 142–154. Springer, Heidelberg (2009). https://doi.org/10.1007/978-3-642-04238-6_14
31. Kim, H., Jin, H., Somenzi, F.: Disequality management in integer difference logic via finite instantiations. JSAT 3(1–2), 47–66 (2007)
32. King, T., Barrett, C., Dutertre, B.: Simplex with sum of infeasibilities for SMT. In: Proceedings of FMCAD 2013, pp. 189–196 (2013)
33. Li, C.M., Li, Y.: Satisfying versus falsifying in local search for satisfiability. In: Cimatti, A., Sebastiani, R. (eds.) SAT 2012. LNCS, vol. 7317, pp. 477–478. Springer, Heidelberg (2012). https://doi.org/10.1007/978-3-642-31612-8_43
34. Lopes, N.P., Monteiro, J.: Automatic equivalence checking of programs with uninterpreted functions and integer arithmetic. Int. J. Softw. Tools Technol. Transfer 18(4), 359–374 (2015). https://doi.org/10.1007/s10009-015-0366-1
35. McCarthy, J.: Towards a mathematical science of computation. In: Colburn, T.R., Fetzer, J.H., Rankin, T.L. (eds) Program Verification. Studies in Cognitive Systems, vol 14. Springer, Dordrecht. https://doi.org/10.1007/978-94-011-1793-7_2
36. Niemetz, A., Preiner, M., Biere, A.: Precise and complete propagation based local search for satisfiability modulo theories. In: Chaudhuri, S., Farzan, A. (eds.) CAV 2016. LNCS, vol. 9779, pp. 199–217. Springer, Cham (2016). https://doi.org/10.1007/978-3-319-41528-4_11
37. Nieuwenhuis, R., Oliveras, A.: DPLL(T) with exhaustive theory propagation and its application to difference logic. In: Etessami, K., Rajamani, S.K. (eds.) CAV 2005. LNCS, vol. 3576, pp. 321–334. Springer, Heidelberg (2005). https://doi.org/10.1007/11513988_33
38. Nieuwenhuis, R., Oliveras, A., Tinelli, C.: Solving SAT and SAT modulo theories: from an abstract Davis-Putnam-Logemann-Loveland procedure to DPLL(T). J. ACM 53(6), 937–977 (2006)
39. Pnueli, A., Rodeh, Y., Strichman, O., Siegel, M.: The small model property: how small can it be? Inf. Comput. 178(1), 279–293 (2002)
40. Roselli, S.F., Bengtsson, K., Åkesson, K.: SMT solvers for job-shop scheduling problems: models comparison and performance evaluation. In: Proceedings of CASE 2018, pp. 547–552 (2018)
41. Sebastiani, R.: Lazy satisfiability modulo theories. JSAT 3(3–4), 141–224 (2007)
42. Selman, B., Kautz, H.A., Cohen, B., et al.: Local search strategies for satisfiability testing. In: Cliques, Coloring, and Satisfiability, vol. 26, pp. 521–532 (1993)
43. Seshia, S.A., Lahiri, S.K., Bryant, R.E.: A hybrid SAT-based decision procedure for separation logic with uninterpreted functions. In: Proceedings of DAC 2003, pp. 425–430 (2003)

44. Strichman, O., Seshia, S.A., Bryant, R.E.: Deciding separation formulas with SAT. In: Brinksma, E., Larsen, K.G. (eds.) CAV 2002. LNCS, vol. 2404, pp. 209–222. Springer, Heidelberg (2002). https://doi.org/10.1007/3-540-45657-0_16
45. Talupur, M., Sinha, N., Strichman, O., Pnueli, A.: Range allocation for separation logic. In: Alur, R., Peled, D.A. (eds.) CAV 2004. LNCS, vol. 3114, pp. 148–161. Springer, Heidelberg (2004). https://doi.org/10.1007/978-3-540-27813-9_12
46. Thornton, J., Pham, D.N., Bain, S., Ferreira, V., Jr.: Additive versus multiplicative clause weighting for SAT. In: Proceedings of AAAI 2004, pp. 191–196 (2004)
47. Wang, C., Gupta, A., Ganai, M.: Predicate learning and selective theory deduction for a difference logic solver. In: Proceedings of DAC 2006, pp. 235–240 (2006)

Reasoning About Data Trees Using CHCs

Marco Faella[1] and Gennaro Parlato[2(✉)]

[1] University of Naples Federico II, Naples, Italy
m.faella@unina.it
[2] University of Molise, Campobasso, Italy
gennaro.parlato@unimol.it

Abstract. Reasoning about data structures requires powerful logics supporting the combination of structural and data properties. We define a new logic called MSO-D *(Monadic Second-Order logic with Data)* as an extension of standard MSO on trees with predicates of the desired data logic. We also define a new class of *symbolic data tree automata* (SDTAs) to deal with data trees using a simple machine. MSO-D and SDTAs are both Turing-powerful, and their high expressiveness is necessary to deal with interesting data structures. We cope with undecidability by encoding SDTA executions as a system of CHCs *(Constrained Horn Clauses)*, and solving the resulting system using off-the-shelf solvers. We also identify a fragment of MSO-D whose satisfiability can be effectively reduced to the emptiness problem for SDTAs. This fragment is very expressive since it allows us to characterize a variety of data trees from the literature, solving certain infinite-state games, etc. We implement this reduction in a prototype tool that combines an MSO decision procedure over trees (MONA) with a CHC engine (Z3), and use this tool to conduct several experiments, demonstrating the effectiveness of our approach across different problem domains.

1 Introduction

Reasoning about linear or tree-like data structures requires very expressive logics that allow combining structural and data properties. Logical characterizations of common data structures often impose restrictions on the structural part, which are intertwined with constraints on the data part. For example, in a *binary search tree* (BST) the data values are organized in the form of a binary tree, where the numerical value associated with each node is greater than or equal to all the values stored in its left sub-tree and smaller than all those in its right sub-tree. Logical characterisations of data structures may also require the calculation of measures concerning parts of the structure such as size or height. Think of *red-black trees* (RBT), a type of BST with additional constraints, such as "every path from a given node to any of its descendant leaves goes through the same number

This work was partially supported by INDAM-GNCS 2020-2021, and by AWS 2021 Amazon Research Awards.

The authors dedicate this paper to their advisor Margherita Napoli.

S. Shoham and Y. Vizel (Eds.): CAV 2022, LNCS 13372, pp. 249–271, 2022.
https://doi.org/10.1007/978-3-031-13188-2_13

of black nodes". Similarly, for AVL trees we need to impose that the heights of the sub-trees rooted in the children of any node differ by a maximum of one.

As a first contribution, we define a new logic called MSO-D *(Monadic Second-Order logic with Data)* as an extension of standard MSO on binary trees with data constraints. The MSO component of the logic allows us to express structural properties, while the data constraint component allows us to impose properties on the data associated with the nodes. Constraints on data are expressed by predicates from a desired data logic that is completely agnostic to the underlying tree structure. We connect the two components by means of uninterpreted functions that map each node of the tree to a data item. An example of an MSO-D formula that defines BSTs is:

$$\forall x . \forall y . \Big(\big(path_l(x,y) \rightarrow val(x) \geq val(y)\big) \wedge \big(path_r(x,y) \rightarrow val(x) < val(y)\big) \Big), \quad (1)$$

where x and y are first-order variables ranging over the set of nodes, $path_l(x,y)$ (resp., $path_r(x,y)$) is an MSO formula expressing that "y is in the left (resp., right) sub-tree of x", and val is an uninterpreted function that maps each node of the tree to an integer.

As a second contribution, we define a new class of *symbolic data tree automata* (SDTAs) to recognize languages of data trees using a simple machine. Such automata perform a bottom-up computation starting from the leaves of the data tree. The state of an SDTA is represented by the value of a set of *state variables*, whereas the data trees recognized by the automaton carry another set of *alphabet variables*. The transitions of an SDTA are expressed by joint constraints over state and alphabet variables. For example, BSTs attach to each node a single alphabet variable, say *val*, holding the numerical value of that node. An SDTA recognizing BSTs will use additional state variables to check that the data tree is indeed a BST. In this case, two state variables are sufficient to achieve this goal: one holding the minimum and one holding the maximum value stored in the sub-tree rooted in the current node. Similarly, SDTAs can be designed to recognize the classes of RBTs and AVL trees.

We have to deal with undecidable problems when reasoning about data trees using MSO-D or SDTAs, and this is unavoidable if we want to *(a)* handle trees with data from infinite domains, and *(b)* relate data from different nodes. These two features make SDTAs *Turing-powerful* since they can encode executions of two-counter machines. A similar argument holds for the satisfiability problem of MSO-D, since we can write a formula that allows us to relate data in consecutive nodes. By prohibiting the propagation of unbounded information between nodes, the decidability of relevant decision problems can be recovered (see [11,12] for an account on this). However, these features are both essential to deal with data structures such as BSTs, RBTs, AVL trees, Heaps, etc.

A way to cope with undecidability is to encode the executions of an SDTA as a system of CHCs (*Constrained Horn Clauses*) or, equivalently, as a CLP (*Constraint Logic Program*) [26], and solve the system using efficient off-the-shelf tools. Systems of CHCs correspond to a restricted class of first-order logic, and are a versatile formalism for representing and solving a variety of program verification or model checking problems, including those regarding sequential, concurrent, and functional programs. Efficient algorithms have been proposed for solving systems of CHCs, often leveraging or generalizing techniques developed in the context of automatic program verification [2,21,22]. As a result, CHCs are often used as an intermediate representation in a variety of verification and synthesis tools [6,18,20,23,25,27,29,35]. Here, we follow a similar approach to solve the emptiness problem for SDTAs, and this offers several advantages. First, it provides a separation of concerns, allowing users of our framework to focus only on aspects related to the tree data structure at hand, while giving CHC solver developers a clean framework that can be instantiated using various model checking algorithms and specialized decision procedures. Furthermore, by expressing CHCs in the standard SMT-LIB language, one can take advantage of different CHC engines, whose performance keeps improving year-over-year, as witnessed by the *competition on constrained Horn clauses* CHC-COMP [19].

As a third contribution, we show several results linking the MSO-D satisfiability problem to the emptiness of SDTAs, and thus to the problem of solving a CHC system. A fundamental theorem for the class of regular (word or tree) languages states that a language is regular if and only if it is MSO-definable, i.e., definable by a closed formula (i.e., a sentence) of standard MSO [4,5,14,15,39,41]. Here, we show that if we allow MSO-D data predicates to talk only about the data of a single node, the satisfiability problem can be reduced to the emptiness of SDTAs. Furthermore, both decision problems are decidable in this case [11]. Moreover, we identify a larger undecidable syntactical fragment of MSO-D where the above reduction can still be performed. Namely, we give an effective reduction when the MSO-D formula is of the form $\exists \boldsymbol{x} \forall \boldsymbol{y} \,.\, \varphi(\boldsymbol{x}, \boldsymbol{y})$, where φ can contain additional quantifiers and each data constraint in φ is either unary, or accesses the data in a bounded neighborhood of the nodes referred to by $\boldsymbol{x}$ and at most one of the variables of $\boldsymbol{y}$. We show that this fragment is very expressive as it allows us to characterize a variety of tree data structures from the literature, solve certain infinite-state games, and handle many other potential applications.

As a fourth and final contribution, we have implemented the reduction for the syntactic MSO-D fragment described above in a prototype tool that combines an MSO decision procedure over trees (MONA [28]) with a CHC engine (of the SMT solver Z3 [24,36]). Using this tool we have conducted several experiments to demonstrate the effectiveness and the practicality of our approach.

Organization of the Paper. The rest of the paper is organized as follows. Section 2 defines data trees, while Sect. 3 introduces the MSO-D logic. Section 4 deals with the definition of SDTAs, and Sect. 5 shows that the emptiness problem for SDTAs is undecidable in general but can be solved by off-the-shelf CHC engines. Section 6 shows a reduction from the MSO-D satisfiability problem to the emptiness of SDTAs, for the MSO-D fragment $\exists \boldsymbol{x} \forall \boldsymbol{y} \,.\, \varphi(\boldsymbol{x}, \boldsymbol{y})$. Section 7 describes our prototype implementation and summarises our experimental evaluation. Related work and concluding remarks can be found in Sect. 8 and 9, respectively.

2 Data Trees

Here we formally define *data trees*. We deal with trees that are finite in size and labeled with data from possibly infinite domains. We consider only binary trees (i.e., trees of arity 2) to keep notation to a minimum. However, the methods and approaches presented in the paper apply to any class of trees of fixed arity.

We will use $\mathbb{N}$ to denote the set of all natural numbers, $\mathbb{Z}$ to stand for the set of integers, and $\mathbb{B}$ to represent the set $\{0, 1\}$. For a number $n \in \mathbb{N}$, we write $[n]$ to denote the interval $\{1, \dots, n\}$.

Words. An *alphabet* is a finite set of *symbols*. A *word* w over an alphabet Σ is a finite (possibly empty) sequence $w = a_1 a_2 \dots a_n$ where $a_i \in \Sigma$ for $i \in [n]$. We denote with $|w|$ the *length* of the sequence of symbols forming w. The *empty word*, denoted by ϵ, is the word formed by no symbol. We denote the set of all words over Σ by Σ^*. A *language* L over Σ is any subset of Σ^*. A *prefix* (resp. *suffix*) of a word w is either ϵ, or any sequence $a_1 \dots a_j$ (resp., $a_j \dots a_n$), for some $j \in [n]$. Given two words $a = a_1 a_2 \dots a_n$ and $b = b_1 b_2 \dots b_m$, their *concatenation* denoted ab, is the word $a_1 a_2 \dots a_n b_1 b_2 \dots b_m$. Given a word $w \in \Sigma^*$ and a language $L \subseteq \Sigma^*$, we define $Ext(w, L)$ as the language of all words w' such that ww' is a word in L, i.e., $Ext(w, L) = \{w' \mid ww' \in L\}$.

Trees. A *binary tree* T, or simply a *tree*, is a finite and prefix-closed subset of $\{0, 1\}^*$. We call the elements of T *nodes*, and the node identified by ϵ the *root* of T. The *edge relation* is defined implicitly: for $d \in \{0, 1\}$, if v and vd are both nodes of T, then (v, vd) is an *edge* of T. Further, if d is 0 (resp., 1) we say that vd is the *left* (resp., *right*) *child* of v, and v is the *parent* of vd. A *leaf* is a node with no children, while an *internal node* is a node that is not a leaf. The *height* of T is $\max_{t \in T} |t|$. The *sub-tree* of T rooted at a given node $t \in T$ is $Ext(t, T)$. Further, $Ext(t, T)$ is a *left* (resp., *right*) *sub-tree* of t if $t = t'0$ (resp., $t = t'1$), for some $t' \in T$. The k-th *level* of a tree T consists of the sequence of all $t \in T$, with $|t| = k$, sorted in ascending lexicographic order. Further, the k-th *level* of T is filled *left to right* if it is a prefix of the k-th *level* of $\{0, 1\}^*$.

Data Signatures. Data signatures are like structured data types (a.k.a. *records*) in programming languages: a *data signature* $\mathcal{S}$ is a set of pairs $\{id_i : type_i\}_{i=1\dots n}$. Common types of interest include bounded or unbounded integers (denoted by `int` and $\mathbb{Z}$, resp.), floating point rationals and real numbers (`float` and $\mathbb{R}$), the Boolean type $\mathbb{B}$ and the bit vectors of length k. If a signature contains a single field whose type is a finite alphabet Σ, we call that signature an *enumeration*. An *evaluation* ν of a data signature $\mathcal{S}$ is a map that associates each field name id in $\mathcal{S}$ with a value of the corresponding type, denoted by $\nu.id$. We denote by $L(\mathcal{S})$ the set of all evaluations of $\mathcal{S}$, also called the *language* of $\mathcal{S}$.

Data Trees. A *data tree* with data signature $\mathcal{S}$, or an *$\mathcal{S}$-tree*, is a pair (T, λ) where T is a tree and λ is a labelling function that maps each node $t \in T$ into an evaluation of $\mathcal{S}$, i.e., $\lambda(t) \in L(\mathcal{S})$. Another way of looking at data trees is to think of them as a traditional tree data structure where the data $\lambda(t)$ associated with each node t is structured. Thus, to simplify the notation when λ is clear from the context, we adopt a C-like notation to refer to the value of fields associated with tree nodes: if t is a tree node and id is a field of $\mathcal{S}$, we write $t.id$ as a shorthand for $\lambda(t).id$. If the data signature is an enumeration, we recover the traditional notion of Σ-labelled tree.

Many data structures from the literature can be seen as data trees. Below we give a high-level description of well-known data structures [9]. In addition to using them for motivating purposes, we will also use them as running examples.

Example 1 (Binary Search Trees). A BST is a binary tree where each node stores a key taken from a totally ordered set, with the property that the key stored in each internal node is greater than or equal to all the keys stored in the node's left subtree, and smaller than those in its right subtree. Thus, an appropriate signature for data trees representing BSTs is $\{val : \mathbb{Z}\}$. □

Example 2 (Red-black Trees). An RBT is a binary tree where each internal node stores a numerical value, satisfying the binary search tree property. The leaves do not contain keys or data and they represent a NIL pointer. Each node has a color (red or black), and the following properties hold: *(i)* every leaf is black, *(ii)* if a node is red then both its children are black, and *(iii)* every path from a given node to a descendent leaf contains the same number of black nodes.

Note that while the color is a piece of information stored in the node, the *black height* can instead be computed on demand. Thus, the signature for data trees representing RBTs may be $\{val : \mathbb{Z}, is\_black : \mathbb{B}\}$. □

Example 3 (Max-Heap). A MAX-HEAP is a binary tree where each node stores a key taken from a totally ordered set, say $\mathbb{Z}$, and can be described as an $\mathcal{S}$-tree (T, λ) where $\mathcal{S}$ is a data signature consisting of a single integer field, say $\{key : \mathbb{Z}\}$, that obeys the following two constraints: (i) (*shape property*) T is almost complete, i.e., all its levels are complete, except the last one, that is filled from left to right; and (ii) (*heap property*) the value stored in each node is greater than or equal to the values stored in the node's children.

3 Monadic Second-Order Logic with Data

In this section, we introduce our MSO-D logic to express properties of data trees. We define MSO-D by extending the standard Monadic Second-Order logic on (enumeration) trees (a.k.a. MSO) with constraints on the Data.

Data constraints are formulas in first-order logic (FOL) with equality (here we use standard FOL syntax and semantics [34]). However, since data trees may involve different data types, we will consider formulas with many-sorted signatures as opposed to the classical unsorted version. Specifically, we deal with formulas of a many-sorted first-order theory $\mathcal{D}$ with sorts $data_1, \ldots, data_n$. For each $data_i$, we allow a theory $\mathcal{D}_{data_i}$ whose function symbols have type $data_i^n \to data_i$ and whose relation symbols have type $data_i^m \to \mathbb{B}$, for some n and m. For example, each of these theories can be the theory of *arithmetic, reals, arrays*, etc. From now on, we may refer to $\mathcal{D}$ as the *data theory* of MSO-D.

We also introduce a finite set of *connecting function symbols*, denoted $\mathcal{F}$, which we use to extend the Mso component of our logic with data. Let *nodes* be the sort of the Mso component. Then, each $f \in \mathcal{F}$ is an uninterpreted function symbol with type *nodes* $\rightarrow$ *data$_i$*, for some $i \in [n]$. These functions allow us to model fields that we associate with each node in the tree. In particular, we say that $f \in \mathcal{F}$ models a field of an $\mathcal{S}$-tree if f is also the name of a field in $\mathcal{S}$. Otherwise, f may serve the purpose of endowing tree nodes with extra data fields without these being present in the labels of the data tree. This is a very useful feature for characterizing tree data structures, e.g., we can use $bh \in \mathcal{F}$ to logically characterize the *black height* of nodes in RBTs, even if that information is not part of the data signature of RBTs.

We are now ready to formally define the syntax of Mso-D over $\mathcal{S}$-trees with data theory $\mathcal{D}$ and connecting functions $\mathcal{F}$. We fix countable sets of propositional variables (denoted by p), first-order node variables (denoted by x, y, etc.), and node-set variables (denoted by X, Y, etc.). We assume that $\mathcal{D}$ includes relation symbols $\mathcal{D}^{\text{rel}}$. We also assume that the symbols in $\mathcal{D}$, the variable names, and the symbols in $\mathcal{F}$ do not overlap. Since $\mathcal{D}$ is imported in Mso-D unchanged we do not report its definition here. The remaining components of the syntax of Mso-D$(\mathcal{D}, \mathcal{F}, \mathcal{S})$ are defined by the following grammar:

$$\text{Node terms: } t \stackrel{\text{def}}{=} x \mid t.left \mid t.right$$

$$\text{Formulas: } \varphi \stackrel{\text{def}}{=} p \mid t_1 = t_2 \mid t \in X \mid \exists x \,.\, \varphi \mid \exists X \,.\, \varphi \mid \neg\varphi \mid \varphi \wedge \varphi$$

$$\mid r(f_1(t_1), \ldots, f_k(t_k)) \qquad r \in \mathcal{D}^{\text{rel}}, f_1, \ldots, f_k \in \mathcal{F}$$

where r and $f_1, \ldots, f_k$ are well-typed, i.e., there is an index i such that the type of r is *data$_i^k$*, and for every $j \in [k]$, f_j has type *nodes* $\rightarrow$ *data$_i$*. We denote the set of all variables occurring in φ by $Var(\varphi)$.

An *interpretation* of a formula φ is a pair $(T^\lambda, \mathbb{I})$, where T^λ is an $\mathcal{S}$-tree (T, λ), and $\mathbb{I}$ interprets the remaining symbols of the logic. We interpret the $\mathcal{D}$-component of our theory as we would interpret $\mathcal{D}$ in isolation. Assume that $\mathbb{D}$ is the chosen interpretation of $\mathcal{D}$, with underlying universes D_i for sort *data$_i$*. Also, $\mathbb{I}$ maps each function symbol f in $\mathcal{F}$ with type *nodes* $\rightarrow$ *data$_i$* to a concrete function $\mathbb{I}(f) : T \rightarrow D_i$. Moreover, if f is also the name of a field in $\mathcal{S}$, then we require that $\mathbb{I}(f)$ coincides with the value of the field f in each node of the tree, i.e., $\mathbb{I}(f)(v) = \lambda(v).f$, for every $v \in T$. The satisfaction relation depends also on $\mathbb{D}$, but we omit it here because we consider it fixed.

We interpret the variables in $Var(\varphi)$ by mapping each of them into a subset of nodes of T with the following properties: (i) first-order variables are assigned singletons, and (ii) propositional variables are assigned either all nodes (encoding *true*) or no node at all (encoding *false*). For a set of nodes $S \subseteq T$ and a (first- or second-order) variable $\alpha \in Var(\varphi)$, we denote by $\mathbb{I}[S/\alpha]$ the function that maps α to S, and agrees with $\mathbb{I}$ on all the other variables. Node terms are interpreted as follows:

$$\mathbb{I}(t) = \begin{cases} \mathbb{I}(x) & \text{if } t = x \\ \mathbb{I}(s)0 & \text{if } t = s.\mathit{left} \text{ and } \mathbb{I}(s)0 \in T \\ \mathbb{I}(s)1 & \text{if } t = s.\mathit{right} \text{ and } \mathbb{I}(s)1 \in T \\ \mathbb{I}(s) & \text{otherwise.} \end{cases}$$

Notice that the *.left* and *.right* operators *stutter* on leaves, that is, for all leaves v it holds $v = v.\mathit{left} = v.\mathit{right}$.

The *satisfaction relation* $T^\lambda, \mathbb{I} \models \varphi$ is so defined.

$$
\begin{aligned}
&T^\lambda, \mathbb{I} \models p && \text{iff } \mathbb{I}(p) = T \\
&T^\lambda, \mathbb{I} \models t_1 = t_2 && \text{iff } \mathbb{I}(t_1) = \mathbb{I}(t_2) \\
&T^\lambda, \mathbb{I} \models t \in X && \text{iff } \mathbb{I}(t) \subseteq \mathbb{I}(X) \\
&T^\lambda, \mathbb{I} \models r(f_1(t_1), \dots, f_k(t_k)) && \text{iff } \mathbb{D}(r)(\ \mathbb{I}(f_1)(\mathbb{I}(t_1)), \dots, \mathbb{I}(f_k)(\mathbb{I}(t_k))\ ) \\
&T^\lambda, \mathbb{I} \models \neg\varphi && \text{iff } T^\lambda, \mathbb{I} \not\models \varphi \\
&T^\lambda, \mathbb{I} \models \varphi_1 \wedge \varphi_2 && \text{iff } T^\lambda, \mathbb{I} \models \varphi_1 \text{ and } T^\lambda, \mathbb{I} \models \varphi_2 \\
&T^\lambda, \mathbb{I} \models \exists x . \varphi && \text{iff there exists } v \in T \text{ such that } T^\lambda, \mathbb{I}[\{v\}/x] \models \varphi \\
&T^\lambda, \mathbb{I} \models \exists X . \varphi && \text{iff there exists } S \subseteq T \text{ such that } T^\lambda, \mathbb{I}[S/X] \models \varphi
\end{aligned}
$$

We say that T^λ *satisfies* φ, denoted $T^\lambda \models \varphi$, if there is an interpretation $\mathbb{I}$ such that $T^\lambda, \mathbb{I} \models \varphi$. We define the language of trees satisfying an Mso-D sentence in the usual way. An Mso-D *sentence* is a formula with no free variables. We define the set of all $\mathcal{S}$-trees T^λ satisfying an Mso-D$(\mathcal{D}, \mathcal{F}, \mathcal{S})$ sentence φ by $\mathcal{L}(\varphi)$, i.e., the set of all $\mathcal{S}$-trees T^λ such that $T^\lambda \models \varphi$. A language of trees L is Mso-D$(\mathcal{D}, \mathcal{F}, \mathcal{S})$ *definable* if there exists an Mso-D$(\mathcal{D}, \mathcal{F}, \mathcal{S})$ sentence φ such that $L = \mathcal{L}(\varphi)$.

We recover standard Mso when $\mathcal{S}$ is an enumeration and $\mathcal{D}$ includes a unary relation r_a for each $a \in \Sigma$, whose interpretation is $\{a\}$.

Undecidability of the Satisfiability Problem. The *satisfiability problem* for a given Mso-D$(\mathcal{D}, \mathcal{F}, \mathcal{S})$ sentence φ asks whether $\mathcal{L}(\varphi)$ is empty. Let $\mathcal{D}$ be the theory of linear integer arithmetic. It is easy to model an execution of any given 2-counter machine using a unary data tree whose signature has two fields of type $\mathbb{N}$ to model the counters, and an enumeration field to keep track of the current instruction. Each machine configuration is represented by a node, and we can impose constraints in our logic so that two consecutive nodes in the tree model a machine transition. Likewise, we can also express the property of a halting computation in our logic. Thus, the satisfiability of the Mso-D logic is undecidable, even though the underlying data logic $\mathcal{D}$ is decidable. Of course, by choosing a finite domain for the interpretation of the underlying data logic, we regain decidability in that the problem matches that of the standard Mso.

Examples. We now show various examples to illustrate the expressiveness of Mso-D. We will use the usual predefined abbreviations to denote the remaining propositional connectives ($\varphi_1 \vee \varphi_2$ and $\varphi_1 \to \varphi_2$), the universal quantifier ($\forall \alpha . \varphi \overset{\text{def}}{=} \neg \exists \alpha . \neg \varphi$), $x \neq y \overset{\text{def}}{=} \neg(x = y)$, and the conditional expression ($\varphi ? \varphi_1 : \varphi_2) \overset{\text{def}}{=} (\varphi \wedge \varphi_1) \vee (\neg\varphi \wedge \varphi_2)$. Finally, the following standard Mso predicates will come in handy: $child(x, y)$, $root(x)$, $leaf(x)$, and $path(x, y)$.

*Example 4 (*Mso-D *Characterization of* Bst*s).* We define the characteristic property of Bsts on data trees with data signature $\{val : \mathbb{Z}\}$. We first introduce the auxiliary predicate $path_l(x, y)$ (resp., $path_r(x, y)$) with the meaning "y is in the left (resp., right) sub-tree of x". Using these predicates, we define the Mso-D sentence (1) that says that all values in the left sub-tree of a node x contain values that are smaller than the value in x, and similarly for the right sub-tree.

To demonstrate the use of connecting functions to model auxiliary node fields, we give an alternative way to characterize Bsts. We introduce two auxiliary connecting functions: min and max. We impose constraints to ensure that for each node x in the tree $min(x)$ and $max(x)$ are the minimum and maximum values of the sub-tree rooted in x, respectively. It is straightforward to see that we can impose the Bst property by relating the values in each node with min and max in their children as follows:

$$\psi_{\text{bst}} \stackrel{\text{def}}{=} \forall x . \Big(\big(x \neq x.left \ ? \ min(x) = min(x.left) \wedge max(x.left) \leq val(x)$$
$$: \ min(x) = val(x) \big) \wedge$$
$$\big(x \neq x.right? \ max(x) = max(x.right) \wedge min(x.right) > val(x)$$
$$: \ max(x) = val(x) \big) \ \Big). \quad \square$$

*Example 5 (*Mso-D *characterization of* Rbt*s).* We can also express the defining properties of red-black trees as follows:

(a) Every leaf is black: $\forall x . leaf(x) \rightarrow is\_black(x)$.
(b) If a node is red, both its children are black:

$$\forall x . (\neg is\_black(x)) \rightarrow \big(is\_black(x.left) \wedge is\_black(x.right) \big).$$

(c) Every path from a node to a leaf contains the same number of black nodes. We encode this property as the consistency of the black height data field bh:

$$\forall x . \forall y . \Big(\ \big(\ (\ is\_black(x) \wedge child(y, x)) \rightarrow (bh(y) = bh(x) - 1) \ \big)$$
$$\wedge \big((\neg is\_black(x) \wedge child(y, x)) \rightarrow (bh(y) = bh(x)) \ \big)$$
$$\wedge \big((leaf(x) \wedge \ is\_black(x)) \rightarrow bh(x) = 1 \big)$$
$$\wedge \big((leaf(x) \wedge \neg is\_black(x)) \rightarrow bh(x) = 0 \big) \quad \Big).$$
$$\square$$

Extended Models. Since we are going to build automata corresponding to formulas with free variables, it is convenient to encode the variable interpretation in the tree itself, by expanding the data signature with an extra Boolean flag for each free variable. The flag corresponding to a free variable will be set to 1 in the node(s) that belong to the interpretation of that variable. In detail, for a given interpretation $(T^\lambda, \mathbb{I})$, assume that $Var(\varphi) = \{\alpha_1, \ldots, \alpha_n\}$, we can define an *extended tree* (T, λ^E) with data signature $\mathcal{S}^E = \mathcal{S} \cup \{a_1, \ldots, a_n : \mathbb{B}\}$, where $\lambda^E(u)(a_i) = 1$ iff $u \in \mathbb{I}(\alpha_i)$. Conversely, from an extended tree we can extract the corresponding variable interpretation. For such an extended tree we can write $T^{\lambda^E} \models \varphi$ without mentioning $\mathbb{I}$.

4   Symbolic Data-Tree Automata

In this section, we define a new class of tree automata called *Symbolic Data-Tree Automata*. They generalize traditional bottom-up finite tree automata as they work with data trees. Furthermore, they are symbolic because the alphabet and set of states are defined using evaluations of data signatures, and its transition function is defined through constraints[1] involving states and alphabet.

Definition 1 (SYMBOLIC DATA-TREE AUTOMATA). *A symbolic data-tree automaton, or* SDTA *for short,* $\mathcal{A}$ *is a tuple* $(\mathcal{S}^\Sigma, \mathcal{S}^Q, \psi^F, \Psi^\Delta)$ *where:*

- $\mathcal{S}^\Sigma$ *is the* alphabet data signature *defining the tree alphabet* $\Sigma = L(\mathcal{S}^\Sigma)$;
- $\mathcal{S}^Q$ *is the* state data signature *defining the set of states* $Q = L(\mathcal{S}^Q)$;
- ψ^F *is a unary constraint defining the set of final states* $F \subseteq Q$, *i.e., the set consisting of all elements* $q \in Q$ *such that* $\psi^F(q)$ *evaluates to true;*
- Ψ^Δ *is a tuple of four transition constraints:*

$$\psi_{lr}(q_l, q_r, \sigma, q), \quad \psi_l(q_l, \sigma, q), \quad \psi_r(q_r, \sigma, \ q), \quad \psi_{leaf}(\sigma, q),$$

where q_l, q_r, *and* q *are variables of type* $\mathcal{S}^Q$, *and* σ *is of type* $\mathcal{S}^\Sigma$.

$\mathcal{A}$ accepts $\mathcal{S}^\Sigma$*-trees. A tree* (T, λ) *is accepted by* $\mathcal{A}$ *if there is a total function* $\pi : T \to Q$ *such that for every node* $t \in T$ *the following holds:*

- *t has both children, and* $\psi_{lr}(\,\pi(t0),\ \pi(t1),\ \lambda(t),\ \pi(t)\,)$ *holds;*
- *t has only the left child, and* $\psi_l(\,\pi(t0),\ \lambda(t),\ \pi(t)\,)$ *holds;*
- *t has only the right child, and* $\psi_r(\,\pi(t1),\ \lambda(t),\ \pi(t)\,)$ *holds;*
- *t is a leaf, and* $\psi_{leaf}(\,\lambda(t),\ \pi(t)\,)$ *holds;*
- $\psi^F(\,\pi(\epsilon)\,)$ *holds.*

The language of $\mathcal{A}$, *denoted* $L(\mathcal{A})$, *is the class of all* $\mathcal{S}^\Sigma$*-trees accepted by* $\mathcal{A}$. □

We recover standard tree automata when both data signatures $\mathcal{S}^\Sigma$ and $\mathcal{S}^Q$ are enumerations. In that case, we call $\mathcal{A}$ an *enumeration tree automaton* and we denote it as (Σ, Q, F, Δ), where $\Sigma = L(\mathcal{S}^\Sigma)$, $Q = L(\mathcal{S}^Q)$, and so on.

---

[1] We use the term *constraint* to denote a generic predicate $con(x_1, \ldots, x_k)$ in which the type of variable x_i is some data signature $\mathcal{S}_i$. We deliberately leave the definition of the constraints unspecified, and specify them only when it is necessary to do so.

Example 6 (Symbolic Data-Tree Automaton for Max Heap). We define an SDTA $\mathcal{A}_{bmh}$ where $L(\mathcal{A}_{bmh})$ is the set of all max heaps. The state data signature of $\mathcal{A}_{bmh}$ is $\{h : \mathbb{N}, f : \mathbb{B}, val : \mathbb{N}\}$. We use the h field to store the height of the sub-tree rooted in the node, the f field to store whether the sub-tree rooted in the node is complete with the last level completely filled, and val stores the node's data value. The transition data constraints are as follows:

$$\psi_{leaf}(\sigma, q) \overset{\text{def}}{=} q.h = 1 \wedge q.f \wedge q.val = \sigma.val$$

$$\psi_l(q_l, \sigma, q) \overset{\text{def}}{=} q_l.h = 1 \wedge q.h = 2 \wedge \neg q.f \wedge \sigma.val \geq \sigma_l.val \wedge q.val = \sigma.val$$

$$\psi_{lr}(q_l, q_r, \sigma, q) \overset{\text{def}}{=} (q_l.h - 1 \leq q_r.h \leq q_l.h) \wedge \big(q.f \leftrightarrow (q_l.f \wedge q_r.f \wedge q_l.h = q_r.h)\big)$$
$$\wedge \big(\neg q_l.f \rightarrow (q_r.h < q_l.h \wedge q_r.f)\big) \wedge \big(\neg q_r.f \rightarrow (q_r.h = q_l.h \wedge q_l.f)\big)$$
$$\wedge \ \sigma.val \geq q_l.val \wedge \sigma.val \geq q_r.val \wedge q.val = \sigma.val.$$

For each leaf, we set the height field h to 1, the field f to true, and copy the label of the node into the state field val. Note that all sub-trees of a complete tree are still complete trees. Thus, if a node has only the left child, this child must be a leaf, and we set the parent node's fields accordingly. A node with only the right child leads to a violation of the shape property, thus $\psi_r(q_r, \sigma, q) \overset{\text{def}}{=} \textit{false}$. Finally, we consider the case where the node has both children. Here ψ_{lr} constrains the fields of the state data signature to guarantee their invariants. Specifically, the first two lines enforce the shape property while the last line enforces the heap property and copies the value of the label into the state field val. To conclude, we define ψ^F as a tautology. However, if, for example, we wanted to accept only max heaps of height at least 100 we could have defined $\psi^F(q) \overset{\text{def}}{=} (q.h \geq 100)$. □

5   Solving the Emptiness Problem for SDTAs

The *emptiness problem* for SDTAs consists in determining whether the tree language recognized by a given SDTA $\mathcal{A}$ is empty, i.e., whether $L(\mathcal{A})$ is empty. We first prove that the emptiness problem for SDTAs is undecidable, and then show that it can be reduced to the satisfiability of a system of constrained Horn clauses (CHCs), for which increasingly efficient off-the-shelf semi-procedures exist.

It is well known that the emptiness problem for tree automata is decidable [8]. However, as explained for MSO-D in Sect. 3, as soon as the state data signature involves an unbounded data domain (such as integers or reals) and basic arithmetics (e.g., increment and test for zero), the emptiness problem becomes undecidable. Thus, we have the following.

Theorem 1. *The emptiness problem for SDTAs is undecidable.*

We cope with this negative result by providing a reduction to the satisfiability of a system of CHCs, when the transition constraints of the automaton are defined through quantifier-free first-order logic formulas.

Constrained Horn Clauses. We fix a set R of uninterpreted fixed-arity relation symbols, which represent the unknowns in the system. A *Constrained Horn Clause*, or CHC for short, is a formula of the form $H \leftarrow C \wedge B_1 \wedge \cdots \wedge B_n$ where:

- C is a constraint over some background theory that does not contain any application of predicates in R;
- for every $i \in [n]$, B_i is an application $p(v_1, \ldots, v_k)$ of a relation symbol $p \in R$ to first-order variables $v_1, \ldots, v_k$;
- H is the clause *head* and, similarly to B_i, is an application $p(v_1, \ldots, v_k)$ of a relation symbol $p \in R$ to the first-order variables, or *false*;
- the first-order variables appearing in the signature of the predicates and constraints are all implicitly universally quantified.

A finite set $\mathcal{H}$ of CHCs is a *system*, and it corresponds to the first-order formula obtained by putting all its CHCs in conjunction. We assume that the semantics of constraints is given a priori as a structure. A system $\mathcal{H}$ with relation symbols R is *satisfiable* if there is an interpretation to each predicate in R that makes all clauses in $\mathcal{H}$ valid.

It is a well-known result from constraint logic programming that every system of CHCs $\mathcal{H}$ has a unique minimal model that can be computed as the fixed-point of an operator derived by the clauses of $\mathcal{H}$ [16,26]. This property, which allows us to use a fixed-point semantics for CHC systems, to justify the correctness of the reduction defined below (i.e., Theorem 2).

Reduction. We give a linear time reduction from the emptiness problem for SDTAs to the satisfiability of systems of CHCs. Let $\mathcal{A} = (\mathcal{S}^\Sigma, \mathcal{S}^Q, \psi^F, \Psi^\Delta)$ be an SDTA with $\Psi^\Delta = (\psi_{lr}, \psi_l, \psi_r, \psi_{leaf})$, q_l, q_r and q be structured variables of type $\mathcal{S}^Q$, σ be a struc-

$$
\begin{aligned}
h(q) &\leftarrow \psi_{lr}(q_l, q_r, \sigma, q) \wedge h(q_l) \wedge h(q_r) \\
h(q) &\leftarrow \psi_l(q_l, \sigma, q) \wedge h(q_l) \\
h(q) &\leftarrow \psi_r(q_r, \sigma, q) \wedge h(q_r) \\
h(q) &\leftarrow \psi_{leaf}(\sigma, q) \\
false &\leftarrow \psi^F(q) \wedge h(q)
\end{aligned}
$$

tured variable of type $\mathcal{S}^\Sigma$, and $h(q)$ be an uninterpreted predicate. We map $\mathcal{A}$ into the CHC system $\mathcal{H}_\mathcal{A}$ formed by the CHCs shown on the right.

Theorem 2 (EMPTINESS). *Let $\mathcal{A}$ be an SDTA. Then, $L(\mathcal{A})$ is empty if and only if $\mathcal{H}_\mathcal{A}$ is satisfiable.*

6   From Logic to Automata

In this section, we describe a reduction from the satisfiability problem of MSO-D to the emptiness problem of SDTAs, when the MSO-D formula φ is a sentence in the following form:

$$\varphi = \exists x_1, \ldots, x_n . \forall y_1, \ldots, y_m . \theta, \tag{2}$$

where each data constraint of the formula θ, say $r(f_1(t_1), \ldots, f_k(t_k))$, satisfies one of the following:

- r is unary (i.e., $k = 1$), or
- r depends only on variables $x_1, \ldots, x_n$ and at most one of the variables $y_1, \ldots, y_m$, i.e., $Var(t_1, \ldots, t_k) \subseteq \{x_1, \ldots, x_n, y_i\}$, for some $i \in [m]$.

Notice that θ may contain other quantifiers, but the additional quantified variables can occur only inside unary data constraints. Moreover, it is easy to see that this fragment is closed under positive Boolean combinations (i.e., conjunctions and disjunctions).

This fragment strictly includes the MSO logic with data defined in [11] for data words, which only allows unary data constraints. Below we show that the added expressivity can be used to define and verify properties of a variety of data structures, including those from Examples 4 and 5, and infinite-state games.

In our reduction, we first construct a standard finite-state tree automaton over a finite alphabet (Sect. 6.1), which we then convert to an SDTA (Sect. 6.2).

6.1   Building the Enumerated Tree Automaton

The first step in our reduction from MSO-D to SDTAs is to convert the MSO-D formula φ of type (2) into a formula φ' in standard MSO by *abstracting away* all data constraints. We distinguish two types of data constraints. *Global constraints* refer only to the data of the existentially quantified variables x_i; on a given data tree, once the interpretation of those variables is chosen, each global constraint is either *true* or *false*: it is a global property of the tree. *Local constraints*, instead, additionally refer to a variable, say z, that is not one of $\{x_1, \ldots, x_n\}$; even if the interpretation of $\{x_1, \ldots, x_n\}$ is fixed, the truth of such constraints depends on the interpretation of z. Accordingly, we replace each data constraint in θ, say $r(f_1(t_1), \ldots, f_k(t_k))$, as follows:

Global Constraints. If $Var(t_1, \ldots, t_k) \subseteq \{x_1, \ldots, x_n\}$, we replace all occurrences of the data constraint with a new propositional variable p. We denote by $p_1, \ldots, p_h$ all such propositional variables.

Local Constraints. Otherwise, there is a unique variable $z \in Var(t_1, \ldots, t_k)$ that is *not* one of $\{x_1, \ldots, x_n\}$. We then introduce a new free second-order variable C, and replace each occurrence of the above data constraint with the clause $z \in C$. We denote by $C_1, \ldots, C_l$ all the second-order variables introduced in this process.

Besides the above substitutions, in the resulting MSO formula we leave variables $x_1, \ldots, x_n$ free, so that the models of the formula will carry the interpretation of those variables as extra bits in the node labels (recall the discussion on extended models in Sect. 3). We thus obtain the following MSO formula:

$$\varphi' \stackrel{\text{def}}{=} \forall y_1, \ldots, y_m . \theta'. \tag{3}$$

Since φ' has no data constraints, we can take its data signature to be empty.

Example 7. Consider the formula ψ_{bst} from Example 4 that defines BSTs using auxiliary data *min* and *max*. Since it uses a single universal quantifier, it belongs to the syntactic fragment (2). For the sake of simplicity, consider a stronger formula ψ'_{bst} forcing internal nodes to have two children (a.k.a. a *full* BST):

$$\psi'_{bst} \stackrel{\text{def}}{=} \psi_{bst} \wedge \forall y \,.\, full\_tree(y), \quad \text{where}$$

$$full\_tree(y) \stackrel{\text{def}}{=} \big(\neg leaf(y) \rightarrow (y.left \neq y \wedge y.right \neq y)\big).$$

Now, consider the following true property of full BSTs: the successor of an internal node is the left-most leaf in its right sub-tree. The following formula states the opposite of that property:

$$\psi_{succ} \stackrel{\text{def}}{=} \exists x_1, x_2, x_3 \,.\, \Big(\big(val(x_1) < val(x_2) < val(x_3)\big) \wedge$$

$$\neg leaf(x_1) \wedge leaf(x_3) \wedge left\_only\_path(x_1.right, x_3)\Big).$$

It is easy to see that $\psi'_{bst} \wedge \psi_{succ}$ is equivalent to a formula ψ in our fragment:

$$\exists x_1, x_2, x_3 \,.\, \forall y \,.\, \Big(\big(val(x_1) < val(x_2) < val(x_3)\big) \wedge \neg leaf(x_1) \wedge leaf(x_3)$$

$$\wedge\ left\_only\_path(x_1.right, x_3) \wedge full\_tree(y)$$

$$\wedge\ \big(y \neq y.left \,?\, min(y) = min(y.left) \wedge max(y.left) < val(y) \,:\, min(y) = val(y)\big)$$

$$\wedge\ \big(y \neq y.right \,?\, max(y) = max(y.right) \wedge min(y.right) > val(y) \,:\, max(y) = val(y)\big)\Big).$$

The conversion outlined above turns ψ into the following MSO formula:

$$\forall y \,.\, \Big(p_1 \wedge \neg leaf(x_1) \wedge leaf(x_3) \wedge left\_only\_path(x_1.right, x_3) \wedge full\_tree(y)$$

$$\wedge\ \big(y \neq y.left \,?\, y \in C_1 \,:\, y \in C_2\big) \wedge \big(y \neq y.right \,?\, y \in C_3 \,:\, y \in C_4\big)\Big),$$

where proposition p_1 corresponds to the global constraint $val(x_1) < val(x_2) < val(x_3)$, the second-order variable C_1 corresponds to the local constraint $min(y) = min(y.left) \wedge max(y.left) < val(y)$, and variables $C_2 - C_4$ correspond to the other data constraints in ψ_{bst}. □

We now apply the standard MSO construction to φ', leading to a bottom-up finite-state tree automaton $A_{\varphi'}$ on the alphabet $\Sigma = \{0,1\}^{n+h+l}$, accepting all finite trees that represent interpretations satisfying φ'. The alphabet is Σ because $n + h + l$ is the total number of free variables in φ': n first-order variables x_i, h propositional variables p_i (corresponding to global constraints), and l second-order variables C_i (corresponding to local constraints). We recall the formal statement of this construction below, for more details see [40] and [8].

Theorem 3. *For all MSO formulas φ' on the empty data signature, with free first-order variables $x_1, \ldots, x_n$, propositional variables $p_1, \ldots, p_h$, and second-order variables $C_1, \ldots, C_l$, there is a deterministic bottom-up tree automaton on the alphabet $\{0,1\}^{n+h+l}$ whose language consists of all extended trees T such that $T \models \varphi'$.*

Simplifying Assumptions. To simplify the presentation of the following constructions, we make two simplifying assumptions. First, we assume that all terms appearing in data constraints are variables, and not composite terms like *x.left.right*. Dropping this assumption is technically simple and omitted due to space constraints. Second, we assume that all connecting functions f appearing in data constraints correspond to fields in S. Sentences that satisfy the second assumption have a unique interpretation $\mathbb{I}$, because they have no free variables and the connecting functions must be interpreted as the functions extracting the corresponding field from each node. We discuss how to remove this restriction in Sect. 6.3.

We now establish a relation between Σ-trees accepted by $A_{\varphi'}$, and data trees on the data signature S defined by φ. Denote by $(a_1, \ldots, a_n, b_1, \ldots, b_h, c_1, \ldots, c_l)$ the generic element of Σ. Given a Σ-tree (T, σ) and a variable x_i in φ', we define $node(\sigma, x_i)$ to be the unique node $u \in T$ such that the a_i component of $\sigma(u)$ is 1. In words, the function *node* picks the position in the tree where the Σ-tree activates the bit a_i.

Definition 2. *Consider an* MSO-D *sentence φ of the form* (2) *on the data signature S, and let $\mathbb{I}$ be its unique interpretation. We say that a Σ-tree (T, σ) and an S-tree (T, λ) are consistent iff for all nodes $u \in T$ the following hold:*

1. *For all $i \in [h]$, let $r_i^{\text{glb}}\big(f_i^1(\alpha_i^1), \ldots, f_i^{j_i}(\alpha_i^{j_i})\big)$ be the global constraint from φ corresponding to the propositional variable p_i from φ'. Recall that under the simplifying assumptions each α_i^j is one of $x_1, \ldots, x_n$, and each f_i^j is one of the names of the fields of S. Then, $\sigma(u)(b_i) = 1$ iff the following holds*

$$\mathbb{D}(r_i^{\text{glb}})\big(\mathbb{I}(f_i^1)(node(\sigma, \alpha_i^1)), \ldots, \mathbb{I}(f_i^{j_i})(node(\sigma, \alpha_i^{j_i})) \big).$$

2. *For all $i \in [l]$, let $r_i^{\text{loc}}\big(g_i^1(\beta_i^1), \ldots, g_i^{k_i}(\beta_i^{k_i}), g_i(z_i)\big)$ be the local constraint from φ corresponding to the second-order variable C_i from φ'. Recall that each β_i^j is one of $x_1, \ldots, x_n$, and each g_i^j (as well as g_i) is one of the names of the fields of S. Then, $\sigma(u)(c_i) = 1$ iff the following holds*

$$\mathbb{D}(r_i^{\text{loc}})\big(\mathbb{I}(g_i^1)(node(\sigma, \beta_i^1)), \ldots, \mathbb{I}(g_i^{k_i})(node(\sigma, \beta_i^{k_i})), \mathbb{I}(g_i)(\lambda(u)) \big).$$

The following result states the fundamental relationship between φ and $A_{\varphi'}$.

Theorem 4. *Let φ be an* MSO-D *sentence of the form* (2) *on the data signature S, and let $A_{\varphi'}$ be the corresponding tree automaton described above. For all data trees (T, λ) with data signature S, the following are equivalent:*

1. *it holds $T^\lambda, \mathbb{I} \models \varphi$, where $\mathbb{I}$ is the unique interpretation of φ;*
2. *there exists a tree $(T, \sigma) \in L(A_{\varphi'})$ s.t. (T, λ) and (T, σ) are consistent.*

6.2 Building the Symbolic Data Tree Automaton

We now convert the tree automaton from the previous section into an SDTA that accepts all and only the data trees satisfying the original MSO-D formula φ.

Intuitively, the SDTA mimics the behavior of the tree automaton, and in doing so, it enforces the data constraints contained in φ. The information about which constraints should be true and which should be false at every node is encoded in the alphabet $\Sigma = \{0,1\}^{n+h+l}$ of the tree automaton. In detail, if $(a_1,\ldots,a_n,b_1,\ldots,b_h,c_1,\ldots,c_l)$ is a generic symbol from the alphabet, the b_i's encode the truth value of the global constraints, and the c_i's encode the truth value of the local constraints. However, the *data* on which to evaluate those constraints comes from different sources. The global constraints are evaluated only on the *guessed* data for the existentially quantified variables $x_1,\ldots,x_n$, whereas the local constraints also access the data of the current node.

Finally, the a_i component of the alphabet encodes the actual position of each x_i in the current tree (i.e., a_i is 1 only in the node that is the interpretation of x_i). So, when $a_i = 1$ the symbolic automaton checks that the guessed data evaluation for x_i corresponds to the data in the current node.

Let $A_{\varphi'} = (\Sigma, Q, F, \Delta)$ be the tree automaton from Sect. 6.1, we now define the SDTA $\mathcal{A}_\varphi = (\mathcal{S}, \mathcal{S}^Q, \psi^F, \Psi^\Delta)$. First, notice that the alphabet data signature $\mathcal{S}$ coincides with that of the original MSO-D formula. We then set the state data signature $\mathcal{S}^Q$ to $\{state : Q\} \cup \{id^i : type \mid (id : type) \in \mathcal{S}, i = 1\ldots n\}$, i.e., $\mathcal{S}^Q$ contains an enumerated data field representing the state of the tree automaton $A_{\varphi'}$, and n copies of each data field in $\mathcal{S}$. These copies are used to store the guessed data evaluations for the existentially quantified variables x_i from (2). For a symbolic state $q \in L(\mathcal{S}^Q)$ and $i \in [n]$, we denote by $q[x_i]$ the i-th projection of q on $\mathcal{S}$, i.e., the evaluation that assigns to each field id in $\mathcal{S}$ the value $q.id^i$. The acceptance constraint $\psi^F(q)$ is simply defined as $q.state \in F$.

Regarding the transition constraints Ψ^Δ, we will focus only on the case of nodes with two children, since the other cases are similar. Let (s_l, s_r, a, s) be a transition in $A_{\varphi'}$, where $a = (a_1,\ldots,a_n,b_1,\ldots,b_h,c_1,\ldots,c_l) \in \Sigma$. We add the following implicant to the transition constraint ψ_{lr}:

$$\Big\{ \quad q_l.state = s_l \wedge q_r.state = s_r \wedge q.state = s \tag{4a}$$

$$\wedge \bigwedge_{i\in[n]} \big(q[x_i] = q_l[x_i] \wedge q[x_i] = q_r[x_i]\big) \quad \wedge \bigwedge_{\{i\,|\,a_i=1\}} (q[x_i] = \sigma) \tag{4b}$$

$$\wedge \bigwedge_{i\in[h]} \Big[(b_i = 1) \leftrightarrow \mathbb{D}(r_i^{\text{glb}})\big(q[\alpha_i^1].f_i^1, \ldots, q[\alpha_i^{j_i}].f_i^{j_i}\big)\Big] \tag{4c}$$

$$\wedge \bigwedge_{i\in[l]} \Big[(c_i = 1) \leftrightarrow \mathbb{D}(r_i^{\text{loc}})\big(q[\beta_i^1].g_i^1, \ldots, q[\beta_i^{k_i}].g_i^{k_i}, \sigma.g_i\big)\Big] \quad \Big\}$$
$$\implies \psi_{lr}(q_l, q_r, \sigma, q). \tag{4d}$$

The above conjuncts can be explained as follows: (4a) mimics the state change in the discrete transition, the first part of (4b) states that the n copies of the data fields held by the symbolic automaton are uniform over the whole tree, the second part of (4b) additionally states that the i-th copy of the data fields coincides with the data σ in the unique node where the discrete automaton

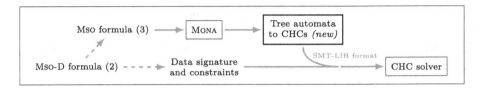

Fig. 1. Architecture of the prototype implementation. Dashed transformations are performed manually, but could be automated by an MSO-D parser.

prescribes $a_i = 1$, (4c) enforces the i-th global constraint r_i^{glb} in all nodes where the discrete automaton prescribes $b_i = 1$, and finally (4d) enforces the local constraints when the c_i component of the discrete alphabet is 1.

Theorem 5. *Let φ be an MSO-D sentence of the form (2) and let $\mathcal{A}_\varphi$ be the corresponding SDTA described above. We have $\mathcal{L}(\varphi) = L(\mathcal{A}_\varphi)$.*

6.3 Supporting Auxiliary Data

So far, we have assumed that all connecting function symbols f appearing in the data constraints correspond to fields in $\mathcal{S}$. In other words, all data constraints refer to data fields that are present in the trees. However, our logic also supports connecting function symbols that do not correspond to fields in the data signature. In that case, the interpretation is free to assign any value to $f(u)$, for each node u in the data tree. Thus, the SDTA $\mathcal{A}_\varphi$ must accept a data tree if there exists an interpretation for those functions that satisfies the formula. To achieve this effect, let $\{f_i\}_{i=1...k}$ be the set of connecting function symbols occurring in φ and not corresponding to data fields in $\mathcal{S}$, where f_i has type $nodes \to data_i$. Define the extended data signature

$$\mathcal{S}' = \mathcal{S} \cup \{f_i : data_i\}_{i=1...k}.$$

We enrich the state data signature of $\mathcal{A}_\varphi$ as follows:

$$\mathcal{S}^Q = \{state : Q\} \cup \{name^i : type \mid (name : type) \in \mathcal{S}', i = 0 \ldots n\}.$$

Compared to the original definition from Sect. 6.2, we store an extra copy of the data fields, identified by index 0, representing the data in the current node. Moreover, all copies include the auxiliary data fields. It is straightforward to adapt the constraint Ψ^Δ from Sect. 6.2 to support such auxiliary data fields.

7   Implementation and Experiments

We implemented a prototype toolchain supporting our framework as shown in Fig. 1. Instead of developing an MSO-D parser, we provide an MSO formula already in the form (3), and supply the data constraints and the data signature for the formula in a separate file, directly in the SMT-LIB format. Next, we convert the Mso formula into an equivalent tree automaton, and in turn into a system of CHCs (as described in Sect. 5). We used Z3 v4.8.10 (64bit for Windows 10) [36] as the CHC solver, and MONA v1.4 [28] as the Mso-to-automata translator. The only new piece of code required by this implementation is the converter from the MONA tree automaton format to CHCs in the SMT-LIB language, which is a simple one-to-one textual transformation. For the experiments, we used a dedicated machine with 16 GB of physical memory and an AMD Ryzen 7 2700X clocked at 3.7 Ghz, running Windows 10.

7.1 Proving Properties of Tree Data Structures

Consider the property of full Bsts described in Example 7, namely that the successor of an internal node is the left-most leaf in its right subtree. We submitted to our tool the conjunction $\psi'_{bst} \wedge \psi_{succ}$, which would be satisfied only by a full Bst where the successor of an internal node is *not* the left-most leaf in its right subtree (property SUCCESSOR). Once the formula is converted into a system of CHCs, the SMT solver proves satisfiability of the system (and hence, unsatisfiability of the original formula) in less than a second.

Table 1. Mso-D satisfiability experiments (Sect. 7).

Example	Mso-D property	Number of CHCs	Result	Time (Z3)
Rbts	BLACKHEIGHT	76	unsat	0.3"
Full Bsts	SUCCESSOR	945	unsat	0.2"
	STEPMOTHER(1.0)		sat	3'
	STEPMOTHER(1.5)		sat	7' 41"
Cinderella	STEPMOTHER(1.8)	23,387	sat	11' 56"
	STEPMOTHER(2.0)		unsat	1 h 54'
	STEPMOTHER(3.0)		unsat	1 h 16'

For Rbts, we consider the property that there exists an internal node whose black height is less than half of its height (property BLACKHEIGHT). Our approach can prove that this property is unsatisfiable on Rbts in less than a second. Both experiments are summarized in Table 1.

7.2 Solving an Infinite-State Game

Our approach can be used to solve certain infinite-state games, such as the Cinderella-Stepmother game [1,3]. In this software synthesis benchmark, two players share n buckets, each holding up to c units of water. The buckets are positioned in a circle and are initially empty. The game is played in a discrete sequence of turns: when it is Cinderella's turn, she can empty two adjacent buckets. When it is the Stepmother's turn, she can pour water into any subset of buckets, for a total of 1 unit of water. If any of the buckets overflows, Stepmother wins. If the game continues forever with no overflows, Cinderella wins. It can be described as an infinite-state turn-based two-player game of infinite duration with a safety objective (for Cinderella). Notice how not only the game state-space is infinite, but so are the moves available to Stepmother at each step.

Given values for the parameters n and c, we build an MSO-D formula $\varphi_{n,c}$ that is satisfiable if and only if Stepmother wins the game with those parameters. The formula holds true on finite trees representing winning strategies of Stepmother. In other words, a tree that satisfies φ tracks all possible game plays where Stepmother pours water according to a specific deterministic plan and Cinderella takes all possible moves. Due to space constraints, further details on the encoding are deferred to an extended version of this paper.

In our experiments, we fixed the number of buckets n to 5 and checked the satisfiability of $\varphi_{5,c}$ for various values of the capacity c. In Table 1, we denote by STEPMOTHER(c) the formula $\varphi_{5,c}$. Bodlaender et al. [3], among their comprehensive analysis of this game, show that for $n = 5$, the minimum capacity for which Cinderella wins the game is $c = 2$ (see Table 1 in [3]). Their proof for this case is manual. Other cases were settled with the help of an SMT solver, using invariants based on non-trivial insights on the reasonable strategies of Stepmother. On the contrary, our encoding based on MSO-D employs only the rules of the game, with no further constraints on the players' moves.

Our setup successfully solves the game for various values of the capacity. The time needed by the SMT solver is very uneven, ranging from three minutes to a maximum of almost two hours for $c = 2$. That is explained by the fact that $c = 2$ is the hardest case for Cinderella to win the game. Therefore, proving that property requires building a complex winning strategy for Cinderella. Such strategy is embedded in the proof of unsatisfiability, and extracting it would be an interesting exercise beyond the scope of the present paper. When the capacity moves away from the critical threshold in either direction, the solving time visibly decreases.

8   Related Work

Our work is related to many works in the literature in different ways. In addition to the works already mentioned in the introduction, here we focus on those that seem to be closest to the results presented in this paper.

Automata on Infinite Alphabets. Symbolic finite automata (SFAs) [43] and symbolic tree automata (STAs) [42] replace the traditional finite alphabet by a decidable theory of unary predicates over a possibly infinite domain. They predicate over data words and trees, but they do not support storing, comparing, or combining data from different positions in the model, as that leads quickly to undecidability. Symbolic register automata [10] extend SFAs by storing data values in a set of registers. They retain decidability of the emptiness problem by only allowing equality comparisons between registers and input data.

Recently, Shimoda et al. [38] introduced *symbolic automatic relations* (SARs) as a formalism to verify properties of recursive data structures. While both MSO-D and SARs rely on CHCs as a backend, they differ in motivation and purpose. SARs aim at encoding specific properties of interest in a way that reduces the verification effort of the underlying CHC solver, whereas MSO-D is intended to provide a high-level language that can be compiled into CHCs.

Decidable Logics with Data Extensions. In [11], D'Antoni et al. design an extension of WS1S on finite data sequences where data can be examined with arbitrary predicates from a decidable theory, similarly to the capabilities of SFAs. They develop custom representations and algorithms to efficiently solve the satisfiability problem by reducing it to the emptiness of SFAs. Colcombet et al. [7] study a decidable fragment of MSO with data equality, called *rigidly guarded* $MSO^{\sim}$, where data equality constraints of the type $val(x) = val(y)$ can only be checked on a single y-position for each x-position. Constraint LTL [13] is another decidable logic for infinite data words, where data in different positions can be compared for equality and for order. Segoufin [37] provides a wider, albeit slightly outdated, perspective on decidable data logics and automata.

Logics for Automated Reasoning About Heap-Manipulating Programs. Similarly to MSO-D, STRAND [32] is a logic that combines MSO on tree-like graphs with the theory of integers. Although STRAND has a fragment that admits a decidable and efficient decision procedure, it is not sufficiently expressive to state properties of classic data structures such as the balancedness of a tree. Also it does not allow solving the Cinderella-Stepmother game. DRYAD logic [33] is a quantifier-free logic supporting recursion on trees, that is deliberately undecidable but admits a sound, incomplete, and terminating validity procedure, based on *natural* proofs [30]. DRYAD recursive definitions could be expressed by our SDTAs that uses the theories of integers and integer (multi)sets; vice versa, proof techniques developed for DRYAD could be used to check the emptiness of (some) SDTAs.

Infinite-State Games. Many infinite-state reachability games like the Cinderella game of Sect. 7.2 can be encoded in MSO-D, including all the reachability games used in the experiments performed by Farzan and Kincaid [17]. In that paper, the authors present a fully automated but incomplete approach for the (undecidable) class of *linear arithmetic games*. Our approach is incomparable to theirs: on the one hand, the approach proposed in Sect. 7.2 does not extend to all linear arithmetic games, because it assumes that one player has a bounded number of moves; on the other hand, we could easily handle games whose transition relations is not limited to linear arithmetic. Another related approach is presented by Beyene et al. [1], who reduce infinite-state games to CHCs extended with existential quantifiers. Such existential quantifiers are handled with the help of user-provided templates.

9   Conclusions and Future Directions

We presented MSO-D and SDTAs as extensions of MSO on trees and finite-state tree automata, respectively, for the purpose of reasoning about data trees. We have shown that these are versatile and powerful models for reasoning about relevant problems, outside the realm of classical automata theory. We believe that the key idea, namely separating the structural properties of interest from the data constraints, makes it easier to reason about challenging problems.

Several future directions are interesting. First, we may want to investigate theoretical questions about SDTAs, such as closure properties, and whether we can reduce classical automata decision problems to solving a system of CHCs. In addition, it will be interesting to identify more expressive MSO-D fragments that can be reduced to the emptiness of SDTAs.

Secondly, we believe that our results have applications to other areas in verification. We have conducted preliminary studies defining extensions of LTL with data (LTL-D) and, by using the framework developed in this paper and closure properties of SDTAs, obtained LTL-D model checking algorithms for (recursive) programs using scalar variables. Our approach is limited to finite runs only, so it will also be interesting to see how we can extend it to infinite trees and games.

Finally, (enumeration) trees can be used to encode executions of different classes of automata, such as concurrent pushdown automata or concurrent queue systems. It will be interesting to see if our approach can help lift the results of [31] to the corresponding class of concurrent programs.

References

1. Beyene, T., Chaudhuri, S., Popeea, C., Rybalchenko, A.: A constraint-based approach to solving games on infinite graphs. In: POPL 2014, Proceedings of the 41st ACM SIGPLAN-SIGACT Symposium on Principles of Programming Languages, pp. 221–233 (2014)
2. Bjørner, N., Gurfinkel, A., McMillan, K., Rybalchenko, A.: Horn clause solvers for program verification. In: Beklemishev, L.D., Blass, A., Dershowitz, N., Finkbeiner, B., Schulte, W. (eds.) Fields of Logic and Computation II. LNCS, vol. 9300, pp. 24–51. Springer, Cham (2015). https://doi.org/10.1007/978-3-319-23534-9_2
3. Bodlaender, M.H.L., Hurkens, C.A.J., Kusters, V.J.J., Staals, F., Woeginger, G.J., Zantema, H.: Cinderella versus the wicked stepmother. In: Baeten, J.C.M., Ball, T., de Boer, F.S. (eds.) TCS 2012. LNCS, vol. 7604, pp. 57–71. Springer, Heidelberg (2012). https://doi.org/10.1007/978-3-642-33475-7_5
4. Büchi, J.R.: Weak second-order arithmetic and finite automata. Math. Log. Q. **6**(1–6), 66–92 (1960)
5. Büchi, J.R.: On a decision method in restricted second-order arithmetic. In: Proceedings of 1960 International Congress for Logic, Methodology and Philosophy of Science, pp. 1–11. Stanford University Press (1962)
6. Champion, A., Chiba, T., Kobayashi, N., Sato, R.: Ice-based refinement type discovery for higher-order functional programs. J. Autom. Reason. **64**(7), 1393–1418 (2020)
7. Colcombet, T., Ley, C., Puppis, G.: Logics with rigidly guarded data tests. Log. Methods Comput. Sci. **11**(3), 1–56 (2015). https://doi.org/10.2168/LMCS-11(3:10)2015

8. Comon, H., et al.: Tree Automata Techniques and Applications (2008). https://hal.inria.fr/hal-03367725
9. Cormen, T.H., Leiserson, C.E., Rivest, R.L., Stein, C.: Introduction to Algorithms, 3rd edn. MIT Press, Cambridge (2009)
10. D'Antoni, L., Ferreira, T., Sammartino, M., Silva, A.: Symbolic register automata. In: Dillig, I., Tasiran, S. (eds.) CAV 2019. LNCS, vol. 11561, pp. 3–21. Springer, Cham (2019). https://doi.org/10.1007/978-3-030-25540-4_1
11. D'Antoni, L., Veanes, M.: Monadic second-order logic on finite sequences. In: Proceedings of the 44th ACM SIGPLAN Symposium on Principles of Programming Languages, POPL 2017, Paris, France, 18–20 January 2017, pp. 232–245. ACM (2017)
12. D'Antoni, L., Veanes, M.: Automata modulo theories. Commun. ACM 64(5), 86–95 (2021)
13. Demri, S., D'Souza, D.: An automata-theoretic approach to constraint LTL. Inf. Comput. 205(3), 380–415 (2007)
14. Doner, J.: Tree acceptors and some of their applications. J. Comput. Syst. Sci. 4(5), 406–451 (1970)
15. Elgot, C.C.: Decision problems of finite automata design and related arithmetics. Trans. Am. Math. Soc. 98, 21–51 (1961)
16. van Emden, M.H., Kowalski, R.A.: The semantics of predicate logic as a programming language. J. ACM 23(4), 733–742 (1976)
17. Farzan, A., Kincaid, Z.: Strategy synthesis for linear arithmetic games. POPL. Proc. ACM Program. Lang. 2, 61:1–61:30 (2018)
18. Fedyukovich, G., Ahmad, M.B.S., Bodík, R.: Gradual synthesis for static parallelization of single-pass array-processing programs. In: Proceedings of the 38th ACM SIGPLAN Conference on Programming Language Design and Implementation, PLDI 2017, Barcelona, Spain, 18–23 June 2017, pp. 572–585. ACM (2017)
19. Fedyukovich, G., Rümmer, P.: Competition report: CHC-COMP-21. In: Proceedings 8th Workshop on Horn Clauses for Verification and Synthesis, HCVS@ETAPS 2021, Virtual, EPTCS, 28 March 2021, vol. 344, pp. 91–108 (2021)
20. Garoche, P., Kahsai, T., Thirioux, X.: Hierarchical state machines as modular horn clauses. In: Proceedings 3rd Workshop on Horn Clauses for Verification and Synthesis, HCVS@ETAPS 2016, EPTCS, Eindhoven, The Netherlands, 3 April 2016, vol. 219, pp. 15–28 (2016)
21. Grebenshchikov, S., Lopes, N.P., Popeea, C., Rybalchenko, A.: Synthesizing software verifiers from proof rules. In: ACM SIGPLAN Conference on Programming Language Design and Implementation, PLDI 2012, Beijing, China, 11–16 June 2012, pp. 405–416. ACM (2012)
22. Gurfinkel, A., Bjørner, N.: The science, art, and magic of constrained Horn clauses. In: 21st International Symposium on Symbolic and Numeric Algorithms for Scientific Computing, SYNASC 2019, Timisoara, Romania, 4–7 September 2019, pp. 6–10. IEEE (2019)
23. Gurfinkel, A., Kahsai, T., Komuravelli, A., Navas, J.A.: The SeaHorn verification framework. In: Kroening, D., Păsăreanu, C.S. (eds.) CAV 2015. LNCS, vol. 9206, pp. 343–361. Springer, Cham (2015). https://doi.org/10.1007/978-3-319-21690-4_20
24. Hoder, K., Bjørner, N., de Moura, L.: μZ– an efficient engine for fixed points with constraints. In: Gopalakrishnan, G., Qadeer, S. (eds.) CAV 2011. LNCS, vol. 6806, pp. 457–462. Springer, Heidelberg (2011). https://doi.org/10.1007/978-3-642-22110-1_36

25. Hojjat, H., Konečný, F., Garnier, F., Iosif, R., Kuncak, V., Rümmer, P.: A verification toolkit for numerical transition systems. In: Giannakopoulou, D., Méry, D. (eds.) FM 2012. LNCS, vol. 7436, pp. 247–251. Springer, Heidelberg (2012). https://doi.org/10.1007/978-3-642-32759-9_21

26. Jaffar, J., Maher, M.J.: Constraint logic programming: a survey. J. Log. Program. **19**(20), 503–581 (1994)

27. Kahsai, T., Rümmer, P., Sanchez, H., Schäf, M.: JayHorn: a framework for verifying Java programs. In: Chaudhuri, S., Farzan, A. (eds.) CAV 2016. LNCS, vol. 9779, pp. 352–358. Springer, Cham (2016). https://doi.org/10.1007/978-3-319-41528-4_19

28. Klarlund, N., Møller, A.: MONA Version 1.4 User Manual. BRICS, Department of Computer Science, University of Aarhus, Notes Series NS-01-1, January 2001. http://www.brics.dk/mona/

29. Kobayashi, N., Sato, R., Unno, H.: Predicate abstraction and CEGAR for higher-order model checking. In: Proceedings of the 32nd ACM SIGPLAN Conference on Programming Language Design and Implementation, PLDI 2011, San Jose, CA, USA, 4–8 June 2011, pp. 222–233. ACM (2011)

30. Löding, C., Madhusudan, P., Peña, L.: Foundations for natural proofs and quantifier instantiation. Proc. ACM Program. Lang. **2**(POPL), 10:1–10:30 (2018)

31. Madhusudan, P., Parlato, G.: The tree width of auxiliary storage. In: Proceedings of the 38th ACM SIGPLAN-SIGACT Symposium on Principles of Programming Languages, POPL 2011, Austin, TX, USA, 26–28 January 2011, pp. 283–294. ACM (2011)

32. Madhusudan, P., Parlato, G., Qiu, X.: Decidable logics combining heap structures and data. In: Proceedings of the 38th ACM SIGPLAN-SIGACT Symposium on Principles of Programming Languages, POPL 2011, Austin, TX, USA, 26–28 January 2011, pp. 611–622. ACM (2011)

33. Madhusudan, P., Qiu, X., Stefanescu, A.: Recursive proofs for inductive tree data-structures. In: Proceedings of the 39th ACM SIGPLAN-SIGACT Symposium on Principles of Programming Languages, POPL 2012, Philadelphia, Pennsylvania, USA, 22–28 January 2012, pp. 123–136. ACM (2012)

34. Manna, Z., Zarba, C.G.: Combining decision procedures. In: Aichernig, B.K., Maibaum, T. (eds.) Formal Methods at the Crossroads. From Panacea to Foundational Support. LNCS, vol. 2757, pp. 381–422. Springer, Heidelberg (2003). https://doi.org/10.1007/978-3-540-40007-3_24

35. Matsushita, Y., Tsukada, T., Kobayashi, N.: RustHorn: CHC-based verification for rust programs. In: ESOP 2020. LNCS, vol. 12075, pp. 484–514. Springer, Cham (2020). https://doi.org/10.1007/978-3-030-44914-8_18

36. de Moura, L., Bjørner, N.: Z3: an efficient SMT solver. In: Ramakrishnan, C.R., Rehof, J. (eds.) TACAS 2008. LNCS, vol. 4963, pp. 337–340. Springer, Heidelberg (2008). https://doi.org/10.1007/978-3-540-78800-3_24

37. Segoufin, L.: Automata and logics for words and trees over an infinite alphabet. In: Ésik, Z. (ed.) CSL 2006. LNCS, vol. 4207, pp. 41–57. Springer, Heidelberg (2006). https://doi.org/10.1007/11874683_3

38. Shimoda, T., Kobayashi, N., Sakayori, K., Sato, R.: Symbolic automatic relations and their applications to SMT and CHC solving. In: Drăgoi, C., Mukherjee, S., Namjoshi, K. (eds.) SAS 2021. LNCS, vol. 12913, pp. 405–428. Springer, Cham (2021). https://doi.org/10.1007/978-3-030-88806-0_20

39. Thatcher, J.W., Wright, J.B.: Generalized finite automata theory with an application to a decision problem of second-order logic. Math. Syst. Theory **2**(1), 57–81 (1968)

40. Thomas, W.: Automata on infinite objects. In: Van Leeuwen, J. (ed.) Formal Models and Semantics. In: Handbook of Theoretical Computer Science, pp. 133–191. Elsevier, Amsterdam (1990)
41. Trakhtenbrot, B.A.: Finite automata and logic of monadic predicates. Doklady Akademii Nauk SSSR **149**, 326–329 (1961). (in Russian)
42. Veanes, M., Bjørner, N.: Symbolic tree automata. Inf. Process. Lett. **115**(3), 418–424 (2015)
43. Veanes, M., de Halleux, P., Tillmann, N.: Rex: symbolic regular expression explorer. In: 2010 Third International Conference on Software Testing, Verification and Validation, pp. 498–507 (2010)

Verified Erasure Correction in Coq with MathComp and VST

Joshua M. Cohen[✉], Qinshi Wang, and Andrew W. Appel

Princeton University, Princeton, NJ 08544, USA
jmc16@princeton.edu

Abstract. Most methods of data transmission and storage are prone to errors, leading to data loss. Forward erasure correction (FEC) is a method to allow data to be recovered in the presence of errors by encoding the data with redundant parity information determined by an error-correcting code. There are dozens of classes of such codes, many based on sophisticated mathematics, making them difficult to verify using automated tools. In this paper, we present a formal, machine-checked proof of a C implementation of FEC based on Reed-Solomon coding. The C code has been actively used in network defenses for over 25 years, but the algorithm it implements was partially unpublished, and it uses certain optimizations whose correctness was unknown even to the code's authors. We use Coq's Mathematical Components library to prove the algorithm's correctness and the Verified Software Toolchain to prove that the C program correctly implements this algorithm, connecting both using a modular, well-encapsulated structure that could easily be used to verify a high-speed, hardware version of this FEC. This is the first end-to-end, formal proof of a real-world FEC implementation; we verified all previously unknown optimizations and found a latent bug in the code.

Keywords: Reed-Solomon coding · functional correctness verification · interactive theorem proving

1 Introduction

As part of a larger project of ensuring reliable networks, we are applying formal functional-correctness verification to network components: machine-checked proofs that C programs (and, eventually, P4 programs and FPGAs) satisfy their high-level functional specs. When attackers may gain access to the source code and analyze it for bugs and vulnerabilities, we want something stronger than software testing or conventional static analysis: we want a proof that the software works *no matter what input is provided, no matter how dastardly.* And we want a proof that the program works *correctly,* not merely that it does not crash.

One key to reliable networking is *forward erasure correction (FEC):* in a portion of the network in which packets are being lost, add extra parity packets that allow reconstruction of lost packets without retransmission. We use an FEC

S. Shoham and Y. Vizel (Eds.): CAV 2022, LNCS 13372, pp. 272–292, 2022.
https://doi.org/10.1007/978-3-031-13188-2_14

algorithm and C program that have been in active use for over 25 years. The program does many clever and not-so-clever things, and comments indicate that some parts are not fully trusted even by its original authors.

This FEC is a particularly intriguing target for verification because its high-level correctness depends on fairly intricate mathematics—we must reason about polynomials, matrices, and finite fields. Meanwhile, the C implementation's correctness relies on C programming features and careful manipulation of pointers in memory. Thus, we need a tool that can reason at both of these levels. We use the Coq proof assistant, utilizing the Mathematical Components [10] (Math-Comp) library for the high-level reasoning and the Verified Software Toolchain [6] (VST) for the C program verification.[1] Our VST specs are written using *separation logic*, in which we specify precisely what memory is read from and written to as well as all external effects (I/O, system calls, etc.). This gives us a blanket containment property: the C function is guaranteed to only interact with the outside world (memory, OS, etc.) in ways stated in the spec.

Contributions

1. We show that formal verification can prove functional correctness for a C program that uses both intricate mathematics and clever C programming tricks. This is the first formally verified FEC instance that connects a high-level mathematical specification with an efficient, optimized implementation.
2. We formally prove the correctness of a particular version of Reed-Solomon erasure coding, parts of which were unpublished. Further, we prove that an optimization in the C code, a heavily restricted form of Gaussian elimination, is sufficient for this application; this was unknown to the code's authors.
3. For the first time, we utilize both MathComp and VST in the same project. The two libraries differ greatly in types, tactics, and styles of proof; we use both by separating our functional specification into two layers in a process that we expect can be automated.
4. We demonstrate our methods on a real-world C program, verified *as is*, except for two tiny changes, one of which is to fix a latent bug that we discovered.

1.1 Forward Erasure Correction

When transmitting data over a noisy channel, one can use an *error-correcting code*—adding generalized "parity" bits, sending the data across the channel, and then decoding to recover the data if any errors occurred; this technique is known as *forward error correction*. In an *erasure code*, the locations of the missing data are known to the decoder; this allows correction of more errors.

FEC is useful in any network where non-congestion-related packet loss is frequent and retransmission is infeasible or expensive. For instance, wireless networks are especially prone to packet loss due to interference or jamming. More generally,

---

[1] Our Coq proofs and an appendix with expanded definitions, specs, and proofs can be found at github.com/verified-network-toolchain/Verified-FEC/tree/cav22.

errors in network devices due to firmware bugs, misconfiguration, or malware can lead to dropped packets. In these cases, retransmission with TCP is not desirable, because TCP will incorrectly interpret these losses as congestion, grinding the network to a halt. Similarly, applications such as video or audio streaming, often run over UDP, cannot handle retransmission without additional work; moreover, the latency of retransmitting is often too high. Thus, FEC continues to be important in ensuring network reliability.

The algorithm we consider is based on Reed-Solomon [24] coding; it groups the input bits into symbols representing elements of a finite field and interprets the data as a polynomial over this field. Reed-Solomon codes are particularly useful for correcting *burst* errors—errors that occur sequentially—since $n + 1$ consecutive bit errors can only affect at most 2 symbols of length n. Reed-Solomon decoders can be quite complex, both in theory and implementation; many mechanisms have been developed for this purpose. Nevertheless, these codes have been heavily used in applications such as CDs, DVDs, Blu-Ray disks, hard drives, and satellite communications [27].

In the early 1990's, there was a flurry of activity in Reed-Solomon erasure coding. McAuley described [18] and patented [19] a method for FEC based on Reed-Solomon coding for use in network transmission. Rabin [23] described an alternate technique for information dispersal, which was further developed by Preparata [22], Schwarz [25], and others, mainly for use in RAID storage systems; Plank [21] provides a tutorial and explanation. McAuley later wrote a C implementation of FEC for network packets based on this second technique with several further modifications. We will refer to the algorithm implemented by McAuley's C code as the Reed-Solomon Erasure (RSE) code.

Bellcore (now Peraton Labs) has employed this FEC algorithm (and implementation) successfully in numerous networking projects to support resilient communication, most recently in the DARPA EdgeCT program. McAuley's implementation includes many optimizations and modifications to the core algorithm, including some whose correctness was unknown to the code's authors (Sect. 5.2). It had one bug that we corrected (Sect. 6.6). We have produced a formal, machine-checked proof that this FEC implementation correctly recovers data in the presence of erasures—we proved the *algorithm* correct and proved that the *program* correctly implements it.

1.2 Coq and VST

We use the Coq interactive theorem prover, in which the user states and proves theorems in a higher-order dependently typed logic. These theorems are mechanically checked by the Coq kernel. Proofs can be (semi)automated by Coq's built-in tactics and by user-defined tactic programming.

Coq has been widely used in program verification and formalized mathematics. One particularly important verification effort is CompCert [15], an optimizing C compiler written and proved correct in Coq. That is, CompCert comes with a formal proof that the assembly code generated by the compiler preserves the semantics of the input C program.

VST is a program logic and set of proof automation tools that enables the verification of C programs in Coq. Using VST, one can write a specification for each C function, stating its preconditions (properties that must hold before the function is run) and postconditions (properties that must hold when the function finishes). These properties can involve both C-specific assertions (e.g., about the contents of memory) and arbitrary statements in Coq's logic. Then, using custom tactics and proof automation included with VST, the user can prove in Coq that the C function satisfies its specification.

VST's program logic is proved sound, with a machine-checked proof in Coq. When we prove that McAuley's RSE correctly reconstructs missing packets, the soundness proof guarantees that the assembly-language program generated by the CompCert C compiler really has that behavior. VST is formally proved sound for CompCert, but not for gcc or clang. VST is intended (and believed) to be sound for gcc/clang; its program logic has stricter rules than would be necessary only for soundness w.r.t. CompCert. For example, for signed integer arithmetic, where CompCert is (unfortunately) a refinement of C11 (CompCert wraps while C11 is u.b.), VST imposes the (more abstract) C11 spec. Thus, VST proofs about C programs also provide useful (though less foundational) assurance about programs compiled with other compilers.

While conventional separation logics have spatial conjuncts that are predicates just on memory resources, VST's separation logic has spatial conjunct predicates on both memory locations and the outside world, which one might affect by performing IO or making a system call [17, Section 3]. In our project, none of the VST funspecs mention the outside world in the precondition or postcondition; this means, like any Hoare triple in separation logic, that those functions can neither access nor modify that resource.

Proving that a C program satisfies a specification is quite challenging. We must prove low-level correctness properties (the program does not crash, all memory accesses are valid, etc.) and provide loop invariants and intermediate proofs to prove high-level properties (that the function satisfies its spec). Though VST's proof automation is able to hide some of this complexity, many parts must still be done manually. Dealing with heavily optimized C code that was never intended to be verified makes these tasks substantially more complicated.

Section 2 describes the RSE algorithm, which differs in several ways from the technique described by Rabin, Preparata, and Schwarz. Section 3 explains the different verification tasks, including defining a functional model of the algorithm and showing with VST that the C code implements this model. Section 4 describes the functional model, Sect. 5 discusses the verification of this functional model, including the proof that the algorithm correctly reconstructs missing packets, and Sect. 6 discusses the proofs about the C code. Section 7 and Sect. 8 give related and future work.

2   The RSE Algorithm

Like all Reed-Solomon codes, the algorithm treats input symbols as elements of a finite field and interprets the input sequence of words as the coefficients of a polynomial over this field. However, both the C implementation and the RSE algorithm are more naturally described using linear algebra and matrix operations.

Let D be the input data, which consists of k packets, each of length at most c bytes. If any packets are smaller, fill in the missing entries with zeroes so that D is a $k \times c$ matrix. Let h be the number of parity packets we wish to append. We will be able to reconstruct up to h total packet-drops.

Let k_{max} and h_{max} be (fixed) parameters such that $k \leq k_{max}$ and $h \leq h_{max}$. Let $n_{max} = h_{max} + k_{max}$ (maximum number of packets per batch) and let F be a field such that $|F| > n_{max}$.

2.1   Initialization

First, we generate a Vandermonde matrix of size $h_{max} \times n_{max}$; that is, take n_{max} distinct nonzero elements of F, denoted as $\alpha_1, \alpha_2, ..., \alpha_{n_{max}}$, and generate the following matrix:

$$V = \begin{pmatrix} 1 & 1 & \cdots & 1 \\ \alpha_1 & \alpha_2 & \cdots & \alpha_{n_{max}} \\ \alpha_1^2 & \alpha_2^2 & \cdots & \alpha_{n_{max}}^2 \\ \vdots & \vdots & \vdots & \vdots \\ \alpha_1^{h_{max}-1} & \alpha_2^{h_{max}-1} & \cdots & \alpha_{n_{max}}^{h_{max}-1} \end{pmatrix}$$

Then, we run Gaussian elimination (see Sect. 4.2) on this matrix to get the row-reduced form, which consists of the identity matrix followed by W, the $h_{max} \times k_{max}$ *weight matrix*:

$$V \xrightarrow{\text{Gaussian elim}} \left[I_{h_{max} \times h_{max}} \middle| W \right]$$

2.2   Encoding

The encoder receives as input the data D, a $k \times c$ matrix. Let W' be the submatrix of W consisting of the first h rows and the first k columns. The encoder computes $P = W'D$, an $h \times c$ matrix. These are the parity packets that are sent (along with the original data) to the receiver.

$$W = \left. h \middle\{ \begin{bmatrix} \overbrace{W'}^{k} & \cdots \\ \vdots & \ddots \end{bmatrix} \right. \qquad P = W'D \qquad (1)$$

2.3   Decoding

The decoder is significantly more complicated. However, if no packets are lost, the decoder simply returns the first k packets; only if packets are dropped does the following algorithm need to be invoked. To give some intuition, we will first present the decoder for a special case before giving the full algorithm.

Since this is an erasure code, we know the locations of the missing packets; we also require that the total number of missing packets is at most h.

For a special case, suppose that the last h data packets were lost and all parity packets were received. We can think of the original data D as a block matrix consisting of D_1, the $(k - h) \times c$ matrix of the received data, and D_2, the $h \times c$ matrix of the lost data. Similarly, we can split the $h \times k$ matrix W' (from the encoder) into W_1', consisting of the first $k - h$ columns of W', and W_2', consisting of the rest.

$$
W = h\left\{ \begin{bmatrix} \overbrace{W_1'\ W_2'}^{k-h\quad h} & \cdots \\ \vdots & \vdots & \ddots \end{bmatrix} \right. \qquad D = \begin{matrix} k-h \\ h \end{matrix}\left\{ \begin{bmatrix} \overbrace{D_1}^{c} \\ D_2 \end{bmatrix} \right.
$$

$$
P = W'D = W_1'D_1 + W_2'D_2
$$

From this, the missing data D_2 can be computed using P, D_1, and the parts of W', all of which are known:

$$
D_2 = (W_2')^{-1}(P - W_1'D_1) \tag{2}
$$

The general case is similar, but we need to define the relevant submatrices more carefully. Let xh be the number of missing data packets. We must have received at least xh parity packets (or else the total number of missing packets is more than h). Let P' be the submatrix of P consisting of the first xh received parity packets. This time, we let W_1' be the $xh \times (k - xh)$ submatrix of W' whose rows consist of the locations of the xh found parity packets and whose columns consist of the $k - xh$ locations of the received data. Let W_2' be the $xh \times xh$ submatrix of W' whose rows consist of the locations of the xh found parities and whose columns consist of the locations of the missing data. Finally, D_1 and D_2 are still defined such that D_1 contains the received rows and D_2 contains the missing rows. This time, these rows need not be contiguous. These definitions reduce to the previous ones in the special case considered above.

By the definitions of the above submatrices, Eq. 2 still holds (except that we replace P with P'), so we can find the missing data D_2 by computing $(W_2')^{-1}(P' - W_1'D_1)$.

This decoder is only well defined if W_2' is invertible. W_2' is dynamically chosen based on the found parities and missing data, so we must show a stronger claim that any square submatrix up to size $h \times h$ of W is invertible. Proving this was the crucial step in the functional model verification, described in Sect. 5.1.

As noted in Sect. 1.1, this algorithm is a modified version of the technique described by Rabin, Preparata, Schwarz, and others. The main difference is the use of the static weight matrix in RSE; all the others assume that the Vandermonde matrix has dimensions $h \times (k + h)$ and exactly h packets are lost. Thus, their needed correctness property is weaker; it requires only that any $h \times h$ submatrix of W is invertible.

3   Verification Structure

The verification consists of two distinct tasks: we prove that the RSE algorithm is correct (i.e., the decoder recovers the original data in the presence of errors) and that the C program truly implements this algorithm. These two tasks are quite different; the first is purely mathematical and involves proofs about linear algebra, while the second involves implementation details and C-language verification conditions. To separate these tasks and make the proofs more modular, we define a *functional model*, a purely functional program written in Coq that implements the RSE algorithm. This functional model is inefficient but easy to reason about in Coq. Then we use VST to prove that the C program refines this functional model. Finally, we compose these two parts to produce a formal proof that the C implementation of this erasure code is correct.

Separating the functional specification and the VST proofs is a common paradigm; it has been used to verify SHA-256 hashing [4], HMAC-DRBG cryptographic random number generation [28], and floating-point numerical programming [5]. This approach provides a clear formal specification independent of any implementation; we can reuse the same functional model and its correctness proofs to verify another implementation of this algorithm (for instance, an FPGA version). It makes verification more flexible; we can prove further properties later simply by adding additional lemmas about the functional model. It makes the proofs shorter and clearer; we can tell which parts are needed for the core correctness proofs and which are implementation-specific. Finally, it permits a separation of expertise: the person who proves mathematical theorems about the functional model need not know anything about C programming or VST verification, and the person who proves C refinement in VST need not know why the functional model accomplishes the high-level goals.

Our functional model was written in Gallina, the functional programming language embedded in Coq, using the Mathematical Components (MathComp) library for formalized mathematics. MathComp contains definitions and theorems about groups, rings, fields, vector spaces, matrices, polynomials, graphs, and other mathematical objects.

In fact, we define two functional models—a high-level version uses Math-Comp's abstract and dependent types of matrices, polynomials, and the like, while a low-level version uses concrete types such as list (list byte), which VST can use to represent memory contents. Translating between these types is nontrivial (because of all the dependent types in MathComp), so we separate the type conversion proofs from both the high-level mathematical reasoning and the low-level VST refinement proof. This makes the proofs more modular and helps to improve the readability of the resulting formalization. The translation is largely mechanical and we expect that it could be automated; we focus on the high-level functional model and the VST refinement proofs.

4   Functional Model

4.1   The Encoder and Decoder

We translate Eq. 1 into the language of Coq/MathComp:

Definition encoder (h k c max_h max_n : nat) (Hh: h $\leq$max_h) (Hk: k $\leq$max_n)
      (weights : 'M[F]_(max_h, max_n)) (input : 'M[F]_(k, c)) :=
  (mxsub (fun (x : 'I_h) $\Rightarrow$ widen_ord Hh x)
      (fun (x : 'I_k) $\Rightarrow$ rev_ord (widen_ord Hk x)) weights) *m input.

'M[F]_(x, y) denotes a matrix of size $x \times y$ over field F and *m denotes matrix multiplication. The type 'I_n represents an ordinal, a natural number in the range $[0, n-1]$. The encoder takes in the parameters h, k, c, h_{max}, and n_{max} (all defined as in §2), the $h_{max} \times n_{max}$ weight matrix, the $k \times c$ data matrix, and proofs that h and k are bounded appropriately. mxsub creates a submatrix from an input matrix by selecting rows and columns via user-specified functions. widen_ord is needed to handle some dependent type casting; it has no computational content and can be ignored. Finally, rev_ord selects the "opposite" ordinal; for x : 'I_k, rev_ord x = k − x − 1. Therefore, this function selects the first h rows and the last k columns (in reverse order) of the weight matrix and multiplies this by the input. This differs from the algorithm in Sect. 2.2, which selects the first k columns. The overall algorithm's correctness is not affected as long as we choose the matrices W_1' and W_2' in the decoder to be consistent, but this change makes the model consistent with the C implementation (see Sect. 6.2).

The decoder (Eq. 2) can be similarly translated into MathComp; we omit the full definition, but note that we defined the decoder more generally than needed: it is defined over any field and over any Vandermonde matrix on distinct elements of that field.

4.2   Gaussian Elimination

Gaussian elimination, or row reduction, is a well known algorithm in linear algebra for solving systems of linear equations, finding matrix inverses, and calculating determinants. The C code includes an implementation of Gaussian elimination, used to row-reduce the Vandermonde matrix to produce the weight matrix and to invert W_2' in the decoder. Thus, we need to define a corresponding functional model.

Gaussian elimination proceeds by applying a sequence of elementary row operations—swapping two rows, multiplying a row by a scalar, and adding a scalar multiple of one row to another row—to a matrix until it is in row-echelon form, which for full-rank matrices (including all relevant matrices in this application) means that the left hand side becomes the identity matrix. Crucially, these row operations preserve invertibility because each corresponds to left multiplication by an (invertible) elementary matrix.

The order of the row operations may vary; Algorithm 1 describes one concrete implementation of Gaussian elimination (we use 0-indexing to be consistent with

---

ALGORITHM 1: GAUSSIAN ELIMINATION

On input A, an $m \times n$ matrix:
  $r \leftarrow 0; \quad c \leftarrow 0$
  while $r < m$ and $c < n$ **do**
    if for all i such that $r \le i < m$, $A_{i,c} = 0$ **then**
      $c \leftarrow c + 1$
    else
      $i \leftarrow$ the first index s.t. $r \le i < m$ and $A_{i,c} \ne 0$
      Swap rows r and i
      For all $0 \le j < m$, if $A_{j,c} \ne 0$, multiply row j by $A_{j,c}^{-1}$
      For all $0 \le j < m$, $j \ne r$, if $A_{j,c} \ne 0$, subtract row r from row j
      $r \leftarrow r + 1; \quad c \leftarrow c + 1$
    end if
  end while
  for $r = 0$ **to** $r = m - 1$ **do**
    Let c be the index of the first nonzero entry in row r if one exists
    Multiply row r by $A_{r,c}^{-1}$
  end for

MathComp). While translating this into MathComp is largely straightforward, it turns out that the C program does not actually implement Algorithm 1. Rather, rows are never swapped and at each iteration, all entries in column c must be nonzero.

The following excerpt from the C code, with the original comments, shows the error checks to ensure this condition. The code is mainly interesting for the error checks and comments, but we briefly detail how it works: the while guard value never changes; instead for current column k, the code iterates through rows w. The second conditional checks if matrix element (w, k) is nonzero for swapping (but returns an error because swapping is not implemented), while the first conditional breaks out of the loop with an error when w has reached the last row.

```
while (*(q − k) == 0){   /* if zero */
  if (++w == i_max){
    return (FEC_ERR_TRANS_FAILED); /* failed */
  }
  if (*(p + (w * j_max) + j_max − 1 − k) != 0){
    /* swap rows */
    return (FEC_ERR_TRANS_SWAP_NOT_DONE); /* Not done yet! */
  }
}
```

The "swap rows" and "Not done yet!" messages suggest that the authors intended to (eventually) implement the full algorithm. The error checks indicate that the authors were not sure if these errors could be triggered.

We will call this algorithm "Restricted" Gaussian elimination (Algorithm 2). Once again, defining this function in MathComp is not difficult, but proving that this limited form of Gaussian elimination suffices was a major part of the functional model verification (Sect. 5.2).

ALGORITHM 2: RESTRICTED GAUSSIAN ELIMINATION

On input A, an $m \times n$ matrix:
$r \leftarrow 0$
while $r < m$ **do**
　For all $0 \leq j < m$, if $A_{j,r} = 0$, return ERROR
　For all $0 \leq j < m$, multiply row j by $A_{j,r}^{-1}$
　For all $0 \leq j < m$, $j \neq r$, subtract row r from row j
　$r \leftarrow r + 1$
end while
for $r = 0$ **to** $r = m - 1$ **do**
　Multiply row r by $A_{r,r}^{-1}$
end for

4.3 Field Operations

The encoder, decoder, and Gaussian elimination work over any field, but the C implementation uses the field $GF(2^8)$, which we must define. Mathematically, this field is isomorphic to $\mathbb{F}_2[x]/(1 + x^2 + x^3 + x^4 + x^8)$. That is, the elements of this field are polynomials of degree at most 7 with coefficients in $\mathbb{F}_2$ (the field of two elements), and all operations are performed modulo $1 + x^2 + x^3 + x^4 + x^8$. The choice of $\mathbb{F}_2$ is important; it allows us to represent polynomials as sequences of bits. Since the polynomials are of degree at most 7, all field elements can be represented as bytes.

This field and its construction are well understood; while MathComp did not include the construction of finite fields via quotients, we were able to define and prove general results about primitive polynomials and the finite field's construction without much issue. Then, we can prove correct the method the C code uses to populate the lookup tables used to compute in this field (Sect. 6.4).

One difficulty in using this field is the difference between the polynomials we used to define the field and the bytes that we would like to represent as field elements. To avoid manually converting everywhere, we defined another field structure directly on the byte type and used Coq's Canonical Structures.

5 Verifying the Functional Model

5.1 Decoder Correctness

To prove the RSE algorithm correct, we need to prove that the decoder actually reconstructs the original packets. That is, if the data and parity packets that were marked as "received" are correct and there are at most h missing packets, then running the decoder on the received packets should recover the original data. We state this in Coq below:

Theorem decoder_correct: $\forall$ (h xh : nat) (Hh: xh $\leq$ h) (data : 'M[F]_(k, c))
(input: 'M[F]_(k, c)) (parities: 'M[F]_(h, c)) (missing_packets : seq 'I_k)
(found_parities : seq 'I_h) (Hhh: h $\leq$ max_h) (x_h : 'I_h),
($*$ Only the rows in [missing_packets] are incorrect $*$)
($\forall$ (x: 'I_k) (y: 'I_c), x \notin missing_packets $\rightarrow$ data x y = input x y) $\rightarrow$
($*$ All found parity packets were produced by the encoder $*$)
($\forall$ (x: 'I_h) (y: 'I_c), x \in found_parities $\rightarrow$
        parities x y = (encoder Hhh k_leq_n weights data) x y) $\rightarrow$
($*$ We have xh unique missing packets and found parities $*$)
uniq missing_packets $\rightarrow$
uniq found_parities $\rightarrow$
size missing_packets = xh $\rightarrow$
size found_parities = xh $\rightarrow$
($*$ Then, the decoder recovers the original data $*$)
decoder xh input parities missing_packets found_parities Hhh x_h = data.

This theorem is expressed entirely in terms of MathComp matrices and operations; it does not rely on the C implementation at all. Its proof requires two main tasks: showing that W_2' is invertible and proving that the sequence of operations in the decoder is sufficient to recover the original data. The second task is fairly straightforward; we compare the matrices elementwise. Thus, the main challenge comes from proving the invertibility of the submatrix W_2'.

Proving the Invertibility of W_2'. Recall that W_2' is a dynamically chosen submatrix of W, the right submatrix of the row-reduced Vandermonde matrix V. Therefore, we want to prove the following theorem (any_submx_unitmx):

Theorem 1. *Let V be an $m \times n$ row-reduced Vandermonde matrix on distinct elements. Let $m \leq n$ and $z \leq \min(m, n - m)$. Let Y be the submatrix of V formed by taking z rows of V and z of the last $(n - m)$ columns of V. Then Y is invertible.*

Formally proving this theorem in Coq is quite complicated, partly because Math-Comp does not include many of the definitions and results that we need. Namely, we need to define and prove properties about row operations and Vandermonde matrices, including the following well-known property (vandermonde_unitmx):

Theorem 2. *Let V be an $n \times n$ Vandermonde matrix on distinct nonzero elements. Then V is invertible.*

The proof relies on the fact that a degree n polynomial with $n + 1$ zeroes is identically zero, a fact already included in MathComp. This marks the only direct use of polynomial properties (other than in the finite field construction); the rest of the results are purely based on linear algebra.

Note that the only property we required of the weight matrix W was that every $z \times z$ submatrix is invertible. Row-reduced Vandermonde matrices satisfy this property, but any other matrix that satisfies this property could be used, and the encoding-decoding scheme would still be correct.

5.2   Gaussian Elimination

Proving full Gaussian elimination (Algorithm 1) correct is fairly standard (though nontrivial to formalize completely in Coq), since the algorithm is very well-understood.

The real challenge is to determine the conditions under which RGE (Algorithm 2) will return the same result as Algorithm 1. It is easy to see that if the ERROR case is never reached, then the two algorithms are equivalent. But it is not at all obvious how to avoid triggering the error. Invertibility is a necessary but quite insufficient condition; for instance, the restricted algorithm fails on diagonal and triangular matrices. Therefore, we had two tasks: determine the class of matrices for which RGE works correctly and prove that the matrices used in the RSE algorithm are in this class.

For the first task, we needed to determine when certain elements will be zero or nonzero at a given step in Gaussian elimination. This is difficult, since the elements are constantly changing; instead, we transformed the condition into a statement about the invertibility of certain submatrices, since Gaussian elimination preserves invertibility.

During the rth step of Gaussian elimination (assuming no error was reached), the $r \times r$ upper-left submatrix is a diagonal matrix with nonzero elements along the diagonal; all other elements in the first r columns are zero. With this, we defined the submatrix C_k^r (for $k < r$) as the submatrix of A consisting of the first r rows and the first $r + 1$ columns except column k. Then, for $k < r$, $A_{k,r} \neq 0$ exactly when C_k^r is invertible (we prove this by showing that the rows of C_k^r are linearly independent). We can do something similar for $k \geq r$; this time we consider R_k^r, defined to be the submatrix of A consisting of the first $r+1$ columns and rows $\{0, 1, \ldots r - 1, k\}$. Similarly, R_k^r is invertible iff $A_{k,r} \neq 0$. We will say that A is *strongly invertible* if, for all $0 \leq r < m$, C_k^r is invertible for all $k < r$ and R_k^r is invertible for all $k \geq r$. Finally, we prove that RGE is equivalent to full Gaussian elimination iff input A is strongly invertible.

Note that this condition requires a particular set of m^2 submatrices of the input $m \times n$ matrix to be invertible, quite a difficult condition to satisfy. However, in this application, Gaussian elimination is applied to only two kinds of matrices: the matrices W_2' in the decoder and a Vandermonde matrix on $x^{n_{max}-2}, \ldots, x^2, x, 1$ (where x is the primitive element of the field). The strong invertibility of each ultimately follows from properties of Vandermonde matrices: the result for the first matrix follows from Theorem 1, while the result for the second is harder to show, but ultimately follows from repeated applications of Theorem 2 and use of the fact that the field elements are consecutive powers of the primitive element. With this, we proved the previously unknown result that RGE suffices for this application and that the errors shown in Sect. 4.2 are never reached.

6   Verifying the Implementation

The C code consists of five primary functions with the following signatures:

```
// Populate the field lookup tables
void fec_generate_math_tables(void)
// (Restricted) Gaussian elimination on the i_max × j_max matrix p
int fec_matrix_transform(unsigned char *p, unsigned char i_max,
   unsigned char j_max)
// Generate weight matrix (row−reduced Vandermonde matrix)
void fec_generate_weights(void)
// Encode the data by appending h parity packets to the k data packets in pdata.
// plen is an array of the lengths of the data packets.
// pstat is a flag, all are initially FEC_FLAG_KNOWN.
int fec_blk_encode(int k, int h, int c, unsigned char **pdata, int *plen, char *pstat)
// Decode the packets in pdata. The ith flag in pstat is FEC_FLAG_WANTED if
// the ith packet is missing, otherwise FEC_FLAG_KNOWN
int fec_blk_decode (int k, int c, unsigned char **pdata, int *plen, char *pstat)
```

Each of these functions has a corresponding VST specification. We first describe key implementation differences and verification challenges, then discuss the specs for selected functions in Sect. 6.4 and Sect. 6.5.

6.1   Implementation Differences from Algorithm

Broadly, the C code implements the RSE algorithm from Sect. 2 with the parameters $k_{max} = 127$ and $h_{max} = 128$ (as well as a bound of 16000 on c, but this does not affect the correctness). However, neither this algorithm nor the functional model precisely align with the C implementation. Instead, the implementation makes a few changes, and we must prove that these changes do not modify the algorithm's behavior:

– The code uses Restricted Gaussian Elimination rather than Gaussian elimination; see Sect. 5.2.
– The encoder described in Sect. 2.2 takes W' to be the submatrix consisting of the first h rows and the first k columns. But the implementation takes the last k columns in reverse order (and likewise for the decoder) because of how the weight matrix is arranged in memory.
– In the decoder, rather than computing $P - W'_1 D_1$ with a multiplication followed by a subtraction, the implementation does this via a single larger multiplication, taking advantage of the fact that the left hand side of the weight matrix is the identity. The result of the computation is equivalent (though this is not completely trivial), but it is unclear why the authors chose this.
– Due to the representation of matrices in memory, the decoder computes the last matrix multiplication by implicitly reversing the rows of the first matrix and the columns of the second one. Equivalence with standard matrix multiplication is not too hard to prove thanks to MathComp's utilities for iterated summations.

- The code takes as input a sequence of variable-length packets, and we want to recover the original data once the decoder has finished. The RSE algorithm only describes how to generate the recovered packets, but the implementation has to put each packet pointer in its correct position in the packet array and ensure that the length for each packet is correct. The functional model includes filling in missing packets, but it uses matrices of uniform length.

6.2 Implementation-Specific Verification Challenges

Aside from differences between the algorithm and implementation, the C code, first written 25 years ago and last modified over 15 years ago, does several things that make it poorly suited to verification:

- Matrices are represented in memory very inconsistently: as pointers, global 2D arrays, local 2D arrays treated as though they were 1D arrays, and arrays of pointers to each row. The C code freely converts between these types; therefore, we had to prove several general results in VST to improve support for 2D arrays and pointer arithmetic. For example, to convert between 1D and 2D arrays, we prove that a 2D array in memory containing Coq list-of-lists l is equal to storing a 1D array containing concat l, all of the inner lists of l concatenated together. This lemma is generic and will be added to VST for future use. For dealing with arrays of pointers, we used VST's iter_sepcon, which represents iterated separating conjunction over a collection of predicates, and we proved lemmas allowing us to extract and modify a single element of the collection. Additionally, we needed several smaller lemmas and tactics for handling the resulting pointer-equality proof obligations arising from these type conversions and for simplifying the pointer comparisons in loop guards, which we plan to contribute to VST in order to improve the handling of pointer arithmetic.
- Field multiplication is frequently called in a loop, so it was written as a macro rather than a function. VST's front end expands macros, so we would have to prove the correctness of multiplication every time it is used. To avoid this, we changed the macro to a function. This did not have any effect on performance; at gcc optimization level O2 and O3, the performance was the same, and at level O3, the function was inlined.
- The C function for the decoder includes about 30 local variables (including stack-allocated arrays with tens of thousands of elements) and several layers of nested loops; VST became quite slow due to the extremely large context. This required significant proof engineering to make verification feasible, including the use of opaque constants to stop giant arrays from being unfolded and heavy use of the *frame rule*, which allows one to "frame out" parts of the context which are not needed and recover them later, to verify each loop independently.
- The code accesses memory using an inconsistent mix of pointer arithmetic, array indexing, and combinations of both. The VST proof obligations are different in these cases, and we need some auxiliary assertions about equality of memory locations and pointer arithmetic to reason about these dereferences.

6.3   VST Specifications

A C specification in VST looks like:

DECLARE f
WITH $\vec{v}$
PRE [$param\_typs$]
  PROP(p_1) PARAMS($params$) GLOBALS($globs$) SEP(s_1)
POST [ret_ty]
  PROP(p_2) RETURN(ret) SEP(s_2)

where f is the function name, $param\_typs$ are the C function parameter types, ret_ty is the C return type, $params$ are the (symbolic) values of the function parameters, $globs$ are the global variables, and ret is the (symbolic) return value. The entire PRE block represents the precondition, which must hold before the function is run. The POST block is the postcondition, which is true after the function finishes. $p1$ and $p2$ are propositions in Coq's logic, while $s1$ and $s2$ are propositions in separation logic—they describe the contents of memory. Finally, the variables $\vec{v}$ in the WITH clause are logical variables, abstract mathematical values to which the precondition and postcondition can refer.

6.4   Verifying fec_generate_math_tables

The first C function is fec_generate_math_tables, the function that generates the power, logarithm, and inverse tables for the field elements. This function, like the others, is interesting because of how it modifies memory, not because of what it returns; thus the interesting part of the VST spec is the SEP clause. The precondition's SEP clause says that the global array _fec_2_index (the power table) initially stores fec_n zeroes. In the postcondition, this global array now stores the Coq list byte_pows, which we define as the powers of field element x (the ith entry contains x^i). We have similar Coq lists and pre- and post-conditions for the log table and inverse table.

Proving that the field table generation is correct is largely straightforward, given the field definitions described in Sect. 4.3. However, there were two main complications. The first comes from the method of populating the tables: compute x^i for all $0 \le i < 256$ by repeatedly multiplying the result by x in each iteration (this can be implemented efficiently as a bitwise shift left and an xor). The correctness of this method relies on the fact that the modulus polynomial is primitive (i.e., the smallest n such that the modulus polynomial divides $x^n - 1$ is 255), and is not trivial to show in Coq.

Separately, although in the functional model we prove results for arbitrary fields and irreducible polynomials, here we need to show that several specific polynomials are irreducible and primitive (several field sizes are allowed by the code, although only one is used). Both of these conditions require showing that a polynomial is not divisible by a set of polynomials, so the easiest way to show this is by direct computation along with a proof that this computation is sufficient. However, MathComp polynomials are opaque and not computable (dividing two MathComp polynomials results in a hanging computation), so we needed to define concrete, computable polynomials and operations and relate them to their MathComp equivalents. Then, we can prove that the particular polynomials that the C code uses satisfy all needed properties.

6.5 Verifying fec_blk_decode

The function spec for fec_blk_decode is quite long; it consists of many tedious preconditions to ensure that the input packets are stored correctly in memory, that the length and packet status arrays correspond to the actual packets in memory, and that the various integer parameters are within their correct bounds. The list of preconditions is long; however, these functions are called by client functions that do packet-handling and buffer management, and the verification of *those* functions will check that they do indeed set up their inputs correctly (see Sect. 8).

We focus on a key part of the spec: the precondition's SEP clause includes the predicate iter_sepcon_arrays packet_ptrs packets, which states that the Coq list packets is stored in memory at the given pointers. In the postcondition's SEP clause, this becomes iter_sepcon_arrays packet_ptrs (decoder_list k c packets parities stats lengths parbound). In other words, after the function is run, the contents of the packet memory are represented by the *low-level functional model* of the decoder (the version that uses concrete types that VST can understand rather than opaque MathComp types).

Our decoder_correct theorem (Sect. 5.1) states that the *high-level functional model* correctly reconstructs the missing packets that were originally given to the encoder. Lemma decoder_list_correct lowers that result to the low-level functional model, using some injectivity results between the two models.

Thus, a client of the code can compose the VST spec and the correctness theorem to prove that, after fec_blk_decode is run, as long as the received packets and parities were correct, the missing data is recovered and the original data is now stored in memory (see Sect. 8).

6.6 Implementation Bug

While verifying fec_matrix_transform, we discovered a bug in the following code:

```
q = (p + (i * j_max) + j_max − 1);
m = q − j_max;
for (n = q; n > m; n−−) {
    //loop body
}
```

Here, i ranges from 0 to i_max, and p is a pointer to the input matrix. The problem is, when $i = 0$, q points to p + j_max − 1 and thus m points to p − 1. By the C standard and the semantics of CompCert C, the comparison n > m is undefined behavior. In fact, in C11, even the line q − j_max is undefined behavior [12, Section 6.5.6, #8].

This may seem harmless, but 21st-century C compilers optimize under the assumption that the program does not exhibit undefined behavior. A compiler can assume that $m = q - j\_max$ cannot be reached when $i = 0$, and it may mangle the loop body "knowing" that $i \neq 0$. This has caused problems for systems code [26], and the solution is to avoid writing C programs with undefined behavior.

Fortunately, VST's machine-checked proof of soundness makes it impossible to prove a C program correct that contains undefined behavior (unless ruled out by a function precondition). The loop test $n > m$ cannot be verified in VST, since undefined behavior cannot be ruled out.

Without formal methods, this type of bug is quite difficult to find: it depends on subtle C semantics, today's static analyzers won't catch it,[2] and testing cannot catch it until (in some future year) an optimizing C compiler gets more aggressive. VST provides blanket assurance against this entire class of errors.

Moreover, because VST uses separation logic, we specify exactly what effects the code is allowed to have. Thus, in principle, this kind of verification is 100% resistant to adversarial attacks that try and put exploits into code provided that those exploits can be defined as a functional property of the C code (such as which memory addresses it accesses, what system calls it makes, etc.). But our methods cannot defend against side-channel attacks.

7   Related Work

Verification of Network Middleboxes. Through several recent efforts, verification of network functions running in the dataplane has become increasingly feasible. Software dataplane verification [9] uses symbolic execution to prove certain low-level properties (such as memory safety) about programs written with Click, a popular framework for configuring routers and writing network functions. Gravel [31] uses symbolic execution and SMT solvers to verify many middlebox-specific properties of Click programs, including functional correctness. VigNAT [30] uses a mix of symbolic execution and proof checking to verify a Network Address Translation (NAT) implementation in C; this approach requires the use of a specialized data structure library and annotations on the C program but is quite automated overall. Vigor [29] builds on VigNAT to extend similar methods to more general network function verification. It uses a simpler but less expressive specification language, enabling fully automatic verification. Vigor and VigNAT use Verifast [13], a separation-logic-based tool for verifying C programs that is more automated than VST but is not connected to a proof assistant; this makes functional model proofs much more difficult.

These tools are considerably more automated than our work, but face significant restrictions on the type of code they can verify: none can verify code with

---

[2] "Conceptually, this undefined-behavior optimization bug is possible to trigger with STACK's approach [26]. But, as for the current implementation of STACK, the answer is likely no, because it depends on LLVM to do loop unrolling/inlining … and I doubt LLVM would do either …." (Xi Wang, e-mail of May 23, 2022).

arbitrary unbounded loops, pointer arithmetic, or use of complex data structures. More importantly, none could handle the mathematical reasoning needed to prove the correctness of the functional model and ensure that the FEC correctly reconstructs packets.

Verification of Error-Correcting Codes. Since error-correcting codes are both ubiquitous and quite complex to implement correctly, there has been a long line of research in formalizing various codes. Most of these efforts take the form of either automated hardware verification of digital circuits or recent efforts to create formalized libraries of error-correcting codes. We believe that our work is the first to connect a high-level, mathematical specification with an efficient implementation.

Error-correcting codes are hard to verify with automated methods such as model checking and BDDs because of the large state space and the complexity of the algorithms. Some recent efforts [8] have used automated hardware verification tools to verify (non-Reed-Solomon) ECCs, but they can handle very few bit errors. BLUEVERI [16] is a tool for verifying hardware implementations of finite field operations and was applied to Reed-Solomon codes. It can handle more errors (up to almost a dozen bits), but requires extensive manual effort and knowledge of hardware implementation details.

In a separate vein, several recently-developed libraries of formalized coding theory are similar to the functional model in our work, but are not connected to an efficient implementation. Most notably, Affeldt, Garrigue, and Saikawa have developed a Coq library for error-correcting codes, including Hamming and acyclic LDPC [1], Reed-Solomon [2], and BCH [3] codes. This library is built atop MathComp, and includes many theoretical results about each of these codes as well as specific encoders and decoders. Ideally, we would have liked to use this library as part of our functional model, but the implementation we verified differs significantly from standard Reed-Solomon coding, which corrects errors rather than erasures. Their library's Euclidean-algorithm-based decoding is extremely different from the decoder in RSE.

In Lean, a coding theory library called Cotoleta was developed and used to prove results about Levenshtein distance [14] and Hamming(7,4) codes [11]. Separately, Hamming(7,4) and $\frac{1}{2}$-rate convolutional codes were verified in the ACL2 theorem prover [20] with a particular focus on correcting memory errors; these codes were verified against a particular memory model. Both of these projects focused on verifying concrete-sized codes; thus they did not require the same level of abstraction or general mathematical reasoning as our work.

8   Future Work

In a real system, the encoder and decoder verified in this work are called by clients who handle receiving packets, assigning them to batches, and maintaining various data structures. We are currently working to verify a real-world version of such a system. This will permit a single, clean, end-to-end correctness result;

right now, we have separate results for the decoder's correctness and the C program refinement which must be composed together. However, the specification of such a system introduces new challenges; it must reason about packet streams and network-specific features such as headers, timeouts, and packet reordering.

This C implementation of RSE has been useful in several projects at Bellcore/Telcordia/Peraton even though it cannot run at modern packet bit rates. We believe that a line-rate FPGA implementation of the finite-field matrix-multiply partial step is possible, and we are designing an API by which this could be controlled by a C program or a P4 program. Such an FPGA could be proved correct by a layered proof. The top layer would be our MathComp proof with no changes. The bottom layer could be proved using a Coq tool for hardware synthesis and functional-correctness verification, such as Kôika [7].

9   Conclusion

We have presented an efficient, real-world C implementation of Reed-Solomon forward erasure correction that we formally verified using the Coq proof assistant and the Verified Software Toolchain. The code was verified with only minor changes; one macro was turned into a function for ease of verification and one bug that caused undefined behavior was fixed. While the code has been in use for over 25 years, the correctness of certain parts of the underlying algorithm, a modified form of Reed-Solomon erasure coding, were still ill-understood, including a very restricted form of Gaussian elimination. We were able to use Coq's Mathematical Components library to completely verify the correctness of this algorithm and VST to prove that the C code, with its various optimizations and modifications, correctly implements this algorithm. This demonstrates that tools like VST allow us to verify real-world, dusty-deck programs in C, even those whose correctness depends on a broad base of mathematics and those with numerous low-level optimizations. We believe this can be a viable approach to connect efficient low-level code with sophisticated high-level reasoning, enabling reliable software components for networks and other systems.

Appendix

The appendix to this paper can be found in our git repo (see footnote 1) in doc/Appendix.pdf.

References

1. Affeldt, R., Garrigue, J.: Formalization of error-correcting codes: from Hamming to modern coding theory. In: Urban, C., Zhang, X. (eds.) ITP 2015. LNCS, vol. 9236, pp. 17–33. Springer, Cham (2015). https://doi.org/10.1007/978-3-319-22102-1_2
2. Affeldt, R., Garrigue, J., Saikawa, T.: Formalization of Reed-Solomon codes and progress report on formalization of LDPC codes. In: 2016 International Symposium on Information Theory and Its Applications (ISITA), pp. 532–536 (2016)

3. Affeldt, R., Garrigue, J., Saikawa, T.: A library for formalization of linear error-correcting codes. J. Autom. Reason. **64**(6), 1123–1164 (2020). https://doi.org/10.1007/s10817-019-09538-8
4. Appel, A.W.: Verification of a cryptographic primitive: SHA-256. ACM Trans. Program. Lang. Syst. **37**(2), 1–31 (2015). https://doi.org/10.1145/2701415
5. Appel, A.W., Bertot, Y.: C floating-point proofs layered with VST and Flocq. J. Formaliz. Reason. **13**(1), 1–16 (2020). https://doi.org/10.6092/issn.1972-5787/11442
6. Appel, A.W., et al.: Program Logics for Certified Compilers. Cambridge University Press, Cambridge (2014)
7. Bourgeat, T., Pit-Claudel, C., Chlipala, A.: The essence of Bluespec: a core language for rule-based hardware design. In: PLDI'20: Proceedings of the 41st ACM SIGPLAN Conference on Programming Language Design and Implementation, pp. 243–257 (2020)
8. Devarajegowda, K., Servadei, L., Han, Z., Werner, M., Ecker, W.: Formal verification methodology in an industrial setup. In: 2019 22nd Euromicro Conference on Digital System Design (DSD), pp. 610–614 (2019). https://doi.org/10.1109/DSD.2019.00094
9. Dobrescu, M., Argyraki, K.: Software dataplane verification. In: 11th USENIX Symposium on Networked Systems Design and Implementation (NSDI 14), pp. 101–114. USENIX Association, Seattle, April 2014
10. Gonthier, G., Mahboubi, A., Tassi, E.: A Small Scale Reflection Extension for the Coq system. Research Report RR-6455, Inria Saclay Ile de France (2015). https://hal.inria.fr/inria-00258384
11. Hagiwara, M., Nakano, K., Kong, J.: Formalization of coding theory using lean. In: 2016 International Symposium on Information Theory and Its Applications (ISITA), pp. 522–526 (2016)
12. ISO: ISO/IEC 9899:2011 Information technology – Programming languages – C, December 2011. http://www.open-std.org/jtc1/sc22/wg14/www/docs/n1548.pdf
13. Jacobs, B., Piessens, F.: The VeriFast program verifier (2008)
14. Kong, J., Webb, D.J., Hagiwara, M.: Formalization of insertion/deletion codes and the Levenshtein metric in lean. In: 2018 International Symposium on Information Theory and Its Applications (ISITA), pp. 11–15 (2018)
15. Leroy, X.: Formal verification of a realistic compiler. Commun. ACM **52**(7), 107–115 (2009). https://doi.org/10.1145/1538788.1538814
16. Lvov, A., Lastras-Montaño, L.A., Paruthi, V., Shadowen, R., El-Zein, A.: Formal verification of error correcting circuits using computational algebraic geometry. In: 2012 Formal Methods in Computer-Aided Design (FMCAD), pp. 141–148 (2012)
17. Mansky, W., Honoré, W., Appel, A.W.: Connecting higher-order separation logic to a first-order outside world. In: ESOP 2020. LNCS, vol. 12075, pp. 428–455. Springer, Cham (2020). https://doi.org/10.1007/978-3-030-44914-8_16
18. McAuley, A.J.: Reliable broadband communication using a burst erasure correcting code. In: Proceedings of the ACM Symposium on Communications Architectures & Protocols, SIGCOMM 1990, New York, NY, USA, pp. 297–306 (1990). https://doi.org/10.1145/99508.99566
19. McAuley, A.J.: Forward error correction code system. U.S. Patent 5,115,436 (1992)
20. Naseer, M., Ahmad, W., Hasan, O.: Formal verification of ECCs for memories using ACL2. J. Electron. Test. **36**(5), 643–663 (2020). https://doi.org/10.1007/s10836-020-05904-2
21. Plank, J.S.: A tutorial on Reed-Solomon coding for fault-tolerance in RAID-like systems. Softw. Pract. Exp. **27**(9), 995–1012 (1997)

22. Preparata, F.P.: Holographic dispersal and recovery of information. IEEE Trans. Inf. Theory **35**(5), 1123–1124 (2006). https://doi.org/10.1109/18.42233
23. Rabin, M.O.: Efficient dispersal of information for security, load balancing, and fault tolerance. J. ACM **36**(2), 335–348 (1989). https://doi.org/10.1145/62044.62050
24. Reed, I.S., Solomon, G.: Polynomial codes over certain finite fields. J. Soc. Ind. Appl. Math. **8**, 300–304 (1960)
25. Schwarz, T., Buckhard, W.: RAID organization and performance. In: [1992] Proceedings of the 12th International Conference on Distributed Computing Systems, pp. 318–325 (1992). https://doi.org/10.1109/ICDCS.1992.235025
26. Wang, X., Zeldovich, N., Kaashoek, M.F., Solar-Lezama, A.: Towards optimization-safe systems: analyzing the impact of undefined behavior. In: Proceedings of the Twenty-Fourth ACM Symposium on Operating Systems Principles, SOSP 2013, pp. 260–275. Association for Computing Machinery (2013). https://doi.org/10.1145/2517349.2522728
27. Wicker, S.B., Bhargava, V.K.: Reed-Solomon Codes and Their Applications. Wiley-IEEE Press (1999)
28. Ye, K.Q., Green, M., Sanguansin, N., Beringer, L., Petcher, A., Appel, A.W.: Verified correctness and security of mbedTLS HMAC-DRBG. In: Proceedings of the 2017 ACM SIGSAC Conference on Computer and Communications Security, CCS 2017, New York, NY, USA, pp. 2007–2020 (2017). https://doi.org/10.1145/3133956.3133974
29. Zaostrovnykh, A., et al.: Verifying software network functions with no verification expertise. In: Proceedings of the 27th ACM Symposium on Operating Systems Principles, SOSP 2019, New York, NY, USA, pp. 275–290 (2019). https://doi.org/10.1145/3341301.3359647
30. Zaostrovnykh, A., Pirelli, S., Pedrosa, L., Argyraki, K., Candea, G.: A formally verified NAT. In: Proceedings of the Conference of the ACM Special Interest Group on Data Communication, SIGCOMM 2017, New York, NY, USA, pp. 141–154 (2017). https://doi.org/10.1145/3098822.3098833
31. Zhang, K., Zhuo, D., Akella, A., Krishnamurthy, A., Wang, X.: Automated verification of customizable middlebox properties with Gravel. In: 17th USENIX Symposium on Networked Systems Design and Implementation (NSDI 20), pp. 221–239. USENIX Association, Santa Clara, CA, February 2020. https://www.usenix.org/conference/nsdi20/presentation/zhang-kaiyuan

End-to-End Mechanized Proof
of an eBPF Virtual Machine
for Micro-controllers

Shenghao Yuan[1]([⊠])[iD], Frédéric Besson[1][iD], Jean-Pierre Talpin[1][iD],
Samuel Hym[2], Koen Zandberg[4], and Emmanuel Baccelli[3,4][iD]

[1] Inria, Rennes, France
{shenghao.yuan,frederic.besson,
jean-pierre.talpin}@inria.fr
[2] University of Lille, CNRS, Centrale Lille,
UMR 9189 CRIStAL, 59000 Lille, France
samuel.hym@univ-lille.fr
[3] Freie Universität Berlin, Berlin, Germany
[4] Inria, Saclay, France
{koen.zandberg,emmanuel.baccelli}@inria.fr

Abstract. RIOT is a micro-kernel dedicated to IoT applications that
adopts eBPF (extended Berkeley Packet Filters) to implement so-called
femto-containers. As micro-controllers rarely feature hardware memory
protection, the isolation of eBPF virtual machines (VM) is critical to
ensure system integrity against potentially malicious programs. This
paper shows how to directly derive, within the Coq proof assistant, the
verified C implementation of an eBPF virtual machine from a Gallina
specification. Leveraging the formal semantics of the CompCert C compiler, we obtain an end-to-end theorem stating that the C code of our
VM inherits the safety and security properties of the Gallina specification. Our refinement methodology ensures that the isolation property
of the specification holds in the verified C implementation. Preliminary
experiments demonstrate satisfying performance.

Keywords: Mechanized proof · Virtual machines · Fault isolation

1 Introduction

Hardware-enforced memory isolation (*e.g.*, Trustzone, Sanctum [6], Sancus [30])
is often not available on micro-controller units (MCU) which usually trade
coarse-grain isolation for price and performance. To mitigate development variability and cost, common practices for MCU operating system design (RIOT [3],
FreeRTOS, TinyOS, Fushia, and others [14]) advise to run all the device's code
stack in a shared memory space, which can only be reasonably safe if that code
can be trusted. While standard in safety-critical system design, such a trust
requirement is oftentimes unsuitable for networked MCUs, where the extensibility of the OS kernel at runtime is an essential functionality. When system

© The Author(s) 2022
S. Shoham and Y. Vizel (Eds.): CAV 2022, LNCS 13372, pp. 293–316, 2022.
https://doi.org/10.1007/978-3-031-13188-2_15

reconfiguration does not affect the entire network (via, *e.g.,* leader election), extensibility can easily be provided offline, by employing library OSs or unikernels [24], to reconfigure network endpoints independently (*e.g.,* cloud apps). Otherwise, the best solution is to load and execute system extensions (configurations, protocols, firewalls, etc.) as assembly-level Wasm [13] or Berkeley Packet Filters [25] scripts using an interpreter or a Just-In-Time (JIT) compiler on the target device.

Femto-Containers. RIOT adopts the extended Berkeley Packet Filters (eBPF) and tailors it to resource-constrained MCUs by implementing so-called femto-containers: tiny virtual machine instances interpreting eBPF scripts. Compared to more expressive languages, like Wasm, experiments show that RIOT's eBPF implementation, rBPF, requires less memory [39]. The Linux kernel features an eBPF JIT compiler whose security depends on a sophisticated online verifier [29]. As an MCU architecture cannot host such a large verifier, executing JIT code would imply delegation of trust to a third-party, offline, verifier. The alternative is to rely on a defensive VM. Though a VM may be slower than a JIT, it can run untrusted, erroneous, adversary code in an open, and possibly hostile environment, and still isolate faults to protect its host's integrity.

Approach and Goals. This paper investigates an approach that trades high performance on low-power devices for defensive programming and low memory footprint. Our primary goal is to prevent faults that could compromise host devices and, by extension, force networked devices to reboot and resynchronize (*i.e.,* fault tolerance protocols). To maximize trust in the implementation of rBPF, our refinement methodology allows the verified extraction of C code directly from its mechanically proved definition in Gallina, the functional language embedded in the Coq proof assistant [4].

Method. To mechanically prove the correctness of an interpreter, a conventional approach consists in defining the reference semantics in a proof assistant and in showing that an executable optimized interpreter produces the same output. In this paper, our goal is to verify the interpreter of the virtual rBPF instruction set, implemented with the system programming language C. To this aim, we introduce a direct, end-to-end, validation workflow. The semantics of the source instruction set is directly defined by monadic functional terms in our proof assistant. We prove that this semantics enforces safety and security requirements regarding memory isolation and control-flow integrity. Then, C code is automatically derived from these monadic functional terms to implement the expected virtual machine. We prove that the extracted C code has the same stateful behavior as the monadic specification. Our method uses a monadic subset of Gallina of sufficient expressiveness to specify rBPF's semantics, supports the verified extraction of equivalent Clight [20] code, while provably implementing all required defensive runtime checks.

Plan. The rest of the paper is organized as follows. Section 2 states our contributions. Section 3 provides background on BPF and its variants, CompCert and the ∂x code extraction tool. Section 4 presents our workflow to formally refine monadic Gallina programs into C programs. Section 5 defines the proof model of our virtual machine: its semantics, consistency and isolation theorems. Section 6 refines the proof model of our femto-container into a synthesis model ready for code generation with CompCert. Section 7 proves the refinement between the synthesis and implementation models. Section 8 introduces our verified verifier which establishes the invariants needed by the VM. Section 9 case studies the performance of our generated VM implementation with respect to off-the-shelf RIOT femto-containers. Section 10 presents related works and Sect. 11 concludes.

2   Contributions

Implementing a fault-isolating virtual machine for MCUs faces two major challenges. One is to embed the VM inside the MCU's micro-kernel and, hence, to minimize its code size and execution environment. A second challenge is to minimize the verification gap between its proof model and the running code. We address these challenges and present the first end-to-end verification and synthesis of a full-scale, real-world, virtual machine for the BPF instruction set family: CertrBPF, an interpreter tailored to the hardware and resources constraints of MCU architectures running the RIOT operating system. CertrBPF employs a workflow of proof-oriented programming using the functional language Gallina embedded in the proof assistant Coq. The verified refinement and extraction of an executable C program is performed directly from its proof model. We report the successful integration of CertrBPF into the open source IoT operating system RIOT and the evaluation of its performance against micro-benchmarks.

A Certified rBPF Interpreter. CertrBPF is a verified model and implementation of rBPF in Coq. We formalize the syntax and semantics of all rBPF instructions, implement a formal model of its interpreter (femto-container), complete the proof of critical properties of our model, and extract and verify CompCert C code from this formalization. This method allows us to obtain a fully verified virtual machine. Not only is the Gallina specification of the VM proved kernel- and memory-isolated using the proof assistant, but the direct interpretation of its intended semantics as CompCert C code is, itself, verified correct. This yields a fully verified binary program of maximum security and minimal memory footprint and reduced the Trusted Computing Base (TCB): CertrBPF, a memory-efficient kernel-level virtual machine that isolates runtime software faults using defensive code and does not necessitate offline verification.

End-to-End Proof Workflow. An obvious choice is to use the existing Coq extraction mechanism to compile the Gallina model into OCaml. The downside of this approach is that Coq extraction has to be trusted. Moreover the OCaml runtime needs to be trimmed down to fit space requirements of our target architecture and also becomes part of the TCB. Our ambition is instead to minimize the verification gap and provide an end-to-end security proof linking our Gallina model to, bare-metal, extracted C code. Our intended TCB is hence restricted to the Coq type-checker, the C semantics of the CompCert compiler and a pretty-printer for the generated C Abstract Syntax Tree (AST).

To reach this goal, our starting point is a model of the rBPF semantics written in Gallina. We use this proof model to certify that all the memory accesses are valid and isolated to dedicated memory areas, thus ensuring isolation. From this proof model, we then derive a synthesis model of which we extract an executable version in Clight, that we finally prove to perform the same state transitions.

Systems Integration and Micro-benchmarks. We integrate CertrBPF as a drop-in replacement of the current, non-verified, rBPF interpreter in the RIOT operating system. We then comparatively evaluate the performance of CertrBPF integrated in RIOT, running on various 32-bit micro-controller architectures. Our benchmarks demonstrate that, in practice, CertrBPF not just gains security, but reduces memory footprint as well as execution time.

3   Background

This section describes essential features of rBPF, of the CompCert compiler, and of the ∂x code generation tool, that are required by our refinement methodology.

BPF, eBPF and rBPF. Originally, the purpose of Berkeley Packet Filters [25] (BPF) was network packet filtering. The Linux community extended it to provide ways to run custom in-kernel VM code, hooked into various subsystems, for varieties of purposes beyond packet filtering [10]. eBPF was then ported to micro-controllers, yielding RIOT's specification: rBPF [38]. Just as eBPF, rBPF is designed as a 64-bit register-based VM, using fixed-size 64-bit instructions and a reduced instruction set architecture. rBPF uses a fixed-size stack (512 bytes) and defines no heap interaction, which limits the VM memory overhead in RAM. The rBPF specification, however, does not define special registers or interrupts for flow control, nor support virtual memory: the host device's memory is accessed directly and only guarded using permissions.

The CompCert Verified Compiler. CompCert [18] is a C compiler that is both programmed and proved correct using the Coq proof assistant. The compiler is structured into passes using several intermediate languages. Each intermediate language is equipped with a formal semantics and each pass is proved to preserve the observational behavior of programs.

The Clight Intermediate Language. Clight [20] is a pivotal language which condenses the essential features of C using a minimal syntax. The Verified Software Toolchain (VST) [2] verifies C programs at the Clight level that are obtained by the CLIGHTGEN tool. Though we do not reuse the proof infrastructure of VST, we are reusing CLIGHTGEN in order to get a Clight syntax from a C program.

CompCert Values and Memory Model [19,20]. The memory model and the representation of values are shared across all the intermediate languages of CompCert. The set of values *val* is defined as follows:

$$val \ni v::= Vint(i) \mid Vlong(i) \mid Vptr(b, o) \mid Vundef \mid \ldots$$

A value $v \in val$ can be a 32-bit integer $Vint(i)$; a 64-bit integer $Vlong(i)$, a pointer $Vptr(b, o)$ consisting of a block identifier b and an offset o, or the undefined value $Vundef$. The undefined value $Vundef$ represents an unspecified value and is not, strictly speaking, an undefined behavior. Yet, as most of the C operators are strict in $Vundef$, and because branching over $Vundef$ or de-referencing $Vundef$ are undefined behaviors, our proofs will ensure the absence of $Vundef$. CompCert values also include floating-point numbers; they play no role in the current development. CompCert's memory consists of a collection of separate arrays. Each array has a fixed size determined at allocation time and is identified by an uninterpreted block $b \in block$. The memory provides an API for loading values from memory and storing values in memory. Operations are parameterised by a memory chunk k which specifies how many bytes should be written or read and how to interpret bytes as a value $v \in val$.

For instance, the memory chunk $Mint32$ specifies a 32-bit value and $Mint64$ a 64-bit value. The function $load \ k \ m \ b \ o$ takes a memory chunk k, a memory m, a block b and an offset o. Upon success, it returns a value v obtained from the memory by reading bytes from the block b starting at index o. Similarly, the function $store \ k \ m \ b \ o \ v$ takes a memory chunk k, a memory m, a block b, an offset o and a value v. Upon success, it returns an updated memory m' which is identical to m except that the block b contains the value v encoded into bytes according to the chunk k starting at offset o. The isolation properties offered by CompCert memory regions are worth mentioning: $load$ and $store$ operations fail (return $None$) for invalid offsets o and invalid permissions.

The ∂x tool. ∂x emerged from the toolchain used to design and verify the Pip proto-kernel [15]. Its aim was to allow writing most of Pip's source code in Gallina in a style as close to C as possible. ∂x extracts C code from a Gallina source program in the form of a CompCert C AST. The goal of ∂x is to provide C programmers with readily reviewable code and thus avoid misunderstanding between those working on C/assembly modules (that access hardware) and those working on Coq modules (the code and proofs). To achieve this, ∂x handles a C-like subset of Gallina. The functions that are to be converted to C rely on a monad to represent the side effects of the computation, such as modifications to the CPU state. Yet ∂x does not mandate a particular monad for code extraction.

∂x 's Workflow. ∂x proceeds in two steps. First, given a list of Gallina functions, or whole modules, it generates an intermediate representation (IR) for the subset of Gallina it can handle. The second step is to translate this IR into a CompCert C AST. Since Coq has no built-in reflection mechanism, the first step is written in Elpi [8], using the Coq-Elpi plugin [37]. That step can also process external functions (appearing as `extern` in the extracted C code) to support separate compilation with CompCert. In order to obtain an actual C file, ∂x also provides a small OCaml function that binds the extracted C AST to CompCert's C pretty-printer. Even though the ∂x language is a small subset of Gallina, it

inherits much expressivity from the use of Coq types to manipulate values. For example, we can use bounded integers (*i.e.*, the dependent pair of an integer with the proof that it is within some given range), that can be faithfully and efficiently represented as a single `int` in C. To this end, ∂x expects a configuration mapping Coq types to C.

∂x Memory Management. A major design choice in the C-like subset of Gallina used by ∂x is memory management: its generated code executes without garbage collection. This affects the Coq types that can actually be used in ∂x: recursive inductive types, such as lists, cannot automatically be converted. However, this Gallina subset is particularly relevant to programs in which one wants to precisely control memory management and decide how to represent data structures in memory. This is typically the case of an operating system or, in our case, the rBPF virtual machine.

4   A Workflow for End-to-End Verification in Coq

This section gives an overview of our methodology to derive a verified C implementation from a Gallina specification. In the following sections, the methodology will be instantiated to derive the C implementation of a fault-isolating rBPF virtual machine and its verifier. Our approach provides an end-to-end correctness proof, within the Coq proof assistant, that reduces the hurdle of reasoning directly over the C code.

As shown in Fig. 1, the original rBPF C implementation is first formalized by a proof model in Gallina, and the verification of expected properties (*e.g.*, safety) is performed within the Coq proof assistant. This specification is then refined into an optimized (and equivalent) synthesis model ready for C-code extraction.

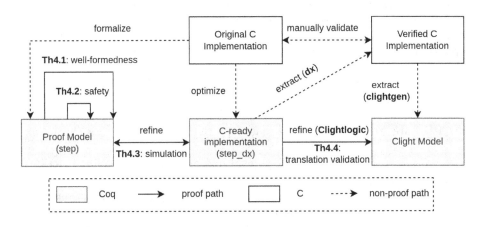

Fig. 1. End-to-end verification and synthesis workflow

The refinement and optimization principle employed by our method consists of deriving a C-ready implementation, in Gallina, that is as close as possible to the expected target C code. This principle allows to i) prove optimizations correct, ii) improve the performance of the extracted code and, iii) facilitate review and validation of extracted code with the system designers. From the C-ready Gallina implementation, we leverage ∂x to automatically generate C code and verify it: i) the generated C code is first parsed as a CompCert Clight model by the CLIGHTGEN tool of VST and ii) it is proved to refine the source Gallina model in Coq using translation validation. Because ∂x generates C code in a syntax-directed manner, a minimal *Clightlogic* is designed to facilitate the refinement proof. The rest of the section explains these different steps in details.

Proof-Oriented Specification. Our specification takes the form of an executable abstract machine in monadic form. It uses the standard option-state monad M.

$$M \; a \; state := state \rightarrow \mathbf{option}(a \times state)$$
$$returnM : a \rightarrow M \; a \; state := \lambda a.\lambda st.\mathbf{Some}(a, st)$$
$$bindM : M \; a \; state \rightarrow (a \rightarrow M \; b \; state) \rightarrow M \; b \; state :=$$
$$\lambda A.f.\lambda s.\mathbf{match} \; A \; s \; \mathbf{with} \mid \mathbf{None} \Rightarrow \mathbf{None} \mid \mathbf{Some}(x, s') \Rightarrow (f \; x) \; s'$$

In the remainder, we write $\emptyset$ for **None** and $\lfloor x \rfloor$ for **Some** x.

The monad threads the state along computations to model its in-place update. The safety property of the machine is implemented as an inline monitor: any violation leads to an unrecoverable error, *i.e.*, the unique error represented by $\emptyset$. One step of the machine has the following signature:

$$step : M \; r \; state$$

where r is the type of the result. The *step* function implements a defensive semantics, checking the absence of error, dynamically. For our rBPF interpreter (see Sect. 5), the absence of error ensures that the rBPF code only performs valid instructions. In particular, all memory accesses are restricted to a sandbox specified as a list of memory regions. Function *step* is part of the TCB and, therefore, a mis-specification could result, after refinement, in an invalid computation. The purpose of the error state is to specify state transitions that would escape the scope of the safety property and, therefore, shall never be reachable from a well-formed state $st \in wf \subseteq \mathcal{P}(state)$. We require well-formedness to be an inductive property of the *step* function.

Theorem 1 (Well-formedness). *The step function preserves well-formedness.*

$$\forall st, st', r. \; st \in wf \wedge step \; st = \lfloor (r, st') \rfloor \Rightarrow st' \in wf$$

We also require that well-formedness is a sufficient condition to prevent the absence of error and, therefore, the safety of computations.

Theorem 2 (Safety). *The step function is safe, i.e., a well-formed state never leads to an error.*

$$\forall st. \; st \in wf \Rightarrow step \; st \neq \emptyset$$

C-Ready Implementation. Our methodology consists in refining the *step* function into an interpreter *step*$_{\partial x}$ complying with the requirements of ∂x. As ∂x performs syntax-directed code generation, the efficiency of the extracted code crucially depends on *step*$_{\partial x}$. In order to preserve the absence of errors, we need a simulation relation between the *step* and *step*$_{\partial x}$ functions. A direct consequence of the simulation thoerem is that *step*$_{\partial x}$ never raises an error.

Theorem 3 (Simulation).   *Given simulation relations $Rs \subseteq$ state $\times$ state' and $Rr \subseteq r \times r'$, the function step$_{\partial x}$ simulates the function step.*

$$\forall s_1, s_1', s_2, r.(s_1, s_2) \in Rs \wedge step\ s_1 = \lfloor r, s_1' \rfloor \Rightarrow \exists s_2', r'. \bigwedge \begin{cases} step_{\partial x}\ s_2 = \lfloor r', s_2' \rfloor \\ (s_1', s_2') \in Rs \\ (r, r') \in Rr \end{cases}$$

Translation Validation of C Code. The next stage consists in refining the *step*$_{\partial x}$ function into a Clight program by relying on ∂x to get a C program and on the CLIGHTGEN tool to get a Clight *step*$_C$ program (see Sect. 6). As this pass is not trusted, we require the following translation validation theorem.

Theorem 4 (Translation Validation).   *Given a simulation relation $Rs \subseteq$ state' $\times$ val $\times$ mem and a relation $Rr \subseteq$ res $\times$ val, the Clight code step$_C$ refines the function step$_{\partial x}$:*

$$\forall r, s, s', v, k, m.(s, v, m) \in Rs \Rightarrow step_{\partial x}\ s = \lfloor (r, s') \rfloor \Rightarrow$$
$$\exists m', r'.Callstate(step_C, [v], k, m) \to^{*t} ReturnState(r', call\_cont(k), m') \wedge$$
$$(s', v, m') \in Rs \wedge (r, r') \in Rr$$

Theorem 4 states that, if *step*$_{\partial x}$ *s* runs without error and returns a result (r, s'), then, the Clight function *step*$_C$ successfully runs with argument v and, after a finite number of execution steps, returns a result r' and a memory m' that preserve the refinement relations. In our encoding, the unique argument v is a pointer to the memory allocated region refining the interpreter state and k represents the continuation of the computation. A corollary of Theorem 4 is that the Clight code *step*$_C$ is free of undefined behaviors. In particular, all memory accesses are valid. As the memory model does not allow to forge pointers, this yields a strong isolation property. In the remainder of this paper, for our rBPF virtual machine, we prove all the aforementioned properties within the Coq proof assistant.

5   A Proof-Oriented Virtual Machine Model

For our proof model, we define an explicit syntax for rBPF. We also define the state of the interpreter and semantic functions, in particular those implementing dynamic security checks. The rBPF instruction set, Fig. 2, features binary arithmetic and logic operations, negation, (un)conditional jumps relative to an offset, operations to load/store values from/to registers/memory, function calls, and termination. There are eleven 64-bit registers $\{R0, \ldots, R10\}$; an immediate is 32-bit wide and an offset is 16-bit wide.

(Operands)	$dst, reg \in registers$, $src \in registers \cup immediate$
	$imm \in immediate$, $ofs \in offset$
(Chunk)	$chk ::= byte \mid halfword \mid word \mid doublewords$
(Operators)	$op ::= add \mid sub \mid mul \mid div \mid and \mid or \mid$
	$lsh \mid rsh \mid mod \mid xor \mid mov \mid arsh$
	$cmp ::= eq \mid neq \mid lt \mid gt \mid le \mid ge \mid set \mid slt \mid sgt \mid sle \mid sge$
(Instruction)	$ins ::=$ Exit $\mid$ Call $imm \mid$ Neg $dst \mid$ Ja $ofs \mid$ Jump cmp dst src ofs
	$\mid$ Alu op dst $src \mid$ Load chk dst reg $ofs \mid$ Store chk dst src ofs

Fig. 2. Core syntax of rBPF instruction set

Machine State. A semantic state st is a tuple $\langle I, L, R, F, M, MRs \rangle$ consisting of a sequence of instructions I, the current location L, registers R, an interpreter flag F, a memory M and a specification of available memory regions MRs. The flag F characterizes the state of the rBPF interpreter. It may be i) a normal state, written F_n; ii) a final state, written F_t; iii) or an error state, written F_e. An error state $f \in F_e$ means that the defensive checks of the interpreter have detected that an invalid behavior is about to occur.

A memory region $mr = \langle start, size, p, ptr \rangle \in MRs$ associates a permission $p \in \{Readable, Writable\}$ to the address range $[start, start + size)$. We make the link between concrete physical addresses and the CompCert memory model using the pointer ptr $(= Vptr\ b\ 0)$ where the block b is the abstract representation of the address $start$. We write $I(L)$ for the instruction located at the program counter L. $R[r]$ retrieves the value of the register r in the register map R. Functions alu and cmp reuse the CompCert's operators over the val type. The alu function returns $\emptyset$ if an error occurs, *e.g.*, division by zero. Functions $load$ and $store$ are those of CompCert's memory model (see Sect. 3).

$$\textbf{alu} : op \rightarrow val \rightarrow val \rightarrow option\ val \qquad \textbf{cmp} : cmp \rightarrow val \rightarrow val \rightarrow bool$$
$$\textbf{load} : chk \rightarrow mem \rightarrow block \rightarrow Z \rightarrow option\ val$$
$$\textbf{store} : chk \rightarrow mem \rightarrow block \rightarrow Z \rightarrow val \rightarrow option\ mem$$

Dynamic Checks. Function $check\_alu$ dynamically checks the validity of an arithmetic to avoid *div-by-zero* and *undefined-shift* errors. For division instructions, $check\_alu$ mandates the second argument to be non-zero. For arithmetic and logical shift instructions, the second argument has to be below $n \in \{32, 64\}$ depending on whether the ALU instruction operates on 32 or 64 bit operands. For simplicity, the paper only considers 64-bit ALU instructions but CertrBPF also has the 32-bit variants.

$$check\_alu(op, v) \stackrel{\text{def}}{=} \begin{cases} v \neq 0 & \text{if } op \in \{div, mod\} \\ 0 \leq v < n & \text{if } op \in \{lsh, rsh, arsh\} \\ true & \text{otherwise} \end{cases}$$

Function $check\_mem$ returns a valid pointer ($Vptr\ b\ ofs$) if there exists a unique memory region mr in MRs such that i) the permission $mr.perm$ is at least *Readable* for Load and *Writable* for Store, *i.e.*, $mr.perm \geq p$; ii) the offset ofs is aligned, *i.e.*, $ofs\%Z(chk) = 0$; iii) in bounds, *i.e.*, $ofs \leq max\_unsigned - Z(chk)$, iv) and the interval $[ofs, hi\_ofs)$ is in the range of mr. Otherwise, $check\_mem$

returns the null pointer $Vnullptr$. The function $Z(chk)$ maps memory chunks $byte$, $halfword$, $word$ and $double$ to 1, 2, 4, and 8, respectively.

$$check\_mem(p, chk, addr, MRs) \overset{\text{def}}{=} \textbf{if } \exists! \; mr \in MRs, b.$$
$$\textbf{let } ofs = addr - mr.start \textbf{ and } hi\_ofs = ofs + Z(chk) \textbf{ in}$$
$$(mr.ptr == Vptr \; b \; 0) \wedge (mr.perm \geq p) \wedge (ofs\%Z(chk) == 0) \wedge$$
$$(ofs \leq max\_signed - Z(chk)) \wedge (0 \leq ofs \wedge hi\_ofs < mr.size))$$
$$\textbf{then } Vptr \; b \; ofs \textbf{ else } Vnullptr$$

Semantics. Functions *interp* and *sem* formalize the implementation of our proof model M_p in the Coq proof assistant by defining a monadic interpreter of rBPF. The top-level recursion *interp* processes a (monotonically decreasing) *fuel* argument and a state s. The function *sem* processes individual instructions $I(L_{pc})$. *MRs* and I are read-only. During normal execution, the flag remains F_n. If the flag turns to F_t or F_e while processing an instruction, execution stops. For instance, if *fuel* reaches zero, the flag turns to F_e. We write $s.F$ for the value of field F in record s and $s\{F = v\}$ updates it to v.

```
interp = λfuel s. if fuel == 0 then ⌊((), s{F=Fₑ})⌋ else
    match sem s with
    | ⌊((), t)⌋ => if t.F≠ Fₙ then ⌊((), t)⌋
                    else interp (fuel-1) t{L = t.L+1}
    | ∅ => ∅

sem = λs. match s.I(s.L) with
| Exit => ⌊((), s{F = Fₜ})⌋
| Call imm => let f_ptr = bpf_get_call imm in
                if f_ptr == Vnullptr then ⌊((), s{F = Fₑ})⌋
                else ⌊((), s{R0 = exec_function f_ptr})⌋
| Ja ofs => ⌊((), s{L = s.L+ofs})⌋
| Jump c dst ofs => if cmp(c, s.R[dst], s.R[src])
                    then ⌊((), s{L = s.L+ofs})⌋ else ⌊((), s)⌋
| Neg dst => ⌊((), s{R[dst]= ¬ s.R[dst]})⌋
| Alu op dst src => if check_alu(op, s.R[src]) then
                    match alu(op, s.R[dst], s.R[src]) with
                    | ⌊v⌋ => ⌊((), s{R[dst] = v})⌋ | ∅ => ∅
                    else ⌊((), s{F = Fₑ})⌋
| Load chk dst reg ofs =>
  match check_mem(Readable, chk, s.R[reg]+ofs, s.MRs) with
  | Vptr b ofs => match load(chk, s.M, b, ofs) with
                    | ⌊v⌋ => ⌊((), s{R[dst] = v})⌋ | ∅ => ∅
  | _ => ⌊((), s{F = Fₑ})⌋
| Store chk dst src ofs =>
  match check_mem(Writable, chk, s.R[dst]+ofs, s.MRs) with
  | Vptr b ofs => match store(chk, s.M, b, ofs, S.R[src]) with
                    | ⌊N⌋ => ⌊((), s{M = N})⌋ | ∅ => ∅
  | _ => ⌊((), s{F = Fₑ})⌋
| _ => ⌊((), s{F = Fₑ})⌋
```

Result $\emptyset$ marks transitions to crash states that are proved unreachable given our carefully crafted definitions of the `check_alu` and `check_mem` functions. Note that the interpreter *interp* does not check the range of branching offsets (*i.e.*, `0 <=s.L< length(s.I)`) and register-out-of-bounds. This properties are statically verified, once and for all, by the verifier of Sect. 8.

Exit terminates the program with flag F_t. The *Call* instruction selects (using *bpf_get_call*) the trusted system API service designated by an immediate number *imm*. It then calls the chosen service if available (*i.e.*, not a null pointer). Unconditional jump *Ja* increments the *pc* by *ofs* and a conditional *Jump* does so when *cmp(c, src, dest)* holds. For an arithmetic operation Alu *op dst src*, *check_alu* first checks the validity of *op* with source *src*, evaluates *op* against destination *dst* using *alu*, stores the result *v* in register *dst*. For simplicity, we omit the case of immediate *srcs*. If the result is $\emptyset$, so becomes the monadic state (undefined behavior). Our definition of *check_alu*, and well-formedness conditions (see Sect. 5.1) ensures that this will never happen and that, in case of error, the execution terminates with flag F_e. Similarly, the semantics of memory instructions (*Load-Store*) validates memory accesses using the *check_mem* function. Its definition ensures the absence of undefined behaviors.

5.1 Proof of Software-Fault Isolation

Our proof model M_p formalizes the semantics of rBPF. It is implemented in Coq using Gallina. Assessing its correctness consists of proving two essential properties: i) the well-formedness of the virtual machine's state, that is, its registers, memory and verifier invariants, and ii) software-fault isolation, that is, the isolation of all transitions to a crash state $\emptyset$ using runtime safety checks (*e.g.*, *check_mem*), ergo the impossibility of a transition to an undefined behavior.

The register invariant states that all registers contain 64-bit integer values. This rules out 32-bit integers, *Vundef* but also pointers and floating-point numbers, for which the **alu** function may be undefined.

Definition 1 (register_inv). $\forall r \in registers.\exists l.R[r] = Vlong\ l$

As expected, the memory consistency invariant is a bit more elaborate. It states that each CompCert memory region *mr* register 8-bit integer blocks *b* of memory *m*, designated by a pointer *mr.ptr* to the 32-bit physical *mr.start* address of *b*, the 32-bit *mr.size* of *b* and at least *Readable* permissions *mr.perm* across $[0, size)$. Finally, every two regions point to disjoint physical address spaces in *m* (as per CompCert's memory regions for *mr'.ptr* $\neq$ *mr.ptr*).

Definition 2 (memory_inv). $\forall mr \in MRs,\ m.\ \exists b, start, size.\ s.t.$

$mr.ptr = Vptr\ b\ 0\ \wedge\ Mem.valid\_block\ m\ b\ \wedge\ is\_byte\_block\ b\ m\ \wedge$
$mr.start = Vint\ start\ \wedge\ mr.size = Vint\ size\ \wedge\ mr.perm \geq Readable\ \wedge$
$Mem.range\_perm\ m\ b\ 0\ (Int.unsigned\ size)\ Cur\ mr.perm\ \wedge$
$(\forall mr' \in MRs, mr' \neq mr \rightarrow mr'.ptr \neq mr.ptr)$

Linux eBPF has a verifier to statically analyze eBPF programs and only accept those which are free of undefined behaviors. Our CertrBPF's verifier, introduced in Sect. 8, ensures the weaker invariant given by Definition 3. The invariant stipulates the minimal pre-condition so that the interpreter can safely run a sequence of instructions I. More precisely, the invariant states that each instruction $I[i]$ references registers within the range $[0, 10]$ and that the target of every jump instruction is within the program range *i.e.*, $0 \leq i + ofs + 1 \leq length(I) - 1$.

Definition 3 (verifier_inv). $\forall i,\ I,\ ofs.\ 0 \leq i \leq length(I) - 1 \rightarrow$
$0 \leq get\_dst(I[i]) \leq 10\ \wedge\ 0 \leq get\_src(I[i]) \leq 10\ \wedge$
$((I[i] = Ja\ ofs \vee I[i] = Jump\ \_\_\_\ ofs) \rightarrow 0 \leq i + ofs + 1 \leq length(I) - 1)$

These three invariants implement well-formedness as proposed in Sect. 4. Therefore, the following Coq Theorem *sem_preserve_inv* proves Theorem 1 and states that well-formedness is preserved by the *interp* function. Similarly, Theorem *inv_ensure_no_undef* proves Theorem 2. This proves that the dynamic checks of the model M_p are sufficient to ensure the absence of error. In particular, all memory accesses are valid and performed within the dedicated memory regions. As a result, our model ensures software fault isolation. The corollary of Theorems *sem_preserve_inv* and *inv_ensure_no_undef* is that our virtual machine, obtained by refinement of the proof model, will always isolate code from other memory regions of the operating system and never crash it.

```
Theorem sem_preserve_inv:  ∀ (st st': state) (fuel: nat)
    (Hinv: register_inv st ∧ memory_inv st ∧ verifier_inv st)
    (Hsem: interp fuel st = ⌊(tt, st')⌋),
        register_inv st' ∧ memory_inv st' ∧ verifier_inv st'.
Theorem interp_no_undef:  ∀ (st: state) (fuel: nat)
    (Hinv: register_inv st ∧ memory_inv st ∧ verifier_inv st),
        interp fuel st ≠ ∅ .
```

6   A Synthesis-Oriented eBPF Interpreter

The coding style of the proof model M_p is quite different from the original RIOT implementation in C and lacks optimizations used in the latter to improve runtime performance. The synthesis model M_s firstly refines M_p into an optimized, safe and behaviorally equivalent monadic model which is then automatically transformed into an effectful implementation model M_c using ∂x.

Synthesis Model M_s. M_s refines our proof model by following the principle "make M_s as close as possible to the expected target C code". M_s also refines Coq types because each Coq inductive type may correspond to several C types (*e.g.*, *Vint/Vlong* to *signed* or *unsigned*, 32-bit or 64-bit). The case of *Vptr* is particularly delicate, as the target type contextually relies on bit-size and signedness. To sort this out, we rename Coq types to match the correct C type. For example, *val64_t, valu32_t, vals32_t* are *Val* types mapped to unsigned long long, unsigned int and int, respectively.

Equivalence. Both M_p and M_s use the same monadic state *st* as in Sect. 5. Hence, the simulation relation $R \subseteq st \times st$, required by Theorem 3, is equality. As a result, we prove the stronger result that both *interp* : *nat* $\rightarrow$ *M unit*, the M_p interpreter, and *interp_dx* : *nat* $\rightarrow$ *M unit*, the M_s interpreter, denote the exact same function.

```
Theorem equivalence_relation: ∀ (st: state) (fuel: nat),
    interp fuel st = interp_dx fuel st.
```

∂x configuration and Implementation model M_c. To extract the implementation model, we supply *∂x* with our monad *M* and a mapping relation from Gallina to C, Table 1.

Table 1. Mapping relation from Gallina to C

	Gallina	C
Types	*reg/sint32_t/valptr8_t* ...	*unsigned int/int/unsigned char* ...*
Constructions	*true/Int.repr(-2)/F_n* ...	*1/-2/0...*
Constants	*Val.addl/subl/mull/Z.eqb* ...	*+/-/*/==/* ...
Functions	*eval_pc: M sint32_t* ...	*int eval_pc(struct state *)* ...
Code struct	*if-then-else, match-pattern* ...	*if-else, switch-case* ...

Inductive types map to C types, *e.g.*, *reg* to *unsigned int* (note that a many-to-one relation from Gallina to C is legal). Gallina constructs and constant functions map to C operators and constants, *e.g.*, '*Val.addl*' to '+', '*Int.repr*(−2)' and '*true*' to '−2' and '1', etc. Gallina functions map to C functions. For any function operating the monadic state, the target C function has an additional argument *st* of type *struct state∗* which corresponds to the implicit state of the monad. Gallina's *match-pattern* translates to C's *switch-case*, etc.

Code Extraction with ∂x. The extracted C implementation preserves the structure of the original Gallina code, and the extracted C functions directly operate on actual memory locations as CompCert memory operations map to C expressions with a dereference. Consider the example of the step_mem_st_reg function.

```
Definition step_mem_st_reg (src: val64_t) (addr: valu32_t) (op: int8_t):
    M unit :=
  do opcode_st <- get_opcode_mem_st_reg op;
  match opcode_st with
  | op_BPF_STXW =>
    do addr_ptr <- check_mem Writable Mint32 addr;
      if eq_ptr_null addr_ptr then
        upd_flag BPF_ILLEGAL_MEM
      else (** i.e. Mem.storev Mint32 addr_ptr src *)
        do _ <- store_mem_reg Mint32 addr_ptr src; returnM tt
  ...
```

CompCert's Byte *int8_t* is mapped to *unsigned char*. Constructs *op_BPF_STXW*,
BPF_ ILLEGAL_MEM and *Writable* are respectively mapped to '99', '-2' and
'2U'. The constant function eq_ptr_null is translated into an operation to check
whether a pointer is null. The 'match opcode_st with' is extracted to 'switch
(opcode_st) case'. Functions step_mem_st_reg, check_mem and store_mem_reg
in C have an additional monadic argument *st*.

```
void step_mem_st_reg(struct bpf_state* st, unsigned long long
    src, unsigned int addr, unsigned char op){
  unsigned char opcode_st;
  unsigned char *addr_ptr;
  opcode_st = get_opcode_mem_st_reg(op);
  switch (opcode_st) {
    case 99:
      addr_ptr = check_mem(st, 2U, 4U, addr);
      if (addr_ptr == 0) {
        upd_flag(st, -2); return;
      } else { // i.e. *(unsigned int *) addr_ptr = src
        store_mem_reg(st, 4U, addr_ptr, src); return;
      }
    ...
```

7   Simulation Proof of the C rBPF Virtual Machine

In this section, we explain how to establish Theorem 4 for the Clight code of our
virtual machine, derived from ∂x, and compiled into a Clight AST in Coq using
the CLIGHTGEN tool.

Simulation Relation. A crucial ingredient of Theorem 4 is the simulation relation
between the Gallina state monad and the Clight state which is essentially made
of a CompCert memory. The Gallina state comprises a CompCert memory that
models the various memory regions available to the rBPF program. This memory
may also contain other blocks that are not modified by the virtual machine
but represent other kernel data-structures. The simulation relation stipulates
that such blocks also exist in the Clight memory and have the same content.
The Clight memory contains additional blocks (*i.e., state_block, ins_block* and

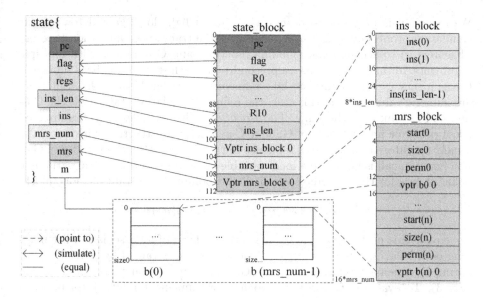

Fig. 3. Simulation relation R between st_{rbpf}, left, and rBPFClight, right.

mrs_block) to model the other fields of the Gallina state. The layout and content of those blocks are depicted in Fig. 3.

Solid arrows in Fig. 3 are simulation relations between $state\_block$ and st_{rbpf}. Solid lines are the equalities between the rBPF memory m and blocks in rBPF-Clight memory. Dashed lines indicate relations of pointers to blocks in CompCert memory. The encoding exploits the fact that each field of the Gallina state has a known length. Thus, every field can be encoded as a continuous sub-block. As a result, the program counter is obtained from the first 4 bytes: loading a memory chunk of type $Mint32$ at offset 0 retrieves the pc field of the Gallina state. The next 4 bytes encode the enumerated type flag. Here, each constructor of type flag is assigned an integer. The next 11×64 bits are used to encode the register bank of the Gallina state.

$$Rs(state, state\_block, m) \stackrel{\text{def}}{=} \begin{cases} st_{rbpf}.pc & = load\ Mint32\ m_{clight}\ state\_block\ 0 \\ st_{rbpf}.flag & = load\ Mint32\ m_{clight}\ state\_block\ 4 \\ st_{rbpf}.R0 & = load\ Mint64\ m_{clight}\ state\_block\ 8 \\ \dots \end{cases}$$

The next elements of the Clight block represent the lists of instructions and of memory regions. In a functional language, lists are potentially of unbounded length and have a polymorphic type. Here, our lists always have fixed lengths and elements of fixed size. As a result, a list is directly encoded by a field specifying its length followed by a pointer to its memory block. The elements of the list are stored continuously in the pointed block.

Systematic Proof of Simulation. Since the ∂x tool is syntax-directed, there is a systematic correspondence between the source Gallina and the target C code.

We exploit this property to design a minimal Clight logic geared toward our simulation proof. Our *Clightlogic* generalizes the translation validation theorem (Theorem 4) to accommodate Gallina functions and C functions with multiple arguments. In that case, we have a precondition which states that the Gallina and C arguments are linked pairwise by a refinement relation. Most of the arguments are numeric values and, in this case, the refinement relation states that the Gallina and C values are the same. The *Clightlogic* also provides a syntax-directed proof principle for each pair of Gallina/C syntactic construct. For instance, the *bindM* operator translates to a sequence in the C code. Also, the result of a Gallina function call is bound to a local variable in C. Moreover, the local variable v below stands for the monadic state in C and points to the state memory block.

$$\partial x(bindM\ f\ (\lambda x.g)) = (vx = f_C(v); g_C(v, vx))$$

To exploit this pattern, our invariants take the form of an association list mapping each local variable to a set of C values that is obtained by partially evaluating a refinement relation with the Gallina value computed by the function (Fig. 3). To evaluate f, one needs to have a refinement relation Rs between the Gallina state st and the C value of v in memory m. Now, suppose that $fst = \lfloor r, st' \rfloor$. Since f_C is a correct refinement of f, relations $Rs(st', v, m')$ and $Rr(r, x)$ hold for the value x of the local variable vx in the current environment. We conclude by mapping $vx \mapsto Rr\ r$ and use this invariant to refine g by g_C.

The translation validation theorem proves a forward simulation relation from Coq to Clight. A backward simulation relation can be constructed as Gallina programs are functions and Clight is *determinate*.

8   CertrBPF Verifier

Linux eBPF's compiler and runtime system do not enforce type or memory safety. Instead, safety is verified prior to execution using a static analyzer that checks programs validity. As both the size and complexity cannot fit the requirements of an MCU architecture, CertrBPF instead provides a simple (linear time) but formally verified verifier, CertrBPF-verifier, which ensures the invariant *verifier_inv* (Definition 3). Accordingly, it scans an input rBPF program (*i.e.*, a list of 64-bit bytecode instructions) and rejects it when: i) a source or destination register is greater than 10. ii) the offset of a jump instruction is out of the instruction sequence bounds. iii) or the last instruction is not the *Exit* instruction (opcode 0x95).

Static verification of these properties allows the interpreter to skip unnecessary dynamic checks. Our verifier adopts the same end-to-end verification method as the interpreter, Sect. 4. The virtual machine state in CertrBPF-verifier is a strict subset of the interpreter's state: $st_v = \langle I, M \rangle$ consists of a sequence of instructions I and a memory M.

```
Theorem verifier_well_formedness_and_safety :
  ∀ (st: verifier_state) (b: bool),
    verifier st = ⌊(b , st)⌋.
Theorem verifier_imply_inv :
  ∀ (st: verifier_state) (st': state)
    (Hinclude: st ⊂ st') (Hpre : verifier st = ⌊(true, st)⌋),
      verifier_inv st'.
```

Theorem *verifier_well_formedness_and_safety* proves both Theorem 1 and Theorem 2. The verifier has the following properties: i) no assumption (every state is well-formed); ii) never crashes (safety); iii) never modifies the VM state. In addition, the Coq theorem *verifier_imply_inv* states that if the *verifier* returns *true*, *verifier_inv* holds. Considering that the verifier's proof and synthesis models are exactly the same, the simulation relation $R_v \subseteq st_v \times st_v$ required by Theorem 3 is equality. CertrBPF-verifier reuses the *Clightlogic* to prove the simulation proof of its C implementation.

9   Evaluation: Case Study of RIOT's Femto-Containers

We integrate CertrBPF as a drop-in replacement for the existing non-verified module optimized for size (vanilla-rBPF) in the IoT operating system RIOT to provide the expected femto-container functionalities [39].

Implementation. The proof model of the interpreter (Sect. 5) consists of 2.4k lines of Coq code and the corresponding isolation proof (Sect. 5.1) is more than 4.8k lines long. The synthesis model, Sect. 6, is approx. 3.2k lines long and the equivalence theorem is completed by 0.6k proof code. The final step (Sect. 7) includes 10.8k translation validation proofs between the Gallina specification and the extracted Clight model. As for the CertrBPF verifier (Sect. 8), the proof and synthesis models sport 1.4k lines of Coq code. The corresponding proofs are more than 0.5k long and the last simulation proof is about 8.3k long. In addition, the *Clightlogic* implementation has 4.4k lines of Coq code.

Experimental Evaluation Setup. Our experimental objects are the original non-verified rBPF interpreter (*i.e.*, vanilla-rBPF) and the automatically extracted and verified CertrBPF interpreter (without RIOT's API). We carry out our measurements on a selected set of popular, commercial, off-the-shelf low-power IoT hardware, representative of modern 32-bit micro-controller architectures and boards: i) Nordic nRF52840 (Arm Cortex-M); ii) Espressif WROOM-32 (Espressif ESP32); iii) Sipeed Longan Nano GD32VF103CBT6 (RISC-V). All code is compiled with GCC using size optimization enabled and the -foptimize-sibling-calls GCC option to remove all tail-recursive calls and thus bound the stack size. This is critical to our isolation theorem as it relies on the implicit

CompCert assumption that the stack cannot overflow. To avoid a possible mismatch between the CompCert semantics and the GCC semantics, we also pass the following options: i) `-fwrapv`, `-fwrapv-pointer` mean that both signed and pointer arithmetic wrap around according to the two's-complement encoding; ii) `-fno-strict-aliasing` means that there is no aliasing assumption.

Results. We first evaluate the memory footprint of the CertrBPF interpreter, compared to vanilla-rBPF. We measure i) *Flash size*: all read-only data, including the actual code; ii) *Stack*: the approximate ram used for stack space; iii) *Context*: the static RAM. In terms of Flash, our measurements show that CertrBPF actually reduces the footprint by 47% on RISC-V and by 35% on ESP32, and a 10% decrease on Cortex-M. In terms of stack requirements, CertrBPF reduces the footprint by 33% on Cortex-M, by 22% on RISC-V, and by 4% on ESP32. The context memory, however, increases from 92B to 144B on all platforms.

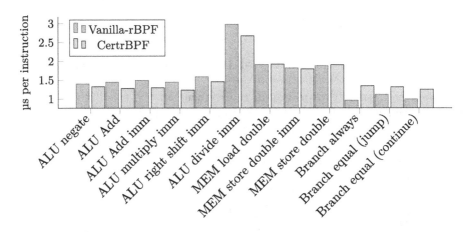

Fig. 4. Time per instructions on the Cortex-M4 platform

Next, we micro-benchmark the performance of core operations: single instructions from the arithmetic logic unit (ALU), for memory access (MEM) and branch instructions, with a mix of register and immediate value for the operands, Fig. 4. These results are averages over 1000 single identical instruction calls with a single return statement to make the application exit.

Finally, we benchmark the performance of actual IoT data processing, hosted in a femto-container with RIOT running on our selected hardware. In this use case, a sliding window average is performed within the femto-container, on available sensor data points. Figure 5 shows the performance we measured depending on the size of the window. We use this as blueprint for computation load scaling.

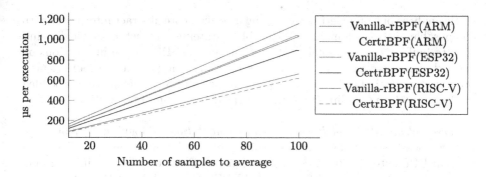

Fig. 5. Sliding window average on Cortex-M, ESP32, and RISC-V.

Key Take-Away. We observe that CertrBPF generally decreases the memory footprint. One reason is that calls to the RIOT API are currently not supported by CertrBPF. We observe, Fig. 4, that the execution slow-down is acute for Branch instructions, on Cortex-M. However, on all other platforms (RISC-V, ESP32 and Cortex-M), our micro-benchmarks show that most instructions enjoy speed-up with CertrBPF compared to vanilla-rBPF. This behavior is also visible in our sensor data processing benchmark, Fig. 5, where CertrBPF performs better than vanilla-rBPF on three platforms. All in all, CertrBPF gains both security and reduces memory footprint as well as execution time.

10   Related Works

Methodologies for Systems and Compilers Verification. The verification of compilers [18], static analyzers [16], and operating systems [12,17] have been the subjects of vast development and verification efforts due to the sheer code size of the artifacts at stake. These full-scale case studies gave rise to new strategies and methodologies to address the challenge of verifying large software. One such approach is Cogent [35] which aims at developing verified applications on top of the SeL4 [17] micro-kernel. Cogent [35] consists of a functional language with linear types to specify source programs and produces C code with Isabelle/HOL proof information. It provides a framework to prove that the extracted C code refines a high-level Isabelle/HOL functional correctness specification in the Isabelle/HOL proof assistant. Our method differs from co-specification in Cogent in that it is direct: it directly translates Coq specifications into C code and performs the end-to-end verification in Coq. CertiKOS [12] uses a multi-layered, refinement-based, and modular definition of a micro-kernel from its low-level memory model to its user-level interface and services. It is adopted in SeKVM [22], a layered Linux KVM hypervisor architecture for multiprocessor hardware. The CompCert project [18] adopted this "divide-and-conquer" strategy to decompose the verification of a full-scale ANSI C compiler into that of its successive transformations from source program to machine code, compositionally verifying each of the translation steps bisimilar. Its related static analyser, Verasco [16], employs static analysis of CompCert C code using a verified core abstract interpreter with composable abstract domains. Our problem statement is methodologically simpler: to build a safe and small VM that interprets rBPF virtual instructions on networked micro-controllers. We choose the radical approach of proof-oriented programming (à la Low* [34], Vale [5]) to prove an rBPF interpreter embedded in Coq correct and to directly extract verified code from its definition.

Background on BPF and Its Verified Implementations. Mogul et al. [26] introduce a stack-based virtual machine to interpret packet filters into the BSD kernel that BPF extended to 32-bit instructions. BPF gained adoption in the Linux community and became eBPF (extended BPF), a virtual 64-bit RISC-like architectures. To our knowledge, verification of BPF runtime systems has mainly focused on JIT translation for operation on micro-kernels. Myreen [28] verifies a JIT compiler targeting x86 for a stack language using the HOL4 proof assistant. The generated code only preserves the semantics of the source code but does not ensure any isolation property. Porncharoenwase et al. [33] use CompCert to extract an OCaml translator from BPF to assembly code, verified using the proof assistant Coq, using the OCaml runtime, an assembler, and a linker as TCB. Van Geffen et al. [11] present an optimized JIT compiler for Linux BPF with automated static analysis onboard, assuming offline verification using the Linux BPF verifier as TCB. For field deployment on networks of micro-controllers (IoT), all the above approaches would require a trusted, offline BPF verifier and, additionally, a secure upload protocol to sign verified scripts and perform authenticated uploads on target devices, which motivates our approach to use a fault-proof virtual machine instead.

Background on Verified Virtual Machines. Lochbihler [23] presents the verified implementation of a virtual machine modeling the semantics, memory model and byte-code semantics of Java, all by using the proof methodology of translation validation [18,32]. Desharnais and Brunthaler [7] propose the formal verification of an optimized and secure Javascript interpreter in Isabelle/HOL. Its proof methodology is based on concepts of bisimulation. The interpreter targets optimal security and run-time performance. To target MCU devices, our rBPF VM instead seeks optimal run-time memory footprint, to support the expected capability of dynamically running several isolated services on a small device with shared memory. Zhang et al. [40] present a different and ambitious workflow using the deductive programming environment Why3 [9] to specify a virtual machine of Etherium byte-code (EVM) and verify functional correctness of smart contracts against it. The EVM is extracted to OCaml binary code, yielding a TCB consisting of the OCaml runtime and the implementation of Eth's protocols.

Background on Converting Gallina Programs into Executables. Just as the proof-oriented approach advocated by dependently-typed functional languages like F* mentioned in Sect. 2, there are various alternatives to ∂x for extracting executables from Gallina programs. To begin with, Coq comes with a builtin extraction mechanism [21] that generates OCaml, Haskell or Scheme. This path has a rather large TCB (Coq extraction and a compiler). CertiCoq [1] is an ongoing project aiming at generating CompCert C code from Gallina using a specific IR and several passes. Once this effort is completed, it will allow one to rely on a small TCB. Œuf [27] is another tool to compile Gallina to C. It considers a carefully chosen subset of Gallina to tackle the tricky issue of verifying the reflection of Gallina into an AST. Both CertiCoq and Œuf, however, require a garbage collector and define how Coq inductives are represented at runtime. Codegen [36] converts Gallina to C with the goal of maximizing performance by, *e.g.*, allowing the user to control how Coq values are represented at runtime. Rupicola [31] considers an original and promising approach which regards a compiler as a partial decision procedure: it consists of a proof search procedure, which may fail, or else exhibit a target program in bedrock2 (a C-like low-level language AST embedded in Coq) with a proof of equivalence. It has, at present, only been tested for small algorithms. We chose to use ∂x for its simplicity and because it does not increase our TCB. It shares with Codegen the capability to configure the representation of values. Unlike Codegen, it produces C code that is structurally identical to source code. This direct and traceable translation simplifies the verification of generated code w.r.t. source programs, and facilitates source program optimisations.

11   Conclusion and Future Works

This paper uses a refinement methodology to directly derive a verified C implementation of rBPF, the implementation of BPF hosted by the RIOT operating system, from a Gallina specification in Coq. All the refinement steps are mechanically verified using the Coq proof assistant to minimize the TCB. We prove our rBPF virtual machine to isolate software faults and not to produce runtime errors. Performances are at par with the vanilla rBPF implementation in RIOT.

Our future works aim at instantiating our proof workflow to a (fault-isolating) JIT compiler, one challenge being that Linux's approach of using a verifier will not be feasible on resource-constrained devices, and another being that certain operations might only be expressible in assembly code. This calls for further studies on ways to substantially improve the efficiency of our VM.

Acknowledgments. The authors wish to thank the anonymous reviewers for their feedback and suggestions. This work is partly funded by Inria Challenge RIOT-fp, the ANR/BMBF project TinyPART, and the H2020 project Sparta.

Artifacts. The source code and proofs of our virtual machine, its generated code and benchmark data are available on https://gitlab.inria.fr/syuan/rbpf-dx/-/tree/CAV22-AE.

References

1. Anand, A., et al.: Certicoq : a verified compiler for Coq. In: CoqPL (2017)
2. Appel, A.W., et al.: Program logics for certified compilers. In: CUP (2014)
3. Baccelli, E., et al.: RIOT: an open source operating system for low-end embedded devices in the IoT. IoT J. 5(6), 4428–4440 (2018)
4. Bertot, Y., Castéran, P.: Interactive theorem proving and program development. In: Coq'Art: The Calculus of Inductive Constructions. Springer, Heidelberg (2013). https://doi.org/10.1007/978-3-662-07964-5
5. Bond, B., et al.: Vale: verifying high-performance cryptographic assembly code. In: USENIX Security, pp. 917–934 (2017)
6. Costan, V., Lebedev, I., Devadas, S.: Sanctum: minimal hardware extensions for strong software isolation. In: USENIX Security, pp. 857–874. USENIX (2016)
7. Desharnais, M., Brunthaler, S.: Towards efficient and verified virtual machines for dynamic languages. In: CPP, pp. 61–75. ACM (2021)
8. Dunchev, C., Guidi, F., Sacerdoti Coen, C., Tassi, E.: ELPI: fast, embeddable, λ prolog interpreter. In: Davis, M., Fehnker, A., McIver, A., Voronkov, A. (eds.) LPAR 2015. LNCS, vol. 9450, pp. 460–468. Springer, Heidelberg (2015). https://doi.org/10.1007/978-3-662-48899-7_32
9. Filliâtre, J.-C., Paskevich, A.: Why3 — Where Programs Meet Provers. In: Felleisen, M., Gardner, P. (eds.) ESOP 2013. LNCS, vol. 7792, pp. 125–128. Springer, Heidelberg (2013). https://doi.org/10.1007/978-3-642-37036-6_8
10. Fleming, M.: A thorough introduction to eBPF. Linux Weekly News (2017)
11. Van Geffen, J., Nelson, L., Dillig, I., Wang, X., Torlak, E.: Synthesizing JIT compilers for In-Kernel DSLs. In: Lahiri, S.K., Wang, C. (eds.) CAV 2020. LNCS, vol. 12225, pp. 564–586. Springer, Cham (2020). https://doi.org/10.1007/978-3-030-53291-8_29
12. Gu, R., et al.: Certikos: an extensible architecture for building certified concurrent os kernels. In: OSDI, pp. 653–669. USENIX (2016)
13. Haas, A., et al.: Bringing the web up to speed with webassembly. In: PLDI, pp. 185–200. ACM (2017)
14. Hahm, O., Baccelli, E., Petersen, H., Tsiftes, N.: Operating systems for low-end devices in the Internet of Things: a survey. IoT J. 3(5), 720–734 (2016)
15. Jomaa, N., Torrini, P., Nowak, D., Grimaud, G., Hym, S.: Proof-oriented design of a separation kernel with minimal trusted computing base. In: AVOCS, vol. 76. Electronic Communications of the EASST (2018)
16. Jourdan, J.H., Laporte, V., Blazy, S., Leroy, X., Pichardie, D.: A formally-verified C static analyzer. In: POPL, pp. 247–259. ACM (2015)
17. Klein, G., et al.: seL4: formal verification of an OS kernel. In: SOSP, p. 207. ACM Press (2009)
18. Leroy, X.: Formal verification of a realistic compiler. Commun. ACM 52(7), 107–115 (2009)
19. Leroy, X., Appel, A.W., Blazy, S., Stewart, G.: The CompCert Memory Model, Version 2. Research Report RR-7987, INRIA (2012)
20. Leroy, X., Blazy, S.: Formal verification of a C-like memory model and its uses for verifying program transformations. JAR 41(1), 1–31 (2008)
21. Letouzey, P.: A new extraction for Coq. In: Geuvers, H., Wiedijk, F. (eds.) TYPES 2002. LNCS, vol. 2646, pp. 200–219. Springer, Heidelberg (2003). https://doi.org/10.1007/3-540-39185-1_12

22. Li, S.W., Li, X., Gu, R., Nieh, J., Hui, J.Z.: Formally verified memory protection for a commodity multiprocessor hypervisor. In: USENIX Security, pp. 3953–3970. USENIX (2021)
23. Lochbihler, A.: A machine-checked, type-safe model of Java concurrency: language, virtual machine, memory model, and verified compiler. Ph.D. thesis, Karlsruhe Institute of Technology (2012)
24. Madhavapeddy, A., et al.: Unikernels: library operating systems for the cloud. In: ASPLOS, pp. 461–472. ACM (2013)
25. McCanne, S., Jacobson, V.: The BSD packet filter: a new architecture for user-level packet capture. In: Usenix Winter Conference, vol. 46, pp. 259–270. USENIX (1993)
26. Mogul, J., Rashid, R., Accetta, M.: The packer filter: an efficient mechanism for user-level network code. In: SOSP, pp. 39–51. ACM (1987)
27. Mullen, E., Pernsteiner, S., Wilcox, J.R., Tatlock, Z., Grossman, D.: Œuf: minimizing the Coq extraction TCB. In: CPP, pp. 172–185. ACM (2018)
28. Myreen, M.O.: Verified just-in-time compiler on x86. In: POPL, pp. 107–118. ACM (2010)
29. Nelson, L., Geffen, J.V., Torlak, E., Wang, X.: Specification and verification in the field: applying formal methods to BPF just-in-time compilers in the Linux kernel. In: OSDI, pp. 41–61. USENIX (2020)
30. Noorman, J., et al.: Sancus: low-cost trustworthy extensible networked devices with a zero-software trusted computing base. In: USENIX Security, pp. 479–498. USENIX (2013)
31. Pit-Claudel, C., Philipoom, J., Jamner, D., Erbsen, A., Chlipala, A.: Relational compilation for performance-critical applications. In: PLDI. ACM (2022)
32. Pnueli, A., Siegel, M., Singerman, E.: Translation validation. In: Steffen, B. (ed.) TACAS 1998. LNCS, vol. 1384, pp. 151–166. Springer, Heidelberg (1998). https://doi.org/10.1007/BFb0054170
33. Porncharoenwase, S., Bornholt, J., Torlak, E.: Fixing code that explodes under symbolic evaluation. In: Beyer, D., Zufferey, D. (eds.) VMCAI 2020. LNCS, vol. 11990, pp. 44–67. Springer, Cham (2020). https://doi.org/10.1007/978-3-030-39322-9_3
34. Protzenko, J., et al.: Verified low-level programming embedded in F*. In: PACMPL 1(ICFP), pp. 17:1–17:29 (2017). https://doi.org/10.1145/3110261
35. Rizkallah, C., et al.: A framework for the automatic formal verification of refinement from COGENT to C. In: Blanchette, J.C., Merz, S. (eds.) ITP 2016. LNCS, vol. 9807, pp. 323–340. Springer, Cham (2016). https://doi.org/10.1007/978-3-319-43144-4_20
36. Tanaka, A.: Coq to C translation with partial evaluation. In: PEPM@POPL, pp. 14–31. ACM (2021)
37. Tassi, E.: Coq-Elpi, Coq plugin embedding Elpi (2021). https://github.com/LPCIC/coq-elpi
38. Zandberg, K., Baccelli, E.: Minimal virtual machines on IoT microcontrollers: the case of Berkeley Packet Filters with rBPF. In: PEMWN, pp. 1–6. IEEE (2020)
39. Zandberg, K., Baccelli, E.: Femto-Containers: DevOps on Microcontrollers with Lightweight Virtualization & Isolation for IoT Software Modules (2021), preprint
40. Zhang, X., Li, Y., Sun, M.: Towards a formally verified EVM in production environment. In: Bliudze, S., Bocchi, L. (eds.) COORDINATION 2020. LNCS, vol. 12134, pp. 341–349. Springer, Cham (2020). https://doi.org/10.1007/978-3-030-50029-0_21

Hemiola: A DSL and Verification Tools to Guide Design and Proof of Hierarchical Cache-Coherence Protocols

Joonwon Choi(✉), Adam Chlipala, and Arvind

MIT CSAIL, Cambridge, USA
joonwonc@alum.mit.edu, {adamc,arvind}@csail.mit.edu

Abstract. Cache-coherence protocols have been one of the greatest challenges in formal verification of hardware, due to their central complication of executing multiple memory-access transactions concurrently within a distributed message-passing system. In this paper, we introduce Hemiola, a framework embedded in Coq that guides the user to design protocols that never experience inconsistent interleavings while handling transactions concurrently. The framework provides a DSL, where any protocol designed in the DSL always satisfies the serializability property, allowing a user to verify the protocol assuming that transactions are executed one-at-a-time. Hemiola also provides a novel invariant proof method, for protocols designed in Hemiola, that only requires considering execution histories without interleaved memory accesses. We used Hemiola to design and prove hierarchical MSI and MESI protocols as case studies. We also demonstrated that the case-study protocols are hardware-synthesizable, by using a compilation/synthesis toolchain targeting FPGAs.

Keywords: formal verification · cache coherence · proof assistants

1 Introduction

Programming languages and compilers help engineers describe each system at the most expedient level of abstraction. The process of experimenting with new languages is most familiar from the software world, but hardware designers also benefit from it. Of course, Verilog and VHDL themselves are significant steps up from direct circuit descriptions. Some families of hardware languages go further, in roughly the sense that, say, Java goes further than C, providing abstractions that simplify reasoning about modular design. The rule-based hardware languages like Bluespec [23] allow hardware designers to *imagine* that system modules take turns executing local atomic state-change rules, with *no concurrency*. In reality, parallel execution is essential for performance, and compilers for these languages rely on static analysis to extract parallelism soundly.

Roughly speaking, a rule in Bluespec and its relatives must run within a single clock cycle. What happens when we want to simplify reasoning about

© The Author(s) 2022
S. Shoham and Y. Vizel (Eds.): CAV 2022, LNCS 13372, pp. 317–339, 2022.
https://doi.org/10.1007/978-3-031-13188-2_16

longer-running processes? A prime example is a cache-coherence protocol. A memory hierarchy is a distributed system, with many caches communicating through explicit message passing, requiring at least as many clock cycles as the longest dependency chain of message exchanges. The logic is notoriously difficult to get right. One reason is that many memory requests from processor cores may be handled simultaneously. One cache may be working on one request, while a neighboring cache is working on a different request. Might there be abstractions that remove this complication from the hardware designer's thought process, much as Bluespec allows the same designer to pretend that different hardware components do not execute state-change logic in parallel?

We answer affirmatively in presenting *Hemiola*, the first hardware-description language that presents cache-coherence transactions *as if they run atomically*, while realizing the usual parallel performance gains. We define a transaction as all the activity within the memory system in response to a single request from a processor core or other user of the memory. One request may trigger a flurry of activity in the protocol, but the designer may at least pretend that no other request is active in the same period.

The foundation of Hemiola is identifying *commonalities across practical cache-coherence protocols* and embodying them in a domain-specific language (DSL). We fix a notion of node hierarchy and message-passing channels, enumerating *rule templates* capturing relevant communication patterns. Protocols are then described in terms of single-cycle, per-cache rules, each instantiated from a template. Crucially, a locking discipline is built into the language and handled automatically by the templates.

In addition to the DSL, Hemiola provides formal tools significantly easing verification of all cache-coherence protocols designed in it. The DSL is embedded in the Coq proof assistant and has a fully machine-checked proof of soundness, formalized as *serializability*: any state invariant preserved with one-transaction-at-a-time execution is also preserved in true parallel execution. The serializability property is once-and-for-all at the language level, freeing protocol designers from needing to reason about interleavings among transactions. In a sense, our work takes techniques that have been used for *per-protocol* verification and lifts them to apply at the level of a DSL, so that no verification effort need be expended on them per-protocol.

To sum up, the contribution of this paper consists of two parts[1]:

- We discover a set of topology and lock conditions that ensures *serializability*, extracted from usual cache-coherence protocol designs. We then identify a DSL, where every protocol defined in this language ensures serializability by-construction, backed up with mechanized Coq proof (Sect. 3). Lastly, we formalize how serializability helps prove global invariants, by using the novel notion of *predicate messages* in distributed protocols (Sect. 4).
- We provide the complete correctness proofs of hierarchical cache-coherence protocols (Sect. 5) using Hemiola. Our case studies are the first complete

---

[1] Our framework and case studies are available as open source: https://github.com/mit-plv/hemiola. Choi's dissertation [9] goes into additional detail.

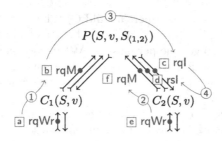

Fig. 1. A simple MSI directory protocol and its rule-execution cases

mechanized proofs that share a large segment of reusable proofs across various cache-coherence protocols. We also demonstrate that the case-study protocols are hardware-synthesizable, by using a compilation/synthesis toolchain in Hemiola (Sect. 6).

2   A Motivating Example

Before introducing our proposed method to design and verify cache-coherence protocols, we provide a simple motivating example to explain the typical challenges and how we suggest to handle them. For simplicity, in this section, we will consider a protocol handling only *a single memory location*. We will see it is still nontrivial to design a correct protocol.

The overall goal of cache coherence is to preserve coherence among multiple candidate values in a memory subsystem. In other words, if the system is coherent, then it should behave like an atomic memory. Figure 1 shows caches and network channels for a directory-based MSI protocol. There are three caches (P, C_1, and C_2), and each of them has its own status (**M**odified, **S**hared, or **I**nvalid) and data (v). In this MSI protocol, a cache can read/write the data with the M status, only read with S, and cannot read/write with I. The parent P additionally has a data structure called a *directory* to track the statuses of the children. For example, a directory might be $S_{\langle 1,2 \rangle}$, meaning that both C_1 and C_2 have S status, in some logical snapshot of state.

Caches communicate through ordered channels, shown as ($\rightarrowtail$) in the figure. Child caches (C_1 and C_2) have channels to receive and respond to requests from processor cores. There are three types of channels between a parent and a child: one channel is for parent-to-child messages, and the other two channels are for child-to-parent requests and responses. It is natural to wonder why two separate child-to-parent channels are required; we will see the reason very soon.

Figure 1 also depicts some example state-transition cases depending on the cache statuses. In this setting, all the caches run concurrently by repeatedly executing *rules* that make atomic, local state transitions. A rule may take some messages from input channels, perform a state transition, and put messages in output channels. A rule may also have a precondition, blocking use of that rule when the precondition does not hold.

A rule execution ① is a case where a child C_1 takes a request ⓐ rqWr from a processor to write data, but it does not have M status and thus further requests to the parent (ⓑ rqM) to get the permission. At this moment, in many practical cache-coherence-protocol designs, C_1 changes its status to a *transient state* SM to record its current status (S) and the next expected status (M) and to make *any further processor requests stall*.

Due to the concurrent execution of caches, we might have another rule executed at the same time. ② is executed concurrently with ①, where C_2 also takes a processor request ⓔ rqWr and sends ⓕ rqM to the parent as well. Since ① and ② happened at the same time, the parent P needs to decide which request to deal with. Suppose that it decided to handle ⓑ rqM first.

③ presents the next execution by P, taking the input message ⓑ rqM and making an invalidation request (ⓒ rqI) to the other child C_2 to change its status to I. This request is required, since when a child has M, the others should not be able to read/write the data. The parent, at this moment, changes its directory status to a transient state to disallow any other requests from the children (e.g., ⓕ rqM), since otherwise it will handle two rqM messages simultaneously, which might lead to an incoherent state – two M statuses in the caches.

Lastly, ④ shows the case that C_2 handles the invalidation request (ⓒ rqI). A number of corner cases should be handled carefully in this step:

- Since C_2 requested ⓕ rqM, it has a transient state SM when ⓒ rqI arrives. It should still be able to handle this invalidation request even in the transient state (while any processor requests stall). In this case, C_2 accepts ⓒ rqI and changes its transient state to IM. We see that transient states should be fine-grained enough to distinguish which requests to handle.
- Due to the existence of ⓕ rqM, if we had a single channel from a child to a parent, a deadlock would occur. P cannot take ⓕ rqM since it is in a transient state after making an invalidation request. It cannot take ⓓ rsI as well, since the response is not at the head of the ordered channel. This case shows the necessity of having multiple channels between a child and a parent.

A so-called three-channel system has been widely used and regarded as a good choice to make the design correct and live [33,34]. While there are other possible correct topology and network settings, the cases shown in Fig. 1 at least demonstrate that it is nontrivial to construct one of them. Note that the three-channel system is *logical* in the sense that the actual hardware implementation may use various hardware components that can simulate the requirements.

In terms of making a protocol design correct, transient states, topology, and network settings contribute to make *interleavings* correct. Considering the sequence of rule executions [①; ③; ④] (in red) as an execution flow – we will later call it a *transaction* – to handle a processor request ⓐ rqWr, we see that the other execution flow (in blue) could not happen after ②, which is for another processor request ⓔ rqWr. As explained above case-by-case, proper transient states and network channels made ⓕ rqM stall. This mechanism to ensure safe interleavings is called *noninterference* [11,18], which ensures that no other transactions spuriously affect state transitions by an ongoing transaction.

Hemiola in a Nutshell. If transient states, proper topology, and network settings are essential for designing a correct protocol, can we craft a DSL where *only conformant protocols are expressible?*

That is exactly what we did with Hemiola. The Hemiola DSL helps designers design cache-coherence protocols in a safe way. Instead of requiring designers to use transient states coupled to a protocol, we discover *general* stall conditions that by themselves ensure noninterference and form those conditions as conceptual locks. The stall conditions are *extracted and abstracted* from the usual transient states, so they can apply to practical protocols.

For instance, a designer may write a rule for ① without any DSL support like the left rule in the following code:

```
 1 system memoryMSI {
 2   cache C1 {
 3     state status: MSI, value: valueT, in_transition: TrsMSI
 4     ...
 5     // Without any DSL support          |    // Using the Hemiola DSL
 6     rule getMRqUpUp {                    |    rule getMRqUpUp from template rquu {
 7       msgIn = procToC1.deq();            |      receive rqWr();
 8       assert (msgIn.id == rqWr);         |      assert (status == S);
 9       assert (!in_transition);           |      send rqM();
10       assert (status == S);              |    }
11       in_transition <= SM;               |
12       c1ToPRq.enq({id: rqM, val: 0}); }  |
13 } }
```

Note that a designer has to find proper input/output channels (`procToC1` and `c1ToPRq`) and check/set a proper transient state (`in_transition`) in order to define the rule.

On the other hand, the left rule can be written more easily by using the Hemiola DSL as the right rule. Instead of using explicit channels and transient states, the right rule just uses the `rquu` *rule template* (where `rquu` stands for request-up-up). The rule templates employ *proven-safe* network structures and automatically check/set/release associated locks, so users can design protocols without worrying about incorrect use of network channels, locks, etc.

3   The Hemiola Domain-Specific Language

As explained in Sect. 2, in designing a cache-coherence protocol, it is nontrivial to make concurrent execution of transactions correct. In this section, we introduce the Hemiola DSL to ease that burden. While conventional approaches deal with transient states directly to derive noninterference per-state, the Hemiola DSL limits protocols to satisfy *abstract conditions* that can guarantee noninterference by-construction. The conditions have already been mentioned in Sect. 2 – network topology and locking mechanisms extracted from transient states of practical cache-coherence protocols.

Notations. An overline (e.g., $\bar{l}$) denotes a list. [] and $(\bar{l} + e)$ denote nil and single-element append, respectively. $\oplus \bar{l}$ flattens the list of lists $\bar{l}$ with repeated concatenation. $(\overline{l_1} + \overline{l_2})$, $(\overline{l_1} - \overline{l_2})$, and $(\overline{l_1} \# \overline{l_2})$ denote append, subtraction, and disjointness of lists, respectively. We use the same operation $(+)$ for the single-element and general append. Regarding a list of key-value pairs as a finite map, we override notations for lists. For example, $(M + \bar{l})$ updates multiple key-value pairs in a finite map M. Moreover, we overload the same operation $(M + (k, v))$ for a single update for simplicity. $(\overline{s.\mathsf{fd}})$ is used as a shorter notation for $(\mathsf{List.map}\ (\lambda s.\ s.\mathsf{fd})\ \bar{s})$. We use $\langle \cdot \rangle$ to denote a struct and use a name (e.g., $s.\mathsf{fd}$) to access a field value.

3.1   Syntax

The Hemiola DSL is similar to well-known rule-based hardware-description languages (HDLs) such as Bluespec [23], Kami [10], and Kôika [4]. A notable difference is that rule descriptions are restricted by predesigned *rule templates* to avoid spurious interleavings among transactions.

A *system* $S ::= \langle \overline{C}, \overline{i_{\mathsf{in}}}, \overline{i_{\mathsf{rq}}}, \overline{i_{\mathsf{rs}}} \rangle$ is the biggest unit of the language; it consists of caches $(\overline{C})$ and channel indices for internal messages $(\overline{i_{\mathsf{in}}})$ and external (processor) inputs$(\overline{i_{\mathsf{rq}}})$/outputs$(\overline{i_{\mathsf{rs}}})$. A *cache* $C ::= \langle i, s_{\mathsf{init}}, \overline{r} \rangle$ consists of its index (unique within a system), an initial state (s_{init}), and rules $(\overline{r})$. A *rule* (r) makes state transitions within the cache, and it is always defined by one of the rule templates provided by the language.

Each rule template must be instantiated with a rule index (should be unique within a cache), a precondition, and a transition function, where the types of the precondition and transition vary by template. A precondition of a rule template usually takes input messages and a (partial) current cache state and decides whether the rule can be executed or not. A transition function takes the same arguments in general but returns the next cache state and output messages. Neither state transition nor input-messages consumption happens if the precondition does not hold. We will introduce the detailed rule-template forms in the next section (Sect. 3.2).

A *message* $m ::= \langle \mathsf{ty}, \mathsf{id}, \mathsf{val} \rangle$ is composed of a Boolean message type (request or response), a message ID (effectively from an enumeration of message kinds), and a value. We use *value* to refer to the set of legal contents of memory addresses. A pair $im ::= (i, m)$ is used sometimes to represent a message m in a channel with an index i.

3.2   Rule Templates

The Hemiola DSL follows syntax and semantics of traditional rule-based HDLs, but the major difference is that Hemiola further restricts the way of describing rules, which itself guarantees noninterference among transactions.

Topology and Network Requirements. First of all, Hemiola requires that the caches in a given system form a tree topology. Most cache-coherent memory subsystems follow this topology, where leaf nodes correspond to L1 caches, and the root corresponds to the main memory. A child and its parent in the tree communicate using the three channels shown in Sect. 2.

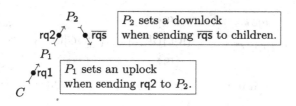

Fig. 2. Locking mechanism in Hemiola

Note that the topology and network settings are required *logically*; the actual hardware implementation may use various hardware components (e.g., finite-capacity FIFOs or buses) that can simulate the requirements.

Locking Mechanism. We saw in Sect. 2 why transient states are required to ensure noninterference in cache-coherence protocols. Revisiting the issue described in Fig. 1, a child should be able to handle an invalidation request from the parent even if it is in a transient state (SM), and after handling the request it changes its transient state to IM.

Hemiola supports a locking mechanism reflecting this discovery; the locking is more general in that the framework looks at whether the message is from the parent or a child. This mechanism is still enough to describe practical cache-coherence protocols and sufficient to ensure noninterference.

In particular, Hemiola employs two kinds of locks: *uplocks and downlocks*. We say a cache is uplocked (or downlocked) when it holds an uplock (or downlock), respectively. Figure 2 depicts the locking mechanism in Hemiola. An uplock is set when a cache (P_1 in the figure) makes an upward request to its parent (P_2); it is released when the cache gets a corresponding response from the parent. The cache cannot make any further upward requests while uplocked. On the contrary, a downlock is set when a cache (P_2 in the figure) makes a downward request(s) to some of its children; similarly it is released when the cache gets corresponding response(s) from the child requestee(s). The cache cannot make any further downward requests while downlocked.

Now every cache defined in Hemiola *does not need to set transient states* to consider all possible combinations among stable statuses. For instance, instead of setting a transient state SM, it is now desirable to maintain its status S and *set an uplock* to record it just made an upward request. We emphasize that the Hemiola locks *do not enforce more restrictions* on protocols than what is enforced by transient states; e.g., as an uplock makes certain messages like rqS and rqM stall, a transient state SM makes them stall as well.

Each cache defined by Hemiola has a semantic lock state holding a lock type (uplock or downlock) and related messages/indices. The user, however, does not need to deal with this lock state while using the DSL; locks are managed implicitly by Hemiola.

Note that the DSL supports design of single-cache-line protocols, and thus the uplock and downlock are assigned per-line. The single-line protocol is then

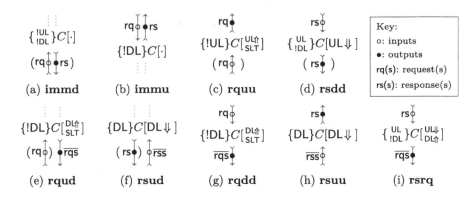

Fig. 3. Rule templates in Hemiola

naturally extended to all cache lines using a protocol compiler that will be introduced in Sect. 6. This approach is sound in terms of correctness, since a transaction does not affect coherence for the other lines.

The Nine Rule Templates. Hemiola provides a set of rule templates for describing protocols in a way that guarantees noninterference by-construction. Figure 3 presents the nine rule templates. Each diagram has the form $\{P\}C[Q]$ and arrows (representing the directions of messages; e.g., a downward arrow indicates messages from a parent) with circles (○ for inputs and ● for outputs) and labels representing requests (rq(s)) and responses (rs(s)). It means that the rule template is for a cache C, requires input messages (○) with the message types determined by the label, has a precondition P, performs a state transition Q, and generates output messages (●). The precondition and state transition are implicit in the sense that they are automatically checked and performed, respectively, whenever the rule is executed. Note that some rule templates may make local state transitions without any input/output messages (input/output messages marked with parentheses in Fig. 3).

UL, DL, !UL, and !DL in a precondition indicate that the cache should be uplocked, downlocked, uplock-free, and downlock-free, respectively. UL⇑, DL⇑, UL⇓, and DL⇓ in a state transition indicate setting an uplock, setting a downlock, releasing an uplock, and releasing a downlock, respectively. SLT annotates that the rule template forbids any state modification beside locking.

The rule templates are carefully designed to avoid any spurious interleavings among transactions. We see a number of cases that are worth analyzing:

- **immu** and **rqdd** show that a cache can handle a downward request even when uplocked. These rules do not have a precondition that the cache should be uplock-free. This relaxation is necessary to avoid a deadlock.
- **rsdd** says that in order to handle a response from the parent, the cache should be downlock-free. This precondition is required to ensure noninterference.
- **rsrq** forces the order of a traversal, saying that the traversal for the outer caches must be done before traversing the inner caches. This rule is used when

$$
\text{SSilent:}\ \frac{}{s \xrightarrow[S]{l_\epsilon} s} \qquad \text{SIns:}\ \frac{\overline{im} \neq [] \qquad \overline{im}.i \subseteq S.\overline{i_{\mathrm{rq}}}}{\langle \overline{c}, M \rangle \xrightarrow[S]{l_{\mathrm{in}}(\overline{im})} \langle \overline{c}, M + \overline{im} \rangle}
$$

$$
\text{SOuts:}\ \frac{\overline{im} \neq [] \qquad \overline{im} \subseteq M.\mathsf{hds} \qquad \overline{im}.i \subseteq S.\overline{i_{\mathrm{rs}}}}{\langle \overline{c}, M \rangle \xrightarrow[S]{l_{\mathrm{out}}(\overline{im})} \langle \overline{c}, M - \overline{im} \rangle}
$$

$$
\text{SInt:}\ \frac{\begin{array}{ccc} S = \langle \overline{C}, \overline{i_{\mathrm{in}}}, \overline{i_{\mathrm{rq}}}, \overline{i_{\mathrm{rs}}} \rangle & C \in S.\overline{C} & r \in C.\overline{r} \\ \overline{im^{\mathrm{ins}}}.i \subseteq S.\overline{i_{\mathrm{in}}} \cup S.\overline{i_{\mathrm{rq}}} & \overline{c}[C.i] = c_1 & \overline{im^{\mathrm{ins}}} \subseteq M.\mathsf{hds} \\ r.p\,(c_1, \overline{im^{\mathrm{ins}}}) & r.t\,(c_1, \overline{im^{\mathrm{ins}}}) = (c_2, \overline{im^{\mathrm{outs}}}) \\ \overline{im^{\mathrm{outs}}}.i \subseteq S.\overline{i_{\mathrm{in}}} \cup S.\overline{i_{\mathrm{rs}}} & \overline{im^{\mathrm{ins}}}.i\ \#\ \overline{im^{\mathrm{outs}}}.i \end{array}}{\langle \overline{c}, M \rangle \xrightarrow[S]{l_{\mathrm{int}}(C.i, r.i, \overline{im^{\mathrm{ins}}}, \overline{im^{\mathrm{outs}}})} \left\langle \begin{array}{c} \overline{c} + (C.i, c_2), \\ M - \overline{im^{\mathrm{ins}}} + \overline{im^{\mathrm{outs}}} \end{array} \right\rangle}
$$

Fig. 4. Transition steps of the Hemiola DSL

a transaction needs to traverse all the caches in the system, e.g., invalidating all the other caches to obtain the M status. The forced order is important to avoid a deadlock.

4   Verification in Hemiola

We have introduced the Hemiola DSL in Sect. 3 and provided an intuition that rule templates ensure general noninterference, i.e., interleavings among any transactions are safe. That said, we have not yet showed how the rule templates guarantee such noninterference in a formal way. We also have not explained how noninterference eases the verification of cache-coherence protocols.

In this section, we provide the semantics of the Hemiola DSL and the formal meaning of general noninterference called *serializability*. We then introduce our novel approach to proving invariants called *predicate messages*, which eliminates the burden of considering interference while proving invariants.

4.1   Semantics of the Hemiola DSL

A system in Hemiola follows so-called "one-rule-at-a-time semantics" [4,5,10,34], i.e., any state transition by concurrent rule executions can be interpreted as a serial execution of rules. Thus, it is fair to consider that a state transition happens by executing a single rule.

Transition Steps. Figure 4 describes the complete semantics for transition steps of the Hemiola DSL. The semantics for a step is presented as a judgment $s_0 \xrightarrow[S]{l} s_1$, where S is the system to execute, s_0 is a prestate, s_1 is a poststate, and l is a label generated by the state transition. The state of a system (in domain $\mathbb{S}$)

is a pair $\langle \overline{c}, M \rangle$ of cache states ($\overline{c}$) and message states (M). Cache states are represented in a finite map from cache indices to cache states, and message states are represented in a finite map from channel indices to ordered queues of messages.

Rule [SSilent] represents the case where no state transition happens in the current step; an empty label (l_ϵ) is generated in this case. From now on, we assume that all the input/output messages used in the step definitions do not share the same channel, i.e., (List.NoDup$\overline{im.i}$). [SIns] describes the case for external input messages coming to the system; an external-inputs label ($l_{in}(\overline{im})$) is generated in this case. [SOuts] describes the opposite case, for output messages being released to the external world, generating an external-outputs label ($l_{out}(\overline{im})$).

Lastly, [SInt] deals with a state transition by a rule (r) in a cache (C). It nondeterministically chooses a cache and a rule in the cache, checks that the precondition holds, and applies the transition to update the state of the system; an internal label ($l_{int}(C.i, r.i, \overline{im}^{ins}, \overline{im}^{outs})$) is generated in this case, which records a cache index, a rule index, input messages, and output messages. Note that the semantics is based on ordered channels, so messages are *enqueued* and *dequeued* in each state-transition case.

The step semantics is naturally lifted to one for *multiple steps*, presented as a judgment $s_0 \xRightarrow[S]{\overline{l}} s_1$, where $\overline{l}$ is a sequence of labels generated by executions of the steps in order. We will sometimes call such a sequence of labels a *history*.

We say that a state s is *reachable* iff there is a history $\overline{l}$ such that $S_{init} \xRightarrow[S]{\overline{l}} s$ holds, where S_{init} is the initial state of the system S. We use a simpler notation $S \Rightarrow s$ for reachable states. We also call such a history $\overline{l}$ *legal*, denoted as $S \xRightarrow{\overline{l}} \bullet$. We call $\mathcal{I} : \mathbb{S} \to \mathbb{P}^2$ an *invariant* over a system S if $\mathcal{I}$ holds for all reachable states, i.e., $\forall s. (S \Rightarrow s) \to \mathcal{I}(s)$.

Behaviors and Correctness. A system S has a behavior $\lfloor \overline{l} \rfloor$ (denoted as $S \Downarrow \lfloor \overline{l} \rfloor$) iff $S_{init} \xRightarrow[S]{\overline{l}} s$ holds, where $\lfloor \cdot \rfloor$ filters out silent (l_ϵ) and internal (l_{int}) labels so only the external parts remain. We call such a sequence of labels a *trace*. Lastly, we say that a system I ("implementation") trace-refines another system S ("specification"), written as $I \sqsubseteq S$, iff every trace of I is also a trace of S:

$$I \sqsubseteq S \triangleq \forall \overline{t}. \ I \Downarrow \overline{t} \to S \Downarrow \overline{t}.$$

In order to prove trace refinement, we usually establish a *simulation relation* [6] between the implementation and the spec states and prove that the relation is preserved over steps, and it is crucial to state and prove proper invariants of the implementation for the simulation proof. Since the invariant proof is indeed the most significant part of the whole correctness proof, in this paper we would like to focus on how Hemiola helps a user state and prove invariants.

---

[2] $\mathbb{P}$ is Prop in Coq, which can reasonbly be interpreted as Boolean in this paper.

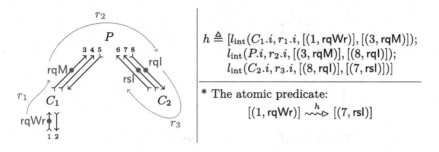

Fig. 5. An example of an atomic history

4.2 Serializability in Hemiola

Serializability [3,28] is a celebrated notion of concurrency correctness. While each transaction in a system affects multiple values, serializability guarantees that interleaved execution of such transactions is correct in that the effect (state change) is the same as if the transactions were executed serially, i.e., *atomically in some order with no interleaving*.

In order to define serializability formally, we first provide basic definitions of atomic histories and transactions. A history h is *atomic* iff it satisfies the predicate $(\overline{im^{\mathrm{init}}} \overset{h}{\leadsto} \overline{im^{\mathrm{end}}})$ with *initial messages* $\overline{im^{\mathrm{init}}}$ and *live messages* $\overline{im^{\mathrm{end}}}$, constructed inductively by the following two cases:

- Any singleton history with an internal label is an atomic history with its input and output messages as initial and live messages, respectively.
- If h is an atomic history, $(h+l)$ is also an atomic history if l *consumes* its input messages from the live messages of h. The new live messages are constructed by subtracting the input messages and adding the output messages of l to the previous live messages.

Figure 5 presents an atomic history already shown in Fig. 1. h is generated by executions of three rules, $r_1 \in C_1.\overline{r}$, $r_2 \in P.\overline{r}$, and $r_3 \in C_2.\overline{r}$. Rule r_1 takes an input message $(1, \mathsf{rqWr})$ (from the channel with index 1) as an initial message of the history. Rule r_2 takes $(3, \mathsf{rqM})$, the output message from r_1. Finally, r_3 takes $(8, \mathsf{rql})$, the output message from r_2. Summing up all the rule executions, by the definition of an atomic history we get the predicate lower-right in Fig. 5.

This example shows that an atomic history intuitively captures a *transaction flow* triggered by the initial messages. Note that an atomic history does not need to be completed, e.g., h in the example is incomplete in the sense that the live message (rsl) is not a response sent to an external channel.

We call an atomic history $(\overline{im^{\mathrm{init}}} \overset{h}{\leadsto} \overline{im^{\mathrm{end}}})$ a *transaction* if its initial messages are external requests $(\overline{im^{\mathrm{init}}}.i \subseteq S.\overline{i_{\mathrm{rq}}})$; we denote it as $S \diagup h$.

With a clear notion of transactions, we can now easily define sequential histories and serializability. A history h is *sequential* iff the history is a concatenation of transactions:

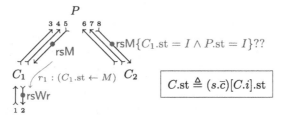

Fig. 6. Interference breaks a predicate message

$$\text{Sequential } S \; h \triangleq \exists \bar{t}. \; (\forall t \in \bar{t}. \; S \swarrow t) \wedge h = \oplus \bar{t}.$$

A legal history h is *serializable* in the system S iff there exists a sequential history that reaches the same state:

$$\text{Serializable } S \; h \triangleq \forall s. \; S_{\mathsf{init}} \xRightarrow{h}_{S} s \rightarrow \exists h_{\mathsf{seq}}. \; \text{Sequential } S \; h_{\mathsf{seq}} \wedge S_{\mathsf{init}} \xRightarrow{h_{\mathsf{seq}}}_{S} s.$$

A system S is *serializable* iff every legal history is serializable:

$$\text{Serializable } S \triangleq \forall h. \; \text{Serializable } S \; h.$$

4.3   Predicate Messages

Now we discuss how to exploit our notion of serializability: how does it help prove global invariants of a system? In proving the correctness of a cache-coherence protocol, it is very common to state an invariant like "an important property holds *whenever the system includes a certain message in a certain channel.*" We call such an invariant a *predicate message*, giving the intuition of messages that logically carry predicates that must be true so long as those messages remain in play. More formally, $S \vdash im\{P\} \triangleq \forall s. \; (S \Rightarrow s) \rightarrow im \in s.M \rightarrow P(s)$, where $s.M$ refers to the message state of the system. We will write just $im\{P\}$ when the system S is clear from context, also often using a shorter version $id\{P\}$ (considering only messages with a given ID) when it is not ambiguous.

Figure 6 presents an example of a predicate message. When a child C_2 is about to handle a response message rsM, which is a permission to change the cache status to M, we expect the parent and the other child C_1 to have I status (like $\{C_1.\text{st} = I \wedge P.\text{st} = I\}$ in the figure). However, between the sending of that message and receipt by C_2, the predicate may be broken *by another transaction*; for instance, the predicate no longer holds if a state transition happens by $r_1 \in C_1$, which takes another $(5, \text{rsM})$ and updates the status of C_1 to M.

Investigating this corner case carefully, we find that actually no two different rsM messages can be in the system at the same time. It implies that now the predicate message for rsM should have a much-more-complicated form, which considers *all possible noninterference cases*. The complete desired predicate message for $(8, \text{rsM})$ will then look like:

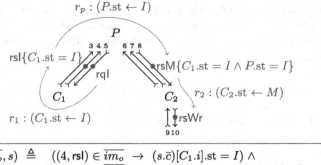

$$\mathcal{I}_A\,(\overline{im_o}, s) \triangleq \quad ((4, \mathsf{rsl}) \in \overline{im_o} \ \rightarrow\ (s.\bar{c})[C_1.i].\mathsf{st} = I) \wedge$$
$$((8, \mathsf{rsM}) \in \overline{im_o} \ \rightarrow\ (s.\bar{c})[C_1.i].\mathsf{st} = I \wedge (s.\bar{c})[P.i].\mathsf{st} = I)$$

Fig. 7. Predicate messages defined as an atomic invariant

$$(8, \mathsf{rsM}) \left\{ \begin{array}{l} C_1.\mathsf{st} = I \ \wedge\ P.\mathsf{st} = I \ \wedge\ \textit{// The original predicate} \\ \textit{// Noninterference with another transaction to get M from } C_1 \\ (7, \mathsf{rsl}) \notin s.M \ \wedge\ (5, \mathsf{rsM}) \notin s.M \ \wedge \\ \cdots\textit{// More noninterference cases will be required} \end{array} \right\}$$

It is indeed a burden to consider all possible interleavings per predicate message. We would not have faced such a complication if we could ensure that no other transactions interfere while handling a transaction. Serializability guarantees exactly that simplification, and Hemiola provides a way of designing and proving predicate messages in the simpler form, *not taking any interference into account*.

Our novel approach to employing predicate messages in atomic histories begins with formalizing the notion of atomic invariants. We say that $\mathcal{I}_A :$ $\overline{\mathbb{IM}} \times \mathbb{S} \rightarrow \mathbb{P}$ is an *atomic invariant* iff $\mathcal{I}_A\,(\overline{im_o}, s_1)$ holds for any atomic history h with $s_0 \overset{h}{\underset{S}{\Rightarrow}} s_1$ and $\overline{im_i} \overset{h}{\rightsquigarrow} \overline{im_o}$.

Figure 7 shows an example of predicate messages defined in an atomic history, formalized as an atomic invariant. An atomic invariant $\mathcal{I}_A$ is a conjunction of clauses $(im \in \overline{im_o} \rightarrow P(s))$, each claiming that the predicate P holds when im is in *the live messages* $\overline{im_o}$. We can prove that the atomic invariant $\mathcal{I}_A$ holds by induction on state-transition steps through the atomic history in the figure:

- The initial step of the atomic history is the one by r_1. The live messages are $[(4, \mathsf{rsl})]$. Since r_1 changes the status of C_1 to I, it is straightforward to prove $\mathcal{I}_A$.
- The next step is by r_p, and at this point the live messages are $[(8, \mathsf{rsM})]$. By the induction hypothesis, we obtain the predicate message $(4, \mathsf{rsl})\{C_1.\mathsf{st} = I\}$. Since r_p changes the status of P to I, we can prove the predicate for $(8, \mathsf{rsM})$.
- The last step is by r_2, and the live messages are $[(10, \mathsf{rsWr})]$. $\mathcal{I}_A$ trivially holds here since it does not contain any predicate for $(10, \mathsf{rsWr})$.

Note that the invariant proof was straightforward since no other state transitions interfere with an atomic history.

How do atomic invariants help prove conventional invariants? If the system S is serializable, by definition, for every reachable state there is a sequential history that reaches the same state. Since the sequential history is a concatenation of transactions, an invariant can be proven *by showing that any transaction preserves it*.

Since a transaction is an (external) atomic history, we can make use of corresponding atomic invariants. In other words, we can employ both conventional/atomic invariants ($\mathcal{I}$ and $\mathcal{I}_A$) to prove the ones for the next state (s_{i+1}):

$$\mathcal{I}_A\left(\overline{m_i}, s_i\right) \wedge \mathcal{I}(s_i) \rightarrow \left(\mathcal{I}_A\left(\overline{m_{i+1}}, s_{i+1}\right) \wedge \mathcal{I}(s_{i+1})\right).$$

For instance, in proving a cache-coherence protocol, we usually want to have an invariant claiming that at most one node of the system has M status at a time. The predicate messages defined in Fig. 7 will play a crucial role here, e.g., the one for $(8, \mathsf{rsM})$ says that C_1 and P both have I status, which means that the state transition by $(r_2 : C_2.\mathsf{st} \leftarrow M)$ preserves the invariant. We will see more comprehensive uses of predicate messages in our case studies (Sect. 5).

4.4 Serializability Guarantee by the Hemiola DSL

The biggest contribution of the Hemiola framework includes the serializability proof. The highest-level theorem simply claims that use of good topology (OnTree S t) and the rule templates (GoodRules S t) guarantees serializability:

$$\forall S, t.\ \mathsf{OnTree}\ S\ t \wedge \mathsf{GoodRules}\ S\ t \rightarrow \mathsf{Serializable}\ S.$$

In the proof we used a well-established technique called commuting reductions [15], showing that any interleaving transactions can be serialized by performing a finite number of reductions. Interested readers are referred to Choi's dissertation [9], which describes more details of the proof.

5 Case Studies: Hierarchical MSI and MESI Protocols

In this section we explain how we designed, specified, and formally proved the correctness of the following three hierarchical cache-coherence protocols: inclusive/noninclusive MSI protocols and a noninclusive MESI protocol. Each protocol is *parameterized by a tree* that decides the topology of the memory subsystem. In other words, whenever we instantiate the tree parameter, we get a cache-coherence design and its correctness proof *for free*.

The protocols are directory-based and support arbitrary evictions. The inclusive MSI protocol requires back-invalidation to maintain the cache-line inclusion [30]. The noninclusive protocols employ the noninclusive-cache inclusive-directory (NCID) [38] structure to optimize cache space.

We will introduce common points among our case-study protocols. Particularly, we focus on *how predicate messages are used* (introduced in Sect. 4.3) to ease the invariant proofs required to prove protocol correctness. More details about the correctness proofs are provided in Choi's dissertation [9].

5.1   Cache States

A cache state consists of a status, a value, a directory, and a Boolean called an ownership bit. A status is either M, E, S, or I. The MESI protocol applies further optimizations to the MSI protocol: if a cache line has E status, then the line is exclusive to the cache but also clean.

A directory contains a status of its children called a directory status and a list of child-cache indices that have the directory status. An L1 cache does not have a directory since it has no children.

The *ownership bit* decides whether the cache is responsible for writing the value back to the parent when evicted. The ownership bit intuitively constrains which caches can have valid status; we will see how this intuition is formalized as an invariant in Sect. 5.3.

5.2   Protocol Description with Rule Templates

We present a number of rule descriptions, used in our case studies, that employ the rule templates provided in Hemiola. Each rule template is defined in Coq, taking in several parameters and generating a rule. We exploited Coq's notation mechanism to define each rule template compactly.

```
1  rule l1GetMRqUpUp from template rquu {
2    receive rqWr();
3    assert (status != M);
4    send rqM();
5  }
```

The above code presents an actual rule definition in an L1 cache, starting with an invocation of a particular rule template rquu, which takes an upward request (to the cache) and sends a further request to the parent. This rule receives a message with the ID rqWr from the processor core[3] to get a write permission. This rule template also requires to write down the precondition (assert) and the output message (send). In this example the cache simply forwards rqM to the parent. As explained in Sect. 3.2, the rquu rule template does not allow any state transition except locking – the template automatically sets an uplock.

```
1  rule l1DownIRsUpDownM from template rsud {
2    receive downRsI();
3    hold {rsbTo, rqM()};
4    status <= I;
5    dir <= M [rsbTo];
6    owned <= false;
7    send rsM();
8  }
```

The above rule presents another case that sends the response to the child who requested rqM. Template rsud says that the rule takes responses from children and responds back to the original child requestor. The rule receives the response message with the ID downRsI. In order to execute this rule, the cache should hold

---

[3] It is a rule defined in an L1 cache, thus an upward request is from the core.

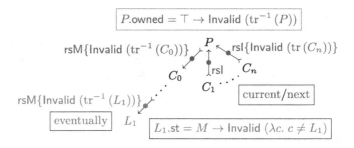

Fig. 8. Use of predicate messages in the case-study protocols

a downlock containing the index of the original requestor (`rsbTo`) and the request message with the ID `rqM`, acting like an assertion for the lock state.

As a state transition, this rule sets its status to `I`, sets the directory status to `M` by adding the requestor, and sets the ownership bit as false since the requestor will make the value dirty after it obtains `M`. It also sends a response (`rsM`) to the requestor. Lastly, the downlock is released *automatically and implicitly* by the `rsud` rule template.

```
1  rule liGetSImmME from template immd {
2    receive rqS() from cidx;
3    assert (status == E || status == M);
4    assert (dir.status == I);
5    status <= I;
6    dir <= E [cidx];
7    send rsE(value);
8  }
```

The above rule is for the MESI protocol, fired when an intermediate cache gets a request from a child to read the data, while the parent has status `E` or `M`. In this case, instead of responding with `rsS`, the cache sends `rsE` to provide `E`. Once the original requestor obtains `E` status, it can both read and write.

5.3 Invariant Proof Using Predicate Messages

Now we present how predicate messages (introduced in Sect. 4.3) are used to prove a nontrivial invariant required for all of our three case-study protocols.

Figure 8 shows a coordination between predicate messages and conventional invariants. Suppose that an L1 cache (shown as L_1 in gray in the figure) requested to the parent to get the `M` status. When it finally handles the response rsM, it should know all the other caches (except itself) have been invalidated to prove the desired invariant about `M` (denoted as L_1.st $= M \rightarrow$ Invalid $(\lambda c.\ c \neq L_1)$). This proof case can be supported using the predicate message for rsM, stating Invalid $(\mathrm{tr}^{-1}(C))$ (the caches outside of the subtree rooted to C are invalid) when the message goes to C. Since L_1 is a leaf node in the tree, it is trivial to prove Invalid $(\mathrm{tr}^{-1}(L_1)) \rightarrow$ Invalid $(\lambda c.\ c \neq L_1)$, so we see an example of a predicate message helping prove a conventional invariant.

Figure 8 also shows another coordination to prove a predicate message. When a child C_i sends the invalidation response rsI, it should know that all the caches inside the subtree of C_i have been invalidated (denoted as Invalid $(\mathrm{tr}\,(C_i))$). When the parent P subsequently handles the responses, it responds with rsM to the original requestor (C_0 in the figure), requiring to prove Invalid $(\mathrm{tr}^{-1}\,(C_0))$, the predicate message for rsM.

While P also changes its status to I in this state transition, how do we infer that the caches outside P have already been invalidated, which is required to prove the predicate over rsM? In this case, we should know that 1) P has the ownership bit true (from a simple cache-level invariant of P) and 2) the caches outside of a cache with ownership bit set should have I status (denoted as $P.\mathsf{owned} = \top \rightarrow$ Invalid $(\mathrm{tr}^{-1}\,(P))$) as an invariant. Combining all the predicates and the state transition by P, we can prove the next predicate message for rsM to the original requestor C_0.

6 Compilation and Synthesis to Hardware

So far we have dealt with cache-coherence protocols for a single line. In order to build a hardware-synthesizable multiline implementation, we developed a compiler that takes a single-line Hemiola protocol and generates a multiline implementation described in Kami [10].

Kami is a hardware formal-verification framework, where its own HDL and proof tools are defined in Coq, allowing users to design, specify, verify, and synthesize their hardware components. Since Kami already has a hardware-synthesis toolchain, we can just compile a Hemiola program to Kami and use the toolchain to run it on FPGAs.

6.1 Compilation of Hemiola Protocols

The compiler uses prebuilt hardware components described in Kami. One of them is NCID [38], whose interfaces include asynchronous read and write of the line status and value. Another prebuilt component holds a *finite* number of miss-status holding registers (MSHRs), whose abstract interface includes registering, updating, and releasing MSHRs with respect to their types (uplock or downlock) and locking addresses. The compiler also takes a cache configuration as an argument to set the capacity of a cache, the number of MSHRs, etc.

One of the biggest differences between a source Hemiola protocol and the target Kami implementation is that the target accesses multiple lines *asynchronously*. In the source protocol, a single-line value is read (or written) *immediately*, whereas in the target the value is accessed first by making a read (or write) request to a cache and next by handling the response. In order to optimize such line accesses, the compiler uses a prebuilt pipeline to deal with multiple line accesses in parallel.

6.2 Synthesis of Hemiola Protocols

Once we have obtained a multiline cache-coherence protocol implementation from the compiler, we can use Kami's synthesis toolchain to transliterate it to a Bluespec [23] implementation and synthesize it to load on an FPGA.

Before synthesis, we first evaluated two Hemiola protocols, Hemiola$_2$ and Hemiola$_3$, instantiated from our hierarchical noninclusive MESI protocol described in Sect. 5, using the Bluespec simulator. Hemiola$_3$ is a 3-level protocol, consisting of four 32 KB 4-way set-associative L1 caches, two 128 KB 8-way L2 caches, and a 512 KB 16-way last-level cache. Hemiola$_2$ is 2-level, consisting of four L1 caches and the last-level cache. Each line holds 32 bytes in all the protocols. We compared the performance with an existing Bluespec implementation, RiscyOO [37], featuring a 2-level inclusive MESI protocol with self-invalidation [30]. We set the cache sizes of RiscyOO the same as for Hemiola$_2$.

Figure 9 shows the performance result. We measured performance by counting the number of transactions performed in 5×10^5 simulation cycles, with various workloads that make random requests but mimic some amount of temporal/spatial locality of memory accesses. Though one should not draw too many conclusions from the precise measurements, the result shows that the Hemiola protocols are competitive with a practical implementation coded by hand.

Next we synthesized the Hemiola protocols, also shown in Fig. 9. We used Xilinx's Virtex-7 VC707 FPGA [1] for synthesis. Each protocol uses a minimal clock length that can safely cover its critical path. Both Hemiola$_3$ and Hemiola$_2$ stayed within the FPGA's budget of lookup tables (LUTs) and flip-flops (FFs). We performed tandem verification covering over 10^9 memory requests for each protocol on the FPGA, by connecting it to a tester module that generates a random workload and a reference memory to check its safety and liveness.

Performance (#trs/cycle)	all-shared	pair-shared	ex:sh=1:1	ex:sh=4:1
Hemiola$_3$	0.259	0.868	0.506	0.764
Hemiola$_2$	0.270	0.800	0.637	0.913
RiscyOO	0.336	0.791	0.637	0.988

	Clock length	Critical path	#LUTs	#FFs
Hemiola$_2$	40 ns	36.861 ns	126,714	41,203
Hemiola$_3$	40 ns	37.608 ns	240,034	61,011

Fig. 9. Evaluation and synthesis of Hemiola protocols

Optimization and verification of the cache-controller design are nontrivial; the pipeline requires correct stall logic, which is as sophisticated as the logic in pipelined processors. While the verification of the pipeline is one of our future-work directions, we see it as orthogonal to the verification of cache-coherence protocols, our focus with Hemiola.

7   Related Work

Model Checking. Model checking has long been widely used to verify cache-coherence protocols. Various model checkers like Murphi [12], SMV [20], and TLA+ [13,14] have been used.

In order to overcome the usual state-space-explosion problem, model checkers have developed noninterference lemmas to deal with the state-space explosion by interleavings [11,18]. In order to obtain effective lemmas, a number of approaches used descriptions in terms of transactions (called "message flows") [24,31,32]. Instead of looking at each transaction, Hemiola provides serializability that guarantees noninterference among any transactions defined on top of the framework.

In order to verify cache-coherence protocols with arbitrary numbers of cores (but no hierarchy), parameterization has been used in designing and model-checking the protocols [2,35,36]. Since Hemiola is built on Coq, we can take full advantage of parameterization, and indeed the framework supports verification of cache-coherence protocols with an arbitrary tree shape as a parameter.

In order to increase scalability further, recent approaches used modularity in protocol design and successfully verified hierarchical cache-coherence protocols [7,8,16,17]. The enforced modularity, however, made it hard to design and verify noninclusive protocols. [7,8] tried to solve this problem using assume-guarantee reasoning and history variables, while still maintaining the concept of compositional verification, but faced state-space explosion again, and thus they just verified a two-level MSI protocol with three L2 caches. [16,17] have developed the Neo theory as a safe way to compose "subtrees" of caches to have a hierarchical protocol. They argued it is possible to verify noninclusive protocols in the Neo framework when a directory is still inclusive but did not provide the actual design and proof. We provided the proofs of hierarchical noninclusive cache-coherence protocols in Hemiola, without any such restrictions.

Another notable success of cache-coherence verification employed program synthesis to generate a protocol for a given atomic specification [25,26]. The ProtoGen/HieraGen synthesizer can generate various hierarchical protocols including 3-hop protocols and even unconventional protocols like TSO-CC but does not support noninclusive protocols as well. Furthermore, they used Murphi to verify synthesized protocols, but in ProtoGen [26] they only succeeded up to three caches without exhausting memory, and in HieraGen [25] they succeeded only with the root, two cache-H, and two cache-L nodes. Since Hemiola supports noninclusive protocols but not 3-hop ones, we see protocol-design-space coverage between Hemiola and ProtoGen/HieraGen as incomparable. That said, in terms of verification, Hemiola provides a much higher level of formal assurance by allowing verification of protocols with arbitrary tree topologies.

Theorem Proving. Theorem proving also has been used to verify cache-coherence protocols. A number of works proved correctness of specific protocols [22,29]. A recent success was a proof of a hierarchical MSI protocol with an arbitrary tree topology using Coq [34], but it was not structured to promote streamlined reuse of results for other protocols. It also included rather complex and ad-hoc invariants that needed to characterize transient states.

Another notable project designed a modular-specification approach for cache coherence, verifying each cache against the spec while generating/proving invariants automatically, using the Ivy verification tool [19,21,27]. While in Hemiola a user should state and prove invariants manually, the framework provides serializability as a large essential invariant that can be reused by various protocols, and then invariants become easier to prove on top of it.

8   Conclusion

We have developed a framework called Hemiola for simplified design and formal proof of cache-coherence protocols. The template-based DSL ensures that the only protocols that can be expressed are those that admit a form of per-memory-access serializability. On top of the framework, we proved the correctness of hierarchical MSI and MESI protocols as case studies, demonstrating that Hemiola indeed eases proof burden. We also built a protocol compiler and demonstrated these protocol implementations running on FPGAs.

Acknowledgements. We thank our reviewers for their feedback and detailed comments. This work was supported by the Defense Advanced Research Projects Agency (DARPA) under Grant No. HR001118C0018. The U.S. Government is authorized to reproduce and distribute reprints for Governmental purposes notwithstanding any copyright notation thereon. The views and conclusions contained herein are those of the authors and should not be interpreted as necessarily representing the official policies or endorsements, either expressed or implied, of DARPA or the U.S. Government.

References

1. 7 Series FPGAs Configurable Logic Block - User Guide, September 2016. https://www.xilinx.com/support/documentation/user_guides/ug474_7Series_CLB.pdf
2. Banks, C.J., Elver, M., Hoffmann, R., Sarkar, S., Jackson, P., Nagarajan, V.: Verification of a lazy cache coherence protocol against a weak memory model. In: FMCAD 2017, Austin, TX, pp. 60–67 (2017) http://dl.acm.org/citation.cfm?id=3168451.3168470
3. Bernstein, P.A., Hadzilacos, V., Goodman, N.: Concurrency Control and Recovery in Database Systems. Addison-Wesley Longman Publishing Co., Inc. (1987)
4. Bourgeat, T., Pit-Claudel, C., Chlipala, A., Arvind: The essence of Bluespec: a core language for rule-based hardware design. In: PLDI, New York, NY, USA, pp. 243–257 (2020). https://doi.org/10.1145/3385412.3385965
5. Braibant, T., Chlipala, A.: Formal verification of hardware synthesis. In: Sharygina, N., Veith, H. (eds.) CAV 2013. LNCS, vol. 8044, pp. 213–228. Springer, Heidelberg (2013). https://doi.org/10.1007/978-3-642-39799-8_14

6. Brookes, S.D., Rounds, W.C.: Behavioural equivalence relations induced by programming logics. In: Diaz, J. (ed.) ICALP 1983. LNCS, vol. 154, pp. 97–108. Springer, Heidelberg (1983). https://doi.org/10.1007/BFb0036900

7. Chen, X.: Verification of hierarchical cache coherence protocols for futuristic processors. Ph.D. thesis, USA (2008)

8. Chen, X., Yang, Y., Gopalakrishnan, G., Chou, C.T.: Efficient methods for formally verifying safety properties of hierarchical cache coherence protocols. Form. Methods Syst. Des. **36**(1), 37–64 (2010). https://doi.org/10.1007/s10703-010-0092-y

9. Choi, J.: Structural design and proof of hierarchical cache-coherence protocols. Ph.D. thesis (2021). https://hdl.handle.net/1721.1/130759

10. Choi, J., Vijayaraghavan, M., Sherman, B., Chlipala, A., Arvind: Kami: a platform for high-level parametric hardware specification and its modular verification. In: Proc. ACM Program. Lang. **1**(ICFP), 24:1–24:30 (2017). https://doi.org/10.1145/3110268

11. Chou, C.-T., Mannava, P.K., Park, S.: A simple method for parameterized verification of cache coherence protocols. In: Hu, A.J., Martin, A.K. (eds.) FMCAD 2004. LNCS, vol. 3312, pp. 382–398. Springer, Heidelberg (2004). https://doi.org/10.1007/978-3-540-30494-4_27

12. Dill, D.L.: The Mur ϕ verification system. In: Alur, R., Henzinger, T.A. (eds.) CAV 1996. LNCS, vol. 1102, pp. 390–393. Springer, Heidelberg (1996). https://doi.org/10.1007/3-540-61474-5_86

13. Joshi, R., Lamport, L., Matthews, J., Tasiran, S., Tuttle, M., Yu, Y.: Checking cache-coherence protocols with TLA+. Form. Methods Syst. Des. **22**(2), 125–131 (2003). https://doi.org/10.1023/A:1022969405325

14. Lamport, L.: Specifying Systems: The TLA+ Language and Tools for Hardware and Software Engineers. Addison-Wesley Longman Publishing Co., Inc. (2002)

15. Lipton, R.J.: Reduction: a method of proving properties of parallel programs. Commun. ACM **18**(12), 717–721 (1975). https://doi.org/10.1145/361227.361234

16. Matthews, O., Bingham, J., Sorin, D.J.: Verifiable hierarchical protocols with network invariants on parametric systems. In: FMCAD 2016, pp. 101–108. FMCAD Inc, Austin (2016)

17. Matthews, O., Sorin, D.J.: Architecting hierarchical coherence protocols for push-button parametric verification. MICRO 2017, pp. 477–489 (2017). https://doi.org/10.1145/3123939.3123971

18. McMillan, K.L.: Verification of infinite state systems by compositional model checking. In: Pierre, L., Kropf, T. (eds.) CHARME 1999. LNCS, vol. 1703, pp. 219–237. Springer, Heidelberg (1999). https://doi.org/10.1007/3-540-48153-2_17

19. McMillan, K.: Modular specification and verification of a cache-coherent interface. FMCAD 2016, pp. 109–116. FMCAD Inc, Austin (2016). http://dl.acm.org/citation.cfm?id=3077629.3077651

20. McMillan, K.L.: Symbolic Model Checking. Kluwer Academic Publishers, USA (1993)

21. McMillan, K.L., Padon, O.: Ivy: a multi-modal verification tool for distributed algorithms. In: Lahiri, S.K., Wang, C. (eds.) CAV 2020. LNCS, vol. 12225, pp. 190–202. Springer, Cham (2020). https://doi.org/10.1007/978-3-030-53291-8_12

22. Moore, J. Strother.: An ACL2 proof of write invalidate cache coherence. In: Hu, Alan J.., Vardi, Moshe Y.. (eds.) CAV 1998. LNCS, vol. 1427, pp. 29–38. Springer, Heidelberg (1998). https://doi.org/10.1007/BFb0028728, http://dl.acm.org/citation.cfm?id=647767.733778

23. Nikhil, R.: Bluespec system verilog: efficient, correct RTL from high level specifications, pp. 69–70 (2004). https://doi.org/10.1109/MEMCOD.2004.1459818

24. O'Leary, J., Talupur, M., Tuttle, M.R.: Protocol verification using flows: an industrial experience. In: FMCAD 2009, pp. 172–179 (2009). https://doi.org/10.1109/FMCAD.2009.5351126
25. Oswald, N., Nagarajan, V., Sorin, D.J.: HieraGen: automated generation of concurrent, hierarchical cache coherence protocols. In: ISCA 2020, pp. 888–899 (2020). https://doi.org/10.1109/ISCA45697.2020.00077
26. Oswald, N., Nagarajan, V., Sorin, D.J.: ProtoGen: automatically generating directory cache coherence protocols from atomic specifications. In: ISCA 2018, Piscataway, NJ, USA, pp. 247–260 (2018) https://doi.org/10.1109/ISCA.2018.00030
27. Padon, O., McMillan, K.L., Panda, A., Sagiv, M., Shoham, S.: Ivy: safety verification by interactive generalization. SIGPLAN Not. **51**(6), 614–630 (2016). https://doi.org/10.1145/2980983.2908118
28. Papadimitriou, C.: The Theory of Database Concurrency Control. Computer Science Press Inc., USA (1986)
29. Park, S., Dill, D.L.: Verification of FLASH cache coherence protocol by aggregation of distributed transactions. In: SPAA 1996, pp. 288–296. ACM, New York (1996). https://doi.org/10.1145/237502.237573
30. Ros, A., Kaxiras, S.: Complexity-effective multicore coherence. In: PACT 2012, pp. 241–252. Association for Computing Machinery, New York (2012). https://doi.org/10.1145/2370816.2370853
31. Sethi, D., Talupur, M., Malik, S.: Using flow specifications of parameterized cache coherence protocols for verifying deadlock freedom. In: Cassez, F., Raskin, J.-F. (eds.) ATVA 2014. LNCS, vol. 8837, pp. 330–347. Springer, Cham (2014). https://doi.org/10.1007/978-3-319-11936-6_24
32. Talupur, M., Tuttle, M.R.: Going with the flow: parameterized verification using message flows. In: FMCAD 2008 (2008)
33. Vijayaraghavan, M.: Modular verification of hardware systems. Ph.D. thesis (2016). http://hdl.handle.net/1721.1/106096
34. Vijayaraghavan, M., Chlipala, A., Arvind, Dave, N.: Modular deductive verification of multiprocessor hardware designs. In: Kroening, D., Păsăreanu, C. (eds.) CAV 2015. LNCS, vol. 9207, pp. 109–127. Springer, Cham (2015). https://doi.org/10.1007/978-3-319-21668-3_7
35. Zhang, M., Bingham, J.D., Erickson, J., Sorin, D.J.: PVCoherence: designing flat coherence protocols for scalable verification. In: HPCA 2014, pp. 392–403 (2014). https://doi.org/10.1109/HPCA.2014.6835949
36. Zhang, M., Lebeck, A.R., Sorin, D.J.: Fractal coherence: scalably verifiable cache coherence. In: MICRO 2010, USA, pp. 471–482 (2010). https://doi.org/10.1109/MICRO.2010.11
37. Zhang, S., Wright, A., Bourgeat, T., Arvind, A.: Composable building blocks to open up processor design. In: MICRO 2018, pp. 68–81 (2018). https://doi.org/10.1109/MICRO.2018.00015
38. Zhao, L., Iyer, R., Makineni, S., Newell, D., Cheng, L.: NCID: a non-inclusive cache, inclusive directory architecture for flexible and efficient cache hierarchies. In: CF 2010, New York, NY, USA, pp. 121–130 (2010). https://doi.org/10.1145/1787275.1787314

Machine Learning

Specification-Guided Learning of Nash Equilibria with High Social Welfare

Kishor Jothimurugan[✉], Suguman Bansal, Osbert Bastani, and Rajeev Alur

University of Pennsylvania, Philadelphia, USA
kishor@seas.upenn.edu

Abstract. Reinforcement learning has been shown to be an effective strategy for automatically training policies for challenging control problems. Focusing on non-cooperative multi-agent systems, we propose a novel reinforcement learning framework for training joint policies that form a Nash equilibrium. In our approach, rather than providing low-level reward functions, the user provides high-level specifications that encode the objective of each agent. Then, guided by the structure of the specifications, our algorithm searches over policies to identify one that provably forms an ϵ-Nash equilibrium (with high probability). Importantly, it prioritizes policies in a way that maximizes social welfare across all agents. Our empirical evaluation demonstrates that our algorithm computes equilibrium policies with high social welfare, whereas state-of-the-art baselines either fail to compute Nash equilibria or compute ones with comparatively lower social welfare.

1 Introduction

Reinforcement learning (RL) is an effective strategy for automatically synthesizing controllers for challenging control problems. As a consequence, there has been interest in applying RL to multi-agent systems. For example, RL has been used to coordinate agents in cooperative systems to accomplish a shared goal [22]. Our focus is on non-cooperative systems, where the agents are trying to achieve their own goals [17]; for such systems, the goal is typically to learn a policy for each agent such that the joint strategy forms a Nash equilibrium.

A key challenge facing existing approaches is how tasks are specified. First, they typically require that the task for each agent is specified as a reward function. However, reward functions tend to be very low-level, making them difficult to manually design; furthermore, they often obfuscate high-level structure in the problem known to make RL more efficient in the single-agent [14] and cooperative [22] settings. Second, they typically focus on computing an arbitrary Nash equilibrium. However, in many settings, the user is a social planner trying to optimize the overall social welfare of the system, and most existing approaches are not designed to optimize social welfare.

We propose a novel multi-agent RL framework for learning policies from high-level specifications (one specification per agent) such that the resulting

---

The extended version of this paper can be found at [3].

© The Author(s) 2022
S. Shoham and Y. Vizel (Eds.): CAV 2022, LNCS 13372, pp. 343–363, 2022.
https://doi.org/10.1007/978-3-031-13188-2_17

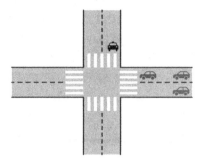

Fig. 1. Intersection Example

joint policy (i) has high social welfare, and (ii) is an ϵ-Nash equilibrium (for a given ϵ). We formulate this problem as a constrained optimization problem where the goal is to maximize social welfare under the constraint that the joint policy is an ϵ-Nash equilibrium.

Our algorithm for solving this optimization problem uses an enumerative search strategy. First, it enumerates candidate policies in decreasing order of social welfare. To ensure a tractable search space, it restricts to policies that conform to the structure of the user-provided specification. Then, for each candidate policy, it uses an explore-then-exploit self-play RL algorithm [4] to compute *punishment strategies* that are triggered when some agent deviates from the original joint policy. It also computes the maximum benefit each agent derives from deviating, which can be used to determine whether the joint policy augmented with punishment strategies forms an ϵ-Nash equilibrium; if so, it returns the joint policy.

Intuitively, the enumerative search tries to optimize social welfare, whereas the self-play RL algorithm checks whether the ϵ-Nash equilibrium constraint holds. Since this RL algorithm comes with PAC (Probably Approximately Correct) guarantees, our algorithm is guaranteed to return an ϵ-Nash equilibrium with high probability. In summary, our contributions are as follows.

- We study the problem of maximizing social welfare under the constraint that the policies form an ϵ-NE. To the best of our knowledge, this problem has not been studied before in the context of learning (beyond single-step games).
- We provide an enumerate-and-verify framework for solving the said problem.
- We propose a verification algorithm with a probabilistic soundness guarantee in the RL setting of probabilistic systems with unknown transition probabilities.

Motivating Example. Consider the road intersection scenario in Fig. 1. There are four cars; three are traveling east to west and one is traveling north to south. At any stage, each car can either move forward one step or stay in place. Suppose each car's specification is as follows:

- *Black car:* Cross the intersection before the green and orange cars.
- *Blue car:* Cross the intersection before the black car and stay a car length ahead of the green and orange cars.
- *Green car:* Cross the intersection before the black car.
- *Orange car:* Cross the intersection before the black car.

We also require that the cars do not crash into one another.

Clearly, not all agents can achieve their goals. The next highest social welfare is for three agents to achieve their goals. In particular, one possibility is that all cars except the black car achieve their goals. However, the corresponding joint policy requires that the black car does not move, which is not a Nash equilibrium—there is always a gap between the blue car and the other two cars behind, so the black car can deviate by inserting itself into the gap to achieve its own goal. Our algorithm uses self-play RL to optimize the policy for the black car, and finds that the other agents cannot prevent the black car from improving its outcome in this way. Thus, it correctly rejects this joint policy. Eventually, our algorithm computes a Nash equilibrium in which the black and blue cars achieve their goals.

1.1   Related Work

Multi-agent RL. There has been work on learning Nash equilibria in the multi-agent RL setting [1,12,13,21,23,24]; however, these approaches focus on learning an arbitrary equilibrium and do not optimize social welfare. There has also been work on studying weaker notions of equilibria in this context [9,27], as well as work on learning Nash equilibria in two agent zero-sum games [4,20,26].

RL from High-Level Specifications. There has been recent work on using specifications based on temporal logic for specifying RL tasks in the single agent setting; a comprehensive survey may be found in [2]. There has also been recent work on using temporal logic specifications for multi-agent RL [10,22], but these approaches focus on cooperative scenarios in which there is a common objective that all agents are trying to achieve.

Equilibrium in Markov Games. There has been work on computing Nash equilibrium in Markov games [17,25], including work on computing ϵ-Nash equilibria from logical specifications [6,7], as well as recent work focusing on computing welfare-optimizing Nash equilibria from temporal specifications [18,19]; however, all these works focus on the planning setting where the transition probabilities are known. Checking for existence of Nash equilibrium, even in deterministic games, has been shown to be NP-complete for reachability objectives [5].

Social Welfare. There has been work on computing welfare maximizing Nash equilibria for bimatrix games, which are two-player one-step Markov games with known transitions [8,11]; in contrast, we study this problem in the context of general Markov games.

2   Preliminaries

2.1   Markov Game

We consider an n-agent Markov game $\mathcal{M} = (\mathcal{S}, \mathcal{A}, P, H, s_0)$ with a finite set of states $\mathcal{S}$, actions $\mathcal{A} = A_1 \times \cdots \times A_n$ where A_i is a finite set of actions available to agent i, transition probabilities $P(s' \mid s, a)$ for $s, s' \in \mathcal{S}$ and $a \in \mathcal{A}$, finite horizon H, and initial state s_0 [20]. A *trajectory* $\zeta \in \mathcal{Z} = (\mathcal{S} \times \mathcal{A})^* \times \mathcal{S}$ is a finite sequence $\zeta = s_0 \xrightarrow{a_0} s_1 \xrightarrow{a_1} \cdots \xrightarrow{a_{t-1}} s_t$ where $s_k \in \mathcal{S}$, $a_k \in \mathcal{A}$; we use $|\zeta| = t$ to denote the length of the trajectory ζ and $a_k^i \in A_i$ to denote the action of agent i in a_k.

For any $i \in [n]$, let $\mathcal{D}(A_i)$ denote the set of distributions over A_i—i.e., $\mathcal{D}(A_i) = \{\Delta : A_i \to [0,1] \mid \sum_{a_i \in A_i} \Delta(a_i) = 1\}$. A *policy* for agent i is a function $\pi_i : \mathcal{Z} \to \mathcal{D}(A_i)$ mapping trajectories to distributions over actions. A policy π_i is *deterministic* if for every $\zeta \in \mathcal{Z}$, there is an action $a_i \in A_i$ such that $\pi_i(\zeta)(a_i) = 1$; in this case, we also use $\pi_i(\zeta)$ to denote the action a_i. A *joint policy* $\pi : \mathcal{Z} \to \mathcal{D}(A)$ maps finite trajectories to distributions over joint actions. We use $(\pi_1, \ldots, \pi_n)$ to denote the joint policy in which agent i chooses its action in accordance to π_i. We denote by $\mathcal{D}_\pi$ the distribution over H-length trajectories in $\mathcal{M}$ induced by π.

We consider the reinforcement learning setting in which we do not know the probabilities P but instead only have access to a simulator of $\mathcal{M}$. Typically, we can only sample trajectories of $\mathcal{M}$ starting at s_0. Some parts of our algorithm are based on an assumption which allows us to obtain sample trajectories starting at any state that has been observed before. For example, if taking action a_0 in s_0 leads to a state s_1, we assume we can obtain future samples starting at s_1.

Assumption 1. *We can obtain samples from $P(\cdot \mid s, a)$ for any previously observed state s and any action a.*

2.2   Specification Language

We consider the specification language SPECTRL to express agent specifications. We choose SPECTRL since there is existing work on leveraging the structure of SPECTRL specifications for single-agent RL [16]. However, we believe our algorithm can be adapted to other specification languages as well.

Formally, a SPECTRL specification is defined over a set of *atomic predicates* $\mathcal{P}_0$, where every $p \in \mathcal{P}_0$ is associated with a function $[\![p]\!] : \mathcal{S} \to \mathbb{B} = \{\texttt{true}, \texttt{false}\}$; we say a state s *satisfies* p (denoted $s \models p$) if and only if $[\![p]\!](s) = \texttt{true}$. The set of *predicates* $\mathcal{P}$ consists of conjunctions and disjunctions of atomic predicates. The syntax of a predicate $b \in \mathcal{P}$ is given by the grammar $b ::= p \mid (b_1 \wedge b_2) \mid (b_1 \vee b_2)$, where $p \in \mathcal{P}_0$. Similar to atomic predicates, each predicate $b \in \mathcal{P}$ corresponds to a function $[\![b]\!] : \mathcal{S} \to \mathbb{B}$ defined naturally over Boolean logic. Finally, the syntax of SPECTRL is given by[1]

$$\phi ::= \texttt{achieve } b \mid \phi_1 \texttt{ ensuring } b \mid \phi_1; \phi_2 \mid \phi_1 \texttt{ or } \phi_2,$$

where $b \in \mathcal{P}$. Each specification ϕ corresponds to a function $[\![\phi]\!] : \mathcal{Z} \to \mathbb{B}$, and we say $\zeta \in \mathcal{Z}$ satisfies ϕ (denoted $\zeta \models \phi$) if and only if $[\![\phi]\!](\zeta) = \texttt{true}$. Letting ζ be a finite trajectory of length t, this function is defined by

$\zeta \models \texttt{achieve } b$	if $\exists\, i \leq t,\; s_i \models b$
$\zeta \models \phi \texttt{ ensuring } b$	if $\zeta \models \phi$ and $\forall\, i \leq t,\; s_i \models b$
$\zeta \models \phi_1; \phi_2$	if $\exists\, i < t,\; \zeta_{0:i} \models \phi_1$ and $\zeta_{i+1:t} \models \phi_2$
$\zeta \models \phi_1 \texttt{ or } \phi_2$	if $\zeta \models \phi_1$ or $\zeta \models \phi_2$.

Intuitively, the first clause means that the trajectory should eventually reach a state that satisfies the predicate b. The second clause says that the trajectory should satisfy specification ϕ while always staying in states that satisfy b. The third clause says that the trajectory should sequentially satisfy ϕ_1 followed by ϕ_2. The fourth clause means that the trajectory should satisfy either ϕ_1 or ϕ_2.

2.3   Abstract Graphs

SPECTRL specifications can be represented by *abstract graphs* which are DAG-like structures in which each vertex represents a set of states (called subgoal regions) and each edge represents a set of concrete trajectories that can be used to transition from the source vertex to the target vertex without violating safety constraints.

Definition 1. An *abstract graph* $\mathcal{G} = (U, E, u_0, F, \beta, \mathcal{Z}_{\text{safe}})$ is a directed acyclic graph (DAG) with vertices U, (directed) edges $E \subseteq U \times U$, initial vertex $u_0 \in U$, final vertices $F \subseteq U$, subgoal region map $\beta : U \to 2^S$ such that for each $u \in U$, $\beta(u)$ is a subgoal region,[2] and *safe trajectories* $\mathcal{Z}_{\text{safe}} = \bigcup_{e \in E} \mathcal{Z}_{\text{safe}}^e \cup \bigcup_{f \in F} \mathcal{Z}_{\text{safe}}^f$, where $\mathcal{Z}_{\text{safe}}^e \subseteq \mathcal{Z}$ denotes the safe trajectories for edge $e \in E$ and $\mathcal{Z}_{\text{safe}}^f \subseteq \mathcal{Z}$ denotes the safe trajectories for final vertex $f \in F$.

Intuitively, (U, E) is a standard DAG, and u_0 and F define a graph reachability problem for (U, E). Furthermore, β and $\mathcal{Z}_{\text{safe}}$ connect (U, E) back to the original MDP $\mathcal{M}$; in particular, for an edge $e = u \to u'$, $\mathcal{Z}_{\text{safe}}^e$ is the set of safe trajectories in $\mathcal{M}$ that can be used to transition from $\beta(u)$ to $\beta(u')$.

Definition 2. A trajectory $\zeta = s_0 \xrightarrow{a_0} s_1 \xrightarrow{a_1} \cdots \xrightarrow{a_{t-1}} s_t$ in $\mathcal{M}$ satisfies the abstract graph $\mathcal{G}$ (denoted $\zeta \models \mathcal{G}$) if there is a sequence of indices $0 = k_0 \leq k_1 < \cdots < k_\ell \leq t$ and a path $\rho = u_0 \to u_1 \to \cdots \to u_\ell$ in $\mathcal{G}$ such that

---

[1] Here, achieve and ensuring correspond to the "eventually" and "always" operators in temporal logic.

[2] We do not require that the subgoal regions partition the state space or that they be non-overlapping.

- $u_\ell \in F$,
- for all $z \in \{0, \ldots, \ell\}$, we have $s_{k_z} \in \beta(u_z)$,
- for all $z < \ell$, letting $e_z = u_z \to u_{z+1}$, we have $\zeta_{k_z:k_{z+1}} \in \mathcal{Z}_{\text{safe}}^{e_z}$, and
- $\zeta_{k_\ell:t} \in \mathcal{Z}_{\text{safe}}^{u_\ell}$.

The first two conditions state that the trajectory should visit a sequence of subgoal regions corresponding to a path from the initial vertex to some final vertex, and the last two conditions state that the trajectory should be composed of subtrajectories that are safe according to $\mathcal{Z}_{\text{safe}}$.

Prior work shows that for every SPECTRL specification ϕ, we can construct an abstract graph $\mathcal{G}_\phi$ such that for every trajectory $\zeta \in \mathcal{Z}$, $\zeta \models \phi$ if and only if $\zeta \models \mathcal{G}_\phi$ [16]. Finally, the number of states in the abstract graph is linear in the size of the specification.

2.4   Nash Equilibrium and Social Welfare

Given a Markov game $\mathcal{M}$ with unknown transitions and SPECTRL specifications $\phi_1, \ldots, \phi_n$ for the n agents respectively, the score of agent i from a joint policy π is given by

$$J_i(\pi) = \Pr_{\zeta \sim \mathcal{D}_\pi} [\zeta \models \phi_i].$$

Our goal is to compute a *high-value* ϵ-Nash equilibrium in $\mathcal{M}$ w.r.t these scores. Given a joint policy $\pi = (\pi_1, \ldots, \pi_n)$ and an alternate policy π_i' for agent i, let (π_{-i}, π_i') denote the joint policy $(\pi_1, \ldots, \pi_i', \ldots, \pi_n)$. Then, a joint policy π is an ϵ-*Nash equilibrium* if for all agents i and all alternate policies π_i', $J_i(\pi) \geq J_i((\pi_{-i}, \pi_i')) - \epsilon$. Our goal is to compute a joint policy π that maximizes the social welfare given by

$$\texttt{welfare}(\pi) = \frac{1}{n} \sum_{i=1}^n J_i(\pi)$$

subject to the constraint that π is an ϵ-Nash equilibrium.

3   Overview

Our framework for computing a high-welfare ϵ-Nash equilibrium consists of two phases. The first phase is a *prioritized enumeration* procedure that learns deterministic joint policies in the environment and ranks them in decreasing order of social welfare. The second phase is a *verification phase* that checks whether a given joint policy can be extended to an ϵ-Nash equilibrium by adding punishment strategies. A policy is returned if it passes the verification check in the second phase. Algorithm 1 summarizes our framework.

For the enumeration phase, it is impractical to enumerate all joint policies even for small environments, since the total number of deterministic joint policies is $\Omega(|\mathcal{A}|^{|\mathcal{S}|^{H-1}})$, which is $\Omega(2^{n|\mathcal{S}|^{H-1}})$ if each agent has atleast two actions. Thus,

---

Algorithm 1 HIGHNASHSEARCH

Inputs: Markov game (with unknown transition probabilities) $\mathcal{M}$ with n-agents, agent specifications $\phi_1, \ldots, \phi_n$, Nash factor ϵ, precision δ, failure probability p.

Outputs: ϵ-NE, if found.

1: PrioritizedPolicies ← PRIORITIZEDENUMERATION($\mathcal{M}, \phi_1, \ldots, \phi_n$)
2: **for** joint policy $\pi \in$ PrioritizedPolicies **do**
3:    // Can π be extended to an ϵ-NE?
4:    isNash, τ ← VERIFYNASH($\mathcal{M}, \pi, \phi_1, \cdots, \phi_n, \epsilon, \delta, p$)
5:    **if** isNash **then return** $\pi \bowtie \tau$ // Add punishment strategies
6: **return** No ϵ-NE found

---

in the prioritized enumeration phase, we apply a specification-guided heuristic to reduce the number of joint policies considered. The resulting search space is independent of $|\mathcal{S}|$ and H, depending only on the specifications $\{\phi_i\}_{i \in [n]}$. Since the transition probabilities are unknown, these joint policies are trained using an efficient compositional RL approach.

Since the joint policies are trained cooperatively, they are typically not ϵ-Nash equilibria. Hence, in the verification phase, we use a probably approximately correct (PAC) procedure (Algorithm 2) to determine whether a given joint policy can be modified by adding *punishment strategies* to form an ϵ-Nash equilibrium. Our approach is to reduce this problem to solving two-agent zero-sum games. The key insight is that for a given joint policy to be an ϵ-Nash equilibrium, unilateral deviations by any agent must be successfully punished by the coalition of all other agents. In such a *punishment game*, the deviating agent attempts to maximize its score while the coalition of other agents attempts to minimize its score, leading to a competitive min-max game between the agent and the coalition. If the deviating agent can improve its score by a margin $\geq \epsilon$, then the joint policy cannot be extended to an ϵ-Nash equilibrium. Alternatively, if no agent can increase its score by a margin $\geq \epsilon$, then the joint policy (augmented with punishment strategies) is an ϵ-Nash equilibrium. Thus, checking if a joint policy can be converted to an ϵ-Nash equilibrium reduces to solving a two-agent zero-sum game for each agent. Each punishment game is solved using a self-play RL algorithm for learning policies in min-max games with unknown transitions [4], after converting specification-based scores to reward-based scores. While the initial joint policy is deterministic, the punishment strategies can be probabilistic.

Overall, we provide the guarantee that with high probability, if our algorithm returns a joint policy, it will be an ϵ-Nash equilibrium.

4   Prioritized Enumeration

We summarize our specification-guided compositional RL algorithm for learning a finite number of deterministic joint policies in an unknown environment under Assumption 1. These policies are then ranked in decreasing order of their (estimated) social welfare.

Fig. 2. Abstract Graph of black car.

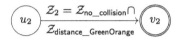

Fig. 3. Abstract Graph of blue car.

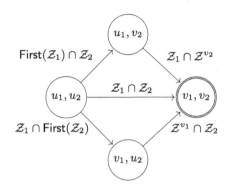

Fig. 4. Product Abstract Graph of black and blue cars. $\mathcal{Z}^{v_1}$ and $\mathcal{Z}^{v_2}$ refer to safe trajectories after the black and blue cars have reached their final states, respectively.

Our learning algorithm harnesses the structure of specifications, exposed by their abstract graphs, to curb the number of joint policies to learn. For every set of *active agents* $B \subseteq [n]$, we construct a product abstract graph, from the abstract graphs of all active agents' specifications. A property of this product is that if a trajectory ζ in $\mathcal{M}$ corresponds to a path in the product that ends in a final state then ζ satisfies the specification of *all* active agents. Then, our procedure learns one joint policy for every path in the product graph that reaches a final state. Intuitively, policies learned using the product graph corresponding to a set of active agents B aim to maximize satisfaction probabilities of all agents in B. By learning joint policies for every set of active agents, we are able to learn policies under which some agents may not satisfy their specifications. This enables learning joint policies in non-cooperative settings. Note that the number of paths (and hence the number of policies considered) is independent of $|\mathcal{S}|$ and H, and depends only on the number of agents and their specifications.

One caveat is that the number of paths may be exponential in the number of states in the product graph. It would be impractical to naïvely learn a joint policy for every path. Instead, we design an efficient compositional RL algorithm that learns a joint policy for each edge in the product graph; these edge policies are then composed together to obtain joint policies for paths in the product graph.

4.1   Product Abstract Graph

Let $\phi_1, \ldots, \phi_n$ be the specifications for the n-agents, respectively, and let $\mathcal{G}_i = (U_i, E_i, u_0^i, F_i, \beta_i, \overline{\mathcal{Z}}_{\text{safe},i})$ be the abstract graph of specification ϕ_i in the environment $\mathcal{M}$. We construct a product abstract graph for every set of active agents in $[n]$. The product graph for a set of active agents $B \subseteq [n]$ is used to learn joint policies which satisfy the specification of all agents in B with high probability.

Definition 3. *Given a set of agents* $B = \{i_1, \ldots, i_m\} \subseteq [n]$, *the product graph* $\mathcal{G}_B = (\overline{U}, \overline{E}, \overline{u}_0, \overline{F}, \overline{\beta}, \overline{\mathcal{Z}}_{\text{safe}})$ *is the asynchronous product of* $\mathcal{G}_i$ *for all* $i \in B$, *with*

- $\overline{U} = \prod_{i \in B} U_i$ *is the set of product vertices,*
- *An edge* $e = (u_{i_1}, \ldots, u_{i_m}) \to (v_{i_1}, \ldots, v_{i_m}) \in \overline{E}$ *if at least for one agent* $i \in B$ *the edge* $u_i \to v_i \in E_i$ *and for the remaining agents,* $u_i = v_i$,
- $\overline{u}_0 = (u_0^{i_1}, \ldots, u_0^{i_m})$ *is the initial vertex,*
- $\overline{F} = \Pi_{i \in B} F_i$ *is the set of final vertices,*
- $\overline{\beta} = (\beta_{i_1}, \ldots, \beta_{i_m})$ *is the collection of concretization maps, and*
- $\overline{\mathcal{Z}}_{\text{safe}} = (\overline{\mathcal{Z}}_{\text{safe},i_1}, \ldots, \overline{\mathcal{Z}}_{\text{safe},i_m})$ *is the collection of safe trajectories.*

We denote the i-th component of a product vertex $\overline{u} \in \overline{U}$ by u_i for agent $i \in B$. Similarly, the i-th component in an edge $e = \overline{u} \to \overline{v}$ is denoted by $e_i = u_i \to v_i$ for $i \in B$; note that e_i can be a self loop which is not an edge in $\mathcal{G}_i$. For an edge $e \in \overline{E}$, we denote the set of agents $i \in B$ for which $e_i \in E_i$, and not a self loop, by $\text{progress}(e)$.

Abstract graphs of the black car and the blue car from the motivating example are shown in Figs. 2 and 3 respectively. The vertex v_1 denotes the subgoal region $\beta_{\text{black}}(v_1)$ consisting of states in which the black car has crossed the intersection but the orange and green cars have not. The subgoal region $\beta_{\text{blue}}(v_2)$ is the set of states in which the blue car has crossed the intersection but the black car has not. $\mathcal{Z}_1$ denotes trajectories in which the black car does not collide and $\mathcal{Z}_2$ denotes trajectories in which the blue car does not collide and stays a car length ahead of the orange and green cars. The product abstract graph for the set of active agents $B = \{\text{black, blue}\}$ is shown in Fig 4. The safe trajectories on the edges reflect the notion of *achieving* a product edge which we discuss below.

A trajectory $\zeta = s_0 \xrightarrow{a_0} s_1 \xrightarrow{a_1} \cdots \xrightarrow{a_{t-1}} s_t$ *achieves* an edge $e = \overline{u} \to \overline{v}$ in $\mathcal{G}_B$ if all progressing agents $i \in \text{progress}(e)$ reach their target subgoal region $\beta_i(v_i)$ along the trajectory and the trajectory is safe for all agents in B. For a progressing agent $i \in \text{progress}(e)$, the initial segment of the rollout until the agent reaches its subgoal region should be safe with respect to the edge e_i. After that, the rollout should be safe with respect to every future possibility for the agent. This is required to ensure continuity of the rollout into adjacent edges in the product graph $\mathcal{G}_B$. For the same reason, we require that the entire rollout is safe with respect to all future possibilities for non-progressing agents. Note that we are not concerned with non-active agents in $[n] \backslash B$. In order to formally define this notion, we need to setup some notation.

For a predicate $b \in \mathcal{P}$, let the set of safe trajectories w.r.t. b be given by $\mathcal{Z}_b = \{\zeta = s_0 \xrightarrow{a_0} s_1 \xrightarrow{a_1} \cdots \xrightarrow{a_{t-1}} s_t \in \mathcal{Z} \mid \forall \, 0 \leq k \leq t, s_k \models b\}$. It is known that safe trajectories along an edge in an abstract graph constructed from a SPECTRL specification is either of the form $\mathcal{Z}_b$ or $\mathcal{Z}_{b_1} \circ \mathcal{Z}_{b_2}$, where $b, b_1, b_2 \in \mathcal{P}$ and $\circ$ denotes concatenation [16]. In addition, for every final vertex f, $\mathcal{Z}_{\text{safe}}^f$ is of the form $\mathcal{Z}_b$ for some $b \in \mathcal{P}$. We define First as follows:

$$\text{First}(\mathcal{Z}') = \begin{cases} \mathcal{Z}_b, & \text{if } \mathcal{Z}' = \mathcal{Z}_b \\ \mathcal{Z}_{b_1}, & \text{if } \mathcal{Z}' = \mathcal{Z}_{b_1} \circ \mathcal{Z}_{b_2} \end{cases}$$

We are now ready to define the notion of satisfiability of a product edge.

Definition 4. A rollout $\zeta = s_0 \xrightarrow{a_0} s_1 \xrightarrow{a_1} \cdots \xrightarrow{a_{t-1}} s_k$ achieves an edge $e = \overline{u} \to \overline{v}$ in $\mathcal{G}_B$ (denoted $\zeta \models_B e$) if

1. for all progressing agents $i \in \text{progress}(e)$, there exists an index $k_i \leq k$ such that $s_{k_i} \in \beta_i(v_i)$ and $\zeta_{0:k_i} \in \mathcal{Z}^{e_i}_{\text{safe},i}$. If $v_i \in F_i$ then $\zeta_{k_i:k} \in \mathcal{Z}^{v_i}_{\text{safe},i}$. Otherwise, $\zeta_{k_i:k} \in \text{First}(\mathcal{Z}^{v_i \to w_i}_{\text{safe},i})$ for all $w_i \in \text{outgoing}(v_i)$. Furthermore, we require $k_i > 0$ if $u_i \neq u_0^i$.
2. for all non-progressing agents $i \in B \backslash \text{progress}(e)$, if $u_i \notin F_i$, $\zeta \in \text{First}(\mathcal{Z}^{u_i \to w_i}_{\text{safe},i})$ for all $w_i \in \text{outgoing}(u_i)$. Otherwise (if $u_i \in F_i$), $\zeta \in \mathcal{Z}^{u_i}_{\text{safe},i}$

We can now define what it means for a trajectory to achieve a path in the product graph $\mathcal{G}_B$.

Definition 5. Given $B \subseteq [n]$, a rollout $\zeta = s_0 \to \cdots \to s_t$ achieves a path $\rho = \overline{u}_0 \to \cdots \to \overline{u}_\ell$ in $\mathcal{G}_B$ (denoted $\zeta \models_B \rho$) if there exists indices $0 = k_0 \leq k_1 \leq \cdots \leq k_\ell \leq t$ such that (i) $\overline{u}_\ell \in \overline{F}$, (ii) $\zeta_{k_z:k_{z+1}}$ achieves $\overline{u}_z \to \overline{u}_{z+1}$ for all $0 \leq z < \ell$, and (iii) $\zeta_{k_\ell:t} \in \mathcal{Z}^{u_{\ell,i}}_{\text{safe},i}$ for all $i \in B$.

Theorem 2. Let $\rho = \overline{u}_0 \to \overline{u}_1 \to \cdots \to \overline{u}_\ell$ be a path in the product abstract graph $\mathcal{G}_B$ for $B \subseteq [n]$. Suppose trajectory $\zeta \models_B \rho$. Then $\zeta \models \phi_i$ for all $i \in B$.

That is, joint policies that maximize the probability of achieving paths in the product abstract graph $\mathcal{G}_B$ have high social welfare w.r.t. the active agents B.

4.2 Compositional RL Algorithm

Our compositional RL algorithm learns joint policies corresponding to paths in product abstract graphs. For every $B \subseteq [n]$, it learns a joint policy π_e for each edge in the product abstract graph $\mathcal{G}_B$, which is the (deterministic) policy that maximizes the probability of achieving e from a given initial state distribution. We assume all agents are acting cooperatively; thus, we treat the agents as one and use single-agent RL to learn each edge policy. We will check whether any deviation to this co-operative behaviour by any agent can be punished by the coalition of other agents in the verification phase. The reward function is designed to capture the reachability objective of progressing agents and the safety objective of all active agents.

The edges are learned in topological order, allowing us to learn an induced state distribution for each product vertex $\overline{u}$ prior to learning any edge policies from $\overline{u}$; this distribution is used as the initial state distribution when learning outgoing edge policies from $\overline{u}$. In more detail, the distribution for the initial vertex of $\mathcal{G}_B$ is taken to be the initial state distribution of the environment; for every other product vertex, the distribution is the average over distributions

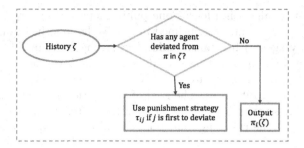

Fig. 5. π_i augmented with punishment strategies.

induced by executing edge policies for all incoming edges. This is possible because the product graph is a DAG.

Given edge policies Π along with a path $\rho = \overline{u}_0 \rightarrow \overline{u}_1 \rightarrow \cdots \rightarrow \overline{u}_\ell = \overline{u} \in \overline{F}$ in $\mathcal{G}_B$, we define a *path policy* π_ρ to navigate from $\overline{u}_0$ to $\overline{u}$. In particular, π_ρ executes $\pi_{e[z]}$, where $e[z] = \overline{u}_z \rightarrow \overline{u}_{z+1}$ (starting from $z = 0$) until the resulting trajectory achieves $e[z]$, after which it increments $z \leftarrow z + 1$ (unless $z = \ell$). That is, π_ρ is designed to achieve the sequence of edges in ρ. Note that π_ρ is a finite-state deterministic joint policy in which vertices on the path correspond to the memory states that keep track of the index of the current policy. This way, we obtain finite-state joint policies by learning edge policies only.

This process is repeated for all sets of active agents $B \subseteq [n]$. These finite-state joint policies are then ranked by estimating their social welfare on several simulations.

5 Nash Equilibria Verification

The prioritized enumearation phase produces a list of path policies which are ranked by the total sum of scores. Each path policy is deterministic and also finite state. Since the joint policies are trained cooperatively, they are typically not ϵ-Nash equilibria. Thus, our verification algorithm not only tries to prove that a given joint policy is a ϵ-Nash equilibrium, but also tries to modify it so it satisfies this property. In particular, our verification algorithm attempts to modify a given joint policy by adding *punishment strategies* so that the resulting policy is an ϵ-Nash equilibrium.

Concretely, it takes as input a finite-state deterministic joint policy $\pi = (M, \alpha, \sigma, m_0)$ where M is a finite set of *memory states*, $\alpha : \mathcal{S} \times \mathcal{A} \times M \rightarrow M$ is the memory update function, $\sigma : \mathcal{S} \times M \rightarrow \mathcal{A}$ maps states to (joint) actions and m_0 is the initial policy state. The *extended memory update function* $\hat{\alpha} : \mathcal{Z} \rightarrow M$ is given by $\hat{\alpha}(\epsilon) = m_0$ and $\hat{\alpha}(\zeta s_t a_t) = \alpha(s_t, a_t, \hat{\alpha}(\zeta))$. Then, π is given by $\pi(\zeta s_t) = \sigma(s_t, \hat{\alpha}(\zeta))$. The policy π_i of agent i simply chooses the ith component of $\pi(\zeta)$ for any history ζ.

The verification algorithm learns one punishment strategy $\tau_{ij} : \mathcal{Z} \rightarrow \mathcal{D}(A_i)$ for each pair (i, j) of agents. As outlined in Fig. 5, the modified policy for agent i uses π_i if every agent j has taken actions according to π_j in the past. In case some agent j' has taken an action that does not match the output of $\pi_{j'}$, then agent i uses the punishment strategy τ_{ij}, where j is the agent that deviated the earliest (ties broken arbitrarily). The goal of verification is to check if there is a set of punishment strategies $\{\tau_{ij} \mid i \neq j\}$ such that after modifying each agent's policy to use them, the resulting joint policy is an ϵ-Nash equilibrium.

5.1   Problem Formulation

We denote the set of all punishment strategies of agent i by $\tau_i = \{\tau_{ij} \mid j \neq i\}$. We define the composition of π_i and τ_i to be the policy $\tilde{\pi}_i = \pi_i \bowtie \tau_i$ such that for any trajectory $\zeta = s_0 \xrightarrow{a_0} \cdots \xrightarrow{a_{t-1}} s_t$, we have

- $\tilde{\pi}_i(\zeta) = \pi_i(\zeta)$ if for all $0 \leq k < t$, $a_k = \pi(\zeta_{0:k})$—i.e., no agent has deviated so far,
- $\tilde{\pi}_i(\zeta) = \tau_{ij}(\zeta)$ if there is a k such that (i) $a_k^j \neq \pi_j(\zeta_{0:k})$ and (ii) for all $\ell < k$, $a_\ell = \pi(\zeta_{0:\ell})$. If there are multiple such j's, an arbitrary but consistent choice is made (e.g., the smallest such j).

Given a finite-state deterministic joint policy π, the verification problem is to check if there exists a set of punishment strategies $\tau = \bigcup_i \tau_i$ such that the joint policy $\tilde{\pi} = \pi \bowtie \tau = (\pi_1 \bowtie \tau_1, \ldots, \pi_n \bowtie \tau_n)$ is an ϵ-Nash equilibrium. In other words, the problem is to check if there exists a policy $\tilde{\pi}_i$ for each agent i such that (i) $\tilde{\pi}_i$ follows π_i as long as no other agent j deviates from π_j and (ii) the joint policy $\tilde{\pi} = (\tilde{\pi}_1, \ldots, \tilde{\pi}_n)$ is an ϵ-Nash equilibrium.

5.2   High-Level Procedure

Our approach is to compute the best set of punishment strategies τ^* w.r.t. π and check if $\pi \bowtie \tau^*$ is an ϵ-Nash equilibrium. The best punishment strategy against agent j is the one that minimizes its incentive to deviate. To be precise, we define the best response of j with respect to a joint policy $\pi' = (\pi_1', \ldots, \pi_n')$ to be $\mathrm{br}_j(\pi') \in \arg\max_{\pi_j''} J_j(\pi_{-j}', \pi_j'')$. Then, the best set of punishment strategies τ^* w.r.t. π is one that minimizes the value of $\mathrm{br}_j(\pi \bowtie \tau)$ for all $j \in [n]$. To be precise, define $\tau[j] = \{\tau_{ij} \mid i \neq j\}$ to be the set of punishment strategies *against* agent j. Then, we want to compute τ^* such that for all j,

$$\tau^* \in \arg\min_\tau J_j((\pi \bowtie \tau)_{-j}, \mathrm{br}_j(\pi \bowtie \tau)). \tag{1}$$

We observe that for any two sets of punishment strategies τ, τ' with $\tau[j] = \tau'[j]$ and any policy π_j', we have $J_j((\pi \bowtie \tau)_{-j}, \pi_j') = J_j((\pi \bowtie \tau')_{-j}, \pi_j')$. This is because, for any τ, punishment strategies in $\tau \backslash \tau[j]$ do not affect the behaviour of the joint policy $((\pi \bowtie \tau)_{-j}, \pi_j')$, since no agent other than agent j will deviate from π. Hence, $\mathrm{br}_j(\pi \bowtie \tau)$ as well as $J_j((\pi \bowtie \tau)_{-j}, \mathrm{br}_j(\pi \bowtie \tau))$ are independent of $\tau \setminus \tau[j]$; therefore, we can separately compute $\tau^*[j]$ (satisfying Eq. 1) for each j and take $\tau^* = \bigcup_j \tau^*[j]$. The following theorem follows from the definition of τ^*.

Theorem 3. *Given a finite-state deterministic joint policy* $\pi = (\pi_1, \ldots, \pi_n)$*, if there is a set of punishment strategies* τ *such that* $\pi \bowtie \tau$ *is an* ϵ*-Nash equilibrium, then* $\pi \bowtie \tau^*$ *is an* ϵ*-Nash equilibrium, where* τ^* *is the set of best punishment strategies w.r.t.* π*. Furthermore,* $\pi \bowtie \tau^*$ *is an* ϵ*-Nash equilibrium iff for all* j*,*

$$J_j((\pi \bowtie \tau^*)_{-j}, \mathrm{br}_j(\pi \bowtie \tau^*)) - \epsilon \leq J_j(\pi \bowtie \tau^*) = J_j(\pi).$$

Thus, to solve the verification problem, it suffices to compute (or estimate), for all j, the optimal deviation scores

$$\mathrm{dev}_j^\pi = \min_{\tau[j]} \max_{\pi_j'} J_j((\pi \bowtie \tau)_{-j}, \pi_j'). \tag{2}$$

5.3 Reduction to Min-Max Games

Next, we describe how to reduce the computation of optimal deviation scores to a standard self-play RL setting. We first translate the problem from the specification setting to a reward-based setting using *reward machines*.

Reward Machines. A *reward machine (RM)* [14] is a tuple $\mathcal{R} = (Q, \delta_u, \delta_r, q_0)$ where Q is a finite set of states, $\delta_u : \mathcal{S} \times \mathcal{A} \times Q \to Q$ is the state transition function, $\delta_r : \mathcal{S} \times Q \to [-1, 1]$ is the reward function and q_0 is the initial RM state. Given a trajectory $\zeta = s_0 \xrightarrow{a_0} \ldots \xrightarrow{a_{t-1}} s_t$, the reward assigned by $\mathcal{R}$ to ζ is $\mathcal{R}(\zeta) = \sum_{k=0}^{t-1} \delta_r(s_k, q_k)$, where $q_{k+1} = \delta_u(s_k, a_k, q_k)$ for all k. For any SPECTRL specification ϕ, we can construct an RM such that the reward assigned to a trajectory ζ indicates whether ζ satisfies ϕ.

Theorem 4. *Given any* SPECTRL *specification* ϕ*, we can construct an RM* $\mathcal{R}_\phi$ *such that for any trajectory* ζ *of length* $t + 1$*,* $\mathcal{R}_\phi(\zeta) = \mathbf{1}(\zeta_{0:t} \models \phi)$*.*

For an agent j, let $\mathcal{R}_j$ denote $\mathcal{R}_{\phi_j} = (Q_j, \delta_u^j, \delta_r^j, q_0^j)$. Letting $\tilde{\mathcal{D}}_\pi$ be the distribution over length $H+1$ trajectories induced by using π, we have $\mathbb{E}_{\zeta \sim \tilde{\mathcal{D}}_\pi}[\mathcal{R}_j(\zeta)] = J_j(\pi)$. The deviation values defined in Eq. 2 are now min-max values of expected reward, except that it is not in a standard min-max setting since the policy of every non-deviating agent $i \neq j$ is constrained to be of the form $\pi_i \bowtie \tau_i$. This issue can be handled by considering a product of $\mathcal{M}$ with the reward machine $\mathcal{R}_j$ and the finite-state joint policy π. The following theorem follows naturally.

Theorem 5. *Given a finite-state deterministic joint policy* $\pi = (M, \alpha, \sigma, m_0)$*, for any agent* j*, we can construct a simulator for an augmented two-player zero-sum Markov game* $\mathcal{M}_j^\pi$ *(with rewards) which has the following properties.*

- *The number of states in* $\mathcal{M}_j^\pi$ *is at most* $2|S||M||Q_j|$*.*
- *The actions of player 1 is* $\tilde{A}_j$*, and the actions of player 2 is* $\mathcal{A}_{-j} = \prod_{i \neq j} A_i$*.*

Algorithm 2 VERIFYNASH

Inputs: Finite-state deterministic joint policy π, specifications ϕ_j for all j, Nash factor ϵ, precision δ, failure probability p.

Outputs: True or False along with a set of punishment strategies τ.

1: existsNE ← True
2: $\tau \leftarrow \emptyset$
3: $\tilde{\mathcal{M}} \leftarrow$ BFS-ESTIMATE$(\mathcal{M}, \delta, p)$ // Only run if $\mathcal{M}$ has not been estimated before.
4: **for** agent $j \in \{1, \ldots, n\}$ **do**
5:     $\mathcal{R}_j \leftarrow$ CONSTRUCTRM(ϕ_j)
6:     $\tilde{\mathcal{M}}_j \leftarrow$ CONSTRUCTGAME$(\tilde{\mathcal{M}}, j, \mathcal{R}_j, \pi)$
7:     $\tilde{\text{dev}}_j \leftarrow \min_{\bar{\pi}_2} \max_{\bar{\pi}_1} \bar{J}^{\tilde{\mathcal{M}}_j}(\bar{\pi}_1, \bar{\pi}_2)$
8:     $\bar{\pi}_2^* \leftarrow \arg\min_{\bar{\pi}_2} \max_{\bar{\pi}_1} \bar{J}^{\tilde{\mathcal{M}}_j}(\bar{\pi}_1, \bar{\pi}_2)$
9:     existsNE ← existsNE $\wedge$ $(\tilde{\text{dev}}_j \leq J_j(\pi) + \epsilon - \delta)$
10:    $\tau \leftarrow \tau \cup$ PUNSTRAT$(\bar{\pi}_2^*)$
11: **return** existsNE, τ

- *The min-max value of the two player game corresponds to the deviation cost of j, i.e.,*

$$\text{dev}_j^{\pi} = \min_{\bar{\pi}_2} \max_{\bar{\pi}_1} \bar{J}_j^{\pi}(\bar{\pi}_1, \bar{\pi}_2),$$

where $\bar{J}_j^{\pi}(\bar{\pi}_1, \bar{\pi}_2) = \mathbb{E}\left[\sum_{k=0}^{H} R_j(\bar{s}_k, a_k) \mid \bar{\pi}_1, \bar{\pi}_2\right]$ is the expected sum of rewards w.r.t. the distribution over $(H+1)$-length trajectories generated by using the joint policy $(\bar{\pi}_1, \bar{\pi}_2)$ in $\mathcal{M}_j^{\pi}$.

- *Given any policy $\bar{\pi}_2$ for player 2 in $\mathcal{M}_j^{\pi}$, we can construct a set of punishment strategies $\tau[j] =$ PUNSTRAT$(\bar{\pi}_2)$ against agent j in $\mathcal{M}$ such that*

$$\max_{\bar{\pi}_1} \bar{J}_j^{\pi}(\bar{\pi}_1, \bar{\pi}_2) = \max_{\pi_j'} J_j((\pi \bowtie \tau[j])_{-j}, \pi_j').$$

Given an estimate $\tilde{\mathcal{M}}$ of $\mathcal{M}$, we can also construct an estimate $\tilde{\mathcal{M}}_j^{\pi}$ of $\mathcal{M}_j^{\pi}$.

We omit the superscript π from $\mathcal{M}_j^{\pi}$ when there is no ambiguity. We denote by CONSTRUCTGAME$(\tilde{\mathcal{M}}, j, \mathcal{R}_j, \pi)$ the product construction procedure that constructs and returns $\tilde{\mathcal{M}}_j^{\pi}$.

5.4   Solving Min-Max Games

The min-max game $\mathcal{M}_j$ can be solved using self-play RL algorithms. Many of these algorithms provide probabilistic approximation guarantees for computing the min-max value of the game. We use a model-based algorithm, similar to the one proposed in [4], that first estimates the model $\mathcal{M}_j$ and then solves the game in the estimated model.

One approach is to use existing algorithms for reward-free exploration to estimate the model [15], but this approach requires estimating each $\mathcal{M}_j$ separately. Under Assumption 1, we provide a simpler and more sample-efficient algorithm, called BFS-ESTIMATE, for estimating $\mathcal{M}$. BFS-ESTIMATE performs a search over the transition graph of $\mathcal{M}$ by exploring previously seen states in a breadth first manner. When exploring a state s, multiple samples are collected by taking all possible actions in s several times and the corresponding transition probabilities are estimated. After obtaining an estimate of $\mathcal{M}$, we can directly construct an estimate of $\mathcal{M}_j^\pi$ for any π and j when required. Letting $|Q| = \max_j |Q_j|$ and $|M|$ denote the size of the largest finite-state policy output by our enumeration algorithm, we get the following guarantee.

Theorem 6. *For any $\delta > 0$ and $p \in (0, 1]$, BFS-ESTIMATE$(\mathcal{M}, \delta, p)$ computes an estimate $\tilde{\mathcal{M}}$ of $\mathcal{M}$ using $O\left(\frac{|\mathcal{S}|^3 |M|^2 |Q|^4 |\mathcal{A}| H^4}{\delta^2} \log\left(\frac{|\mathcal{S}||\mathcal{A}|}{p}\right)\right)$ sample steps such that with probability at least $1 - p$, for any finite-state deterministic joint policy π and any agent j,*

$$\left| \min_{\bar{\pi}_2} \max_{\bar{\pi}_1} \bar{J}^{\tilde{\mathcal{M}}_j^\pi}(\bar{\pi}_1, \bar{\pi}_2) - \boldsymbol{dev}_j^\pi \right| \leq \delta,$$

where $\bar{J}^{\tilde{\mathcal{M}}_j^\pi}(\bar{\pi}_1, \bar{\pi}_2)$ is the expected reward over length $H+1$ trajectories generated by $(\bar{\pi}_1, \bar{\pi}_2)$ in $\tilde{\mathcal{M}}_j^\pi$. Furthermore, letting $\bar{\pi}_2^* \in \arg\min_{\bar{\pi}_2} \max_{\bar{\pi}_1} \bar{J}^{\tilde{\mathcal{M}}_j}(\bar{\pi}_1, \bar{\pi}_2)$ and $\tau[j] = \text{PUNSTRAT}(\bar{\pi}_2^*)$, we have

$$\left| \max_{\bar{\pi}_1} \bar{J}^{\tilde{\mathcal{M}}_j^\pi}(\bar{\pi}_1, \bar{\pi}_2^*) - \max_{\pi_j'} J_j((\pi \bowtie \tau[j])_{-j}, \pi_j') \right| \leq \delta. \tag{3}$$

The min-max value of $\tilde{\mathcal{M}}_j^\pi$ as well as $\bar{\pi}_2^*$ can be computed using value iteration. Our full verification algorithm is summarized in Algorithm 2. It checks if $\tilde{\boldsymbol{dev}}_j \leq J_j(\pi) + \epsilon - \delta$ for all j, and returns True if so and False otherwise. It also simultaneously computes the punishment strategies τ using the optimal policies for player 2 in the punishment games. Note that BFS-ESTIMATE is called only once (i.e., the first time VERIFYNASH is called) and the obtained estimate $\tilde{\mathcal{M}}$ is stored and used for verification of every candidate policy π. The following soundness guarantee follows from Theorem 6.

Corollary 1 (Soundness). *For any $p \in (0, 1]$, $\varepsilon > 0$ and $\delta \in (0, \varepsilon)$, with probability at least $1 - p$, if HIGHNASHSEARCH returns a joint policy $\tilde{\pi}$ then $\tilde{\pi}$ is an ϵ-Nash equilibrium.*

6 Complexity

In this section, we analyze the time and sample complexity of our algorithm in terms of the number of agents n, size of the specification $|\phi| = \max_{i \in [n]} |\phi_i|$, number of states in the environment $|\mathcal{S}|$, number of joint actions $|\mathcal{A}|$, time horizon H, precision δ and the failure probability p.

Sample Complexity. It is known [16] that the number of edges in the abstract graph $\mathcal{G}_i$ corresponding to specification ϕ_i is $O(|\phi_i|^2)$. Hence for any set of active agents B, the number of edges in the product abstract graph $\mathcal{G}_B$ is $O(|\phi|^{2|B|})$.

Hence total number of edge policies learned by our compositional RL algorithm is $\sum_{B \subseteq [n]} O((|\phi|^2)^{|B|}) = O((|\phi|^2 + 1)^n)$. We learn each edge using a fixed number of sample steps C, which is a hyperparameter.

The number of samples used in the verification phase is the same as the number used by BFS-ESTIMATE. The maximum size of a candidate policy output by the enumeration algorithm $|M|$ is at most the length of the longest path in a product abstract graph. Since the maximum path length in a single abstract graph $\mathcal{G}_i$ is bounded by $|\phi_i|$ and at least one agent must progress along every edge in a product graph, the maximum length of a path in any product graph is at most $n|\phi|$. Also, the number of states in the reward machine $\mathcal{R}_j$ corresponding to $|\phi_j|$ is $O(2^{|\phi_j|})$. Hence, from Theorem 6 we get that the total number of sample steps used by our algorithm is $O\big((|\phi|^2 + 1)^n C + \frac{2^{4|\phi|}|\mathcal{S}|^3 n^2 |\phi|^2 |\mathcal{A}| H^4}{\delta} \log\big(\frac{|\mathcal{S}||\mathcal{A}|}{p}\big)\big)$.

Time Complexity. As with sample complexity, the time required to learn all edge policies is $O((|\phi|^2 + 1)^n (C + |\mathcal{A}|))$ where the term $|\mathcal{A}|$ is added to account for the time taken to select an action from $\mathcal{A}$ during exploration (we use Q-learning with ε-greedy exploration for learning edge policies). Similarly, time taken for constructing the reward machines and running BFS-ESTIMATE is $O(\frac{2^{4|\phi|}|\mathcal{S}|^3 n^2 |\phi|^2 |\mathcal{A}| H^4}{\delta} \log\big(\frac{|\mathcal{S}||\mathcal{A}|}{p}\big))$.

The total number of path policies considered for a given set of active agents B is bounded by the number of paths in the product abstract graph $\mathcal{G}_B$ that terminate in a final product state. First, let us consider paths in which exactly one agent progresses in each edge. The number of such paths is bounded by $(|B||\phi|)^{|B||\phi|}$ since the length of such paths is bounded by $|B||\phi|$ and there are at most $|B||\phi|$ choices at each step—i.e., progressing agent j and next vertex of the abstract graph $\mathcal{G}_{\phi_j}$. Now, any path in $\mathcal{G}_B$ can be constructed by merging adjacent edges along such a path (in which at most one agent progresses at any step). The number of ways to merge edges along such a path is bounded by the number of groupings of edges along the path into at most $|B||\phi|$ groups which is bounded by $(|B||\phi|)^{|B||\phi|}$. Therefore, the total number of paths in $\mathcal{G}_B$ is at most $2^{2|B||\phi|\log(n|\phi|)}$. Finally, the total number of path policies considered is at most $\sum_{B \subseteq [n]} 2^{2|B||\phi|\log(n|\phi|)} \leq ((n|\phi|)^{2|\phi|} + 1)^n = O(2^{2n|\phi|\log(2n|\phi|)})$.

Now, for each path policy π, the verification algorithm solves $\tilde{\mathcal{M}}_j^\pi$ using value iteration which takes $O(|\tilde{\mathcal{S}}||\mathcal{A}|Hf(|\mathcal{A}|)) = O(2^{|\phi|}n|\phi||\mathcal{S}||\mathcal{A}|Hf(|\mathcal{A}|))$ time, where $f(|\mathcal{A}|)$ is the time required to solve a linear program of size $|\mathcal{A}|$. Also accounting for the time taken to sort the path policies, we arrive at a time complexity bound of $2^{O(n|\phi|\log(n|\phi|))}\mathrm{poly}(|\mathcal{S}|, |\mathcal{A}|, H, \frac{1}{p}, \frac{1}{\delta})$.

It is worth noting that the procedure halts as soon as our verification procedure successfully verifies a policy; this leads to early termination for cases where there is a high value ϵ-Nash equilibrium (among the policies considered). Furthermore, our verification algorithm runs in polynomial time and therefore one could potentially improve the overall time complexity by reducing the search space in the prioritized enumeration phase—e.g., by using domain specific insights.

7   Experiments

We evaluate our algorithm on finite state environments and a variety of specifications, aiming to answer the following:

- Can our approach be used to learn ϵ-Nash equilibria?
- Can our approach learn policies with high social welfare?

We compare our approach to two baselines described below, using two metrics: (i) the social welfare welfare(π) of the learned joint policy π, and (ii) an estimate of the minimum value of ϵ for which π forms an ϵ-Nash equilibrium:

$$\epsilon_{\min}(\pi) = \max\{J_i(\pi_{-i}, \mathrm{br}_i(\pi)) - J_i(\pi) \mid i \in [n]\}.$$

Here, $\epsilon_{\min}(\pi)$ is computed using single agent RL (specifically, Q-learning) to compute $\mathrm{br}_i(\pi)$ for each agent i.

Environments and Specifications. We show results on the *Intersection environment* illustrated in Fig. 1, which consists of k-cars (agents) at a 2-way intersection of which k_1 and k_2 cars are placed along the N-S and E-W axes, respectively. The state consists of the location of all cars where the location of a single car is a non-negative integer. 1 corresponds to the intersection, 0 corresponds to the location one step towards the south or west of the intersection (depending on the car) and locations greater than 1 are to the east or north of the intersection. Each agent has two actions. STAY stays at the current position. MOVE decreases the position value by 1 with probability 0.95 and stays with probability 0.05. We consider specifications similar to the ones in the motivating example.

Baselines. We compare our NE computation method (HIGHNASHSEARCH) to two approaches for learning in non-cooperative games. The first, MAQRM, is an adaption of the reward machine based learning algorithm proposed in [22]. MAQRM was originally proposed for cooperative multi-agent RL where there is a single specification for all the agents. It proceeds by first decomposing the specification into individual ones for all the agents and then runs a Q-learning-style algorithm (QRM) in parallel for all the agents. We use the second part of their algorithm directly since we are given a separate specification for each agent. The second baseline, NVI, is a model-based approach that first estimates transition probabilities, and then computes a Nash equilibrium in the estimated game using value iteration for stochastic games [17]. To promote high social welfare, we select the highest value Nash solution for the matrix game at each stage of value iteration. Note that this greedy strategy may not maximize social welfare. Both MAQRM and NVI learn from rewards as opposed to specification; thus, we supply rewards in the form of reward machines constructed from the specifications. NVI is guaranteed to return an ϵ-Nash equilibrium with high probability, but MAQRM is not guaranteed to do so.

Table 1. Results for all specifications in Intersection Environment. Total of 10 runs per benchmark. Timeout = 24 h.

Spec.	Num. of agents	Algorithm	welfare(π) (avg ± std)	$\epsilon_{min}(\pi)$ (avg ± std)	Num. of terminated runs	Avg. num. of sample steps (in millions)
ϕ^1	3	HIGHNASHSEARCH	**0.33 ± 0.00**	**0.00 ± 0.00**	10	1.78
		NVI	0.32 ± 0.00	**0.00 ± 0.00**	10	1.92
		MAQRM	0.18 ± 0.01	0.51 ± 0.01	10	2.00
ϕ^2	4	HIGHNASHSEARCH	**0.55 ± 0.10**	**0.01 ± 0.02**	10	11.53
		NVI	0.04 ± 0.01	0.02 ± 0.01	10	12.60
		MAQRM	0.12 ± 0.01	0.20 ± 0.03	10	15.00
ϕ^3	4	HIGHNASHSEARCH	**0.49 ± 0.01**	**0.00 ± 0.01**	10	11.26
		NVI	0.45 ± 0.01	**0.00 ± 0.01**	10	12.60
		MAQRM	0.11 ± 0.01	0.22 ± 0.02	10	15.00
ϕ^4	3	HIGHNASHSEARCH	0.90 ± 0.15	**0.00 ± 0.00**	10	2.16
		NVI	**0.98 ± 0.00**	**0.00 ± 0.00**	4	2.18
		MAQRM	0.23 ± 0.01	0.39 ± 0.04	10	2.00
ϕ^5	5	HIGHNASHSEARCH	**0.58 ± 0.02**	**0.00 ± 0.00**	10	62.17
		NVI	0.05 ± 0.01	0.01 ± 0.01	7	80.64
		MAQRM	Timeout	Timeout	0	Timeout

Results. Our results are summarized in Table 1. For each specification, we ran all algorithms 10 times with a timeout of 24 h. Along with the average social welfare and ϵ_{min}, we also report the average number of sample steps taken in the environment as well as the number of runs that terminated before timeout. For a fair comparison, all approaches were given a similar number of samples from the environment.

Nash Equilibrium. Our approach learns policies that have low values of ϵ_{min}, indicating that it can be used to learn ϵ-Nash equilibria for small values of ϵ. NVI also has similar values of ϵ, which is expected since NVI provides guarantees similar to our approach w.r.t. Nash equilibria computation. On the other hand, MAQRM learns policies with large values of ϵ_{min}, implying that it fails to converge to a Nash equilibrium in most cases.

Social Welfare. Our experiments show that our approach consistently learns policies with high social welfare compared to the baselines. For instance, ϕ^3 corresponds to the specifications in the motivating example for which our approach learns a joint policy that causes both blue and black cars to achieve their goals. Although NVI succeeds in learning policies with high social welfare for some specifications (ϕ^1, ϕ^3, ϕ^4), it fails to do so for others (ϕ^2, ϕ^5). Additional experiments (see extended version [3]) indicate that NVI achieves similar social welfare as our approach for specifications in which all agents can successfully achieve their goals (cooperative scenarios). However, in many other scenarios in which only some of the agents can fulfill their objectives, our approach achieves higher social welfare.

8 Conclusions

We have proposed a framework for maximizing social welfare under the constraint that the joint policy should form an ϵ-Nash equilibrium. Our approach involves learning and enumerating a small set of finite-state deterministic policies in decreasing order of social welfare and then using a self-play RL algorithm to check if they can be extended with punishment strategies to form an ϵ-Nash equilibrium. Our experiments demonstrate that our approach is effective in learning Nash equilibria with high social welfare.

One limitation of our approach is that our algorithm does not have any guarantee regarding optimality with respect to social welfare. The policies considered by our algorithm are chosen heuristically based on the specifications, which may lead to scenarios where we miss high welfare solutions. For example, ϕ^2 corresponds to specifications in the motivating example except that the blue car is not required to stay a car length ahead of the other two cars. In this scenario, it is possible for three cars to achieve their goals in an equilibrium solution if the blue car helps the cars behind by staying in the middle of the intersection until they catch up. Such a joint policy is not among the set of policies considered; therefore, our approach learns a solution in which only two cars achieve their goals. We believe that such limitations can be overcome in future work by modifying the various components within our enumerate-and-verify framework.

Acknowledgements. We thank the anonymous reviewers for their helpful comments. This work is supported in part by NSF grant 2030859 to the CRA for the CIFellows Project, ONR award N00014-20-1-2115, DARPA Assured Autonomy award, NSF award CCF 1723567 and ARO award W911NF-20-1-0080.

References

1. Akchurina, N.: Multi-agent reinforcement learning algorithm with variable optimistic-pessimistic criterion. In: ECAI, vol. 178, pp. 433–437 (2008)
2. Alur, R., Bansal, S., Bastani, O., Jothimurugan, K.: A framework for transforming specifications in reinforcement learning. arXiv preprint arXiv:2111.00272 (2021)
3. Alur, R., Bansal, S., Bastani, O., Jothimurugan, K.: Specification-guided learning of Nash equilibria with high social welfare (2022). https://arxiv.org/abs/2206.03348
4. Bai, Y., Jin, C.: Provable self-play algorithms for competitive reinforcement learning. In: Proceedings of the 37th International Conference on Machine Learning (2020)

5. Bouyer, P., Brenguier, R., Markey, N.: Nash equilibria for reachability objectives in multi-player timed games. In: Gastin, P., Laroussinie, F. (eds.) CONCUR 2010. LNCS, vol. 6269, pp. 192–206. Springer, Heidelberg (2010). https://doi.org/10. 1007/978-3-642-15375-4_14

6. Chatterjee, K.: Two-player nonzero-sum ω-regular games. In: Abadi, M., de Alfaro, L. (eds.) CONCUR 2005. LNCS, vol. 3653, pp. 413–427. Springer, Heidelberg (2005). https://doi.org/10.1007/11539452_32

7. Chatterjee, K., Majumdar, R., Jurdziński, M.: On nash equilibria in stochastic games. In: Marcinkowski, J., Tarlecki, A. (eds.) CSL 2004. LNCS, vol. 3210, pp. 26–40. Springer, Heidelberg (2004). https://doi.org/10.1007/978-3-540-30124-0_6

8. Czumaj, A., Fasoulakis, M., Jurdzinski, M.: Approximate nash equilibria with near optimal social welfare. In: Twenty-Fourth International Joint Conference on Artificial Intelligence (2015)

9. Greenwald, A., Hall, K., Serrano, R.: Correlated Q-learning. In: ICML, Vol.3, pp. 242–249 (2003)

10. Hammond, L., Abate, A., Gutierrez, J., Wooldridge, M.: Multi-agent reinforcement learning with temporal logic specifications. In: International Conference on Autonomous Agents and MultiAgent Systems, pp. 583–592 (2021)

11. Hazan, E., Krauthgamer, R.: How hard is it to approximate the best nash equilibrium? In: Proceedings of the Twentieth Annual ACM-SIAM Symposium on Discrete Algorithms, SODA 2009, pp. 720–727. Society for Industrial and Applied Mathematics (2009)

12. Hu, J., Wellman, M.P.: Nash Q-learning for general-sum stochastic games. J. Mach. Learn. Res. 4(Nov), 1039–1069 (2003)

13. Hu, J., Wellman, M.P., et al.: Multiagent reinforcement learning: theoretical framework and an algorithm. In: ICML, vol. 98, pp. 242–250. Citeseer (1998)

14. Icarte, R.T., Klassen, T., Valenzano, R., McIlraith, S.: Using reward machines for high-level task specification and decomposition in reinforcement learning. In: International Conference on Machine Learning, pp. 2107–2116. PMLR (2018)

15. Jin, C., Krishnamurthy, A., Simchowitz, M., Yu, T.: Reward-free exploration for reinforcement learning. In: International Conference on Machine Learning, pp. 4870–4879. PMLR (2020)

16. Jothimurugan, K., Bansal, S., Bastani, O., Alur, R.: Compositional reinforcement learning from logical specifications. Adv. Neural Inf. Proc. Syst. **34**, 10026–10039 (2021)

17. Kearns, M., Mansour, Y., Singh, S.: Fast planning in stochastic games. In: Proceedings of the Sixteenth Conference on Uncertainty in Artificial Intelligence, pp. 309–316 (2000)

18. Kwiatkowska, M., Norman, G., Parker, D., Santos, G.: Equilibria-based probabilistic model checking for concurrent stochastic games. In: ter Beek, M.H., McIver, A., Oliveira, J.N. (eds.) FM 2019. LNCS, vol. 11800, pp. 298–315. Springer, Cham (2019). https://doi.org/10.1007/978-3-030-30942-8_19

19. Kwiatkowska, M., Norman, G., Parker, D., Santos, G.: PRISM-games 3.0: stochastic game verification with concurrency, equilibria and time. In: Lahiri, S.K., Wang, C. (eds.) CAV 2020. LNCS, vol. 12225, pp. 475–487. Springer, Cham (2020). https://doi.org/10.1007/978-3-030-53291-8_25

20. Littman, M.L.: Markov games as a framework for multi-agent reinforcement learning. In: Machine Learning Proceedings 1994, pp. 157–163. Elsevier (1994)

21. Littman, M.L.: Friend-or-foe Q-learning in general-sum games. In: ICML, vol. 1, pp. 322–328 (2001)

22. Neary, C., Xu, Z., Wu, B., Topcu, U.: Reward machines for cooperative multi-agent reinforcement learning (2021)
23. Perolat, J., Strub, F., Piot, B., Pietquin, O.: Learning nash equilibrium for general-sum Markov games from batch data. In: Proceedings of the 20th International Conference on Artificial Intelligence and Statistics (2017)
24. Prasad, H., LA, P., Bhatnagar, S.: Two-timescale algorithms for learning nash equilibria in general-sum stochastic games. In: Proceedings of the 2015 International Conference on Autonomous Agents and Multiagent Systems, pp. 1371–1379 (2015)
25. Shapley, L.S.: Stochastic games. Proc. Nat. Acad. Sci. **39**(10), 1095–1100 (1953)
26. Wei, C.Y., Hong, Y.T., Lu, C.J.: Online reinforcement learning in stochastic games. In: Proceedings of the 31st International Conference on Neural Information Processing Systems, pp. 4994–5004 (2017)
27. Zinkevich, M., Greenwald, A., Littman, M.: Cyclic equilibria in markov games. Adv. Neural Inf. Proc. Syst. **18**, 1641 (2006)

Synthesizing Fair Decision Trees
via Iterative Constraint Solving

Jingbo Wang$^{(\boxtimes)}$, Yannan Li, and Chao Wang

University of Southern California, Los Angeles, CA 90089, USA
jingbow@usc.edu

Abstract. Decision trees are increasingly used to make socially sensitive decisions, where they are expected to be both accurate and fair, but it remains a challenging task to optimize the learning algorithm for fairness in a predictable and explainable fashion. To overcome the challenge, we propose an iterative framework for choosing decision attributes, or *features*, at each level by formulating *feature selection* as a series of mixed integer optimization problems. Both fairness and accuracy requirements are encoded as numerical constraints and solved by an off-the-shelf constraint solver. As a result, the trade-off between fairness and accuracy is quantifiable. At a high level, our method can be viewed as a generalization of the entropy-based greedy search techniques such as `CART` and `C4.5`, and existing fair learning techniques such as `IGCS` and `MIP`. Our experimental evaluation on six datasets, for which *demographic parity* is used as the fairness metric, shows that the method is significantly more effective in reducing bias than other methods while maintaining accuracy. Furthermore, compared to non-iterative constraint solving, our iterative approach is at least 10 times faster.

1 Introduction

Decision trees are one of the most widely used machine learning models in statistical analysis, data mining and decision making. Compared to other predictive models such as deep neural networks, decision trees have the advantage of being easily understandable by humans, which makes them a favorite building block in systems that require interpretability [34]. However, when they are used to make socially sensitive decisions in business, finance and law enforcement, decision trees may introduce bias against certain groups [16]. In this context, a widely used group fairness metric is *demographic parity* [11,38], also known as the *80% rule* [8]. Bias against demographic groups, in general, comes from two sources. First, historical data used to learn models may be biased. Second, learning algorithms may be biased even if they operate on unbiased data.

State-of-the-art decision tree learning algorithms such as `CART` and `C4.5` [10, 29], which are the ones used by popular machine learning toolkits, rely on a

---

This work was partially funded by the U.S. National Science Foundation grants CNS-1813117 and CNS-1702814.

S. Shoham and Y. Vizel (Eds.): CAV 2022, LNCS 13372, pp. 364–385, 2022.
https://doi.org/10.1007/978-3-031-13188-2_18

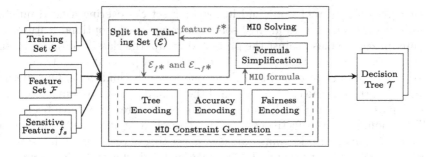

Fig. 1. SFTREE – our symbolic method for synthesizing a fair decision tree.

greedy search technique that is optimized solely for high learning speed and classification accuracy. Since they do not consider fairness as an optimization requirement at all, they often produce decision trees that are severely biased. To mitigate the bias, modifications have been proposed to make the greedy search discrimination-aware [24] (e.g., IGCS). Unfortunately, these modifications are not always effective as shown by our own experimental evaluation in Sect. 5 and, more importantly, the impact of *ad hoc* modifications is often unpredictable and difficult to explain.

Meanwhile, there is a line of work in operational research that formulates decision tree learning as a mixed-integer optimization (MIO) problem [7,35]. Given a finite set $\mathcal{F}$ of decision attributes, or features, and a maximum tree depth K, the set of all possible decision trees is captured symbolically as a set of numerical constraints, which is then fed to a solver to compute the *globally-optimal* decision tree. While optimality was defined initially to minimize the tree size and accuracy loss [7,35], later on, fairness was added as a goal of the optimization [1,5]. However, the approach remains largely theoretical due to its limited scalability: since the entire decision tree must be encoded as a monolithic MIO problem, only small training datasets (with sample sizes in the 1000s) and small decision trees (with depths up to 4 or 5) can be handled [2,7].

To overcome the limitations of the existing approaches, we propose an *iterative constraint solving* technique for synthesizing decision trees in a practically efficient fashion while simultaneously optimizing for fairness and accuracy. Instead of encoding the decision tree as a monolithic MIO formula, we break it down to a series of small steps to avoid the scalability bottleneck. Specifically, starting from the root node, we use constraint solving to conduct a depth-bounded look-ahead search at each level of the decision tree, to compute the best feature. Within the look-ahead search, we encode both fairness and accuracy requirements explicitly as numerical constraints, to make the fairness-accuracy trade-off not only predictable but also easy to explain.

The overall flow of our method, SFTREE, is shown in Fig. 1. Given a set of training examples ($\mathcal{E}$), a set of features ($\mathcal{F}$), and a sensitive feature ($f_s \in \mathcal{F}$) as input, SFTREE returns the synthesized decision tree ($\mathcal{T}$) as output. Internally, SFTREE encodes the hierarchical structure of a partial decision tree symbolically starting from the current node and its training set $\mathcal{E}$, covering a fixed number of tree levels. Then, it uses an MIO solver to compute the optimal feature, f^*, that minimizes the bias against the protected group, the classification error, and the tree size. Assuming that $f^* \in \{0, 1\}$ is a Boolean predicate, the training set is partitioned into subsets $\mathcal{E}_{f^*}$ and $\mathcal{E}_{\neg f^*}$, one for each child node. Our method iteratively partitions the child nodes until the training subset becomes empty, or all examples in $\mathcal{E}$ belong to the same class, or all features in $\mathcal{F}$ have been used.

To demonstrate its effectiveness, we have implemented SFTREE and evaluated it on six supervised learning datasets, consisting of three small datasets and three large ones. Since the small datasets can be handled even by the monolithic MIO approach (named MIP [1]) to obtain globally-optimal and fair solutions, we used them to evaluate the quality of decision trees learned by our method. The large datasets, which are out of the reach of MIP, were used to evaluate scalability. For comparison, we also evaluated CART [27], a mainstream decision tree learning algorithm, and IGCS [24], a discrimination-aware learning algorithm.

The experimental results show that, among all methods (CART, IGCS, MIP, and SFTREE), SFTREE produces the best overall solution in terms of fairness and accuracy. In contrast, CART produces unfair decision trees in most cases and, while IGCS does well on the small datasets, it produces mostly unfair decision trees for the large datasets. Neither CART nor IGCS is effective in satisfying the well-known *80% Rule* [8] for demographic parity [11,38]. In contrast, SFTREE satisfies the *80% Rule* in all cases. In terms of scalability, MIP fails to handle any of the large datasets, while SFTREE handles all of them. In fact, among all four methods, SFTREE is the only one that produces fair and accurate decision trees for datasets with >40,000 training samples.

To sum up, this paper makes the following contributions:

- We propose an iterative constraint-solving method for synthesizing fair decision trees:
  - By formulating feature selection as a series of mixed integer optimization subproblems, we make the constraints efficiently solvable.
  - By encoding fairness and accuracy explicitly as symbolic constraints, we make the trade-off quantifiable and easy to explain.
- We demonstrate the advantages of SFTREE over existing approaches (CART, IGCS, and MIP) using six popular datasets in the fairness literature.

The remainder of this paper is organized as follows. In Sect. 2, we review the basics of decision tree learning and group fairness. In Sect. 3, we present our method. In Sect. 4, we present generalization and performance enhancement techniques. In Sect. 5, we present our experimental results. After reviewing the related work in Sect. 6, we give our conclusions in Sect. 7.

2 Background

2.1 Training Dataset $\mathcal{E}$

The training dataset is a finite set of examples, $\mathcal{E} = \{(x_i, y_i)\}$, where $i \in \mathcal{N}$ is the index, input $x_i = \langle f_1, \ldots, f_k \rangle$ is a vector of features, and output y_i is a class

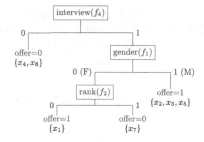

i	Input(x_i)				Output(y_i)
	gender(f_1)	rank(f_2)	experi(f_3)	interv(f_4)	offer
1	0	0	1	1	1
2	1	0	1	1	1
3	1	1	0	1	1
4	0	1	0	0	0
5	1	1	0	1	1
6	1	0	1	0	0
7	0	1	0	1	0

Fig. 2. An example training dataset $\mathcal{E}$ (left) and the related decision tree $\mathcal{T}$ (right).

label. Let $\mathcal{F}$ be the set of all features. For ease of comprehension, let us assume for now that all input features and the output class label are Boolean. In this case, every input $x_i \in \{0,1\}^k$ is a k-bit vector in the feature space, the output $y_i \in \{0,1\}$ is a bit, and a decision tree trained using $\mathcal{E}$ is a k-input Boolean function. To make the presentation clear, we may also use $y_i \in \{-,+\}$ instead of $y_i \in \{0,1\}$ as the output, where $-$ means "no" and $+$ means "yes".

Figure 2 shows a training set $\mathcal{E}$, where each row in the table represents an example. The input features are a job candidate's *gender* (0 = Female, 1 = Male), *college rank* (0 = Low, 1 = High), *experience* (0 = No, 1 = Yes), and *interview score* (0 = Not-Good, 1 = Good), while the output shows whether the job is offered (0 = No, and 1 = Yes). At the root of the decision tree, for instance, the input goes to the left branch when ($f_4 = 0$) and to the right branch when ($f_4 = 1$). The example illustrates three important notions associated with the training set: (1) partition of $\mathcal{E}$ (2) entropy, and (3) conditional entropy.

Partition. Given a set $\mathcal{E}$ and a feature f_j, we can partition $\mathcal{E}$ into subsets $\mathcal{E}_{f_j=0}$ and $\mathcal{E}_{f_j=1}$, or $\mathcal{E}_{\neg f_j}$ and $\mathcal{E}_{f_j}$, respectively, in shorthand notation. Here, $\mathcal{E}_{\neg f_j} = \{(x_i, y_i) \in \mathcal{E} \mid f_j(x_i) = 0\}$ consists of examples whose f_j is 0, and $\mathcal{E}_{f_j} = \{(x_i, y_i) \in \mathcal{E} \mid f_j(x_i) = 1\}$ consists of examples whose f_j is 1. By definition, we have $\mathcal{E}_{\neg f_j} \subseteq \mathcal{E}$ and $\mathcal{E}_{f_j} \subseteq \mathcal{E}$, $\mathcal{E}_{\neg f_j} \cap \mathcal{E}_{f_j} = \varnothing$ and $\mathcal{E}_{\neg f_j} \cup \mathcal{E}_{f_j} = \mathcal{E}$.

For our example in Fig. 2, partitioning the dataset by *gender* (f_1) results in subsets $\mathcal{E}_{f_1=F} = \mathcal{E}_{\neg f_1} = \{(x_1,y_1)(x_4,y_4)(x_7,y_7)\}$ and $\mathcal{E}_{f_1=M} = \mathcal{E}_{f_1} = \{(x_2,y_2)(x_3,y_3)(x_5,y_5)(x_6,y_6)\}$.

Entropy. The diversity (or purity) of a set $\mathcal{E}$ may be measured by Shannon entropy. Let $|\mathcal{E}^+|$ be the number of examples in $\mathcal{E}$ with positive output label, and $|\mathcal{E}^-|$ be the number of examples with negative output label. The percentage of positive examples is $|\mathcal{E}^+|/|\mathcal{E}|$, and the percentage of negative examples is $|\mathcal{E}^-|/|\mathcal{E}|$. Thus, the entropy is $H(\mathcal{E}) = -\frac{|\mathcal{E}^+|}{|\mathcal{E}|} log(\frac{|\mathcal{E}^+|}{|\mathcal{E}|}) - \frac{|\mathcal{E}^-|}{|\mathcal{E}|} log(\frac{|\mathcal{E}^-|}{|\mathcal{E}|})$.

For our example in Fig. 2, since $|\mathcal{E}^-| = 3$ and $|\mathcal{E}^+| = 4$, the entropy is $H(\mathcal{E}) = -\frac{3}{7}log(\frac{3}{7}) - \frac{4}{7}log(\frac{4}{7}) \approx 0.985$.

Conditional Entropy. Given a partition of the set $\mathcal{E}$ by the feature f_j, the entropy of each subset, $\mathcal{E}_{\neg f_j}$ or $\mathcal{E}_{f_j}$, is defined similarly. For our example, since $\mathcal{E}_{\neg f_1}$ has 2/3 negative examples and 1/3 positive examples, the entropy is $H(\mathcal{E}_{\neg f_1}) = -\frac{2}{3}log(\frac{2}{3}) - \frac{1}{3}log(\frac{1}{3}) = 0.918$. Similarly, since $\mathcal{E}_{f_1}$ has $1/4$ negative examples and $3/4$ positive examples, the entropy is $H(\mathcal{E}_{f_1}) = -\frac{1}{4}log(\frac{1}{4}) - \frac{3}{4}log(\frac{3}{4}) = 0.811$.

The conditional entropy of $\mathcal{E}$, with respect to f_j, is defined as follows:

$$H(\mathcal{E} \mid f_j) = \frac{|\mathcal{E}_{\neg f_j}|}{|\mathcal{E}|}H(\mathcal{E}_{\neg f_j}) + \frac{|\mathcal{E}_{f_j}|}{|\mathcal{E}|}H(\mathcal{E}_{f_j})$$

For our running example, since there are 3 female and 4 male candidates, we have $|\mathcal{E}_{\neg f_1}|/|\mathcal{E}| = 3/7$ and $|\mathcal{E}_{f_1}|/|\mathcal{E}| = 4/7$. Thus, the conditional entropy is $H(\mathcal{E} \mid f_1) = \frac{3}{7}H(\mathcal{E}_{\neg f_1}) + \frac{4}{7}H(\mathcal{E}_{f_1}) \approx 0.857$.

The difference between $H(\mathcal{E})$ and $H(\mathcal{E} \mid f_j)$ is called the *information gain*, a metric for evaluating how effective f_i is in separating positive examples from negative examples in $\mathcal{E}$. For our example, since $H(\mathcal{E}) \approx 0.985$ and $H(\mathcal{E} \mid f_1) \approx 0.857$, the information gain (of partitioning $\mathcal{E}$) by *gender (f_1)* is $0.985 - 0.857 = 0.128$. In contrast, the information gain by *interview (f_4)* is $0.985 - 0.516 = 0.469$. Thus, f_4 is more effective as a decision attribute.

Real-Valued Features. It is important to note that, while the above examples use Boolean features, our method is more general in that it allows all features have real values, i.e., $x_i \in [0,1]^k$ instead of $x_i \in \{0,1\}^k$. We accomplish this by applying one-hot encoding to any categorical feature and normalizing any real-valued feature to the $[0,1]$ domain. Thus, the branch predicates become $(f_j < b_v)$ and $(f_j \geqslant b_v)$, instead of $(f_j = 0)$ and $(f_j = 1)$, where $b_v \in (0,1]$ is a threshold computed by our method. For example, if f_j is the (normalized) salary and $b_v = 0.5$, the branch predicates are $(f_j < 0.5)$ and $(f_j \geqslant 0.5)$.

2.2   Decision Tree Learning

A decision tree $\mathcal{T}$ is a binary tree consisting of a set of nodes and a set of edges. Let the set of nodes be $\mathcal{V} \cup \mathcal{L}$, where $\mathcal{V}$ is the subset of branch nodes (including the root) and $\mathcal{L}$ is the subset of leaf nodes. Let E be the set of edges between these nodes. A path in $\mathcal{T}$ is a sequence of nodes and edges, denoted $v_0, e_1, v_1 \ldots v_n, e_n, l_n$, where v_0 is the root, l_n is a leaf node, $v_1 \ldots v_n$ are the internal nodes, and $e_1, \ldots, e_n$ are the edges.

Each edge has a branch condition. The edge is activated only if the condition holds for a given input x. In Fig. 2, for example, the left-most path of the decision tree has the condition $f_4(x) = 0$ and output *offer* $= 0$, while the right-most path has the condition $(f_4(x) = 1) \wedge (f_1(x) = M)$ and output *offer* $= 1$.

Given a training set $\mathcal{E} = \{(x_i, y_i)\}$, where x_i is an input and y_i is the known output, mainstream algorithms aim to learn a decision tree $\mathcal{T}$ that minimizes the classification error. They also aim to minimize the tree size which, in general, allows $\mathcal{T}$ to generalize well on the test examples.

The Baseline Algorithm. Algorithm 1 shows the top-level procedure of these mainstream algorithms. It takes the training set $\mathcal{E}$ and the feature set $\mathcal{F}$ as input, and returns a decision tree ($\mathcal{T}$) as output. These mainstream algorithms use a

---

Algorithm 1. The baseline decision tree learning procedure $\mathcal{T} = \text{DTL}(\mathcal{E}, \mathcal{F})$.

1: **Input:** training set $\mathcal{E} = \{(x_1, y_1), \ldots, (x_n, y_n)\}$ and feature set $\mathcal{F} = \{f_1, f_2, \ldots, f_k\}$
2: **Output:** decision tree $\mathcal{T}$
3: **if** all examples in $\mathcal{E}$ have the same label $l = \text{LABEL}(\mathcal{E})$
4:    **return** $\mathcal{T} = \text{LeafNode}(l)$
5: **else if** $\mathcal{F} = \varnothing$ and the most common label of $\mathcal{E}$ is $l^* = \text{MostCommonLabel}(\mathcal{E})$
6:    **return** $\mathcal{T} = \text{LeafNode}(l^*)$
7: **else if** $\mathcal{E} = \varnothing$ and in $\mathcal{E}.\text{parent}$, we have $l^* = \text{MostCommonLabel}(\mathcal{E}.\text{parent})$
8:    **return** $\mathcal{T} = \text{LeafNode}(l^*)$
9: **else**
10:    $\mathcal{T} = \text{BranchNode}(f^*)$, where $f^* = \text{FindNextFeature}(\mathcal{E}, \mathcal{F})$
11:    **foreach** value $i \in \{0, 1\}$ of the chosen feature f^*
12:       $\mathcal{T}_i = \text{DTL}(\mathcal{E}_{f^*=i}, \mathcal{F} \setminus \{f^*\})$
13:       Add an edge from $\mathcal{T}$ to $\mathcal{T}_i$ with label $(f^*(x) = i)$
14: **return** $\mathcal{T}$

Algorithm 2. Subroutine $\text{FindNextFeature}(\mathcal{E}, \mathcal{F})$ used in CART.

1: Let $H(\mathcal{E}) := -\sum_{l \in \{-,+\}} \frac{|\mathcal{E}^l|}{|\mathcal{E}|} \log(\frac{|\mathcal{E}^l|}{|\mathcal{E}|})$ ▷ Entropy
2: Let $H(\mathcal{E} \mid f) := \sum_{i \in \{0,1\}} \frac{|\mathcal{E}_{f=i}|}{|\mathcal{E}|} H(\mathcal{E}_{f=i})$ ▷ Conditional Entropy
3: **return** $f^* = \text{argmax}_{f \in \mathcal{F}} H(\mathcal{E}) - H(\mathcal{E} \mid f)$

---

greedy method to recursively select decision attributes from $\mathcal{F}$ and use them to partition the training set $\mathcal{E}$. At each step, it selects the best feature f^* using the subroutine FINDNEXTFEATURE.

In CART, for example, FINDNEXTFEATURE is entropy-based, to maximize the information gain of partitioning $\mathcal{E}$ by f as shown in Algorithm 2. While this is fast and often leads to high classification accuracy, it does not consider fairness and thus often produces biased decision trees. In this work, we use *iterative constraint solving* to overcome the limitation.

After f^* is computed by FINDNEXTFEATURE, Algorithm 1 uses it to partition the training set $\mathcal{E}$, and recursively process the two subsets: $\text{DTL}(\mathcal{E}_{f^*=0}, \mathcal{F} \setminus \{f^*\})$ and $\text{DTL}(\mathcal{E}_{f^*=1}, \mathcal{F} \setminus \{f^*\})$. The recursion ends when

- all training examples in the set $\mathcal{E}$ have the same class label (*Lines 3–4*);
- there are no features left in $\mathcal{F}$ to split $\mathcal{E}$ further (*Lines 5–6*); or
- the set $\mathcal{E}$ is empty (*Lines 7–8*).

2.3   Fairness Metric

Given a training set $\mathcal{E}$ and a sensitive feature $f_s \in \mathcal{F}$, e.g., race or gender, the goal is to construct a decision tree $\mathcal{T}$ that maximizes classification accuracy while minimizing bias. The metric concerned in this work, *demographic parity* [11,38], comes from the legal guideline in the United States for avoiding employment discrimination. Known as the *80% rule* [8], it says the percentage at which

Algorithm 3. Subroutine FINDNEXTFEATURE($\mathcal{E}, \mathcal{F}$) in our method.

1: Let f_s be the sensitive feature
2: $(O, \Phi) = \text{DTLENCODING}(\mathcal{E}, \mathcal{F}, f_s)$
3: $f^* = \text{MIOSOLVER}(O, \Phi)$
4: **return** f^*

candidates from one protected group are offered jobs should be at least 80% of the percentage at which candidates from another group are offered jobs.

This is formalized using the fairness index, $F_s(\mathcal{T}, \mathcal{E})$, defined as follows:

$$F_{f_s}(\mathcal{T}, \mathcal{E}) = \frac{Pr[\mathcal{T}(x) = + \mid f_s(x) = 0]}{Pr[\mathcal{T}(x) = + \mid f_s(x) = 1]} \tag{1}$$

where $Pr[\mathcal{T}(x) = + \mid f_s(x) = 0]$, or $Pr^+_{\neg f_s}$ in short, is the probability of positive examples under the condition $f_s(x) = 0$, and $Pr[\mathcal{T}(x) = + \mid f_s(x) = 1]$, or $Pr^+_{f_s}$ in short, is the probability of positive examples under the condition $f_s(x) = 1$. Thus, we have $Pr^+_{\neg f_s} = \frac{|\{x \in \mathcal{E} \mid f_s(x)=0 \wedge \mathcal{T}(x)=+\}|}{|\{x \in \mathcal{E} \mid f_s(x)=0\}|}$ and $Pr^+_{f_s} = \frac{|\{x \in \mathcal{E} \mid f_s(x)=1 \wedge \mathcal{T}(x)=+\}|}{|\{x \in \mathcal{E} \mid f_s(x)=1\}|}$.

Demographic parity means $0.8 \leqslant F_s(\mathcal{T}, \mathcal{E}) \leqslant (1/0.8) = 1.25$. For the example in Fig. 2, since $F_{f_1}(\mathcal{T}, \mathcal{E}) = 0.44$ for *gender* (f_1), the tree fails to satisfy the *80% rule* due to bias against female. The bias is explicit in that f_1 is actually used in the edge labels of the right most two paths of the decision tree. However, even if f_1 is not used in $\mathcal{T}$ explicitly, $\mathcal{T}$ may still be biased against female, for example, if other non-sensitive features (or their combinations) are statistically correlated to f_1 and, as a result, introduce bias against female. This is the reason why mitigating bias during decision tree learning is a challenging task.

3 Our Method

To minimize the bias and, at the same time, maximize the classification accuracy, we proposed to follow the top-level procedure in Algorithm 1, but formulate *feature selection* as a series of mixed-integer optimization (MIO) subproblems.

As shown in Algorithm 3, each of our MIO subproblems consists of an objective function O and a constraint Φ, and the solution is an assignment of the numerical variables (shared by O and Φ) that minimizes O while satisfying Φ. In the remainder of this section, we present our symbolic encoding of the objective function, O, and the constraint, Φ, respectively.

3.1 The Objective Function O

We define the function as $O := O_{accu} + \alpha O_{tree} - \beta O_{fair}$, consisting of components for accuracy loss (O_{accu}), tree size (O_{tree}), and fairness score (O_{fair}), respectively. The constants, α and β, are used to make trade-offs. In our implementation, α is fixed to $1/(2^{K+1}-2)$ while β is the optimal value in $[0,1]$ selected using n-fold cross-validation.

Specifically, we test the values 0.02, 0.04, 0.06, ... to 1.00 and, for each fold of the dataset, we compute the objective function and choose β with the minimal objective value. In general, a bigger β means more fairness. Our experiments show that, as β gets larger, O_{fair} remains constant initially and then starts increasing while O_{accu} remains constant, and then O_{accu} starts increasing.

Since the decision tree structure is not known *a priori*, we encode a complete binary tree while allowing all branch and leaf nodes to be activated or de-activated. Recall that $\mathcal{L}$ is the subset of leaf nodes, $\mathcal{V}$ is the subset of branch nodes, $l \in \mathcal{L}$ denotes a leaf node, and $v \in \mathcal{V}$ denotes a branch node.

Tree Size $(O_{tree} := \sum_{v \in \mathcal{V}} p_v)$. We assign a variable p_v to each branch node $v \in \mathcal{V}$, to indicate if a feature is used to split v. Thus, $p_v = 1$ means v is split, while $p_v = 0$ means v is not split. To get a valid decision tree, p_v must be constrained also by formula Φ (Sect. 3.2) . Assuming the number of p_v variables is $|\mathcal{V}|$, the tree size is the number of p_v variables with value 1.

Accuracy Loss $(O_{accu} := \frac{1}{|\mathcal{L}|} \sum_{l \in \mathcal{L}} L_l)$. We assign a variable L_l to each leaf node $l \in \mathcal{L}$ to represent the misclassification error at l. Since we start with a complete tree, each leaf node corresponds to a distinct path. The actual value of L_l is defined by formula Φ (Sect. 3.3). Assuming the number of L_l variables is $|\mathcal{L}|$, the accuracy loss is measured by averaging the L_l values.

Fairness Score $(O_{fair} := F)$. We assign a variable F to represent the overall fairness score of the decision tree. The value of F is defined by formula Φ (Sect. 3.4) according to the definition of demographic parity.

Next, we present our encoding of formula $\Phi := \Phi_{tree} \wedge \Phi_{accu} \wedge \Phi_{fair}$, where Φ_{tree} encodes the hierarchical structure of the tree, Φ_{accu} encodes the accuracy requirement, and Φ_{fair} encodes the fairness requirement. They share variables with O_{tree}, O_{accu} and O_{fair} in the objective function, such as p_v, L_l, and F. Note that, since the constraint will be solved by an off-the-shelf MIO solver, Φ must be encoded as a conjunction of equality/inequality constraints. If *logical-or* operators are needed, they must be converted to equality/inequality operators.

3.2 Encoding of the Decision Tree (Φ_{tree})

Given a node, which may be the root of the decision tree under construction, or any of its branch nodes, we consider a depth-K *complete binary tree* rooted at that node. Since it is a complete binary tree, there are precisely $T_K = 2^{K+1} - 1$ nodes with indices $1 \ldots T_K$ and, for any node n, the left and right child nodes have indices $2n$ and $2n + 1$, respectively. Furthermore, the set of leaf nodes is $\mathcal{L} = \{2^K, 2^K + 1 \ldots 2^{K+1} - 1\}$, where $|\mathcal{L}| = 2^K$, and the set of branch nodes is $\mathcal{V} = \{1, 2 \ldots 2^K - 1\}$, where $|\mathcal{V}| = 2^K - 1$.

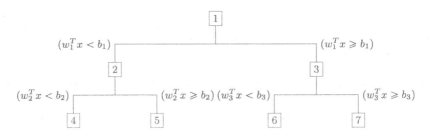

Fig. 3. Example of a complete binary tree, where $\mathcal{V} = \{1, 2, 3\}$ are branch nodes, $\mathcal{L} = \{4, 5, 6, 7\}$ are leaf nodes, and the decision thresholds b_1, b_2 and b_3 belong to $[0, 1]$. (Color figure online)

- Every leaf node $l \in \mathcal{L}$ has an output class label, and the path from root to l represents a classification rule, which assigns any input x that goes through the path to the output class.
- Every branch node $v \in \mathcal{V}$ has a vector w_v of bits for selecting the feature. Thus, at most one bit in w_v is 1, and $w_v[i] = 1$ means feature f_i is selected. For input x, the value of the selected feature is $f_i(x) = w_v^T x$.
- When node v is split by a feature, its outgoing edges are labeled $(w_v^T x < b_v)$ and $(w_v^T x \geqslant b_v)$, respectively. Here, $b_v \in (0, 1]$ is a symbolic threshold. When $f_i(x) = w_v^T x$ is a Boolean feature and $b_v = 1$, for example $(w_v^T x < 1)$ means $f_i(x) = 0$, and $(w_v^T x \geqslant 1)$ means $f_i(x) = 1$.

Figure 3 shows a depth-2 binary tree whose branch nodes are colored in *teal* and leaf nodes are colored in *red*. The thresholds b_1, b_2 and b_3 may be either 0 or a value in $(0, 1]$: only when they are non-zero, the corresponding nodes are split by features.

For instance, when b_2 is set to 1, if edge condition $(w_2^T x < 1)$ holds, input x goes to the left child, and if $(w_2^T x \geqslant 1)$ holds, x goes to the right child. When b_2 is set to 0, however, since edge condition $(w_2^T x < 0)$ is always false and $(w_2^T x \geqslant 0)$ is always true, input x always goes to the right child. In other words, $b_2 = 0$ disallows splitting at node $v = 2$.

Symbolic Variables. To model how a feature splits the training set, we define some symbolic variables first.

- **Input ($\mathbf{x}_{ij}$):** We use $\mathbf{x}_{ij}$ to model the j-th feature of the i-th input in $\mathcal{E}$. Thus, $i \in [1 \ldots n]$, $j \in [1 \ldots k]$, $n = |\mathcal{E}|$, and $k = |\mathcal{F}|$. The value of $\mathbf{x}_{i,j}$ may be any real number from 0 to 1, i.e., $\mathbf{x}_{i,j} \in [0, 1]$.
- **Split (p_v):** For every branch node $v \in \mathcal{V}$, we use p_v to model if v is split by a feature. The value of p_v is either 0 (no) or 1 (yes).
- **Selection (w_{vj}):** We use w_{vj} to model if the j-th feature is selected by node $v \in \mathcal{V}$. The value of w_{vj} is either 0 (no) or 1 (yes). Since both w and x are k-bit vectors, $w_v^T x$ is the value of the selected feature for a given input x.
- **Threshold (b_v):** We use b_v to control the activation of branch conditions at node $v \in \mathcal{V}$. When $b_v = 0$, input x always goes to the right child since

condition $(w_v^T x < 0)$ is unsatisfiable. Otherwise, x goes to the left child when $(w_v^T x < b_v)$, and to the right child when $(w_v^T x \geq b_v)$.

- **Input Association** (z_{it}): We use z_{it} to model if the i-th input, x_i, is associated with node $t \in \{\mathcal{L} \vee \mathcal{V}\}$. The value of z_{it} is either 0 (no) or 1 (yes).
- **Empty Association** (I_t): For every leaf node $t \in \mathcal{L}$, we use I_t to model if t has any associated input. The value of I_t is either 0 (no) or 1 (some).

Formula Φ_{tree}. We define the formula as $\Phi_{tree} := \Pi_{split} \wedge \Pi_{edge} \wedge \Pi_{leaf} \wedge \Pi_{branch}$ where Π_{split} encodes how features are used to split branch nodes, Π_{edge} encodes the constraints on edges, Π_{leaf} encodes the constraints on leaf nodes, and Π_{branch} encodes the constraints on branch nodes.

Subformula Π_{split}. We construct Π_{split} by constraining p_v, w_{vj}, and b_v:

1. If $p_v = 1$, meaning $v \in \mathcal{V}$ is split, we require $(\sum_{j \in \{1,...,k\}} w_{vj} = 1)$ to ensure exactly one feature is selected. We also require $(b_v > 0)$ to activate the branch conditions on the outgoing edges, $(w_v^T x < b_v)$ and $(w_v^T x \geq b_v)$.
2. If $p_v = 0$, meaning v is not split, we require $(\sum_{j \in \{1,...,k\}} w_{vj} = 0)$ to ensure no feature is selected, and $(b_v = 0)$ to de-activate the left branch. That is, input x always goes to the right, while the left subtree stops growing.

Thus, we have $\Pi_{split} := \bigwedge_{v \in \mathcal{V}} (\sum_{j \in \{1,...,k\}} w_{vj} = p_v) \wedge (0 \leq b_v \leq p_v)$.

Subformula Π_{edge}. We construct Π_{edge} by constraining the p_v variables: If node $v \in \mathcal{V}$ stops splitting, its child nodes also stop splitting. That is, when $p_v = 0$, both p_{2v} and p_{2v+1} must also be 0.
Thus, we have $\Pi_{edge} = \bigwedge_{v \in \mathcal{V}} (p_v \geq p_{2v}) \wedge (p_v \geq p_{2v+1})$.

Subformula Π_{leaf}. We construct Π_{leaf} by constraining variables z_{it} and I_t:

1. For each input x_i, where $i \in \{1,...,n\}$ and $n = |\mathcal{E}|$, we require that x_i is associated with exactly one leaf node $l \in \mathcal{L}$, i.e., $(\sum_{l \in \mathcal{L}} z_{il} = 1)$.
2. If $I_l = 0$, meaning no input is associated with l, we require that $(z_{il} = 0)$ for all $i \in \{1,...,n\}$. This is encoded as $\bigwedge_{l \in \mathcal{L}} (z_{il} \leq I_l)$.

Thus, we have $\Pi_{leaf} := \bigwedge_{i \in \{1,...,n\}} (\sum_{l \in \mathcal{L}} z_{il} = 1) \wedge \bigwedge_{l \in \mathcal{L}} (z_{il} \leq I_l)$.

Subformula Π_{branch}. We construct Π_{branch} by constraining w_{vj}, b_v, and z_{it}:

1. In a complete binary tree, the depth-d nodes are $v \in \{2^d, ..., 2^{d+1} - 1\}$. Since exactly one of them is associated with input x_i, we require that condition $\Pi_{br1} := (\sum_{v \in \{2^d,...,2^{d+1}-1\}} z_{iv} = 1)$ holds.
2. At each node $v \in \mathcal{V}$, since input x_i is associated with either the left child $L = 2v$ or the right child $R = 2v + 1$, but not both, we require that the following three conditions hold:
   - $\Pi_{br2} := \bigwedge_{v \in \{2^d,...,2^{d+1}-1\}} (z_{iv} = z_{i(2v)} + z_{i(2v+1)})$
   - $\Pi_{br3} := \bigwedge_{v \in \{2^d,...,2^{d+1}-1\}} (\sum_{j \in \{1,...,k\}} w_{vj} x_{ij} - \gamma_L (1 - z_{iL}) < b_v)$
   - $\Pi_{br4} := \bigwedge_{v \in \{2^d,...,2^{d+1}-1\}} (\sum_{j \in \{1,...,k\}} w_{vj} x_{ij} + (1 - z_{iR}) \geq b_v)$

Thus, we have $\Pi_{branch} := \bigwedge_{i \in \{1,...,n\}} \bigwedge_{d \in \{1,...,K-1\}} (\Pi_{br1} \wedge \Pi_{br2} \wedge \Pi_{br3} \wedge \Pi_{br4})$.

Explanation of Π_{br3} and Π_{br4}. What we would like to encode in Π_{br3} is the fact that branch condition $(\sum w_{vj} x_{ij} < b_v)$ may be either TRUE (x_i goes to the left child L when $z_{iL} = 1$ and $b_v \in (0, 1]$) or FALSE (x_i goes to the right child R when $z_{iL} = 0$ and $b_v \in (0, 1]$, or when $b_v = 0$). However, since off-the-shelf MIO solvers do not support *logical-or* operators, we have to encode these different scenarios in a single inequality constraint. This is accomplished by adding a slack value, $-\gamma_L(1 - z_{iL})$, to the branch condition. Similarly, in Π_{br4}, we add a slack value, $(1 - z_{iR})$, to the branch condition $(\sum w_{vj} x_{ij} \geqslant b_v)$.

3.3   Encoding of the Accuracy Requirement (Φ_{accu})

To minimize the accuracy loss defined in $O_{accu} := \frac{1}{|\mathcal{L}|} \sum_{l \in \mathcal{L}} L_l$ (Sect. 3.1), we need to constrain the L_l variables in Φ_{accu} such that L_l models the misclassification error at the leaf node $l \in \mathcal{L}$. In the depth-K complete binary tree, there are $|\mathcal{L}| = 2^K$ leaf nodes. For each leaf node l, variable L_l represents the number of misclassified examples $(x_i, y_i) \in \mathcal{E}$: it is misclassified if the given output y_i does not match the predicted output $\mathcal{T}(x_i)$.

The formula $\Phi_{accu} := \Phi_p \wedge \Phi_N \wedge \Phi_\theta \wedge \Phi_{loss}$ consists of four subformulas.

Subformula Φ_P. For each $(x_i, y_i) \in \mathcal{E}$, where $i \in \{1, \ldots, n\}$ and $n = |\mathcal{E}|$, and for each output value $m \in \{0, 1\}$, we use p_{im} to model if $(y_i = m)$. The value of p_{im}, which is either 0 or 1, is $const_{im} := (y_i = m) ? 0 : 1$.

Thus, we have $\Phi_p := \bigwedge_{i=1}^n \bigwedge_{m=0}^1 (p_{im} = const_{im})$.

Subformula Φ_N. We use variable N_l to represent the number of examples associated with leaf node l, and N_{lm} to represent those with output value m.

Thus, we have $\Phi_N := \bigwedge_{l \in \mathcal{L}} (N_l = \sum_{i=1}^n z_{il}) \wedge (N_{lm} = \frac{1}{2} \sum_{i=1}^n z_{il}(1 + p_{im}))$.

Subformula Φ_θ. According to Lines 5–8 of Algorithm 1, each leaf node has an output class label $\theta_l = \text{argmax}_{m \in \{0,1\}} N_{lm}$. Since **argmax** cannot be directly encoded, we define a matrix of θ_{lm} variables in $\{0, 1\}$, where $\theta_{lm} = 1$ means the output label of node l is m. By definition, only one θ_{lm} variable can be 1.

Thus, we have $\Phi_\theta := \bigwedge_{l \in \mathcal{L}} (\sum_{m \in \{0,1\}} \theta_{lm} = 1)$.

Subformula Φ_{loss}. Assuming that m is the output label predicted by the leaf node l. The misclassification error, L_l, is equal to the number of examples associated with l, denoted N_l, minus the number of examples that have the most common label m, denoted $\text{max}_{m \in \{0,1\}} N_{lm}$.

To avoid **max/min** in $L_l = N_l - \text{max}_{m \in \{0,1\}} N_{lm} = \text{min}_{m \in \{0,1\}} (N_l - N_{lm})$, we use θ_{lm} variables and constant $n = |\mathcal{E}|$ to rewrite the constraint as :

$$(L_l \geqslant 0) \wedge \bigwedge_{m \in \{0,1\}} (L_l \geqslant N_l - N_{lm} - n(1 - \theta_{lm})) \wedge (L_l \leqslant N_l - N_{lm} + n\theta_{lm})$$

Thus, we have $\Phi_{loss} := \bigwedge_{l \in \mathcal{L}} ((L_l \geqslant 0) \wedge \bigwedge_{m \in \{0,1\}} (L_l \geqslant N_l - N_{lm} - n(1 - \theta_{lm})) \wedge (L_l \leqslant N_l - N_{lm} + n\theta_{lm}))$.

3.4 Encoding of the Fairness Requirement

Formula $\Phi_{fair} := \Phi_{F_s} \wedge \Phi_{FM}$ has two subformulas. Here, Φ_{F_s} encodes the fairness index and Φ_{FM} encodes the constraints on variables used in Φ_{F_s}.

According to Eq. 1 (Sect. 2.3), the fairness index is defined as $F_s = (Pr^+_{\neg f_s}/Pr^+_{f_s})$, where f_s is a sensitive feature such that $f_s(x)$, for any input $x \in \mathcal{E}$, may be 0 or 1 (e.g., female and male) while $\mathcal{T}(x) = +$ means the output generated by $\mathcal{T}$ is positive (e.g., a job is offered). According to the *"80% rule"*, demographic parity is achieved if F_s is above 80%. In this work, our goal is to find a solution that (1) satisfies ($F_s > 0.8$) and, at the same time (2) maximizes the value of F_s.

However, the definition of F_s shown in Eq. 1 has division operators, which are not supported by off-the-shelf MIO solvers. Furthermore, the divisor part of the equation varies even for a fixed set $\mathcal{E}$ of examples, which makes the encoding a challenging task. To overcome the challenge, we refine the definition of as follows:

$$\frac{Pr^+_{f_s=0}}{Pr^+_{f_s=1}} = \frac{|\{x \in \mathcal{E} \mid f_s(x) = 0, \mathcal{T}(x) = +\}| \, / \, |\{x \in \mathcal{E} \mid f_s(x) = 0\}|}{|\{x \in \mathcal{E} \mid f_s(x) = 1, \mathcal{T}(x) = +\}| \, / \, |\{x \in \mathcal{E} \mid f_s(x) = 1\}|} = \frac{S_0^+/S_0}{S_1^+/S_1} \tag{2}$$

For each of the four components, we create a symbolic variable. Variable S_0 represents the number of examples whose sensitive feature has the value 0 (e.g., *female*) for the *gender (f_1)* feature. Variable S_0^+ represents the number of examples in S_0 that have the positive output (e.g., a job is offered). Variable S_1 represents the number of examples whose sensitive feature has the value 1 (e.g., *male*) for the *gender (f_1)* feature. Variable S_1^+ represents the number of examples in S_1 that have the positive output.

Subformula Φ_{F_s}. We use Φ_{F_s} to enforce the *80% rule*: $F_s = \frac{S_0^+/S_0}{S_1^+/S_1} \geqslant 0.8$. Assuming $S_0 > 0$, $S_0^+ > 0$, $S_1 > 0$, and $S_1^+ > 0$, we encode the rule as follows:

$$\Phi_{F_s} := (S_0^+ \times S_1 - 0.8 \times S_0 \times S_1^+ \geqslant 0)$$

There are two advantages of this encoding. First, the resulting constraint can be solved by off-the-shelf MIO solvers, whereas a direct encoding of Eq. 2 cannot. Second, the value of ($S_0^+ \times S_1 - 0.8 \times S_0 \times S_1^+$) increases as F_s increases; therefore, it can be used as part of the objective function, O_{fair}, to maximize F_s.

Subformula Φ_{FM}. We use Φ_{FM} to constrain the variables S_0, S_0^+, S_1, and S_1^+. Toward this end, we need to define the following variables:

- S_{0i}: We use variable $S_{0i} \in \{0,1\}^n$ to model if the value of $f_s(x_i)$ is 0. Thus, we require $S_{0i} = 1$ when $f_s(x_i) = 0$, and $S_{0i} = 0$ otherwise.
- S_{0il}^+: We use variable $S_{0il}^+ \in \{0,1\}^{n \times |\mathcal{L}|}$ to model, at each leaf node $l \in \mathcal{L}$, if $x_i \in \mathcal{E}$ is given the positive output. Thus, we require $S_{0il}^+ = 1$ when the following condition holds, and $S_{0il}^+ = 0$ otherwise:

$$(\theta_{lm} = 1 \ \wedge \ m = 1 \ \wedge \ z_{il} = 1 \ \wedge \ S_{0i} = 1)$$

In the condition above, ($\theta_{lm} = 1$) means the output label produced by the leaf node l is m, and ($m = 1$) means m is the positive output ("+").

– S_{1i} and S_{1il}^+: We define variables S_{1i} and S_{1il}^+ similar to S_{0i} and S_{0il}^+.

Thus, we have $\Phi_{FM} := (S_0 = \sum_{i \in \{1,...,n\}} S_{0i}) \wedge (S_0^+ = \sum_{i \in \{1,...,n\}} \sum_{l \in \mathcal{L}} S_{0il}^+) \wedge$ $(S_1 = \sum_{i \in \{1,...,n\}} S_{1i}) \wedge (S_1^+ = \sum_{i \in \{1,...,n\}} S_{1il}^+)$.

Putting It All Together. Recall that, in Sect. 3.3, we have constrained the accuracy loss, L_l, in the objective function O_{accu}, and defined the objective function O_{tree} in Sect. 3.1, which is used to minimize the tree size and thus reduce over-fitting. As for the objective function O_{fair} (Sect. 3.1), we define the fairness score as follows: $F = (S_0^+ \times S_1 - 0.8 \times S_0 \times S_1^+)$.

Thus, we have the entire MIO problem as follows:

$$\text{minimize} \quad \frac{1}{|\mathcal{L}|} \sum_{l \in \mathcal{L}} L_l + \alpha \sum_{v \in \mathcal{V}} p_v - \beta F \quad (3)$$
$$\text{subject to} \quad \Phi_{accu}(L_l) \wedge \Phi_{tree}(p_v) \wedge \Phi_{fair}(F)$$

4 Generalization and Performance Enhancement

In this section, we first explain how our method relates to various existing algorithms (Sect. 4.1). Next, we present techniques for speeding up constraint solving while maintaining the quality of the solution (Sect. 4.2). Finally, we show that, beyond *demographic parity*, our method can encode other group fairness metrics, such as *equal opportunity* and *equal odds* (Sect. 4.3).

4.1 Relating to Existing Algorithms

Recall that our method performs feature selection by symbolically encoding a depth-K binary tree, to perform a bounded look-ahead search of the optimal feature using the MIO solver. For ease of presentation, let us call the selected feature *depth-K optimal*, where $K \in \{1, \ldots, +\infty\}$.

Depth-1 Optimal. When $K = 1$, the tree consists of the root node only and, as a result, look-ahead search is disabled. In this case, our method is the same as a purely greedy search method. Depending on whether fairness is encoded, there are two cases.

– Without the fairness component, our method would compute the *depth-1 optimal* feature that minimizes only the tree size and the accuracy loss. This is similar to mainstream decision tree learning algorithms such as CART.
– With the fairness component, our method would compute the *depth-1 optimal* feature that minimizes the tree size and the accuracy loss, and maximizes the fairness score. This is similar to IGCS [24], an discrimination-aware technique for learning decision trees.

Our experimental evaluation (in Sect. 5) shows that neither CART nor IGCS is effective in improving fairness, especially for larger datasets, primarily due to their inability to look beyond the current node.

Depth-∞ Optimal. When K is set to a sufficiently-large number, our method is able to find the globally optimal feature for not only the root node, but also other nodes in the decision tree. Thus, it would compute the entire decision tree in one shot.

- Without the fairness component, our method would act like the technique introduced by Bertsimas and Dunn [7], which laid the ground work for encoding an optimal classification tree as a monolithic MIO problem.
- With the fairness component, our method would act like MIP, a fair learning technique introduced by Aghaei et al. [1].

Our experimental evaluation (in Sect. 5) shows that the computational overhead of the monolithic MIO approach or MIP is too high to be practically useful. We discuss how to set the value of K in our method in the next subsection.

4.2 Performance Enhancement

We propose two techniques for speeding up our method by (1) choosing the K value adaptively and (2) sampling the training examples in $\mathcal{E}$.

Choosing the K Value Adaptively. There is a trade-off between looking further ahead and reducing the constraint solving time. Given $n = |\mathcal{E}|$ training examples, and 2^K leaf nodes in a depth-K binary tree, the number of decision variables (such as S_{0il}) would be $(n \times 2^K)$. Since mixed-integer optimization is NP-hard, the complexity of constraint solving is $O(2^{n \times 2^K})$. Empirically, we have found that Gurobi, a state-of-the-art solver, may take 1–2 h to solve a problem for $n = 1000$ training examples and tree depth $K = 7$—this is consistent with prior experimental results, e.g., Bertsimas and Dunn [7]. Unfortunately, supervised learning datasets in practice often bring as many as 50,000 training examples to the root node of a decision tree, although the number decreases gradually and may reach 0 for some leaf nodes. Therefore, setting K to 7, or any predetermined value, would not work well in practice.

Instead, we propose to set the K value adaptively. Given a time-out limit (T/O) for learning a decision tree, we start with a relatively small K value, say $K = 2$, to synthesize a decision tree. Then, we increase the K value to synthesize a better decision tree. We keep increasing the K value as long as the time limit is not yet reached, and the quality of the decision tree is improved. We measure the quality of the tree using the value of the objective function, O, which consists of the tree size, the accuracy loss, and the fairness score.

Sampling the Training Examples. We propose to reduce the size of the constraints in Φ by sampling the training examples in $\mathcal{E}$, before using them to construct the formula Φ. Our experience shows that sampling can reduce the value of n significantly and, at the same time, maintaining the quality of the MIO solution. For the adult dataset, which has $48,842$ training examples, even with a small K value, the symbolic constraints would take more than 1 h to solve.

Algorithm 4. Subroutine FINDNEXTFEATURE($\mathcal{E}, \mathcal{F}$) with our enhancement.

1: Let f_s be the sensitive feature
2: **if** $|\mathcal{E}| \leqslant 8000$ **then** $(O, \Phi) =$ DTLENCODING($\mathcal{E}, \mathcal{F}, f_s$)
3: **else** $(O, \Phi) =$ DTLENCODING($\mathcal{E}|_{sampled}, \mathcal{F}, f_s$)
4: **return** $f^* =$ MIOSOLVER(O, Φ)

Empirically, we have observed that the feature computed by depth-K look-ahead using 8,000 randomly-chosen examples is almost as good as the feature computed using all examples. Based on this observation, we set the threshold ($n \leqslant 8000$), i.e., at most 8,000 examples from $\mathcal{E}$ are used in the symbolic constraints in Algorithm 4, where $\Phi =$ DTLENCODING($\mathcal{E}, \mathcal{F}, f_s$) is invoked if $|\mathcal{E}| \leqslant 8000$. Otherwise, $\mathcal{E}$ is replaced by the randomly-sampled subset $\mathcal{E}|_{sampled}$.

Our sampling method is not directly applicable to the original MIP approach because, if sampled data are used as input, the MIP solving procedure would permanently discard the rest of the data, which would significantly degrade its accuracy. In contrast, sampling in our method only causes the rest of the data to be ignored temporarily (for this particular node) but, for the child nodes in the subtree, the entire data will still be used in the subsequent computation.

4.3 Encoding Other Group Fairness Metrics

Beyond *demographic parity*, there are two popular metrics for group fairness, of which one is *equal opportunity* and the other is *equalized odds*.

Equal Opportunity. In addition to the sensitive feature f_s, there is a decision-critical feature f_c. Let $P^+_{f_s=0, f_c=1} = \frac{|x \in \mathcal{E} \mid f_s(x)=0, f_c(x)=1, T(x)=+|}{|x \in \mathcal{E} \mid f_s(x)=0, f_c(x)=1|} = \frac{S^+_0}{S_0}$ and $P^+_{f_s=1, f_c=1} = \frac{|x \in \mathcal{E} \mid f_s(x)=1, f_c(x)=1, T(x)=+|}{|x \in \mathcal{E} \mid f_s(x)=1, f_c(x)=1|} = \frac{S^+_1}{S_1}$. A decision tree T satisfies *equal opportunity* if the following condition holds (for a small ϵ).

$$P^+_{f_s=1, f_c=1} - P^+_{f_s=0, f_c=1} \leqslant \epsilon \tag{4}$$

In our method, Eq. 4 may be encoded as $\Phi_{eq} := S^+_1 S_0 - S^+_0 S_1 - \epsilon S_0 S_1 \leqslant 0$, to replace Φ_{F_s} in the fairness requirement $\Phi_{fair} := \Phi_{F_s} \wedge \Phi_{FM}$. The definitions of variables S_0, S^+_0, S_1 and S^+_1 are analogous to that in Sect. 3.4. Similarly, we can define fairness decision variables S_{0i}, S_{0il}, S_{1i}, and S_{1il}. For example, the value of S_{0i} is set to 1 if $f_s(x_i) = 0 \wedge f_c(x_i) = 1$ and is set to 0 otherwise.

Equalized Odds. To satisfy *equalized odds*, we must satisfy Eq. 4, as well as the condition below:

$$P^+_{f_s=1, f_c=0} - P^+_{f_s=0, f_c=0} \leqslant \epsilon. \tag{5}$$

Since Eq. 5 can be encoded similarly to Eq. 4, the details are omitted for brevity.

Table 1. Comparing our method with existing methods on small benchmarks.

Benchmark	SFTree (ours)		CART [27]		IGCS [24]		MIP [1]	
	Accuracy	Fairness	Accuracy	Fairness	Accuracy	Fairness	Accuracy	Fairness
German Fold1	77.5%	0.82	83.0%	0.65	74.0%	0.84	80.5%	0.82
German Fold2	80.5%	0.81	85.0%	0.67	78.5%	**0.78**	83.5%	0.82
German Fold3	76.0%	0.84	79.0%	0.71	73.5%	0.80	78.5%	0.84
German Fold4	81.0%	0.80	83.5%	0.65	76.0%	0.84	81.0%	0.89
German Fold5	80.5%	0.81	85.0%	0.66	77.0%	0.81	83.0%	0.81
Salary Fold1	81.8%	0.82	90.9%	0.59	81.8%	0.82	81.8%	0.82
Salary Fold2	72.7%	0.83	90.9%	0.57	81.8%	**0.77**	81.8%	0.84
Salary Fold3	72.7%	0.83	81.8%	0.62	72.7%	0.83	81.8%	0.83
Salary Fold4	81.8%	0.82	90.9%	0.61	81.8%	0.82	81.8%	0.82
Salary Fold5	81.8%	0.81	81.8%	0.57	72.7%	**0.73**	72.7%	0.83
Student Fold1	71.2%	0.84	75.9%	0.58	72.1%	**0.78**	72.8%	0.87
Student Fold2	70.3%	0.81	75.1%	0.63	69.3%	0.82	72.8%	0.85
Student Fold3	70.9%	0.81	73.6%	0.57	71.4%	0.81	73.6%	0.85
Student Fold4	69.1%	0.82	75.1%	0.61	69.3%	**0.77**	71.3%	0.84
Student Fold5	71.5%	0.84	77.5%	0.53	72.0%	0.81	75.1%	0.84

5 Experiments

We have implemented our method, SFTREE, using Python, Julia 1.5.1 [15], and
Gurobi 9.03 [21], where Julia is used to encode the MIO constraints and Gurobi is
used to solve the constraints. We compared SFTREE with three state-of-the-art
techniques: CART, which is a mainstream algorithm for decision tree learning,
IGCS, which is a discrimination-aware learning algorithm, and MIP, which is a
monolithic MIO approach to learning fair tress. We conducted all experiments
with Catalina running on a macOS with 2.4 GHz 8-Core CPU and 64G RAM.

Benchmarks. Our evaluation uses six popular benchmarks from the fairness
literature. They are divided to three small datasets and three large datasets.
Since the small datasets can be handled by the less-scalable but more-accurate
MIP to obtain globally optimal solutions, they are useful in evaluating the quality
of our method. The large datasets, in contrast, are out of the reach of MIP and
thus useful in evaluating the scalability of our method.

- Among the small datasets, German [23] (predicting credit risks) has 1000 training examples and 20 features; Student [12] (predicting student performance)
  has 649 training examples and 33 features; and Salary [36] (predicting the
  salary level) has 52 training examples and 16 features. In these datasets, the
  sensitive feature is *gender*.
- Among the large datasets, Adult [14] (predicting the earning power) has
  48,842 training examples and 14 features (with *race* as the sensitive feature);
  Default [37] (predicting loan default risk) has 30,000 training examples and
  23 features (with *gender* as the sensitive feature); and Compas [13] (predicting
  the recidivism risk) has 10,500 training examples and 16 features (with *race*
  as the sensitive feature).

Table 2. Comparing our method with existing methods on large benchmarks.

Benchmark	SFTree (ours)		CART [27]		IGCS [24]		MIP [1]	
	Accuracy	Fairness	Accuracy	Fairness	Accuracy	Fairness	Accuracy	Fairness
Adult Fold1	80.3%	0.81	83.0%	0.54	82.8%	**0.51**	-	-
Adult Fold2	77.4%	0.86	80.0%	0.57	81.9%	**0.68**	-	-
Adult Fold3	75.7%	0.84	79.8%	0.57	81.3%	**0.72**	-	-
Adult Fold4	78.1%	0.83	82.1%	0.55	83.0%	**0.62**	-	-
Adult Fold5	77.1%	0.86	82.6%	0.55	75.7%	**0.68**	-	-
Default Fold1	80.5%	0.81	84.7%	0.64	81.3%	**0.77**	-	-
Default Fold2	84.7%	0.81	86.3%	0.61	84.0%	**0.73**	-	-
Default Fold3	80.5%	0.83	83.2%	0.66	82.7%	**0.75**	-	-
Default Fold4	78.8%	0.85	84.1%	0.64	81.5%	**0.73**	-	-
Default Fold5	81.4%	0.82	83.9%	0.64	81.7%	**0.71**	-	-
Compas Fold1	86.4%	0.89	92.8%	0.63	86.7%	0.81	-	-
Compas Fold2	89.8%	0.96	92.5%	0.61	87.5%	0.83	-	-
Compas Fold3	85.3%	0.94	90.4%	0.67	88.9%	**0.74**	-	-
Compas Fold4	87.2%	0.96	92.6%	0.63	92.0%	**0.61**	-	-

During learning, we apply the standard 5-fold cross validation expect for `Compas`, to which we apply 4-fold cross validation to be consistent with prior work.

Results on the Small Benchmarks. We compare the quality of the decision trees learned by our method and three existing methods on the small benchmarks. The results are shown in Table 1, where Column 1 shows name of the dataset, Columns 2–3 shows the result of our method in terms of accuracy and fairness, computed by cross-validation, Columns 4–5 show the result of `CART`, Columns 6–7 show the result of `IGCS`, and Columns 8–9 show the result of `MIP`. Since the datasets are small, `MIP` is able to compute the best solutions: without violating the *80% Rule*, it maximizes accuracy.

The result shows that, overall, `CART` has the best accuracy but the worst fairness score. `IGCS` improves over `CART`, but still violates the *80% Rule* in 5 out of the 15 cases. In contrast, `SFTree` satisfies the fairness requirement in all 15 cases and, at the same time, achieves high accuracy. Furthermore, it runs more than 10 times faster than `MIP`.

Results on the Large Benchmarks. We use these benchmarks to evaluate both the quality and the scalability of our method. Table 2 shows the result of the quality comparison, which has the same format as Table 1. `CART` has the highest accuracy but fails to satisfy the fairness requirement in all 14 cases. Although `IGCS` is somewhat effective for the small benchmarks in Table 1, here, it fails to satisfy the fairness requirement in 12 of the 14 cases. In contrast, our method is the only one that satisfies the fairness requirement in all cases and, at the same time, has accuracy comparable to `CART` and `IGCS`.

Table 3 shows the execution time comparison. `MIP` times out in all 14 cases (`T/O = 3h`), while our method finishes each within 1 h. Thus, our method runs more than 10 times faster than `MIP`. Although `CART` and `IGCS` are faster, they are equivalent to depth-1 look-ahead search in our method and, due to the limited ability to look ahead, they almost never satisfy the fairness requirement.

Table 3. Comparing the run time of methods on large benchmarks (T/O = 3h).

Benchmark	SFTree	CART [27]	IGCS [24]	MIP [1]	Benchmark	SFTree	CART [27]	IGCS [24]	MIP [1]
Adult Fold1	2064s	39s	40s	T/O	Default Fold1	2499s	28s	28s	T/O
Adult Fold2	2119s	39s	39s	T/O	Default Fold2	2478s	29s	29s	T/O
Adult Fold3	2075s	39s	40s	T/O	Default Fold3	2526s	29s	29s	T/O
Adult Fold4	2090s	39s	40s	T/O	Default Fold4	2536s	28s	29s	T/O
Adult Fold5	2091s	39s	39s	T/O	Default Fold5	2531s	28s	29s	T/O
Compas Fold1	2115s	15s	16s	T/O	Compas Fold2	2137s	15s	15s	T/O
Compas Fold3	2129s	15s	15s	T/O	Compas Fold4	2166s	15s	15s	T/O

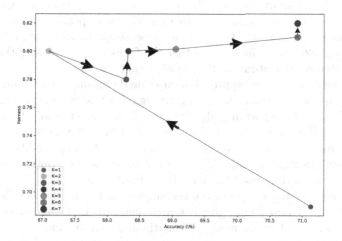

Fig. 4. How accuracy and fairness of the learned decision tree change with the K value for the *Student* dataset. For each $K = 1, \ldots, 7$, we plot the fairness and accuracy scores.

Evaluating the Impact of the K-value. We have also evaluated how the K value affects the quality of the learned decision tree using the `Student Fold1` benchmark. Since the benchmark is small enough, we set K to fixed values $1, \ldots, 7$ instead of letting it adapt, so we can assess the impact. Figure 4 shows the result, where the x-axis is accuracy and the y-axis is the fairness score. Thus, the closer a dot is to the right-top corner, the higher the overall quality is. The result shows that the quality of our solution increases dramatically as the K value increases from 1 to 7, due to the increasingly deeper look-ahead search.

Summary of Additional Results. While we have also evaluated the scalability of our method with respect to the dataset size, we omit the results for brevity and instead provide a summary. What we have found is that, as the dataset gets larger, the execution time of our method increases modestly at first, and then stops increasing after a threshold is reached. This is due to the use of performance enhancement techniques presented in Sect. 4. Thus, our method does not have scalability issues. In fact, among all four methods, SFTREE is the only one that consistently produces fair and accurate decision trees for datasets with >40,000 training samples.

6 Related Work

At a high level, our method can be viewed as an *in-processing* approach to mitigating bias in machine learning models. Broadly speaking, there are three approaches: *pre-processing* [17, 25, 31], *in-processing* [11, 19, 24, 30, 33] and *post-processing* [18, 22], depending on whether the focus is on de-biasing the training data, the learning algorithm, or the classification output.

Since the *pre-processing* approach focuses on de-biasing the training data [17, 25, 31], it is applicable to any machine learning model; however, it cannot remove bias introduced by the learning algorithms, which is problematic because, even if the training data is not biased, learning algorithms may introduce new bias. While the *post-processing* approach can remove such bias by modifying the predicted output [18, 22], the result is often hard to predict and difficult to explain. In contrast, our method does not have these limitations.

Compared to other *in-processing* techniques for fair learning decision trees, including IGCS [24] and similar greedy search methods [11, 19, 30, 33], our method has the advantage of being more systematic and quantifiable. This is because we encode both accuracy and fairness requirements explicitly as numerical constraints. Thus, it would be easy to explain, at every step, why a feature is chosen over another feature, and quantify how much more effective it is in minimizing bias and accuracy loss at the same time. Compared to the monolithic constraint solving approach, including MIP [1] and similar methods [5, 35], our method has the advantage of being significantly more scalable.

Our method differs from the recent work of Torfah et al. [32] in that their method uses a small training set sampled from a known distribution and thus does not need techniques such as incremental solving. Furthermore, their method assumes the decision predicates are given, but in our method, the predicates are synthesized from real-valued features. Finally, our fairness constraint is also different from the explainability constraint.

Besides synthesis, there are techniques for improving fairness by repairing an existing machine learning model [4, 9, 20, 26], and techniques for verifying that an existing machine learning model is indeed fair, e.g., by using probabilistic analysis methods [3, 6, 28]. While these techniques are related, they differ from our method in that they cannot synthesize new decision trees from training data while ensuring the decision trees are fair by construction.

7 Conclusion

We have presented a method for synthesizing a fair and accurate decision tree, by formulating feature section as a series of mixed-integer optimization problems and solve them using an off-the-shelf constraint solver. The method is flexible in expressing group fairness metrics including *demographic parity, equal opportunity,* and *equal odds.* On popular datasets, it is able to learn decision trees that satisfy the fairness requirement and, at the same time, achieve a high classification accuracy.

References

1. Aghaei, S., Azizi, M.J., Vayanos, P.: Learning optimal and fair decision trees for non-discriminative decision-making. In: AAAI Conference on Artificial Intelligence (2019)
2. Aghaei, S., Gómez, A., Vayanos, P.: Strong optimal classification trees. CoRR abs/2103.15965 (2021). https://arxiv.org/abs/2103.15965
3. Albarghouthi, A., D'Antoni, L., Drews, S., Nori, A.V.: FairSquare: probabilistic verification of program fairness. In: Proceedings of the ACM on Programming Languages (OOPSLA), pp. 1–30 (2017)
4. Albarghouthi, A., D'Antoni, L., Drews, S.: Repairing decision-making programs under uncertainty. In: International Conference on Computer Aided Verification (2017)
5. Azizi, M.J., Vayanos, P., Wilder, B., Rice, E., Tambe, M.: Designing fair, efficient, and interpretable policies for prioritizing homeless youth for housing resources. In: International Conference on the Integration of Constraint Programming, Artificial Intelligence, and Operations Research (2018)
6. Bastani, O., Zhang, X., Solar-Lezama, A.: Probabilistic verification of fairness properties via concentration. In: Proceedings of the ACM on Programming Languages (OOPSLA) (2019)
7. Bertsimas, D., Dunn, J.: Optimal classification trees. Mach. Learn. **106**(7), 1039–1082 (2017)
8. Biddle, D.: Adverse Impact and Test Validation: A Practitioner's Guide to Valid and Defensible Employment Testing. Routledge, London (2017)
9. Bolukbasi, T., Chang, K.W., Zou, J.Y., Saligrama, V., Kalai, A.T.: Man is to computer programmer as woman is to homemaker? Debiasing word embeddings. In: Advances in Neural Information Processing Systems (2016)
10. Breiman, L., Friedman, J.H., Olshen, R.A., Stone, C.J.: Classification and Regression Trees. Routledge, New York (2017)
11. Calders, T., Kamiran, F., Pechenizkiy, M.: Building classifiers with independency constraints. In: IEEE International Conference on Data Mining Workshops (2009)
12. Cortez, P., Silva, A.M.G.: Using data mining to predict secondary school student performance (2008)
13. Dieterich, W., Mendoza, C., Brennan, T.: COMPAS risk scales: demonstrating accuracy equity and predictive parity. Northpointe Inc. (2016)
14. Dua, D., Karra Taniskidou, E.: UCI machine learning repository. School of Information and Computer Science (2017). http://archive.ics.uci.edu/ml
15. Dunning, I., Huchette, J., Lubin, M.: JuMP: a modeling language for mathematical optimization. SIAM Rev. **59**(2), 295–320 (2017)

16. Dwork, C., Hardt, M., Pitassi, T., Reingold, O., Zemel, R.S.: Fairness through awareness. In: Innovations in Theoretical Computer Science (2012)
17. Feldman, M., Friedler, S.A., Moeller, J., Scheidegger, C., Venkatasubramanian, S.: Certifying and removing disparate impact. In: ACM SIGKDD International Conference on Knowledge Discovery and Data Mining (2015)
18. Fish, B., Kun, J., Lelkes, Á.D.: A confidence-based approach for balancing fairness and accuracy. In: SIAM International Conference on Data Mining (2016)
19. Friedler, S.A., Scheidegger, C., Venkatasubramanian, S., Choudhary, S., Hamilton, E.P., Roth, D.: A comparative study of fairness-enhancing interventions in machine learning. In: Conference on Fairness, Accountability, and Transparency (2019)
20. Grari, V., Ruf, B., Lamprier, S., Detyniecki, M.: Achieving fairness with decision trees: an adversarial approach. Data Sci. Eng. **5**(2), 99–110 (2020)
21. Gurobi Optimization, LLC: Gurobi optimizer reference manual (2021). https://www.gurobi.com
22. Hardt, M., Price, E., Srebro, N.: Equality of opportunity in supervised learning. In: Annual Conference on Neural Information Processing Systems (2016)
23. Hofmann, H.: Statlog (German Credit Data) Data Set (2021). https://archive.ics.uci.edu/ml/datasets/statlog+(german+credit+data)
24. Kamiran, F., Calders, T., Pechenizkiy, M.: Discrimination aware decision tree learning. In: IEEE International Conference on Data Mining (2010)
25. Kamiran, F., Karim, A., Zhang, X.: Decision theory for discrimination-aware classification. In: IEEE International Conference on Data Mining (2012)
26. Kamishima, T., Akaho, S., Asoh, H., Sakuma, J.: Fairness-aware classifier with prejudice remover regularizer. In: Flach, P.A., De Bie, T., Cristianini, N. (eds.) ECML PKDD 2012. LNCS (LNAI), vol. 7524, pp. 35–50. Springer, Heidelberg (2012). https://doi.org/10.1007/978-3-642-33486-3_3
27. Lewis, R.J.: An introduction to classification and regression tree (CART) analysis. In: Annual Meeting of the Society for Academic Emergency Medicine (2000)
28. Meyer, A., Albarghouthi, A., D'Antoni, L.: Certifying robustness to programmable data bias in decision trees. In: Advances in Neural Information Processing Systems (2021)
29. Quinlan, J.R.: C4.5: Programs for Machine Learning. Elsevier, Amesterdam (2014)
30. Raff, E., Sylvester, J., Mills, S.: Fair forests: regularized tree induction to minimize model bias. In: AAAI/ACM Conference on AI, Ethics, and Society (2018)
31. Thanh, B.L., Ruggieri, S., Turini, F.: k-NN as an implementation of situation testing for discrimination discovery and prevention. In: ACM SIGKDD International Conference on Knowledge Discovery and Data Mining (2011)
32. Torfah, H., Shah, S., Chakraborty, S., Akshay, S., Seshia, S.A.: Synthesizing pareto-optimal interpretations for black-box models. In: International Conference on Formal Methods in Computer Aided Design (2021)
33. Valdivia, A., Sánchez-Monedero, J., Casillas, J.: How fair can we go in machine learning? Assessing the boundaries of accuracy and fairness. Int. J. Intell. Syst. **36**(4), 1619–1643 (2021)
34. Verma, A., Murali, V., Singh, R., Kohli, P., Chaudhuri, S.: Programmatically interpretable reinforcement learning. In: International Conference on Machine Learning (2018)
35. Verwer, S., Zhang, Y.: Learning decision trees with flexible constraints and objectives using integer optimization. In: International Conference on AI and OR Techniques in Constraint Programming for Combinatorial Optimization Problems (2017)

36. Weisberg, S.: Applied Linear Regression. Wiley, Hoboken (2005)
37. Yeh, I.C., Lien, C.H.: The comparisons of data mining techniques for the predictive accuracy of probability of default of credit card clients. Exp. Syst. Appl. **36**(2), 2473–2480 (2009)
38. Zafar, M.B., Valera, I., Rogriguez, M.G., Gummadi, K.P.: Fairness constraints: mechanisms for fair classification. In: Artificial Intelligence and Statistics (2017)

SMT-Based Translation Validation
for Machine Learning Compiler

Seongwon Bang[1], Seunghyeon Nam[1], Inwhan Chun[1], Ho Young Jhoo[1],
and Juneyoung Lee[2]($\boxtimes$) iD

[1] Seoul National University, Seoul, Korea
{seongwon.bang,seunghyeon.nam,inwhan.chun,
hoyoung.jhoo}@sf.snu.ac.kr
[2] CryptoLab, Seoul, Korea
aqjune@cryptolab.co.kr

Abstract. Machine learning compilers are large software containing complex transformations for deep learning models, and any buggy transformation may cause a crash or silently bring a regression to the prediction accuracy and performance. This paper proposes an SMT-based translation validation framework for Multi-Level IR (MLIR), a compiler framework used by many deep learning compilers. It proposes an SMT encoding tailored for translation validation that is an over-approximation of the FP arithmetic and reduction operations. It performs abstraction refinement if validation fails. We also propose a new approach for encoding arithmetic properties of reductions in SMT. We found mismatches between the specification and implementation of MLIR, and validated high-level transformations for `SqueezeNet`, `MobileNet`, and `text_classification` with proper splitting.

1 Introduction

Machine learning compilers play a crucial role in the deep learning ecosystem. Their primary goal is to lower high-level tensor operations into fast machine instructions. To boost the speed of training and inference, they utilize several optimizations. Tensors' layouts may be changed for spatial locality, and loops lowered from tensor operations may be fused and offloaded into GPUs if beneficial. Any bug in the optimizations may cause a crash or silently bring a regression to the prediction accuracy and performance.

However, verifying machine learning compilers is a challenging goal. Opensource compilers like XLA, Glow, and MLIR are being updated daily. As their intermediate representations (IRs) are for internal uses, they are sometimes underspecified, making their formalization hard. Furthermore, programmers want to boost the performance at the expense of precision by allowing unsafe arithmetic properties such as associativity of addition.

Supplementary Information The online version contains supplementary material available at https://doi.org/10.1007/978-3-031-13188-2_19.

S. Shoham and Y. Vizel (Eds.): CAV 2022, LNCS 13372, pp. 386–407, 2022.
https://doi.org/10.1007/978-3-031-13188-2_19

Recently, SMT-based automatic translation validation has gained attention [33] because it fits well with fast-moving industrial compilers. Translation validation is an approach to checking whether a specific compilation is correct by inspecting the source (input) and target (output) programs. To cover a variety of compiler optimizations, it uses an SMT solver which is an automatic theorem prover for first-order logic. Using an SMT solver allows us to quickly explore possible semantics for IRs by implementing them and validating compilations of various programs.

A key challenge is how to make SMT solvers prove the verification condition in a reasonable time. To use an SMT solver, the given problem must not be too complex. Bit-vector and uninterpreted function (UF) theories are well-supported by the majority of solvers, whereas floating-point numbers are not [14]. This implies that finding an efficient encoding for tensors and their operations is important for practical validation of machine learning compilers.

In this paper, we propose an SMT-based translation validation framework for Multi-Level IR (MLIR). MLIR is a compiler framework for facilitating the modular development of domain-specific compilers by sharing IRs and relevant transformations. MLIR is primarily used by TensorFlow, TFLite, and IREE. More deep learning frameworks like PyTorch are adding supports for MLIR.

Our goal is to validate high-level, target-independent intraprocedural transformations in MLIR. These include lowering high-level tensor operations to loops, bufferizing tensors, simplifying tensor/buffer operations, and simple loop optimizations. Our tool does not receive hints about the ongoing transformation from the compiler.

The list of contributions of our paper is as follows:

- The first SMT-based translation validation for MLIR (Sect. 3).
- An abstract representation of FP arithmetic for translation validation (Sect. 4).
- An SMT encoding of tensor operations and loops as well as fast encoding of arithmetic properties of reduction operations (Sect. 5).
- Validation of compilation of three deep learning models as well as hundreds of unit tests in MLIR (Sect. 7).
- A discovery of several ambiguities in the semantics of MLIR (Sect. 7).

2   Multi-level Intermediate Representation (MLIR)

The MLIR project is an open-source compiler infrastructure that facilitates the modular development of domain-specific compilers by sharing reusable parts. The reusable parts are dialects and relevant compiler transformations. A dialect is a subset of a compiler's intermediate representation language. An intermediate representation (IR) program in MLIR is expressed using one or more dialects. They are ultimately lowered into the input languages of low-level code generation frameworks such as LLVM IR or SPIR-V through first-class dialects. We will introduce several core dialects in MLIR, which are also our targets for validation.

Dialects for Tensors. The `tensor` and `tosa` (Tensor Operator Set Architecture) dialects define the tensor type and operations. Pre-trained machine learning models can be lowered to them via importers.

A tensor type consists of an element type and dimensions. The tensor dimensions can be dynamic, which are retrievable in runtime. Its elements can be accessed through, e.g., `tensor.extract` with valid indices. Tensor registers do not alias each other and are in the static single assignment (SSA) form. `tosa` provides a set of operations commonly employed by deep neural networks, such as a convolution or pooling.

```
// f32 is the float type in C
func @calc(%img : tensor<2x64x64x3xf32>,
        %filter : tensor<16x3x6x3xf32>) {
%c0 = arith.constant -0.0 : f32
%bias = tensor.from_elements %c0, ... , %c0
                    : tensor<16xf32>
%res = tosa.conv2d(%img, %filter, %bias)
        ...->tensor<2x62x59x16xf32>
return %res : tensor<2x62x59x16xf32>
}
```

(a) A convolution operation.

```
#col_major = affine_map<(d0, d1)->(d1*3+d0)>
func @example(%arg0 : memref<2x3xf32>,
    %arg1 : memref<2x3xf32, #col_major>) {
...
}
```

(b) Two `memref` arguments.

```
#map0 = affine_map<(d0, d1, d2)->(d0, d2)>
#map1 = affine_map<(d0, d1, d2)->(d2, d1)>
#map2 = affine_map<(d0, d1, d2)->(d0, d1)>
// i32 is the 32-bit int type in C
%output = linalg.generic {
// #map0, #map1: maps for %A, %B
// #map2:       a map for %C
indexing_maps = [#map0, #map1, #map2],
iterator_types = ["parallel", "parallel",
                            "reduction"]}
ins(%A, %B : tensor<16x8xi32>,
                tensor<8x32xi32>)
outs(%C : tensor<16x32xi32>) {
^bb0(%a: i32, %b: i32, %c: i32):
    %ab  = arith.muli %a, %b : i32
    %res = arith.addi %c, %ab : i32
    linalg.yield %res : i32
} -> tensor<16x32xi32>
```

(c) `%C+%A×%B` in `linalg`.

Fig. 1. Dialects for tensors and buffers in MLIR.

The @calc function in Fig. 1(a) takes two tensor arguments, performs convolution (`tosa.conv2d`), and returns the result. The input bias and output tensor are stored at tensor-typed virtual registers `%bias` and `%res`. Note that different dialects – `tensor`, `tosa`, and `arith` (dialect for simple arithmetic operations) – can exist in one IR program.

MemRef Dialect. The `memref` dialect has a type for memory references (which is also called `memref`) and relevant operations. The `memref` type is similar to a pointer type in C but has richer information than that. It has a layout map that maps multidimensional, logical indices into a one-dimensional, physical address[1]. It is used to create a view of a specific memory region in the form of a tensor. It supports arbitrary access patterns such as strided accesses or a transposed view. MLIR transformations assume that the layout map is injective.

Figure 1(b) shows two `memref` arguments with different layout maps. `%arg0` has a default row-major layout map. On the other hand, `%arg1` has a column-major layout map meaning that `%arg1[i][j]` is located at offset $(i + j \times 3)$ from the reference point. The values multiplied by offsets d0, d1 (1 and 3 in `#col_major`) are called strides.

---

[1] Its domain can also be multidimensional in general, but we do not support the case.

Linalg Dialect. The `linalg` dialect contains various loop-like operations on tensors and buffers. `linalg` operations are more primitive than `tosa`'s and can be performed on buffers.

In `linalg`, one can represent a generic loop in a structured form using the `linalg.generic` operation. Each loop explicitly takes input tensors or buffers as its operands. The loop's indexing maps describe which elements are chosen at each iteration. The elements chosen from the inputs at an iteration are represented as input arguments of the loop body region.

The loop body yields a value at each iteration, and the results constitute the output elements. A loop that takes an output buffer writes the resulting elements to the buffer. A loop that takes an output tensor stores the resulting tensor in a new tensor register, which can later be used as another input tensor.

Figure 1(c) shows how to represent %C + %A × %B for three matrices %A, %B, and %C in `linalg.generic`. %C and the resulting tensor (%output)'s shapes must be the same. The `linalg.generic` is a triple nested loop that has three induction variables d0, d1, d2. The `indexing_maps` describe which elements of the tensors are retrieved in each iteration. The retrieved elements are assigned into block arguments %a, %b, and %c of the loop body. The loop body performs integral multiplication (`arith.muli`) followed by addition (`arith.addi`) and yields it to the next iteration which again becomes %c. `iterator_type` shows that the third (innermost) loop is a reduction loop because it is doing summation, whereas the two outer loops can be parallelized.

`linalg` is the source and target dialect of several key transformations. First, `tosa`'s operations can be lowered into the combination of `linalg`'s operations on tensors. Second, bufferization on `linalg`'s operations changes their tensor operands into buffers. Third, the `linalg.generic` loops can be optimized into fused `linalg.generic` loops or simpler operations. Fourth, conversions from `linalg` to lower level dialects yield for loops (`affine`, `scf`) or control-flow graphs (`standard`).

Transformations in MLIR. MLIR provides transformations that (1) convert the input programs written in high-level dialects into the low-level ones, or (2) optimize the input program into more efficient form. Except for those that intentionally change the input program's behavior, transformations must preserve the behavior.

3   Overview

In this section, we introduce `mlir-tv`, a translation validation framework for MLIR. Like other frameworks [22,33,36,41,42], `mlir-tv` takes two programs written in the IR and checks whether the transformation is correct. Since `mlir-tv` targets intraprocedural transformations, functions in the two programs with the same signature are checked pairwisely. `mlir-tv` relies on an SMT solver to automatically prove that the transformation is correct or find a counterexample if incorrect.

`mlir-tv` symbolically encodes each MLIR instruction in a function and emits its final state in a logical formula. After encoding the final states of the source and target functions f_{src} and f_{tgt}, `mlir-tv` checks a refinement predicate using an SMT solver. The predicate states that for any input state I consisting of an initial memory and argument values, $f_{\mathrm{src}}(I) \sqsupseteq f_{\mathrm{tgt}}(I)$ must hold where $\sqsupseteq$ is a refinement relation between two final states (Sect. 6.3). If the SMT solver finds an input that breaks the refinement, `mlir-tv` concludes that the compiler transformation is incorrect. If the SMT solver proves that such input does not exist, the transformation is correct.

3.1 Abstraction for Floating-Point Arithmetic

For practical validation of tensor transformations, it is crucial to efficiently represent floating-point (FP) arithmetic in SMT. SMT-LIB 2 formally supports IEEE-754 [10] under the name of the FPA theory [37]. SMT solvers supporting the FPA theory typically simulate the hardware implementation of the FP arithmetic by representing their bits as boolean variables and converting FP operations into boolean expressions (called *bit-blasting*) [13]. Then, the formula can be efficiently solved using their highly optimized SAT solvers.

However, there are two challenges in using the FPA theory to prove transformations on tensors. First, encoding FP arithmetic in SMT is expensive because solvers internally yield large expressions. Also, a significant portion of tensor transformations does not require such precise encoding. For example, bufferization is agnostic to the representation of the underlying values because its goal is *moving* the virtual registers to memory buffers correctly. Second, machine learning compilers want to support transformations that are incorrect under IEEE-754 for performance. We cannot simply rely on FPA in this case because it will invalidate the transformations.

To address these concerns, `mlir-tv` abstractly encodes the FP operations (Sect. 4). We find an abstract domain for FP numbers that is *specific* to the transformation to validate. It uses over-approximations meaning that a successful validation implies the correctness of the transformation. If it is not validated, `mlir-tv` refines the abstraction and try validation again (Sect. 6.3).

3.2 The Formal Semantics of Dialects

Since there is no official formal semantics for MLIR dialects yet, we read the textual specification of MLIR dialects and represented them in the encoding function. The function returns the final state in SMT expressions. Therefore, it implicitly defines the big-step formal semantics of the dialects in MLIR. Also, the function contains encoding rules for each instruction, which implicitly represent its small-step semantics.

Note that we are not proposing new formal semantics for unsafe FP arithmetic. We assume that there exists a valid FP semantics that satisfies certain arithmetic properties. The concrete semantics of FP operations is hidden under the uninterpreted functions used for the abstract encoding. The semantics of unsafe FP arithmetic is often explained using nondeterministic execution [11] and encoding it in SMT requires universal quantification which is expensive.

4   Encoding Floating-Point Numbers and Tensors

To overcome the challenges described in Sect. 3.1, we devise an abstract encoding of FP arithmetic tailored for translation validation. In this abstract encoding, an FP number is represented as a bit-vector that is typically smaller than its original bit width. The operations on FP numbers are represented as UFs satisfying arithmetic properties like commutativity. Our encoding does not miss bugs because it is an over-approximation of the FP arithmetic. On the other hand, validation failure does not always mean that the transformation is wrong.

4.1   Abstract Domain of Floating-Point Numbers

We begin with defining an abstract domain for FP numbers that is specific to the transformation to validate. We count the number of distinct FP numbers that are required to express at least one counterexample if the transformation is incorrect. As a result, if it is possible to prove that no counterexample is found in this abstract domain, no concrete counterexample can exist.

Consider a transformation that swaps the two operands of FP addition. An invocation of the source function (top) can observe at most three distinct FP numbers because it has three FP registers %a, %b, and %c_src. Similarly, the target function (below) can observe at most three different numbers. The number of distinct FP numbers required to validate the transformation is not greater than $4 = 3 + 3 - 2$ since two of those are shared as arguments.

```
// The source function
func @f(%a: f32, %b: f32) {
  %c_src = addf %a, %b: f32
  return %c_src: f32
}
```

```
// The target function
func @f(%a: f32, %b: f32) {
  %c_tgt = addf %b, %a: f32
  return %c_tgt: f32
}
```

After counting the number, we abstractly represent the values of FP registers and constants using bit-vectors. For the above example, 2 bits are enough in theory because $4 \leq 2^2$. We will use notation $[\![\%a]\!]$ to represent the abstract bit-vector value of %a. In SMT, two bit-vector variables are declared for %a and %b because they can be any value, and %c_src and %c_tgt are defined as expressions with respect to the variables.

Defining Operations. To abstractly define addf, we declare a UF for addition. If the arithmetic properties of addition are ignored, $[\![\text{addf}(\%a, \%b)]\!]$ may be defined as $\text{addf}_{\text{SMT}}([\![\%a]\!], [\![\%b]\!])$ where the definition of UF addf_{SMT} is arbitrarily determined by the SMT solver. Since the solver's goal is to find a counterexample, it will try to find a definition of addf_{SMT} that breaks the transformation. If the solver couldn't find one, the transformation is correct under any definition of FP addition.

Note that validating the above example requires encoding commutativity 'addf$_\text{SMT}$([%a], [%b]) = addf$_\text{SMT}$([%b], [%a])'. Instead of using an expensive universal quantification, we encode addition as 'addf$'_\text{SMT}$(x, y) & addf$'_\text{SMT}$(y, x)' where & is the bitwise and operation and addf$'_\text{SMT}$ is another UF. Without loss of generality, it encodes all possible commutative functions[2].

To encode the result of operations on $\pm 0, \pm 1, \pm$fMAX (finite max), $\pm\infty$ and NaN, we use the ite (if-then-else) expression in SMT. For example, to encode 'NaN + y = NaN', the expression is wrapped with an ite that checks if one of the inputs is NaN. Combined with the commutativity encoding, the expression for $x + y$ becomes as follows. 'x is NaN' is the SMT formula checking x is NaN by inspecting x's abstract representation which will be described later.

$$\text{ite}(x \text{ is NaN} \vee y \text{ is NaN}, \quad \text{NaN}, \quad \text{addf}'_\text{SMT}(x, y) \ \& \ \text{addf}'_\text{SMT}(y, x))$$

Using UFs and ites, we abstractly encode $+, -, \times, /$ and x^y. Subtraction is defined as an addition of the negated second operand. Division is not equivalent to multiplication of the inversed operand due to the existence of subnormal values. Therefore, it is encoded using a separate UF.

Comparisons, $|x|$ and $-x$ are precisely encoded because our bit-vector representation natively supports them. Their representation will be described below.

Bit-vector Structure. A bit-vector for FP consists of a sign bit (SB) at its most significant bit and magnitude bits (MB) at the entire lesser significant bits. They represent the sign and the order of absolute value of the original number, respectively. Therefore, comparing the magnitudes of two finite FP numbers is equivalent to simply comparing their MBs. If MB$[1 \ldots |\text{MB}| - 1]$ are all set to 1, the original value is ∞ (MB$[0] = 0$) or NaN value (1). Unlike IEEE-754 [10] which have multiple NaN values per sign, we have one representation per sign[3].

The bit-vector representation of an FP constant number is a concatenation of the sign bit and magnitude bits which is a bit-vector variable in SMT. The bit-vector variables are given preconditions so that a constant with a larger absolute value is guaranteed to have larger MB.

Supporting Floating Point Casts. To support FP casts, MB is further split into three parts: limit bits (LB), truncated bits (TB), and precision bits (PB) in descending significance order. These parts determine the result of casting the value into a smaller FP type. LB represents the overflow condition. If LB is 0, a cast to the smaller size yields a finite value. If not, it yields $\pm\infty$. TB represents the magnitude floored to the target type. Its bit width is equivalent to the bit width of MB of the smaller type. PB represents the offset from the floored value. If PB is 0, the value is truncated to the exact value without loss of precision. Otherwise, the value must be rounded, and the direction is determined by a UF

---

[2] We describe its formal proof in our online supplementary material [5].

[3] We chose this policy because respecting the bits invalidates several transformations in LLVM and the behavior of processors canonicalizing NaN values [33].

returning boolean. Extension is done by copying MB to TB and filling LB and PB with 0^4.

4.2   Encoding Tensors

In SMT, a tensor is represented as an array expression from the address space-sized bit-vector to the element type. A multidimensional tensor is encoded as a one-dimensional array in row-major order. The dimension sizes of dynamically shaped tensor arguments are encoded as bit-vector variables. The number of elements of a tensor cannot exceed the size of the address space.

For each tensor argument in MLIR function, a new SMT array variable is assigned because its value can be fully arbitrary. The results of tensor operations are encoded as lambda expressions in SMT which is described in Sect. 5.1.

Uninitialized Tensors. A tensor may contain uninitialized elements. In SMT, a tensor carries another boolean array that indicates uninitialized elements.

We define accessing uninitialized elements as an undefined behavior (UB) for the following reason. During bufferization, `linalg.init_tensor` operation that returns an uninitialized tensor is lowered into `memref.alloc`. The `memref.alloc` operation is then converted into a `malloc` call in LLVM IR, reading uninitialized bytes of which and using them may raise UB.

Tensor arguments in MLIR are assumed to be fully initialized. `linalg`'s `init_tensor` is the only operation that creates an uninitialized tensor. Operations like `tensor.insert` can create a partially initialized tensor.

4.3   Calculating the Bit Width

The bit width of the abstract representation of FP numbers is decided by the number of float registers and constants. Since all FP registers can store distinct FP numbers, the number of different FP numbers that may appear during the source and target program execution is bounded by the number of FP registers and distinct constants.

However, an operation that does not return an FP number can internally observe an unseen number. For example, suppose `is_int(x)` that returns true if float `x` is an integral value. Given an UF $floor_{SMT}(x)$ that returns an abstract float with its decimal truncated, this operation can be encoded as '`x == `$floor_{SMT}(x)$', which hides an unseen number in $floor_{SMT}(x)$.

Therefore, we count the number of UFs applied to abstract FP numbers while encoding the source and target instructions. The size of the BV field is $\lceil \log_2 N \rceil$ where N is the number of applied UFs added by the number of FP arguments as well as distinct constants of the source and target functions. From the above example, `is_int(x)` must increment N even if it returns boolean because $floor_{SMT}(x)$ can return an unseen FP value.

---

[4] We describe the full encoding of constants of different types and other details in our online supplementary material [5].

```
func @f(%x, %y: tensor<8xf32>) {    func @f(%x, %y: tensor<8xf32>,    func @f(...) -> f32 {
  %z_src = tosa.add %x, %y                %i: index) -> f32 {           %x_i, %y_i = %x[%i], %y[%i]
  return %z_src                       %z_src = tosa.add %x, %y         %z_src_i = addf %x_i, %y_i
}                                     %z_src_i = %z_src[%i]            return %z_src_i
                                      return %z_src_i               }
                                    }


func @f(%x, %y: tensor<8xf32>) {    func @f(%x, %y: tensor<8xf32>,    func @f(...) -> f32 {
  %z_tgt = tosa.add %y, %x                %i: index) -> f32 {           %x_i, %y_i = %x[%i], %y[%i]
  return %z_tgt                       %z_tgt = tosa.add %y, %x         %z_tgt_i = addf %y_i, %x_i
}                                     %z_tgt_i = %z_tgt[%i]            return %z_tgt
                                      return %z_tgt                 }
                                    }

            (a)                                 (b)                              (c)
```

Fig. 2. Reducing elementwise tensor operations into scalar operations.

Considering Tensors and Memory. In general, a tensor with M elements must increase N by M because it can have M different floats. To reduce the bound, we again rely on the fact that finding only *one* counter-example is enough. If that counter-example is a tensor, one mismatched element is sufficient.

If all tensor operations in functions are elementwise, we can simply ignore tensors' dimensions and count them as FP numbers when evaluating N. Consider the example in Fig. 2(a). To validate that transforming the upper f to the lower f is correct, we must check whether %z_src[i] and %z_tgt[i] are equal for any i. Therefore, we can rewrite the functions into the form in Fig. 2(b) without affecting the correctness of the transformation. Note that the return types of two functions are changed from tensor to float. Since tosa.add is an instruction that performs addf elementwisely, choosing i from tosa.add only requires i'th elements from its input tensors. Therefore, the functions can again be rewritten as in Fig. 2(c). Since only the i'th elements of tensors %x and %y are used, the functions can again be rewritten to take %x_i and %y_i as function arguments instead, which is not depicted in the figure. Therefore, validating the initial pair is equivalent to validating two functions taking and adding two FP numbers.

Given a memref value, one can only access in-bounds locations. Thus, its size is added into N. If all tensor operations are elementwise, it is counted as one.

5   Supporting Tensor Operations and Loops

In this section, we introduce the SMT encoding of tensor operations and loops.

5.1   Encoding Tensor Operations

The result of a tensor operation is encoded as a lambda expression in SMT. For example, a negation of tensor t is encoded as 'lambda i, negate(select(t, i))' where i is a 32 bit-vector variable, 'select(t, i)' selects the i-th element from the SMT array of t, and 'negate(bv)' is an alias for an SMT expression extracting the sign bit of bv and concatenating its negation with its BV bits. Note that it does not check whether i is within the bound of the tensor. It is because the values at out-of-bounds indices cannot affect the program's behavior.

For operations returning a multidimensional tensor, the lambda chooses and returns the element in row-major order. For example, transpose of t whose size is $N \times N$ is encoded as 'lambda i, select(t, $i\%N \times N + i/N$)'.

Encoding Reduction Operations. In general, reduction operations like summation of an array cannot be precisely encoded in SMT-LIB 2. To support them, we abstractly encode the reduction operations using UFs. For example, we declare sum which is a UF taking an array and returning a float number. Since this is an over-approximation, the validation may fail. In this case, we perform abstraction refinement, which will be described in Sect. 6.3.

The out-of-bounds elements of an array are wiped out before applying to UF because they must not affect the result. This is done by wrapping the input array with lambda and select. The select returns the value that do not affect the result of the reduction (e.g., -0.0 for a summation) if the index is out of bounds.

Tensor Operations and Undefined Behavior. The documentation was not clear about the behavior of a program violating the assumptions that tensor operations expect at runtime. The violations include out-of-bounds access, size mismatch of the dynamic-shaped tensors, and reading an uninitialized element. If it is defined as having well-defined side effects such as calling exit, dead tensor operations cannot be freely removed and lowering to LLVM IR whose behavior may be undefined cannot be explained. Therefore, we define them as UB.

5.2 Encoding Loops

In MLIR, linalg loops are typically generated from high-level tensor operations. Compared to loops in general programs, they are simple and syntactically provide rich information. The loop consists of instructions without side-effect (modulo UB), and linalg loops explicitly state input/output tensors' index mappings as well as parallelizable induction variables. Therefore, we can construct the output tensor or buffer without synthesizing loop invariants.

```
#id = affine_map<(d0, d1) -> (d0, d1)>
#transposed = affine_map<(d0, d1) -> (d1, d0)>

// %C = %A + %B^T, %C's shape = %out's shape
%C = linalg.generic {indexing_maps = [#id, #transposed, #id],
                     iterator_types = ["parallel", "parallel"]}
    ins(%A, %B : tensor<?x?xf32>) outs(%out : tensor<?x?xf32>) {
^bb0(%a: f32, %b: f32, %unused: f32):
  %c = arith.addf %a, %b: f32
  linalg.yield %c : f32
} -> tensor<?x?xf32>
```

Consider the above loop that adds tensors %A and %B^T. Indexing maps (#id, #transposed, #id) are mappings from two induction variables (hence a doubly nested loop) to the indices of input (%A, %B) and output (%out) tensors. The loop body shows that the initial value of %out is not used. Since iterations over each dimension have no dependency because they are parallel (iterator_types), we can conclude that %out[i][j] = %A[i][j] + %B[j][i].

In this section, we propose an encoding of loops in linalg using the lambda theory and a universal quantification. Encoding a loop in linalg starts with finding loop bounds. Loop bounds are determined by matching the ranges of the indexing maps with the tensor (buffer) sizes. Then, the loop body which yields the element of the resulting tensor is encoded. If the output type is tensor, the resulting tensor is encoded in lambda in row-major order. If the output type is buffer, the memory locations are accordingly updated.

For the above example, the yielded result at each iteration is described as a lambda expression with two parameters: 'lambda (d_0, d_1), add(%A$[d_0, d_1]$, %B$[d_1, d_0]$)'. Then, the output tensor %C is encoded as a lambda with a single parameter i. It selects $(i\,/\,N, i\,\%\,N)$ from the first lambda where N is %out's width.

Determining Loop Bounds. If the sizes of %A and %B are larger than that of %out, should the linalg.generic raise UB or add parts of the inputs?

To find its valid semantics, the first transformation to consider is linalg's conversion from linalg.generic to a canonical for loop in another dialect. The conversion generates a for loop with the upper bounds of induction variables explicitly given. The conversion sequentially visits the indexing maps, and finds the first dimension that exactly matches. Exact matching means that the range of the indexing map must be identity, not e.g., d0 + 1. If such dimension cannot be found, the linalg.generic is considered syntactically invalid.

The second transformation is the canonicalization of linalg.generic. If a linalg.generic loop iterates over the input tensors and simply returns the elements, its output is replaced with the input tensors regardless of the input/output tensors' shapes. However, if we determine the loop bounds only by the shape of the first matched tensor, this transformation cannot be justified when input tensors have different sizes.

Therefore, we encode the loop bounds of linalg.generic as follows. First, we find loop bounds according to the algorithm of the first transformation (generic to for). For the above example, the upper bounds of d0 and d1 are the dimension's sizes of %A because the first indexing map is for %A. Second, all input tensors' shapes must match the determined loop bounds, otherwise UB. In the case of the above example, %A, %B and %out's shapes must be equal.

Encoding Loops on Buffers. If inputs/outputs are buffers, tensors are loaded from the inputs, the loop is performed on the tensors, and the resulting tensor is stored into the output buffer. The input and output buffers of linalg.generic must be disjoint (Sect. 6.2). If the output buffer's layout map is identity, the output memory block is updated using lambda. If not, a fresh SMT array for the updated block is created, and the equalities between old/new elements of the block and the output tensor are encoded using forall quantifications.

Encoding Reduction Loops. Induction variables which have "`parallel`" in the `iterator_types` attribute must appear as the parameters of the SMT lambda expression. Other variables, however, must be accordingly encoded. To encode reduction loops, we syntactically match the operand of the last `yield` and use the corresponding UF for the reduction (Sect. 5.1). This worked well in practice because the reduction loops in MLIR had common patterns.

5.3 Supporting Arithmetic Properties of Reductions

Floating-point addition and multiplication are not associative, but programmers sometimes want to boost performance at the expense of precision by allowing compiler optimizations that rely on the property. To encode the property, the definition of addition and multiplication must be different from IEEE-754 because using it causes inconsistency in the underlying logic.

Then, what is the semantics of $x + y + z$? One possible solution is that its evaluation nondeterministically yields either $(x+y)+z$ or $x+(y+z)$ [11]. However, encoding the semantics in SMT requires introducing quantified variables.

Therefore, as described in Sect. 5.1, we start from abstractly encoding reduction operations in UFs. For example, UF `sum` takes an array $[x, y, z]$ and returns its summation. A question is how to encode their arithmetic properties like $\mathtt{sum}([\mathtt{sum}([x,y]),z]) = \mathtt{sum}([x,\mathtt{sum}([y,z])])$. We introduce a new technique that works when the length of the input array is constant. This technique is not specific to a summation but can be applied to any reduction.

Encoding Commutativity. The first arithmetic property to consider is commutativity: '$\mathtt{sum}([...,x,...,y,...]) = \mathtt{sum}([...,y,...,x,...])$'.

A straightforward solution is to use the multiset theory. Two `sum`s are considered equal if the multisets converted from input arrays are equal. For the solvers that do not support the multiset theory, a multiset can be simulated using an array taking an element and returning its count. However, this multiset-based approach does not scale well (Sect. 7.3). We conjecture that existing algorithms in the solvers are not good at checking the equality of two multisets (cvc5)/counter arrays (Z3).

We suggest a hash-based approach for encoding the multiset equality. Our approach begins with defining a hash function F on an array. If two arrays are equal, their hash values must be equal. The inverse holds when the range of F is sufficiently large. It only uses the theory of UF and BV, which are cheap.

To define F, we define another hash function f on floating-point numbers. $F(A)$ is defined as a summation of hash values of its elements $\sum_{x \in A} f(x)$. By the arithmetic property of bit-vector addition, $F(A) = F(A')$ if A' is a permutation of A. The inverse direction also holds. We prove that if $F(A) = F(A')$ for any f, A' is a permutation of A.

Theorem 1. *Given A and A' that are arrays of type T, if $\forall f . \sum_{x\in A} f(x) = \sum_{x\in A'} f(x)$ where $f \in T \to BV(\lceil \log_2 max(|A|, |A'|)\rceil)$, A' is a permutation of A.*

Proof. Let's assume that $count(S, x)$ is the number of x in multiset S. For example, $count(\{1, 1, 3\}, 1)$ is 2. We first prove the following lemma.

Lemma 1. *Given two multisets S and S', $S = S'$ holds if*

$$\forall g, \left(\sum_{x\in S} count(S, x) \times g(x) \right) = \left(\sum_{x\in S'} count(S', x) \times g(x) \right)$$

where $g \in T \to BV(\lceil \log_2 max(|S|, |S'|)\rceil)$.

Proof. Assume that $g_k(x)$ is a function that returns 1 if $x = k$ and 0 otherwise. By picking each element of S as k and $g = g_k$, $S = S'$ holds.   □

Assume that S is a multiset from array A and S' from A'. From the assumption $\forall f . \sum_{x\in A} f(x) = \sum_{x\in A'} f(x)$, we can derive $\forall g, \left(\sum_{x\in S} count(S, x) \times g(x)\right) = \left(\sum_{x\in S'} count(S', x) \times g(x)\right)$. Then, we can apply the lemma. By the conclusion of the lemma, the two multisets are equal, hence A is a permutation of A'.   □

For each pair of two sum function calls appearing in the source and target, their equality is encoded as a constraint. Since $P \implies Q$ iff $\neg Q \implies \neg P$, the universal quantification in the Theorem 1 can be converted into an existential form '$\texttt{sum}(A) \neq \texttt{sum}(A') \implies \exists f . \sum_{x\in A} f(x) \neq \sum_{x\in A'} f(x)$'. Since $\exists f$ can be moved out, the precondition is quantifier-free.

Encoding Flattening of a Nested Reduction. By expanding the hash function based approach, we can encode the equality between nested reductions. Consider this equality: '$\texttt{sum}([\texttt{sum}(A), \texttt{sum}(B)]) = \texttt{sum}(A +\!\!+ B)$'.

Since the array $[\texttt{sum}(A), \texttt{sum}(B)]$ is not a permutation of $A +\!\!+ B$, the previous encoding does guarantee that the two summations are equivalent. To support this case, given a hash function F and summation $\texttt{sum}(A)$, we add a precondition $F(\texttt{sum}(A)) = \sum_{x\in A} F(x)$. That is, the hash value of $\texttt{sum}(A)$ is equivalent to the summation of hash values of $x \in A$.

Note that the hash function is individually defined per a pair of summations in the programs. This causes additional preconditions for each hash pair to relate inner and outer summation. We reduce the number of preconditions by unifying hash functions into one[5].

6   Encoding Memory and Refinement

MLIR has several dialects providing memory operations, such as $\texttt{memref}$, $\texttt{affine}$, and $\texttt{bufferization}$. We propose a memory model for these dialects. Also, we illustrate our SMT encoding for the model.

---

[5] Due to the limited space, we prove that the unified hash function's range must not be smaller than $[0, p^2 n)$ where p is the number of summation pairs and n is the maximum size of an array in our online supplementary material [5].

6.1   Memory Model

Memory Block. A memory is made up of smaller memory blocks in our memory model. A memory block is a unit of a memory allocation, and is either created by `memref.alloc`, `memref.alloca`, clone-like operations of `bufferization`, or defining a global variable. `memref.alloca` allocates a block at stack whereas `memref.alloc` has no such constraint. `memref.dealloc` frees the block.

A memory block is uniquely identified with a block id. Its properties consist of the number of elements, block type, writability, liveness, and the list of elements with the list of booleans indicating whether each element is initialized. The block type is a boolean value which shows whether it is created by `memref.alloc`. Allocating instruction creates a new memory block which is initially alive, writable, and fully uninitialized. The clone-like operation marks the source block with permanent read-only. The behavior of accessing a dead block is undefined, and also accessing an uninitialized element is undefined behavior. This decision is described in Sect. 4.2 as well.

Memory Reference. The `memref` type is a reference to a specific memory area. It consists of the pointing block's id, block offset, layout map, dimension sizes of the pointing area, and a flag indicating whether it is a view reference. A block offset may be non-zero because `memref` allows creating an aliased reference via `memref.view`, which may not point to the head of the block. `memref` may point to an out-of-bounds area of the block, and accessing that area is UB.

Loading a tensor from `memref` is well-defined if (1) the referenced area is within the bounds of the memory block, (2) the block is alive (i.e. not deallocated yet), and (3) the visited offsets are fully initialized. Writing a tensor is well-defined if the area is in-bounds and the block is alive and writable.

6.2   Encoding the Memory Model

The properties of memory blocks are encoded as SMT variables `size`, `writable`, `liveness`, `block_type`, `elements`, `initialized`. By default, all properties are defined as SMT variables because we cannot make any assumption on how and when a block is created in general. If the block's definition is visible (e.g., it is a global variable), they are initialized with literals in SMT. `elements` and `initialized` are encoded as SMT arrays from the offset to the value and boolean.

The number of blocks necessary to validate the transformation is determined via static analysis, which is described in [30]. The number is bounded because we do not support loops containing allocating operations. This works in practice because allocations are usually located outside of the loops. After the analysis, each block and property declares one SMT variable. The blocks for global variables and allocating operations are assigned constant block ids.

Local and Non-local Blocks. We adopt the notion of local and non-local blocks from [30]. Local blocks are created by the allocating instructions that belong to the validated function, whereas non-local blocks are not. Only the non-local blocks are checked at the refinement of final states. We do not consider escaped local blocks because (1) memref cannot have memref as its element type, and (2) we do not support call instructions.

Encoding Memory Access. The SMT encodings of memory load/store operations follow the encodings described in [30]. The result of loading a value from memref %m is encoded as ite(%m.bid $= 0$, arr$_0$[%m.ofs], ite(%m.bid $= 1, \ldots$)) where arr$_0$ has the elements of memory block 0. Storing a value to memref updates the elements of possibly aliased blocks with ites.

Encoding disjointnesses of two memref accesses – which is required by several buffer operations – is hard in general because a memref can point to non-contiguous locations in arbitrary patterns. Therefore, we support encoding a disjointness of memrefs with trivial, row-major layout maps only, raising an error otherwise.

6.3   Compiler Correctness and Abstraction Refinement

Finally, we compare the final states of the source and target functions. A final state is defined as (ub, m, v) where ub is UB, m is the memory, and v is the return value. A final state refines another, or $(ub, m, v) \sqsupseteq (ub', m', v')$, if (1) ub is true, or (2) $ub = ub' \wedge v = v'^6 \wedge m$ refines m'. A memory m refines m' if for non-local blocks (b, b') with same id in the source and target, if (1) reading b at offset o is successful, so does the access to o at b', and (2) if b is writable, so does b'. For any input state I consisting of an initial memory and argument values, $f_{\mathrm{src}}(I) \sqsupseteq f_{\mathrm{tgt}}(I)$ must hold where $f(I)$ denotes the final state of function f. In SMT, the formula is inverted to remove the outermost quantification.

Abstraction Refinement. To make validations cheap on average, we progressively refine the abstraction scheme that describes the abstraction level of encodings. Abstraction refinement happens when a validation fails or timeouts.

In the first round, the integer and FP dot operations are encoded using independent UFs which are not related to a summation. Also, FP numbers of different types are independently encoded and casts are defined as full UFs. If validation fails, the dot operations are encoded as a composition of a summation and multiplications, and the encoding for casts described in Sect. 4.1 is used. If this also fails, summations of arrays having small constant numbers of elements are unrolled into a sequence of additions and validated again. This validates, for example, folding sum($[1.0, 2.0]$) into $1.0 + 2.0$.

---

[6] For floats, NaNs of different signs are considered equivalent. For memrefs, we do not support references to local blocks because it needs universal quantifications [30]. Validating functions returning such values may result in false alarms.

Our abstraction cannot validate the constant folding optimization in general. To address this, `mlir-tv` provides a command-line option for using IEEE-754. It disables the unsafe properties on reductions because they are not compatible.

7 Implementation and Evaluation

`mlir-tv` consists of 8,900 lines of C++ codes. It supports 25 `tosa` ops, 11 `memref` ops, 13 `linalg` ops, 10 `tensor` ops, 29 `arith` ops, 3 `bufferization` ops, and 8 other ops. `mlir-tv` uses Z3 4.8.13 and cvc5 0.0.3 as a solver, with 30 s timeout. The experiments in this section are performed using Z3 because Z3 showed better performance than cvc5 in `mlir-tv`'s sanity tests. We used the Apple M1 CPU and 16 GB RAM with a fixed version of MLIR (`b5a0f0f`, 26/Dec).

We wrote 57 function pairs to check that it validates correct transformations and finds counterexamples for wrong pairs. From these tests, we observed that using the abstract encoding was 13.6x faster on average than the concrete IEEE-754 encoding. Shrinking the bit width of abstract FP (Sect. 4.3) was important because it brought 2.2x speedup compared to simply using 32 bits.

7.1 Validating MLIR Unit Tests

We validated the unit tests in the official MLIR project using `mlir-tv`. The unit tests (1) apply specific transformations to small, pre-defined MLIR programs, and (2) check whether the output programs syntactically match the test patterns. Using `mlir-tv`, we validated that the outputs of the transformations preserved the semantics of the inputs as well. We bounded the size of dynamic-shaped tensors to 100 to avoid timeouts. Bugs in tests with such tensors may have been missed.

Among the MLIR's unit tests, which consist of 2,467 function pairs in total, `mlir-tv` validated 433 tests, raised timeout for 8 tests, and failed for 8 tests. Validating the tests did not require encoding the unsafe arithmetic properties for reductions, but we are aware of uncovered transformations that require them.

We could find several issues in the semantics of MLIR dialects.

Signed Zero, NaN and $-\infty$. The `tosa.conv2d` and `tosa.depthwise_conv2d` operations are lowered to `linalg.pad_tensor` with the input tensors padded with +0.0. Also, we found that MLIR was folding $x + (+0.0)$ into x. However, this is incorrect since (1) $x + (+0.0) \neq x$ if $x = -0.0$ and (2) the `tosa` specification [6] states that an FP type must support signed zero. This problem was also found from `tosa.fully_connected` and `tosa.reduce_sum` operations whose lowered loops fill the initial tensors with +0.0. We reported these issues to the LLVM community. After the report, $x + (+0.0) \rightarrow x$ folding has been fixed [1]. We also found that lowering `tosa.clamp` and `tosa.max_pool2d` does not preserve their outputs if the inputs contain a NaN and $-\infty$ value.

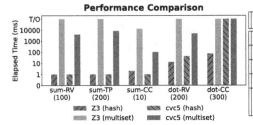

Name	Transformation
sum-RV	$\Sigma \mathrm{rev}(X) \to \Sigma X$
sum-TP	$\Sigma X^T \to \Sigma X$
sum-CC	$\Sigma(\Sigma X_1, \Sigma X_2) \to \Sigma(X_1 + \!\!+ X_2)$
dot-RV	$\mathrm{rev}(X_1) \cdot \mathrm{rev}(X_2) \to X_1 \cdot X_2$
dot-CC	$X_1 \cdot X_2 + X_3 \cdot X_4 \to$ $(X_1 + \!\!+ X_3) \cdot (X_2 + \!\!+ X_4)$

Fig. 3. (a) A graph showing the effectiveness of our encoding of unsafe arithmetic properties of reduction operations. The numbers below the labels indicate the sizes of input tensors. The Y-axis shows the running time of `mlir-tv`. Timeout is 30,000 ms. (b) Descriptions of the test cases. X is a 1D or 2D tensor, Σ is a summation, rev is a reverse, $\cdot$ is a dot product, and $+\!\!+$ is a concatenation.

`memref` **Operations and Read-Only Blocks.** We couldn't find a good semantics for `linalg.fill` with a `memref` reference to a read-only memory block given as its operand. If `linalg.fill` with a read-only `memref` raises UB, it cannot explain the `linalg-bufferize` transformation because it creates `linalg.fill` with its `memref` operand pointing to a read-only block. If it is well-defined, it cannot explain the `linalg-generalize-named-ops` transformation because this converts `linalg.fill` into a loop storing a value to the pointer.

We found that `buffer-deallocation` transformation was introducing UB. It inserts `memref.dealloc` to free the unused result of `memref.clone`. But, mutating the result of `clone` is UB according to the specification.

Also, it was not clearly stated in the document when `memref.clone` makes the referenced location read-only. We discussed this issue in the online LLVM Discussion Forums, and the document was fixed to clearly state that it is immediately after the operation that the block becomes read-only [2].

7.2 Validating Compilation of Deep Learning Models

We compiled the TFLite models of `text_classification_v2`, `SqueezeNet` [25] and `MobileNet` [24], taken from the official TensorFlow website [7,8], by running them through `tosa-to-linalg`, `tosa-to-standard`, `canonicalize`, `fuse-elementwise-ops`, `tensor-constant-bufferize`, `linalg-bufferize`, `tensor-bufferize` transformations. To address validation failures of `tosa-to-linalg` due to the problem in `tosa`'s ± 0.0 handling, we tweaked `mlir-tv` so that it recognizes $+0.0$ used by certain operations as -0.0 instead.

To validate them in a reasonable time, we split the source and target programs into smaller functions. Since the networks did not have complex control flows other than loops, splitting was not very hard. The split functions contain an average 9.5 to 11.6 instructions. All transformations were validated correctly in `text_classification_v2`, but the last two transformations were failed in the other models since they have unsupported operations.

7.3 Performance Evaluation of Hash-Based Encoding

We compared the performance of our hash-based encoding to the multiset-based encoding. In the latter encoding, two reductions are assumed to be equal if the multisets converted from the input arrays are equal. For cvc5, we used its native multiset theory. For Z3, we simulated multisets by defining an array that counts the numbers of elements. We set QF_AUFBV logic to Z3 by default and used ALL logic only when the solver failed. For cvc5, we used HO_AUFBV and HO_ALL logic respectively. We ran tests 10 times and calculated their average execution times. The timeout was set to 30 s.

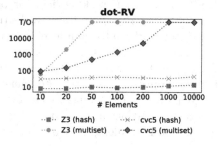

Fig. 4. Running times of dot-RV by tensor size. Timeout is 30,000 ms.

Our hash-based encoding was faster than multiset-based encoding in overall cases (Figs. 3 and 4). cvc5's multiset theory performed better than the Z3's array encoding, but was still slower than the hash-based encoding. The hash-based encoding showed consistent running time regardless of tensor size.

8 Related Work

Verifying Programs with Floating-Points. Strategies for verifying programs using FP arithmetic (FPA) vary with their goals and background theories. Several works using abstract interpretation [29], SMT solvers [23,40] or computer algebra systems [31] target checking round-off errors of FP operations automatically. Axiomatizing and verifying FPA in theorem provers [12] enable us to make analysis sound and complete, but they require significant efforts.

To realize bit-precise FP reasoning in SMT, one can use a bit-vector representation of FP numbers (bit-blasting). Since bit-blasting can generate large and complex formulae, researchers have tried to find better FP abstraction. [15] presents an abstraction technique using either large or reduced precision of FPA. UppSAT [44] proposes an abstraction framework including fixed-point and real arithmetic. SymFPU [13] gives an effective yet correct bit-vector encoding of FPA considering various types and special cases of IEEE 754.

Verifying Programs Using Arrays. Several works have proposed their approaches to embedding the theory of arrays [34] into SMT solvers. [21,35] consider array read and write terms as uninterpreted functions, and regard the theory of array as axioms. FreqHorn [20] and SPACER [26] utilize constrained Horn clauses (CHC) engines. [27] analyzes array programs with broader theories by translating the axioms of the theory of array into the CHC format.

Yet another approach uses mathematical induction-based techniques to reason about array-manipulating programs with loops. [16] verify the validity of a given parameterized Hoare triple where the length of array N is used as a parameter of the pre- and post-condition.

Machine Learning Compilers. Optimizing deep learning specific workloads has been a major working field for both hardware vendors [3,4] and software developers. [9,19] These frameworks translate neural-net representations in several frameworks into high-level computation graphs. Then, they optimize the graphs via well-known optimizations such as operator fusion or data layout transformation. Recent works allow optimization of dynamic workloads [38,45] and supports optimizations for heterogeneous systems [43].

[39] surveyed the bugs in DL compilers. They reported that the high-level IR transformations are the most buggy ones and stated that finding wrong code generation is challenging and should receive more attention.

Compiler Verification. [11] relaxes FPA semantics since a compiler can ignore strict IEEE-754 behavior like fast-math optimizations in LLVM. They propose Icing which is a language allowing IEEE 754-unsafe FPA optimizations, and CakeML [28] which is a verified compiler with the optimizations. [32] proposes a verified tensor optimizer whose optimizations can be explored via Coq's tactics.

As for translation validation (TV), [18] proposes a practical TV framework for Halide which is a language for processing arrays. To support fast-math optimizations, it mainly uses Z3's type for real numbers. For general-purpose compilers, many different tools have been developed [36]. Alive2 [33], LLVM-MD [42] and Peggy [41] validate the transformations in LLVM using various techniques. The SMT memory model for Alive2 [30] uses a technique that is similar to our approach in order to bound the number of memory blocks. Some TV tools [17,22] split the original programs and validate the smaller pairs.

9   Conclusion

We propose `mlir-tv`, an SMT-based translation validation framework for MLIR. It abstractly encodes the FP arithmetic and reduction operations in SMT. Since the abstraction is an over-approximation, `mlir-tv` does not miss bugs unless a flag for bounding the size of dynamically shaped tensors is given. If validation fails, `mlir-tv` tries again with refined abstractions. We also propose a hash-based approach for encoding arithmetic properties of reductions, which outperformed a multiset-based one. `mlir-tv` found several mismatches between the specification and implementation of MLIR from the unit tests. Finally, `mlir-tv` validated high-level transformations for three pretrained DL models.

Acknowledgements. The authors thank Chung-Kil Hur, Nuno P. Lopes and anonymous reviewers for their feedbacks on previous versions of this paper. We thank Jiun Kim for helping our experiments by writing useful scripts. We also thank Hong-Seok Kim, Jieung Kim, Hyunchul Park, Inho Seo and engineers from Google for their precious comments. Seunghyeon Nam, Inwhan Chun and Ho Young Jhoo were supported by the Basic Science Research Program through the National Research Foundation of Korea under Project Number 2020R1A2C2011947.

References

1. https://reviews.llvm.org/D114127
2. https://reviews.llvm.org/D106258
3. Arm NN SDK. https://www.arm.com/products/silicon-ip-cpu/ethos/arm-nn
4. NVIDIA TensorRT. https://developer.nvidia.com/tensorrt
5. Supplementary material. https://doi.org/10.5281/zenodo.6615676
6. Tensor operator set architecture (TOSA) v0.23.0. https://developer.mlplatform. org/w/tosa/?v=19
7. TensorFlow Lite Examples: Text classification. https://www.tensorflow.org/lite/ examples/text_classification/overview
8. TensorFlow Lite: Hosted models. **TensorFlow Lite: Hosted models**
9. XLA: Optimizing compiler for machine learning. https://www.tensorflow.org/xla
10. IEEE standard for floating-point arithmetic: IEEE Std 754-2008, pp. 1–70 (2008). https://doi.org/10.1109/IEEESTD.2008.4610935
11. Becker, H., Darulova, E., Myreen, M.O., Tatlock, Z.: Icing: supporting fast-math style optimizations in a verified compiler. In: Dillig, I., Tasiran, S. (eds.) CAV 2019. LNCS, vol. 11562, pp. 155–173. Springer, Cham (2019). https://doi.org/10.1007/ 978-3-030-25543-5_10
12. Boldo, S., et al.: Flocq: a unified library for proving floating-point algorithms in Coq. In: 2011 IEEE 20th Symposium on Computer Arithmetic, pp. 243–252 (2011)
13. Brain, M., Schanda, F., Sun, Y.: Building better bit-blasting for floating-point problems. In: Vojnar, T., Zhang, L. (eds.) TACAS 2019. LNCS, vol. 11427, pp. 79–98. Springer, Cham (2019). https://doi.org/10.1007/978-3-030-17462-0_5
14. Brain, M., Niemetz, A., Preiner, M., Reynolds, A., Barrett, C., Tinelli, C.: Invertibility conditions for floating-point formulas. In: Dillig, I., Tasiran, S. (eds.) CAV 2019. LNCS, vol. 11562, pp. 116–136. Springer, Cham (2019). https://doi.org/10. 1007/978-3-030-25543-5_8
15. Brillout, A., et al.: Mixed abstractions for floating-point arithmetic. In: 2009 Formal Methods in Computer-Aided Design, pp. 69–76 (2009)
16. Chakraborty, S., Gupta, A., Unadkat, D.: DIFFY: inductive reasoning of array programs using difference invariants. In: Silva, A., Leino, K.R.M. (eds.) CAV 2021. LNCS, vol. 12760, pp. 911–935. Springer, Cham (2021). https://doi.org/10.1007/ 978-3-030-81688-9_42
17. Churchill, B., et al.: Semantic program alignment for equivalence checking. In: PLDI (2019). https://doi.org/10.1145/3314221.3314596
18. Clément, B., et al.: End-to-end translation validation for the halide language. Proc. ACM Program. Lang. **6**(OOPSLA1), 1–30 (2022). https://doi.org/10.1145/ 3527328
19. Cyphers, D.S., et al.: Intel nGraph: an intermediate representation, compiler, and executor for deep learning. arXiv arXiv:1801.08058 (2018)
20. Fedyukovich, G., Prabhu, S., Madhukar, K., Gupta, A.: Quantified invariants via syntax-guided synthesis. In: Dillig, I., Tasiran, S. (eds.) CAV 2019. LNCS, vol. 11561, pp. 259–277. Springer, Cham (2019). https://doi.org/10.1007/978-3-030-25540-4_14
21. Ganesh, V., Dill, D.L.: A decision procedure for bit-vectors and arrays. In: Damm, W., Hermanns, H. (eds.) CAV 2007. LNCS, vol. 4590, pp. 519–531. Springer, Heidelberg (2007). https://doi.org/10.1007/978-3-540-73368-3_52
22. Gupta, S., Rose, A., Bansal, S.: Counterexample-guided correlation algorithm for translation validation. Proc. ACM Prog. Lang. **4**(OOPSLA), 1–29 (2020). https:// doi.org/10.1145/3428289

23. Haller, L., et al.: Deciding floating-point logic with systematic abstraction. In: 2012 Formal Methods in Computer-Aided Design, pp. 131–140 (2012)
24. Howard, A.G., et al.: MobileNets: efficient convolutional neural networks for mobile vision applications. CoRR abs/1704.04861 (2017)
25. Iandola, F.N., et al.: SqueezeNet: AlexNet-level accuracy with 50x fewer parameters and <1 mb model size. arXiv arXiv:1602.07360 (2016)
26. Komuravelli, A., Gurfinkel, A., Chaki, S.: SMT-based model checking for recursive programs. In: Biere, A., Bloem, R. (eds.) CAV 2014. LNCS, vol. 8559, pp. 17–34. Springer, Cham (2014). https://doi.org/10.1007/978-3-319-08867-9_2
27. Komuravelli, A., et al.: Compositional verification of procedural programs using horn clauses over integers and arrays. In: Proceedings of the 15th Conference on Formal Methods in Computer-Aided Design, pp. 89–96. FMCAD Inc., Austin, Texas (2015)
28. Kumar, R., et al.: CakeML: a verified implementation of ML. In: Proceedings of the 41st ACM SIGPLAN-SIGACT Symposium on Principles of Programming Languages, pp. 179–191. Association for Computing Machinery, New York (2014)
29. Kästner, D., et al.: Astrée: Proving the absence of runtime errors. In: Embedded Real Time Software and Systems (2010)
30. Lee, J., Kim, D., Hur, C.-K., Lopes, N.P.: An SMT encoding of LLVM's memory model for bounded translation validation. In: Silva, A., Leino, K.R.M. (eds.) CAV 2021. LNCS, vol. 12760, pp. 752–776. Springer, Cham (2021). https://doi.org/10.1007/978-3-030-81688-9_35
31. Lee, W., Sharma, R., Aiken, A.: On automatically proving the correctness of math.h implementations. Proc. ACM Program. Lang. 2(POPL), 1–32 (2018)
32. Liu, A., Bernstein, G.L., Chlipala, A., Ragan-Kelley, J.: Verified tensor-program optimization via high-level scheduling rewrites. Proc. ACM Program. Lang. 6(POPL), 1–28 (2022). https://doi.org/10.1145/3498717
33. Lopes, N.P., et al.: Alive2: bounded translation validation for LLVM. In: PLDI (2021). https://doi.org/10.1145/3453483.3454030
34. McCarthy, J.: Towards a mathematical science of computation. In: IFIP Congress (1962)
35. de Moura, L., Bjørner, N.: Generalized, efficient array decision procedures. In: 2009 Formal Methods in Computer-Aided Design, pp. 45–52 (2009)
36. Necula, G.C.: Translation validation for an optimizing compiler. In: PLDI (2000). https://doi.org/10.1145/349299.349314
37. Rümmer, P., Wahl, T.: An SMT-LIB theory of binary floating-point arithmetic. In: SMT 2010 Workshop (2010)
38. Shen, H., et al.: Nimble: efficiently compiling dynamic neural networks for model inference. In: Smola, A., Dimakis, A., Stoica, I. (eds.) Proceedings of Machine Learning and Systems, vol. 3, pp. 208–222 (2021)
39. Shen, Q., et al.: A comprehensive study of deep learning compiler bugs. In: Proceedings of the 29th ESEC/FSE 2021, pp. 968–980. Association for Computing Machinery, New York (2021)
40. Solovyev, A., Baranowski, M.S., Briggs, I., Jacobsen, C., Rakamarić, Z., Gopalakrishnan, G.: Rigorous estimation of floating-point round-off errors with symbolic Taylor expansions. ACM Trans. Program. Lang. Syst. 41(1), 1–39 (2019). https://doi.org/10.1145/3230733
41. Stepp, M., et al.: Equality-based translation validator for LLVM. In: CAV (2011). https://doi.org/10.1007/978-3-642-22110-159
42. Tristan, J.B., et al.: Evaluating value-graph translation validation for LLVM. In: PLDI (2011). https://doi.org/10.1145/1993316.1993533

43. Yadav, R., Aiken, A., Kjolstad, F.: DISTAL: the distributed tensor algebra compiler (2022)
44. Zeljić, A., Backeman, P., Wintersteiger, C.M., Rümmer, P.: Exploring approximations for floating-point arithmetic using UppSAT. In: Galmiche, D., Schulz, S., Sebastiani, R. (eds.) IJCAR 2018. LNCS (LNAI), vol. 10900, pp. 246–262. Springer, Cham (2018). https://doi.org/10.1007/978-3-319-94205-6_17
45. Zhu, K., et al.: DISC: A dynamic shape compiler for machine learning workloads. arXiv arXiv:2103.05288 (2021)

Verifying Fairness in Quantum Machine Learning

Ji Guan[1(✉)], Wang Fang[1,2], and Mingsheng Ying[1,3]

[1] State Key Laboratory of Computer Science,
Institute of Software, Chinese Academy of Sciences,
Beijing 100190, China
{guanj,fangw,yingms}@ios.ac.cn
[2] University of Chinese Academy of Sciences,
Beijing 100049, China
[3] Department of Computer Science and Technology,
Tsinghua University, Beijing 100084, China

Abstract. Due to the beyond-classical capability of quantum computing, quantum machine learning is applied independently or embedded in classical models for decision making, especially in the field of finance. Fairness and other ethical issues are often one of the main concerns in decision making. In this work, we define a formal framework for the fairness verification and analysis of quantum machine learning decision models, where we adopt one of the most popular notions of fairness in the literature based on the intuition—any two similar individuals must be treated similarly and are thus unbiased. We show that quantum noise can improve fairness and develop an algorithm to check whether a (noisy) quantum machine learning model is fair. In particular, this algorithm can find bias kernels of quantum data (encoding individuals) during checking. These bias kernels generate infinitely many bias pairs for investigating the unfairness of the model. Our algorithm is designed based on a highly efficient data structure—Tensor Networks—and implemented on Google's TensorFlow Quantum. The utility and effectiveness of our algorithm are confirmed by the experimental results, including income prediction and credit scoring on real-world data, for a class of random (noisy) quantum decision models with 27 qubits (2^{27}-dimensional state space) tripling (2^{18} times more than) that of the state-of-the-art algorithms for verifying quantum machine learning models.

Keywords: Quantum Machine Learning · Fairness Verification · Quantum Noise · Quantum Decision Model

1 Introduction

Quantum Machine Learning: Google's quantum supremacy (or advantage) experiment demonstrated that a quantum computer *Sycamore* with 53 noisy superconducting qubits can do a specific calculation, namely sampling, in 200 s

S. Shoham and Y. Vizel (Eds.): CAV 2022, LNCS 13372, pp. 408–429, 2022.
https://doi.org/10.1007/978-3-031-13188-2_20

that would take (arguably) 10,000 years on the largest classical computer using existing Algorithms [1]. More recently, a quantum computer *Jiuzhang* with 76 noisy photonic qubits was used to perform a type of Boson sampling in 20 s that would require 600 million years for a classical computer [2]. These experiments mark the beginning of the Noisy Intermediate-Scale Quantum (NISQ) computing era, where quantum computers with tens-to-hundreds of qubits become a reality, but quantum noise still cannot be avoided.

Quantum machine learning is believed to be a far frontrunner in setting a path for practical beyond-classical applications of NISQ quantum devices. This stimulates the fast development of various quantum machine learning (see [3] for a review). Stepping into industries, Google recently built up a framework *TensorFlow Quantum* for the design and training of quantum machine learning within its well-known classical machine learning platform—*TensorFlow* [4].

Classical machine learning has led to automated decision models assuming a significant role in making real-world decisions, especially in finance [5]. Such (financial) decision tasks are known to face the curse of dimensionality as there are too many features available to model customers/users. Principal component analysis (PCA) is one of the most popular methods for dimensionality reduction. It was recently shown that quantum PCA Algorithm [6] can run exponentially faster on a quantum processor. At the same time, the training process of quantum machine learning could be sped up exponentially (compared with classical training) by using quantum PCA to implement iterative gradient descent methods for network training [7]. It is worth noting that this quantum approach is generic in the sense that it can be applied to various types of neural networks, including shallow, convolutional, and recurrent networks, and thus can mitigate the high complexity issue of classical training. Because of these reasons, quantum machine learning has been introduced to be applied independently or embedded in classical decision-making models, e.g. fraud detection (in transaction monitoring) [8,9], credit assessments (risk scoring for customers) [10,11], and recommendation systems for content dissemination [12] (see reviews [13,14] for more information). Similar to the classical counterparts, the quantum models are trained on individuals' information, e.g. saving, employment, salary (encoded as quantum data).

Fairness in Machine Learning: It is well-known that classical decision models are prone to discriminating against users/consumers on the basis of characteristics such as race and gender [15], and have even led to legal mandates of ensuring *fairness*. To develop fair models, various attempts have been made to precisely define and quantify fairness. They broadly fall into two categories: *group* and *individual* fairness. Group fairness aims to achieve through statistical parity the same outcomes across different protected groups (e.g. gender or race) [16,17], whereas individual fairness advocates treating similar individuals similarly (receiving the similar outcomes) [18] (see [19,20] for various definitions of fairness and discussions about their relationship). The computer science community has endeavoured to check and avoid bias in classical decision models in the sense of different types of fairness (e.g. [18,19,21]). In particular, several verifiers for formal analysis and fairness verification have been designed and implemented, including FairSquare [22], VeriFair [23] and Justicia [24].

Inevitably, the same issue of fairness arises in the quantum models too. Furthermore, as quantum machine learning is principled by quantum mechanics, which is usually hard to explain to the end-users, it is even more important to verify fairness when a decision is made by a quantum machine learning algorithm. However, to the best of our knowledge, the verification problem of fairness in quantum algorithms has not yet been touched.

Contributions of this Paper: In this work, we define a formal framework so that the fairness of quantum machine learning decision models can be verified and analyzed in a principled way. Our *design decision* is as follows: we focus on individual fairness—*treating similar individuals similarly* [18]. The trace distance—one of the most widely used quantities in quantum information [25, Section 9.2]—is chosen as the metric for measuring the similarity of quantum data (individuals) in defining fairness. Our main technical contributions include:

(1) **Problem Reduction**: We prove that for a given (noisy) quantum decision model, checking the fairness can be reduced to a variant of distinguishing quantum measurements (states), a fundamental problem in quantum information. We resolve this specific variant problem by finding the maximum difference between the eigenvalues of the matrices generated by quantum measurements. As a corollary, we show that quantum noise can improve fairness.

(2) **Algorithm**: Based on (1), an algorithm is developed to exactly and efficiently check whether or not a quantum machine learning decision model is fair. A special strength of this algorithm is that it can identify *bias kernels* during the checking, and these kernels generate infinitely many *bias pairs*, that is, two similar quantum data that are not treated similarly. Then these bias pairs can be used to investigate the bias of the decision model.

(3) **Case Studies**: The effectiveness of our algorithm is confirmed by experiments on quantum (noisy) decision models with 8 or 9 quantum bits (qubits) for income prediction and credit scoring on real-world data. In particular, its efficiency is shown by a class of random quantum decision models with 27 qubits, which works on a 2^{27}-dimensional state space. The state-of-the-art verification algorithm [26] for quantum machine learning was only able to deal with (the robustness with) 9 qubits. Our experiments can be considered a big step toward the demanded number (≥ 50) of qubits in practical applications of the NISQ era.

1.1 Related Works and Challenges

To put our work in an appropriate context, let us further discuss some related works and the challenges we face in this paper.

Classical Versus Quantum Models: In order to identify and mitigate the bias of classical machine learning decision models, an algorithm for maximizing utility with fairness guarantee was proposed [18]. Then the strategy of searching input data with linear and integral constraints is employed in a verifier for proving individual fairness of a given decision model [21]. The verifier is sound but not complete in general. But in the case of linear models, it is exact (both sound and complete) if the worst-case exponential time is allowed. However, although quantum decision models are always linear, the above technique cannot be directly generalized from the classical case to the quantum case. The main obstacle here is that the corresponding constraints in the quantum models are nonlinear, and thus searching the data set in a linear domain is ineffective in the quantum case. In this paper, we surmount this obstacle by reducing the quantum fairness verification problem to determining the distinguishability of a quantum measurement, which is independent of input data. Then we resolve the latter by eigenvalue analysis with polynomial time in the dimension of input quantum data. As a result, our algorithm is exact (sound and complete) and efficient.

Fairness Versus Robustness: As in the classical case, the individual fairness considered in this paper can be thought of as a kind of global robustness [21]. This will be formally discussed in Sect. 3. In the last few years, quite a few papers have been devoted to (adversarial) robustness verification of quantum machine learning (e.g. [26–28]), where a verifier is given a nominal input quantum datum and it checks robustness in a neighborhood of that particular input datum. However, the techniques developed in these works cannot be directly generalized to solve our problem of fairness verification, because we are required to check a global property. Instead, we transfer the impact of the evolution of the quantum machine learning model on input quantum data to quantum measurements.

Efficiency: As the dimension of input data increases exponentially with the number of qubits, efficiency is always a key issue in the verification of quantum machine learning models. The state-of-the-art algorithms for robustness verification mentioned above can only cope with quantum machine learning models with 9 qubits[1]. In this paper, we boost the scale up to 27 qubits on a small server, which represents a big step toward the demand in practical applications of NISQ devices (≥ 50 qubits). The speedup originates from not only the high efficiency of our algorithm but also the based data structure we adopted— *Tensor Network* [29]—which can exploit the locality and regularity of the underlying circuits of quantum decision models and thus further optimize the algorithm.

2   Quantum Decision Models

For convenience of the reader, in this section, we review the setup of quantum (machine learning) decision models in their most basic form.

Classical Models: In the classical world, a *classification decision model* is a mapping $f_c : \mathcal{C} \to \mathcal{O}$, where $\mathcal{C}$ is a set of data to be classified, and $\mathcal{O}$ is a set of outcomes corresponding to the classes we are interested in; for example

---

[1] The experiments of [26] were performed on a personal computer and the size is at most 8 qubits. We have estimated and tested the same experiments on the server we used in this paper and only 9 qubits can be handled.

$\mathcal{O} = \{0,1\}$ in the simplest non-trivial (binary) case. Such a model f_c can be generalized to be a randomized mapping $f_r : \mathcal{C} \to \mathcal{D}(\mathcal{O})$, where $\mathcal{D}(\mathcal{O})$ denotes the set of probability distributions over $\mathcal{O}$. f_r is known as a *regression decision model* to predict distributions and naturally describes a randomized classification procedure: to classify $x \in \mathcal{C}$, choose an outcome $o \in \mathcal{O}$ according to the distribution $f_r(x)$. For example, o is chosen as the outcome corresponding to the maximum probability of $f_r(x)$. Therefore, the basic form of a classical decision model is a randomized mapping $f = f_r$ ($f = f_c$ when f is degenerated to be a deterministic mapping).

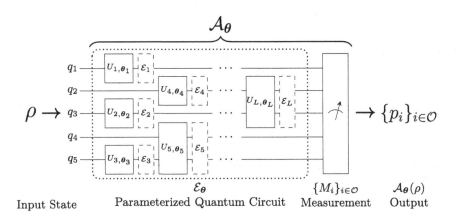

Fig. 1. Noisy Quantum (Machine Learning) Decision Model

Quantum Models: Due to the statistical nature of quantum mechanics, a quantum decision model is inherently a randomized mapping $\mathcal{A} : \mathcal{D}(\mathcal{H}) \to \mathcal{D}(\mathcal{O})$. Here $\mathcal{D}(\mathcal{H})$ is the set of *quantum states* (data) and to be specific later. Inspired by the classical models, $\mathcal{A}$ is not predefined but initialized as $\mathcal{A}_\theta$ by a parameterized quantum circuit $\mathcal{E}_\theta$ (see Fig. 1) with a set of free parameters $\theta = \{\theta_j\}_{j=1}^L$. Following the training strategy of classical machine learning, $\mathcal{A}_\theta$ is trained on a set of input quantum states (training dataset) by tuning θ subject to some loss function $\mathcal{L}(\theta)$.

In the following, we explain the noisy quantum decision model from the left side to the right one of Fig. 1. For the details of the training process, we refer to a comprehensive review paper [30].

Input State ρ : The input state of the model is a quantum *mixed state* ρ, which is mathematically modelled by a positive semi-definite complex matrix, written as $\rho \geq 0$, with unit trace[2]. ρ admits a decomposition form[3]: $\rho = \sum_k p_k \psi_k$

---

[2] ρ has unit trace if $\text{tr}(\rho) = 1$, where trace $\text{tr}(\rho)$ of ρ is defined as the summation of diagonal elements of ρ.

[3] This kind of decomposition is generally infinitely many, and one instance is eigendecomposition, i.e., p_k and $|\psi_k\rangle$ are eigenvalues and eigenvectors of ρ, respectively.

where $\{p_k\}$ is a probability distribution and each ψ_k is a rank-one positive semi-definite matrix, i.e., $\psi_k = |\psi_k\rangle\langle\psi_k|$. Here, $|\psi_k\rangle$ is a unit vector and $\langle\psi_k|$ is the entry-wise conjugate transpose of $|\psi_k\rangle$, i.e., $\langle\psi_k| = |\psi_k\rangle^\dagger$. Physically, $|\psi_k\rangle$ represents a *pure state*, and ρ represents an ensemble $\{(p_k, |\psi_k\rangle)\}_k$, often called a mixed state, meaning that ρ is at $|\psi_k\rangle$ with probability p_k. In particular, if $\rho = \psi$ for some pure state $|\psi\rangle$, then the ensemble is deterministic; that is, it is degenerated to a singleton $\{(1, \psi)\}$. In general, the statistical feature of ρ may result from quantum noise, which is unavoidable in the current NISQ era, from the surrounding environment.

Example 1 (Qubits – Quantum Bits). A pure state of a single qubit q is described by a 2-dimensional unit vector and in the Dirac notation it can be written as:

$$|\psi\rangle = \begin{pmatrix} a \\ b \end{pmatrix} = a|0\rangle + b|1\rangle \text{ for } |0\rangle = \begin{pmatrix} 1 \\ 0 \end{pmatrix}, |1\rangle = \begin{pmatrix} 0 \\ 1 \end{pmatrix} \text{ and } |a|^2 + |b|^2 = 1,$$

and ensembles $\{(\frac{1}{2}, |0\rangle), (\frac{1}{2}, |+\rangle)\}$ and $\{(\frac{1}{6}, |1\rangle), (\frac{5}{6}, |\phi\rangle)\}$ of q are represented by the same 2-by-2 mixed state

$$\rho = \frac{1}{4}\begin{pmatrix} 3 & 1 \\ 1 & 1 \end{pmatrix} = \frac{1}{2}|0\rangle\langle0| + \frac{1}{2}|+\rangle\langle+| = \frac{1}{6}|1\rangle\langle1| + \frac{5}{6}|\phi\rangle\langle\phi|,$$

where $|+\rangle = \frac{1}{\sqrt{2}}(|0\rangle + |1\rangle)$ and $|\phi\rangle = \frac{1}{\sqrt{10}}(3|0\rangle + |1\rangle)$.

For a system of multiple qubits $q_1, ..., q_n$, the state space is a 2^n-dimensional Hilbert (linear) space, denoted by $\mathcal{H}$. As a result, pure and mixed states on $\mathcal{H}$ are 2^n-dimensional unit vectors and $2^n \times 2^n$ positive semi-definite matrices with unit trace, respectively. It is worth noting that *the dimension 2^n of the state space $\mathcal{H}$ of quantum states is exponentially increasing with the number n of qubits.* Thus, describing a quantum system with a large number of qubits and verifying its properties on a classical computer is challenging. For our purpose of verifying fairness in quantum machine learning, we adopt a compact data structure—*Tensor Networks*—to mitigate this issue (see this in Sect. 6).

Parameterized Quantum Circuit $\mathcal{E}_\theta$: Several different types of parameterized quantum circuits have been proposed; e.g. quantum neural networks (QNNs) [31] and quantum convolutional neural networks (QCNNs) [32]. Basically, $\mathcal{E}_\theta$ consists of a sequence of quantum operations: $\mathcal{E}_\theta = \mathcal{E}_{d,\theta_d} \circ \cdots \circ \mathcal{E}_{1,\theta_1}$. For each input quantum state ρ, the output of the circuit is $\mathcal{E}_\theta(\rho) = \mathcal{E}_{d,\theta_d}(\ldots \mathcal{E}_{2,\theta_2}(\mathcal{E}_{1,\theta_1}(\rho)))$. In the current NISQ era, each component $\mathcal{E}_{i,\theta_i}$ is:

- either a parameterized quantum gate $\mathcal{U}_{i,\theta_i}$ (the full boxes in Fig. 1) with $\mathcal{U}_{i,\theta_i}(\rho) = U_{i,\theta_i}\rho U_{i,\theta_i}^\dagger$, where U_{i,θ_i} is a unitary matrix with parameters θ_i, i.e., $U_{i,\theta_i}^\dagger U_{i,\theta_i} = U_{i,\theta_i}U_{i,\theta_i}^\dagger = I$ (the identity matrix), and $U_{i,\theta_i}^\dagger$ is the entry-wise conjugate transpose of U_{i,θ_i};
- or a quantum noise $\mathcal{E}_i$ (the dashed boxes in Fig. 1). Mathematically, it can be described by a family of Kraus matrices $\{E_{ij}\}$ [25]: $\mathcal{E}_i(\rho) = \sum_j E_{ij}\rho E_{ij}^\dagger$ with $\sum_j E_{ij}^\dagger E_{ij} = I$. Briefly, $\mathcal{E}_i$ is represented as $\mathcal{E}_i = \{E_{ij}\}$.

Note that in constructing a quantum machine learning model, only quantum gate $\mathcal{U}_{i,\theta_i}$ is parameterized, and noises $\mathcal{E}_i$ are not because they come from the outside environment.

It should be pointed out that, in a practical model, as shown in Fig. 1, each quantum operation $\mathcal{E} = \mathcal{E}_{i,\theta_i}$ non-trivially applies on one or two qubits. For example, if $\mathcal{E}$ only works on the first qubit, then $\mathcal{E} = \mathcal{E}_1 \otimes \mathrm{id}_2 \otimes \ldots \otimes \mathrm{id}_n$ and $\mathcal{E}(\rho_1 \otimes \rho_2 \otimes \ldots \otimes \rho_n) = \mathcal{E}_1(\rho_1) \otimes \rho_2 \otimes \ldots \otimes \rho_n$, where ρ_i is the mixed state applied on qubit q_i and tensor product $\rho_1 \otimes \rho_2 \otimes \ldots \otimes \rho_n$ is the joint state of multiple qubits $q_1, \ldots, q_n$. This locality feature will be exploited by Tensor Networks to optimize our verification algorithm for fairness in the Evaluation Section—Sect. 6.

Example 2. Consider the 1-qubit noise model: $\mathcal{E}_U(\rho) = (1 - p)\rho + pU\rho U^\dagger$ where $0 \leq p \leq 1$ is a probability and U is a unitary matrix. It includes the following typical noises depending on the choice of U: $U = X$ for bit flip, $U = Z$ for phase flip and $U = Y = \imath XZ$ for bit-phase flip [25, Section 8.3], where I, X, Y, Z are *the Pauli matrices:*

$$X = \begin{pmatrix} 0 & 1 \\ 1 & 0 \end{pmatrix}, \; Y = \begin{pmatrix} 0 & -\imath \\ \imath & 0 \end{pmatrix}, \; Z = \begin{pmatrix} 1 & 0 \\ 0 & -1 \end{pmatrix}, \; I = \begin{pmatrix} 1 & 0 \\ 0 & 1 \end{pmatrix},$$

where $\imath$ denotes imaginary unit. The depolarizing noise combines the above three kinds of noise: $\mathcal{E}_D(\rho) = (1 - p)\rho + p\frac{I}{2} = (1 - \frac{3p}{4})\rho + \frac{p}{4}(X\rho X + Y\rho Y + Z\rho Z)$.

Measurement $\{M_i\}_{i \in \mathcal{O}}$: At the end of parameterized quantum circuit $\mathcal{E}_\theta$, we cannot directly read out the output $\mathcal{E}_\theta(\rho)$. The only way allowed by quantum mechanics to extract classical information from $\mathcal{E}_\theta(\rho)$ is through a quantum measurement, which is mathematically modeled by a set $\{M_i\}_{i \in \mathcal{O}}$ of matrices with $\mathcal{O}$ being the set of possible outcomes and $\sum_{i \in \mathcal{O}} M_i^\dagger M_i = I$. This observing process is probabilistic: for the measurement on state $\mathcal{E}_\theta(\rho)$, an outcome $i \in \mathcal{O}$ is obtained with probability $p_i = \mathrm{tr}(M_i \mathcal{E}_\theta(\rho) M_i^\dagger)$[4]. Therefore, the output of quantum machine learning model $\mathcal{A}_\theta$ upon an input ρ is a probability distribution $\mathcal{A}_\theta(\rho) = \{p_i : p_i = \mathrm{tr}(M_i \mathcal{E}_\theta(\rho) M_i^\dagger)\}$, as depicted at the rightmost of Fig. 1.

In this paper, we focus on the well-trained quantum machine learning models (i.e., θ has been tuned), so we ignore the θ in $\mathcal{E}_\theta$ and $\mathcal{A}_\theta$. Now, we can formally specify quantum decision model $\mathcal{A}$ as follows:

Definition 1. *A quantum decision model $\mathcal{A} = (\mathcal{E}, \{M_i\}_{i \in \mathcal{O}})$ is a randomized mapping:*

$$\mathcal{A} : \mathcal{D}(\mathcal{H}) \to \mathcal{D}(\mathcal{O}) \qquad \mathcal{A}(\rho) = \{\mathrm{tr}(M_i \mathcal{E}(\rho) M_i^\dagger)\}_{i \in \mathcal{O}} \quad \forall \rho \in \mathcal{D}(\mathcal{H}),$$

where $\mathcal{E}$ is a super-operator on Hilbert space $\mathcal{H}$, and $\{M_i\}_{i \in \mathcal{O}}$ is a quantum measurement on $\mathcal{H}$ with $\mathcal{O}$ being the set of measurement outcomes (classical information) we are interested in.

---

[4] After measuring $\mathcal{E}_\theta(\rho)$ with outcome $i \in \mathcal{O}$, the state $\mathcal{E}_\theta(\rho)$ will be collapsed (changed) to $\rho_i' = M_i \mathcal{E}_\theta(\rho) M_i^\dagger / p_i$. As we can see, the post-measurement state ρ_i' is dependent on the measurement outcome i. This special property is vitally different from the classical computation.

Like their classical counterparts, quantum decision models are usually classified into two categories: *regression* and *classification* models. Regression models generally predict a value/quantity, whereas classification models predict a label/class. More specifically, a regression model $\mathcal{A}_\mathcal{R}$ uses the output of $\mathcal{A}$ directly as the predicted value of the regression variable $\rho \in \mathcal{D}(\mathcal{H})$. That is $\mathcal{A}_\mathcal{R}(\rho) = \mathcal{A}(\rho)$ for all $\rho \in \mathcal{D}(\mathcal{H})$. In the classical world, regression models have been successfully applied to many real-world applications, such as stock market prediction and object detection. Quantum regression models were recently used to predict molecular atomization energies [33] and the demonstration of IBM's programming platform—Qiskit [34, Variational Quantum Regression]. On the other hand, classification model $\mathcal{A}_\mathcal{C}$ further uses the measurement outcome probability distribution $\mathcal{A}(\rho)$ to sign a class label on the input state ρ. The most common way is as follows:

$$\mathcal{A}_\mathcal{C} : \mathcal{D}(\mathcal{H}) \to \mathcal{O} \qquad \mathcal{A}_\mathcal{C}(\rho) = \arg\max_i \mathcal{A}(\rho)_i \quad \forall \rho \in \mathcal{D}(\mathcal{H}), i \in \mathcal{O},$$

where $\mathcal{A}(\rho)_i$ denotes the i-th element of distribution $\mathcal{A}(\rho)$. Classical classification models have broad applications in our daily life, such as face recognition and medical image classification. Quantum classification models have been used to implement quantum phase recognition [32] and cluster excitation detection [4] from real-world physical problems, and fraud detection [8] in finance.

As we saw above, although classical and quantum decision models f and $\mathcal{A}$ are both randomized mappings, the input data to them and their procedure of processing the data are fundamentally different. These differences make that the techniques for verifying classical models cannot be directly applied to quantum models and we have to develop new techniques for the latter.

3   Defining Fairness

As discussed in the Introduction, an important issue in classical machine learning is: how fair is the decision made by machines? The same issue exists for quantum machine learning. Intuitively, the fairness of quantum decision model $\mathcal{A}$ is to treat all input states equally, i.e., there is not a pair of two closed input states that has a large difference between their corresponding outcomes. Formally,

Definition 2 (Bias Pair). *Suppose we are given a quantum decision model* $\mathcal{A} = (\mathcal{E}, \{M_i\}_{i \in \mathcal{O}})$, *two distance metrics* $D(\cdot, \cdot)$ *and* $d(\cdot, \cdot)$ *on* $\mathcal{D}(\mathcal{H})$ *and* $\mathcal{D}(\mathcal{O})$, *respectively, and two small enough threshold values* $1 \geq \varepsilon, \delta > 0$. *Then* (ρ, σ) *is said to be an* (ε, δ)-*bias pair if the following is true*

$$[D(\rho, \sigma) \leq \varepsilon] \wedge [d(\mathcal{A}(\rho), \mathcal{A}(\sigma)) > \delta]. \tag{1}$$

The first condition in (1) indicates that the distance between input states ρ and σ is within ε, and the second condition shows the difference between outcomes $\mathcal{A}(\rho)$ and $\mathcal{A}(\sigma)$ is beyond δ. Sometimes, without any ambiguity, (ρ, σ) is called a bias pair if ε and δ are preset.

Definition 3 (Fair Model). *Let* $\mathcal{A} = (\mathcal{E}, \{M_i\}_{i \in \mathcal{O}})$ *be a decision model. Then* $\mathcal{A}$ *is* (ε, δ)-*fair if there is no any* (ε, δ)-*bias pair.*

The intuition behind this notion of fairness is that small or non-significant perturbation of a sample ρ to σ (i.e. $D(\rho, \sigma) \leq \varepsilon$) must not be treated "differently" by a fair model. The choice of input distance function $D(\cdot, \cdot)$ identifies the perturbations to be considered non-significantly, while the choice of the output distance function $d(\cdot, \cdot)$ limits the changes allowed to the perturbed outputs in the model.

Fairness Implying Robustness: As the same in the classical situation [21], robustness of quantum machine learning is a special case of fairness defined above. Formally, robustness is defined on a specific state ρ: given a quantum model $\mathcal{A} = (\mathcal{E}, \{M_i\}_{i \in \mathcal{O}})$, ρ is (ε, δ)-robust if for all $\sigma \in \mathcal{D}(\mathcal{H})$, $D(\rho, \sigma) \leq \varepsilon$ implies $d(\mathcal{A}(\rho), \mathcal{A}(\sigma)) \leq \delta$. In contrast, fairness is established on all quantum states: $\mathcal{A}$ is (ε, δ)-fair if and only if ρ is (ε, δ)-robust for all states $\rho \in \mathcal{D}(\mathcal{H})$. So, *fairness implies robustness and can be thought of as global robustness.*

Choice of Distances: The reader should have noticed that the above definition of fairness for quantum decision models is similar to that for classical decision models. But an intrinsic distinctness between them comes from the choice of distances $D(\cdot, \cdot)$ and $d(\cdot, \cdot)$. In the classical case, the distances define the similarity between individuals and their appropriate choices have been intensively discussed [18]. One of the most used distances is total variation distance, measuring the closeness of individuals encoded by probability distributions. In this paper, we use it as $d(\cdot, \cdot)$ for measurement outcome distributions in Definition 1 and choose $D(\cdot, \cdot)$ to be the trace distance. Trace distance is essentially a generalization of total variation distance, and has been widely used by the quantum computation and quantum information community to define the closeness of quantum states [25, Section 9.2]. Formally, for two quantum states $\rho, \sigma \in \mathcal{D}(\mathcal{H})$,

$$D(\rho, \sigma) = \frac{1}{2}\mathrm{tr}(|\rho - \sigma|),$$

where $|\rho - \sigma| = \Delta_+ + \Delta_-$ if $\rho - \sigma = \Delta_+ - \Delta_-$ with $\mathrm{tr}(\Delta_+ \Delta_-) = 0$ and $\Delta_\pm$ being positive semi-definite matrix. On the other hand, for two probability distributions $p = \{p_i\}_{i \in \mathcal{O}}$, $q = \{q_i\}_{i \in \mathcal{O}}$ over $\mathcal{O}$, $d(p, q) = \frac{1}{2}\sum_i |p_i - q_i|$. In particular, for the measurement outcome distributions, we have:

$$d(\mathcal{A}(\rho), \mathcal{A}(\sigma)) = \frac{1}{2}\sum_i |\mathrm{tr}(M_i^\dagger M_i \mathcal{E}(\rho - \sigma))|.$$

If ρ and σ are both diagonal matrices, i.e., $\rho = \mathrm{diag}(p_1, \cdots, p_{|\mathcal{O}|})$ and $\sigma = \mathrm{diag}(q_1, \cdots, q_{|\mathcal{O}|})$, then $D(\rho, \sigma) = d(p, q)$.

4   Characterizing Fairness

In this section, we give a characterization of fairness in terms of the Lipschitz constant and clarify its relationship with quantum noises.

4.1 Fairness and Lipschitz Constant

The Lipschitz constant has been widely used in classical machine learning for applications ranging from robustness and fairness certification of classifiers to stability analysis of closed-loop systems with reinforcement learning controllers (e.g. [35,36]). In this subsection, we show that there also exists a close connection between the Lipschitz constant and fairness in the quantum setting. Let us start from an observation:

Lemma 1. *Let $\mathcal{A} = (\mathcal{E}, \{M_i\}_{i \in \mathcal{O}})$ be a quantum decision model. Then*

$$d(\mathcal{A}(\rho), \mathcal{A}(\sigma)) \leq D(\rho, \sigma). \tag{2}$$

Proof. See Appendix A in [37] for the proof.

The above lemma indicates that quantum decision model $\mathcal{A}$ is automatically (ε, δ)-fair whenever $\varepsilon = \delta$. Furthermore, we see that $\mathcal{A}$ is unconditionaly *Lipschitz continuous*: there exists a constant $K > 0$ ($K \leq 1$ by Lemma 1) such that for all $\rho, \sigma \in \mathcal{D}(\mathcal{H})$,

$$d(\mathcal{A}(\rho), \mathcal{A}(\sigma)) \leq KD(\rho, \sigma). \tag{3}$$

As usual, K is called a *Lipschitz constant* of $\mathcal{A}$. Furthermore, the smallest K, denoted by K^*, is called the (best) Lipschitz constant of $\mathcal{A}$.

In the context of quantum machine learning, the following theorem shows that K^* actually measures the fairness of decision model $\mathcal{A}$, i.e., the best (maximum) ratio of δ and ε in a fair model, and the states ψ, ϕ achieving K^* can be used to find bias pairs in fairness verification.

Theorem 1. *1. Given a quantum decision model $\mathcal{A} = (\mathcal{E}, \{M_i\}_{i \in \mathcal{O}})$ and $1 \geq \varepsilon, \delta > 0$, $\mathcal{A}$ is (ε, δ)-fair if and only if $\delta \geq K^*\varepsilon$.*
2. If $\mathcal{A}$ is not (ε, δ)-fair, then (ψ, ϕ) achieving K^* is a bias kernel; that is, for any quantum state $\sigma \in \mathcal{D}(\mathcal{H})$, (ρ_ψ, ρ_ϕ) is a bias pair where

$$\rho_\psi = \varepsilon\psi + (1 - \varepsilon)\sigma \qquad \rho_\phi = \varepsilon\phi + (1 - \varepsilon)\sigma. \tag{4}$$

Proof (Outline). The "if" direction of the first claim is derived by the definitions of (ε, δ)-fairness and K^* together with (3). The "only if" direction of the first claim and the second claim are both based on the existence of pure states $|\psi\rangle$ and $|\phi\rangle$ achieving K^*: $d(\mathcal{A}(\psi), \mathcal{A}(\phi)) = K^*D(\psi, \phi)$. The detailed proof is presented in Appendix B in [37].

4.2 Fairness and Noises

In this subsection, we turn to consider the relation between fairness and noise. Let us first examine a simple example. Assume a noiseless quantum decision model $\mathcal{A} = (\mathcal{U}, \{\mathcal{M}_i\}_{i \in \mathcal{O}})$ where $\mathcal{U}$ is a unitary operator, i.e., $\mathcal{U} = \{U\}$ for some unitary matrix U. The 1-qubit depolarizing noise in Example 2 can be generalized to a large-size system with the following form:

$$\mathcal{E}(\rho) = (1 - p)\rho + p\frac{I}{N} \qquad \forall \rho \in \mathcal{D}(\mathcal{H}),$$

where $0 \leq p \leq 1$ and N is the dimension of the state space $\mathcal{H}$ of the system. By introducing it into $\mathcal{A}$, we obtain a noisy model $\mathcal{A}_{\mathcal{E}} = (\mathcal{E} \circ \mathcal{U}, \{\mathcal{M}_i\}_{i \in \mathcal{O}})$. Let K^* and $K^*_{\mathcal{E}}$ be the Lipschitz constants of $\mathcal{A}$ and $\mathcal{A}_{\mathcal{E}}$, respectively. A calculation (with the help of Theorem 3 below) yields:

$$K^*_{\mathcal{E}} = (1 - p)K^*. \tag{5}$$

Theorem 1 indicates that the less the Lipschitz constant is, the fairer the quantum machine learning model will be. So, depolarizing noise improves fairness by the order of $(1 - p)$. By the way, it was shown in [38] that depolarizing noise can improve the robustness of quantum machine learning. This result can be strengthened by using (5) to quantitatively characterize the robustness improvement.

The observation in the above example can actually be generalized to the following:

Theorem 2. *Let $\mathcal{A} = (\mathcal{U}, \{\mathcal{M}_i\}_{i \in \mathcal{O}})$ be a quantum decision model. Then for any quantum noise represented by a super-operator $\mathcal{E}$, we have $K^*_{\mathcal{E}} \leq K^*$, where K^* and $K^*_{\mathcal{E}}$ are the Lipschitz constants of $\mathcal{A}$ and $\mathcal{A}_{\mathcal{E}} = (\mathcal{E} \circ \mathcal{U}, \{\mathcal{M}_i\}_{i \in \mathcal{O}})$.*

Proof (Outline). The proof of this theorem mainly depends on the observation that the range of $\mathcal{A}_{\mathcal{E}}$ is a subset of the range of $\mathcal{A}$, i.e. $\{\mathcal{E} \circ \mathcal{U}(\rho) : \rho \in \mathcal{D}(\mathcal{H})\} \subseteq \{\mathcal{U}(\rho) : \rho \in \mathcal{D}(\mathcal{H})\} = \mathcal{D}(\mathcal{H})$. Subsequently, by Definition 2 of fairness, the output distributions of $\mathcal{A}_{\mathcal{E}}$ are contained in that of $\mathcal{A}$. A restatement of this theorem in terms of quantum states (measurements) distinguishability and its full proof are presented in Appendix C in [37].

Remark 1. The above theorem indicates that adding noises at the end of noiseless computation can always improve fairness. Indeed, this is also true when the noises appear in the middle (after any gate in the circuit).

5   Fairness Verification

In this section, we develop an algorithm for the fairness verification of quantum decision models based on the theoretical results obtained in the last section. Formally, the major problem concerned in this paper is the following:

Problem 1 (Fairness Verification Problem). Given a quantum decision model $\mathcal{A}$ and $1 \geq \varepsilon, \delta > 0$, check whether or not $\mathcal{A}$ is (ε, δ)-fair. If not then (at least) one bias pair (ρ, σ) is provided.

5.1   Computing the Lipschitz Constant

First of all, we note that essentially, Theorem 1 gives a verification condition for fairness in terms of the Lipschitz constant K^*. Therefore, computing K^* is crucial for fairness verification. However, this problem is much more difficult than that in the classical counterpart as discussed in Subsect. 1.1. The following theorem provides a method to compute the Lipschitz constant K^* by evaluating the eigenvalues of certain matrices.

Theorem 3. *1. Given a quantum decision model* $\mathcal{A} = (\mathcal{E}, \{M_i\}_{i \in \mathcal{O}})$. *The Lipschitz constant* K^* *is:*

$$K^* = \max_{A \subseteq \mathcal{O}}[\lambda_{\max}(M_A) - \lambda_{\min}(M_A)] \text{ with } M_A = \sum_{i \in A} \mathcal{E}^\dagger(M_i^\dagger M_i),$$

where $\mathcal{E}^\dagger$ *is the conjugate map[5] of* $\mathcal{E}$, *and* $\lambda_{\max}(M_A)$ *and* $\lambda_{\min}(M_A)$ *are the maximum and minimum eigenvalues of positive semi-definite matrix* M_A, *respectively.*

2. Furthermore, let $A^* \subseteq \mathcal{O}$ *be an optimal solution of reaching the Lipschitz constant, i.e.,*

$$A^* = \arg\max_{A \subseteq \mathcal{O}}[\lambda_{\max}(M_A) - \lambda_{\min}(M_A)]$$

and $|\psi\rangle$ *and* $|\phi\rangle$ *be two normalized eigenvectors corresponding to the maximum and minimum eigenvalues of* M_{A^*}, *respectively. Then we have*

$$d(\mathcal{A}(\psi), \mathcal{A}(\phi)) = K^* D(\psi, \phi) = K^*,$$

where $\psi = |\psi\rangle\langle\psi|$ *and* $\phi = |\phi\rangle\langle\phi|$.

Proof (Outline). This theorem can be proved by reducing the problem of calculating the Lipschitz constant to determining the distinguishability of a quantum measurement. Then we claim that the distinguishability is the maximum difference between the eigenvalues of the matrices generated by the measurement. The details are quite involved, and we postpose them into Appendix C in [37].

Based on the above theorem, we are able to develop Algorithm 1 for computing the Lipschitz constant K^*. The correctness and complexity are provided in the next subsection.

5.2   Fairness Verification Algorithm

Now we are ready to present our main algorithm—Algorithm 2—for verifying fairness of quantum decision models.

To see the correctness of Algorithm 2, let us first note that the second part of Theorem 3 shows that K^* can be achieved by $d(\mathcal{A}(\psi), \mathcal{A}(\phi))$ for two mutually orthogonal quantum (pure) states ψ and ϕ. On the other hand, the second part of Theorem 1 asserts that such states ψ and ϕ form a bias kernel. Moreover, since state $\sigma \in \mathcal{D}(\mathcal{H})$ in (4) is arbitrary and $\mathcal{D}(\mathcal{H})$ is an infinite set, infinitely many bias pairs can be generated from this kernel.

To analyze the complexities of Algorithm 2 and its subroutine—Algorithm 1, we first see by Theorem 1 that for evaluating the (ε, δ)-fairness of quantum decision model $\mathcal{A}$, the Lipschitz constant K^* is sufficient and necessary. Thus the first step (Line 1) of Algorithm 2 is to call Algorithm 1 to compute K^* by the mean of Theorem 3. The complexity of Algorithm 1 mainly attributes to computing $W_i = \sum_{j \in \mathcal{J}} E_j^\dagger M_i^\dagger M_i E_j$ for each $i \in \mathcal{O}$, and for each $A \subseteq \mathcal{O}$, $\sum_{i \in A} W_i$

---

[5] $\mathcal{E}^\dagger(\rho) = \sum_{j \in \mathcal{J}} E_j^\dagger \rho E_j$ if $\mathcal{E}$ admits Kraus matrix form $\mathcal{E}(\rho) = \sum_{j \in \mathcal{J}} E_j \rho E_j^\dagger$.

Algorithm 1. Lipschitz($\mathcal{A}$)

Input: A quantum decision model $\mathcal{A} = (\mathcal{E} = \{E_j\}_{j \in \mathcal{J}}, \{M_i\}_{i \in \mathcal{O}})$ on a Hilbert space $\mathcal{H}$ with dimension N.
Output: The Lipschitz constant K^* and (ψ, ϕ) as in Theorem 3.
1: **for each** $i \in \mathcal{O}$ **do**
2:     $W_i = \mathcal{E}^\dagger(M_i^\dagger M_i) = \sum_{j \in \mathcal{J}} E_j^\dagger M_i^\dagger M_i E_j$
3: **end for**
4: $K^* = 0$, $A^* = \emptyset$ be an empty set and $M_{A^*} = \mathbf{0}$, zero matrix.
5: **for each** $A \subseteq \mathcal{O}$ **do**
6:     $M_A = \sum_{i \in A} W_i$ and $K_A = \lambda_{\max}(M_A) - \lambda_{\min}(M_A)$
7:     **if** $K_A > K^*$ **then**
8:         $K^* = K_A$, $A^* = A$ and $M_{A^*} = M_A$
9:     **end if**
10: **end for**
11: $|\psi\rangle$ and $|\phi\rangle$ are obtained two normalized eigenvectors corresponding to the maximum and minimum eigenvalues of M_{A^*}, respectively.
12: **return** K^* and (ψ, ϕ)

Algorithm 2. FairVeriQ($\mathcal{A}, \varepsilon, \delta$)

Input: A quantum decision model $\mathcal{A} = (\mathcal{E} = \{E_j\}_{j \in \mathcal{J}}, \{M_i\}_{i \in \mathcal{O}})$ on a Hilbert space $\mathcal{H}$ with dimension N, and real numbers $1 \geq \varepsilon, \delta > 0$.
Output: **true** indicates $\mathcal{A}$ is (ε, δ)-fair or **false** with a bias kernel pair (ψ, ϕ) indicates $\mathcal{A}$ is not (ε, δ)-fair.
1: $(K^*, (\psi, \phi))$=Lipschitz($\mathcal{A}$)   // Call Algorithm 1
2: **if** $\delta \geq K^* \varepsilon$ **then**
3:     **return true**
4: **else**
5:     **return false** and (ψ, ϕ)
6: **end if**

---

and its maximum and minimum eigenvalues (and the corresponding eigenvectors for $A = A^*$ at the end). The former calculation needs $O(N^5)$ as the multiplication of $N \times N$ matrices needs $O(N^3)$ operations, and the number $|\mathcal{J}|$ of the Kraus operators $\{E_j\}_{j \in \mathcal{J}}$ of $\mathcal{E}$ can be at most N^2 [39, Chapter 2.2]; the complexity of the latter one is $O(2^{|\mathcal{O}|}|\mathcal{O}|N^2)$ since the number of subsets of $\mathcal{O}$ is $2^{|\mathcal{O}|}$, $|A| \leq |\mathcal{O}|$ for any $A \subseteq \mathcal{O}$ and computing maximum and minimum eigenvalues with corresponding eigenvectors of $N \times N$ matrix costs $O(N^2)$. Therefore, the total complexity of Algorithm 1 is $O(N^5 + 2^{|\mathcal{O}|}|\mathcal{O}|N^2)$. After that, in Lines 2-6, we simply compare δ and $K^* \varepsilon$ to answer the fairness verification problem. So, Algorithm 2 shares the same complexity with Algorithm 1.

Theorem 4. *The worst case complexities of Algorithms 1 and 2 are both $O(N^5 + 2^{|\mathcal{O}|}|\mathcal{O}|N^2)$, where N is the dimension of input Hilbert state space $\mathcal{H}$ and $|\mathcal{O}|$ is the number of the measurement outcome set $\mathcal{O}$.*

Like their classical counterparts, quantum machine learning models usually downscale large-dimension input data to small-size outputs. This means that the number $|\mathcal{O}|$ of the measurement outcome set $\mathcal{O}$ is far smaller than the dimension N of input Hilbert state space $\mathcal{H}$. It is even a constant 2 in most real-world tasks for binary decisions/classifications, such as income prediction and credit scoring (see the examples in Sect. 6), and in this case, the complexities of Algorithms 1 and 2 are both $O(N^5)$. However, the dimension N is exponential in the number n of the input qubits, i.e., $N = 2^n$. Thus the complexity turns out to be $O(2^{5n})$. In verification of classical models, this *state-space explosion problem* [40] can be mitigated by using some custom-made data structures to capture the features of the underlying data, e.g. Binary Decision Diagrams (BDDs) [41]. In the quantum case, we cross this difficulty by employing a quantum data structure—*Tensor Networks (TNs)*, originating from quantum many-body physics—to exploit the locality and regularity of the circuits representing quantum machine learning models. As a result, quantum models with up to $n = 27$ qubits can be handled by our verification algorithm.

6   Evaluation

In this section, we evaluate the efficiency of our verification algorithm (Algorithm 1) on noisy quantum decision models. The algorithm is implemented on *TensorFlow Quantum* [4]—a platform of Google for designing and training quantum machine learning algorithms. Then we test it by verifying the fairness of two groups of examples:

- *Small-scale models trained from real-world data* (Subsect. 6.1): There is still no public benchmarks for quantum decision models. We choose two publicly available financial datasets, *German Credit Data* [42] and *Adult Income Dataset* from *Diverse Counterfactual Explanations Dataset* [43] and train small-scale quantum models from them on TensorFlow Quantum. Then we evaluate the Lipschitz constant K^* of the trained models by Algorithm 1.
- *Medium-scale models* (Subsect. 6.2): Medium-scale models (10–30 qubits) are difficult to be trained on TensorFlow Quantum with a personal computer or a small server since the simulated quantum noises lead to large-size (up to $2^{30} \times 2^{30}$) matrix manipulations. Thus we turn to using a model from the tutorial of TensorFlow Quantum as a seed to generate a group of medium-scale models. The efficiency of our algorithm is then demonstrated on these models with randomly sampled parameters.

All source codes can be found at: https://github.com/Veri-Q/Fairness. All our experiments are carried out on a server with Intel Xeon Platinum 8153 @ 2.00 GHz $\times$ 256 Processors, 2048 GB Memory and no dedicated GPU. The machine runs Centos 7.7.1908 and each experiment is run with at most 80 processors. We use the NumPy and Google TensorNetwork [44] Python packages to compute Lipschitz constants and bias kernels for small-scale models and medium-scale models, respectively. These two packages have their own advantages in different sizes.

6.1   A Practical Application in Finance

Adult Income Dataset. The original version of this dataset is extracted from the 1994 Census database by Barry Becker [45]. We use the modified version of the adult income dataset by DiCE [43]. Each individual in this modified dataset has 8 features and the classification whether the income exceeds $50,000/year or not. We randomly select 1,000 and 400 data from the training dataset and test dataset contained in this modified dataset, respectively. The task of the quantum decision model task is to predict whether an individual's income exceeds $50,000/year or not.

German Credit Dataset. This dataset contains 1,000 loan applicants with 20 features and the classification whether they are considered as having good credit risk or not (Creditability). It provides 500 applicants for the training and 500 applicants for the test. By using the p-value with creditability for each variable [46], we have 9 features (e.g., Account Balance, Payment Status) left as significant predictors. The task of the quantum model to be trained is to classify whether the person has good credit risk or not.

These datasets contain some categorical features, which are transformed into different integer numbers for further operations. Then we have $n \in \{8, 9\}$ numbering features in total and use the following data-encoding feature map:

$$\boldsymbol{x} = (x_1, x_2, \ldots, x_n) \mapsto |\psi(\boldsymbol{x})\rangle = \bigotimes_{j=1}^{n} X^{x_j} |0\rangle$$

for Pauli matrix X defined in Example 2 to encode an n-dimensional feature vector $\boldsymbol{x}$ (each dimension is normalized by its maximum value) to an n-qubits quantum state $\psi(\boldsymbol{x}) = |\psi(\boldsymbol{x})\rangle\langle\psi(\boldsymbol{x})|$.

Models: For the quantum decision model, we choose the basic rotation and entangling building blocks [47] to construct parameterized quantum circuits (see Fig. 2). In the rotation block, without any ambiguity, we directly use X and Z to represent parameterized X-rotation $e^{-i\frac{\theta_1}{2}X}$ and parameterized Z-rotation $e^{-i\frac{\theta_2}{2}Z}$ on one qubit, respectively. It is worth noting that the parameterized $(Z\text{-}X\text{-}Z)$-rotation induces universal gates on each qubit [25, Theorem 4.1], and thus the expressiveness of the models on one qubit is ensured. In the entangling block, XX stands for the parameterized $(X \otimes X)$-rotation $e^{-i\frac{\theta_3}{2}X \otimes X}$ on two qubits. The entangling block can create entanglement between each qubit. Here entanglement is a unique feature of quantum models to express the interactions of qubits. The model is constructed by alternately using these two blocks with a quantum measurement M at the end of the model.

Since TensorFlow Quantum is inefficient in training noisy models, we only use 3 rotation blocks and 2 entangling blocks in the training models. In addition, to

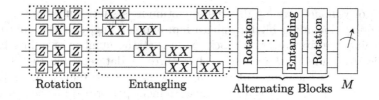

Fig. 2. Parameterized Quantum Circuits for Quantum Finance Decision Models.

Table 1. Experimental results of Lipschitz constant K^* of the trained models.

Dataset	Noise		Accuracy		K^*	Time
	type	probability	train	test		
	None		0.732	0.686	1.0000×10^0	\
	Phase flip	10^{-4}	0.726	0.692	9.9997×10^{-1}	2.36s
		10^{-3}	0.724	0.714	9.9800×10^{-1}	2.02s
		10^{-2}	0.704	0.708	9.6918×10^{-1}	1.94s
	Depolarizing	10^{-4}	0.709	0.686	9.9977×10^{-1}	2.77s
		10^{-3}	0.701	0.712	9.9789×10^{-1}	2.93s
German Credit		10^{-2}	0.709	0.682	9.7916×10^{-1}	3.44s
	Bit flip	10^{-4}	0.712	0.728	9.9975×10^{-1}	2.27s
		10^{-3}	0.710	0.690	9.9743×10^{-1}	2.47s
		10^{-2}	0.724	0.678	9.7981×10^{-1}	2.05s
	Mixed noise	10^{-4}	0.710	0.704	9.9980×10^{-1}	2.15s
		10^{-3}	0.731	0.682	9.9834×10^{-1}	2.08s
		10^{-2}	0.731	0.692	9.7021×10^{-1}	1.95s
	None		0.777	0.770	1.0000×10^0	\
	Phase flip	10^{-4}	0.784	0.767	9.9992×10^{-1}	0.44s
		10^{-3}	0.771	0.770	9.9805×10^{-1}	0.51s
		10^{-2}	0.773	0.767	9.8057×10^{-1}	0.48s
	Depolarizing	10^{-4}	0.774	0.767	9.9987×10^{-1}	0.57s
		10^{-3}	0.781	0.767	9.9867×10^{-1}	0.58s
Adult Income (DiCE)		10^{-2}	0.779	0.767	9.8667×10^{-1}	0.69s
	Bit flip	10^{-4}	0.780	0.767	9.9980×10^{-1}	0.57s
		10^{-3}	0.777	0.767	9.9800×10^{-1}	0.49s
		10^{-2}	0.778	0.770	9.8117×10^{-1}	0.54s
	Mixed noise	10^{-4}	0.762	0.720	9.9987×10^{-1}	0.68s
		10^{-3}	0.752	0.720	9.9812×10^{-1}	0.67s
		10^{-2}	0.759	0.720	9.7647×10^{-1}	0.67s

simulate noisy models, we put different quantum noises introduced in Example 2 on each qubit, including bit flip, phase flip, depolarizing, and the mixtures of them, behind the first rotation block. Note that the number of qubits for the models is the same as the number of features of datasets due to the above choice of the data-encoding feature map. The final measurement $M = \{M_0 = I \otimes |0\rangle\langle 0|, M_1 = I \otimes |1\rangle\langle 1|\}$ is a local measurement performed on the last qubit. With the binary classification task, the loss function we choose is binary cross-entropy: $-\frac{1}{N} \sum_{j=1}^{N} c_j \cdot \log \bar{c}_j + (1 - c_j) \log(1 - \bar{c}_j))$, where N is the size of the batch fixed in the training process, c_j is the true label and $\bar{c}_j$ is the outcome of the measurement. All models are well trained and achieve around 70% train and test accuracy (see Column "Accuracy" in Table 1), matching that of the previously used classical and quantum finance decision models (e.g. [10,21]).

Evaluation Details and Results: The results of evaluating Algorithm 1 on the models trained from different datasets and different quantum noises are presented in Table 1. For different datasets, we train noise-free models to serve as the baseline for training and test accuracy (see Row "None"). Furthermore, different types of noise are added with different levels of probabilities. We list the Lipschitz constant K^* and the running time of Algorithm 1 aided by NumPy for each column. It can be seen that the higher level of noise's probability, the smaller value of constant K^*. Therefore, the claim of quantum noise improving fairness in Sect. 4.2 is confirmed by the numerical results. This is also observed in Table 2 later.

6.2   Scalability in the NISQ Era

Models: To reflect an actual application in the NISQ era, we choose not to randomly generate a parameterized quantum circuit model. Instead, we expanded the existing example of Quantum Convolutional Neural Network (QCNN) [32] in the QCNN tutorial[6] of TensorFlow Quantum from 8 qubits (see Fig. 3) to 27 qubits. In the experiment, we use the QCNN model with one convolution layer and one pooling layer. The noise is applied between convolution and pooling layers on each qubit. The final measurement is $M = \{M_0 = I \otimes |0\rangle\langle 0|, M_1 = I \otimes |1\rangle\langle 1|\}$ performed on the last qubit with a gate U appended before. Since training a noisy model of this size is currently intractable on TensorFlow Quantum, the parameters in the model are all randomly sampled.

---

[6] https://tensorflow.google.cn/quantum/tutorials/qcnn.

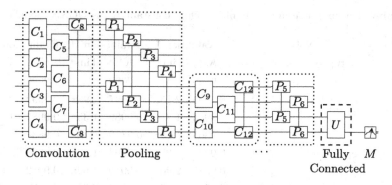

Fig. 3. The QCNN model in the tutorial of TensorFlow Quantum. Each C_i in the convolution layer is a parameterized 2-qubit gate to find a new state between adjacent qubits. Each P_i in the pooling layer is also a parameterized 2-qubit gate with another form that attempts to extract the information of two qubits into a single qubit.

Evaluation Details and Results: We choose the models with 25 and 27 qubits to run experiments. Since the parameters are randomly sampled, for each noise with different levels of probability, we generate the model and evaluate the Lipschitz constant K^* for 3 times. However, because a $2^{25} \times 2^{25}$ or $2^{27} \times 2^{27}$ complex matrix consumes a huge amount of memory, it is not feasible to directly use Algorithm 1 as the previous experiment, where we represent the M_A in Algorithm 1 as a matrix and use the package NumPy to evaluate eigenvalue. We instead use a tensor network [48] to represent the M_A and the subroutine of evaluating eigenvalue in Algorithm 1 is implemented with the basic power method for eigenvalue problem [49] by using TensorNetwork package. Although there are some packages for sparse matrix in Python that can collaborate with TensorNetwork, their implementation for computing eigenvalues still consumes a huge amount of memory. The evaluation results on QCNN models with randomly sampled parameters and different quantum noises are listed in Table 2. These results prove that our fairness verification algorithm is efficient and can handle 27-qubit quantum decision models on a small server. For further exploring the scalability of our verification algorithm, we also test on 29-qubit QCNN models; Please see Appendix D in [37] for the results.

Last but not least, it is worth noting that in all experiments, we also obtain bias kernels by Algorithm 1 at the running time presented in Tables 1 and 2, but as they are large-size (up to 2^{27}-dimensional) vectors, we do not show them.

Table 2. Experimental results of Lipschitz constant K^* of QCNN models.

#Qubits	Noise		Evaluation I		Evaluation II		Evaluation III	
	type	probability	K^*	Time	K^*	Time	K^*	Time
25	None		1.0000	\	1.0000	\	1.0000	\
	Phase flip	10^{-4}	0.9998	2.15m	0.9997	1.92m	0.9999	2.12m
		10^{-3}	0.9983	1.71m	0.9982	1.35m	0.9987	1.10m
		10^{-2}	0.9865	1.75h	0.9870	54.49m	0.9831	39.07m
	Depolarizing	10^{-4}	0.9998	2.22m	0.9998	1.59m	0.9998	2.38m
		10^{-3}	0.9985	2.46m	0.9980	1.62m	0.9982	2.04m
		10^{-2}	0.9824	2.33m	0.9802	2.53m	0.9809	1.77m
	Bit flip	10^{-4}	0.9997	1.74m	0.9998	1.60m	0.9999	2.15m
		10^{-3}	0.9986	2.44m	0.9980	1.80m	0.9991	2.37m
		10^{-2}	0.9943	1.78h	0.9854	20.78m	0.9919	49.36m
	Mixed noise	10^{-4}	0.9998	3.68m	0.9998	1.34m	0.9998	1.94m
		10^{-3}	0.9980	1.66m	0.9966	2.06m	0.9983	0.96m
		10^{-2}	0.9901	37.24m	0.9861	1.95h	0.9759	6.03m
27	None		1.0000	\	1.0000	\	1.0000	\
	Phase flip	10^{-4}	0.9999	6.75m	0.9998	7.34m	0.9998	8.62m
		10^{-3}	0.9980	6.66m	0.9977	9.55m	0.9981	6.56m
		10^{-2}	0.9896	7.64m	0.9839	54.12m	0.9709	4.45m
	Depolarizing	10^{-4}	0.9998	6.10m	0.9998	6.89m	0.9998	6.77m
		10^{-3}	0.9981	4.51m	0.9985	5.34m	0.9978	21.75m
		10^{-2}	0.9809	1.20h	0.9767	6.48m	0.9773	8.48m
	Bit flip	10^{-4}	0.9998	6.52m	0.9999	5.39m	0.9999	6.86m
		10^{-3}	0.9986	4.38m	0.9984	7.96m	0.9971	10.37m
		10^{-2}	0.9917	5.03h	0.9894	4.15h	0.9854	3.90h
	Mixed noise	10^{-4}	0.9998	6.67m	0.9998	5.19m	0.9997	10.39m
		10^{-3}	0.9976	7.06m	0.9976	5.91m	0.9986	6.62m
		10^{-2}	0.9806	7.70m	0.9850	7.98m	0.9881	6.02h

7   Conclusion

In this work, we initiate the studies on algorithmic verification of fairness of
quantum machine learning decision models. In particular, we showed that this
verification problem can be reduced to computing the Lipschitz constant of the
decision models, and then resolved the latter by introducing and estimating single measurement distinguishability. Based on these theoretical results, we developed an algorithm that can verify the (ε, δ)-fairness of quantum decision models
and provides useful bias kernels for explaining the unfairness of the models.

An interesting topic for future research is how to improve the results presented in this paper for training quantum decision models with fairness guarantee. On the other hand, further investigations are required to better understand the bias kernels detected by our verification algorithm, especially through more experiments on real-world applications.

Acknowledgments. Ji Guan would like to thank Jiayi Chen for her linguistic assistance during the preparation of this paper. This work was partly supported by the National Key R&D Program of China (Grant No: 2018YFA0306701), the National Natural Science Foundation of China (Grant No: 61832015).

References

1. Arute, F., et al.: Quantum supremacy using a programmable superconducting processor. Nature **574**(7779), 505–510 (2019)
2. Zhong, H.-S., Wang, H., Deng, Y.-H., Chen, M.-C., Peng, L.-C., Luo, Y.-H., Qin, J., Dian, W., Ding, X., Yi, H., et al.: Quantum computational advantage using photons. Science **370**(6523), 1460–1463 (2020)
3. Biamonte, J., Wittek, P., Pancotti, N., Rebentrost, P., Wiebe, N., Lloyd, S.: Quantum machine learning. Nature **549**(7671), 195–202 (2017)
4. Google. Tensorflow Quantum. https://www.tensorflow.org/quantum, (Accessed 2021)
5. Dixon, M.F., Halperin, I., Bilokon, P.: Machine Learning in Finance. Springer, Cham (2020). https://doi.org/10.1007/978-3-030-41068-1
6. Lloyd, S., Mohseni, M., Rebentrost, P.: Quantum principal component analysis. Nature Phys. **10**(9), 631–633 (2014)
7. Rebentrost, P., Schuld, M., Wossnig, L., Petruccione, F., Lloyd, S.: Quantum gradient descent and Newton's method for constrained polynomial optimization. New J. Phys. **21**(7), 073023 (2019)
8. Liu, N., Rebentrost, P.: Quantum machine learning for quantum anomaly detection. Phys. Rev. A **97**(4), 042315 (2018)
9. Di Pierro, A., Incudini, M.: Quantum machine learning and fraud detection. In: Dougherty, D., Meseguer, J., Mödersheim, S.A., Rowe, P. (eds.) Protocols, Strands, and Logic. LNCS, vol. 13066, pp. 139–155. Springer, Cham (2021). https://doi.org/10.1007/978-3-030-91631-2_8
10. Garc´Ia, R., Cahue, J., Pavas, S.: Credit risk scoring with a supervised quantum classifier, May 2020
11. Milne, A., Rounds, M., Goddard, P.: Optimal feature selection in credit scoring and classification using a quantum annealer. White Paper 1Qbit (2017)
12. Kerenidis, I., Prakash, A.: Quantum recommendation systems (2016). arXiv preprint arXiv:1603.08675
13. Egger, D.J., et al.: Quantum computing for finance: state-of-the-art and future prospects. IEEE Trans. Quant. Eng. **1**, 1–24 (2020)
14. Orus, R., Mugel, S., Lizaso, E.: Quantum computing for finance: overview and prospects. Rev. Phys. **4**, 100028 (2019)
15. Flores, A.W., Bechtel, K., Lowenkamp, C.T.: False positives, false negatives, and false analyses: A rejoinder to machine bias: there's software used across the country to predict future criminals. and it's biased against blacks. Fed. Probation **80**, 38 (2016)

16. Calders, T., Kamiran, F., Pechenizkiy, M.: Building classifiers with independency constraints. In: 2009 IEEE International Conference on Data Mining Workshops, pp. 13–18. IEEE (2009)
17. Pedreshi, D., Ruggieri, S., Turini, F.: Discrimination-aware data mining. In: Proceedings of the 14th ACM Sigkdd International Conference On Knowledge Discovery and Data Mining, pp. 560–568 (2008)
18. Dwork, C., Hardt, M., Pitassi, T., Reingold, O., Zemel, R.: Fairness through awareness. In: Proceedings of the 3rd Innovations in Theoretical Computer Science Conference, pp. 214–226 (2012)
19. Barocas, S., Hardt, M., Narayanan, A.: Fairness and Machine Learning. fairmlbook.org, (2019). http://www.fairmlbook.org
20. Binns, R.: On the apparent conflict between individual and group fairness. In: Proceedings of the 2020 Conference on Fairness, Accountability, and Transparency, pp. 514–524 (2020)
21. John, P.G., Vijaykeerthy, D., Saha, D.: Verifying individual fairness in machine learning models. In: Conference on Uncertainty in Artificial Intelligence, PMLR, pp. 749–758 (2020)
22. Albarghouthi, A., D'Antoni, L., Drews, S., Nori, A.V.: Fairsquare: probabilistic verification of program fairness. In: Proceedings of the ACM on Programming Languages (OOPSLA), vol. 1, pp. 1–30 (2017)
23. Bastani, O., Zhang, X., Solar-Lezama, A.: Probabilistic verification of fairness properties via concentration. In: Proceedings of the ACM on Programming Languages (OOPSLA), vol. 3, pp. 1–27 (2019)
24. Ghosh, B., Basu, D., Meel, K.S.: Justicia: a stochastic SAT approach to formally verify fairness. In: AAAI, pp. 7554–7563. AAAI Press (2021)
25. Nielsen, M.A., Chuang, I.L.: Quantum computation and quantum information. Cambridge University Press (2010)
26. Guan, J., Fang, W., Ying, M.: Robustness verification of quantum classifiers. In: Silva, A., Leino, K.R.M. (eds.) CAV 2021. LNCS, vol. 12759, pp. 151–174. Springer, Cham (2021). https://doi.org/10.1007/978-3-030-81685-8_7
27. Liu, N., Wittek, P.: Vulnerability of quantum classification to adversarial perturbations. Phys. Rev. A 101(6), 062331 (2020)
28. Weber, M., Liu, N., Li, B., Zhang, C., Zhao, Z.: Optimal provable robustness of quantum classification via quantum hypothesis testing. NPJ Quant. Inf. 7(1), 1–12 (2021)
29. Biamonte, J., Bergholm, V.: Tensor networks in a nutshell (2017). arXiv preprint arXiv:1708.00006
30. Cerezo, M., et al.: Variational quantum algorithms. Nature Rev. Phys. 3(9), 625–644 (2021)
31. Beer, K.: Training deep quantum neural networks. Nature Commun. 11(1), 1–6 (2020)
32. Cong, I., Choi, S., Lukin, M.D.: Quantum convolutional neural networks. Nature Phys. 15(12), 1273–1278 (2019)
33. Reddy, P., Bhattacherjee, A.B.: A hybrid quantum regression model for the prediction of molecular atomization energies. Mach. Learn. Sci. Technol. 2(2), 025019 (2021)
34. IBM. Learn quantum computation using Qiskit. https://qiskit.org/textbook/preface.html, (Accessed 2021)
35. Fazlyab, M., Robey, A., Hassani, H., Morari, M., Pappas, G.: Efficient and accurate estimation of Lipschitz constants for deep neural networks. In: Advances in Neural Information Processing Systems, vol. 32 (2019)

36. Szegedy, C., et al.: Intriguing properties of neural networks. In: Bengio, Y., LeCun, Y., (eds.) 2nd International Conference on Learning Representations, ICLR 2014, Banff, AB, Canada, pp. 14–16 April 2014. Conference Track Proceedings (2014)
37. Supplemental Material: Verifying Fairness in Quantum Machine Learning. https://doi.org/10.5281/zenodo.6612720
38. Yuxuan, D., Hsieh, M.-H., Liu, T., Tao, D., Liu, N.: Quantum noise protects quantum classifiers against adversaries. Phys. Rev. Res. 3(2), 023153 (2021)
39. Wolf, M.M.: Quantum channels & operations: Guided tour (2012). https://www-m5.ma.tum.de/foswiki/pub/M5/Allgemeines/MichaelWolf/QChannelLecture.pdf
40. Baier, C., Katoen, J.-P.: Principles of model checking. MIT Press (2008)
41. Akers, S.B.: Binary decision diagrams. IEEE Trans. Comput. 27(06), 509–516 (1978)
42. UCI Machine Learning Repository. Statlog (german credit data) data set. https://archive.ics.uci.edu/ml/datasets/Statlog+%28German+Credit+Data%29/, (Accessed 2021)
43. Mothilal, R.K., Sharma, A., Tan, C.: Explaining machine learning classifiers through diverse counterfactual explanations. In: Proceedings of the 2020 Conference on Fairness, Accountability, and Transparency, January 2020
44. Roberts, C., et al.: Tensornetwork: a library for physics and machine learning (2019). https://tensornetwork.readthedocs.io/en/latest/index.html
45. Kohavi, R., Becker. B.: Uci machine learning repository, adult data set. https://archive.ics.uci.edu/ml/datasets/adult, (Accessed 2021)
46. The Pennsylvania State University. Analysis of german credit data. https://online.stat.psu.edu/stat508/book/export/html/796, (Accessed 2021)
47. Zhu, D., et al.: Training of quantum circuits on a hybrid quantum computer. Sci. Adv. 5(10), eaaw9918 (2019)
48. Bridgeman, J.C., Chubb, C.T.: Hand-waving and interpretive dance: an introductory course on tensor networks. J. Phys. A: Math. Theor. 50(22), 223001 (2017)
49. Bai, Z., Demmel, J., Dongarra, J., Ruhe, A., van der Vorst, H.: Templates for the Solution of Algebraic Eigenvalue Problems. Society for Industrial and Applied Mathematics (2000)

MoGym: Using Formal Models for Training and Verifying Decision-making Agents

Timo P. Gros[1], Holger Hermanns[1,2], Jörg Hoffmann[1], Michaela Klauck[1(✉)], Maximilian A. Köhl[1(✉)], and Verena Wolf[1]

[1] Saarland University, Saarland Informatics Campus, Saarbrücken, Germany
[2] Institute of Intelligent Software, Guangzhou, China
{timopgros,hermanns,hoffmann,klauck,koehl,wolf}@cs.uni-saarland.de

Abstract. MoGym, is an integrated toolbox enabling the training and verification of machine-learned decision-making agents based on formal models, for the purpose of sound use in the real world. Given a formal representation of a decision-making problem in the JANI format and a reach-avoid objective, MoGym (a) enables training a decision-making agent with respect to that objective directly on the model using reinforcement learning (RL) techniques, and (b) it supports rigorous assessment of the quality of the induced decision-making agent by means of deep statistical model checking (DSMC). MoGym implements the standard interface for training environments established by OpenAI Gym, thereby connecting to the vast body of existing work in the RL community. In return, it makes accessible the large set of existing JANI model checking benchmarks to machine learning research. It thereby contributes an efficient feedback mechanism for improving in particular reinforcement learning algorithms. The connective part is implemented on top of Momba. For the DSMC quality assurance of the learned decision-making agents, a variant of the statistical model checker MODES of the MODEST TOOLSET is leveraged, which has been extended by two new resolution strategies for non-determinism when encountered during statistical evaluation.

Keywords: Formal Methods · Statistical Model Checking · Reinforcement Learning

1 Introduction

Making optimal decisions in an uncertain environment is the crux of many practical problems. Reinforcement Learning (RL) is a popular method to compute near-optimal policies for sequential decision-making problems [60]. In the last years, RL algorithms that approximate optimal decision policies by training deep

---

Authors are listed alphabetically. This work was partially supported by the German Research Foundation (DFG) under grant No. 389792660 as part of TRR 248, by the European Regional Development Fund (ERDF), and by the Key-Area Research and Development Program Grant 2018B010107004 of Guangdong Province.

S. Shoham and Y. Vizel (Eds.): CAV 2022, LNCS 13372, pp. 430–443, 2022.
https://doi.org/10.1007/978-3-031-13188-2_21

neural networks have exhibited unprecedented performance in various tasks [47]. However, the expressivity of these models makes them difficult to interpret or to be checked for consistency for some desired properties. This is an impediment to the use of such representations in safety-critical applications [61]. In addition, the environment of the decision-making agent executing the policy during training is typically specified implicitly in the form of simulation code. In the academic context, for instance the Arcade Learning Environment is widely used, which provides game simulators for different ATARI 2006 benchmarks [6].

If one strives for a principled understanding of the power of RL algorithms or of the properties of a specific learned agent in the (possibly uncertain) environment, a formal, mathematically precise and unambiguous description of the *training environment* appears central. The formal methods community has developed appropriate language concepts for the description of such environment models. Their advantage lies in their succinctness and modularity as well as their underlying mathematically rigorous formal semantics based on stochastic process models such as Markov Decision Processes (MDPs) [53], the main semantic object of probabilistic model checking [40]. A widespread format to describe MDP models of environments is the JANI format [14], providing a modular, automata-like syntax, supported by several model checkers, like Storm, the MODEST TOOLSET, EPMC [29,30,33], and via a translation also by PRISM [41].

This paper presents MoGym, a toolbox that bridges the gap between formal methods and RL by enabling (a) formally specified training environments to be used with machine-learned decision-making agents, and (b) the rigorous assessment of the quality of learned agents. For (a), it implements and extends the OpenAI Gym API [11], which is the widely used standard interface for deep reinforcement learning [16,26,35,50,55]. MoGym is based on Momba [39], a Python toolbox for dealing with quantitative models from construction to analysis centered around JANI. MoGym can process JANI models for the description of a training environment and, based on the induced formal MDP semantics, makes it possible to train agents using popular RL algorithms.

For (b), the environment format itself is accessible to state-of-the-art model checkers. This enables probabilistic model checking of a specific agent acting in the environment specified by the model. This can be crucial to determining if further training improves the agent's quality and, whenever synthesis of the optimal agent is feasible, it allows a comparison of the agent's behavior to the optimal one. As such, the environment provides a stable and fully controllable training and checking context to assert the safety risk induced by an agent during and after training. More concrete, MoGym leverages deep statistical model checking (DSMC) [20,21]. As shown in these works on DSMC, the quality assessment of an agent during training is not trivial and can especially not always be derived from the observed training returns. Hence, analyzing the quality of the decision-making agents after training clearly is of interest [20,21], especially for badly interpretable agent structures such as neural networks (NN). In DSMC this is done by using the decision-making agent as an oracle resolving the non-determinism in the MDP specifying the environment. When resolving

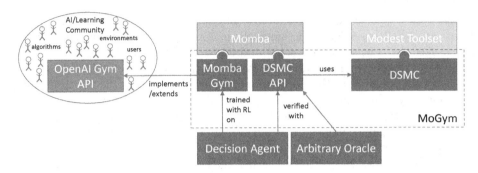

Fig. 1. The architecture of MoGYM and its components

the non-determinism, a Markov chain results on which the probability of satisfying a given reach-avoid objective can be calculated. A prominent technique for doing so with very low memory requirements is statistical model checking (SMC) [5,7,32,34,44,64,67]. The satisfaction probability for the reach-avoid objective calculated using statistics based on a set of simulation runs of the resulting Markov chain, can serve as an indicator of the quality of the decision-making agent for solving the reach-avoid task it was originally trained on.

MoGYM comprises the following components:

- *Momba Gym*, newly implemented on top of Momba [39]. It implements and extends the OpenAI Gym API [11] for deep reinforcement learning. Momba Gym can be used to load a specified formal model together with a reach-avoid objective given by a JANI file [14] and then train a decision-making agent on it, which interacts in the environment given by the formal model.
- The *DSMC API*, also newly implemented on top of Momba. It includes a Python API to use the DSMC functionality [20,21] of the MODEST TOOLSET [13,30].
- *DSMC* implemented in the MODEST TOOLSET. In prior work [20,21], we implemented Deep Statistical Model Checking for specific networks and purposes, only. With this work, we extend the statistical model checker MODES [13] of the MODEST TOOLSET to be able to handle any formal MDP model given in one of the input languages of the toolset, and any neural network of arbitrary structure, as well as arbitrary oracles connected via a function. With the DSMC functionality it is possible to statistically model check the probability with which formal properties, i.e., reach-avoid objectives, are fulfilled by the decision-making agent, respectively oracle.

Figure 1 shows how the different parts of MoGYM are interconnected. First, a decision-making agent can be trained on a formal model and a reach-avoid property, defined in a JANI model, against the OpenAI Gym API by using Momba Gym with different reinforcement learning techniques, which can be implemented and defined by the user. Afterwards, the trained agent can be verified w.r.t. reach-avoid objectives by invoking the DSMC API, which makes use of the DSMC extension of the statistical model checker MODES. Alternatively, the training step can be skipped, or can be done in any other way, and an arbitrary external oracle can be checked.

We are not aware of any other work that enables a direct connection of formal verification models and reinforcement learning that directly allows the analysis of different RL agents for a variety of verification benchmarks.

Outline of the paper. In Sect. 2 we describe the Momba Gym Python API and explain how MoGym is used to train agents on existing JANI MDPs. Sect. 3 presents the DSMC API of Momba, and discusses its use to assess the quality of decision-making agents or arbitrary oracles via DSMC, together with the new DSMC functionality of MODES. In Sect. 4 we provide empirical insight into the full functionality of MoGym. Sect. 5 concludes the paper.

A preview of the Jupyter Notebook demonstrating the code we used to execute the experiments shown in the paper can be found online. It will later be part of the full artifact for the tool paper.

2 Formal Models as Training Environments

At the heart of MoGym is an implementation of the OpenAI Gym API in *Momba Gym*, which now enables the usage of JANI models as training environments. OpenAI Gym [11] constitutes *the* standard API for interfacing environments with different reinforcement learning algorithms enabling their comparison and fostering development of new techniques. It is widely used by both, algorithms that interact with the interface [16, 26, 35, 50, 55], as well as various benchmarks that implement (and sometimes extend) the interface [3, 15, 18, 62, 63, 66]. With Momba Gym, MoGym provides an extension of this API for general JANI MDP models equipped with reach-avoid properties. JANI is a JSON-based format for exchanging formal models between tools [14]. It is the standard format in the quantitative verification community and directly supported by state-of-the-art tools, like Storm [33], the MODEST TOOLSET [30], and EPMC [29]. Translations from and to other languages such as the PRISM language [41, 42], Modest [28] and even the planning language PPDDL [36, 37] exist.

A JANI model is a network of interacting automata with variables. Each automaton consists of a set of *locations* and a set of probabilistic *edges* from a *source* location to possibly multiple *destination* locations. Edges can be labeled with *edge labels* and annotated, depending on the destination, with assignments to variables. The *transitions* of the network are then obtained by synchronizing the automata, i.e., in every transition, potentially multiple automata participate with one edge, respectively. For our purposes, we assume that a decision-making agent controls a single automaton in the network, i.e., resolves the non-determinism of this automaton. Fig. 2 exemplifies the construction of an automata network from two automata: a controlled automaton (a) and a non-controlled automaton (b). Depending on which of the edges of automaton (b) is taken, the probability of ending up in state b is either 1.0 (action α) or 0.2 (action β). The final composition (c) is then the product of both automata synchronizing over the shared edge labels α and β. Controlling automaton (a) here

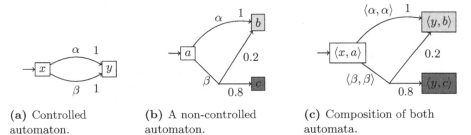

(a) Controlled automaton.

(b) A non-controlled automaton.

(c) Composition of both automata.

Fig. 2. Networks of interacting automata.

implies selecting which of the transitions in the final compositional does happen. By choosing the edge labeled with α, the transition $\langle \alpha, \alpha \rangle$ in the composition is selected and analogously for β. The choice of α in the controlled automaton obviously is the one maximizing the probability of reaching the green state $\langle y, b \rangle$ in the composition (c). In fact, the state is reached with certainty. Technically, this approach would extend to a multi-agent setting where different agents resolve the non-determinism in different parts of the model. We plan to provide a multi-agent setting in future work and assume here that all non-determinism not resolved by the controlled automaton is resolved uniformly.[1]

For training an agent in an environment, the OpenAI Gym API requires the definition of an *action space* and an *observation space*. In response to receiving observations from the observation space, the trained agent makes a decision from the action space. To enable the usage of general JANI MDP models as environments, an action space and observation space have to be extracted from the model. Depending on the model, there are multiple ways to do so. Momba Gym implements different strategies for this extraction. For the action space, edges of the controlled automaton can be selected by index or by label. For the observation space, (i) only global variables, (ii) global variables and local variables of the controlled automaton, or (iii) all variables can be declared as observable.[2] Other strategies can easily be added to Momba Gym.

Whenever the agent makes a decision in response to an observation, the decision is mapped to an edge of the controlled automaton and then to a transition of the network. If present, other non-deterministic influences are resolved uniformly at random, as mentioned above. In this case, the user receives a warning message so that this is taken into account when inspecting the results. After taking the respective transition, the environment continues the trace through the model until a state is reached where the agent can make a decision again.

Momba Gym supports reach-avoid properties of the form $\phi \, \mathbf{U} \, \psi$ where ϕ and ψ are propositional logic formulas over the model's states. $\phi \, \mathbf{U} \, \psi$ encodes the property that a state satisfying ψ is reached eventually and that ϕ holds on all states prior to reaching ψ. In a *bad state*, which should be avoided, ψ is not

---

[1] That is, each of the remaining non-deterministic options is considered equiprobable. MoGym can easily be extended with other mechanisms to resolve non-determinism.

[2] For more details about those strategies see https://momba.dev/gym/.

satisfied and (i) there are no remaining transitions or (ii) ϕ is violated. In a *goal state* ψ is satisfied. To apply RL techniques, Momba Gym supports providing a *reward structure* specifying the reward for reaching a goal, the (usually negative) reward for reaching a bad state, the reward for taking a decision neither leading to a goal nor to a bad state (usually zero), and the reward for taking a non-applicable decision. Using the Momba Gym API integrated in Momba, one can create a training environment from an arbitrary JANI MDP model as follows:

```
from momba import jani, gym
model = jani.load_model(JANI_SOURCE)
# ...
env = gym.create_generic_env(model, automaton)
```

In this command, `automaton` is the automaton the agent controls. The function `create_generic_env` takes additional optional parameters specifying the strategy for the extraction of the action and observation space (i.e., by index or by label, see above) as well as the reward structure (by defining the four reward values indicated above) and parameters of the JANI model. The resulting `env` implements the OpenAI Gym API such that it can be directly used to train an agent for the given property using arbitrary RL algorithms based on the OpenAI Gym API. Thereby, Momba Gym makes JANI MDP models accessible to the RL community to train and evaluate their algorithms on. The implementation of the Momba Gym environment uses the explicit state space exploration engine of Momba which is written in Rust. It is sufficiently performant such that it can be used to train different agents using state-of-the-art RL algorithms.

Momba Gym extends the OpenAI Gym API with the ability to *fork* the environment and query the applicable actions. The former is useful for algorithms based on *Monte-Carlo Tree Search (MTS)* [12], known to act favorably on prominent benchmarks, like Atari Games [24]. Further, MTS forms the basis of DeepMind's famous algorithms around AlphaGo and AlphaZero [57].

In addition to the general Momba Gym API, we provide exemplary code to train an agent for an arbitrary formal model. While we ourselves implemented *deep Q-learning* [47], MoGym is open to any (deep) reinforcement learning algorithm. Using our implementation of deep Q-learning, enables training of a decision-making agent for an arbitrary JANI MDP model.[3] We note however that deep RL is known to be hyperparameter sensitive [45], so intensive tweaking of hyperparameters might be needed for the learning to work. In this regard our deep Q-learning implementation is no exception.

3   Verifying Agents Using Statistical Model Checking

If given a formal model and a decision-making agent trained on it, MoGym supports verification by deep statistical model checking. To this end, the DSMC API of MoGym implements two functions, one for verifying arbitrary agents in the form of Python functions and one for verifying PyTorch neural networks.

---

[3] Details will be included in the artifact of the paper.

Both functions rely on our DSMC extension of the statistical model checker MODES [13] of the MODEST TOOLSET [30], which accepts both forms of decision entities, and returns the reach-avoid probability calculated by the model checker.

Statistical model checking is based on Monte-Carlo simulation [56, 65]. Using statistics, a probability estimate is derived from a set of simulation runs, regarding the satisfaction of a reach-avoid property, the error of which is bounded by a confidence interval. This is determined by the probability of the error in the computation being larger than ϵ is smaller than δ: $P(error > \epsilon) < \delta$. For SMC to be applicable, the non-determinism of the model needs to be resolved [8, 13]. In our DSMC setting this is done by the agent and otherwise resolved uniformly, i. e., equiprobable across all options (see Sect. 2). The computed reach-avoid probability can serve as an indicator of the overall quality of the decisions made by the agent [20]. The DSMC implementation in MODES provides the same functionality regarding the observation space (global and/or local variables) and action space (select by index or label) as the Momba Gym training infrastructure described in Sect. 2.

As mentioned above, MODES can deal with two variants of decision-making agents. An arbitrary Python function mapping observations to decisions can be checked with the DSMC API of MoGym by executing:

```
gym.checker.check_oracle(oracle, model, automaton)
```

Here, `oracle` is the Python function implementing the decision-making agent. Notably, this is not limited to trained agents in any way. Any arbitrary Python function with an appropriate signature can be used. The other parameters are analogous to `create_generic_env`. In particular, `check_oracle` also allows optionally specifying a strategy for extracting the action and observation spaces (see above).

While `check_oracle` involves executing Python code, a more efficient approach is available when the decision-making agent is a PyTorch neural network. In this case, the network can directly be verified with `check_nn`:

```
gym.checker.check_nn(nn, model, automaton)
```

To this end, we assume that the network is a sequence of layers. The function `check_nn` extracts these layers from the provided neural network `nn` and exports them in a JSON-based format. The neural network is then loaded by MODES and used for model checking without calling back into the Python runtime. With the help of TorchSharp [25] (a .NET library providing access to the library that powers PyTorch) our extension of MODES supports networks with arbitrary dimensions and activation functions.

Alternatively to the DSMC API provided by MoGym, it is also possible to invoke MODES on the command line to check a NN or to connect it to an arbitrary decision-making agent via a socket connection. The agent could be any program taking the information of the observation space as input and sending an action decision back.

4   Experimental Insights

With MoGym it is now possible to train agents and assess their quality for arbitrary JANI MDP models by evaluating them using the DSMC extension of the statistical model checker MODES. In the following, we demonstrate all parts of the workflow when MoGym is used from training to evaluation. For our case studies, the training was performed by using a well-established standard RL algorithm, the deep Q-learning algorithm [47].

Benchmarks. Working with MoGym starts with devising a formal model to train a decision-making agent on. For example, the *Quantitative Verification Benchmark Set* (QVBS) [31] contains JANI models originally collected for competitions among quantitative verification tools. With the help of MoGym they are now accessible for use in the learning community. For our case studies, we selected three MDP benchmarks from the QVBS: *cdrive.2*, *elevators* and *firewire_dl*. With respect to the observation spaces, we use the Momba Gym API default setting, in which only global variables are observable.

In *cdrive.2* a car drives in a city modeled using locations connected by roads with traffic lights. The car should reach a destination without an accident [10]. In the *elevators* case, a certain number of elevators is available to transport coins to a predefined level. An elevator can fall down on a lower level [10,38]. The *firewire_dl* benchmark models the leader election protocol in the Tree Identify Protocol of the IEEE 1394 High Performance Serial Bus [43,59].

Another popular benchmark is Racetrack, which has been adopted for decision making under uncertainty in many works [2,4,9,19,46,51,52]. In Racetrack, a vehicle needs to be driven on a discretized grid track towards a goal as fast as possible without crashing. A preview of the Jupyter Notebook showing the code we used for the experiments, which will later be part of the tool paper's artifact, is available online.

Training. We trained agents for all of the considered benchmarks by using the calls to the Momba Gym API as introduced in Sect. 2, which can be inspected in Sect. 2.1 and 2.2 of the Jupyter notebook.

Fig. 3 (a) and (b) shows the training progress of *cdrive.2* and *Racetrack*, respectively, depicted in blue. The training for *cdrive.2* took around 1 *min*, and for *Racetrack* about 22 *min*, on a standard laptop. In contrast to these two benchmarks, learning for *elevators* and *firewire_dl* failed. During training, the agent was able to reach the goal, but the NN was not able to generalize.

Verification. For *cdrive.2* and *Racetrack*, the training return increases over the number of training episodes and is quite stable at the end. The training return is commonly regarded as an estimator of the training progress [47,48]. Here it appears to indicate that the quality of the trained neural networks does neither increase nor decrease from a certain episode on.

However, we now can use DSMC to check the actual quality of the trained agents, i.e., we can determine how high the probability is that they indeed

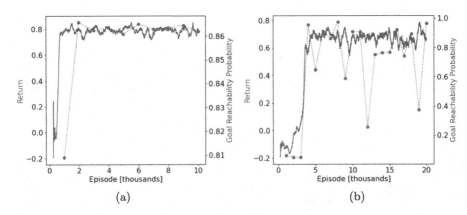

Fig. 3. Blue: Training curve showing sliding mean of the training return, i.e., the accumulated discounted reward over the last 500 training episodes, on the left y-axis. Note the different scale for (a) and (b). Red: Goal reachability probability on the right y-axis. Both are plotted over the number of training episodes on the x-axis. (a) Shows results for *cdrive.2* and (b) for *Racetrack*.

reach the goal in their respective environments defined by the MDP model. We do so by making use of the DSMC API of MoGym, introduced in Sect. 3 using MODES as backend. We check the goal reachability probability of the NN policies extracted every 1000 training episodes as shown in Sect. 2.1 and 2.2 of the Jupyter notebook.

As depicted by Fig. 3, the return during training is not as expressive as expected. While the training return is relatively consistent for both *cdrive.2* and *Racetrack*, the goal reachability probability (depicted in the red points) over training is not. In contrast, it both increases and decreases over the training episodes. So, the training return alone turns out not to be a good indicator for deciding which of the extracted policies actually is the best one. For *cdrive.2* (Fig. 3 (a)), this can be considered as fine tuning, as most of the policies perform near-optimal. In contrast, for *Racetrack* (Fig. 3 (b)), we observe a huge difference between the policies, including near-optimal policies as well as policies with a goal reachability probability of only about 20%. These deeper insights regarding the neural networks' quality are only possible by using DSMC.

Having selected the best policy for each benchmark, the analysis yields a goal reachability probability of 86.57% for *cdrive.2*, where a policy acting optimally would reach the goal with a probability of 86.45%.[4] The optimal value has been calculated with the exhaustive probabilistic model checking engine MCSTA [27] of the MODEST TOOLSET. The goal reachability probability of the best NN policy

---

[4] Note that the goal reachability probability of the NN policies is estimated by statistical model checking. Thus, even though it might seem surprising at first sight, it is of course possible that the analysis of our policy yields a slightly higher goal reachability probability than optimally possible as long as this is within the given confidence interval. We use $P(error > \epsilon) < \delta$, where $\epsilon = 0.01$ and $\delta = 0.05$, i.e., a confidence of 95%.

of the trained agent for *Racetrack* is 97.30% where the optimal policy reaches the goal with a probability of 99.99%.

5 Conclusion and Future Work

We presented MoGym, an integrated toolbox to train, analyze and verify decision-making agents on formal models. These formal models are made available through Momba Gym, which implements and extends the well-established OpenAI Gym API for arbitrary reinforcement learning techniques. Using these techniques to obtain NNs or, alternatively, some general decision-making agents, they can then be rigorously verified with DSMC using the new extension of MODES. The approach is open to all JANI MDPs and MODES can in principle handle arbitrary fully connected and even convolutional networks.

On the basis of the QVBS and *Racetrack*, we showed how the toolchain of MoGym works. As presented, our formal-model-based approach enables deeper insights for specified properties than non-formal, implicitly defined simulation-based environments.

In the future, we want to address the problem which caused the training for *elevators* and *firewire_dl* to fail. Given the successes of deep RL across many diverse environments [1,23,47,49,54,57,58], one is tempted to expect it to work well on the considered environments [22,31], too. Still, deep reinforcement learning is known to perform badly in domains with large action spaces [17], and we suspect this to be the root of the problem we observe. The action structures arising in networks of automata are of a specific kind. Rooted in process algebra, their main role is to enable and orchestrate synchronization across automata, and this is indeed the case for the JANI models *elevators* and *firewire_dl*. A more meaningful construction of an action space of compositional models suitable for learning appears needed.

Furthermore, the extension of our tool to other model types and an extension to control all of the modeled automata, making the learning task a multi-agent one, would clearly be of interest. Apart from that, we plan to build upon MoGym to develop DSMC techniques further. With DSMC Evaluation Stages [21] it has already been shown that DSMC can be applied during deep RL to determine state space regions with weak performance to concentrate on them during the learning process. With the help of MoGym this technique can now be done much more integrated and there is room for further implementations into this direction in our tool chain.

References

1. Agostinelli, F., McAleer, S., Shmakov, A., Baldi, P.: Solving the Rubik's Cube with Deep Reinforcement Learning and Search. Nature M. Intel. pp. 356–363 (2019)
2. Baier, C., Christakis, M., Gros, T.P., Groß, D., Gumhold, S., Hermanns, H., Hoffmann, J., Klauck, M.: Lab conditions for research on explainable automated decisions. In: TAILOR 2020. pp. 83–90 (2020)

3. Bard, N., et al.: The hanabi challenge: A new frontier for ai research. Artificial Intelligence **280**, 103216 (2020)
4. Barto, A.G., Bradtke, S.J., Singh, S.P.: Learning to act using real-time dynamic programming. Artificial Intelligence **72**(1), 81–138 (1995)
5. Basu, A., Bensalem, S., Bozga, M., Caillaud, B., Delahaye, B., Legay, A.: Statistical Abstraction and Model-Checking of Large Heterogeneous Systems. In: FORTE 2010. vol. 6117, pp. 32–46. Springer (2010)
6. Bellemare, M.G., Naddaf, Y., Veness, J., Bowling, M.: The arcade learning environment: An evaluation platform for general agents. JAIR **47**, 253–279 (2013)
7. Bogdoll, J., Fioriti, L.M.F., Hartmanns, A., Hermanns, H.: Partial order methods for statistical model checking and simulation. In: FORTE 2011. vol. 6722, pp. 59–74. Springer (2011)
8. Bogdoll, J., Hartmanns, A., Hermanns, H.: Simulation and Statistical Model Checking for Modestly Nondeterministic Models. In: GI/ITG Conf. Measurement, Modelling, and Eval. Comp. Sys. Depend. Fault Tol. pp. 249–252. Springer (2012)
9. Bonet, B., Geffner, H.: Labeled RTDP: improving the convergence of real-time dynamic programming. In: ICAPS. pp. 12–21 (2003)
10. Bonet, B., Givan, B.: Non-Deterministic Planning Track of the 2006 IPC. http://idm-lab.org/wiki/icaps/ipc2006/probabilistic/ (2006), acc. Oct., 13, 2021
11. Brockman, G., Cheung, V., Pettersson, L., Schneider, J., Schulman, J., Tang, J., Zaremba, W.: Openai gym. CoRR **abs/1606.01540** (2016)
12. Browne, C.B., et al.: A survey of monte carlo tree search methods. IEEE Trans. Comp. Intel. and AI in Games **4**(1), 1–43 (2012)
13. Budde, C.E., D'Argenio, P.R., Hartmanns, A., Sedwards, S.: A statistical model checker for nondeterminism and rare events. In: TACAS. pp. 340–358 (2018)
14. Budde, C.E., Dehnert, C., Hahn, E.M., Hartmanns, A., Junges, S., Turrini, A.: JANI: Quantitative model and tool interaction. In: TACAS. pp. 151–168 (2017)
15. Côté, M.A., et al.: Textworld: A learning environment for text-based games. In: Workshop on Computer Games. pp. 41–75. Springer (2018)
16. Doshi-Velez, F., Kim, B.: Towards a rigorous science of interpretable machine learning. arXiv preprint arXiv:1702.08608 (2017)
17. Dulac-Arnold, G., et al.: Deep reinforcement learning in large discrete action spaces. arXiv preprint arXiv:1512.07679 (2015)
18. Fan, L., Zhu, Y., Zhu, J., Liu, Z., Zeng, O., Gupta, A., Creus-Costa, J., Savarese, S., Fei-Fei, L.: Surreal: Open-source reinforcement learning framework and robot manipulation benchmark. In: Conf. Robot Learning. pp. 767–782. PMLR (2018)
19. Gros, T.P., Groß, D., Gumhold, S., Hoffmann, J., Klauck, M., Steinmetz, M.: TraceVis: Towards Visualization for Deep Statistical Model Checking. In: Int. Symp. Leveraging Applications of Formal Methods, Verification and Validation (2020)
20. Gros, T.P., Hermanns, H., Hoffmann, J., Klauck, M., Steinmetz, M.: Deep statistical model checking. In: FORTE 2020. pp. 96–114 (2020)
21. Gros, T.P., Höller, D., Hoffmann, J., Klauck, M., Meerkamp, H., Wolf, V.: DSMC evaluation stages: Fostering robust and safe behavior in deep reinforcement learning. In: QEST. pp. 197–216 (2021)
22. Gros, T.P., Höller, D., Hoffmann, J., Wolf, V.: Tracking the race between deep reinforcement learning and imitation learning. In: QEST 2020. vol. 12289, pp. 11–17. Springer (2020)
23. Gu, S., Holly, E., Lillicrap, T., Levine, S.: Deep Reinforcement Learning for Robotic Manipulation with Asynchronous Off-policy Updates. In: 2017 IEEE Int. Conf. robotics and automation (ICRA). pp. 3389–3396. IEEE (2017)

24. Guo, X., Singh, S., Lee, H., Lewis, R.L., Wang, X.: Deep learning for real-time atari game play using offline monte-carlo tree search planning. In: Advances in neural information processing systems. pp. 3338–3346 (2014)
25. Gustafsson, N., et al.: TorchSharp. https://github.com/dotnet/TorchSharp (2021), accessed on Sept., 22, 2021
26. Haarnoja, T., Zhou, A., Abbeel, P., Levine, S.: Soft actor-critic: Off-policy maximum entropy deep reinforcement learning with a stochastic actor. In: Int. conf. ML. pp. 1861–1870. PMLR (2018)
27. Hahn, E.M., Hartmanns, A.: A comparison of time- and reward-bounded probabilistic model checking techniques. In: SETTA 2016. pp. 85–100 (2016)
28. Hahn, E.M., Hartmanns, A., Hermanns, H., Katoen, J.: A compositional modelling and analysis framework for stochastic hybrid systems. Formal Methods Syst. Des. **43**(2), 191–232 (2013)
29. Hahn, E.M., Li, Y., Schewe, S., Turrini, A., Zhang, L.: iscasmc: A web-based probabilistic model checker. In: FM 2014. pp. 312–317 (2014)
30. Hartmanns, A., Hermanns, H.: The Modest Toolset: An integrated environment for quantitative modelling and verification. In: TACAS 2014. pp. 593–598 (2014)
31. Hartmanns, A., Klauck, M., Parker, D., Quatmann, T., Ruijters, E.: The Quantitative Verification Benchmark Set. In: TACAS 2019. pp. 344–350 (2019)
32. Hartmanns, A., Timmer, M.: On-the-Fly Confluence Detection for Statistical Model Checking. In: NFM 2013
33. Hensel, C., Junges, S., Katoen, J.P., Quatmann, T., Volk, M.: The probabilistic model checker storm. Int. Jour. on Software Tools for Technology Transfer (2021)
34. Hérault, T., Lassaigne, R., Magniette, F., Peyronnet, S.: Approximate probabilistic model checking. In: VMCAI 2004. vol. 2937, pp. 73–84. Springer (2004)
35. Ho, J., Ermon, S.: Generative adversarial imitation learning. Advances in neural information processing systems **29**, 4565–4573 (2016)
36. Hoffmann, J., Hermanns, H., Klauck, M., Steinmetz, M., Karpas, E., Magazzeni, D.: Let's learn their language? A case for planning with automata-network languages from model checking. In: AAAI 2020. pp. 13569–13575 (2020)
37. Klauck, M., Steinmetz, M., Hoffmann, J., Hermanns, H.: Bridging the gap between probabilistic model checking and probabilistic planning: Survey, compilations, and empirical comparison. J. Artif. Intell. Res. **68**, 247–310 (2020)
38. Koehler, J., Schuster, K.: Elevator control as a planning problem. In: 5. Int. Conf. Art. Intel. Planning Sys. pp. 331–338. AAAI (2000)
39. Köhl, M.A., Klauck, M., Hermanns, H.: Momba: JANI meets python. In: TACAS. pp. 389–398 (2021)
40. Kwiatkowska, M.Z., Norman, G., Parker, D.: Stochastic model checking. In: SFM 2007, Advanced Lectures. pp. 220–270. LNCS 4486 (2007)
41. Kwiatkowska, M.Z., Norman, G., Parker, D.: PRISM 4.0: Verification of probabilistic real-time systems. In: 23. CAV 2011. pp. 585–591 (2011)
42. Kwiatkowska, M.Z., Norman, G., Parker, D.: The PRISM benchmark suite. In: 9. QEST 2012. pp. 203–204 (2012)
43. Kwiatkowska, M.Z., Norman, G., Sproston, J.: Probabilistic model checking of deadline properties in the IEEE 1394 firewire root contention protocol. Formal Aspects Comput. **14**(3), 295–318 (2003)
44. Legay, A., Delahaye, B., Bensalem, S.: Statistical Model Checking: An Overview. In: Runtime Verification - 1. RV 2010. vol. 6418, pp. 122–135. Springer (2010)
45. Liessner, R., Schmitt, J., Dietermann, A., Bäker, B.: Hyperparameter optimization for deep reinforcement learning in vehicle energy management. In: ICAART (2). pp. 134–144 (2019)

46. McMahan, H.B., Gordon, G.J.: Fast exact planning in Markov decision processes. In: ICAPS. pp. 151–160 (2005)
47. Mnih, V., et al.: Human-level Control through Deep Reinforcement Learning. Nature **518**, 529–533 (2015)
48. Mnih, V., et al.: Asynchronous methods for deep reinforcement learning. In: Int. conf. machine learning. pp. 1928–1937. PMLR (2016)
49. Nazari, M., Oroojlooy, A., Snyder, L., Takac, M.: Reinforcement learning for solving the vehicle routing problem. In: Advances in Neural Inf. Proc. Sys. 31, pp. 9839–9849. Curran Associates, Inc. (2018)
50. Pathak, D., Agrawal, P., Efros, A.A., Darrell, T.: Curiosity-driven exploration by self-supervised prediction. In: Int. conf. ML. pp. 2778–2787. PMLR (2017)
51. Pineda, L.E., Lu, Y., Zilberstein, S., Goldman, C.V.: Fault-tolerant planning under uncertainty. In: IJCAI. pp. 2350–2356 (2013)
52. Pineda, L.E., Zilberstein, S.: Planning under uncertainty using reduced models: Revisiting determinization. In: ICAPS 2014 (2014)
53. Puterman, M.L.: Markov Decision Processes: Discrete Stochastic Dynamic Programming. Wiley (1994)
54. Sallab, A.E., Abdou, M., Perot, E., Yogamani, S.: Deep Reinforcement Learning Framework for Autonomous Driving. Electronic Imaging **2017**(19), 70–76 (2017)
55. Schulman, J., Wolski, F., Dhariwal, P., Radford, A., Klimov, O.: Proximal policy optimization algorithms. arXiv preprint arXiv:1707.06347 (2017)
56. Sen, K., Viswanathan, M., Agha, G.: On Statistical Model Checking of Stochastic Systems. In: CAV. pp. 266–280 (2005)
57. Silver, D., et al.: Mastering the Game of Go Without Human Knowledge. Nature **550**(7676), 354–359 (2017)
58. Silver, D., et al.: A General Reinforcement Learning Algorithm That Masters Chess, Shogi, and Go Through Self-play. Science **362**(6419), 1140–1144 (2018)
59. Stoelinga, M., Vaandrager, F.W.: Root contention in IEEE 1394. In: 5. AMAST Workshop, ARTS'99. vol. 1601, pp. 53–74. Springer (1999)
60. Sutton, R.S., Barto, A.G.: Reinforcement Learning: An Introduction. Adaptive computation and machine learning, The MIT Press, second edn. (2018)
61. Verma, A., Murali, V., Singh, R., Kohli, P., Chaudhuri, S.: Programmatically interpretable reinforcement learning. In: Int. Conf. on ML. PMLR (2018)
62. Waschneck, B., Reichstaller, A., Belzner, L., Altenmüller, T., Bauernhansl, T., Knapp, A., Kyek, A.: Optimization of global production scheduling with deep reinforcement learning. Procedia Cirp **72**, 1264–1269 (2018)
63. Xia, F., Zamir, A.R., He, Z., Sax, A., Malik, J., Savarese, S.: Gibson env: Real-world perception for embodied agents. In: IEEE Conf. Computer Vision and Pattern Recognition. pp. 9068–9079 (2018)
64. Younes, H.L.S., Simmons, R.G.: Probabilistic verification of discrete event systems using acceptance sampling. In: CAV 2002. vol. 2404, pp. 223–235. Springer (2002)
65. Younes, H.L., Kwiatkowska, M., Norman, G., Parker, D.: Numerical vs. Statistical Probabilistic Model Checking: An Empirical Study. In: TACAS. pp. 46–60. Springer (2004)
66. Yu, T., Quillen, D., He, Z., Julian, R., Hausman, K., Finn, C., Levine, S.: Meta-world: A benchmark and evaluation for multi-task and meta reinforcement learning. In: Conf. Robot Learning. pp. 1094–1100. PMLR (2020)
67. Zuliani, P., Platzer, A., Clarke, E.M.: Bayesian statistical model checking with application to Stateflow/Simulink verification. FM Sys. Des. **43**(2), 338–367 (2013)

Synthesis and Concurrency

Synthesis and Analysis of Petri Nets
from Causal Specifications

Mateus de Oliveira Oliveira[✉]

University of Bergen, Bergen, Norway
mateus.oliveira@uib.no

Abstract. Petri nets are one of the most prominent system-level formalisms for the specification of causality in concurrent, distributed, or multi-agent systems. This formalism is abstract enough to be analyzed using theoretical tools, and at the same time, concrete enough to eliminate ambiguities that would arise at implementation level. One interesting feature of Petri nets is that they can be studied from the point of view of true concurrency, where causal scenarios are specified using partial orders, instead of approaches based on interleaving.

On the other hand, message sequence chart (MSC) languages, are a standard formalism for the specification of causality from a purely behavioral perspective. In other words, this formalism specifies a set of causal scenarios between actions of a system, without providing any implementation-level details about the system.

In this work, we establish several new connections between MSC languages and Petri nets, and show that several computational problems involving these formalisms are decidable. Our results fill some gaps in the literature that had been open for several years. To obtain our results we develop new techniques in the realm of slice automata theory, a framework introduced one decade ago in the study of the partial order behavior of bounded Petri nets. These techniques can also be applied to establish connections between Petri nets and other well studied behavioral formalisms, such as the notion of Mazurkiewicz trace languages.

Keywords: MSC Languages · Mazurkiewicz Traces · Petri Nets

1 Introduction

Petri nets are one of the most prominent system-level formalisms for the specification of causality in concurrent, distributed or multi-agent systems. This formalism is abstract enough to be analyzed using theoretical tools, and at the same time, concrete enough to eliminate ambiguities that would arise at implementation level. One interesting feature of Petri nets is that they can be studied from the point of view of true concurrency, where causal scenarios are specified using partial orders, instead of approaches based on interleaving [18,36]. On the other hand, message sequence chart (MSC) languages [16,19], are a standard formalism for the specification of causality from a purely behavioral perspective. In

© The Author(s) 2022
S. Shoham and Y. Vizel (Eds.): CAV 2022, LNCS 13372, pp. 447–467, 2022.
https://doi.org/10.1007/978-3-031-13188-2_22

other words, this formalism specifies a set of causal scenarios between actions of a system, without providing any implementation-level details about the system.

In this work, we show that given an MSC automaton $\mathcal{M}$ specifying a set of partial orders $\mathcal{L}_{po}(\mathcal{M})$, and a b-bounded Petri net N with causal behavior $\mathcal{P}_{cau}(N)$, it is decidable whether $\mathcal{L}_{po}(\mathcal{M}) \cap \mathcal{P}_{cau}(N) \neq \emptyset$, and whether $\mathcal{L}_{po}(\mathcal{M}) \subseteq \mathcal{P}_{cau}(N)$ (Theorem 8). Additionally, for any given $b \in \mathbb{N}_+$, one can synthesize a b-bounded Petri net N that best captures the behavior specified by $\mathcal{M}$ (Theorem 9). More specifically, $\mathcal{L}_{po}(\mathcal{M}) \subseteq \mathcal{P}_{cau}(N)$, and there is no other b-bounded Petri net N' such that $\mathcal{L}_{po}(\mathcal{M}) \subseteq \mathcal{P}_{cau}(N') \subsetneq \mathcal{P}_{cau}(N)$. Finally, if the MSC automaton $\mathcal{M}$ is *locally synchronized*, a well studied property in the context of MSC language theory [1,19,31], then one can also test whether $\mathcal{P}_{cau}(N) \subseteq \mathcal{L}_{po}(\mathcal{M})$ (Theorem 8).

The feasibility of all computational problems described above have been open even for 1-bounded Petri nets, despite the fact that both Petri nets and MSC languages have been defined several decades ago. The key of our results is a new connection between MSC automata and slice automata, a formalism introduced in [33] in the study of the partial order behavior of bounded Petri nets. More specifically, we show that for each MSC automaton $\mathcal{M}$, one can construct a slice automaton $\mathcal{A}$ such that $\mathcal{L}_{po}(\mathcal{M}) = \mathcal{L}_{po}(\mathcal{A})$ (Theorem 7). A crucial feature of this construction is that it preserves good decidability properties. More precisely, if the input MSC automaton $\mathcal{M}$ is locally synchronized, then the obtained slice automaton $\mathcal{A}$ satisfies a property called saturation, which is crucial for the analysis of the causal behavior of Petri nets against safety specifications. To establish the connection mentioned above, we develop new slice-theoretic machinery of independent interest. In particular, we introduce the notions of slice-traces, and the notion of a locally synchronized slice automaton. In Sect. 8, we show that this new framework can also be used to establish connections between slice automata (and therefore, Petri nets), and the formalism of Mazurkiewicz trace languages [8,12,20,24,28,28], which is another well-studied formalism for the specification of sets of partial orders. In this case, it also holds that our reductions preserve good decidability properties, in the sense that finite automata accepting trace-closed languages are mapped to saturated slice automata.

Related Work. During the last four decades many partial order formalisms have been introduced and several connections have been established between these formalisms [9,13,17,21,25,29,36]. In particular, the expressiveness of finite message-passing automata with a priori unbounded FIFO channels was studied in [5], where it was shown that these automata capture exactly the class of MSC languages that are definable in existential monadic second-order logic interpreted over MSCs. Asynchronous cellular automata for traces were originally introduced by Zielonka [37]. A notion of asynchronous cellular automaton for pomsets without auto-concurrency was devised in [10]. Existentially bounded communicating automata have been considered in [14] where an equivalence was established between communication automata, globally cooperative compositional message sequence graphs and monadic second-order logic. Several connections between communicating automata with bounded channels and Mazurkiewicz traces have been considered in [15]. Generalizations of Mazurkiewicz traces have been considered in [22], and some extensions of message sequence graphs that are suitable for model checking under MSO specifications have been considered in [27]. Series parallel languages have been considered in [26]. It is important to note that the class of partial orders that can be accepted by slice automata are incomparable with the class of series parallel partial orders. On the one hand, series parallel partial orders are not necessarily k-bounded in the sense considered in this work. On the other hand, it is easy to construct k-bounded partial orders that are not series parallel. In particular, for $k \geq 4$, slice automata are able to define k-bounded partial orders whose underlying undirected graph have the complete graph K_4 as a minor, whereas it is known that no such partial order can be series parallel. It is also worth noting that none of the formalisms described in this paragraph are able to represent the causal behavior of arbitrary bounded Petri nets. Generalizations of finite automata accepting infinite words have been considered in several contexts. For instance, regular sets of infinite message sequence charts [23]. Automata over message sequence charts capable of accepting infinite MSCs were studied in [4]. We note that we do not consider automata capable of accepting infinite partial orders in this work.

2 The Causal Semantics of Petri Nets

In this section, we briefly define the classic notion of Petri-nets and describe their partial-order semantics. Within this semantics, partial orders are used to represent the causality between events in concurrent runs of a Petri net.

A Petri net is a tuple $N = (P, T, W, \mathfrak{m}_0)$ where P is a set of *places*, T is a set of *transitions* such that $P \cap T = \emptyset$, $W : (P \times T) \cup (T \times P) \to \mathbb{N}$ is a function that assigns a weight $W(x, y)$ to each element $(x, y) \in (P \times T) \cup (T \times P)$, and $\mathfrak{m}_0 : P \to \mathbb{N}$ is a function that assigns a non-negative integer $m_0(p)$ to each place $p \in P$.

A marking for N is any function of the form $\mathfrak{m} : P \to \mathbb{N}$. Intuitively, a marking $\mathfrak{m}$ assigns a number of tokens to each place of N. The marking $\mathfrak{m}_0$ is called the *initial marking* of N. If $\mathfrak{m}$ is a marking and t is a transition in T, then we say that t is enabled at $\mathfrak{m}$ if $\mathfrak{m}(p) - W(p, t) \geq 0$ for every place $p \in P$. If this is the case, the firing of t yields the marking $\mathfrak{m}'$ which is obtained from $\mathfrak{m}$ by setting $\mathfrak{m}'(p) = \mathfrak{m}(p) - W(p, t) + W(t, p)$ for every place $p \in P$. A firing sequence for N is a mixed sequence of markings and transitions $\mathfrak{s} \equiv \mathfrak{m}_0 \xrightarrow{t_1} \mathfrak{m}_1 \xrightarrow{t_2} \dots \xrightarrow{t_n} \mathfrak{m}_n$ such that for each $i \in \{1, ..., n\}$, t_i is enabled at $\mathfrak{m}_{i-1}$, and $\mathfrak{m}_i$ is obtained from $\mathfrak{m}_{i-1}$ by the firing of t_i. We say that such a firing sequence is b-bounded if for each $i \in \{0, ..., n\}$ and each $p \in P$, $\mathfrak{m}_i(p) \leq b$. We say that N is b-bounded if each of its firing sequences is b-bounded.

The partial order semantics of Petri nets is defined using the notion of Petri-net processes introduced by Goltz and Reisig in [18]. The information about the causality between events is extracted from objects called Petri net *processes*, which encode the production and consumption of tokens along a concurrent run of the Petri net in question. The definition of processes, in turn, is based on the notion of *occurrence net*.

An occurrence net is a DAG $O = (B \, \dot\cup \, V, F)$ where the vertex set $B \, \dot\cup \, V$ is partitioned into a set B, whose elements are called conditions, and a set V, whose elements are called events. The edge set $F \subseteq (B \times V) \cup (V \times B)$ is restricted in such a way that for every condition $b \in B$, $|\{(b, v) \mid v \in V\}| \leq 1$ and $|\{(v, b) \mid v \in V\}| \leq 1$. In other words, conditions in an occurrence net are unbranched. For each condition $b \in B$, we let $InDegree(b)$ denote the number of edges having b as target. A process of a Petri net N is an occurrence net whose conditions are labeled with places of N, and events are labeled with transitions of N. Processes are intuitively used to describe the token game in a concurrent execution of the net.

Definition 1 (Process [18]). *A process of a Petri net $N = (P, T, W, m_0)$ is a labeled DAG $\pi = (B\dot\cup V, F, \rho)$ where $(B\dot\cup V, F)$ is an occurrence net and $\rho : (B \cup V) \to (P \cup T)$ is a labeling function satisfying the following properties.*

1. *Places label conditions and transitions label events: $\rho(B) \subseteq P$ and $\rho(V) \subseteq T$.*
2. *For every $p \in P$, $|\{b : InDegree(b) = 0, \rho(b) = p\}| = m_0(p)$.*
3. *For every $v \in V$, and every $p \in P$, $|\{(b, v) \in F : \rho(b) = p\}| = W(p, \rho(v))$ and $|\{(v, b) \in F : \rho(b) = p\}| = W(\rho(v), p)$.*

Item 1 says that the conditions of a process are labeled with places, while the events are labeled with transitions. Item 2 says that the minimal vertices of the process, are conditions. Intuitively, each of these conditions represent a token in the initial marking of N. Thus for each place p of N the process has $m_0(p)$ minimal conditions labeled with the place p. Item 3, determines that the token game of a process corresponds to the token game defined by the firing of transitions in the Petri net N. Thus if a transition t consumes $W(p, t)$ tokens from place p and produces $W(t, p)$ tokens at place p, then each event labeled with t must have $W(p, t)$ in-neighbours that are conditions labeled with p, and $W(t, p)$ out-neighbours that are conditions labeled with p.

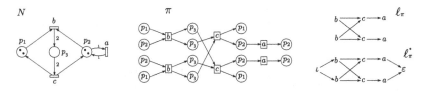

Fig. 1. A 2-bounded Petri net N. A process π of N. The partial order ℓ_π derived from π. The extension $\hat\ell_\pi$ of ℓ_π.

Let $R \subseteq X \times X$ be a binary relation over a set X. We denote by $\mathbf{tc}(R)$ the transitive closure of R. If $\pi = (B \cup V, F, \rho)$ is a process then the *causal order* of π is the partial order $\ell_\pi = (V, \mathbf{tc}(F)|_{V \times V}, \rho|_V)$ which is obtained by taking the transitive closure of F and subsequently by restricting $\mathbf{tc}(F)$ to pairs of events of V. In other words the causal order of a process π is the partial order induced by π on its events.

If $\ell = (V, <, l)$ is a partial order, then we let $\ell^* = (V', <', l')$ be the *extended version* of ℓ, where $V' = V \cup \{v_\iota, v_\varepsilon\}$, $<' = < \cup (\{v_\iota\} \times V) \cup (V \times \{v_\varepsilon\}) \cup \{(v_\iota, v_\varepsilon)\}$, $l'|_V = l$, $l'(v_\iota) = \iota$ and $l'(v_\varepsilon) = \varepsilon$. In other words, ℓ' is obtained from ℓ by the addition of an element v_ι that is smaller than all other elements, and an element v_ε that is greater than all other elements. The addition of these minimal and maximal elements to a partial order are made to avoid the consideration of special cases in some of our future lemmas. All of our results work if ignore this step, but at the expense of more repetitive proofs that deal with corner cases. We denote by $\mathcal{P}_{cau}(N)$ the set of all extended versions of partial orders derived from processes of N: $\mathcal{P}_{cau}(N) = \{\ell_\pi | \pi$ is a process of $N\}$. We say that $\mathcal{P}_{cau}(N)$ is the causal language of N. We observe that several processes of N may correspond to the same partial order in $\mathcal{P}_{cau}(N)$.

Recall that the Hasse diagram of a partial order $\ell = (V, <, l)$ is the DAG $H = (V, E)$ with the smallest number of edges with the property that $< = \mathbf{tc}(E)$. It is a well known result in partial order theory that this DAG is unique. We say that ℓ is a k-partial-order, for some $k \in \mathbb{N}$, if there exist k paths $\mathfrak{p}_1, \ldots, \mathfrak{p}_k$ in H that cover all vertices and edges of H. In other words, $V = \bigcup_i V_i$ and $E = \bigcup_i E_i$ where for each $i \in \{1, \ldots, k\}$, V_i and E_i are the vertex-set and edge-set of the path $\mathfrak{p}_i$ respectively. We note that the paths in the cover are not necessarily vertex-disjoint nor edge-disjoint.

For each $k \in \mathbb{N}$, let $\mathcal{P}_{cau}(N, k)$ denote the set of k-partial-orders which are causal-orders of N. It can be shown that if N is b-bounded, then every causal-order of $N = (P, T, W, \mathfrak{m}_0)$ is a $(b \cdot |P|)$-partial-order. In other words, each causal-order of N can be covered by at most $b \cdot |P|$ paths. This implies that $\mathcal{P}_{cau}(N) = \mathcal{P}_{cau}(N, b \cdot |P|)$.

3   Message Sequence Chart Languages

Message Sequence Charts (MSCs) are a suitable formalism for the representation of the exchange of messages between processes of a concurrent systems. In particular, during the last two decades, MSCs have been used to specify runs of telecommunication protocols. Intuitively, an MSC can be formalized as a partial-order that represents the causality between messages exchanged in a given concurrent run. Infinite families of MSCs, and therefore infinite families of partial-orders, can be specified using equivalent formalisms such as *message sequence graphs*, *hierarchical (or high-level) message sequence charts (HMSCs)* [2,30,32], or *message sequence chart automata* which will be defined below.

We formalize MSCs according to the terminology used in [30]. Let $\mathcal{J}$ be a finite set of processes, also called instances. For each instance $i \in \mathcal{J}$, we associate a finite set of actions $\Sigma_i = \Sigma_i^{int} \cup \Sigma_i^! \cup \Sigma_i^?$. This set is partitioned into a set Σ_i^{int} of *internal actions*, a set $\Sigma_i^! = \{i!j : j \in \mathcal{J}\backslash\{i\}\}$ of *send actions*, and a set $\Sigma_i^? = \{i?j : j \in \mathcal{J}\backslash\{i\}\}$ of *receive actions*. We shall assume that for each two distinct instances $i, j \in \mathcal{J}$, $\Sigma_i \cap \Sigma_j = \emptyset$. The set of actions associated with $\mathcal{J}$ is defined as $\Sigma_{\mathcal{J}} = \bigcup_{i \in \mathcal{J}} \Sigma_i$. Given an action $a \in \Sigma_{\mathcal{J}}$, $Ins(a)$ denotes the unique instance i such that $a \in \Sigma_i$. For each $\Sigma_{\mathcal{J}}$-labeled partial-order $\ell = (V, <, l)$ and each vertex $v \in V$, we let $Ins(v) = Ins(l(v))$ be the instance of $\mathcal{J}$ where the action $l(v)$ occurs. For each $i, j \in \mathcal{J}$ with $i \neq j$, and each subset $X \subseteq V$ we let $\#^{i!j}(X) = |\{v \in X \mid l(v) = i!j\}|$ be the number of messages sent from i to j, and by $\#^{i?j}(X) = \{v \in X \mid l(v) = i?j\}$ be the number of messages received by i which were sent by j. We write $v \leq v'$ as a shortcut for $v < v' \vee v = v'$. For each $v \in V$ we let $\downarrow v = \{v' \mid v' \leq v\}$ be the set of all nodes of ℓ which are smaller or equal to v. We write $v \prec v'$ to indicate that $v < v'$ and for every $u \in V$, $v < u \leq v' \Rightarrow u = v'$. In other words, $v \prec v'$ if v' is an out-neighbour of v in the Hasse diagram of ℓ.

Definition 2 (Message Sequence Chart (MSC)). *Let $\mathcal{J}$ be a set of processes. A message sequence chart over $\mathcal{J}$ is a $\Sigma_{\mathcal{J}}$-labeled partial-order $M = (V, <, l)$ satisfying the following properties.*

1. *For every pair of actions $v, v' \in V$ if $Ins(v) = Ins(v')$ then either $v < v'$, $v' < v$ or $v = v'$.*
2. *For every $i, j \in \mathcal{J}$ with $i \neq j$, $\#^{i!j}(V) = \#^{j?i}(V)$.*
3. *For each $v \in V$ and each $i, j \in \mathcal{J}$, if $l(v) = i!j$ and $l(v') = j?i$ and $\#^{i!j}(\downarrow v) = \#^{j?i}(\downarrow v')$, then $v < v'$.*
4. *If $v \prec v'$ and $Ins(v) \neq Ins(v')$, then*
$$l(v) = i!j, \ l(v') = j?i \ and \ \#^{i!j}(\downarrow v) = \#^{j?i}(\downarrow v').$$

Intuitively, Condition 1 states that actions occurring on the same process are linearly ordered. Condition 2 states that for each two distinct processes i, j, the number of messages send from i to j is equal to the number of messages received by j coming from i. Condition 3 states that for each $n \in \mathbb{N}$, the n-th message sent from i to j is received when the n-th action $j?i$ occurs, i.e., the channels in which these messages are transmitted are assumed to be FIFO. Finally, Condition 4 establishes a causal dependence between send and receive actions from distinct processes.

Let $M = (V, <, l)$ and $M' = (V', <', l')$ be MSCs over $\mathcal{J}$. The composition of M with M' is the MSC $M \circ M' = (V'', <'', l'')$ where $V'' = V \cup V'$, $l'' = l \cup l'$, and $<''$ is the transitive closure of the relation $< \cup <' \cup \{(v, v') \in V \times V' | Ins(v) = Ins(v')\}$.

To define infinite families of partial-orders, we use the notion of *message sequence chart automata* (MSC Automata). Let $\mathbb{M}_{\mathcal{J}}$ be the set of all finite MSCs over $\mathcal{J}$. Here, the set $\mathbb{M}_{\mathcal{J}}$ may be regarded as an (infinite) alphabet of MSCs.

Definition 3. *Let $\mathcal{J}$ be a set of processes. A message sequence chart automaton (MSC automaton) over $\mathcal{J}$ is a finite automaton $\mathcal{M} = (Q, \mathfrak{R}, Q_0, F)$ where Q is finite a set of states, $Q_0 \subseteq Q$ is a set of initial states, F is a set of final states and $\mathfrak{R} \subseteq Q \times \mathbb{M}_{\mathcal{J}} \times Q$.*

We say that a sequence $M_1 M_2 ... M_n$ of MSCs is accepted by $\mathcal{M}$ if there is a sequence $q_0 \xrightarrow{M_1} q_1 \xrightarrow{M_2} ... \xrightarrow{M_n} q_n$ where $q_0 \in Q_0$, $q_n \in F$ and $(q_{i-1}, M_i, q_i) \in \mathfrak{R}$ for each $i \in \{1, ..., n\}$. An MSC automaton generates two languages. At the syntactic level, $\mathcal{L}(\mathcal{M})$ is the set of all sequences $M_1 M_2 ... M_n$ of MSCs accepted by $\mathcal{M}$. At the semantic level,

$$\mathcal{L}_{po}(\mathcal{M}) = \{M_1 \circ ... \circ M_n \mid n \in \mathbb{N}, M_1 ... M_n \in \mathcal{L}(\mathcal{M})\}$$

is the set of all MSCs obtained by composing each sequence of MSCs in $\mathcal{L}(\mathcal{M})$. We note that an MSC language can be represented by an MSC automaton if and only if it can be represented by the more traditionally used message sequence graphs [2,30,32]. Nevertheless, we choose to work with MSC automata due to the fact that the proof of our results will be shorter.

If M is an MSC, then the communication graph of M, denoted by $G(M)$, has the processes of M as vertices, and has one edge e with source in a process p and target in a process q if and only if p sends some message to q in M. We say that M is locally-synchronized if the graph $G(M)$ has a unique non-trivial[1] strongly connected component, and every vertex that is not in such component is isolated. We say that an MSC automaton $\mathcal{M}$ is locally-synchronized if for each loop $q_1 \xrightarrow{M_1} q_2 \xrightarrow{M_2} ... q_n \xrightarrow{M_n} q_1$ in $\mathcal{M}$, the MSC $M_1 \circ M_2 \circ ... \circ M_n$ is locally-synchronized.

The partial-order language accepted by an MSC automaton is linearization-regular [19] if the set of linearizations of partial-orders in $\mathcal{L}_{po}(\mathcal{M})$ can be recognized by a finite automaton over the alphabet $\Sigma_{\mathcal{J}}$. In other words, $\mathcal{L}_{po}(\mathcal{M})$ is linearization-regular if the following set of strings over $\Sigma_{\mathcal{J}}$ is regular in the usual sense of finite automata theory.

$$lin(\mathcal{M}) = \bigcup_{\ell \in \mathcal{L}_{po}(\mathcal{M})} lin(\ell). \tag{1}$$

It can be shown that an MSC language generated by an MSC automaton $\mathcal{M}$ is linearization-regular if and only if $\mathcal{M}$ is locally synchronized.

Theorem 1 ([2,31]). *Let $\mathcal{M}$ be an MSC automaton. Then $\mathcal{L}_{po}(\mathcal{M})$ is linearization-regular if and only if $\mathcal{M}$ is locally-synchronized.*

4   Slice Automata

In this section we define *slices* and *slice automata*. Slice automata will be used to provide a static representation of infinite families of DAGs and infinite families of partial-orders. We note that slices can be related to several formalisms such as, multi-pointed graphs, [11], co-span decompositions [7] and graph transformations [3,6,11,35].

In what follows, T denotes a finite set of labels. A slice $\mathbf{S} = (V, E, l, s, t, [I, C, O])$ is a $(T \cup \mathbb{N})$-labeled DAG where the vertex set $V = I \,\dot\cup\, C \,\dot\cup\, O$ is partitioned into an in-frontier I, a center C and an out-frontier O. The function $l : V \to T \cup \mathbb{N}$ labels the center vertices in C with elements of T, and the in- and out-frontier vertices with positive integers in such a way that $l(I) = \{1, ..., |I|\}$ and

---

[1] A strongly connected component is trivial if it has a unique vertex.

$l(O) = \{1, ..., |O|\}$. We require that each frontier-vertex v in $I \cup O$ is the endpoint of exactly one edge $e \in E$ and that the edges are directed from the in-frontier to the out-frontier. More precisely, for each edge $e \in E$, we assume that $s(e) \in I \cup C$ and that $t(e) \in C \cup O$. We may also speak of a slice $\mathbf{S}$ with frontiers (I, O) to indicate that the in-frontier of $\mathbf{S}$ is I and that the out-frontier of $\mathbf{S}$ is O.

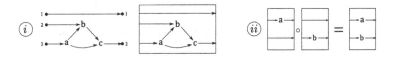

Fig. 2. *i*) A slice and its pictorial representation. *ii*) Composition of slices.

A slice $\mathbf{S}_1 = (V_1, E_1, l_1, s_1, t_1)$ with frontiers (I_1, O_1) can be glued to a slice $\mathbf{S}_2 = (V_2, E_2, l_2, s_2, t_2)$ with frontiers (I_2, O_2) provided $|O_1| = |I_2|$. In this case the glueing gives rise to the slice $\mathbf{S}_1 \circ \mathbf{S}_2 = (V_3, E_3, l_3, s_3, t_3)$ with frontiers (I_1, O_2) which is obtained by taking the disjoint union of $\mathbf{S}_1$ and $\mathbf{S}_2$, and by fusing, for each $i \in \{1, ..., |O_1|\}$, the unique edge $e_1 \in E_1$ for which $l_1(t_1(e_1)) = i$ with the unique edge $e_2 \in E_2$ for which $l_2(s_2(e_2)) = i$. Formally, the fusion of e_1 with e_2 is performed by creating a new edge e_{12} with source $s_3(e_{12}) = s_1(e_1)$ and target $t_3(e_{12}) = t_2(e_2)$, and by deleting e_1 and e_2. Thus in the glueing process the vertices in the glued frontiers disappear.

A *unit slice* is a slice with exactly one vertex in its center. A slice is *initial* if it has empty in-frontier and *final* if it has empty out-frontier. The width of a slice $\mathbf{S}$ with frontiers (I, O) is defined as $w(\mathbf{S}) = \max\{|I|, |O|\}$. A *slice alphabet* is any finite set of slices. In particular, for each finite set of symbols T and each $k \in \mathbb{N}$ we let $\overrightarrow{\Sigma}(k, T)$ be the set of all unit slices $\mathbf{S}$ of width at most k whose center vertex is labeled with an element from T. Observe that the alphabet $\overrightarrow{\Sigma}(k, T)$ is finite and has asymptotically $|T| \cdot 2^{O(k \log k)}$ slices. A sequence $\mathbf{U} = \mathbf{S}_1 \mathbf{S}_2 ... \mathbf{S}_n$ of unit slices is called a unit decomposition if $\mathbf{S}_i$ can be glued to $\mathbf{S}_{i+1}$ for each $i \in \{1, ..., n-1\}$. In this case, we let $\mathring{\mathbf{U}} = \mathbf{S}_1 \circ \mathbf{S}_2 \circ ... \circ \mathbf{S}_n$ be the DAG associated with $\mathbf{U}$, which is obtained by glueing each two consecutive slices in $\mathbf{U}$. The width of $\mathbf{U}$, denoted by $w(\mathbf{U})$, is defined as the maximum width of a slice occurring in $\mathbf{U}$. We let $\overrightarrow{\Sigma}(k, T)^*$ be the set of all sequences of slices over $\overrightarrow{\Sigma}(k, T)$, and $\overrightarrow{\Sigma}(k, T)^{\circledast}$ be the set of all unit decompositions over $\overrightarrow{\Sigma}(k, T)$.

Definition 4 (Slice Automaton). *Let T be a finite set of symbols and let $k \in \mathbb{N}$. A slice automaton over $\overrightarrow{\Sigma}(k, T)$ is a finite automaton $\mathcal{A} = (Q, \mathfrak{R}, q_0, F)$ where Q is a set of states, $q_0 \in Q$ is an initial state, $F \subseteq Q$ is a set of final states, and $\mathfrak{R} \subseteq Q \times \overrightarrow{\Sigma}(k, T) \times Q$ is a transition relation such that for every $q, q', q'' \in Q$ and every $\mathbf{S} \in \overrightarrow{\Sigma}(k, T)$:*

1. if $(q_0, \mathbf{S}, q) \in \mathfrak{R}$ then $\mathbf{S}$ is an initial slice,
2. if $(q, \mathbf{S}, q') \in \mathfrak{R}$ and $q' \in F$, then $\mathbf{S}$ is a final slice,
3. if $(q, \mathbf{S}, q') \in \mathfrak{R}$ and $(q', \mathbf{S}', q'') \in \mathfrak{R}$, then $\mathbf{S}$ can be glued to $\mathbf{S}'$.

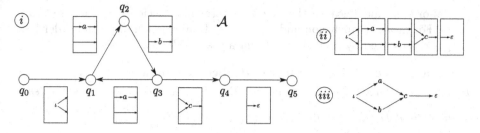

Fig. 3. *i)* A slice automaton $\mathcal{A}$. *ii)* A unit decomposition **U** accepted by $\mathcal{A}$. *iii)* The DAG $\mathring{\mathbf{U}}$ obtained by glueing each two consecutive slices in **U**.

Languages of a Slice Automaton. A slice automaton $\mathcal{A}$ can be used to represent three types of languages. At a syntactic level, we have the slice language $\mathcal{L}(\mathcal{A})$ which consists of the set of all unit decompositions accepted by $\mathcal{A}$.

$$\mathcal{L}(\mathcal{A}) = \{\mathbf{S}_1\mathbf{S}_2...\mathbf{S}_n \mid \mathbf{S}_1\mathbf{S}_2...\mathbf{S}_n \text{ is accepted by } \mathcal{A}\} \tag{2}$$

At a semantic level, we have the graph language $\mathcal{L}_{\mathcal{G}}(\mathcal{A})$ which consists of all DAGs represented by unit decompositions in $\mathcal{L}(\mathcal{A})$, and the partial-order language $\mathcal{L}_{po}(\mathcal{A})$, which consists of all partial-orders which arise as the transitive closure (**tc**) of DAGs in $\mathcal{L}_{\mathcal{G}}(\mathcal{A})$. Formally, the graph language, and the partial-order languages accepted by $\mathcal{A}$ are defined as follows.

$$\mathcal{L}_{\mathcal{G}}(\mathcal{A}) = \{\mathring{\mathbf{U}} \mid \mathbf{U} \in \mathcal{L}(\mathcal{A})\} \qquad \mathcal{L}_{po}(\mathcal{A}) = \{\mathbf{tc}(\mathring{\mathbf{U}}) \mid \mathring{\mathbf{U}} \in \mathcal{L}_{\mathcal{G}}(\mathcal{A})\}. \tag{3}$$

Let H be a DAG whose vertices are labeled with elements from a finite set T. Then we let $\boldsymbol{ud}(H, \overrightarrow{\boldsymbol{\Sigma}}(k,T))$ denote the set of all unit decompositions **U** in $\overrightarrow{\boldsymbol{\Sigma}}(k,T)^{\circledast}$ for which $\mathring{\mathbf{U}} = H$. We say that a slice automaton $\mathcal{A}$ over $\overrightarrow{\boldsymbol{\Sigma}}(k,T)$ is *saturated* if for every DAG $H \in \mathcal{L}_{\mathcal{G}}(\mathcal{A})$ we have that $\boldsymbol{ud}(H, \overrightarrow{\boldsymbol{\Sigma}}(k,T)) \subseteq \mathcal{L}(\mathcal{A})$.

The transitive reduction of a DAG $H = (V, E, l)$ is the (unique) minimal subgraph $\mathbf{tr}(H)$ of H with the same transitive closure as H. Note that $\mathbf{tc}(\mathbf{tr}(H)) = \mathbf{tc}(H)$. We say that a DAG H is transitively reduced if $H = \mathbf{tr}(H)$. Alternatively, we call a transitively reduced DAG a Hasse diagram. We say that a slice automaton $\mathcal{A}$ is transitively reduced if every DAG in $\mathcal{L}_{\mathcal{G}}(\mathcal{A})$ is transitively reduced. Theorem 2 states that any slice automaton $\mathcal{A}$ can be converted into a transitively reduced slice automaton $\mathbf{tr}(\mathcal{A})$ representing the same partial-order language in such a way that the saturation property is preserved.

Theorem 2 ([34]). *Let $\mathcal{A}$ be a slice automaton over $\overrightarrow{\boldsymbol{\Sigma}}(k,T)$. Then one can construct in time $2^{O(k \log k)} \cdot |\mathcal{A}|$ a transitively reduced slice automaton $\mathbf{tr}(\mathcal{A})$ such that $\mathcal{L}_{po}(\mathbf{tr}(\mathcal{A})) = \mathcal{L}_{po}(\mathcal{A})$. Additionally, if $\mathcal{A}$ is saturated, then so is $\mathbf{tr}(\mathcal{A})$.*

Transitively reduced saturated slice automata are important for our setting because they can be used to canonically represent infinite families of partial-orders, and because they enjoy several nice decidability/closure properties. For instance, inclusion and emptiness of intersection of partial-order languages represented by such slice automata are decidable.

Lemma 1 (Properties of Saturated Slice Automata). *Let $\mathcal{A}$ and $\mathcal{A}'$ be transitively-reduced slice automata over $\overrightarrow{\Sigma}(k,T)$. Assume that $\mathcal{A}'$ is saturated.*

1. *It is decidable whether $\mathcal{L}_{po}(\mathcal{A}) \cap \mathcal{L}_{po}(\mathcal{A}') \neq \emptyset$.*
2. *It is decidable whether $\mathcal{L}_{po}(\mathcal{A}) \subseteq \mathcal{L}_{po}(\mathcal{A}')$.*

Additionally, the partial order behavior of bounded Petri nets can be represented using transitively-reduced, saturated slice automata.

Theorem 3 ([33]). *Let $N = (P, T, W, \mathfrak{m}_0)$ be a b-bounded Petri net. Then for each $k \in \mathbb{N}$ one can construct in time $2^{O(|P| \cdot k \cdot \log b \cdot k)} \cdot |T|^{|P|}$ a transitively-reduced, saturated slice automaton $\mathcal{A}(N,k)$ over $\overrightarrow{\Sigma}(k,T)$ such that $\mathcal{L}_{po}(\mathcal{A}(N,k)) = \mathcal{P}_{cau}(N,k)$.*

We note that every partial-order in the causal language of a b-bounded Petri net is a k-partial-order for some $k \leq b \cdot |P|$. Therefore, if we set $\mathcal{A}(N) = \mathcal{A}(N, b \cdot |P|)$ then $\mathcal{L}_{po}(\mathcal{A}(N)) = \mathcal{P}_{cau}(N)$. Finally, synthesis of Petri nets from (any) slice automata is decidable.

Theorem 4 (Synthesis [33]). *Let $\mathcal{A}$ be a slice automaton over $\overrightarrow{\Sigma}(k,T)$. For each $b \in \mathbb{N}$ one can construct a b-bounded Petri net N satisfying the following properties.*

1. *$\mathcal{L}_{po}(\mathcal{A}) \subseteq \mathcal{P}_{cau}(N)$.*
2. *There is no other b-bounded Petri net N' with $\mathcal{L}_{po}(\mathcal{A}) \subseteq \mathcal{P}_{cau}(N') \subsetneq \mathcal{P}_{cau}(N)$.*

5   Weak Saturation

In this section, we introduce the notion of weak-saturation, a relaxation of the notion of saturation that is more suitable for applications involving other partial order formalisms. The main result of this section states that weak-saturated slice automata can be effectively transformed into saturated slice automata.

Let $H = (V, E, l, s, t)$ be a T-labeled DAG and $\omega = (v_1, ..., v_n)$ be a topological ordering of the vertices of H. In other words, ω is a sequence of vertices from H such that for each i, j with $i < j$, there is no edge $e \in E$ with source $s(e) = v_j$ and target $t(e) = v_i$. We say that a unit decomposition $\mathbf{U} = \mathbf{S}_1 \mathbf{S}_2 ... \mathbf{S}_n$ over $\overrightarrow{\Sigma}(k,T)$ is compatible with ω if $\overset{\circ}{\mathbf{U}} = H$ and for each i, v_i is the center vertex of $\mathbf{S}_i$. Note that given a graph H and a topological ordering ω, there may be several unit decompositions of H compatible with ω. We denote by $\boldsymbol{ud}(H, \omega, \overrightarrow{\Sigma}(k,T))$ the set of all unit decompositions of H over $\overrightarrow{\Sigma}(k,T)$ that are compatible with ω. Note that for each graph H, we have that

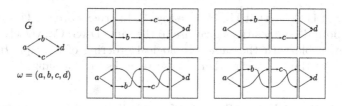

Fig. 4. A graph H, an ordering $\omega = (a, b, c, d)$ of the vertices of H, and all unit decompositions of H compatible with ω. For each unit decompositions $\mathbf{U}, \mathbf{U}'$ in $ud(H, \omega, \vec{\Sigma}(k, T))$, $\mathbf{U}$ is a twisting of $\mathbf{U}'$.

$$ud(H, \vec{\Sigma}(k, T)) = \bigcup_{\omega} ud(H, \omega, \vec{\Sigma}(k, T)) \tag{4}$$

where ω ranges over all topological orderings of H.

Definition 5 (Weak Saturation). *We say that a slice automaton $\mathcal{A}$ is weakly saturated if for each DAG H in $\mathcal{L}_\mathcal{G}(\mathcal{A})$, and each topological ordering ω of H,*

$$\mathcal{L}(\mathcal{A}) \cap ud(H, \omega, \vec{\Sigma}(k, T)) \neq \emptyset.$$

In other words, a slice automaton $\mathcal{A}$ is weakly saturated if for each graph H and each topological ordering ω of H there is at least one unit decomposition of H in $\mathcal{L}(\mathcal{A})$ which is compatible with ω. In Sect. 6 we will show that weak saturation is a decidable property. The following lemma states that each weakly saturated slice automaton can be transformed into a saturated slice automaton representing the same set of DAGs, and therefore the same set of partial-orders.

Lemma 2. *Let $\mathcal{A}$ be a weakly saturated slice automaton over $\vec{\Sigma}(k, T)$. Then one can construct in time $2^{O(k \log k)} \cdot |\mathcal{A}|$ a saturated slice automaton $\mathcal{A}'$ such that $\mathcal{L}_\mathcal{G}(\mathcal{A}) = \mathcal{L}_\mathcal{G}(\mathcal{A}')$.*

Proof. For $w \geq 0$, let $[w] = \{1, ..., w\}$. We let $[0]$ be the empty set $\emptyset$. A permutation of $[w]$ is a bijective mapping $\pi : [w] \to [w]$. We denote by $\emptyset$ the empty permutation $\pi : [0] \to [0]$. Let $\mathbf{S}$ be a slice with frontiers (I, O) and let $\pi : [|I|] \to [|I|]$ and $\pi' : [|O|] \to [|O|]$ be permutations. We denote by $(\pi, \mathbf{S}, \pi')$ the slice that is obtained from $\mathbf{S}$ by permuting the labels of the in-frontier nodes according to π, and by permuting the labels of the out-frontier nodes according to π'.

Let $\mathbf{U} = \mathbf{S}_1 \mathbf{S}_2 ... \mathbf{S}_n$ be a unit decomposition over $\vec{\Sigma}(k, T)$, where each slice $\mathbf{S}_i$ has frontiers (I_i, O_i). Let $\pi_1, ..., \pi_{n-1}$ be a sequence where for each $j \in \{1, ..., n-1\}$, $\pi_j : [|O_j|] \to [|O_j|]$ is a permutation. Then we say that the unit decomposition

$$\mathbf{U}' = (\emptyset, \mathbf{S}_1, \pi_1)(\pi_1, \mathbf{S}_2, \pi_2)...(\pi_n, \mathbf{S}_n, \emptyset)$$

is a twisting of $\mathbf{U}$. Note that $\overset{\circ}{\mathbf{U}} = \overset{\circ}{\mathbf{U}}{}'$ (see Fig. 4). In other words, if $\mathbf{U}$ is a twisting of $\mathbf{U}'$ then both decompositions give rise to the same DAG. Conversely, if $\mathbf{U}$ and $\mathbf{U}'$ are compatible with the same topological ordering of a graph H then $\mathbf{U}$ and $\mathbf{U}'$ are twistings of each other. These remarks are formalized in the next proposition.

Proposition 1. *Let H be a DAG and $\mathbf{U}$ and $\mathbf{U}'$ be unit decompositions of H. Then $\mathbf{U}$ is a twisting of $\mathbf{U}'$ if and only if there is a topological ordering ω of H such that $\mathbf{U}, \mathbf{U}' \in \mathbf{ud}(H, \omega, \overrightarrow{\Sigma}(k, T))$.*

We say that a slice automaton $\mathcal{A}$ over $\overrightarrow{\Sigma}(k, T)$ is *twisted* if whenever a unit decomposition $\mathbf{U}$ belongs to $\mathcal{L}(\mathcal{A})$ then all its twistings also belong to $\mathcal{L}(\mathcal{A})$. Alternatively, in view of Proposition 1, $\mathcal{A}$ is twisted if whenever

$$\mathcal{L}_{\mathcal{G}}(\mathcal{A}) \cap \mathbf{ud}(H, \omega, \overrightarrow{\Sigma}(k, T)) \neq \emptyset$$

for a DAG H and a topological ordering ω of H, we have that $\mathbf{ud}(H, \omega, \overrightarrow{\Sigma}(k, T)) \subseteq \mathcal{L}(\mathcal{A})$. Using Eq. 4 the notion of saturation can be redefined in terms of weak saturation and twisting.

Proposition 2. *Let $\mathcal{A}$ be a slice automaton over $\overrightarrow{\Sigma}(k, T)$. Then $\mathcal{A}$ is saturated if and only if it is both twisted and weakly saturated.*

Therefore, to prove Lemma 2 it is enough to devise a procedure that takes a slice automaton $\mathcal{A}$ and returns a slice automaton $tw(\mathcal{A})$ whose slice language $\mathcal{L}(tw(\mathcal{A}))$ consists of all twisted versions of unit decompositions in $\mathcal{L}(\mathcal{A})$. If $\mathcal{A}$ is weakly saturated, then $tw(\mathcal{A})$ is (fully) saturated.

Let $\mathcal{A} = (Q, \Delta, q^0, F)$. We assume that all states of $\mathcal{A}$ can be reached from the initial state q^0, and reach some final state in F. Let q be a state in Q. We say that the width of q is w if either there is a transition $(q, \mathbf{S}, q')$ such that the in-frontier of $\mathbf{S}$ has size w, or there is a transition $(q', \mathbf{S}, q)$ such that the out-frontier of $\mathbf{S}$ has size w. Note that conditions 1–3 of the definition of slice automaton (Definition 4) ensure that the notion of width of a state is well defined. Now the automaton $tw(\mathcal{A}) = (Q', \Delta', r_0', F')$ is defined as follows:

$$r_0' = q_\emptyset^0 \qquad F' = \{q_\emptyset \mid q \in F\}$$

$$Q' = \{q_\pi \mid \pi : [w(q)] \to [w(q)] \text{ is a permutation.}\} \tag{5}$$

$$\Delta' = \{(q_\pi, (\pi, \mathbf{S}, \pi'), q_{\pi'}) \mid (q, \mathbf{S}, q') \in \Delta, \ q_\pi, q_{\pi'} \in Q'\}$$

It is immediate to check that a unit decomposition $\mathbf{U} = \mathbf{S}_1 \mathbf{S}_2 ... \mathbf{S}_n$ is accepted by $\mathcal{A}$ if and only each twisting $\mathbf{U}' = (\emptyset, \mathbf{S}_1, \pi_1)(\pi_1, \mathbf{S}_2, \pi_2)...(\pi_{n-1}, \mathbf{S}_n, \emptyset)$ is accepted by $\mathcal{A}'$. Therefore, the automaton $tw(\mathcal{A})$ is twisted. Additionally, if $\mathcal{A}$ is weakly saturated, then by Eq. 4 we have that $tw(\mathcal{A})$ is saturated. Finally, we note that the size of $\mathcal{A}'$ is at most $2^{O(k \log k)} \cdot |\mathcal{A}|$, since there can be at most $O(k!) = 2^{O(k \log k)}$ permutations of a set of labels with at most k elements. $\square$

6   Slice Traces

In this section we introduce the notion of slice traces, and use this notion to show that the weak-saturation property for slice automata is decidable. This notion will also be used in Sect. 3 to establish connections between MSC languages and saturated slice languages.

We say that two slice strings $\mathbf{U}, \mathbf{U}' \in \overrightarrow{\Sigma}(k,T)^*$ are locally $\overrightarrow{\Sigma}(k,T)$-equivalent, and denote this fact by $\mathbf{U} \overset{k}{\simeq} \mathbf{U}'$, if there exist $\mathbf{W}, \mathbf{W}' \in \overrightarrow{\Sigma}(k,T)^*$ and $\mathbf{S}_1, \mathbf{S}'_1, \mathbf{S}_2, \mathbf{S}'_2 \in \overrightarrow{\Sigma}(k,T)$ with $\mathbf{S}_1 \circ \mathbf{S}_2 = \mathbf{S}'_1 \circ \mathbf{S}'_2$ such that $\mathbf{U} = \mathbf{W}\mathbf{S}_1\mathbf{S}_2\mathbf{W}'$ and $\mathbf{U}' = \mathbf{W}\mathbf{S}'_1\mathbf{S}'_2\mathbf{W}'$ (Fig. 5).

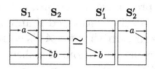

Fig. 5. Local Equivalence. $\mathbf{S}_1\mathbf{S}_2$ is 4-equivalent to $\mathbf{S}'_1, \mathbf{S}'_2$.

We let $\overset{k}{\equiv} \subseteq \overrightarrow{\Sigma}(k,T)^* \times \overrightarrow{\Sigma}(k,T)^*$ be the equivalence relation defined on slice strings by taking the reflexive, symmetric and transitive closure of $\overset{k}{\simeq}$. We note that if $\mathbf{U}$ is a unit decomposition in $\overrightarrow{\Sigma}(k,T)^{\circledast}$ then any slice string $\mathbf{U}'$ that is $\overrightarrow{\Sigma}(k,T)$-equivalent to $\mathbf{U}$ is also a unit decomposition in $\overrightarrow{\Sigma}(k,T)^{\circledast}$, and additionally, $\mathring{\mathbf{U}} = \mathring{\mathbf{U}}'$. We note that there may exist unit decompositions in $\overrightarrow{\Sigma}(k,T)^{\circledast}$ which are not $\overrightarrow{\Sigma}(k,T)$-equivalent but which are $\overrightarrow{\Sigma}(k',T)$-equivalent for some $k' > k$. Nevertheless, the following proposition states that for each k-coverable DAG H, $\overset{k}{\equiv}$-equivalence is already enough to relate any two unit decompositions of H.

Proposition 3. *Let* $\mathbf{U}_1$ *and* $\mathbf{U}_2$ *be unit decompositions in* $\overrightarrow{\Sigma}(k,T)^{\circledast}$ *such that the DAGs* $\mathring{\mathbf{U}}_1$ *and* $\mathring{\mathbf{U}}_2$ *are* k-coverable. *Then* $\mathring{\mathbf{U}}_1 = \mathring{\mathbf{U}}_2$ *if and only if* $\mathbf{U}_1 \overset{k}{\equiv} \mathbf{U}_2$.

There is a substantial difference between our notion of independence, defined on slice alphabets and the notion of independence in Mazurkiewicz trace theory. While the independence relation on slices is determined solely based on the structure of the slices (Fig. 5), without taking into consideration the events that label their center vertices, the Mazurkiewicz independence relation is defined directly on events. As a consequence, once an independence relation I is fixed, the nature of the partial-orders that can be represented as traces with respect to I is restricted. This is valid even for more general notions of traces, such as Diekert's semi-traces [8] and the context dependent traces of [20], in which for instance, partial-orders containing auto-concurrency[2] cannot be represented. In

---

[2] Auto-concurrency is the process of firing two transitions with the same label simultaneously.

our setting, any partial order ℓ labeled over a set of events T may be represented by a slice trace: namely the set of unit decompositions of its Hasse diagram.

Theorem 5. *Let $\mathcal{A}$ be a slice automaton over a slice alphabet $\overrightarrow{\Sigma}(k,T)$ representing a set of k-partial-orders. Then we may effectively determine whether the slice language generated by $\mathcal{A}$ is weakly saturated.*

Proof. Assume without loss of generality that the slice automaton $\mathcal{A}$ is transitively reduced. Otherwise, just apply the transitive reduction algorithm from [34]. Since each partial-order $\ell \in \mathcal{L}_{po}(\mathcal{A})$ is a k-partial-order, the Hasse digram H of ℓ can be covered by k paths. Therefore, by Proposition 3, any unit decomposition of H has width at most k. Now let $tw(\mathcal{A})$ be automaton obtained from $\mathcal{A}$ by applying the twisting procedure in the proof of Lemma 2. Then by Proposition 2 the automaton $\mathcal{A}$ is weakly saturated if and only if $tw(\mathcal{A})$ is saturated. Therefore, it is enough to verify whether $tw(\mathcal{A})$ is saturated. With this in mind, it is enough to test the following condition. If a slice word $w\mathbf{S}_1\mathbf{S}_2u$ is generated by $\mathcal{A}'$ then every word $w\mathbf{S}_1'\mathbf{S}_2'u$ satisfying $\mathbf{S}_1' \circ \mathbf{S}_2' = \mathbf{S}_1 \circ \mathbf{S}_2$ is generated by $\mathcal{A}$ as well. Let $\mathcal{A}'$ be the minimal deterministic slice automaton generating the same slice language as $tw(\mathcal{A})$. Then any unit decomposition $\mathbf{S}_1\mathbf{S}_2 \cdots \mathbf{S}_n \in \mathcal{L}(\mathcal{A}')$ corresponds to a unique computational path in $\mathcal{A}'$. Therefore to verify our condition, we just need to determine whether $\mathcal{A}'$ is "diamond" closed. In other words we need to test whether for each pair of transition rules $q\mathbf{S}_1 r$ and $r\mathbf{S}_2 q'$ of the $\mathcal{A}'$ and each unit decomposition $\mathbf{S}_1'\mathbf{S}_2'$ of $\mathbf{S}_1 \circ \mathbf{S}_2$, $\mathcal{A}'$ has a state r' and transitions $q\mathbf{S}_1'r'$ and $r'\mathbf{S}_2'q'$. Clearly this condition can be verified in polynomial time on the size of $\mathcal{A}'$, since $\mathbf{S}_1 \circ \mathbf{S}_2$ can have at most $2^{O(k \cdot \log k)}$ possible decompositions. $\qquad\square$

7 From MSC Automata to Slice Automata

In this section we define the notion of locally-synchronized slice automata. Let $\mathbf{S}$ be a slice (possibly with several vertices in the center) with k in-frontier vertices $v_1, ..., v_k$ and k out-frontier vertices $u_1, ..., u_k$. For each $i \in \{1, ..., k\}$, we say that a path $\mathfrak{p}_i$ from v_i to u_i is *trivial* if v_i and u_i are the only vertices in $\mathfrak{p}_i$. Let $\mathfrak{p}_1, ..., \mathfrak{p}_k$ be paths such that for each i, $\mathfrak{p}_i$ is a path from v_i to u_i. We let the communication graph $\mathrm{comm}(\mathbf{S}, \mathfrak{p}_1, ..., \mathfrak{p}_k)$ be the directed graph whose vertices are paths in $\{\mathfrak{p}_1, ..., \mathfrak{p}_k\}$, and such that for each $i,j \in \{1, ..., k\}$, there is an edge from $\mathfrak{p}_i$ to $\mathfrak{p}_j$ if either these paths share a vertex or there is an edge with source in some vertex of $\mathfrak{p}_i$ and target in some vertex of $\mathfrak{p}_j$. We say that $\mathbf{S}$ is *locally-synchronized* $\mathrm{comm}(\mathbf{S}, \mathfrak{p}_1, ..., \mathfrak{p}_k)$ has at most one strongly connected component with more than one vertex. Note that trivial paths correspond to isolated vertices. This notion of local synchronization for slices, generalizes the notion of local synchronization for message sequence charts in the sense that processes correspond to paths, and isolated vertices in the communication graph of an MSC correspond to trivial paths.

Definition 6 (Locally-Synchronized Slice Automaton). *A slice automaton $\mathcal{A}$ is locally-synchronized if for every loop $q_1 \xrightarrow{\mathbf{S}_1} q_2 \xrightarrow{\mathbf{S}_2} ... \xrightarrow{\mathbf{S}_{n-1}} q_n \xrightarrow{\mathbf{S}_n} q_1$ in $\mathcal{A}$, the slice $\mathbf{S}_1 \circ \mathbf{S}_2 ... \circ \mathbf{S}_n$ is locally synchronized.*

The next theorem states that any locally-synchronized slice automaton can be transformed further into a saturated slice automaton representing the same partial order language as the original one.

Theorem 6. *Let T be a finite set of symbols, and $k \in \mathbb{N}$. Let $\mathcal{A}$ be a locally-synchronized slice automaton over $\vec{\Sigma}(k, T)$. Then one can construct a saturated slice automaton $\mathcal{A}'$ such that $\mathcal{L}_{po}(\mathcal{A}') = \mathcal{L}_{po}(\mathcal{A})$.*

The following theorem is the main result of this section. It states that MSC automata can be converted into slice automata representing the same partial-order language. Additionally, this conversion transforms locally-synchronized MSC automata into saturated slice automata.

Theorem 7 (From MSC Automata to Slice Automata). *Let $\mathcal{M}$ be an MSC automaton over $\mathcal{J}$. Then one can construct a transitively-reduced slice automaton $\mathcal{A}(\mathcal{M})$ satisfying $\mathcal{L}_{po}(\mathcal{M}) = \mathcal{L}_{po}(\mathcal{A}(\mathcal{M}))$. Furthermore, if $\mathcal{M}$ is locally-synchronized, then $\mathcal{A}(\mathcal{M})$ is saturated.*

Proof. Let $\mathcal{J} = \{1, ..., k\}$ be a set of processes. We let $\mathbf{S}^{\iota}(\mathcal{J})$ be the slice with empty in-frontier $I = \emptyset$, k out-frontier vertices $O = \{v_1, ..., v_k\}$ where each v_i is labeled with the number i, and with a unique vertex v in the center which is connected to each vertex in O. We say that $\mathbf{S}^{\iota}(\mathcal{J})$ is the *initial slice* of $\mathcal{J}$.

Analogously, let $\mathbf{S}^{\varepsilon}(\mathcal{J})$ be the slice with empty out-frontier $O = \emptyset$, k in-frontier vertices $I = \{u_1, ..., u_k\}$ where each u_i is labeled with the number i, and with a unique center vertex v in the center. For each i there is an edge with source in u_i and target in v. We say that $\mathbf{S}^{\varepsilon}(\mathcal{J})$ is the *final slice* of $\mathcal{J}$.

Now let M be an MSC over $\mathcal{J}$. Then we let $\mathbf{S}(M)$ be the slice (not necessarily a unit slice) constructed as follows. $\mathbf{S}(M)$ has k in-frontier vertices $x_1, ..., x_k$, and k out-frontier vertices $y_1, ..., y_k$. Let H be the Hasse diagram of M. Then for each $i \in \{1, ..., k\}$ proceed as follows. If H has no vertex labeled with an element of Σ_i, then add an edge from the in-frontier vertex x_i to the out-frontier vertex y_i. Otherwise, if such a vertex exists, then add an edge from x_i to the (unique) minimal vertex of H labeled with an element of Σ_i, and an edge from the (unique) maximal vertex of H labeled with an element of Σ_i to the out-frontier vertex y_i. Note that the transitive closure of the slice $\mathbf{S}^{\iota}(\mathcal{J}) \circ \mathbf{S}(M) \circ \mathbf{S}^{\varepsilon}(\mathcal{J})$ is precisely the extension of the partial-order M (see Sect. 2). We let $\mathbf{W}(M) = \mathbf{S}_1 \mathbf{S}_2 ... \mathbf{S}_n$ be an arbitrary sequence of unit slices such that $\mathbf{S}(M) = \mathbf{S}_1 \circ \mathbf{S}_2 \circ ... \circ \mathbf{S}_n$.

Now let $\mathcal{M}$ be an MSC automaton over $\mathcal{J}$. We will show how to construct a slice automaton $\mathcal{A}'(\mathcal{M})$ over $\vec{\Sigma}(|\mathcal{J}|, \Sigma_{\mathcal{J}})$ such that $\mathcal{L}_{po}(\mathcal{A}'(\mathcal{M})) = \mathcal{L}_{po}(\mathcal{M})$. The conversion is done as follows. Let M be an MSC with m nodes and let $\mathbf{W}(M) = \mathbf{S}_1 \mathbf{S}_2 ... \mathbf{S}_m$. We replace each transition (q, M, q') in $\mathcal{M}$ by a sequence of transitions

$$(q, \mathbf{S}_1, q_1)(q_1, \mathbf{S}_2, q_2) ... (q_{n-1}, \mathbf{S}_n, q').$$

Now we create an initial state q_ι and add the transition $(q_\iota, \mathbf{S}^\iota(\mathcal{J}), q)$ for each initial state q of $\mathcal{M}$. Analogously, we create a final state q_ε and add the transition $(q, \mathbf{S}^\varepsilon(\mathcal{J}), q_\varepsilon)$ for each final state of $\mathcal{M}$. Now it is immediate to check that $\mathcal{M}$ accepts a sequence $M_1 M_2 ... M_n$ of $MSCs$ if and only if $\mathcal{A}'(\mathcal{M})$ accepts the unit decomposition

$$\mathbf{U} = \mathbf{S}^\iota(\mathcal{J}) \mathbf{W}(M_1) \mathbf{W}(M_2) ... \mathbf{W}(M_n) \mathbf{S}^\varepsilon(\mathcal{J}).$$

This implies that $\mathbf{tc}(\overset{\circ}{\mathbf{U}}) = \ell^*$ where $\ell = M_1 \circ M_2 \circ ... \circ M_n$. Therefore, $\mathcal{L}_{po}(\mathcal{A}'(\mathcal{M})) = \mathcal{L}_{po}(\mathcal{M})$.

Now assume that $\mathcal{L}_{po}(\mathcal{M})$ is linearization-regular. Then by Theorem 1, we may assume that $\mathcal{M}$ is locally-synchronized. Let $\mathbf{W}(M_1) \mathbf{W}(M_2) ... \mathbf{W}(M_n)$ label a loop in $\mathcal{A}'(\mathcal{M})$. Then $M_1 M_2 ... M_n$ labels a loop in $\mathcal{M}$. Since by assumption $\mathcal{M}$ is locally-synchronized, we have that the MSC $M_1 \circ M_2 \circ ... \circ M_n$ is locally-synchronized. This implies that the slice $\mathbf{S}(M_1) \circ \mathbf{S}(M_2) \circ ... \circ \mathbf{S}(M_n)$ is also locally-synchronized. Since a sequence of MSCs $M_1 M_2 ... M_n$ labels a loop in $\mathcal{M}$ if and only if the sequence of unit slices $\mathbf{W}(M_1) \mathbf{W}(M_2) ... \mathbf{W}(M_n)$ labels a loop in $\mathcal{A}'(\mathcal{M})$, we have that $\mathcal{A}'(\mathcal{M})$ is locally-synchronized. Therefore, as a last step we apply Theorem 6 to construct a slice automaton $\mathcal{A}(\mathcal{M})$ which is saturated and has the same partial-order language as $\mathcal{A}'(\mathcal{M})$, and therefore, the same partial-order language as $\mathcal{M}$. □

By combining Theorem 7 with Theorem 3 and Lemma 1, we have the following theorem.

Theorem 8. *Let $\mathcal{M}$ be an MSC automaton over $\mathcal{J}$ and N be b-bounded Petri net with transition set $T = \mathcal{J}$.*

1. *It is decidable whether $\mathcal{L}_{po}(\mathcal{M}) \cap \mathcal{P}_{cau}(N) \neq \emptyset$.*
2. *It is decidable whether $\mathcal{L}_{po}(\mathcal{M}) \subseteq \mathcal{P}_{cau}(N)$.*
3. *If $\mathcal{M}$ is locally synchronized, it is decidable whether $\mathcal{P}_{cau}(N) \subseteq \mathcal{L}_{po}(\mathcal{M})$.*

Proof. Let $\mathcal{A}$ be the slice automaton derived from $\mathcal{M}$ as in Theorem 7. Then $\mathcal{A}$ is transitively-reduced and $\mathcal{L}_{po}(\mathcal{M}) = \mathcal{L}_{po}(\mathcal{A})$. Let $\mathcal{A}'$ be the slice automaton constructed from N as in Theorem 3. Then $\mathcal{A}'$ is transitively-reduced, saturated and $\mathcal{L}_{po}(\mathcal{A}) = \mathcal{P}_{cau}(N)$. By Lemma 1, we have that it is decidable whether $\mathcal{L}_{po}(\mathcal{A}) \cap \mathcal{L}_{po}(\mathcal{A}') \neq \emptyset$ and whether $\mathcal{L}_{po}(\mathcal{A}) \subseteq \mathcal{L}_{po}(\mathcal{A}')$. Finally, if $\mathcal{M}$ is locally synchronized, then $\mathcal{A}$ is saturated, and therefore the inclusion $\mathcal{L}_{po}(\mathcal{A}') \subseteq \mathcal{L}_{po}(\mathcal{A})$ is also decidable. □

By combining Theorem 7 with Theorem 9 we have the following theorem.

Theorem 9 (Synthesis From MSC Automata). *Let $\mathcal{M}$ be an MSC automaton over $\mathcal{J}$. For each $b \in \mathbb{N}$ one can construct a b-bounded Petri net N satisfying the following properties.*

1. $\mathcal{L}_{po}(\mathcal{M}) \subseteq \mathcal{P}_{cau}(N)$.
2. *There is no other b-bounded Petri net N' with $\mathcal{L}_{po}(\mathcal{M}) \subseteq \mathcal{P}_{cau}(N') \subsetneq \mathcal{P}_{cau}(N)$.*

Additionally, if $\mathcal{M}$ is locally synchronized, then one can decide whether $\mathcal{P}_{cau}(N) = \mathcal{L}_{po}(\mathcal{M})$.

Proof. Let $\mathcal{A}$ be the slice automaton of Theorem 7. Then $\mathcal{A}$ is transitively-reduced and $\mathcal{L}_{po}(\mathcal{M}) = \mathcal{L}_{po}(\mathcal{A})$. By Theorem 4, one can construct a b-bounded Petri net N such that $\mathcal{L}_{po}(\mathcal{A}) \subseteq \mathcal{P}_{cau}(N)$, and such that there is no b-bounded Petri net N' with $\mathcal{L}_{po}(\mathcal{A}) \subseteq \mathcal{P}_{cau}(N') \subsetneq \mathcal{P}_{cau}(N)$.

Note that if there is a b-bounded Petri net whose causal behavior is equal to $\mathcal{L}_{po}(\mathcal{A})$, then by minimality, we have that $\mathcal{P}_{cau}(N) = \mathcal{L}_{po}(\mathcal{A})$. Nevertheless, in general it is not possible to verify whether equality is achieved. On the other hand, if $\mathcal{M}$ is locally synchronized, then by Item 3 of Theorem 8, one can also test whether the equality $\mathcal{P}_{cau}(N) \subseteq \mathcal{L}_{po}(\mathcal{A})$ holds.   □

8   From Mazurkiewicz Traces to Slice Languages

In Mazurkiewicz trace theory, partial-orders are represented as equivalence classes of words over an alphabet of events [28]. Given an alphabet T of events and a symmetric and anti-reflexive *independence relation* $I \subseteq T \times T$, a string $\alpha ab\beta$ is defined to be similar to the string $\alpha ba\beta$ ($\alpha ab\beta \simeq \alpha ba\beta$) provided $(a, b) \in I$. A trace is then an equivalence class of the transitive reflexive closure $\simeq^*$ of the relation $\simeq$. We denote by $[\alpha]_I$ the trace corresponding to a string $\alpha \in T^*$.

A partial-order $\ell_I(\alpha)$ is associated with a string $\alpha \in T^*$ of events in the following way: First we consider a dependence DAG $dep_I(\alpha) = (V, E, l)$ that has one vertex $v_i \in V$ labeled by the event α_i for each $i \in \{1, ..., |\alpha|\}$. An edge connects v_i to v_j in E if and only if $i < j$ and $(\alpha_i, \alpha_j) \notin I$. Then $\ell_I(\alpha)$ is the transitive closure of $dep_I(\alpha)$. One may verify that two strings induce the same partial-order if and only if they belong to the same trace. The trace language induced by a string language $\mathcal{L} \subseteq T^*$ with respect to an independence relation I is the set $[\mathcal{L}]_I = \{[\alpha]_I | \alpha \in \mathcal{L}\}$ and the trace closure of $\mathcal{L}$ is the language $\mathcal{L}^I = \cup_{\alpha \in \mathcal{L}} [\alpha]$.

Given a finite automaton $\mathcal{F}$ over an alphabet T and an independence relation $I \subset T \times T$, we denote by $\mathcal{L}(\mathcal{F})$ the regular language defined by $\mathcal{F}$ and by $\mathcal{L}_{po}(\mathcal{F}, \mathcal{I}) = \{\ell_I(\alpha) | \alpha \in \mathcal{L}(\mathcal{F})\}$ the partial-order language induced by $(\mathcal{F}, \mathcal{I})$. We call the pair $(\mathcal{F}, \mathcal{I})$ a Mazurkiewicz pair. We say that $\mathcal{L}(\mathcal{F})$ is trace-closed if $[\alpha]_I \subseteq \mathcal{L}(\mathcal{F})$ for each $\alpha \in \mathcal{L}(\mathcal{F})$. As an abuse of terminology, we may say that the Mazurkiewicz pair $(\mathcal{F}, \mathcal{I})$ is trace-closed.

We let $\hat{\mathcal{L}}_{po}(\mathcal{F}, \mathcal{I}) = \{\hat{\ell} \mid \ell \in \mathcal{L}_{po}(\mathcal{F}, \mathcal{I})\}$ be the set of extensions of partial-orders in $\mathcal{L}_{po}(\mathcal{F}, \mathcal{I})$. We note that extensions are only considered to make the construction of the automaton $\mathcal{A}(\mathcal{F}, \mathcal{I})$ slightly cleaner. With some easy case analysis one can construct slice automata whose partial-order language is $\mathcal{L}_{po}(\mathcal{F}, \mathcal{I})$ instead of $\hat{\mathcal{L}}_{po}(\mathcal{F}, \mathcal{I})$. The next theorem (Theorem 10) states that for any finite automaton $\mathcal{F}$ and independence relation I, one can construct a slice automaton $\mathcal{A}(\mathcal{F}, \mathcal{I})$ whose partial-order language is equal to $\hat{\mathcal{L}}_{po}(\mathcal{F}, \mathcal{I})$.

Theorem 10 (From Traces to Slices). *Let $\mathcal{F}$ be a finite automaton over an alphabet T, and $I \subset T \times T$ an independence relation. Then for some $k \leq |T|^2$ one can construct a transitively-reduced slice automaton $\mathcal{A}(\mathcal{F}, \mathcal{I})$ over $\overrightarrow{\boldsymbol{\Sigma}}(k, T \cup \{\iota, \varepsilon\})$ such that $\mathcal{L}_{po}(\mathcal{A}(\mathcal{F}, \mathcal{I})) = \hat{\mathcal{L}}_{po}(\mathcal{F}, \mathcal{I})$. Additionally, if $(\mathcal{F}, \mathcal{I})$ is trace-closed, then $\mathcal{A}(\mathcal{F}, \mathcal{I})$ is saturated.*

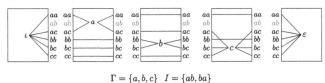

$$\Gamma = \{a, b, c\} \quad I = \{ab, ba\}$$

Fig. 6. Mapping an independence alphabet $(T, \mathcal{I})$ to a slice alphabet $\overrightarrow{\boldsymbol{\Sigma}}(T, \mathcal{I}) \subseteq \overrightarrow{\boldsymbol{\Sigma}}(k, T)$ where $k \leq |T|^2$.

In the remainder of this section we prove Theorem 10. We note that the difficulty in the construction of the automaton $\mathcal{A}(\mathcal{F}, \mathcal{I})$ lies in showing that $\mathcal{A}(\mathcal{F}, \mathcal{I})$ is saturated whenever $\mathcal{L}(\mathcal{F})$ is trace-closed. As a first step in the proof, we will use the independence alphabet $(T, \mathcal{I})$ to construct a slice alphabet $\overrightarrow{\boldsymbol{\Sigma}}(T, \mathcal{I}) = \{\mathbf{S}_a | a \in T\} \cup \{\mathbf{S}_\iota, \mathbf{S}_\varepsilon\}$ with the following property: For each string $\alpha = \alpha_1 \alpha_2 ... \alpha_n \in T^*$ the partial-order defined by the unit decomposition $\mathbf{U}_\alpha = \mathbf{S}_\iota \mathbf{S}_{\alpha_1} \mathbf{S}_{\alpha_2} \cdots \mathbf{S}_{\alpha_n} \mathbf{S}_\varepsilon$ is precisely the extension of the partial-order $\ell_I(\alpha)$ induced by α (Fig. 6).

Let $\rho : T \rightarrow \{1, ..., |T|\}$ be an arbitrary ordering of the elements of T. Let $D = \{ab \mid a, b \in T, \rho(a) \leq \rho(b), (a, b) \notin I\}$ be the set of pairs of non-independent elements of T. Let $\bar{\rho} : D \rightarrow \{1, ..., |D|\}$ be the natural lexicographic ordering induced on D by the ordering ρ. For each symbol $a \in T$ we define the slice $\mathbf{S}_a$ as follows: Both the in-fronter I and the out-frontier O of $\mathbf{S}_a$ have $|D|$ vertices, and the center of $\mathbf{S}_a$ has a unique vertex v_a which is labeled by a. In symbols $I = \{I_{ab} | ab \in D\}$ and $O = \{O_{ab} | ab \in D\}$. For each $ab \in D$, both the in-frontier vertex I_{ab} and the out-frontier vertex O_{ab} are labeled with the number $\bar{\rho}(ab)$. For each pair $bc \in D$ with $a \neq b$ and $a \neq c$ we add an edge to $\mathbf{S}_a$ with source in I_{bc} and target in O_{bc}, and for each pair $ax \in D$ ($xa \in D$) we add an edge with source in I_{ax} (I_{xa}) and target in v_a, and an edge with source in v_a and target in O_{ax} (O_{xa}) (Fig. 6). We associate with the symbol ι an initial slice $\mathbf{S}_\iota$, with center vertex v_ι labeled by ι, and out-frontier O. Analogously, with the symbol ε, we associate a final slice $\mathbf{S}_\varepsilon$ with center vertex v_ε labeled by ε, and in-frontier I. We note that the slice alphabet $\overrightarrow{\boldsymbol{\Sigma}}(T, \mathcal{I})$ is a subset of $\overrightarrow{\boldsymbol{\Sigma}}(k, T \cup \{\iota, \varepsilon\})$ where $k = |D| \leq |T|^2$.

Now let $\alpha = \alpha_1 \alpha_2 ... \alpha_n$ be a string in T, $dep_I(\alpha)$ be the dependence graph of α and $\mathbf{U}_\alpha = \mathbf{S}_\iota \mathbf{S}_{\alpha_1} ... \mathbf{S}_{\alpha_n} \mathbf{S}_\varepsilon$. Let v_i be the i-th vertex of $dep_I(\alpha)$, and u_i be the center vertex of the slice $\mathbf{S}_{\alpha_i}$. Then it is straightforward to check that for each $i, j \in \{1, ..., n\}$ with $i < j$, there is a path from u_i to u_j in the graph $\mathring{\mathbf{U}}_\alpha$ if and only if there is a path from v_i to v_j in $dep_I(\alpha)$. This implies that the partial-order $\mathbf{tc}(\mathring{\mathbf{U}}_\alpha)$ is the extension of the partial-order $\ell_I(\alpha)$ induced by α. In other words, $\mathbf{tc}(\mathring{\mathbf{U}}_\alpha) = \hat{\ell}_I(\alpha)$.

Now, from the pair $(\mathcal{F}, \mathcal{I}) = (Q, \mathfrak{R}, Q_0, F)$ we construct an auxiliary slice automaton $\mathcal{A}'(\mathcal{F}, \mathcal{I}) = (Q', \mathfrak{R}', Q'_0, F')$ as follows. We let $Q' = Q \cup \{q_\iota, q_\varepsilon\}$, $Q'_0 = \{q_\iota\}$, $F' = \{q_\varepsilon\}$, and $\mathfrak{R}' = \{(q_\iota, \mathbf{S}_\iota, q) \mid q \in Q_0\} \cup \{(q, \mathbf{S}_\varepsilon, q_\varepsilon) \mid q \in F\} \cup \{(q, \mathbf{S}_a, q') \mid (q, a, q') \in \mathfrak{R}\}$. Then we have that $\mathcal{F}$ accepts a string α if and only if $\mathcal{A}'(\mathcal{F}, \mathcal{I})$ accepts the unit decomposition $\mathbf{U}_\alpha$. This implies that $\mathcal{L}_{po}(\mathcal{A}'(\mathcal{F}, \mathcal{I})) = \hat{\mathcal{L}}_{po}(\mathcal{F}, \mathcal{I})$.

Now assume that $\mathcal{L}(\mathcal{F})$ is trace closed. Then for each string $\gamma \in [\alpha]_I$, we have that $\gamma \in \mathcal{L}(\mathcal{F})$ and therefore $\mathbf{U}_\gamma \in \mathcal{L}(\mathcal{A}(\mathcal{F}, \mathcal{I}))$. Since for each topological ordering ω of the graph $\overset{\circ}{\mathbf{U}}_\alpha$, there is a $\gamma \in [\alpha]_I$ such that $\mathbf{U}_\gamma$ is compatible with ω, we have that $\mathcal{A}'(\mathcal{F}, \mathcal{I})$ is weakly saturated. Therefore, by Lemma 2 we can construct a saturated slice automaton $\mathcal{A}(\mathcal{F}, \mathcal{I})$ with $\mathcal{L}_{po}(\mathcal{A}(\mathcal{F}, \mathcal{I})) = \mathcal{L}_{po}(\mathcal{A}'(\mathcal{F}, \mathcal{I}))$. $\qquad\square$

9 Conclusion

In this work, we have established connections between the causal semantics of Petri nets and message sequence chart languages. In particular, we showed that message sequence chart automata can be used as a tool for the study of the causal behavior of Petri nets. Despite the fact that each of these formalisms have been defined several decades ago, the connections established in our work were unknown. In order to prove our results we have introduced new slice theoretic machinery of independent interest. In particular, our techniques pave the way for the use of slice automata as a bridge between bounded Petri nets and behavioral formalisms. Further evidence for this assessment is given in Sect. 8, where we show how to map Mazurkiewicz Trace languages to trace languages in such a way that trace closure implies saturation. This means that the results in Theorems 8 and 9 also hold if instead of MSC automata we use Mazurkiewicz pairs.

References

1. Adsul, B., Mukund, M., Kumar, K.N., Narayanan, V.: Causal closure for MSC languages. In: Sarukkai, S., Sen, S. (eds.) FSTTCS 2005. LNCS, vol. 3821, pp. 335–347. Springer, Heidelberg (2005). https://doi.org/10.1007/11590156_27
2. Alur, R., Yannakakis, M.: Model checking of message sequence charts. In: Baeten, J.C.M., Mauw, S. (eds.) CONCUR 1999. LNCS, vol. 1664, pp. 114–129. Springer, Heidelberg (1999). https://doi.org/10.1007/3-540-48320-9_10
3. Bauderon, M., Courcelle, B.: Graph expressions and graph rewritings. Math. Syst. Theory 20(2–3), 83–127 (1987)
4. Bollig, B., Kuske, D.: Muller message-passing automata and logics. Inf. Comput. 206(9–10), 1084–1094 (2008)
5. Bollig, B., Leucker, M.: Message-passing automata are expressively equivalent to EMSO logic. Theor. Comput. Sci. 358(2–3), 150–172 (2006)
6. Brandenburg, F.J., Skodinis, K.: Finite graph automata for linear and boundary graph languages. Theor. Comput. Sci. 332(1–3), 199–232 (2005)

7. Bruggink, H.J.S., König, B.: On the recognizability of arrow and graph languages. In: Ehrig, H., Heckel, R., Rozenberg, G., Taentzer, G. (eds.) ICGT 2008. LNCS, vol. 5214, pp. 336–350. Springer, Heidelberg (2008). https://doi.org/10.1007/978-3-540-87405-8_23

8. Diekert, V.: A partial trace semantics for Petri Nets. Theor. Comput. Sci. **134**(1), 87–105 (1994)

9. Droste, M.: Concurrent automata and domains. Int. J. Found. Comput. Sci. **3**(4), 389–418 (1992)

10. Droste, M., Gastin, P., Kuske, D.: Asynchronous cellular automata for pomsets. Theor. Comput. Sci. **247**(1–2), 1–38 (2000)

11. Engelfriet, J., Vereijken, J.J.: Context-free graph grammars and concatenation of graphs. Acta Informatica **34**, 773–803 (1997)

12. Fanchon, J., Morin, R.: Pomset languages of finite step transition systems. In: Franceschinis, G., Wolf, K. (eds.) PETRI NETS 2009. LNCS, vol. 5606, pp. 83–102. Springer, Heidelberg (2009). https://doi.org/10.1007/978-3-642-02424-5_7

13. Gaifman, H., Pratt, V.R.: Partial order models of concurrency and the computation of functions. In: Proceedings of the 2nd Symposium on Logic in Computer Science (LICS 1987), pp. 72–85 (1987)

14. Genest, B., Kuske, D., Muscholl, A.: A Kleene theorem and model checking algorithms for existentially bounded communicating automata. Inf. Comput. **204**(6), 920–956 (2006)

15. Genest, B., Kuske, D., Muscholl, A.: On communicating automata with bounded channels. Fundamenta Informaticae **80**(1–3), 147–167 (2007)

16. Genest, B., Muscholl, A., Seidl, H., Zeitoun, M.: Infinite-state high-level MSCS: model-checking and realizability. J. Comput. Syst. Sci. **72**(4), 617–647 (2006)

17. Gischer, J.L.: The equational theory of pomsets. Theor. Comput. Sci. **61**, 199–224 (1988)

18. Goltz, U., Reisig, W.: Processes of place/transition-nets. In: Diaz, J. (ed.) ICALP 1983. LNCS, vol. 154, pp. 264–277. Springer, Heidelberg (1983). https://doi.org/10.1007/BFb0036914

19. Henriksen, J.G., Mukund, M., Kumar, K.N., Sohoni, M., Thiagarajan, P.: A theory of regular MSC languages. Inf. Comput. **202**(1), 1–38 (2005)

20. Hoogers, P., Kleijn, H., Thiagarajan, P.: A trace semantics for Petri Nets. Inf. Comput. **117**(1), 98–114 (1995)

21. Jategaonkar Jagadeesan, L., Jagadeesan, R.: Causality and true concurrency: a data-flow analysis of the Pi-Calculus. In: Alagar, V.S., Nivat, M. (eds.) AMAST 1995. LNCS, vol. 936, pp. 277–291. Springer, Heidelberg (1995). https://doi.org/10.1007/3-540-60043-4_59

22. Kuske, D.: Contributions to a trace theory beyond Mazurkiewicz traces (2000)

23. Kuske, D.: Regular sets of infinite message sequence charts. Inf. Comput. **187**(1), 80–109 (2003)

24. Kuske, D., Morin, R.: Pomsets for local trace languages. J. Automata Lang. Combinatorics **7**(2), 187–224 (2002)

25. Langerak, R., Brinksma, E., Katoen, J.-P.: Causal ambiguity and partial orders in event structures. In: Mazurkiewicz, A., Winkowski, J. (eds.) CONCUR 1997. LNCS, vol. 1243, pp. 317–331. Springer, Heidelberg (1997). https://doi.org/10.1007/3-540-63141-0_22

26. Lodaya, K., Weil, P.: Series-parallel languages and the bounded-width property. Theor. Comput. Sci. **237**(1–2), 347–380 (2000)

27. Madhusudan, P., Meenakshi, B.: Beyond message sequence graphs. In: Hariharan, R., Vinay, V., Mukund, M. (eds.) FSTTCS 2001. LNCS, vol. 2245, pp. 256–267. Springer, Heidelberg (2001). https://doi.org/10.1007/3-540-45294-X_22

28. Mazurkiewicz, A.: Trace theory. In: Brauer, W., Reisig, W., Rozenberg, G. (eds.) ACPN 1986. LNCS, vol. 255, pp. 278–324. Springer, Heidelberg (1987). https://doi.org/10.1007/3-540-17906-2_30

29. Montanari, U., Pistore, M.: Minimal transition systems for history-preserving bisimulation. In: Reischuk, R., Morvan, M. (eds.) STACS 1997. LNCS, vol. 1200, pp. 413–425. Springer, Heidelberg (1997). https://doi.org/10.1007/BFb0023477

30. Morin, R.: On regular message sequence chart languages and relationships to Mazurkiewicz trace theory. In: Honsell, F., Miculan, M. (eds.) FoSSaCS 2001. LNCS, vol. 2030, pp. 332–346. Springer, Heidelberg (2001). https://doi.org/10.1007/3-540-45315-6_22

31. Muscholl, A., Peled, D.: Message sequence graphs and decision problems on Mazurkiewicz traces. In: Kutyłowski, M., Pacholski, L., Wierzbicki, T. (eds.) MFCS 1999. LNCS, vol. 1672, pp. 81–91. Springer, Heidelberg (1999). https://doi.org/10.1007/3-540-48340-3_8

32. Muscholl, A., Peled, D., Su, Z.: Deciding properties for message sequence charts. In: Nivat, M. (ed.) FoSSaCS 1998. LNCS, vol. 1378, pp. 226–242. Springer, Heidelberg (1998). https://doi.org/10.1007/BFb0053553

33. de Oliveira Oliveira, M.: Hasse diagram generators and Petri Nets. Fundamenta Informaticae **105**(3), 263–289 (2010)

34. Oliveira Oliveira, M.: Canonizable partial order generators. In: Dediu, A.-H., Martín-Vide, C. (eds.) LATA 2012. LNCS, vol. 7183, pp. 445–457. Springer, Heidelberg (2012). https://doi.org/10.1007/978-3-642-28332-1_38

35. Thomas, W.: Finite-state recognizability of graph properties. Theorie des Automates et Applications **172**, 147–159 (1992)

36. Vogler, W. (ed.): Modular Construction and Partial Order Semantics of Petri Nets. LNCS, vol. 625. Springer, Heidelberg (1992). https://doi.org/10.1007/3-540-55767-9

37. Zielonka, W.: Notes on finite asynchronous automata. RAIRO-Theor. Inform. Appl. **21**(2), 99–135 (1987)

Verifying Generalised and Structural Soundness of Workflow Nets via Relaxations

Michael Blondin[1] , Filip Mazowiecki[2], and Philip Offtermatt[1,2(✉)]

[1] Université de Sherbrooke, Sherbrooke, Canada
philip.offtermatt@usherbrooke.ca
[2] Max Planck Institute for Software Systems,
Saarbrücken, Germany

Abstract. Workflow nets are a well-established mathematical formalism for the analysis of business processes arising from either modeling tools or process mining. The central decision problems for workflow nets are k-soundness, generalised soundness and structural soundness. Most existing tools focus on k-soundness. In this work, we propose novel scalable semi-procedures for generalised and structural soundness. This is achieved via integral and continuous Petri net reachability relaxations. We show that our approach is competitive against state-of-the-art tools.

1 Introduction

Workflow nets are a well-established mathematical formalism for the description of business processes arising from software modelers and process mining (*e.g.*, see [2,3]), and further notations such as UML activity diagrams [4]. More precisely, a workflow net consists of *places* that contain resources, and *transitions* that can consume, create and move resources concurrently. Two designated places, denoted i and f, respectively model the initialization and completion of a process. Workflow nets, which form a subclass of Petri nets, enable the automatic formal verification of business processes. For example, 1-*soundness* states that from the initial configuration $\{i: 1\}$, every reachable configuration can reach the final configuration $\{f: 1\}$. Informally, this means that given any partial execution of a business process, it is possible to complete it properly.

Soundness. The main decision problems concerning workflow nets revolve around soundness properties. The generalisation of 1-soundness to several resources is k-*soundness*. It asks whether from $\{i: k\}$, every reachable configuration can reach $\{f: k\}$ (here, $\{p: k\}$ indicates that place p contains k resources). Intuitively, 1-soundness guarantees that every initialised process terminates, and k-soundness guarantees that k initialised processes working in parallel will all terminate (see

---

An extended version of this paper with an appendix containing the missing proofs can be obtained from https://arxiv.org/abs/2206.02606.

© The Author(s) 2022
S. Shoham and Y. Vizel (Eds.): CAV 2022, LNCS 13372, pp. 468–489, 2022.
https://doi.org/10.1007/978-3-031-13188-2_23

e.g. [1,2]). *Generalised soundness* asks whether k-soundness holds for all $k \geq$ 1. Unlike k-soundness, generalised soundness preserves desirable properties like composition and has other desirable properties for business applications [20]. *Structural soundness* is the existential counterpart of generalised soundness, *i.e.* it asks whether k-soundness holds for some $k \geq 1$. Structural soundness gives information on how many processes can be controlled in parallel [31], moreover, by applying results about structural soundness, one can compute the set of all k for which the workflow net is k-sound [9, Section 7].

These problems are all decidable [1,21,31], but with high complexity: either PSPACE- or EXPSPACE-complete [9]. Most of the (software) tools focus on k-soundness, with an emphasis on $k = 1$. Existing algorithms for generalised and structural soundness rely on Petri net reachability [19,21,31], which was recently shown Ackermann-complete [13,24], so not primitive recursive. In this work, we describe *novel scalable semi-procedures for generalised and structural soundness*.

We focus on "negative instances", *i.e.* where soundness does *not* hold. Let us motivate this. It is known that given a workflow net $\mathcal{N}$, one can iteratively apply simple reduction rules to $\mathcal{N}$. The resulting workflow net $\mathcal{N}'$ is sound iff $\mathcal{N}$ is as well [10,22]. In practice, one infers that $\mathcal{N}$ is sound from the fact that $\mathcal{N}'$ has been reduced to a trivial workflow net where only i and f remain. However, if $\mathcal{N}$ is *not* sound, one obtains some nontrivial $\mathcal{N}'$ that must be verified via some other approach such as model checking. In this work, we provide algorithmic building blocks for this case, where state-space exploration is prohibitive.

Relaxations. This is achieved by considering two reachability relaxations, namely integer reachability and continuous reachability. As their name suggests, these two notions relax some forbidden behaviour of workflow nets. Informally, integer reachability allows for the amount of resources to become temporarily negative, while continuous reachability allows the fragmentation of resources into pieces. Such relaxations possibly introduce spurious behaviour, but enjoy significantly better algorithmic properties (*e.g.*, see [7]). For example, they have been successfully employed for the verification of multi-threaded program skeletons [5,8,15].

Generalised Soundness. Based on these relaxations, we provide two necessary conditions for generalised soundness: *integer boundedness* and *continuous soundness*. The former states that the state-space of a given workflow net is bounded (from above) even under integer reachability. The latter states that a given workflow net is 1-sound under continuous reachability. We show the following for integer boundedness and continuous soundness:

- Well-established classical reduction rules preserve both properties;
- Integer boundedness is testable in polynomial time, and continuous soundness is coNP-complete;
- From a practical viewpoint, they are respectively translatable into instances of linear programming and linear arithmetic (which can be solved efficiently by dedicated tools such as SMT solvers);
- Under a mild computational assumption, continuous soundness implies integer boundedness.

Thus, altogether, in order to check whether a workflow net $\mathcal{N}$ is generalised *unsound*, one may first use classical reduction rules to obtain a smaller workflow net $\mathcal{N}'$; test integer *unboundedness* in polynomial time; and, if needed, move onto testing continuous *unsoundness*.

The fact that continuous reachability can be used to semi-decide generalised soundness is arguably surprising. Using the notation of computation temporal logic (CTL), k-soundness can be rephrased as $\{i\colon k\} \models \forall G\, \exists F\, \{f\colon k\}$. Some other well-studied properties have a similar structure, *e.g.* liveness and home-stateness amount to "$\boldsymbol{m}_{\mathrm{init}} \models \bigwedge_{t \in T} \forall G\, \exists F\, (t \text{ is enabled})$" and "$\boldsymbol{m}_{\mathrm{init}} \models \forall G\, \exists F\, \boldsymbol{m}_{\mathrm{home}}$". It is known that liveness, home-stateness, and other properties such as boundedness and inclusion, *cannot* be approximated continuously [8, Sect. 4]. Yet, generalised soundness quantifies k-soundness universally, and this enables a continuous over-approximation. Consequently, we provide a novel application of continuous relaxations for the efficient verification of properties beyond reachability.

Structural Soundness. The authors of [31] have observed that a property called structural quasi-soundness is a necessary condition for structural soundness. The former states that $\{i\colon k\}$ can reach $\{f\colon k\}$ for some $k \geq 1$. In [31], structural quasi-soundness is reduced to Petri net reachability, which has non primitive recursive complexity. In this work, we show that structural quasi-soundness can be rephrased as continuous reachability. Since the latter can be tested in polynomial time [18], or alternatively via SMT solving [8], this vastly improves the practicability of structural quasi-soundness. We further show that this approach can be adapted so that it provides a lower bound on the first k such that $\{i\colon k\}$ can reach $\{i\colon f\}$. From a practical point of view, this is useful as it can vastly reduce the number of reachability queries to decide structural soundness.

Free-Choice Nets. Many real-world workflow nets have a specific structure where concurrency is restricted. Such nets are known as *free-choice* workflow nets (*e.g.*, see [14] for a book). In particular, free-choice workflow nets allow for the modeling of many features present in common workflow management systems [2]. Generalised soundness is equivalent to 1-soundness for free-choice workflow nets [28]. In this work, we prove that continuous soundness is equivalent to generalised soundness. As a byproduct of our proof, we show that structural soundness is also equivalent to continuous soundness. Altogether, the notions of $\{1\text{-}, \text{generalised}, \text{structural}, \text{continuous}\}$ soundness *all coincide* for free-choice nets. In particular, this means that the continuous relaxation is *exact* and can serve as an efficient addition to the existing algorithmic toolkit.

Experimental Results. To demonstrate the viability of our approach, we have implemented and experimentally evaluated a prototype. As part of our evaluation, we propose several new synthetic instances for generalised and structural soundness, which are hard to decide with naive approaches. Some of these instances involve the composition of workflow nets arising from the modeling of business processes in the IBM WebSphere Business Modeler. Our prototype is competitive against both a state-of-the-art Petri net model checker, and a workflow net analyzer. In particular, our approach exhibits better signs of scalability.

Organization. The paper follows the structure of this introduction. Section 2 introduces notation, workflow nets and some properties. Section 3 defines integer and continuous relaxations, and further shows that they are preserved under reduction rules. Sections 4, 5, 6 present the aforementioned results on generalised soundness, structural soundness and free-choice nets. Section 7 provides experimental results. Section 8 concludes. Some proofs are deferred to an appendix.

2   Preliminaries

We use $\mathbb{Z}$, $\mathbb{N}$, $\mathbb{Q}$ and $\mathbb{Q}_{\geq 0}$ to respectively denote the integers, the naturals (including 0), the rationals and the nonnegative rationals (including 0). Let $x, y \in \mathbb{Q}^S$ be vectors over a finite set S. We write $x \leq y$ if $x[s] \leq y[s]$ for all $s \in S$. We write $x < y$ if $x \leq y$ and $x[s] < y[s]$ for some $s \in S$. We extend addition and subtraction to vectors, *i.e.* $(x + y)[s] := x[s] + y[s]$ and $(x - y)[s] := x[s] - y[s]$ for all $s \in S$. We define $\mathrm{supp}(x) = \{s \in S \mid x[s] \neq 0\}$. Given $c \in \mathbb{Q}$, $c \in \mathbb{Q}^S$ denotes the vector such that $c[s] = c$ for all $s \in S$.

2.1   Petri Nets

A *Petri net* $\mathcal{N}$ is a triple (P, T, F), where P is a finite set of *places*; T is a finite set of *transitions*, such that $T \cap P = \emptyset$; and $F \colon ((P \times T) \cup (T \times P)) \to \{0, 1\}$ is a set of *arcs*. For readers familiar with Petri nets, note that arc weights are not allowed, *i.e.* the weights are always 1. A *marking* is a vector $m \in \mathbb{N}^P$ such that $m[p]$ denotes the number of *tokens* in place p. We denote markings listing nonzero values, *e.g.* $m = \{p_1 : 1\}$ means $m[p_1] = 1$ and $m[p] = 0$ for $p \neq p_1$.

Let $t \in T$. We define the *pre-vector* of t as ${}^\bullet t \in \mathbb{N}^P$, where ${}^\bullet t[p] := F(p, t)$. We define its *post-vector* symmetrically with $t^\bullet[p] := F(t, p)$. The *effect* of t is denoted as $\Delta(t) := t^\bullet - {}^\bullet t$. We say that a transition t is *enabled* at a marking m if $m \geq {}^\bullet t$. If this is the case, then t can be *fired* at m, which results in a marking m' such that $m' := m + \Delta(t)$. We write $m \to^t$ to denote that t is *enabled* at m, and we write $m \to^t m'$ whenever we care about the marking m' resulting from the firing. We further write $m \to m'$ to denote that $m \to^t m'$ for some $t \in T$.

We say that a sequence of transitions $\pi = t_1 \cdots t_n$ is a *run*. We extend the notion of effect, enabledness and firing from transitions to runs in a straightforward way. The *effect* of a run is defined as the sum of the effects of its transitions, that is, $\Delta(\pi) := \Delta(t_1) + \ldots + \Delta(t_n)$. The run π is enabled at m, denoted as $m \to^\pi$, if $m \to^{t_1} m_1 \to^{t_2} m_2 \cdots \to^{t_{n-1}} m_{n-1} \to^{t_n}$ for some markings $m_1, m_2, \ldots, m_{n-1}$. Furthermore, firing π from m leads to m', denoted as $m \to^\pi m'$, if $m \to^\pi$ and $m' = m + \Delta(\pi)$. We denote the reflexive and transitive closure of $\to$ by $\to^*$.

A pair $(\mathcal{N}, m)$, where $\mathcal{N}$ is a Petri net and m is a marking of $\mathcal{N}$, is called a *marked Petri net*. We write $\mathrm{Reach}(\mathcal{N}, m) := \{m' \mid m \to^* m'\}$ to denote the set of markings reachable from m in $\mathcal{N}$.

A marked Petri net $(\mathcal{N}, m)$ is *bounded* if there exists $b \in \mathbb{N}$ such that $m' \in \mathrm{Reach}(\mathcal{N}, m)$ implies $m'[p] \leq b$ for all $p \in P$. It is further *safe* if $b = 1$. We say *unbounded* and *unsafe* for "not bounded" and "not safe".

Sometimes, we argue about transformations on Petri nets which take as an input a Petri net $\mathcal{N}$ and output a Petri net $\mathcal{N}'$. We say that such a transformation *preserves* some property if $\mathcal{N}$ satisfies that property iff $\mathcal{N}'$ satisfies it.

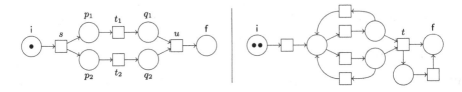

Fig. 1. Example of two Petri nets: respectively $\mathcal{N}_{\text{left}}$ and $\mathcal{N}_{\text{right}}$.

Example 1. The left-hand side of Fig. 1 illustrates a Petri net $\mathcal{N}_{\text{left}} = (P, T, F)$ where $P := \{\mathsf{i}, p_1, p_2, q_1, q_2, \mathsf{f}\}$, $T := \{s, t_1, t_2, u\}$, and F is depicted by arcs, *e.g.* $F[\mathsf{i}, s] = 1$ and $F[s, \mathsf{i}] = 0$. The Petri net is marked by $\{\mathsf{i} \colon 1\}$, *i.e.* with one token in place i. We have $\{\mathsf{i} \colon 1\} \to^s \{p_1 \colon 1, p_2 \colon 1\} \to^{t_1 t_2} \{q_1 \colon 1, q_2 \colon 1\} \to^u \{\mathsf{f} \colon 1\}$. ◁

2.2 Workflow Nets

A workflow net $\mathcal{N}$ is a Petri net [1] such that:

- there is a designated *initial place* i such that $t^{\bullet}[\mathsf{i}] = 0$ for all $t \in T$;
- there is a designated *final place* $\mathsf{f} \neq \mathsf{i}$ such that ${}^{\bullet}t[\mathsf{f}] = 0$ for all $t \in T$; and
- each place and transition lies on at least one path from i to f in the underlying graph of $\mathcal{N}$, *i.e.* (V, E) where $V := P \cup T$ and $(u, v) \in E$ iff $F(u, v) \neq 0$.

We say that $\mathcal{N}$ is:

- *k-sound* if for all $\boldsymbol{m} \in \text{Reach}(\mathcal{N}, \{\mathsf{i} \colon k\})$ it is the case that $\boldsymbol{m} \to^* \{\mathsf{f} \colon k\}$ [1];
- *generalised sound* if $\mathcal{N}$ is k-sound for all $k \in \mathbb{N}_{\geq 1}$ [20, Def. 3],
- *structurally sound* if $\mathcal{N}$ is k-sound for some $k \in \mathbb{N}_{\geq 1}$ [6].

Example 2. Figure 1 depicts two workflow nets: $\mathcal{N}_{\text{left}}$ and $\mathcal{N}_{\text{right}}$. The former is generalised sound, but the latter is not. Indeed, from $\{\mathsf{i} \colon 1\}$, transition t cannot be enabled (as transitions preserve the sum of all tokens). Both workflow nets are structurally sound. Indeed, $\mathcal{N}_{\text{right}}$ is 2-sound as it is always possible to redistribute the two tokens so that t can be fired in order to reach $\{\mathsf{f} \colon 2\}$. ◁

3 Reachability Relaxations

Fix a Petri net $\mathcal{N} = (P, T, F)$. We describe the two aforementioned relaxations.

Integer Reachability. An *integral marking* is a vector $\boldsymbol{m} \in \mathbb{Z}^P$. Any transition $t \in T$ is *enabled* in $\boldsymbol{m} \in \mathbb{Z}^P$, and *firing* t leads to $\boldsymbol{m}' := \boldsymbol{m} + \Delta(t)$, denoted $\boldsymbol{m} \to_{\mathbb{Z}}^t \boldsymbol{m}'$. We define $\boldsymbol{m} \to_{\mathbb{Z}} \boldsymbol{m}'$ and $\boldsymbol{m} \to_{\mathbb{Z}}^* \boldsymbol{m}'$ analogously to the standard setting but w.r.t. $\to_{\mathbb{Z}}^t$ rather than $\to^t$. Similarly, $\mathbb{Z}\text{-Reach}(\mathcal{N}, m) := \{m' \in \mathbb{Z}^P \mid m \to_{\mathbb{Z}}^* m'\}$. As transitions are always enabled, the order of a firing sequence is irrelevant. In particular, $m \to_{\mathbb{Z}}^* m'$ iff there exists $x \in \mathbb{N}^T$ such that $m' = m + \sum_{t \in T} x[t] \cdot \Delta(t)$. Thus, integer reachability amounts to integer linear programming. Moreover, it is NP-complete [12].

Continuous Reachability. A *continuous marking* is a vector $m \in \mathbb{Q}_{\geq 0}^P$. Let $\lambda \in (0, 1]$. We say that λt is *enabled* in m, denoted $m \to_{\mathbb{Q}_{\geq 0}}^{\lambda t}$, if $m \geq \lambda \cdot {}^\bullet t$. In this context, λ is called the *scaling factor*. Furthermore, we denote by $m \to_{\mathbb{Q}_{\geq 0}}^{\lambda t} m'$ that λt is enabled in m, and that its *firing* results in $m' := m + \lambda \cdot \Delta(t)$. A sequence of pairs of scaling factors and transitions is called a *continuous run*.

The notations $m \to_{\mathbb{Q}_{\geq 0}} m'$ and $m \to_{\mathbb{Q}_{\geq 0}}^* m'$ are defined analogously to the discrete case but with respect to $\to_{\mathbb{Q}_{\geq 0}}^{\lambda t}$ rather than $\to^t$ (the internal factors λ can differ). Similarly, $\mathbb{Q}_{\geq 0}\text{-Reach}(\mathcal{N}, m) := \{m' \mid m \to_{\mathbb{Q}_{\geq 0}}^* m'\}$ denotes the markings continuously reachable from m. For example, for $\mathcal{N}_{\text{left}}$ from Fig. 1 and $\pi := \frac{1}{2}s\frac{1}{4}t_1$, we have $\{i : 1\} \to_{\mathbb{Q}_{\geq 0}}^\pi \{i : 1/2, p_1 : 1/4, p_2 : 1/2, q_1 : 1/4\}$. It is known that continuous reachability, namely determining whether $m \to_{\mathbb{Q}_{\geq 0}}^* m'$, given $m, m' \in \mathbb{Q}_{\geq 0}^P$, can be checked in polynomial time [18].

Let us establish the following helpful lemma similar to [18, Lemma 12(1)].

Lemma 1. *Let* m, m' *be continuous markings. It is the case that* $m \to_{\mathbb{Q}_{\geq 0}}^* m'$ *iff there exists* $b \in \mathbb{N}_{\geq 1}$ *such that* $b \cdot m \to^* b \cdot m'$.

3.1   Preservation Under Reduction Rules

In [10], the authors present six reduction rules, denoted $R_1, \ldots, R_6$, that generalize the existing reduction rules of [27]. In the following, we show that these reduction rules preserve natural properties for the two reachability relaxations. This means we will be able to check these properties on a reduced workflow net and get the same results as on the original one.

Formally, the rules simplify a given workflow net $\mathcal{N} = (P, T, F)$. In particular, the places of the resulting workflow net $\mathcal{N}' = (P', T, F')$ form a subset of P. Let us fix a domain $\mathbb{D} \in \{\mathbb{N}, \mathbb{Z}, \mathbb{Q}_{\geq 0}\}$ and let $P' \subseteq P$. For ease of notation, we write $P'' = P \setminus P'$ to denote the (possibly empty) set of removed places. Rules never remove the initial and output places, *i.e.* $i, f \in P'$. We denote by $\pi \colon \mathbb{D}^P \to \mathbb{D}^{P'}$ the obvious projection function, and by $\pi_0 \colon \mathbb{D}^{P'} \to \mathbb{D}^P$ the "reverse projection" which fills new places with 0. Formally, $\pi_0(m)[p'] := m[p']$ for all $p' \in P'$ and $\pi_0(m)[p''] := 0$ for all $p'' \in P''$.

In [10], the authors prove that the rules preserve generalised soundness. This of course implies that they preserve k-soundness for all k. The technical proposition below will be helpful in the forthcoming sections to show the preservation of useful properties based on reachability relaxations.

Proposition 1. *Let $\mathcal{N} = (P, T, F)$ be a workflow net, and let $\mathbb{D} \in \{\mathbb{N}, \mathbb{Z}, \mathbb{Q}_{\geq 0}\}$. Let $\mathcal{N}' = (P', T', F')$ be a workflow net obtained by applying a reduction rule R_i to $\mathcal{N}$, where $P = P' \cup P''$. The following holds.*

- *Rule R_1. We have $P'' = \{p\}$. There exists a nonempty set $R' \subseteq P'$ such that if $\{\mathrm{i}\colon 1\} \to_{\mathbb{D}}^* m$ in $\mathcal{N}$, then $m[p] = \sum_{r \in R'} m[r']$. Moreover, $m \to_{\mathbb{D}}^* n$ in $\mathcal{N}$ iff $\pi(m) \to_{\mathbb{D}}^* \pi(n)$ in $\mathcal{N}'$.*
- *Rules R_2 and R_3. We have $P'' = \emptyset$ and $m \to_{\mathbb{D}}^* n$ in $\mathcal{N}$ iff $m \to_{\mathbb{D}}^* n$ in $\mathcal{N}'$.*
- *Rules R_4 and R_5. We have $P'' = \{p\}$. For all m' and n', $m' \to_{\mathbb{D}}^* n'$ in $\mathcal{N}'$ iff $\pi_0(m') \to_{\mathbb{D}}^* \pi_0(n')$ in $\mathcal{N}$. Further, for all $t \in T$ and $p' \in P'$: either ${}^\bullet t[p] = 1$ implies ${}^\bullet t[p'] = 0$; or $t^\bullet[p] = 1$ implies $t^\bullet[p'] = 0$. Also, for $\mathbb{D} \neq \mathbb{Z}$, if $\exists m : \{\mathrm{i}\colon 1\} \to_{\mathbb{D}}^* m \not\to_{\mathbb{D}}^* \{\mathrm{f}\colon 1\}$ holds in $\mathcal{N}$, then $\exists m' : \{\mathrm{i}\colon 1\} \to_{\mathbb{D}}^* m' \not\to_{\mathbb{D}}^* \{\mathrm{f}\colon 1\}$ holds in $\mathcal{N}'$.*
- *Rule R_6. We have $P'' = \{p_2, \ldots, p_k\}$. There exists $p_1 \in P'$ such that for all $n \in P^{\mathbb{D}}$, if $\sum_{i=1}^k m[p_i] = \sum_{i=1}^k n[p_i]$ and $n[p'] = m[p']$ for $p' \in P' \setminus \{p_1\}$, then $m \to_{\mathbb{D}}^* n$. Moreover, if $m[p_i] = n[p_i] = 0$ for $i > 1$, then $m \to_{\mathbb{D}}^* n$ in $\mathcal{N}$ iff $\pi(m) \to_{\mathbb{D}}^* \pi(n)$ in $\mathcal{N}'$.*

4   Using Relaxations For Generalised Soundness

In this section, we explain how reachability relaxations can be leveraged in order to semi-decide generalised soundness of workflow nets. More precisely, we state two necessary conditions for a workflow net to be generalised sound: one phrased in terms of integer reachability, and one in terms of continuous reachability. Furthermore, for each condition we: (1) show that it is preserved under reduction rules, and (2) establish its computational complexity. Overall, this means that to conclude that a given workflow net $\mathcal{N}$ is *not* generalised sound, one may first reduce $\mathcal{N}$, and *then* efficiently test for one of these two necessary conditions.

For integer boundedness, we need the mild assumption of nonredundancy. Let $\mathcal{N} = (P, T, F)$ be a workflow net. We say that a place $p \in P$ is *nonredundant*[1] if there exist $k \in \mathbb{N}_{\geq 1}$ and $m \in \mathbb{N}^P$ such that $\{\mathrm{i}\colon k\} \to^* m$ and $m[p] \geq 1$. It is known (and simple to see) that redundant places can be removed from a workflow net without changing whether it is generalised sound. Moreover, testing whether a place is nonredundant can be done in polynomial time. Indeed, by Lemma 1, it amounts to testing for the existence of some $m \in \mathbb{Q}_{\geq 0}^P$ such that $\{\mathrm{i}\colon 1\} \to_{\mathbb{Q}_{\geq 0}}^* m$ and $m[p] > 0$. The latter is known as a *coverability* query and it can be checked in polynomial time [18]. Thus, in order to test whether a given workflow net is generalised sound, one can first remove its redundant places. We call a workflow net without redundant places a *nonredundant workflow net*.

4.1   Integer Unboundedness

Recall that a marked Petri net $(\mathcal{N}, m)$ is *bounded* if there exists $b \in \mathbb{N}$ such that $m' \in \mathrm{Reach}(\mathcal{N}, m)$ implies $m' \leq b$. It is well-known that any 1-sound workflow

---

[1] This notion is adapted from batch workflow nets considered in [21].

net must be bounded from $\{i: 1\}$ [1]. In particular, this means that boundedness is a necessary condition for generalised soundness. However, testing boundedness has extensive computational cost as it is EXPSPACE-complete [11, 29]. Consider the relaxed property of *integer boundedness*. It is defined as boundedness, but where "$m' \in \text{Reach}(\mathcal{N}, m)$" is replaced with "$m' \in \mathbb{Z}\text{-Reach}(\mathcal{N}, m) \cap \mathbb{N}^P$".

Proposition 2 ([9, Lemma 5.9]). *Let $\mathcal{N}$ be a nonredundant workflow net. If $(\mathcal{N}, \{i: 1\})$ is integer unbounded, then $\mathcal{N}$ is not generalised sound.*

Proposition 3. *The reduction rules from [10] preserve integer unboundedness.*

Next, we establish the complexity of integer unboundedness in two steps. The first step, in the next proposition, shows that testing integer boundedness amounts to a simple condition, independent of the initial marking. The second step shows the condition can be translated into a linear program over $\mathbb{Q}$, rather than $\mathbb{N}$. As a corollary, integer unboundedness is testable in polynomial time.

Proposition 4. *A marked Petri net $(\mathcal{N}, m)$ is integer unbounded iff there exists a marking $m' > 0$ such that $0 \rightarrow_{\mathbb{Z}}^* m'$ (independent of m).*

Proof. Let $\mathcal{N} = (P, F, T)$ be a Petri net and let $m \in \mathbb{N}^P$.

$\Rightarrow$) By assumption, there exist $m_0, m_1, \ldots \in \mathbb{Z}\text{-Reach}(\mathcal{N}, m) \cap \mathbb{N}^P$ such that, for every $i \in \mathbb{N}$, it is the case that $m_i \not\leq i$. Since $(\mathbb{N}^P, \leq)$ is well-quasi-ordered, there exist indices $i_0, i_1, \ldots$ such that $m_{i_j} \leq m_{i_k}$ for all $j < k$. Without loss of generality, we can assume that $m_{i_j} < m_{i_k}$ for all $j < k$, as we could otherwise extract such a subsequence. Recall that each $m_{i_\ell} \in \mathbb{Z}\text{-Reach}(\mathcal{N}, m)$. Let $\pi_\ell \in T^*$ be such that $m \rightarrow_{\mathbb{Z}}^{\pi_\ell} m_{i_\ell}$. Let $x_\ell \in \mathbb{N}^T$ be the vector such that $x_\ell(t)$ indicates the number of occurrences of transition t in π_ℓ. Since $(\mathbb{N}^T, \leq)$ is well-quasi-ordered, there exist $j < k$ such that $x_j \leq x_k$. Let $m' := m_{i_k} - m_{i_j}$ and $\pi := \prod_{t \in T} t^{(x_k[t] - x_\ell[t])}$. We have $0 \rightarrow_{\mathbb{Z}}^{\pi} m' > 0$ as desired since:

$$m' = m_{i_k} - m_{i_j} = (m + \Delta(\pi_k)) - (m + \Delta(\pi_\ell)) = \Delta(\pi_k) - \Delta(\pi_\ell)$$
$$= \sum_{t \in T} x_k[t] \cdot \Delta(t) - \sum_{t \in T} x_\ell[t] \cdot \Delta(t) = \sum_{t \in T} (x_k - x_\ell)[t] \cdot \Delta(t) = \Delta(\pi).$$

$\Leftarrow$) By assumption $0 \rightarrow_{\mathbb{Z}}^{\pi} m' > 0$. In particular, this means that $m \rightarrow_{\mathbb{Z}}^{\pi} m + m' \rightarrow_{\mathbb{Z}}^{\pi} m + 2m' \rightarrow_{\mathbb{Z}} \cdots$. Therefore, $(\mathcal{N}, m)$ is not integer bounded. $\square$

Proposition 5. *A marked Petri net $(\mathcal{N}, m)$, where $\mathcal{N} = (P, T, F)$, is integer unbounded iff this system has a solution: $\exists x \in \mathbb{Q}_{\geq 0}^T : \sum_{t \in T} x[t] \cdot \Delta(t) > 0$. In particular, given a workflow net $\mathcal{N}$, testing integer boundedness of $(\mathcal{N}, \{i: 1\})$ can be done in polynomial time.*

4.2   Continuous Soundness

Let us now introduce a continuous variant of 1-soundness based on continuous reachability. We prove that this variant, which we call *continuous soundness*, is a necessary condition for generalised soundness, and preserved by reduction rules. Moreover, we show that continuous soundness is coNP-complete, and relates to integer boundedness.

We say that a workflow net $\mathcal{N}$ is *continuously sound* if for all continuous markings $m \in \mathbb{Q}_{\geq 0}$-Reach$(\mathcal{N}, \{i: 1\})$ it is the case that $m \to_{\mathbb{Q}_{\geq 0}}^* \{f: 1\}$.

Theorem 1. *Continuous unsoundness implies generalised unsoundness.*

Proof. Let $\mathcal{N} = (P, T, F)$ be a workflow net that is not continuously sound. By definition of continuous soundness, there exists some continuous marking $m \in \mathbb{Q}_{\geq 0}^P$ such that $\{i: 1\} \to_{\mathbb{Q}_{\geq 0}}^* m$ and $m \not\to_{\mathbb{Q}_{\geq 0}}^* \{f: 1\}$. By Lemma 1, there exists $b \in \mathbb{N}_{\geq 1}$ such that $\{i: b\} \to^* b \cdot m$. Furthermore, by Lemma 1, $b \cdot m \not\to^* \{f: b\}$. This means that $\mathcal{N}$ is not b-sound, and consequently not generalised sound. □

Proposition 6. *The reduction rules from [10] preserve continuous soundness.*

Theorem 2. *Continuous soundness is coNP-complete. Moreover, coNP-hardness holds even if the underlying graph of the given workflow net is acyclic.*

Proof (of membership in coNP). The *inclusion problem* consists in determining whether, given Petri nets $\mathcal{N}$ and $\mathcal{N}'$ over a common set of places, and markings m and m', it is the case that $\mathbb{Q}_{\geq 0}$-Reach$(\mathcal{N}, m) \subseteq \mathbb{Q}_{\geq 0}$-Reach$(\mathcal{N}', m')$. The inclusion problem is known to be coNP-complete [8, Prop. 4.6].

Let $\mathcal{N} = (P, T)$ be a workflow net. Let $\mathcal{N}^{-1} = (P, T^{-1})$ be defined as $\mathcal{N}$ but with its transitions reversed, *i.e.* where $T^{-1} := \{t^{-1} \mid t \in T\}$ with $^\bullet(t^{-1}) := t^\bullet$ and $(t^{-1})^\bullet := {}^\bullet t$. It is the case that $m \to_{\mathbb{Q}_{\geq 0}}^* m'$ in $\mathcal{N}$ iff $m' \to_{\mathbb{Q}_{\geq 0}}^* m$ in $\mathcal{N}^{-1}$. Observe that $\mathcal{N}$ is continuously sound iff the following holds for all m:

$$m \in \mathbb{Q}_{\geq 0}\text{-Reach}(\mathcal{N}, \{i: 1\}) \implies \{f: 1\} \in \mathbb{Q}_{\geq 0}\text{-Reach}(\mathcal{N}, m).$$

So, as $\{f: 1\} \in \mathbb{Q}_{\geq 0}$-Reach$(\mathcal{N}, m)$ is equivalent to $m \in \mathbb{Q}_{\geq 0}$-Reach$(\mathcal{N}^{-1}, \{f: 1\})$, continuous soundness holds iff $\mathbb{Q}_{\geq 0}$-Reach$(\mathcal{N}, \{i: 1\}) \subseteq \mathbb{Q}_{\geq 0}$-Reach$(\mathcal{N}^{-1}, \{f: 1\})$. As inclusion can be tested in coNP, membership follows.

□

Proof (of coNP-hardness). We give a reduction from the problem of determining whether a Boolean formula in disjunctive normal form (DNF) is a tautology. We adapt a construction from [30] used to show that soundness in acyclic workflow nets is coNP-hard. The proof is more challenging under the continuous semantics as several variable valuations and clauses can be simultaneously used.

The reduction is depicted in Fig. 2 for $\varphi = (x_1 \wedge x_2 \wedge \neg x_4) \vee (\neg x_1 \wedge x_3 \wedge x_4)$. In general, let $\varphi = \bigvee_{j \in [1..k]} C_j$ be a Boolean formula in DNF with k clauses over variables $x_1, \ldots, x_m$. We define a workflow net $\mathcal{N}_\varphi = (P, T, F)$.

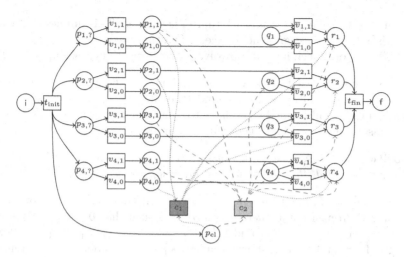

Fig. 2. A workflow net $\mathcal{N}_\varphi$ such that $\mathcal{N}_\varphi$ is continuously sound iff $\varphi = (x_1 \wedge x_2 \wedge \neg x_4) \vee (x_1 \wedge x_3 \wedge x_4)$ is a tautology. Places and transitions contain their names (not values). Arcs corresponding to the first and second clauses are respectively dotted and dashed.

Definition. The places are defined as $P := \{\mathrm{i}, p_{\mathrm{cl}}, \mathrm{f}\} \cup P_{\mathrm{var}} \cup P_{\mathrm{clean}}$, where $P_{\mathrm{var}} := \bigcup_{i \in [1..m]} \{p_{i,?}, p_{i,1}, p_{i,0}\}$ and $P_{\mathrm{clean}} := \bigcup_{i \in [1..m]} \{q_i, r_i\}$. The transitions are defined as $T := \{t_{\mathrm{init}}, t_{\mathrm{fin}}\} \cup T_{\mathrm{var}} \cup T_{\mathrm{clauses}} \cup T_{\overline{\mathrm{var}}}$, where

$$T_{\mathrm{var}} := \bigcup_{i \in [1..m]} \{v_{i,1}, v_{i,0}\}, T_{\mathrm{clauses}} := \{c_i \mid i \in [1..k]\} \text{ and } T_{\overline{\mathrm{var}}} := \bigcup_{i \in [1..m]} \{\overline{v}_{i,1}, \overline{v}_{i,0}\}.$$

Let us explain how $\mathcal{N}_\varphi$ is *intended* to work. Transition t_{init} enables the initialization of variables and the selection of a clause that satisfies φ, i.e. ${}^\bullet t_{\mathrm{init}} := \{\mathrm{i}: 1\}$ and $t_{\mathrm{init}}^\bullet := \{p_{i,?}: 1 \mid i \in [1..m]\} + \{p_{\mathrm{cl}}: 1\}$. A token in place $p_{i,b}$ indicates that variable x_i has been assigned value b (where "?" indicates "none"). Consequently, we have ${}^\bullet v_{i,b} := p_{i,?}$ and $v_{i,b}^\bullet := p_{i,b}$ for each $i \in [1..m]$ and $b \in \{0, 1\}$.

Transition c_j consumes a token associated to each literal of clause C_j, *i.e.* ${}^\bullet c_j := \{v_{i,1} \mid x_i \in C_j\} + \{v_{i,0} \mid \neg x_i \in C_j\}$. A token in place q_i indicates that variable x_i is not needed anymore (due to some satisfied clause). A token in place r_i indicates that variable x_i has been discarded. Therefore, transition c_j produces these tokens: $c_j^\bullet := \{q_i \mid x_i \notin C_j \wedge \neg x_i \notin C_j\} + \{r_i \mid x_i \in C_j \vee \neg x_i \in C_j\}$.

Transition $\overline{v}_{i,b}$ discards variable x_i, i.e. ${}^\bullet \overline{v}_{i,b} := \{p_{i,b}, q_i\}$ and ${}^\bullet \overline{v}_{i,b} := \{q_i\}$. Once each variable is discarded, transition t_{fin} terminates the execution, i.e. ${}^\bullet t_{\mathrm{fin}} := \{r_i \mid i \in [1..m]\}$ and $t_{\mathrm{fin}}^\bullet := \{\mathrm{f}: 1\}$.

Correctness. Note that under $\to_{\mathbb{Q}_{\geq 0}}^*$, the workflow net needs not to proceed as described. Indeed, it could, e.g., assign half a token to $p_{i,0}$ and half a token to $p_{i,1}$. Similarly, several clauses can be used, with distinct scaling factors. Nonetheless, $\mathcal{N}_\varphi$ is continuously sound iff φ is a tautology.

$\Rightarrow$) Let $b_1, \ldots, b_m \in \{0, 1\}$. Let $\pi := t_{\mathrm{init}} v_{1,b_1} \cdots v_{m,b_m}$. We have: $\{\mathrm{i}: 1\} \to_{\mathbb{Q}_{\geq 0}}^\pi \{v_{i,b_i}: 1 \mid i \in [1..m]\} + \{p_{\mathrm{cl}}: 1\}$. Since $\mathcal{N}_\varphi$ is continuously sound by assumption, there must exists some $j \in [1..k]$ such that c_j is enabled. This implies that clause C_j is satisfied by the assignment. Hence, φ is a tautology.

$\Leftarrow$) The proof is technical and involves several invariants (see appendix). □

We may now prove that any nonredundant workflow net that is integer unbounded is also continuously unsound (the reverse is not necessarily true). Therefore, integer unboundedness relates to continuous soundness much like continuous unsoundness relates to generalised soundness.

Proposition 7. *Let $\mathcal{N}$ be a nonredundant workflow net and $\boldsymbol{m} \in \mathbb{N}^P$. If $(\mathcal{N}, \boldsymbol{m})$ is integer unbounded, then $\mathcal{N}$ is not continuously sound.*

Proof. Let $\mathcal{N} = (P, T, F)$ and $\boldsymbol{m} \in \mathbb{N}^P$ be such that $(\mathcal{N}, \boldsymbol{m})$ is not integer bounded. By Proposition 4, there exists $\boldsymbol{m}' > \boldsymbol{0}$ such that $\boldsymbol{0} \to_{\mathbb{Z}}^* \boldsymbol{m}'$. By nonredundancy, there exist $\lambda \in \mathbb{N}_{\geq 1}$ and $\boldsymbol{m}'' \in \mathbb{N}^P$ such that $\{\mathsf{i}\colon \lambda\} \to^* \{\mathsf{f}\colon 1\} + \boldsymbol{m}''$.

In [21, Lemma 12], it is shown that $\{\mathsf{i}\colon k\} \to_{\mathbb{Z}}^* \boldsymbol{n}$ implies the existence of some $\ell \in \mathbb{N}$ such that $\{\mathsf{i}\colon k + \ell\} \to^* \{\mathsf{f}\colon \ell\} + \boldsymbol{n}$. By invoking this lemma with $k := 0$ and $\boldsymbol{n} := \boldsymbol{m}'$, we obtain $\{\mathsf{i}\colon \ell\} \to^* \{\mathsf{f}\colon \ell\} + \boldsymbol{m}'$ for some $\ell \in \mathbb{N}$.

Altogether, $\{\mathsf{i}\colon \lambda + \ell\} \to^* \{\mathsf{f}\colon \lambda + \ell\} + \boldsymbol{m}' + \boldsymbol{m}''$. Since $\lambda + \ell \geq 1$, Lemma 1 yields $\{\mathsf{i}\colon 1\} \to_{\mathbb{Q}_{\geq 0}}^* \{\mathsf{f}\colon 1\} + \boldsymbol{m}'''$ where $\boldsymbol{m}''' := (1/(\lambda + \ell))\boldsymbol{m}'$. As every transition of a workflow net produces at least one token, this contradicts the fact that $\mathcal{N}$ is continuously sound. Indeed, it is impossible to fully get rid of $\boldsymbol{m}''' > \boldsymbol{0}$. □

5   Using Relaxations For Structural Soundness

A workflow net $\mathcal{N}$ is *k-quasi-sound* if $\{\mathsf{i}\colon k\} \to^* \{\mathsf{f}\colon k\}$. Furthermore, $\mathcal{N}$ is *structurally quasi-sound* if it is k-quasi-sound for some $k \in \mathbb{N}_{\geq 1}$.

As observed in [31], structural quasi-soundness is a necessary condition for structural soundness. The notion of structural quasi-soundness is naturally generalised to an arbitrary Petri net $\mathcal{N} = (P, T, F)$. Given markings $\boldsymbol{m}, \boldsymbol{m}' \in \mathbb{N}^P$, we say that $\boldsymbol{m}$ *structurally reaches* $\boldsymbol{m}'$ in $\mathcal{N}$ if $k \cdot \boldsymbol{m} \to^* k \cdot \boldsymbol{m}'$ for some $k \in \mathbb{N}_{\geq 1}$. A workflow net is structurally quasi-sound iff $\boldsymbol{m} := \{\mathsf{i}\colon 1\}$ structurally reaches $\boldsymbol{m}' := \{\mathsf{f}\colon 1\}$. So, the observation of [31] can be rephrased as follows.

Proposition 8. *Let $\mathcal{N}$ be a workflow net. If $\{\mathsf{i}\colon 1\}$ does not structurally reach $\{\mathsf{f}\colon 1\}$ in $\mathcal{N}$, then $\mathcal{N}$ is not structurally sound.*

The problem of structural quasi-soundness can be reduced to an instance of the Petri net reachability problem [31, Lemma 2.1]. Intuitively, the reduction produces a Petri net that nondeterministically chooses multiples of $\{\mathsf{i}\colon 1\}$ and $\{\mathsf{f}\colon 1\}$ for which to check reachability. Such an approach has a prohibitive computational cost as Petri net reachability is Ackermann-complete. However, we observe that structural reachability, and hence structural quasi-soundness, is equivalent to continuous reachability by Lemma 1.

Proposition 9. *Let $\mathcal{N} = (P, T, F)$ be a Petri net, and let $\boldsymbol{m}, \boldsymbol{m}' \in \mathbb{N}^P$ be markings. It is the case that $\boldsymbol{m}$ structurally reaches $\boldsymbol{m}'$ iff $\boldsymbol{m} \to_{\mathbb{Q}_{\geq 0}}^* \boldsymbol{m}'$.*

For a workflow net $\mathcal{N} = (P, T, F)$, let $k_\mathcal{N} \in \mathbb{N}_{\geq 1} \cup \{\infty\}$ be the smallest number for which $\mathcal{N}$ is $k_\mathcal{N}$-quasi-sound. Then $\mathcal{N}$ is structurally sound iff $k_\mathcal{N} \neq \infty$ and $\mathcal{N}$ is $k_\mathcal{N}$-sound [31, Thm 2.1]. By Proposition 9, $k_\mathcal{N} \neq \infty$ can be checked in polynomial time via a continuous reachability query. Moreover, a lower bound on $k_\mathcal{N}$ can be obtained by computing $k_{\mathcal{N},\mathbb{Z}} \in \mathbb{N}_{\geq 1} \cup \{\infty\}$, defined as the smallest value such that $\{i\colon k\} \to_\mathbb{Z}^* \{f\colon k\}$. We obtain a better bound by defining $k_{\mathcal{N},\mathbb{Q}_{\geq 0}} \in \mathbb{N}_{\geq 1} \cup \{\infty\}$ as the smallest value for which there is a continuous run $\pi = \lambda_1 t_1 \cdots \lambda_n t_n$ such that $\{i\colon k\} \to_{\mathbb{Q}_{\geq 0}}^\pi \{f\colon k\}$ and $\pi \in \mathbb{N}^T$, where $\pi[t] := \sum_{i \in [1..n]: t_i = t} \lambda_i$. Values $k_{\mathcal{N},\mathbb{Z}}$ and $k_{\mathcal{N},\mathbb{Q}_{\geq 0}}$ can respectively be computed by a translation to integer linear programming, and a decidable optimization modulo theory.

Proposition 10. *Let $\mathcal{N}$ be a workflow net. It is the case that $k_{\mathcal{N},\mathbb{Z}} \leq k_{\mathcal{N},\mathbb{Q}_{\geq 0}} \leq k_\mathcal{N}$. Moreover, $k_{\mathcal{N},\mathbb{Z}}$ can be computed from an integer linear program $\mathcal{P}$; $k_{\mathcal{N},\mathbb{Q}_{\geq 0}}$ can be obtained by computing $\min k \in \mathbb{N}_{\geq 1} : \varphi(k)$ where φ is a formula from the existential fragment of mixed linear arithmetic φ, i.e. $\exists FO(\mathbb{Q}, \mathbb{Z}, <, +)$; and both $\mathcal{P}$ and φ are constructible in polynomial time from $\mathcal{N}$.*

6   Free-Choice Workflow Nets

Let $\mathcal{N} = (P, T, F)$ be a Petri net. We say that $\mathcal{N}$ is *free-choice* if for any $s, t \in T$, it is the case that either $\mathrm{supp}({}^\bullet s) \cap \mathrm{supp}({}^\bullet t) = \emptyset$ or ${}^\bullet s = {}^\bullet t$. For example, the nets $\mathcal{N}_{\mathrm{left}}$ and $\mathcal{N}_{\mathrm{right}}$ from Fig. 1 are respectively free-choice and not free-choice.

It is known that generalised soundness is equivalent to 1-soundness in free-choice workflow nets [28]. We will show that the same holds for structural soundness, and that, surprisingly, for continuous soundness as well. This means that notions of soundness collapse for free-choice nets. This is proven in the forthcoming Lemma 2 and Theorem 3, which form one of the main theoretical contributions of this work.

Let $(\mathcal{N}, m)$ be a marked Petri net. We say that a transition t is *quasi-live* in $(\mathcal{N}, m)$ if there exists m' such that $m \to^* m' \to^t$. Similarly, we say that a transition t is *live* in $(\mathcal{N}, m)$ if for all m' such that $m \to^* m'$, t is quasi-live in $(\mathcal{N}, m')$. In words, quasi-liveness states that there is at least one way to enable t, and liveness states that t can always be re-enabled. The set of *quasi-live* and *live* transitions of $(\mathcal{N}, m)$ are defined respectively as $F(m) := \{t \in T \mid t \text{ is quasi-live in } (\mathcal{N}, m)\}$ and $L(m) := \{t \in T \mid t \text{ is live in } (\mathcal{N}, m)\}$.

Lemma 2. *Let $\mathcal{N} = (P, T, F)$ be a free-choice Petri net, let $c \in \mathbb{N}_{\geq 1}$, and let $m \in \mathbb{N}^P$. The following statements hold.*

1. *There exists a marking m' such that $m \to^* m'$ and $L(m') = F(m')$.*
2. *If $L(m) = F(m)$, then $L(c \cdot m) = F(c \cdot m) = F(m)$.*
3. *If $L(c \cdot m) = F(c \cdot m)$, $c \cdot m \to^* \{f\colon c\}$ and $(\mathcal{N}, c \cdot m)$ is bounded, then $m = \{f\colon 1\}$.*

Lemma 3. *Let $\mathcal{N}$ be a workflow net. If $\mathcal{N}$ is continuously sound, then $(\mathcal{N}, \{i\colon k\})$ is bounded for all $k \in \mathbb{N}_{\geq 1}$.*

Theorem 3. *Let $\mathcal{N}$ be a free-choice workflow net. These statements are equivalent: (1) $\mathcal{N}$ is 1-sound, (2) $\mathcal{N}$ is generalised sound, (3) $\mathcal{N}$ is structurally sound, and (4) $\mathcal{N}$ is continuously sound.*

Proof. (1) $\Rightarrow$ (2). This was shown in [28].

(2) $\Rightarrow$ (3). By definition, if $\mathcal{N}$ is k-sound for all k, then it is for some k.

(2) $\Rightarrow$ (4). By Theorem 1.

(3) $\Rightarrow$ (1). Let $k \in \mathbb{N}_{\geq 1}$ be such that $\mathcal{N}$ is k-sound. Let $\boldsymbol{m} \in \mathbb{N}^P$ be such that $\{\mathsf{i}\colon 1\} \to^* \boldsymbol{m}$. By Lemma 2(1), there is a marking $\boldsymbol{m}' \in \mathbb{N}^P$ such that $\boldsymbol{m} \to^* \boldsymbol{m}'$ and $F(\boldsymbol{m}') = L(\boldsymbol{m}')$. By Lemma 2(2), we have $L(k \cdot \boldsymbol{m}') = F(k \cdot \boldsymbol{m}') = F(\boldsymbol{m}')$.

By k-soundness, $(\mathcal{N}, \{\mathsf{i}\colon k\})$ must be bounded [9, Proposition 3.2 and Lemma 3.6]. Thus, since $\{\mathsf{i}\colon k\} \to^* k \cdot \boldsymbol{m} \to^* k \cdot \boldsymbol{m}'$, it is also the case that $(\mathcal{N}, k \cdot \boldsymbol{m}')$ is bounded. By k-soundness, $k \cdot \boldsymbol{m}' \to^* \{\mathsf{f}\colon k\}$. By invoking Lemma 2(3) with $c := k$, we conclude that $\boldsymbol{m}' = \{\mathsf{f}\colon 1\}$. So, $\mathcal{N}$ is 1-sound as $\{\mathsf{i}\colon 1\} \to^* \boldsymbol{m} \to^* \boldsymbol{m}' = \{\mathsf{f}\colon 1\}$.

(4) $\Rightarrow$ (1). Assume that $\mathcal{N}$ is continuously sound. Let $\boldsymbol{m} \in \mathbb{N}^P$ be a marking such that $\{\mathsf{i}\colon 1\} \to^* \boldsymbol{m}$. By Lemma 2(1), there exists $\boldsymbol{m}' \in \mathbb{N}^P$ such that $\boldsymbol{m} \to^* \boldsymbol{m}'$ and $L(m') = F(m')$. Clearly, $\{\mathsf{i}\colon 1\} \to^*_{\mathbb{Q}_{\geq 0}} \boldsymbol{m}'$ and by continuous soundness $\boldsymbol{m}' \to^*_{\mathbb{Q}_{\geq 0}} \{\mathsf{f}\colon 1\}$. By Lemma 1, there exists $b \in \mathbb{N}_{\geq 1}$ such that $b \cdot \boldsymbol{m}' \to^* \{\mathsf{f}\colon b\}$.

By Lemma 3, continuous soundness of $\mathcal{N}$ implies that $(\mathcal{N}, b \cdot \boldsymbol{m}')$ is bounded, as $\{\mathsf{i}\colon b\} \to^* b \cdot \boldsymbol{m}'$. Since $L(m') = F(m')$, it follows from Lemma 2(2) that $L(b \cdot \boldsymbol{m}') = F(b \cdot \boldsymbol{m}')$. By invoking Lemma 2(3) with $c := b$, we derive $\boldsymbol{m}' = \{\mathsf{f}\colon 1\}$. Therefore, $\mathcal{N}$ is 1-sound as $\{\mathsf{i}\colon 1\} \to^* \boldsymbol{m} \to^* \boldsymbol{m}' = \{\mathsf{f}\colon 1\}$. $\qquad\square$

7   Experimental Evaluation

We implemented our approaches for generalised and structural soundness in C#.[2] We test continuous soundness via SMT solving. More precisely, we use an existential $\psi_{\mathcal{N}}$ formula of linear arithmetic, i.e. $\mathsf{FO}(\mathbb{Q}, <, +)$, from [8]. This formula is such that $\psi(\boldsymbol{m}, \boldsymbol{m}')$ holds iff $\boldsymbol{m} \to^*_{\mathbb{Q}_{\geq 0}} \boldsymbol{m}'$ in $\mathcal{N}$. Continuous soundness amounts to the $\exists\forall$-formula $\psi_{\mathcal{N}}(\{\mathsf{i}\colon 1\}, \boldsymbol{m}) \wedge \neg\psi_{\mathcal{N}}(\boldsymbol{m}, \{\mathsf{f}\colon 1\})$. To solve such formulas, we use Z3 [26]. We further use Z3 to decide structural quasi-soundness and compute $k_{\mathcal{N}, \mathbb{Q}_{\geq 0}}$ (see Proposition 10), again via the formulas of [8].

We evaluated our prototype implementation on a standard benchmark suite used regularly in the literature, and a novel suite of synthetic instances where generalised or structural soundness are hard to decide with a naive approach.

We compared with two established tools for soundness: LoLA (v2.0) [35], and Woflan [33].[3] The latter can only decide *classical* soundness (1-soundness + quasi-liveness). Nonetheless, we use quasi-live instances, so for which 1-soundness and classical soundness are equivalent. We further use a transformation to reduce the verification of k-soundness to the one of 1-soundness [9, Lemma 3.6]. On the

---

[2] The implementation can be obtained from https://doi.org/10.6084/m9.figshare.19721674.v2.

[3] A version of Woflan suitable for running without user interaction was provided, via personal communication, by its maintainer.

other hand, LoLA can directly decide k-soundness. To do so, we start from $\{i: k\}$ and check a CTL formula of the form $\forall G \exists F \left((\boldsymbol{m}[f] = k) \wedge \bigwedge_{p \neq f} \boldsymbol{m}[p] = 0 \right)$.

Experiments were run on an 8-Core Intel® Core™ i7-7700 CPU @ 3.60 GHz with Ubuntu 18.04. We limited memory to ~ 8 GB, and time to 120 s for each instance. Tools were called from a Python script. For LoLA and our implementation, we used the *time* module to measure time. Running Woflan involves some overhead, so we instead take the total verification time reported by Woflan itself.

7.1 Free-Choice Benchmark Suite

The benchmark suite encompasses 1386 free-choice Petri nets that represent business processes modeled in the IBM WebSphere Business Modeler. It was originally presented in [16], and has been studied frequently in the literature [10, 17]. These nets are not workflow nets by our definition, but can be transformed using a known procedure [23]. Intuitively, the nets are workflow nets with multiple final places, and the procedure adds a dedicated output place and ensures that the resulting workflow net represents the desired behaviour. However, roughly 1% of the nets are not workflow nets by our definition even after the procedure, as they contain nodes that are not on a path from i to f. We removed these nets.

We further checked each net for safety using LoLA and dropped unsafe nets. Recall that $(\mathcal{N}, \{i: 1\})$ is sound if each reachable marking has at most one token per place. Unsafe instances can be dropped as unsafety implies 1-unsoundness in free-choice nets [34, Thm. 4.2 and 4.4], and as existing methods for checking safety, *e.g.* via state-space exploration with partial order reductions, are very efficient (here needing a mean of 3 ms). Thus, we considered safe instances only. Among the 1386 instances, 1382 are workflow nets, and 977 are further safe.

We also invoked an implementation of the reduction rules of [10] to reduce the size of all instances.[4] As discussed in the introduction, the rules can reduce some instances to trivially sound nets. However, even the size of nontrivial reduced instances tends to be small, with an average number of places and transitions of roughly 14, while three quarters of nets have at most 18 places and transitions. This is small enough that a complete state-splace enumeration is often feasible, in particular as the nets are safe and especially LoLA utilizes powerful partial order reductions for such nets. As we want to focus on scalability, we chained instances to produce challenging synthetic nets based on real-world instances. This is a natural way of constructing workflow nets, intuitively, the final process can be composed of many subtasks. It can be seen as a special case of refinement operations, studied in the context of generalised soundness [20].

The chaining procedure merges two workflow nets $\mathcal{N} = (P, T, F)$ and $\mathcal{N}' = (P', T', F')$ into $\mathcal{N}'' := (P'', T'', F'')$ where $P'' := P \cup P'$, $T'' := T \cup T' \cup \{t_{aux}\}$ with F'' as $F' + F''$ extended with $^\bullet t_{aux}[f] := 1$, $t_{aux}^\bullet[i'] := 1$, and $^\bullet t_{aux}[p] := t_{aux}^\bullet[p'] := 0$ for other entries. It is readily seen that this construction (1) produces a free-choice net if both $\mathcal{N}$ and $\mathcal{N}'$ are free-choice; and (2) preserves safety.

---

[4] At time of writing, an implementation is available at https://github.com/LoW12/Hadara-AdSimul.

This way, we generated large instances by using $\ell \in \{1, 21, 41, \ldots, 401\}$ randomly chosen unreduced safe instances from the benchmark suite as inputs to be chained into one instance, then reduced that instance. For each number ℓ, we produced 20 combined nets, with a fresh random choice each time, in order to have a more representative collection of nets for ℓ. This resulted in 420 instances, of which 405 are nontrivial after applying reduction rules.

A caveat is that such large nets may seem unlikely to arise in practice. It seems a human designer would avoid designing highly complex processes corresponding to Petri nets with thousands of places. However, process models are not only explicitly written by humans, but also machine-generated, *e.g.* by mining event logs (see [32] for a book on the topic). In particular, being free-choice is preserved by chaining, so a large free-choice net may "hide" and combine several less complex processes, which might necessitate analyzing large workflow nets.

Results. We checked the safe free-choice instances obtained as explained above for 1-soundness using LoLA, Woflan and our implementation of continuous soundness. The results are shown on the left of Fig. 3. The right-hand side of the figure provides an overview over the sizes of the nets. In each case, N refers to the number of original instances that were chained to create each instance.

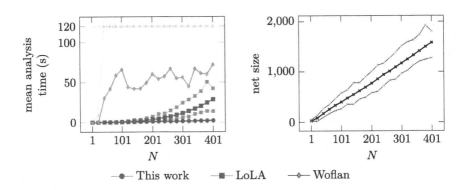

Fig. 3. Experiments on chained free-choice instances. The x-value denotes the number N of chained nets. Dark thick lines denote the mean, and light thin lines of the same color denote the minimum and maximum, respectively. For Woflan, the minimum line is slightly below the line of this work. For this work, the minimum and maximum lines are very close to the mean. *Left:* The y-value denotes time for checking soundness of the 20 nets for each N. Marks on the gray line at 120 s denote timeouts. *Right:* The y-value denotes the size of generated nets. (Color figure online)

The results show that state-space exploration via LoLA is very fast for moderate sizes, but does not scale as well. Continuous soundness is in fact outperformed by LoLA for $N \leq 100$, but scales much better, showing essentially linear growth in the given data range. For instance, continuous soundness takes a mean of 0.25 s for $N = 1$, a mean of 1.07 s for $N = 201$, and a mean of 2.28 s for $N = 401$.

Woflan performs very well on the original instances, but times out frequently for larger instances. Woflan checks so-called S-coverability [34]. This is fast on many instances, even large ones, but starts running into the exponential-time worst case when instances get larger. For $N = 1$ and $N = 21$, Woflan does not ever time out, while it times out for roughly half of the instances in the range from $N = 201$ to $N = 401$. Overall, we infer that for large free-choice workflow nets, deciding soundness by checking continuous soundness can outperform existing techniques, while the procedure is still competitive on moderate instances.

7.2   Synthetic Instances

In the previously discussed benchmark suite, nets are free-choice. So structural and generalised soundness are equivalent by Theorem 3. We considered including a second suite of 590 non-free-choice Petri nets that represent processes of the SAP reference model [25]. However them turn out to be 1-quasi-sound but not 1-sound, so they represent trivial cases for generalised and structural soundness: simply checking 1-soundness, or 1-quasi-soundness and then 1-soundness, decides all instances. It's also worth mentioning that none of the 590 SAP instances are continuously sound, so all of them can be shown to not be generalised sound by checking continuous soundness, without having to check 1-soundness.

In order to have a wider variety of challenging instances, we introduce several families of synthetic workflow nets. The nets are simple to understand, but have large numbers of reachable marking, so are challenging for approaches relying on state-space exploration, *e.g.* model checking.

Encoding Arc Weights. To simplify the presentation, we describe synthetic instances utilizing arcs with weights. For benchmarking, we removed the arc weights and instead input equivalent weightless nets. To do so, we used an encoding that simulates exponentially large weights by polynomially many transitions and places (the encoding is explained in ??). It preserves (quasi-)soundness, but significantly increases the number of reachable markings. Indeed, our synthetic instances are mostly trivial to solve by enumerating reachable markings when arcs have weights, but become much harder to decide when the encoding is used.[5] While much of the literature on workflow nets does not consider nets with arc weights, implicit structural encodings can occur in practice.

Generalised Soundness
Benchmark Instances. We introduce a synthetic family of nets where generalised soundness appears to be challenging. The family $\{\mathcal{N}_c\}_{c \in \mathbb{N}_{\geq 1}}$ is defined at the top of Fig. 4. Parameter $c \in \mathbb{N}_{\geq 1}$ is the smallest value for which $\mathcal{N}_c$ is c-unsound. From $\{i: c\}$, the sequence $t_i^c t_r^{c+1}$ can be fired, which leads to the deadlock $\{r: c+$

---

[5] It is deliberately used to make instances challenging, not to ensure compatibility with LoLA or Woflan, as both support arc weights.

1}. Yet, when starting with $k < c$ tokens in i, and firing t_i^k, transitions t_r and t_f can only be fired exactly k times, and $\{f: k\}$ will be reached.

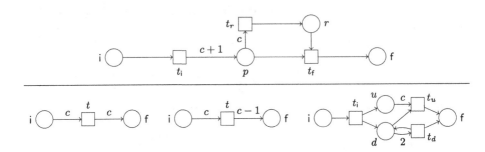

Fig. 4. *Top:* A workflow net $\mathcal{N}_c$ that is c-unsound and k-sound for all $k \in [1..c-1]$. *Bottom:* Three families of instances. *Bottom left:* $\mathcal{N}_{\text{sound-}c}$ is quasi-sound and ℓc-sound for all $\ell \in \mathbb{N}_{\geq 1}$. *Bottom center:* $\mathcal{N}_{\neg\text{quasi-}c}$ is not structurally quasi-sound. *Bottom right:* $\mathcal{N}_{\neg\text{sound-}c}$ is ℓc-quasi-sound for all $\ell \in \mathbb{N}_{\geq 1}$, but not structurally sound.

The naive approach to decide generalised soundness is to check k-soundness for all k until a counterexample is found or a bound is exceeded. It is known that if a counterexample exists, then there also is one of size at most exponential [9, Lemma 5.6 and 5.8]. The approach we chose for semi-deciding generalised soundness is to check continuous soundness. Recall that continuous soundness is a necessary (albeit not sufficient) condition, as shown in Theorem 1.

In our evaluation, we used Woflan and LoLA to check generalised soundness of the family for different c by checking 1-sound, ..., c-soundness, and compared the result to the time needed for testing continuous soundness. Our main goal is to evaluate whether checking continuous soundness is efficient enough to serve as an inexpensive way to witness generalised unsoundness for nontrivial instances.

Results. Figure 5 depicts the results. Woflan and LoLA show good performance for small values of c, but do not scale well to larger values. They respectively time out for $c \geq 5$ and $c \geq 8$. The instances are not free-choice, so LoLA and Woflan need to explore the state-space for each $k \leq c$, which becomes infeasible. For $c \geq 14$, Woflan cannot even check 1-soundness within the time limit. LoLA can check 1- and 2-soundness for $c \leq 28$, but cannot handle 2-soundness for larger c. Continuous soundness is efficiently verifiable even for $c = 40$. In particular, we need less than 5 s on all instances. The greatest time is at $c = 33$. Further, at most 1 s is needed on 34 out of 40 instances (mean of 0.6 s).

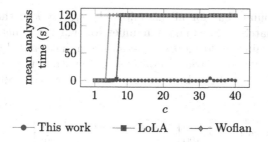

Fig. 5. Time to check generalised soundness of $\mathcal{N}_c$ for different values of c. Marks on the gray line at 120 s denote timeouts. (Color figure online)

Structural Soundness

Benchmark Instances. For structural soundness, recall that our decision procedure is based on checking structural quasi-soundness and obtaining some lower bound for the smallest number for which the net is quasi-sound. Thus, we want to test on both benchmark instances that are structurally quasi-sound and those that are not. We introduce three families of non-free-choice nets for which structural soundness appears challenging. These instances are defined at the bottom of Fig. 4. We respectively denote them $\mathcal{N}_{\text{sound-}c}$ (left), $\mathcal{N}_{\neg\text{quasi-}c}$ (center) and $\mathcal{N}_{\neg\text{sound-}c}$ (right). We claim that: $\mathcal{N}_{\text{sound-}c}$ is ℓc-sound for all $\ell \in \mathbb{N}_{\geq 1}$; $\mathcal{N}_{\neg\text{quasi-}c}$ is not structurally quasi-sound; $\mathcal{N}_{\neg\text{sound-}c}$ is ℓc-quasi-sound for all $\ell \in \mathbb{N}_{\geq 1}$, not k-quasi-sound for any other number $k \in \mathbb{N}_{\geq 1}$, and not structurally sound.

For the experiments, our goal is twofold. First, we want to evaluate whether utilizing continuous reachability to decide structural quasi-soundness is more efficient than using the known reduction to reachability described in [31, Lemma 2.1]. Woflan does not directly support checking reachability, so we only compare with LoLA. Second, we want to evaluate whether the lower bound for the smallest number for which the net is quasi-sound, which we dubbed $k_{\mathcal{N},\mathbb{Q}_{\geq 0}}$ towards the end of Sect. 5, is close to the actual smallest number, dubbed $k_{\mathcal{N}}$.

A caveat of this evaluation is that we evaluate only on our synthetic instances, and that computing $k_{\mathcal{N},\mathbb{Q}_{\geq 0}}$ is only one step in deciding structural soundness. However, we think that the evaluation on these hard synthetic instances can give insights into the applicability on nontrivial real-world instances.

Results. Figure 6 compares the time needed to verify structural reachability for LoLA and our prototype. For small instances, LoLA sometimes performs very well, but we scale better for large values. Of particular note is that in the absence of quasi-soundness, LoLA will generate an infinite state-space, so will generally run out of time or memory. In particular, LoLA times out for all c on $N_{\neg\text{quasi-}c}$. It also times out for $c \geq 32$ on $N_{\neg\text{sound-}c}$. On the other hand, continuous soundness never times out for the given values of c. In fact, when we tested continuous soundness for much larger values of c, we found that our implementation of continuous reachability decides structural quasi-soundness for $N_{\neg\text{quasi-}c}$ in under $2s$ for $c = 20\ 000\ 000$.

We further found that for all instances, $k_{\mathcal{N},\mathbb{Q}_{\geq 0}} = k_{\mathcal{N}}$, that is, our lower bound exactly matches the smallest number for which the net is quasi-sound. Thus, it only remains to decide $k_{\mathcal{N},\mathbb{Q}_{\geq 0}}$-quasi-soundness and $k_{\mathcal{N},\mathbb{Q}_{\geq 0}}$-soundness in order to decide structural soundness. This is in contrast to the naive approach, which starts at $k = 1$ and checks k-quasi-soundness for each value up to $k_{\mathcal{N},\mathbb{Q}_{\geq 0}}$.

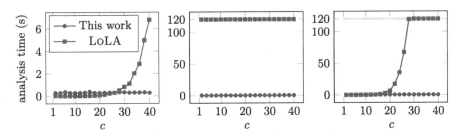

Fig. 6. Time taken vs parameter c for checking structural quasi-soundness using the reduction to reachability, and utilizing our approach to compute $k_{\mathcal{N},\mathbb{Q}_{\geq 0}}$, for each of the three families at the bottom of Fig. 4: $\mathcal{N}_{\text{sound-}c}$ *(left)*, $\mathcal{N}_{\neg\text{quasi-}c}$ *(center)*, $\mathcal{N}_{\neg\text{sound-}c}$ *(right)*. Note that the axis ranges differ. Marks on the gray line at 120 s denote timeouts. (Color figure online)

8   Conclusion

In this work, we have shown how reachability relaxations allow to efficiently semi-decide generalised and structural soundness. Our approach combines nicely with reduction rules, as they all preserve relaxations. In particular, we have introduced continuous soundness as an approximation of generalised soundness, and shown that it coincides with other types of soundness for free-choice nets.

As part of future work, we plan to migrate our prototype into the process mining framework ProM, to make the algorithms available to practitioners.

Acknowledgements. We thank Dirk Fahland and Eric Verbeek for their help with Woflan. Michael Blondin was supported by a Discovery Grant from the Natural Sciences and Engineering Research Council of Canada (NSERC), and by the Fonds de recherche du Québec - Nature et technologies (FRQNT).

References

1. van der Aalst, W.M.P., et al.: Verification of workflow nets. In: Azéma, P., Balbo, G. (eds.) ICATPN 1997. LNCS, vol. 1248, pp. 407–426. Springer, Heidelberg (1997). https://doi.org/10.1007/3-540-63139-9_48
2. van der Aalst, W.M.P.: The application of Petri nets to workflow management. J. Circuits Syst. Comput. 8(1), 21–66 (1998). https://doi.org/10.1142/S0218126698000043

3. van der Aalst, W.M.P., et al.: Workflow verification: finding control-flow errors using Petri-net-based techniques. In: van der Aalst, W., Desel, J., Oberweis, A. (eds.) Business Process Management. LNCS, vol. 1806, pp. 161–183. Springer, Heidelberg (2000). https://doi.org/10.1007/3-540-45594-9_11

4. van der Aalst, W.M.P., van Hee, K.M.: Workflow Management: Models, Methods, and Systems. Cooperative Information Systems. MIT Press, Cambridge (2002)

5. Athanasiou, K., Liu, P., Wahl, T.: Unbounded-thread program verification using thread-state equations. In: Olivetti, N., Tiwari, A. (eds.) IJCAR 2016. LNCS (LNAI), vol. 9706, pp. 516–531. Springer, Cham (2016). https://doi.org/10.1007/978-3-319-40229-1_35

6. Barkaoui, K., Petrucci, L.: Structural analysis of workflow nets with shared resources. In: Proceedings of Workflow Management: Net-Based Concepts, Models, Techniques and Tools (WFM), vol. 98/7, pp. 82–95 (1998)

7. Blondin, M.: The ABCs of Petri net reachability relaxations. ACM SIGLOG News **7**(3) (2020). https://doi.org/10.1145/3436980.3436984

8. Blondin, M., Finkel, A., Haase, C., Haddad, S.: The logical view on continuous Petri nets. ACM Trans. Comput. Log. (TOCL) **18**(3), 24:1–24:28 (2017). https://doi.org/10.1145/3105908

9. Blondin, M., Mazowiecki, F., Offtermatt, P.: The complexity of soundness in workflow nets. In: Proceedings of 37th Symposium on Logic in Computer Science (LICS) (2022)

10. Bride, H., Kouchnarenko, O., Peureux, F.: Reduction of workflow nets for generalised soundness verification. In: Bouajjani, A., Monniaux, D. (eds.) VMCAI 2017. LNCS, vol. 10145, pp. 91–111. Springer, Cham (2017). https://doi.org/10.1007/978-3-319-52234-0_6

11. Cardoza, E., Lipton, R.J., Meyer, A.R.: Exponential space complete problems for Petri nets and commutative semigroups: preliminary report. In: Proceedings of 8th Annual ACM Symposium on Theory of Computing (STOC), pp. 50–54 (1976). https://doi.org/10.1145/800113.803630

12. Chistikov, D., Haase, C., Halfon, S.: Context-free commutative grammars with integer counters and resets. Theor. Comput. Sci. **735**, 147–161 (2018). https://doi.org/10.1016/j.tcs.2016.06.017

13. Czerwinski, W., Orlikowski, L.: Reachability in vector addition systems is Ackermann-complete. In: Proceedings of 62nd Annual IEEE Symposium on Foundations of Computer Science (FOCS) (2021, to appear)

14. Desel, J., Esparza, J.: Free Choice Petri Nets. Cambridge University Press, Cambridge (1995). https://doi.org/10.1017/CBO9780511526558

15. Esparza, J., Ledesma-Garza, R., Majumdar, R., Meyer, P., Niksic, F.: An SMT-based approach to coverability analysis. In: Biere, A., Bloem, R. (eds.) CAV 2014. LNCS, vol. 8559, pp. 603–619. Springer, Cham (2014). https://doi.org/10.1007/978-3-319-08867-9_40

16. Fahland, D., et al.: Instantaneous soundness checking of industrial business process models. In: Dayal, U., Eder, J., Koehler, J., Reijers, H.A. (eds.) BPM 2009. LNCS, vol. 5701, pp. 278–293. Springer, Heidelberg (2009). https://doi.org/10.1007/978-3-642-03848-8_19

17. Favre, C., Völzer, H., Müller, P.: Diagnostic information for control-flow analysis of workflow graphs (a.k.a. free-choice workflow nets). In: Chechik, M., Raskin, J.-F. (eds.) TACAS 2016. LNCS, vol. 9636, pp. 463–479. Springer, Heidelberg (2016). https://doi.org/10.1007/978-3-662-49674-9_27

18. Fraca, E., Haddad, S.: Complexity analysis of continuous Petri nets. Fundamenta Informaticae **137**(1), 1–28 (2015). https://doi.org/10.3233/FI-2015-1168

19. van Hee, K., Oanea, O., Sidorova, N., Voorhoeve, M.: Verifying generalized soundness of workflow nets. In: Virbitskaite, I., Voronkov, A. (eds.) PSI 2006. LNCS, vol. 4378, pp. 235–247. Springer, Heidelberg (2007). https://doi.org/10.1007/978-3-540-70881-0_21

20. van Hee, K., Sidorova, N., Voorhoeve, M.: Soundness and separability of workflow nets in the stepwise refinement approach. In: van der Aalst, W.M.P., Best, E. (eds.) ICATPN 2003. LNCS, vol. 2679, pp. 337–356. Springer, Heidelberg (2003). https://doi.org/10.1007/3-540-44919-1_22

21. van Hee, K., Sidorova, N., Voorhoeve, M.: Generalised soundness of workflow nets is decidable. In: Cortadella, J., Reisig, W. (eds.) ICATPN 2004. LNCS, vol. 3099, pp. 197–215. Springer, Heidelberg (2004). https://doi.org/10.1007/978-3-540-27793-4_12

22. Hoffmann, P.E.: Workflow nets: reduction rules and games. Ph.D. thesis, Technische Universität München (2017)

23. Kiepuszewski, B., ter Hofstede, A.H.M., van der Aalst, W.M.P.: Fundamentals of control flow in workflows. Acta Informatica 39(3), 143–209 (2003). https://doi.org/10.1007/s00236-002-0105-4

24. Leroux, J.: The reachability problem for Petri nets is not primitive recursive. In: Proceedings of 62nd Annual IEEE Symposium on Foundations of Computer Science (FOCS) (2021, to appear)

25. Mendling, J., et al.: Faulty EPCs in the SAP reference model. In: Dustdar, S., Fiadeiro, J.L., Sheth, A.P. (eds.) BPM 2006. LNCS, vol. 4102, pp. 451–457. Springer, Heidelberg (2006). https://doi.org/10.1007/11841760_38

26. de Moura, L., Bjørner, N.: Z3: an efficient SMT solver. In: Ramakrishnan, C.R., Rehof, J. (eds.) TACAS 2008. LNCS, vol. 4963, pp. 337–340. Springer, Heidelberg (2008). https://doi.org/10.1007/978-3-540-78800-3_24 https://github.com/Z3Prover/z3

27. Murata, T.: Petri nets: properties, analysis and applications. Proc. IEEE 77(4), 541–580 (1989). https://doi.org/10.1109/5.24143

28. Ping, L., Hao, H., Jian, L.: On 1-soundness and soundness of workflow nets. In: Third Workshop on Modelling of Objects, Components, and Agents, p. 21 (2004)

29. Rackoff, C.: The covering and boundedness problems for vector addition systems. Theor. Comput. Sci. 6, 223–231 (1978). https://doi.org/10.1016/0304-3975(78)90036-1

30. Ţiplea, F.L., Bocăneală, C., Chiroşcă, R.: On the complexity of deciding soundness of acyclic workflow nets. IEEE Trans. Syst. Man Cybern. Syst. 45(9), 1292–1298 (2015). https://doi.org/10.1109/TSMC.2015.2394735

31. Ţiplea, F.L., Marinescu, D.C.: Structural soundness of workflow nets is decidable. Inf. Process. Lett. 96(2), 54–58 (2005). https://doi.org/10.1016/j.ipl.2005.06.002

32. van der Aalst, W.: Data science in action. In: Process Mining, pp. 3–23. Springer, Heidelberg (2016). https://doi.org/10.1007/978-3-662-49851-4_1

33. Verbeek, E., van der Aalst, W.M.P.: Woflan 2.0 a Petri-net-based workflow diagnosis tool. In: Nielsen, M., Simpson, D. (eds.) ICATPN 2000. LNCS, vol. 1825, pp. 475–484. Springer, Heidelberg (2000). https://doi.org/10.1007/3-540-44988-4_28

34. Verbeek, H.M.W., Basten, T., van der Aalst, W.M.P.: Diagnosing workflow processes using Woflan. Comput. J. 44(4), 246–279 (2001). https://doi.org/10.1093/comjnl/44.4.246

35. Wolf, K.: Petri Net model checking with LoLA 2. In: Khomenko, V., Roux, O.H. (eds.) PETRI NETS 2018. LNCS, vol. 10877, pp. 351–362. Springer, Cham (2018). https://doi.org/10.1007/978-3-319-91268-4_18

Capture, Analyze, Diagnose: Realizability Checking Of Requirements in FRET

Andreas Katis[1]([✉]) [iD], Anastasia Mavridou[1], Dimitra Giannakopoulou[2], Thomas Pressburger[2]([✉]), and Johann Schumann[1]

[1] Employed by KBR; NASA Ames Research Center, Moffett Field, CA, USA
andreas.katis@nasa.gov
NASA Ames Research Center, Moffett Field, CA, USA
tom.pressburger@nasa.gov

Abstract. Requirements formalization has become increasingly popular in industrial settings as an effort to disambiguate designs and optimize development time and costs for critical system components. Formal requirements elicitation also enables the employment of analysis tools to prove important properties, such as consistency and realizability. In this paper, we present the realizability analysis framework that we developed as part of the Formal Requirements Elicitation Tool (FRET). Our framework prioritizes usability, and employs state-of-the-art analysis algorithms that support infinite theories. We demonstrate the workflow for realizability checking, showcase the diagnosis process that supports visualization of conflicts between requirements and simulation of counterexamples, and discuss results from industrial-level case studies.

1   Introduction

Requirements elicitation is a proactive process which, by capturing the intended behavior of a system at an early stage, safeguards against decisions that could lead to increased development costs and even catastrophic failures. Formal requirements analysis can solidify engineers' confidence in the expressed specification. Our work is concerned with ensuring requirements consistency for system components, as a pre-requisite for subsequent system-level analysis. In particular, we focus on the notion of *realizability*: a realizable set of requirements guarantees that an implementation exists, such that it always behaves in a manner consistent with the specification, no matter what input it receives from its environment. The notion of realizability, first described as implementability by Pnueli and Rosner [47], has since then shaped an entire research area over the specification and synthesis of *reactive systems*.

This paper presents the realizability analysis framework that we have developed as part of NASA's open source tool FRET [3] for writing, understanding, and formalizing requirements. FRET is designed with a strong focus on usability, and is used by several NASA projects to explore the benefits of writing

Dimitra Giannakopoulou contributed to this work prior to joining AWS.

S. Shoham and Y. Vizel (Eds.): CAV 2022, LNCS 13372, pp. 490–504, 2022.
https://doi.org/10.1007/978-3-031-13188-2_24

requirements that can be processed by formal analysis tools [10,17,42,45]. Additionally, FRET has been used by external (to NASA) industrial and research teams, e.g., for the formalization of aircraft engine controller requirements [19]. FRET's realizability framework has two main goals: 1) to implement efficient algorithms for checking realizability, and 2) to provide user support in understanding and correcting sources of unrealizability. With these features, FRET provides an end-to-end solution to capturing, analyzing, and diagnosing requirements.

FRET's realizability framework provides a user-friendly interface for analyzing the requirements of system components. We have designed a graphic environment, in which the user can observe a (potentially) decomposed version of the specification that is sound with respect to realizability, as well as further dive into the task of *diagnosing* unrealizable requirements. Compositional analysis is based on our theoretical framework for checking realizability of a global specification through smaller, more tractable parts [25,43]. The diagnosis process is based on the theoretical work by Könighofer et al. [33,34] on generating minimal conflicts of unrealizability. We adjusted the diagnosis algorithm to support the discovery of all minimal conflicts in a contract, accompanied by a counterexample of unrealizability. The computed artifacts can be visualized as an interactive diagram that depicts the dependencies between requirements and conflicts. Counterexample traces that originate from these conflicts can also be simulated to enhance the understanding of unrealizability sources. For the analysis, we have integrated in FRET state-of-the-art tools with respect to realizability checking modulo infinite theories.

In particular, the contributions of this work are:

- The design and implementation of a realizability checking framework in FRET that tightly integrates the JKIND [23] and KIND 2 [35] analysis tools;
- a diagnosis feature for unrealizability that returns all minimal conflicts and their counterexamples in an easy-to-use, graphical user interface;
- the extension of the simulator component in FRET, to be used for the simulation of conflicting requirements in unrealizable specifications; and
- improvements of the algorithms in our in-house fork of the JKIND model checker, following recent work from the KIND 2 and GenSys [48] tools.

2   Related Work

Table 1 provides a comparison between prominent requirements specification tools that support realizability checking with respect to various aspects, such as support for liveness properties, specification decomposition, algorithms.

Spectra Tools [37] and RATSY [8] are requirements specification tools for reactive synthesis over the General Reactivity of Rank 1 (GR(1)) fragment of LTL. The GR(1) fragment is particularly appealing, because it subsumes a subset of requirements that may appear in real world problems, adheres to the popular Assume-Guarantee paradigm, and a polynomial-time synthesis algorithm exists for it [9,46]. Both tools are limited to finite-state problems, and provide the ability to diagnose unrealizable specifications, primarily through the computation of minimal unrealizable cores [33,40] and counterstrategy synthesis, where an

Table 1. Comparison of requirements specification tools w.r.t. realizability checking.

Tool	Finite State	Infinite State	Decomposition	Liveness	Unrealizable Cores	Algorithms	Backend	Other features
Spectra	✔	✗	✗	✔	✔	BDD-based fixpoint	CUDD + JTLV	Well-separation, Vacuity Checking, Counterstrategies
SpeAR	✔	✔	✗	✗	✗	k-induction	JKIND	N/A
AGREE	✔	✔	✗	✗	✗	k-induction	JKIND	N/A
RATSY	✔	✗	✗	✔	✔	BDD-based fixpoint	CUDD+ NuSMV	Counterstrategies
EARS-CTRL	✔	✗	✗	✗	✗	BDD-based fixpoint	autoCode4	N/A
FRET	✔	✔	✔	✗	✔	k-induction, SMT-based fixpoint	JKIND, KIND 2	Simulation of conflicting requirements

implementation for the environment is generated, such that its actions always lead to the violation of the specification [34,39]. Furthermore, Spectra Tools provide the ability to repair unrealizable specifications [38].

SpeAR [22] and AGREE [14] are tools developed at Collins Aerospace for the purpose of requirements specification and analysis. Realizability checking is provided as a feature in both tools with limited support. Both tools depend on JKIND's k-induction algorithm for realizability checking, which supports infinite-state problems, but is not sound with respect to unrealizable results [24].

EARS-CTRL [36] is yet another requirements specification platform that enables analysis of requirements written in Easy Approach to Requirements Syntax (EARS) [41]. Its realizability checking implementation relies upon autoCode4 [13], and is limited to the GXW subset of LTL [12]. Similar to Spectra Tools and RATSY, its analysis is limited to finite-state problems.

FRET's realizability-checking framework encapsulates desirable features of the aforementioned tools into an interface that is designed for users of varying backgrounds in formal methods. Additionally, it is the only requirements specification tool that provides a powerful decomposition approach to help with analysis performance [25,43]. FRET's realizability framework is powered by the algorithms in JKIND and KIND 2. As such, it can analyze requirements that are as expressive as arbitrary discrete past-time metric LTL (pmLTL) formulas, and which may involve arithmetic expressions over the Linear Integer and Real Arithmetic SMT-LIB logics [7]. In practice, the framework targets analysis of formulas corresponding to requirements written in FRETISH, as presented in the next section. FRETISH requirements correspond to templates that form only a subset of all pmLTL formulas. As long as future FRETISH extensions can be translated into pmLTL, analysis will be supported by the realizability backend.

3   The FRETish Language

In FRET, requirements are written in a restricted natural language called FRETISH [27]. FRET formalizes FRETISH requirements in pmLTL and then

Table 2. Two FSM requirements in FRETISH and pmLTL from Katis et al. [32].

[FSM-006]	FSM shall for 5 ticks satisfy (state = 2 & standby & good) => STATE = 3
	H ((O[<=5] (! (Y TRUE))) -> (state = 2 & standby & good) -> STATE = 3
[FSM-007]	FSM shall within 5 ticks satisfy (state = 2 & supported & good) => STATE = 0
	H ((H (! (state = 2 & supported & good) -> STATE = 0)) -> (O[<5] (! (Y TRUE))))

into Lustre. A FRETISH requirement is described using up to six distinct fields (the * symbol designates mandatory fields): 1) scope specifies the time intervals where the requirement is enforced, 2) condition is a Boolean expression that triggers the response to occur at the time the expression's value becomes true, or is true at the beginning of the scope interval, 3) component* is the system component that the requirement is levied upon, 4) shall* is used to express that the component's behavior must conform to the requirement, 5) timing specifies when the response shall happen, subject to the constraints defined in scope and condition and 6) response* is the Boolean expression that the component's behavior must satisfy.

FRETISH provides 8 scopes: *global, in, before, after, notin, only in, only before*, and *only after*. The scope *global* means *always*; the others are with respect to when the system is in a mode or satisfies a Boolean expression. For example, *In mode M* means the requirement is enforced when the system is in mode M, as determined by the Boolean variable M. Also allowed for scope in place of a single Boolean variable is a Boolean expression, except for *in* which in the expression case is written with *while*; e.g., *While vehicle_mode = hover*. In FRETISH, the optional condition field is introduced by the words *upon, when*, or *if*, which are synonymous in FRETISH, or the word *unless*, which is the same as *when !*. FRETISH provides 10 timings: *immediately, at the next timepoint, always, eventually, never, for N* time steps, *within N* time steps, *after N* time steps, *until bool_expr*, and *before bool_expr*. When the scope is omitted it is taken as *global*; when the condition is omitted, it is taken as true; when the timing is omitted, it is taken as *eventually*. If we consider the condition being omitted as a separate case, there are $8 \times 2 \times 10 = 160$ possible combinations of ⟨*scope, condition, timing*⟩, each formalized as a distinct pmLTL formula template. The templates are generated by an algorithm that has been formally proven to generate formalizations with the intended semantics [15].

Boolean expressions can use the standard logical connectives (!, &, |) and can involve arithmetic relations (=,!=,<,<=,>,>=) and operators (+,−,*,/) over integer and real variables. There are two predefined predicates *preInt* and *preReal* that refer to previous values: the expression *preInt*(*init, n*), for integer expression n, returns the value of n at the previous timepoint; if at the beginning of the trace where there is no previous value, then the value of *init* is returned. Currently, FRETISH does not allow arbitrary nesting of temporal operators, e.g. "*In mode m, before q the system shall ...*". Timed operators with intermediate bounds are also not currently expressible; e.g., the equivalent of H[i,j] p, where i $\neq$ 0.

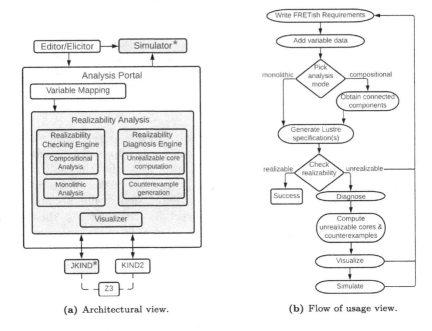

(a) Architectural view.   (b) Flow of usage view.

Fig. 1. Implementation views for realizability checking in FRET.

For the remainder of the paper we use a running example, namely `Finite State Machine (FSM)`, to demonstrate the various aspects of our framework. FSM contains 13 requirements for an abstracted version of an advanced autopilot system, and is part of the Lockheed-Martin Cyber-Physical Challenge Problems [18,32,42]. The requirements capture safety expectations with regards to the autopilot system's state transitions. Table 2 contains two FSM requirements written in FRETISH and their pmLTL formulas, which are generated by FRET.

4 Implementation

Figure 1a shows the architectural components of FRET that communicate with or belong to the *Realizability Analysis* framework.[1] Grayed components illustrate the contributions of this paper. The asterisks in *Simulator* and *JKind* indicate that their existing implementation and features were considerably extended for this work. Arrows show the flow of data between components. All components are implemented in JavaScript using the React, Material-UI and D3 libraries [2,5,6].

FRET requirements are written using the *Editor/Elicitor* component, which also provides semantic explanations in various forms to assist users to clarify subtle semantic issues. The Simulator component provides an interactive visualizer based on graphical signal representation. Given a FRET requirement, it shows

---

[1] The FRET architecture is described in previous work by Giannakopoulou et al. [26].

temporal traces of each of the variables involved as well as the valuation of the requirement for each point in time. The user can interactively modify the input signals, which results in automatically updating the valuation of the requirement and thus, visually inspecting the temporal behavior of the requirement. As part of this work, we extended the Simulator with the following features: 1) the ability to import and export simulation traces, 2) support for numerical expressions, and 3) simultaneous visualization of multiple requirements. We integrated the Simulator in our realizability analysis workflow, to provide the ability to inspect and interact with counterexample traces in unrealizable specifications.

The *Variable Mapping* component collects essential information provided by the user regarding the variables of the requirements, e.g., data types and correspondence to system inputs or outputs. *Realizability Analysis* consists of three sub-components. The *Realizability Checking Engine* is responsible for checking realizability of requirement sets either monolithically or compositionally. Given an unrealizable set of requirements, the *Realizability Diagnosis Engine* implements the algorithm proposed by Könighofer et al. [33,34] to compute all minimal unrealizable sets of requirements, called *minimal unrealizable cores*. For each such core, a counterexample trace is computed that depicts a case under which the environment can lead the system into a deadlocking state. For the computation of minimal conflicts, our implementation uses the *delta-debugging* algorithm [49]. The *Visualizer* implements the user interface that displays analysis results as well as diagnostic results in the case of unrealizable specifications. These results are typically hard to digest in their original form. As such, the visualizer translates the information into an interactive diagram that allows the user to focus on unrealizable cores and inspect or simulate conflicting requirements.

We have integrated into FRET the JKIND [23] and KIND 2 [11] tools for checking realizability. We actively maintain a fork of JKIND [30], because the original repository lacks an implementation for the fixpoint algorithm by Katis et al. [31]. Formerly, the fork implementation relied on the AE-VAL solver's Model-Based Projection algorithm to perform quantifier elimination over forall-exists formulas [20,21]. As part of this work, we have improved its performance by utilizing Z3's [16] quantifier elimination tactics. For instance, for the analysis of FSM the version of JKind using AE-VAL took 1524.82 s [43], whereas our optimization through Z3 dramatically decreased the time to 0.6 s.

The flow of usage of our framework is as follows (Fig. 1b). Once requirements are written in FRETISH and variable information is provided, the user may start the analysis. Realizability can be performed through two different modes: 1) monolithic and 2) compositional, i.e., through the computation of independent sub-specifications, namely connected components. Each connected component is an undirected dependency graph with requirements as vertices and system outputs as edges. Compositional analysis has been proved faster and more prone to return result, compared to the monolithic option [43]. At the next step, the specification is translated to Lustre [29] and fed into JKIND and KIND 2 to perform realizability checking. If the specification is unrealizable, the user can diagnose it using the generated counterexamples, and the FRET simulator.

5   Features Walkthrough

We next demonstrate the features of framework through our running example.

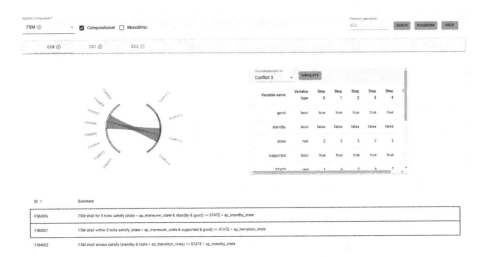

Fig. 2. The realizability checking interface in FRET.

Realizability Checking. Figure 2 provides a snapshot of the overall graphical user interface (GUI) for realizability checking in FRET. As soon as the system component is selected, its connected components (CC) are computed. In the case of FSM, three CCs are identified. The GUI provides a focused view for each one ('CCX' tabs, with X being the corresponding index value), where the user can see which requirements participate in each CC via a table that dynamically grays out unrelated requirements. As soon as the CCs are computed, the realizability checking options become available, i.e., compositional and monolithic.

To check realizability, the user clicks the 'Check' button. Depending on the input specification, four possible answers may be given i.e., the specification is realizable, unrealizable, inconsistent, or the analysis is inconclusive ("unknown" result). Figure 2 shows the results of a compositional check for FSM, where connected components CC0 and CC1 are unrealizable, and CC2 is realizable.

Diagnosing Unrealizability. The compositional results above suggest that the FSM requirements are, as a whole, unrealizable. The next step in the process is to try and understand the source(s) of unrealizability. Since only CC0 and CC1 are unrealizable, it suffices to diagnose these independently. Following Fig. 2, the user selects the 'CC0' tab and clicks the 'Diagnose' button. The computation of minimal unrealizable cores kicks in, as outlined in Sect. 4, identifying 4 cores.

Visualizing Unrealizability. The raw artifacts produced by realizability checking and diagnosis are difficult for the users to digest. Therefore, the ability to visualize data in a user-friendly format is necessary, especially for unrealizable specifications. The core of our proposed solution to visualize unrealizability relies on the use of *chord diagrams* [1]. A chord diagram is a graphic representation of interrelationships between data, where each individual element is placed along the perimeter of a circular construct and relationships are depicted through edges between elements. An important feature of chord diagrams is the ability to maintain a clear representation of dependencies through *hierarchical edge bundling* [28], even when the size of data is large.

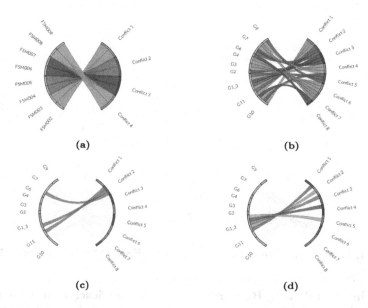

(a)   (b)

(c)   (d)

Fig. 3. (a) Chord Diagram for connected component CC0 in FSM. (b) Chord Diagram for Infusion_Manager. (c) Focused view (one core) for Infusion_Manager. (d) Focused view (one requirement) for Infusion_Manager.

Figure 3a shows the chord diagram that is generated for connected component CC0 in FSM. Requirements and conflicts (i.e., unrealizable cores) define the input data to the chord diagram, which depicts each set using a distinguishable arc on the circular pattern (left and right arc, respectively). Chords, i.e., edges, connect each requirement to the conflicts that it appears in, with each edge being assigned a distinct color that matches the color-coded conflicts.

While hierarchical edge bundling helps us maintain a clear total view, it may be the case that the engineer would like to focus on a particular subset of dependencies, related to either a particular requirement or a specific conflict. We enable this through interactive means where parts of the interface that are not

Table 3. Counterexample for conflicting requirements [**FSM-006**] and [**FSM-007**].

Variable name	Variable type	Step 0	Step 1	Step 2	Step 3	Step 4	Step 5
good	bool	true	true	true	true	true	true
standby	bool	false	false	false	false	false	true
state	int	2	2	2	2	2	2
supported	bool	true	true	true	true	true	true
STATE	int	1	4	5	6	7	0
FSM-006	bool	true	true	true	true	true	false
FSM-007	bool	true	true	true	true	true	true

related to the selected element can be filtered out. Figure 2 shows an instance where the user has already interacted with the chord diagram for CC0, focusing on the unrealizable core containing [**FSM-006**] and [**FSM-007**]. The table of requirements is dynamically sorted so that relevant requirements appear on the top, and are outlined with the color of the corresponding conflict. Additionally, a counterexample witnessing the unrealizability of the conflict is displayed. Table 3 shows the counterexample for requirements [**FSM-006**] and [**FSM-007**].

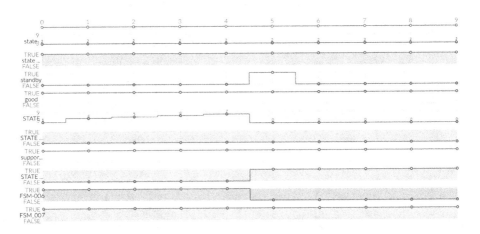

Fig. 4. Simulation of conflicting requirements [**FSM-006**] and [**FSM-007**].

Simulating Conflicting Requirements. Our experience with counterexamples has indicated that a single execution trace is not enough to truly understand interactions between requirements. Therefore, we provide the ability for the user to interact with the set of conflicting requirements by using the FRET simulator, which we have substantially extended to meet our needs in visualizing conflicting requirements. Figure 4 shows how the counterexample (Table 3) for [**FSM-006**] and [**FSM-007**] is displayed in the simulator window: each line shows the values of the input signals as well as the valuation of each of the requirements.

The counterexample in Table 3 is not the only witness to the unrealizability of these requirements. Another example is a trace where requirement [**FSM-006**] holds for 5 consecutive ticks, leading to a violation of requirement [**FSM-007**] at the last tick, assuming that the antecedent of the latter was true at least once within the last 5 ticks. By modifying the values of the input variables, a user may identify additional witnesses to unrealizability causes. Combined with the ability to store and review traces, the simulator makes for an integral element towards understanding and repairing unrealizable specifications.

6   Case Studies

6.1   Lift Plus Cruise Aircraft

This study reports preliminary results on requirements for an autonomous 'lift plus cruise' concept aircraft.[2] This aircraft has a hovering vehicle mode, using its lifting rotors. From the hover mode, it can transition to a flying forward mode, eventually using its rear pusher propeller, and where lift is provided by the wing instead of the lifting rotors. Inbetween the hover and forward modes is a transitional mode which is a phase of concern for the aircraft engineers.

Table 4. FRETISH requirements for Lift Plus Cruise from Katis et al. [32].

[LPC01]	The vehicle **shall** immediately satisfy vehicle_mode = hover
	`H ((! (Y TRUE)) -> vehicle_mode = hover)`
[LPC02]	While vehicle_mode = hover, the vehicle **shall** never satisfy gndspeed > 20.0
	`H ((vehicle_mode = hover) -> (! (gndspeed > 20.0)))`
[LPC03]	While vehicle_mode = hover, the vehicle **shall** eventually satisfy ! rear_propeller
	`(H (((! (vehicle_mode = hover)) & (Y (vehicle_mode = hover))) -> (Y (! ((! (! rear_propeller)) S ((! (! rear_propeller)) & ((vehicle_mode = hover) & ((! (Y TRUE))	(Y (! (vehicle_mode = hover))))))))))) & ((((! (! (vehicle_mode = hover)) & (Y (vehicle_mode = hover)))) S ((! ((! (vehicle_mode = hover)) & (Y (vehicle_mode = hover)))) & ((vehicle_mode = hover) & ((! (Y TRUE))	(Y (! (vehicle_mode = hover)))))))) -> (! ((! ((! rear_propeller) S ((! (! rear_propeller)) & ((vehicle_mode = hover) & ((! (Y TRUE))	(Y (! (vehicle_mode = hover))))))))))`
[LPC04]	The vehicle **shall** always satisfy if (preInt(hover,vehicle_mode) = hover & preReal(0.0,gndspeed) > 15.0) then vehicle_mode = transitional
	`(H (((preInt(hover,vehicle_mode) = hover) & (preReal(0.0,gndspeed) > 15.0)) -> vehicle_mode = transitional))`
[LPC09]	The vehicle **shall** always satisfy if (preInt(hover,vehicle_mode) = transitional & preReal(0.0,airspeed) > 100.0) then vehicle_mode = forward
	`(H (((preInt(hover,vehicle_mode) = transitional) & (preReal(0.0,airspeed) > 100.0)) -> (vehicle_mode = forward)))`

As of this paper, 11 requirements have been formalized in FRET [32]. A subset is shown in Table 4, describing the transition relations and constraints among various vehicle modes and vehicle motion. Requirement **[LPC01]** states that the vehicle starts in hover mode. Requirement **[LPC04]** specifies that if the previous mode is hover, and ground speed is greater than 15 knots, then the vehicle enters transitional mode. Requirement **[LPC09]** states the conditions for transitioning to forward mode. Variables **hover**, **transitional** and **forward** are specified as distinct integer constants. All of the other variables, e.g., **airspeed**, **rear_propeller**, are outputs.

---

[2] We acknowledge discussions with John Kaneshige, Michael Feary and the Revolutionary Vertical Lift Technology team.

The first complete set of FRETISH requirements raised concerns, as realizability checking yielded non-sensical counterexamples, where at least one requirement between [**LPC04**] and [**LPC09**] was violated in the initial state. We quickly identified the issue: both requirements were written using a version of the 'previous' operator `pre` which is undefined at the initial state. We addressed this by introducing the `preInt` and `preReal` operators, which at the initial state return the value of their first argument.

The resulting 11 requirements are in one CC, so we ran analysis in monolithic mode. The requirements are shown to be realizable in about 8 s. As a sanity check for realizability, we experimented with various subsets of the original requirements, as well as adding contradictions. A notable example was omitting [**LPC01**], while modifying [**LPC03**] so that in hover mode, the vehicle must fly faster than 30 knots. This experiment, unexpectedly to us, led to realizability. Further inspection quickly revealed how omitting [**LPC01**] allows the controlled variable `vehicle_mode` to never enter the hover mode. Including [**LPC01**] led to unrealizability with minimal conflict [**LPC01**], [**LPC02**] and [**LPC03**].

6.2   Generic Infusion Pump

This study explores 12 formalized requirements, proven unrealizable by Gacek et al. [24], of the `Infusion_Manager` subcomponent for a Generic Patient Controlled Analgesic (GPCA) infusion pump [44]. The GPCA system originates from the Generic Infusion Pump Research project, a joint effort to identify best software engineering practices in the development of medical devices [4].

Taking advantage of FRETISH's support for system modes (`scope` field), we derived 26 requirements, as opposed to the original 12 [32]. The increased number is a direct product of the declaration of 8 distinct modes, stemming from the system variable $Current\_System\_Mode$, which was originally of integer type. For example, requirement **G1** from Gacek et al.:

$$\mathbf{G1} \overset{\text{def}}{=} (Current\_System\_Mode' \geq 0) \ \wedge \ (Current\_System\_Mode' \leq 8) \ \wedge$$
$$(Current\_System\_Mode' = 0 \Rightarrow \ Commanded\_Flow\_Rate' = 0) \ \wedge$$
$$(Current\_System\_Mode' = 1 \Rightarrow \ Commanded\_Flow\_Rate' = 0)$$

was rewritten into three requirements: $\mathbf{G1_1}$ ensures that the system is in at least one of the 8 modes at any time, while requirements $\mathbf{G1_2}$ and $\mathbf{G1_3}$ ensure that the pump's flow rate is equal to 0 when the system is in mode 0 or 1, respectively. We additionally introduced requirements to ensure mutual exclusion between modes, something that was not needed with a single mode variable. We used KIND 2 to show equivalence between our requirements and the original specification.

Gacek et al. had already shown that the `Infusion_Manager` requirements are unrealizable, verbally attributing unrealizability to a conflict between **G1** and requirement **G7**:

$$\mathbf{G7} \overset{\text{def}}{=} (System\_On \wedge Highest\_Level\_Alarm = 3) \Rightarrow$$
$$(Commanded\_Flow\_Rate' = Flow\_Rate\_KVO)$$

The authors claimed that the requirements are unrealizable because they disagree on the value of output *Commanded_Flow_Rate* under specific conditions. However, FRET's diagnostic procedure provided a different answer, identifying 8 minimal unrealizable cores. Furthermore, the assumed conflict between requirements **G1** and **G7** does not really exist. While the two requirements do disagree on the value for the system output *Commanded_Flow_Rate* under specific circumstances, a realization still exists: one which would never exercise modes 0 or 1! Nevertheless, the report by Gacek et al. was still on the right track, as part of **G1** (FRETISH requirement **G1$_3$**) and **G7** participate in at least one minimal unrealizable core with requirement **G11**, the latter enforcing the system to enter mode 1, given specific system input values:

$$\mathbf{G11} \stackrel{\text{def}}{=} (System\_On \wedge Configured < 1) \Rightarrow Current\_System\_Mode' = 1$$

Figure 3b shows the chord diagram for `Infusion_Manager`, depicting the 8 minimal unrealizable cores. Figures 3c and 3d show resulting states of the diagram after the user interacted with it in order to focus on a specific core, or a specific requirement, respectively.

7   Conclusion

We presented the realizability analysis framework in FRET and demonstrated its interactive GUI, which helps users diagnose unrealizable specifications through visualizations and simulation of conflicts. The framework employs state-of-the-art analysis algorithms that support infinite theories. In the future, we plan to extend the tool with recommendations in the form of environment assumptions.

References

1. Chord diagram. https://www.data-to-viz.com/graph/chord.html
2. D3.js: Data-driven documents. https://d3js.org/
3. FRET: Formal requirements elicitation tool. https://tinyurl.com/ycxe9fv4
4. Generic infusion pump research project. https://rtg.cis.upenn.edu/gip/
5. Material-UI. https://mui.com/
6. React: a javascript library for building user interfaces. https://reactjs.org/
7. Barrett, C., Fontaine, P., Tinelli, C.: The Satisfiability Modulo Theories Library (SMT-LIB) (2016). www.SMT-LIB.org
8. Bloem, R., et al.: RATSY – a new requirements analysis tool with synthesis. In: Touili, T., Cook, B., Jackson, P. (eds.) CAV 2010. LNCS, vol. 6174, pp. 425–429. Springer, Heidelberg (2010). https://doi.org/10.1007/978-3-642-14295-6_37
9. Bloem, R., Jobstmann, B., Piterman, N., Pnueli, A., Sa'ar, Y.: Synthesis of reactive (1) designs. J. Comput. Syst. Sci. **78**(3), 911–938 (2012)
10. Bourbouh, H., et al.: Integrating formal verification and assurance: an inspection rover case study. In: Dutle, A., Moscato, M.M., Titolo, L., Muñoz, C.A., Perez, I. (eds.) NFM 2021. LNCS, vol. 12673, pp. 53–71. Springer, Cham (2021). https://doi.org/10.1007/978-3-030-76384-8_4

11. Champion, A., Mebsout, A., Sticksel, C., Tinelli, C.: The KIND 2 model checker. In: Chaudhuri, S., Farzan, A. (eds.) CAV 2016. LNCS, vol. 9780, pp. 510–517. Springer, Cham (2016). https://doi.org/10.1007/978-3-319-41540-6_29

12. Cheng, C.-H., Hamza, Y., Ruess, H.: Structural synthesis for GXW specifications. In: Chaudhuri, S., Farzan, A. (eds.) CAV 2016. LNCS, vol. 9779, pp. 95–117. Springer, Cham (2016). https://doi.org/10.1007/978-3-319-41528-4_6

13. Cheng, C.-H., Lee, E.A., Ruess, H.: autoCode4: structural controller synthesis. In: Legay, A., Margaria, T. (eds.) TACAS 2017. LNCS, vol. 10205, pp. 398–404. Springer, Heidelberg (2017). https://doi.org/10.1007/978-3-662-54577-5_23

14. Cofer, D., Gacek, A., Miller, S., Whalen, M.W., LaValley, B., Sha, L.: Compositional verification of architectural models. In: Goodloe, A.E., Person, S. (eds.) NFM 2012. LNCS, vol. 7226, pp. 126–140. Springer, Heidelberg (2012). https://doi.org/10.1007/978-3-642-28891-3_13

15. Conrad, E., Titolo, L., Giannakopoulou, D., Pressburger, T., Dutle, A.: A compositional proof framework for FRETish requirements. In: Popescu, A., Zdancewic, S. (eds.) CPP 2022, pp. 68–81. ACM (2022). https://doi.org/10.1145/3497775.3503685

16. de Moura, L., Bjørner, N.: Z3: an efficient SMT solver. In: Ramakrishnan, C.R., Rehof, J. (eds.) TACAS 2008. LNCS, vol. 4963, pp. 337–340. Springer, Heidelberg (2008). https://doi.org/10.1007/978-3-540-78800-3_24

17. Dutle, A., et al.: From requirements to autonomous flight: an overview of the monitoring ICAROUS project. In: Luckcuck, M., Farrell, M. (eds.) FMAS 2020. EPTCS, vol. 329, pp. 23–30. Open Publishing Association (2016). https://doi.org/10.4204/EPTCS.329.3

18. Elliott, C.: An example set of cyber-physical V&V challenges for S5, Lockheed Martin Skunk Works. In: Safe & Secure Systems and Software Symposium (S5) 2016, AFRL (2016). http://mys5.org/Proceedings/2016/Day_2/2016-S5-Day2_0945_Elliott.pdf

19. Farrell, M., Luckcuck, M., Sheridan, O., Monahan, R.: FRETting about requirements: formalised requirements for an aircraft engine controller. In: Gervasi, V., Vogelsang, A. (eds.) Requirements Engineering: Foundation for Software Quality. REFSQ 2022. LNCS, vol. 13216. Springer, Cham (2022). https://doi.org/10.1007/978-3-030-98464-9_9

20. Fedyukovich, G., Gurfinkel, A., Gupta, A.: Lazy but effective functional synthesis. In: Enea, C., Piskac, R. (eds.) VMCAI 2019. LNCS, vol. 11388, pp. 92–113. Springer, Cham (2019). https://doi.org/10.1007/978-3-030-11245-5_5

21. Fedyukovich, G., Gurfinkel, A., Sharygina, N.: Automated discovery of simulation between programs. In: Davis, M., Fehnker, A., McIver, A., Voronkov, A. (eds.) LPAR 2015. LNCS, vol. 9450, pp. 606–621. Springer, Heidelberg (2015). https://doi.org/10.1007/978-3-662-48899-7_42

22. Fifarek, A.W., Wagner, L.G., Hoffman, J.A., Rodes, B.D., Aiello, M.A., Davis, J.A.: SpeAR v2.0: formalized past LTL specification and analysis of requirements. In: Barrett, C., Davies, M., Kahsai, T. (eds.) NFM 2017. LNCS, vol. 10227, pp. 420–426. Springer, Cham (2017). https://doi.org/10.1007/978-3-319-57288-8_30

23. Gacek, A., Backes, J., Whalen, M., Wagner, L., Ghassabani, E.: The JKIND model checker. In: Chockler, H., Weissenbacher, G. (eds.) CAV 2018. LNCS, vol. 10982, pp. 20–27. Springer, Cham (2018). https://doi.org/10.1007/978-3-319-96142-2_3

24. Gacek, A., Katis, A., Whalen, M.W., Backes, J., Cofer, D.: Towards realizability checking of contracts using theories. In: Havelund, K., Holzmann, G., Joshi, R. (eds.) NFM 2015. LNCS, vol. 9058, pp. 173–187. Springer, Cham (2015). https://doi.org/10.1007/978-3-319-17524-9_13

25. Giannakopoulou, D., Katis, A., Mavridou, A., Pressburger, T.: Compositional Realizability Checking within FRET. NASA Technical Memorandum, March 2021
26. Giannakopoulou, D., Pressburger, T., Mavridou, A., Rhein, J., Schumann, J., Shi, N.: Formal requirements elicitation with FRET. In: Mehrdad Sabetzadeh, M., Vogelsang, A., et al. (eds.) REFSQ 2020. CEUR Workshop Proceedings, vol. 2584 (2020)
27. Giannakopoulou, D., Pressburger, T., Mavridou, A., Schumann, J.: Automated formalization of structured natural language requirements. Inf. Softw. Technol. 137, 106590 (2021)
28. Holten, D.: Hierarchical edge bundles: visualization of adjacency relations in hierarchical data. IEEE Trans. Visual. Comput. Graph. 12(5), 741–748 (2006)
29. Jahier, E., Raymond, P., Halbwachs, N.: The Lustre V6 reference manual
30. Katis, A.: JKind fork. https://github.com/andreaskatis/jkind-1
31. Katis, A., et al.: Validity-guided synthesis of reactive systems from assume-guarantee contracts. In: Beyer, D., Huisman, M. (eds.) TACAS 2018. LNCS, vol. 10806, pp. 176–193. Springer, Cham (2018). https://doi.org/10.1007/978-3-319-89963-3_10
32. Katis, A., Mavridou, A., Giannakopoulou, D., Pressburger, T.: Realizability checking of requirements in FRET. NASA Technical Memorandum, June 2021
33. Könighofer, R., Hofferek, G., Bloem, R.: Debugging unrealizable specifications with model-based diagnosis. In: Barner, S., Harris, I., Kroening, D., Raz, O. (eds.) HVC 2010. LNCS, vol. 6504, pp. 29–45. Springer, Heidelberg (2011). https://doi.org/10.1007/978-3-642-19583-9_8
34. Könighofer, R., Hofferek, G., Bloem, R.: Debugging formal specifications: a practical approach using model-based diagnosis and counterstrategies. Int. J. Softw. Tools Technol. Transfer 15(5–6), 563–583 (2013)
35. Larraz, D., Tinelli, C.: Realizability checking of contracts with Kind 2 (2022). https://doi.org/10.48550/ARXIV.2205.09082
36. Lúcio, L., Rahman, S., Cheng, C.-H., Mavin, A.: Just formal enough? Automated analysis of EARS requirements. In: Barrett, C., Davies, M., Kahsai, T. (eds.) NFM 2017. LNCS, vol. 10227, pp. 427–434. Springer, Cham (2017). https://doi.org/10.1007/978-3-319-57288-8_31
37. Maoz, S., Ringert, J.O.: Spectra: a specification language for reactive systems. Softw. Syst. Model. 20(5), 1553–1586 (2021)
38. Maoz, S., Ringert, J.O., Shalom, R.: Symbolic repairs for GR(1) specifications. In: Atlee, J.M., Bultan, T, Whittle, J. (eds.) ICSE 2019, pp. 1016–1026. IEEE/ACM (2019). https://doi.org/10.1109/ICSE.2019.00106
39. Maoz, S., Sa'ar, Y.: Counter play-out: executing unrealizable scenario-based specifications. In: Notkin, D., Cheng, B.H.C., Pohl, K. (eds.) ICSE 2013, pp. 242–251. IEEE (2013). https://doi.org/10.1109/ICSE.2013.6606570
40. Maoz, S., Shalom, R.: Unrealizable cores for reactive systems specifications. In: ICSE 2021, pp. 25–36. IEEE (2021). https://doi.org/10.1109/ICSE43902.2021.00016
41. Mavin, A., Wilkinson, P., Harwood, A., Novak, M.: Easy approach to requirements syntax (EARS). In: RE (2009)
42. Mavridou, A., et al: The ten Lockheed Martin cyber-physical challenges: formalized, analyzed, and explained. In: RE (2020)
43. Mavridou, A., Katis, A., Giannakopoulou, D., Kooi, D., Pressburger, T., Whalen, M.W.: From partial to global assume-guarantee contracts: compositional realizability analysis in FRET. In: Huisman, M., Păsăreanu, C., Zhan, N. (eds.) FM

2021. LNCS, vol. 13047, pp. 503–523. Springer, Cham (2021). https://doi.org/10.1007/978-3-030-90870-6_27

44. Murugesan, A., Sokolsky, O., Rayadurgam, S., Whalen, M., Heimdahl, M., Lee, I.: Linking abstract analysis to concrete design: a hierarchical approach to verify medical CPS safety. In: ICCPS 2014, pp. 139–150. IEEE (2014). https://doi.org/10.1109/ICCPS.2014.6843718

45. Perez, I., Mavridou, A., Pressburger, T., Goodloe, A., Giannakopoulou, D.: Automated translation of natural language requirements to runtime monitors. In: Fisman, D., Rosu, G. (eds.) Tools and Algorithms for the Construction and Analysis of Systems. TACAS 2022. LNCS, vol. 13243. Springer, Cham (2022). https://doi.org/10.1007/978-3-030-99524-9_21

46. Piterman, N., Pnueli, A., Sa'ar, Y.: Synthesis of reactive(1) designs. In: Emerson, E.A., Namjoshi, K.S. (eds.) VMCAI 2006. LNCS, vol. 3855, pp. 364–380. Springer, Heidelberg (2006). https://doi.org/10.1007/11609773_24

47. Pnueli, A., Rosner, R.: On the synthesis of a reactive module. In: POPL 1989, pp. 179–190. ACM (1989). https://doi.org/10.1145/75277.75293

48. Samuel, S., D'Souza, D., Komondoor, R.: GenSys: a scalable fixed-point engine for maximal controller synthesis over infinite state spaces. In: ESEC/FSE 2021, pp. 1585–1589. ACM (2021). https://doi.org/10.1145/3468264.3473126

49. Zeller, A., Hildebrandt, R.: Simplifying and isolating failure-inducing input. IEEE Trans. Softw. Eng. **28**(2), 183–200 (2002)

Information Flow Guided Synthesis

Bernd Finkbeiner[1], Niklas Metzger[1(✉)], and Yoram Moses[2]

[1] CISPA Helmholtz Center of Information Security, Saarbrücken, Germany
{finkbeiner,niklas.metzger}@cispa.de
[2] The Andrew and Erna Viterbi Faculty of Electrical and Computer Engineering
and the Taub Faculty of Computer Science, Technion, Haifa, Israel
moses@technion.ac.il

Abstract. Compositional synthesis relies on the discovery of assumptions, i.e., restrictions on the behavior of the remainder of the system that allow a component to realize its specification. In order to avoid losing valid solutions, these assumptions should be *necessary* conditions for realizability. However, because there are typically many different behaviors that realize the same specification, necessary behavioral restrictions often do not exist. In this paper, we introduce a new class of assumptions for compositional synthesis, which we call *information flow assumptions*. Such assumptions capture an essential aspect of distributed computing, because components often need to act upon information that is available only in other components. The presence of a certain flow of information is therefore often a necessary requirement, while the actual behavior that establishes the information flow is unconstrained. In contrast to behavioral assumptions, which are properties of individual computation traces, information flow assumptions are *hyperproperties*, i.e., properties of sets of traces. We present a method for the automatic derivation of information-flow assumptions from a temporal logic specification of the system. We then provide a technique for the automatic synthesis of component implementations based on information flow assumptions. This provides a new compositional approach to the synthesis of distributed systems. We report on encouraging first experiments with the approach, carried out with the BoSyHyper synthesis tool.

1 Introduction

In *distributed synthesis*, we are interested in the automatic translation of a formal specification of a distributed system's desired behavior into an implementation that satisfies the specification [22]. What makes distributed synthesis far more interesting than the standard synthesis of reactive systems, but also more challenging, is that the result consists of a set of implementations of subsystems, each of which operates based only on partial knowledge of the global system state. While algorithms for distributed synthesis have been studied since the

This work was funded by the German Israeli Foundation (GIF) Grant No. I-1513-407./2019. and by DFG grant 389792660 as part of TRR 248 – CPEC.

S. Shoham and Y. Vizel (Eds.): CAV 2022, LNCS 13372, pp. 505–525, 2022.
https://doi.org/10.1007/978-3-031-13188-2_25

1990s [10,18,22], their high complexity has resulted in applications of distributed synthesis being, so far, very limited.

One of the most promising approaches to making distributed synthesis more scalable is *compositional synthesis* [7,9,14,19,23]. The compositional synthesis of a distributed system with two processes, p and q, avoids the construction of the product of p and q and instead focuses on one process at a time. Typically, it is impossible to realize one process without making certain assumptions about the other process. Compositional synthesis therefore critically depends on finding the assumption that p must make about q, and vice versa: once the assumptions are known, one can build each individual process, relying on the fact that the assumption will be satisfied by the synthesized implementation of the other process. Ideally, the assumptions should be both *sufficient* (i.e., the processes are realizable under the assumptions) and *necessary* (i.e., any implementation that satisfies the specification would also satisfy the assumptions). Without sufficiency, the synthesis cannot find a compositional solution; without necessity, the synthesis loses valid solutions. While sufficiency is obviously checked as part of the synthesis process, it is often impossible to find necessary conditions, because the specifications can be realized by many different behaviors. Any concrete implementation would lead to a specific assumption; however, this implementation is only known once the synthesis is complete, and an assumption that is satisfied by *all* implementations often does not exist.

In this paper, we propose a way out of this chicken-and-egg type of situation. Previous work on generating assumptions for compositional synthesis has focused on *behavioral* restrictions on the environment of a subsystem. We introduce a new class of more abstract assumptions that, instead, focus on the *flow of information*. Consider a system architecture (depicted in Fig. 1a) where two processes a and b are linked by a communication channel c, such that a can write to c and b can read from c. Suppose also that a reads a boolean input in from the environment that is, however, not directly visible to b. We are interested in a distributed implementation for a specification that demands that b should eventually output the value of input in. Since b cannot observe in, its synthesis must rely on the assumption that the value of in will be communicated over the channel c by process a. Expressing this as a *behavioral assumption* is difficult, because there are many different behaviors that accomplish this. Process a could, for example, literally copy the value of in to c. It could also encode the value, for example by writing to c the negation of the value of in. Alternatively, it could delay the transmission of in by an arbitrary number of steps, and even use the length of the delay to encode information about the value of in. Fixing any such communication protocol, by a corresponding behavioral assumption on a, would unnecessarily eliminate potential implementations of b. The minimal assumption that subsystem a must satisfy is in fact an information-flow assumption, namely that b will eventually be able to determine the value of in.

We present a method that derives necessary information flow assumptions automatically. A fundamental difference between behavioral and information flow assumptions is that behavioral assumptions are *trace properties*, i.e., properties of individual traces; by contrast, information flow assumptions are *hyperproperties*, i.e., properties of *sets* of traces. In our example, the assumption that a will eventually communicate the value of in to b is the hyperproperty that any two traces that differ in the value of in must eventually also differ in c. The precise difference between the two traces depends on the communication protocol chosen in the implementation of a; however, any correct implementation of a must ensure that some difference in b's input (on channel c) in the two traces occurs, so that b can then respond with a different output.

Once we have obtained information flow assumptions for all of the subsystems, we proceed to synthesize each subsystem under the assumption generated for its environment. It is important to note that, at this point, the implementation of the environment is not known yet; as a result, we only know *what* information will be provided to process b, but not *how*. This also means that we cannot yet construct an executable implementation of the process under consideration; after all, this implementation would need to correctly decode the information provided by its partner processes. Clearly, we cannot determine how to *decode* the information before we know how the implementation of the sending process *encodes* the information!

Our solution to this quandary is to synthesize a prototype of an implementation for the process that works with *any* implementation of the sender, as long as the sender satisfies the information flow requirement. The prototype differs from the actual implementation in that it has access to the original (unencoded) information. Because of this information the prototype, which we call a *hyper implementation*, can determine the correct output that satisfies the specification. Later, in the actual implementation, the information is no longer available in its original, unencoded form, but must instead be decoded from the communication received from the environment. However, the information flow assumption guarantees that this is actually possible, and access to the original information is, therefore, no longer necessary.

In Sect. 2, we explain our approach in more detail, continuing the discussion of the bit transmission example mentioned above. The paper then proceeds to make the following contributions:

- We introduce the notion of *necessary information flow assumptions* (Sect. 4.1) for distributed systems with two processes and present a method for the automatic derivation of such assumptions from process specifications given in linear-time temporal logic (LTL).
- We strengthen information flow assumptions to the notion of *time-bounded* information flow assumptions (Sect. 4.2), which characterizes information that must be received in finite time. We introduce the notion of *uniform distinguishability* and prove that uniform distinguishability guarantees the necessity of the information flow assumption.
- We introduce the notion of *hyper implementations* (Sect. 5) and provide a synthesis method for their automatic construction. We also explain how to transform hyper implementations into actual process implementations.

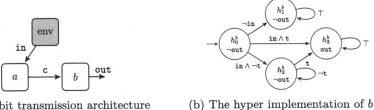

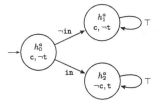

(a) The bit transmission architecture   (b) The hyper implementation of b

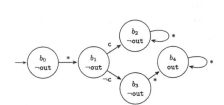

(c) The hyper implementation of a (d) The implementation of b

Fig. 1. The distributed system of the *bit transmission* protocol. The architecture is given in (a), the hyper implementation of b in (b), the hyper implementation of a in(c), and the resulting local implementation of b in (d).

- We present a more restricted *practical approach* (Sect. 6) that simplifies the synthesis for cases where the information flow assumption refers to a finite amount of information.
- Finally, we report on encouraging experimental results (Sect. 7).

2   The Bit Transmission Problem

We use the *bit transmission* example from the introduction to motivate our approach. The example consists of two processes a and b that are combined into the distributed architecture shown in Fig. 1a. Process a observes the (binary) input of the environment through variable in and can communicate with the second process b via a channel (modeled by the shared variable c). Process b observes its own local input from a and has a local output out. We are interested in synthesizing an implementation for our distributed system consisting of two strategies, one for each process, whose combined behavior satisfies the specification. In this example, the specification for process b is to transmit the initial value of in, an input of a, to b's own output; this is expressed by the linear-time temporal logic (LTL) formula $\varphi_b = \text{in} \leftrightarrow \Diamond \text{out}$. The specification does not restrict a's behavior, and so $\varphi_a = true$. Since the value of out is controlled by b, whereas in is determined by the environment and observed by a, this specification forces b to react to an input that b neither observes nor controls. To satisfy the goal, out must remain *false* forever if in is initially *false*, while out must become *true* at least once if in starts with value *true*. Indeed, in order to set out to *true*, process b must *know* that in is initially *true*, which can only be satisfied via information flow from a to b. We can capture this information flow requirement as the following hyperproperty: For every pair of traces that disagree on the initial value of in, process a must (eventually) behave differently on c. The requirement can be expressed in HyperLTL by the formula $\Psi = \forall \pi, \pi'.(\text{in}_\pi \leftrightarrow \text{in}_{\pi'}) \rightarrow \Diamond(\text{c}_\pi \leftrightarrow \text{c}_{\pi'})$. The information flow requirement does not restrict a to behave in a particular manner; the *encoding* of the information about in on the channel c depends on a's behavior. Under the assumption that a will behave according to the information flow requirement Ψ, one can synthesize a solution of b that is correct for every implementation of a. Given its generality, we call such a solution a *hyper implementation*. The hyper implementation of process b is shown in Fig. 1b. Since the point in time when the information is received by b is unknown during the local synthesis process, an additional auxiliary boolean variable t is added to the specification of b. This variable signals that the information has been transmitted and is later derived by a's implementation. Setting out to *true* is only allowed after t is observed by process b. When the hyper implementation is composed with the actual implementation of a, as shown in Fig. 1c, both local specifications are satisfied. The resulting local implementation of b, depicted in Fig. 1d, branches only on local inputs and, together with a, satisfies the specification. While changing state b_0 to b_1, process b cannot distinguish in from ¬in. It has to wait for one time step, i.e., the first difference in outputs of process a, to observe the difference in the shared communication channel. The value of t is obtained from a's implementation and set to *true* with the first difference in c, forbidding the edge from h_0^b to h_3^b in the local implementation of b.

3   Preliminaries

Architectures. For ease of exposition we focus in this paper on systems with two processes. Let $\mathcal{V}$ be a set of variables. An architecture with two black-box processes p and q is given as a tuple $(I_p, I_q, O_p, O_q, I_e)$, where I_p, I_q, O_p, O_q, and I_e are all subsets of $\mathcal{V}$. O_p and O_q are the *output variables* of p and q. O_e are the output variables of the uncontrollable environment. The three sets O_p, O_q and O_e form a partition of $\mathcal{V}$. I_p and I_q are the *input variables* of processes p and q, respectively. For each black-box process, the inputs and outputs are disjoint, i.e., $I_p \cap O_p = \emptyset$ and $I_q \cap O_q = \emptyset$. The inputs I_p and I_q of the black-box processes are all either outputs of the environment or outputs of the other black-box process, i.e., $I_p \subseteq O_q \cup O_e$ and $I_q \subseteq O_p \cup O_e$. We assume that all variables are of boolean type. For a set $V \subseteq \mathcal{V}$, every subset $V' \subseteq V$ defines a *valuation* of V, where the variables in V' have value *true* and the variables in $V \setminus V'$ have value *false*.

Implementations. An implementation of an architecture $(I_p, I_q, O_p, O_q, I_e)$ is a pair (s_p, s_q), consisting of a strategy for each of the two black-box processes. A *strategy* for a black-box process p is a function $s_p : (2^{I_p})^* \rightarrow (2^{O_p})$ that maps finite sequences of valuations of p's input variables (i.e., *histories* of inputs) to a valuation of p's output variables. The (synchronous) *composition* $s_p \| s_q$ of the two strategies is the function $s : (2^{O_e})^* \rightarrow (2^{\mathcal{V}})$ that maps finite sequences of valuations of the environment's output variables to valuations of all variables: we define $s(\epsilon) = s_p(\epsilon) \cup s_q(\epsilon)$ and, for $v \in (2^{O_e})^*, x \in 2^{O_e}$, $s(v \cdot x) = (s_p(f_p(v)) \cup s_q(f_q(v)) \cup x)$, where f_p and f_q map sequences of environment outputs to sequences of process inputs with $f_p(\epsilon) = \epsilon, f_p(v \cdot x) = f_p(v) \cdot ((x \cup s_q(f_q(v))) \cap I_p)$ and $f_q(\epsilon) = \epsilon, f_q(v \cdot x) = f_p(v) \cdot ((x \cup s_p(f_p(v))) \cap I_q)$.

Specifications. Our specifications refer to traces over the set $\mathcal{V}$ of all variables. In general, for a set $V \subseteq \mathcal{V}$ of variables, a *trace* over V is an infinite sequence $x_0 x_1 x_2 \ldots \in (2^V)^\omega$ of valuations of V. A *specification* $\varphi \subseteq (2^{\mathcal{V}})^\omega$ is a set of traces over $\mathcal{V}$. Two traces of disjoint sets $V, V' \subset \mathcal{V}$ can be *combined* by forming the union of their valuations at each position, i.e., $x_0 x_1 x_2 \ldots \sqcup y_0 y_1 y_2 \ldots = (x_0 \cup y_0)(x_1 \cup y_1)(x_2 \cup y_2) \ldots$. Likewise, the *projection* of a trace onto a set of variables $V' \subseteq \mathcal{V}$ is formed by intersecting the valuations with V' at each position: $x_0 x_1 x_2 \ldots \downarrow_{V'} = (x_0 \cap V')(x_1 \cap V')(x_2 \cap V') \ldots$.

For our specification language, we use propositional linear-time temporal logic (LTL) [21], with the set $\mathcal{V}$ of variables as atomic propositions and the usual temporal operators Next $\bigcirc$, Until $\mathcal{U}$, Globally $\square$, and Eventually $\Diamond$. System specifications are given as a conjunction $\varphi_p \wedge \varphi_q$ of two LTL formulas, where φ_p refers only to variables in $O_p \cup O_e$, i.e., the formula relates the outputs of process p to the outputs of the environment, and φ_q refers only to variables in $O_q \cup O_e$. The two formulas represent the *local specifications* for the two black-box processes. An implementation $s = (s_p, s_q)$ defines a set of traces

$$Traces(s_p, s_q) = \{x_0 x_1 \ldots \in (2^O)^\omega \mid x_k = s(i_0 i_1 \ldots i_{k-1}) \text{ for all } k \in \mathbb{N}$$
$$\text{for some } i_0 i_1 i_2 \ldots \in (2^{O_e})^\omega\}.$$

We say that an implementation *satisfies* the specification if the traces of the implementation are contained in the specification, i.e., $Traces(s_p, s_q) \subseteq \varphi$.

The Synthesis Problem. Given an architecture and a specification φ, the synthesis problem is to find an implementation $s = (s_p, s_q)$ that satisfies φ. We say that a specification φ is *realizable* in a given architecture if such an implementation exists, and *unrealizable* if not.

Hyperproperties. We capture information-flow assumptions as hyperproperties. A *hyperproperty over* $\mathcal{V}$ is a set $H \subseteq 2^{(2^{\mathcal{V}})^\omega}$ of sets of traces over $\mathcal{V}$ [6]. An implementation (s_p, s_q) satisfies the hyperproperty H iff its traces are an element of H, i.e., $Traces(s_p, s_q) \in H$. A convenient specification language for hyperproperties is the temporal logic HyperLTL [5]. HyperLTL extends LTL with quantification over trace variables. The syntax of HyperLTL is given by the following grammar $\varphi := \forall \pi. \varphi \mid \exists \pi. \varphi \mid \psi$ and $\psi := v_\pi \mid \neg \psi \mid \psi \wedge \psi \mid \bigcirc \psi \mid \psi \mathcal{U} \psi$ where $v_\pi \in \mathcal{V}$ is a variable and $\pi \in \mathcal{T}$ is a trace variable. Note that the output variables are indexed by trace variables. The quantification over traces makes it possible to express properties like "ψ *must hold on all traces*", which is expressed by $\forall \pi. \psi$. Dually, one can express that "*there exists a trace on which* ψ *holds*", denoted by $\exists \pi. \psi$. The temporal operators are defined as in LTL.

In some cases, a hyperproperty can be expressed in terms of a binary relation on traces. A relation $R \subseteq (2^V)^\omega \times (2^V)^\omega$ of pairs of traces defines the hyperproperty H, where a set T of traces is an element of H iff for all pairs $\pi, \pi' \in T$ of traces in T it holds that $(\pi, \pi') \in R$. We call a hyperproperty defined in this way a *2-hyperproperty*. In HyperLTL, 2-hyperproperties are expressed as formulas with two universal quantifiers and no existential quantifiers. A 2-hyperproperty can equivalently be represented as a set of infinite sequences over the product alphabet Σ^2: for a given 2-hyperproperty $R \subseteq \Sigma^\omega \times \Sigma^\omega$, let $R' = \{(\sigma_0, \sigma_0')(\sigma_1, \sigma_1') \ldots \mid (\sigma_0 \sigma_1 \ldots, \sigma_0' \sigma_1' \ldots) \in R\}$. This representation is convenient for the use of automata to recognize 2-hyperproperties.

4   Necessary Information Flow in Distributed Systems

In reactive synthesis it is natural that the synthesized process reacts to different environment outputs. This is also the case for distributed synthesis, where some outputs of the environment are not observable by a local process and the hidden values must be communicated to the process. In the following we show when such information flow is necessary.

4.1   Necessary Information Flow

Our analysis focuses on pairs of situations for which the specification dictates a *different* reaction from a given black-box process p. Such pairs imply the need for information flow that will enable p to distinguish the two situations: if p cannot distinguish the two situations, it will behave in the same manner in both. Consequently, the specification will be violated, no matter how p is implemented, in at least one of the two situations. A process p needs to satisfy a local specification φ_p, which relates its outputs O_p to the outputs O_e of the environment. (Recall that O_e may contain inputs to the other black-box process.) We are therefore interested in pairs of traces over O_e for which φ_p does *not* admit a common valuation of O_p. We collect such pairs of traces in a *distinguishability relation*, denoted by Δ_p:

Definition 1 (Distinguishability). *Given a local specification φ_p for process p, the* distinguishability relation Δ_p *is the set of pairs of traces over O_e (environment outputs) such that no trace over O_p satisfies φ_p in combination with both traces in the pair. Formally:*

$$\Delta_p = \{(\pi_e, \pi_e') \in (2^{O_e})^\omega \times (2^{O_e})^\omega \mid$$
$$\forall \pi_p \in (2^{O_p})^\omega. \text{ if } \pi_e \sqcup \pi_p \vDash \varphi_p \text{ then } \pi_e' \sqcup \pi_p \nvDash \varphi_p \}$$

By definition of Δ_p, process p must distinguish π_e from π_e', because it cannot respond to both in the same manner. In our running example, Δ_b consists of all pairs of sequences of values of in that differ in the first value of in. Process b must act differently in such situations: if in is initially *true* then b must eventually set out to *true*, while if it starts as *false*, then b must keep out always set to *false*.

In general, a black-box process p must satisfy its specification φ_p despite having only partial access to O_e. The distinguishability relation therefore directly defines an *information flow* requirement: In order to satisfy φ_p, enough information about O_e must be communicated to p via its local inputs I_p to ensure that p can distinguish any pair of traces in Δ_p. We formalize this information flow assumption as the following 2-hyperproperty, which states that if the outputs of the environment in the two traces must be distinguished, i.e., the projection on O_e is in Δ_p, then there must be a difference in the local inputs I_p:

Definition 2 (Information flow assumption). *The* information flow *assumption ψ_p induced by Δ_p is the 2-hyperproperty defined by the relation*

$$R_{\psi_p} = \{(\pi, \pi') \in (2^{\mathcal{V}})^\omega \times (2^{\mathcal{V}})^\omega \mid (\pi{\downarrow}_{O_e}, \pi'{\downarrow}_{O_e}) \in \Delta_p \text{ then } \pi{\downarrow}_{I_p} \neq \pi'{\downarrow}_{I_p}\}$$

In our running example, the information flow assumption for process b requires that on any two executions that disagree on the initial value of in, the values communicated to b over the channel c must differ at some point. Observe that the information flow assumption ψ_p specifies neither how the information is to be encoded on c nor the point in time when the different communication occurs. However, ψ_p requires that the communication differs eventually if the initial values of in are different. Moreover, notice that both Δ_p and ψ_p are determined by p's specification φ_p. The following theorem shows that the information flow assumption ψ_p is a necessary condition, the proof can be found in the full version of this paper [12].

Theorem 1. *Every implementation that satisfies the local specification φ_p for p also satisfies the information flow assumption ψ_p.*

4.2 Time-Bounded Information Flow

We now introduce a strengthened version of the information flow assumption. As shown in Theorem 1, the information flow assumption is a necessary condition for the existence of an implementation that satisfies the specification. Often, however, the information flow assumption is not strong enough to allow for the separate synthesis of individual components in a compositional approach.

Consider again process b in our motivating example. The information flow assumption guarantees that any pair of traces that differ in the initial value of the global input in will differ at some point in the value of the channel c. This assumption is not strong enough to allow process b to satisfy the specification that b must eventually set out to *true* iff the initial value of in is *true*. Suppose that in is *true* initially. Then b must at some point set out to *true*. Process b can only do so when it *knows* that the initial value of in is *true*. The information flow assumption is, however, too weak to guarantee that process b will eventually obtain this knowledge. To see this, consider a hypothetical behavior of process a that sets c forever to *true*, if in is *true* in the first position, and if in is *false* then a keeps c true for $n - 1$ steps, where $n > 0$ is some fixed natural number, before it sets c to *false* at the nth step. This behavior of process a satisfies the information flow assumption for any number n; however, without knowing n, process b does not know how many steps it should wait for in to become *false*. If, at any point in time t, the channel c has not yet been set to *false*, process b can never rule out the possibility that the initial value of in is *true*; it might simply be the case that $t < n$ and, hence, the time when c will be set to *false* still lies in the future of t! Hence, process b can never actually set out to *true*.

To address this, we present a finer version of the distinguishability relation from Definition 1 that we call *time-bounded distinguishability*. Recall that by Definition 1, a pair (π_e, π'_e) is in the distinguishability relation Δ_p if every output sequence π_p for p violates p's specification φ_p when combined with at least one of the input sequences π_e or π'_e. Equivalently, if φ_p is satisfied by π_p combined with π_e, then it is violated when π_p is combined with π'_e. Observe that for p to behave differently in two scenarios, a difference must occur at a finite time t. Clearly, this will only happen if p's input shows a difference in finite time. To capture this, we say that a pair (π_e, π'_e) of environment output sequences is in the *time-bounded* distinguishability relation if the violation with π'_e is guaranteed to happen in finite time. In order to avoid this violation, process p must act in finite time, before the violation occurs on π'_e. We say that a trace π *finitely violates* an LTL formula φ, denoted by $\pi \not\models_f \varphi$, if there exists a finite prefix w of π such that every (infinite) trace extending w violates φ.

Definition 3 (Time-bounded distinguishability). *Given a local specification φ_p for process p, the* time-bounded *distinguishability relation Λ_p is the set of pairs $(\pi_e, \pi'_e) \in (2^{O_e})^\omega \times (2^{O_e})^\omega$ of traces of global inputs such that every trace of local outputs $\pi_p \in O_p$ either violates the specification φ_p when combined with π_e, or finitely violates p's local specification φ_p when combined with π'_e:*

$$\Lambda_p = \{(\pi_e, \pi'_e) \in (2^{O_e})^\omega \times (2^{O_e})^\omega \mid$$
$$\forall \pi_p \in (2^{O_p})^\omega. \ if \ \pi_e \sqcup \pi_p \models \varphi_p \ then \ \pi'_e \sqcup \pi_p \not\models_f \varphi_p \}$$

Note that, unlike the distinguishability relation Δ_p, the *time-bounded* distinguishability relation Λ_p is not symmetric: For (π_e, π'_e), the trace $\pi'_e \sqcup \pi_p$ has to finitely violate φ_p, while the trace $\pi_e \sqcup \pi_p$ only needs to violate φ_p in the infinite evaluation. As a result, the corresponding *time-bounded* information flow assumption will also be asymmetric: we require that on input π_e, process p eventually obtains the knowledge that the input is different from π'_e. For input π'_e we do not impose such a requirement. The intuition behind this definition is that on environment output π'_e, process p must definitely produce some output that does *not* finitely violate φ_p. This output can safely be produced without ever knowing that the input is π'_e. However, on input π_e, it becomes necessary for process p to eventually deviate from the output that would work for π'_e. In order to safely do so, p needs to realize after some finite time that the input is not π'_e. In our running example, π_e would be an input in which in is initially *true*, while π'_e will be one in which it starts out being *false*.

Suppose we have a function $t : (2^{O_e})^\omega \to \mathbb{N}$ that identifies, for each environment output π_e, the time $t(\pi_e)$ by which process p is guaranteed to know that the environment output is not π'_e. We define the information flow assumption for this particular function t as a 2-hyperproperty. Since we do not know t in advance, the time-bounded information flow assumption is the (infinite) union of all 2-hyperproperties corresponding to the different possible functions t.

Definition 4 (Time-bounded information flow assumption). *Given the time-bounded distinguishability relation Λ_p for process p, the* time-bounded information flow assumption χ_p for p is the (infinite) union over the 2-hyperproperties induced by the following relations R_t, for all possible functions $t : (2^{O_e})^\omega \to \mathbb{N}$:

$$R_t = \{(\pi, \pi') \in (2^\mathcal{V})^\omega \times (2^\mathcal{V})^\omega \mid$$
$$\text{if } (\pi\downarrow_{O_e}, \pi'\downarrow_{O_e}) \in \Lambda_p, \text{ then } \pi[0...t(\pi\downarrow_{O_e})]\downarrow_{I_p} \neq \pi'[0...t(\pi\downarrow_{O_e})]\downarrow_{I_p}\}$$

Unlike the information flow assumption (cf. Theorem 1), the *time-bounded* information flow assumption is not in general a necessary assumption. Consider a modification of our motivating example, where there is an additional environment output start, which is only visible to process a, not to process b. The previous specification φ_b is modified so that if in is *true* initially, then out must be *true* two steps after start becomes *true* for the first time; if in is *false* initially, then out must become *false* after two positions have passed since the first time start has become *true*. The specification φ_a ensures that the channel c is set to *true* until start becomes *true*. Clearly, this is realizable: if in is *false* initially, process a sets c to *false* once start becomes *true*, otherwise c stays *true* forever. Process b starts by setting out to *true*. It then waits for c to become *false*, and, if and when that happens, sets out to *false*. In this way, process b accomplishes the correct reaction within two steps after start has occurred. However, the function t required by the time-bounded information flow assumption does not exist, because the time of the communication depends on the environment: the prefix needed to distinguish an environment output π_e, where in is *true* initially from an environment output π'_e, where in is *false* initially, depends on the time when start becomes *true* on π'_e.

We now characterize a set of situations in which the time-bounded information flow requirement is still a necessary requirement. For this purpose we consider time-bounded distinguishability relations where the safety violation occurs after a bounded number of steps. We call such time-bounded distinguishability relations *uniform*; the formal definition follows below.

Definition 5 (Uniform distinguishability). *A time-bounded distinguishability relation Λ_p is* uniform *if for every trace $\pi_e \in (2^{O_e})^\omega$ of global inputs, and every trace $\pi_p \in (2^{O_p})^\omega$ of local outputs of p, there exists a natural number $n \in N$ such that for all $\pi'_e \in (2^{O_e})^\omega$ s.t. $(\pi_e, \pi'_e) \in \Lambda_p$ if $\pi_e \sqcup \pi_p \vDash \varphi_p$ then $\pi'_e \sqcup \pi_p \nvDash_n \varphi_p$.*

Theorem 2. *Let Λ_p be a uniform time-bounded distinguishability relation derived from process p's local specification φ_p. Every computation tree that satisfies φ_p also satisfies the time-bounded information flow assumption χ_p.*

The proof of Theorem 2 can be found in the full version of this paper [12]. The relations presented in this section as well as the uniformity check can be represented by and verified with automata, also shown in [12].

5 Compositional Synthesis

We now use the time-bounded information flow assumptions to split the distributed synthesis problem for an architecture $(I_p, I_q, O_p, O_q, I_e)$ into two separate synthesis problems. The local implementations are then composed and form a correct system, whose decomposition returns the solution for each process.

5.1 Constructing the Hyper Implementations

We begin with the synthesis of local processes. Let Λ_p and Λ_q be the time-bounded distinguishability relations for p and q, and let χ_p and χ_q be the resulting time-bounded information flow assumptions. In the individual synthesis problems, we ensure that process p provides the information needed by process q, i.e., that the implementation of p satisfies χ_q, and, similarly, that q provides the information needed by p, i.e., q's implementation satisfies χ_p.

We carry out the individual synthesis of a process implementation on trees that branch according to the input of the process (including t_p) *and* the environment's output. In such a tree, the synthesized process thus has access to full information. We call this tree a *hyper implementation*, rather than an implementation, because the hyper implementation describes how the process will react to certain information, without specifying *how* the process will receive information. This detail is left open until we know the other process' hyper implementation: at that point, both hyper implementations can be turned into standard strategies, which are trees that branch according to the process' own inputs.

Definition 6 (Hyper implementation). *Let p and q be processes and e be the environment. A $2^{O_e \cup I_p \cup \{t_p\}}$-branching $2^{O_p \cup \{t_q\}}$-labeled tree h_p is a hyper implementation of p.*

Since the hyper implementation has access to the full global information, while the time-bounded information flow assumption only guarantees that the relevant information arrives after some bounded time, the strategy has "too much" information. We compensate for this by introducing a *locality condition*: on two traces $(\pi_e, \pi_e') \in \Lambda_p$ in the distinguishability relation of process p, as long as the input to the process from the external environment is identical, process p's output must be identical until t_p happens (which signals that the bound for the transmission of the information has been reached). For traces $(\pi_e, \pi_e') \notin \Lambda_p$ outside the distinguishability relation, process p's output must be identical until there is a difference in the input to process p or in the value of t_p.

Definition 7 (Locality condition). *Given the time-bounded distinguishability relation Λ_p for process p, the* locality condition η_p *for p is the 2-hyperproperty induced by the following relation R:*

$$R = \{(\pi, \pi') \in (2^{O_e \cup I_p \cup \{t_p\}})^\omega \times (2^{O_e \cup I_p \cup \{t_p\}})^\omega \mid$$
$$\text{if } (\pi\downarrow_{O_e}, \pi'\downarrow_{O_e}) \in \Lambda_p, \text{ then } \pi[0...t]\downarrow_{O_p} = \pi'[0...t]\downarrow_{O_p} \text{ and}$$
$$\text{if } (\pi\downarrow_{O_e}, \pi'\downarrow_{O_e}) \notin \Lambda_p, \text{ then } \pi[0...t']\downarrow_{O_p} = \pi'[0...t']\downarrow_{O_p}\}$$

where t is the smallest natural number such that $\mathbf{t}_p \in \pi[0...t]$ *or* $\pi[0...t] \downarrow_{I_p} \neq$ $\pi'[t] \downarrow_{I_p}$ *(and* ∞ *if no such t exists), and t' is the smallest natural number such that* $\pi[0...t'] \downarrow_{I_p} \neq \pi'[0...t'] \downarrow_{I_p}$ *or* $\pi[0...t'] \downarrow_{\{\mathbf{t}_p\}} \neq \pi'[0...t'] \downarrow_{\{\mathbf{t}_p\}}$ *(and* ∞ *if no such t' exists).*

We now use HyperLTL to formulate the locality condition for process b in our running example. Based on the time-bounded distinguishability relation Λ_b, which relates every trace with $\mathtt{in} = \mathit{true}$ in the first step to all traces on which $\mathtt{in} = \mathit{false}$ holds there, we can write the locality condition:

$$\forall \pi, \pi'.(\mathtt{in}_\pi \wedge \neg\mathtt{in}_{\pi'}) \to ((\mathbf{t}_\pi \vee \mathbf{c}_\pi \leftrightarrow \mathbf{c}_{\pi'}) \mathcal{R}(\mathtt{out}_\pi \leftrightarrow \mathtt{out}_{\pi'}))$$
$$\wedge(\neg(\mathtt{in}_\pi \wedge \neg\mathtt{in}_{\pi'})) \to (\mathbf{t}_\pi \leftrightarrow \mathbf{t}_{\pi'} \vee \mathbf{c}_\pi \leftrightarrow \mathbf{c}_{\pi'}) \mathcal{R}(\mathtt{out}_\pi \leftrightarrow \mathtt{out}_{\pi'}))$$

The order in the formula is analogous to the order in Definition 7. For all pairs of traces that are in the distinguishability relation, i.e., $\mathtt{in}$ is *true* on π and *false* on π', the outputs being equivalent on both traces can only be released by $\mathbf{t}$ on trace π or by a difference in the local inputs ($\mathbf{c}$). Moreover, if the traces are not in the distinguishability relation, i.e., $\neg(\mathtt{in}_\pi \wedge \neg\mathtt{in}_{\pi'})$, then only a difference in $\mathbf{t}$ or $\mathbf{c}$ can release $\mathtt{out}$ to be equivalent on both traces. With the locality condition at hand, we define when a hyper implementation is locally correct:

Definition 8 (Local correctness of hyper implementations). *Let p and q be processes, let φ_p be the local specification of p, let η_p be its locality condition, and let χ_q be the information flow assumption of q. The hyper implementation h_p of p is* locally correct *if it satisfies φ_p, η_p, and χ_q.*

The specification φ_p is a trace property, while η_p and χ_q are hyperproperties. Since all properties that need to be satisfied by the process are guarantees, it is not necessary to assume explicit behaviour of process q to realize process p. Local correctness relies on the guarantee that the other process satisfies the current process' own information flow assumption. Note that both the locality condition and the information flow assumption for p build on the time-bounded distinguishability relation of p.

5.2   Composition of Hyper Implementations

The hyper implementations of each of the processes are locally correct and satisfy the information flow assumptions of the other process respectively. However, the hyper implementations have full information of the inputs and are dependent on the additional variables $\mathbf{t}_p$ and $\mathbf{t}_q$. To construct practically executable local implementations, we first compose the hyper implementations into one strategy.

Definition 9 (Composition of hyper implementations). *Let p and q be two processes with hyper implementations given as infinite $2^{O_e \cup I_p \cup \{\mathbf{t}_p\}}$-branching $2^{O_p \cup \{\mathbf{t}_q\}}$-labeled tree h_p for process p, and an infinite $2^{O_e \cup I_q \cup \{\mathbf{t}_q\}}$-branching $2^{O_p \cup \{\mathbf{t}_p\}}$-labeled tree h_q for process q.*

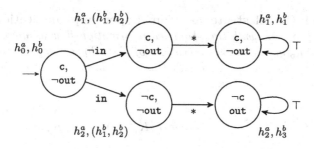

Fig. 2. The composition of the hyper implementations of a in Fig. 1c and b in Fig. 1d. The states are labeled with the combination of states that can be reached for both processes.

Given two hyper implementations h_p and h_q, we define the composition $h = h_p \| h_q$ to be a 2^{O_e}-branching $2^{O_p \cup O_q}$-labeled tree, where $h(v) = (h_p(f_p(v)) \cup h_q(f_q(v))) \cap (O_p \cup O_q)$ and f_p, f_q are defined as follows:

$$f_p(\epsilon) = \epsilon \qquad f_p(v \cdot x) = f_p(v) \cdot ((x \cap I_p) \cup (h_q(f_q(v)) \cap (I_p \cup \{t_p\})))$$
$$f_q(\epsilon) = \epsilon \qquad f_q(v \cdot x) = f_q(v) \cdot ((x \cap I_q) \cup (h_p(f_p(v)) \cap (I_q \cup \{t_q\})))$$

If each hyper implementation satisfies the time-bounded information flow assumption of the other process, then there exists a strategy for each process (given as a tree that branches according to the local inputs of the process), such that the combined behavior of the two strategies corresponds exactly to the composition of the hyper implementations.

The composition of the hyper implementations of the bit transmission protocol is shown in Fig. 2. The initial state is the combination of both process's initial states with the corresponding outputs. We change the state after the value of in is received. While process a directly reacts to in, process b cannot observe its value, and the composition can either be in h_0^b or h_1^b. Both states have the same output. In the next step, process a communicates the value of in by setting c to true or false, such that the loop states h_1^a, h_1^a and h_2^a, h_3^b are reached.

The local strategies of the processes are constructed from the composed hyper implementations. As an auxiliary notion we introduce the *knowledge set*: the set of finite traces in the composition that cannot be distinguished by a process.

Definition 10 (Knowledge set). *Let p and q be two processes with composed hyper implementations $h = h_p \| h_q$. For a finite trace $v \in (2^{I_p})^*$ of inputs to p, we define the knowledge set $K_p(v)$ to be*

$$K_p(v) \triangleq \{w \mid w \text{ is a finite trace of } (2^{O_e})^* \text{ and } f_p(w) = v\}.$$

Lemma 1. *For all $s\, v, v' \in (2^{I_p})^*$, if $K_p(v) = K_p(v')$ then $h(v) \downarrow_{O_p} = h(v') \downarrow_{O_p}$.*

The proof of Lemma 1 can be found in the full version of this paper [12]. The local strategies from the composed hyper implementations are then defined as follows:

Definition 11 (Local strategies from hyper implementations). *Let p and q be two processes with time-bounded information flow assumptions χ_p and χ_q, and $h = h_p \| h_q$ be the composition of their hyper implementations. For $j \in \{p, q\}$ the strategy s_j, represented as a 2^{I_j}-branching 2^{O_j}-labeled tree for process j, is defined as follows:*

$$s_j(\epsilon) = \epsilon \qquad s_j(v) = \begin{cases} \emptyset & \text{if } |K_j(v)| = 0 \\ h(min(K_j(v))) \downarrow_{O_j} & \text{if } |K_j(v)| > 0 \end{cases}$$

where $min(K_j(v))$ is the smallest trace based on an arbitrary order over $K_j(v)$.

The base case of the definition inserts a label for unreachable traces in the composed hyper implementation. For example, the local inputs $I_p \backslash O_e$ are determined by s_q, and not all input words in $(2^{I_q})^*$ are possible. Process p's local strategy s_p can discard these input words. The second case of the definition picks the smallest trace in the knowledge set and computes the outputs from h that are local to a process. Intuitively, the outputs of h have to be the same for every trace that a process considers possible in the composed hyper implementations. We therefore pick one of them, compute the output of the composed hyper-strategy, and restrict the output to the local outputs of the process. The following theorem states the correctness of the construction in Definition 11.

Theorem 3. *Let p and q be two processes with time-bounded information flow assumptions χ_p and χ_q, let $h = h_p \| h_q$ be the composition of their hyper implementations, and s_p and s_q be their local strategies. Then, for all $v \in (2^{O_e})^*$ it holds that $h(v) = s_p(g_p(v)) \cup s_q(g_q(v))$ where g_p, g_q are defined as follows:*

$$g_p(\epsilon) = \epsilon \qquad g_p(v \cdot x) = g_p(v) \cdot ((x \cap I_p) \cup (s_q(g_q(v)) \cap I_p))$$
$$g_q(\epsilon) = \epsilon \qquad g_q(v \cdot x) = g_q(v) \cdot ((x \cap I_q) \cup (s_p(g_p(v)) \cap I_q))$$

The proof is inductive over the words $v \in (2^{O_e})^*$ and can be found in the full version of this paper [12]. Combining all definitions and theorems of the previous sections, we conclude with the following corollary.

Corollary 1. *Let $(I_p, I_q, O_p, O_q, I_e)$ be an architecture and $\varphi = \varphi_p \wedge \varphi_q$ be a specification. If the hyper-strategies h_p and h_q are locally correct, then the implementation (s_p, s_q) satisfies φ.*

6   A More Practical Approach

A major disadvantage of the synthesis approach of the preceding sections is that the hyper implementations are based on the full set of environment outputs; as a result, hyper implementations branch according to inputs that are not actually available; this, in turn, results in our introduction of the locality condition.

In this section, we develop a more practical approach, where the branching is limited to the information that is actually available to a process: this includes any environment output directly visible to the process and, additionally, the information the process is guaranteed to receive according to the information flow assumption. As a result, the synthesis of the process is sound without need for a locality condition. We develop this approach under two assumptions: First, we assume that the time-bounded information flow assumption only depends on environment outputs the sending process can actually see; second, we assume that the time-bounded information flow assumption can be decomposed into a finite set of classes in the following sense: For a trace π of environment outputs, the information class $[\pi]_p$ describes that, on the trace π, the process p eventually needs to become aware that the current trace is in the set $[\pi]$. The information class is obtained by collecting all traces that are *not* related to π in the time-bounded distinguishability relation.

Definition 12 (Information classes). *Given a time-bounded distinguishability relation Λ_p for process p, the* information class $[\pi]_p$ *of a trace π over O_e is the following set of traces:* $\quad [\pi]_p = (2^{O_e})^\omega \setminus \{\pi' \in (2^{O_e})^\omega \mid (\pi, \pi') \in \Lambda_p\}$

The next definition relativizes the specification of the processes for a particular information class, reflecting the fact that the process does not know the actual environment output, but only its information class; hence, the process output needs to be correct for all environment outputs in the information class.

Definition 13 (Relativized specification). *For a process p with specification φ_p and an information class c, the relativized specification $\varphi_{p,c}$ is the following trace property over $(I_p \cap O_e) \cup O_p$:*

$$\varphi_{p,c} = \{\pi_e \sqcup \pi_p \mid \pi_e \in (2^{I_p \cap O_e})^\omega, \pi_p \in (2^{O_p})^\omega \text{ s.t. } \forall \pi'_e \in c. \ \pi'_e \sqcup \pi_p \vDash \varphi_p\}$$

The component specification, which is the basis for the synthesis of the process, must take into account that the process does not know the information class in advance; the behavior of the other process will only eventually reveal the information class. Let IC be the set of information classes for process p. Assume that this set is finite. We now replace the inputs of the process that come from the other process with new auxiliary input channels IC as new inputs. In the hyper implementation, receiving such an input reveals the information class to the process. In the actual implementation, the information class will be revealed by the actual outputs of the other process that are observable for p. The component specification requires that the processes satisfy the relativized specification under the assumption that the information class is eventually received. We encode this assumption as a trace condition ψ, which requires that exactly one of the elements of IC eventually occurs.

Definition 14 (Component specification). *For process p with specification φ_p, the component specification $\langle\varphi_p\rangle$ over $(I_p \cap O_e) \cup IC \cup O_p$ is defined as*

$$\langle\varphi_p\rangle = \{\pi \in (2^{(I_p \cap O_e) \cup IC \cup O_p})^\omega \mid \text{ if } \pi \vDash \psi \text{ then } \pi \vDash \bigwedge_{c \in IC} (\Diamond c \to \varphi_{p,c}\}$$

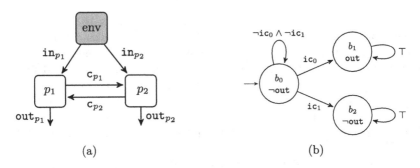

(a)   (b)

Fig. 3. The architecture used for our experiments in (a) where the number outputs, inputs, and communication channels can vary. Figure 3b shows the implementation of process b for its bit transmission component specification.

where ψ is the following trace property over $(I_p \cap O_e) \cup IC \cup O_p$:

$$\psi = \{\pi \in (2^{(I_p \cap O_e) \cup IC \cup O_p})^\omega \mid \exists \pi' \in (2^{O_e})^\omega. \; \pi \downarrow_{I_p \cap O_e} = \pi' \downarrow_{I_p \cap O_e}$$
$$\text{and } \pi \vDash \Diamond[\pi'] \text{ and exactly one element of } IC \text{ occurs on } \pi\}$$

The component specification allows us to replace the locality condition (Definition 7), which is a hyperproperty, with a trace property. Note, however, that the process additionally needs to satisfy the information flow assumption of the other process, which may in general depend on the full set O_e of environment outputs. This would require us to synthesize the process on the full set O_e, and to re-introduce the locality condition. In practice, however, the information flow assumption of one process often only depends on the information of the other process. In this case, it suffices to synthesize each process based only on the locally visible environment outputs.

Figure 3b shows the implementation of b for its component specification $\langle \varphi_b \rangle$. In contrast to its hyper implementation (cf. Fig. 1b), it does not branch according to in and t_p, but only variables in IC. The specification is encoded as the following LTL formula:

$$\langle \varphi_b \rangle = (\Box \neg \mathsf{ic}_0 \vee \Box \neg \mathsf{ic}_1) \wedge \Diamond((\mathsf{ic}_0 \vee \mathsf{ic}_1))$$
$$\rightarrow ((\Diamond \mathsf{ic}_0 \rightarrow \Diamond \mathsf{out}) \wedge (\Diamond \mathsf{ic}_1 \rightarrow \Box \neg \mathsf{out}))$$

The left hand side of the implication represents the assumption ψ, while the right hand side specifies the guarantee for each information class. The composition and decomposition can be performed analogously to the hyper implementations, where we map the value of ic to the values of the communication variables. We construct the automata for component specifications in the full version of this paper [12].

7 Experiments

The focus of our experiments is on the performance of the compositional synthesis approach compared to non-compositional synthesis methods for distributed systems. While the time-bounded information flow assumptions and the component specification can be computed automatically by automata constructions, we have, for the purpose of these experiments, built them manually and encoded them as formulas in HyperLTL or LTL, which were then entered to the BoSy/BoSyHyper [11] synthesis tool[1]. Our experiments are based on the following benchmarks:

- **AC.** *Atomic commit.* The atomic commitment protocol specifies that the output of a local process is set to *true* iff the observable input and the unobservable inputs are *true*. We only consider one round of communication, the initial input determines all values. The parameter shows how many input variables each process receives, Par. = 1 for the running example.
- **EC.** *Eventual commit.* The atomic commit benchmark extended to eventual inputs - if all inputs (independently of each other) eventually become *true*, then there needs to be information flow.
- **SA.** *Send all.* Every input of the sender is relevant for the receiver. If an input is set to true, it will eventually be communicated to the receiver. The parameter represents the number of input values and therefore the number of information classes.

Table 1 shows the performance of the compositional synthesis approach. The column architecture (Arch.) determines for each benchmark if the information flow is directional (dir.) or bidirectional (bidir.). Column (Inflow send) indicates the running time for the sending process; where applicable, column (Inflow rec.) indicates the running time for the synthesis of the process that only receives information. We compare the compositional approach to BoSyHyper, based on a standard encoding of distributed synthesis in HyperLTL (Inc. BoSy), and a specialized tool for distributed synthesis [2] (Distr. BoSy). All experiments were performed on a MacBook Pro with a 2,8 GHz Intel Quad Core processor and 16 GB of RAM. The timeout was 30 min.

Information flow guided synthesis outperforms the standard approaches, especially for more complex components. For example, in the atomic commitment benchmark, scaling in the number of inputs does not impact the synthesis of the local processes, while Distr. BoSy eventually times out, and the running time of Inc. BoSy increases faster than for the information flow synthesis. For all approaches, the Send All benchmark is the hardest one to solve. Here, each input that will eventually be set needs to be eventually sent, which leads to non-trivial communication over the shared variables and an increased state space to memorize the individual inputs. Nevertheless, the information flow guided synthesis outperforms the other approaches and times out with parameter 3

---

[1] The experiments are available at https://doi.org/10.6084/m9.figshare.19697359.

Table 1. The results of the experiments with execution times given in seconds. A cell is highlighted if it was faster than the other approaches, where the sum of synthesis times for both sender and receiver is taken as reference.

Bench.	Arch.	Par.	Inflow send.	Inflow rec.	Distr.BoSy	Inc. BoSy
AC	dir	1	0.92	0.70	**1.41**	2.31
	dir	2	**0.36**	**1.28**	2.86	2.30
	dir	3	**0.92**	**0.68**	2.46	2.55
	dir	4	**0.92**	**0.79**	720.60	3.41
	dir	5	**0.92**	**0.68**	TO	9.27
	bidir	1	1.45	-	**0.96**	9.27
	bidir	2	**2.49**	-	TO	TO
	bidir	3	**79.18**	-	TO	TO
	bidir	4	TO	-	TO	TO
EC	dir	1	0.68	1.87	**0.92**	2.556
	dir	2	0.94	1.85	**0.96**	3.90
	dir	3	**202.09**	TO	TO	TO
	dir	4	TO	TO	TO	TO
	bidir	1	**3.77**	-	4.63	147.46
	bidir	2	TO	-	TO	TO
SA	dir	1	1.31	0.92	2.21	**1.579**
	dir	2	**1.78**	**0.92**	27.47	TO
	dir	3	TO	1.08	TO	TO

because BoSyHyper cannot cope with the number of states needed. Synthesizing a receiver that does not satisfy an information flow assumption is close to irrelevant for every benchmark run. Since these processes are synthesized with local LTL specifications, scaling only in the number of local inputs or information that will eventually be received is easily possible. Notably, these receivers are compatible with any implementation of the sender, whereas the solutions of the other approaches are only compatible for the same synthesis run.

8   Related Work

Compositional synthesis is often studied in the setting of *complete information*, where all processes have access to all environment outputs [9,14,17,19]. In the following, we focus on compositional approaches for the synthesis of distributed systems, where the processes have incomplete information about the environment outputs. Compositionality has been used to improve distributed synthesis in various domains, including reactive controllers [1,16]. Closest to our approach is assume-guarantee synthesis [3,4], which relies on behavioral guarantees of the processs behaviour and assumptions about the behavior of the other processes. Recently, an extension of assume-guarantee synthesis for distributed systems was proposed [20], where the assumptions are iteratively refined. Using a weaker winning condition for synthesis, remorse-free dominance [7] avoids the explicit construction of assumptions and guarantees, resulting in implicit assumptions. A recent approach [13] uses behavioral guarantees in the form of certificates to guide the synthesis process. Certificates specify partial behaviour of each component and are iteratively synthesized. The fundamental difference between all these approaches to the current work is that the assumptions are behavioral. To the best of our knowledge, this is the first synthesis approach based on information-flow assumptions. While there is a rich body of work on the verification of information-flow properties (cf. [8,15,24]), and the synthesis from information-flow properties and other hyperproperties has also been studied before (cf. [11]), the idea of utilizing hyperproperties as assumptions for compositional synthesis of distributed systems is new.

9   Conclusion

The approach introduced in this paper provides the foundation for a new class of distributed synthesis algorithms, where the assumptions refer to the flow of information and are represented as hyperproperties. In many situations, necessary information flow assumptions exist even if there are no necessary behavioral assumptions. There are at least two major directions for future work. The first direction concerns the insight that compositional synthesis profits from the generality of hyperproperties; at the same time, synthesis from hyperproperties is much more challenging than synthesis from trace properties. To address this issue, we have presented the more practical method in Sect. 6, which replaces locality, a hyperproperty, with the component specification, a trace property. However, this method is limited to information flow assumptions that refer to a finite amount of information. It is very common for the required amount of information to be infinite in the sense that the same type of information must be transmitted again and again. We conjecture that our method can be extended to such situations.

A second major direction is the extension to distributed systems with more than two processes. The two-process case has the advantage that the assumptions of one process must be guaranteed by the other. With more than two processes, the localization of the assumptions becomes more difficult or even impossible, if multiple processes have access to the required information.

References

1. Alur, R., Moarref, S., Topcu, U.: Compositional synthesis of reactive controllers for multi-agent systems. In: Chaudhuri, S., Farzan, A. (eds.) CAV 2016. LNCS, vol. 9780, pp. 251–269. Springer, Cham (2016). https://doi.org/10.1007/978-3-319-41540-6_14
2. Baumeister, J.E.: Encodings of bounded synthesis of distributed systems. B.Sc. Thesis, Saarland University (2017)

3. Bloem, R., Chatterjee, K., Jacobs, S., Könighofer, R.: Assume-guarantee synthesis for concurrent reactive programs with partial information. In: Baier, C., Tinelli, C. (eds.) TACAS 2015. LNCS, vol. 9035, pp. 517–532. Springer, Heidelberg (2015). https://doi.org/10.1007/978-3-662-46681-0_50

4. Chatterjee, K., Henzinger, T.A.: Assume-guarantee synthesis. In: Grumberg, O., Huth, M. (eds.) TACAS 2007. LNCS, vol. 4424, pp. 261–275. Springer, Heidelberg (2007). https://doi.org/10.1007/978-3-540-71209-1_21

5. Clarkson, M.R., Finkbeiner, B., Koleini, M., Micinski, K.K., Rabe, M.N., Sánchez, C.: Temporal logics for hyperproperties. In: Abadi, M., Kremer, S. (eds.) POST 2014. LNCS, vol. 8414, pp. 265–284. Springer, Heidelberg (2014). https://doi.org/10.1007/978-3-642-54792-8_15

6. Clarkson, M.R., Schneider, F.B.: Hyperproperties. J. Comput. Secur. **18**(6), 1157–1210 (2010)

7. Damm, W., Finkbeiner, B.: Automatic compositional synthesis of distributed systems. In: Jones, C., Pihlajasaari, P., Sun, J. (eds.) FM 2014. LNCS, vol. 8442, pp. 179–193. Springer, Cham (2014). https://doi.org/10.1007/978-3-319-06410-9_13

8. Dimitrova, R., Finkbeiner, B., Kovács, M., Rabe, M.N., Seidl, H.: Model checking information flow in reactive systems. In: Kuncak, V., Rybalchenko, A. (eds.) VMCAI 2012. LNCS, vol. 7148, pp. 169–185. Springer, Heidelberg (2012). https://doi.org/10.1007/978-3-642-27940-9_12

9. Filiot, E., Jin, N., Raskin, J.-F.: Compositional algorithms for LTL synthesis. In: Bouajjani, A., Chin, W.-N. (eds.) ATVA 2010. LNCS, vol. 6252, pp. 112–127. Springer, Heidelberg (2010). https://doi.org/10.1007/978-3-642-15643-4_10

10. Finkbeiner, B., Schewe, S.: Uniform distributed synthesis. In: Proceedings of the 20th ACM/IEEE Symposium on Logic in Computer Science (LICS), pp. 321–330 (2005)

11. Finkbeiner, B., Hahn, C., Lukert, P., Stenger, M., Tentrup, L.: Synthesizing reactive systems from hyperproperties. In: Chockler, H., Weissenbacher, G. (eds.) CAV 2018. LNCS, vol. 10981, pp. 289–306. Springer, Cham (2018). https://doi.org/10.1007/978-3-319-96145-3_16

12. Finkbeiner, B., Metzger, N., Moses, Y.: Information flow guided synthesis (full version) (2022). https://doi.org/10.48550/ARXIV.2205.12085

13. Finkbeiner, B., Passing, N.: Compositional synthesis of modular systems. In: Hou, Z., Ganesh, V. (eds.) ATVA 2021. LNCS, vol. 12971, pp. 303–319. Springer, Cham (2021). https://doi.org/10.1007/978-3-030-88885-5_20

14. Finkbeiner, B., Passing, N.: Dependency-based compositional synthesis. In: Hung, D.V., Sokolsky, O. (eds.) ATVA 2020. LNCS, vol. 12302, pp. 447–463. Springer, Cham (2020). https://doi.org/10.1007/978-3-030-59152-6_25

15. Finkbeiner, B., Rabe, M.N., Sánchez, C.: Algorithms for model checking HyperLTL and HyperCTL*. In: Kroening, D., Păsăreanu, C.S. (eds.) CAV 2015. LNCS, vol. 9206, pp. 30–48. Springer, Cham (2015). https://doi.org/10.1007/978-3-319-21690-4_3

16. Hecking-Harbusch, J., Metzger, N.O.: Efficient trace encodings of bounded synthesis for asynchronous distributed systems. In: Chen, Y.-F., Cheng, C.-H., Esparza, J. (eds.) ATVA 2019. LNCS, vol. 11781, pp. 369–386. Springer, Cham (2019). https://doi.org/10.1007/978-3-030-31784-3_22

17. Kugler, H., Segall, I.: Compositional synthesis of reactive systems from live sequence chart specifications. In: Kowalewski, S., Philippou, A. (eds.) TACAS 2009. LNCS, vol. 5505, pp. 77–91. Springer, Heidelberg (2009). https://doi.org/10.1007/978-3-642-00768-2_9

18. Kupferman, O., Vardi, M.Y.: Synthesizing distributed systems. In: Logic in Computer Science (LICS) (2001)
19. Kupferman, O., Piterman, N., Vardi, M.Y.: Safraless compositional synthesis. In: Ball, T., Jones, R.B. (eds.) CAV 2006. LNCS, vol. 4144, pp. 31–44. Springer, Heidelberg (2006). https://doi.org/10.1007/11817963_6
20. Majumdar, R., Mallik, K., Schmuck, A., Zufferey, D.: Assume-guarantee distributed synthesis. IEEE Trans. Comput. Aided Des. Integr. Circ. Syst. **39**(11), 3215–3226 (2020). https://doi.org/10.1109/TCAD.2020.3012641
21. Pnueli, A.: The temporal logic of programs. In: 18th Annual Symposium on Foundations of Computer Science, Providence, Rhode Island, USA, 31 October–1 November 1977, pp. 46–57. IEEE Computer Society (1977). https://doi.org/10.1109/SFCS.1977.32
22. Pnueli, A., Rosner, R.: Distributed reactive systems are hard to synthesize. In: 31st Annual Symposium on Foundations of Computer Science, St. Louis, Missouri, USA, 22–24 October 1990, Volume II, pp. 746–757. IEEE Computer Society (1990). https://doi.org/10.1109/FSCS.1990.89597
23. Schewe, S., Finkbeiner, B.: Semi-automatic distributed synthesis. Int. J. Found. Comput. Sci. **18**(1), 113–138 (2007)
24. Yasuoka, H., Terauchi, T.: Quantitative information flow - verification hardness and possibilities. In: Proceedings of the 23rd IEEE Computer Security Foundations Symposium, CSF 2010, Edinburgh, United Kingdom, 17–19 July 2010, pp. 15–27. IEEE Computer Society (2010). https://doi.org/10.1109/CSF.2010.9

Randomized Synthesis for Diversity and Cost Constraints with Control Improvisation

Andreas Gittis, Eric Vin, and Daniel J. Fremont$^{(\boxtimes)}$ (iD)

University of California, Santa Cruz, USA
{agittis,evin,dfremont}@ucsc.edu

Abstract. In many synthesis problems, it can be essential to generate implementations which not only satisfy functional constraints but are also *randomized* to improve variety, robustness, or unpredictability. The recently-proposed framework of control improvisation (CI) provides techniques for the correct-by-construction synthesis of randomized systems subject to hard and soft constraints. However, prior work on CI has focused on qualitative specifications, whereas in robotic planning and other areas we often have quantitative quality metrics which can be traded against each other. For example, a designer of a patrolling security robot might want to know by how much the average patrol time needs to be increased in order to ensure that a particular aspect of the robot's route is sufficiently diverse and hence unpredictable. In this paper, we enable this type of application by generalizing the CI problem to support quantitative soft constraints which bound the expected value of a given cost function, and randomness constraints which enforce diversity of the generated traces with respect to a given label function. We establish the basic theory of labelled quantitative CI problems, and develop efficient algorithms for solving them when the specifications are encoded by finite automata. We also provide an approximate improvisation algorithm based on constraint solving for any specifications encodable as Boolean formulas. We demonstrate the utility of our problem formulation and algorithms with experiments applying them to generate diverse near-optimal plans for robotic planning problems.

1 Introduction

Correct-by-construction synthesis of systems from high-level specifications has become a popular paradigm in fields ranging from circuit design [5] to robotic task planning [25]. Synthesis techniques for many different types of specifications have been developed, especially for temporal logic formulas, which can encode many properties of interest [14]. One less-studied type of specification are *randomness constraints* that require the system's behavior to be sufficiently random, for instance by being close to a uniform distribution over the set of

---

A. Gittis and E. Vin—The two first authors contributed equally to the paper.

© The Author(s) 2022
S. Shoham and Y. Vizel (Eds.): CAV 2022, LNCS 13372, pp. 526–546, 2022.
https://doi.org/10.1007/978-3-031-13188-2_26

allowed behaviors. Such specifications are useful in many applications, as randomness can provide robustness, variety, and unpredictability to a system. For example, fuzz testing tools often use constraints to select classes of inputs which are more likely to trigger bugs, but then search randomly within that class to prevent bias [29]. In robotic planning, a patrolling security robot that uses a fixed plan satisfying its requirements might be vulnerable to exploitation; adding randomness to make its route unpredictable can make exploitation more difficult.

While there has been substantial work on synthesis with stochastic environments (e.g. [2,9]), randomness constraints require the system itself to behave randomly even if the environment is deterministic. Furthermore, unlike most specifications used in synthesis, randomness constraints are properties not of individual behaviors but rather of their distribution, and they cannot be concisely encoded into existing specification formalisms like PCTL [22] and SGL [3]. As a result, synthesis of systems under such constraints requires new techniques.

A recently-proposed paradigm for the correct-by-construction synthesis of systems under randomness constraints is *algorithmic improvisation* [13,15,16]. Algorithmic improvisation comprises a class of synthesis problems whose goal is to construct a randomized algorithm, an *improviser*, satisfying three kinds of constraints: *hard constraints* that the improviser's output must always satisfy, *soft constraints* that need only be satisfied to a certain (tunable) extent, and *randomness constraints* requiring the output to be sufficiently random. These types of constraints correspond to natural requirements arising for example in robot planning: the hard constraints can encode safety or other functional requirements, the soft constraints can encode notions of efficiency or optimality, and the randomness constraints enforce diversity or unpredictability. The original and most-studied form of algorithmic improvisation is the *control improvisation* (CI) problem (introduced in [12] and formalized in [16,17]), where the improviser generates finite sequences of symbols, the hard constraint is a trace property, the soft constraint requires some trace property hold with at least a desired probability, and the randomness constraint puts upper and lower bounds on the probability of individual outputs. Control improvisation and its extensions have been successfully used for musical improvisation [13], robotic planning [19], human modeling subject to constraints [1], and generating synthetic datasets for testing and training cyber-physical systems with machine learning components [18].

However, the prior work on CI is not general enough to cover many randomized synthesis problems of interest, for two reasons. First, many planning, design space exploration, and other problems come with a *cost function* expressing how optimal a particular solution is; in the setting of generating randomized solutions, the most natural soft constraint would be to require that the *expected cost* of a solution should be low, so that we can obtain a diverse set of near-optimal solutions. In a patrolling robot application, for example, the fastest patrol route might be unique and so predictable, and we then want to know by how much we would need to increase the average patrol time in order to enable a sufficiently-diverse set of routes. The prior work on CI cannot provide such an analysis.

Second, while the CI randomness constraint is sufficient to make the improviser's exact output unpredictable, it is *not* sufficient to ensure diversity when many outputs are similar to each other. Continuing our patrolling robot example, suppose that the robot has a choice of two rooms to go through: one room is larger, and so there are (say) 10^6 possible paths through it, vs. only 10^3 through the other room. Even if a perfectly-uniform distribution over all these paths is possible given our other constraints, the robot will end up entering the larger room almost all of the time. But from the point of view of an adversary that wishes to avoid being seen by the robot, the exact path is not relevant: what matters is *which room* the robot will enter, and that is highly predictable. For this application, we need a randomness requirement that enforces diversity not over the output of the improviser, but over some *attribute* of the output.

To enable such applications, in this paper we introduce the concept of *Labelled Quantitative Control Improvisation* (LQCI). This problem extends CI with a soft constraint bounding the expected cost of generated traces, and a randomness constraint requiring near-uniformity of the *label* of a trace, given by an arbitrary label function. We study the theory of LQCI, establishing precise conditions for when an LQCI problem is solvable and a general construction for solving it. We use our construction to develop efficient improvisation algorithms for a broad class of specifications given by finite automata, including common cost functions such as mission time or path length. For specifications not easily encoded to (reasonably-sized) automata, we provide an approximate improvisation algorithm based on constraint solving that handles symbolic specifications encoded as Boolean formulas. We also explore an extension of the LQCI problem for finding the *maximum-entropy* distribution satisfying the other constraints (as in [30]), and develop an algorithm for solving it using convex optimization. Finally, we conduct a case study demonstrating that our approach allows us to formalize and solve realistic robotic planning problems.

In summary, the main contributions of this paper are:

- The labelled quantitative control improvisation problem definition (Sect. 2);
- A characterization of which LQCI problems are solvable, and a general construction for solving them (Sect. 3);
- Efficient improvisation algorithms for finite automata specifications (Sect. 4);
- An approximate algorithm for Boolean formula specifications (Sect. 5);
- An algorithm for maximum-entropy LQCI problems (Sect. 6);
- Experiments using our algorithms for robotic planning (Sect. 7).

We conclude in Sect. 8 with a summary of results and directions for future work. For brevity, we defer full proofs of all results to the Appendix [21].

2   Overview and Problem Definition

In this section we formally define the LQCI problem, first using applications to robotic planning and fuzz testing to motivate various aspects of our definitions. We will return to the robotic planning example for our experiments in Sect. 7.

2.1 Motivating Examples

Robotic Planning. Consider the problem of generating a path for a package delivery robot, where the robot should efficiently visit various drop-off points, visiting charging stations as necessary along the way. Discretizing the world into a grid, we can represent a path as a finite sequence of north, south, east, and west moves. We might have various requirements for such paths, falling into the three types of constraints of a control improvisation problem described above: hard constraints such as completing mission objectives and not navigating into impassable terrain, soft constraints such as preferring shorter paths, and randomness constraints to ensure the chosen path is unpredictable. However, as we saw in Sect. 1, randomness over paths can be less important than randomness over specific features of a path: here, it might be that charging leaves the robot vulnerable for an extended period, so that it is important to limit the extent to which an adversary can predict ahead of time which charging station will be used. If there are 3 charging stations, then all possible paths are divided into 3 classes, and we want the class of a generated path to be unpredictable; we can formalize this as a *label function* which assigns labels to paths, and require that the distribution over labels be close to uniform. Since we do not want to simply pick a single path from each label class, we can also enforce randomness within each class, either by bounding the conditional probabilities of paths (so that no path is too likely relative to others in its class) or by taking the maximum-entropy distribution that satisfies our randomness-over-labels condition (we will return to this approach in Sect. 6).

For efficiency, we want our robot to use routes which are as fast as possible, taking into account varying terrain. We could model this using a *cost function* assigning numerical costs to each path: here, the total time needed to traverse it. However, as mentioned in Sect. 1, prior work on CI can only encode Boolean soft constraints, such as requiring the cost of a path to be at most 5 with probability at least 0.9. While this does allow for some control over the cost, it requires setting an arbitrary threshold, and otherwise ignores the actual values of the cost; thus, a path of cost 6 is treated no differently than a path of cost 10^5. Instead, we want to bound the *expected* cost of a path, so that both the probabilities of individual paths and their absolute costs are taken into account.

Putting all this together, we define our example planning problem as generating paths through the grid worlds in Fig. 1, subject to the following constraints:

Hard Constraint:
    (a) The robot must begin in the start cell **S** and must end in the end cell **E**.
    (b) The robot must visit all package drop-off points **O**.
    (c) The robot must charge at a charging station **C**.
    (d) The robot must not enter impassable locations **X**.

Cost Constraint:
    The expected time to complete the mission must be at most a constant c.

Randomness over Labels:
    For each choice of charging station, the chance that the robot uses that station must be at least λ and at most ρ.

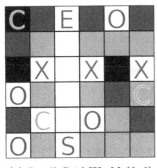
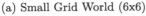

(a) Small Grid World (6x6)

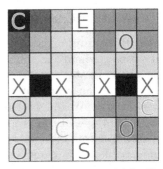

(b) Large Grid World (7x7)

Fig. 1. Grid worlds for our robotic planning example. Darker background indicates higher cost and letters indicate: start and end points (**S**, **E**), impassable locations (**X**), delivery locations (**O**), charging stations (**C**).

Randomness over Words:
  Conditioned on selecting a certain charging station, the probability of picking any path must be at least α and at most β.

  Here, we assume that each grid cell has a cost representing how long it takes to traverse, with the cost of a path (the total mission time) being the sum of the costs of its cells. In Fig. 1, we show higher-cost cells as being darker, with the costs ranging from 0–3 for the small world and 0–10 for the large world. The layout of the map was chosen to admit a variety of different paths, motivated as follows: we envision an impassible river dividing the top and bottom halves of the map, with one low-cost bridge and two high-cost fords. The top-left charging station is a windmill and requires climbing a hill to access; there is also a hydroelectric station next to the river, and an easily-accessible substation near the main north-south road.

Fuzz Testing. Prior work has shown that a variety of programs and protocols can be comprehensively tested by randomly sampling from automata encoding constraints on acceptable tests [11]. LQCI allows us to preserve such guarantees while exercising additional control over which tests are generated.
  As an example, consider the problem of generating randomized network activity for a set of devices communicating over TCP; this could be useful to test robustness of a network monitoring application or network stack. There are a variety of different constraints we might wish to impose on the sequences of packets we generate: each connection should conform to the TCP protocol, so that the tests are meaningful[1]; tests should exhibit a variety of different behaviors

---

[1] We might also want to generate tests that *deviate* from the protocol. This could be done in a variety of ways, e.g. modifying our constraints to allow certain types of deviations, or first generating tests that conform to the protocol and subsequently mutating them.

such as successful/failed connections, interleaving of packets between different connections, etc.; and tests should be as short as possible while still exhibiting these different behaviors, so that we can maximize the number of tests we can perform in a given time. These constraints have trade-offs: for example, tests with failed connections that must be retried will necessarily be longer. As in the robotic planning example, we formulate these requirements as cost and label constraints, which allow us to balance our randomness and control needs.

For concreteness, consider the specific example of generating packet traces for 5 systems communicating over TCP. Our hard constraint can enforce that each connection follows the TCP protocol, using an encoding of the operation of the protocol as a finite automaton [24] (we will present efficient algorithms for LQCI with automata specifications below). Our cost function can assign a cost equal to the length of the trace, so that we prefer shorter sequences (whereas if we simply sampled uniformly from the language of the TCP automaton up to some length, longer sequences would be generated more frequently as there are exponentially more of them). Our label function could use two labels, distinguishing traces with connections that terminate cleanly from those that involve system failures and timeouts (we could also further subdivide into several types of failures). There are many more ways for a connection to fail than to terminate cleanly, and these two classes of traces might have significantly different lengths on average, but we want to ensure that our tests cover both cases adequately. By imposing constraints on the expected cost of a trace, as well as randomness constraints over the label and within each label class, we can control test length while enforcing sufficient diversity among the tests. In fact, we will see below that our LQCI algorithms can find the *minimum-cost* distribution consistent with the randomness constraints, thereby allowing us to test as efficiently as possible given coverage requirements.

2.2   Problem Definition

To formalize synthesis problems like those described above, we define the LQCI problem. Following the definition of CI [16,17], we frame the problem as sampling words over a finite alphabet Σ subject to several constraints. We use the general term *specification* to refer to an encoding of a property of words (a language): for example, a deterministic finite automaton (DFA) is a specification, where the DFA accepts a word if and only if it satisfies the specification; a Boolean formula is another kind of specification. The complexity of the LQCI problem will vary depending on the type of specifications used, as we will see later.

Definition 1. *A Labelled Quantitative Control Improvisation (LQCI) instance over an alphabet Σ is a tuple $\mathcal{C} = (\mathcal{H}, \mathcal{K}, L, m, n, c, \lambda, \rho, \hat{\alpha}, \hat{\beta})$ which contains:*

- *$m, n \in \mathbb{N}$, lower and upper bounds on word length (with $m \leq n$);*
- *$\mathcal{H}$, a hard specification that must be satisfied by all words;*
- *$\mathcal{K} : \Sigma^* \to \mathbb{Q}$, a cost function mapping words to rational costs;*
- *$L : \Sigma^* \to \Omega$, a label function mapping words to a finite set of labels $\Omega = \{\ell_1, \ldots \ell_{|\Omega|}\}$;*

- $c \in \mathbb{Q}^+$, an upper bound on expected cost;
- $\lambda, \rho \in \mathbb{Q}$, lower and upper bounds on the marginal probability of selecting a word with a certain label (with $0 \le \lambda \le \rho \le 1$);
- $\hat{\alpha}_i, \hat{\beta}_i \in \mathbb{Q}$, lower and upper bounds on the conditional probability of words in label class ℓ_i (with $0 \le \hat{\alpha}_i \le \hat{\beta}_i \le 1$ for all i).

We note that the specifications and functions above are abstract, and our definition does not make any assumptions about how they will be encoded in a particular problem. For example, the hard constraint $\mathcal{H}$ over words might be instantiated as the language of a DFA, context-free grammar, etc. Later in the paper we will develop algorithms for solving classes of LQCI instances with specification formalisms that satisfy certain properties.

The restriction to finite traces (via the length bounds m and n) is consistent with prior work on using CI for robotic planning [19]: we frequently want plans that complete within a time limit. Likewise in fuzz testing we want tests of bounded length. Furthermore, as we will see, finite-trace LQCI is still a highly nontrivial problem, so we leave its extension to infinite traces as future work.

Given an LQCI instance, we define several convenient notations:

- $\Sigma^{m:n}$ is all words satisfying the length bounds: $\{w \in \Sigma^* \mid m \le |w| \le n\}$.
- The set of *improvisations* I consists of all words satisfying the length bounds and the hard specification. These are all the words which our improviser is allowed to generate.
- Since the length bounds m, n ensure I is finite, we can consider the image of I under $\mathcal{K}$, which must also be finite. We will refer to this set of *possible costs* as $\Theta = \{\theta_1, \ldots, \theta_{|\Theta|}\}$ (note that enumerating Θ may require an algorithm).
- The *cost class* $I_{i,k}$ consists of all words with label ℓ_i and cost θ_k which satisfy the length bounds and the hard specification, i.e., $\{w \in \Sigma^{m:n} \mid w \in \mathcal{L}(H), L(w) = \ell_i, \mathcal{K}(w) = \theta_k\}$. As the costs of all words in a cost class are equal, we may speak of the *cost* of a cost class without ambiguity.
- The *label class* I_i consists of all words with label ℓ_i as above but any cost, i.e., $\bigcup_{k=1}^{|\Theta|} I_{i,k}$.
- We write $\Pr[X(w) \mid w \leftarrow D]$ for the probability (or $E[\ldots]$ for the expected value) of $X(w)$ given that w is sampled from distribution D.

Definition 2. *Given an LQCI instance $\mathcal{C}$, a distribution D over Σ^* is an* improvising *distribution for that instance if it satisfies the following constraints:*

1. **Hard Constraint:** $\Pr[w \in I \mid w \leftarrow D] = 1$
2. **Cost Constraint:** $E[\mathcal{K}(w) \mid w \leftarrow D] \le c$
3. **Randomness over Labels:** $\forall i \in \{1, \ldots, |\Omega|\}, \lambda \le \Pr[w \in I_i \mid w \leftarrow D] \le \rho$
4. **Randomness over Words:** $\forall i \in \{1, \ldots, |\Omega|\}, \forall y \in I_i,$
   $\hat{\alpha}_i \le \Pr[y = w \mid w \in I_i, w \leftarrow D] \le \hat{\beta}_i$

We say that an LQCI instance is feasible *if there exists an improvising distribution for it (and* infeasible *otherwise). An* improviser *for an LQCI instance is a probabilistic algorithm which takes no input, has finite expected runtime, and whose output distribution is an improvising distribution. Given an LQCI instance C, the* LQCI problem *is then to determine if C is feasible, and, if so, to generate an improviser for C. Finally, an* improvisation scheme *for a class of LQCI instances is a probabilistic algorithm with finite expected runtime that solves the LQCI problem for instances in that class.*

As described in the preceding sections, the goal of our problem definition is to provide formal guarantees about the randomness of improvisations while respecting the various constraints. In some applications, we may simply wish to maximize randomness: then precise control over the randomness parameters for each label class is not needed, and in fact finding values of $\hat{\alpha}_i, \hat{\beta}_i$ which maximize randomness while remaining feasible is nontrivial. Building on our analysis of the basic LQCI problem in the next several sections, in Sect. 6 we will introduce a *maximum-entropy* version of LQCI which directly maximizes randomness without requiring $\hat{\alpha}_i$ and $\hat{\beta}_i$ to be explicitly specified.

3   Feasibility Conditions and the Greedy Construction

In this section, we introduce a greedy construction which will be used to provide necessary and sufficient conditions for an LQCI instance to be feasible. This construction will also form the basis of the improvisation schemes presented later in the paper. For now, we will present the construction without assuming any particular specification formalism and ignoring algorithmic concerns: the description presented here will consider traces one by one and thus be inefficient. The next section will develop efficient implementations of these ideas.

The *greedy LQCI construction* is separated into two phases. In the first phase, the *greedy cost construction*, we define a distribution over each label class individually, greedily optimizing cost by giving as much weight as we can to the cheapest elements while respecting the randomness over words condition. In the second phase, the *greedy label construction*, we define a distribution over labels, greedily assigning maximum marginal probability to the label classes with the cheapest expected costs under the distributions from the first phase while respecting the randomness over labels condition. The intuition is that we want to first make sampling within each label class as cheap as possible, and then sample from the cheapest classes as often as possible, while satisfying the randomness requirements. We will prove below that this greedy approach in fact yields an improvising distribution whenever one exists.

Toy Example. We will begin with a toy example which illustrates the idea and correctness of the greedy construction. Suppose we want to sample from words of length 3 ($m = n = 3$) over the binary alphabet $\Sigma = \{0, 1\}$, subject to the hard constraint that each word must contain at least one 1. We will have two label classes: words with an odd number of 1s will be in label 1, and those with an even number in label 2. The cost of each word will be its integer value in binary. The label parameters will be $\lambda = 0.2$ and $\rho = 1.0$, so that each label must be sampled from with a probability at least 0.2 and at most 1.0. The word randomness parameters will be $\hat{\alpha}_1 = \hat{\alpha}_2 = 0.1$ and $\hat{\beta}_1 = \hat{\beta}_2 = 0.5$, so that when sampling from a particular label class, each word in the class must be selected with probability at least 0.1 and at most 0.5.

Figure 2 shows the greedy construction applied to this LQCI instance. Beginning with label 1, we need to construct a probability distribution over the words 001, 010, 100, and 111. We start by assigning 0.1 to each word, since $\hat{\alpha}_1 = 0.1$. Then we assign as much additional probability as we can (up to $\hat{\beta}_1 = 0.5$) to the cheapest words first until a total of 1 is reached, as shown in the bottom left of Fig. 2. The result is that there are 3 distinct probabilities within the label class: the minimum $\hat{\alpha}_1 = 0.1$, the maximum $\hat{\beta}_1 = 0.5$, and the overflow probability 0.3 on the word 010. This process results in a distribution over label 1 with expected cost 2.2, the minimum achievable while satisfying the randomness over words constraint. A similar process yields a distribution of expected cost 4.1 on label 2. Now that we know the minimum expected cost for each label, we should sample from the cheaper label as frequently as possible. Since $\lambda = 0.2$ and $\rho = 1.0$, we sample from label 2 with probability 0.2 (the minimum allowed) and from label 1 with probability 0.8, yielding a distribution over improvisations with expected cost 2.58. Our analysis will show that this is in fact the minimum possible expected cost over all distributions satisfying conditions (1) (3), and (4) in Definition 2. So if the cost bound c in the LQCI instance is at least this large, then we have an improvising distribution, and otherwise the instance is infeasible.

We now describe the two phases of our construction formally.

The Greedy Cost Construction. For a particular label class $i \in \{1, \ldots, |\Omega|\}$, we proceed as follows. Let $\delta^i = (\delta^i_1, \ldots, \delta^i_{|\Theta|})$ be a list of all the cost classes $I_{i,k}$ with label i, sorted in increasing order of cost. Then fix $o_i = \frac{1 - \hat{\alpha}_i |I_i|}{\hat{\beta}_i - \hat{\alpha}_i}$, whose floor is the maximum number of words that can be assigned $\hat{\beta}_i$ probability (the maximum allowed) while still leaving at least $\hat{\alpha}_i$ probability (the minimum allowed) for each remaining word. Then, moving through the cost classes in the order given by δ^i, we assign $\hat{\beta}_i$ probability to each word in the class, until we get to a class δ^i_r where the cumulative number of words so far (including the new class) would exceed o_i. To this class we assign $\hat{\beta}_i(o_i - \sum_{k=1}^{r-1} |\delta^i_k|) + \hat{\alpha}_i(\sum_{k=1}^{r} |\delta^i_k| - o_i)$ probability (spread uniformly over words in the class), the maximum allowed while leaving exactly $\hat{\alpha}_i$ for each remaining word. Assigning $\hat{\alpha}_i$ to the remaining words, we obtain a distribution D_i over the whole label class I_i.

We note that this process is not well-defined when $\hat{\alpha}_i = \hat{\beta}_i$ (in which case we simply assign probability $\hat{\alpha}_i$ to every word in I_i) or when $\hat{\alpha}_i |I_i| > 1$ (in which case the instance is infeasible due to $\hat{\alpha}_i$ being too large); also, the process does not result in a probability distribution if $\hat{\beta}_i |I_i| < 1$ (in which case the instance is infeasible due to $\hat{\beta}_i$ being too small). Except in these cases, we get a well-defined distribution D_i over I_i which satisfies conditions (1) and (4) of Definition 2. Moreover, the expected cost of D_i is minimal among all such distributions, since it assigns as much weight as possible to the words with lowest cost.

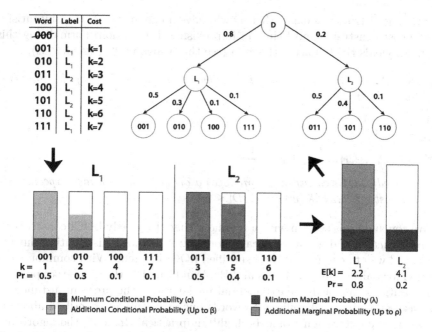

Fig. 2. Applying the greedy LQCI construction to our toy example. Counter-clockwise from upper left: table of improvisations, the greedy cost construction, the greedy label construction, and the final improvising distribution.

The Greedy Label Construction. Given the distributions D_i for each label class I_i from the first stage, we now choose a distribution over labels. Following a similar pattern as before, let δ be a list of the distributions D_i sorted in order of increasing expected cost. Then fix $u = \lfloor \frac{1-|\Omega|\lambda}{\rho-\lambda} \rfloor$, which is the number of label classes that can be assigned probability ρ (the maximum allowed) while still leaving at least λ (the minimum allowed) for each remaining class. We assign ρ probability to the first u label classes in δ. To the next label class we assign probability $1 - \rho u - \lambda(|\Omega| - u - 1)$, the maximum allowed while leaving exactly λ for each remaining label class. Finally, we assign λ to all remaining label classes, and call the resulting distribution over labels $\hat{D}$. Similar to before, this process will be well-defined and result in a distribution when $\frac{1}{\rho} \leq |\Omega| \leq \frac{1}{\lambda}$; otherwise, ρ is too small or λ is too large for condition (3) of Definition 2 to be satisfied.

To complete the construction, we obtain a final distribution D over words by first sampling a label i from $\hat{D}$ and then sampling from D_i. The greedy cost construction ensured that D_i is defined over the class $I_i \subseteq I$ and assigns probability between $\hat{\alpha}_i$ and $\hat{\beta}_i$ to each word, so D will satisfy the hard and randomness over words constraints in Definition 2. The greedy label construction ensures that $\hat{D}$ assigns probability between λ and ρ to each label, so D will also satisfy the randomness over labels constraint. Finally, since each phase selects a distribution of minimal cost amongst those satisfying the corresponding constraints, if *any* improvising distribution exists then D will have no greater cost, thereby satisfying the cost constraint and being an improvising distribution. Formalizing this argument yields the following theorem (see the Appendix [21] for details):

Theorem 1. *An LQCI instance is feasible if and only if all of the following conditions are true:*

1. $\dfrac{1}{\rho} \leq |\Omega| \leq \dfrac{1}{\lambda}$

2. $\forall i \in \{1, \ldots, |\Omega|\}, \ \dfrac{1}{\hat{\beta}_i} \leq |I_i| \leq \dfrac{1}{\hat{\alpha}_i}$

3. *The greedy LQCI construction produces a distribution D whose expected cost is at most c (i.e., $E[\mathcal{K}(w) \mid w \leftarrow D] \leq c$).*

We conclude this section with a reminder that the greedy LQCI construction is a *construction* and not a practical algorithm: it defines a distribution but not a practical way to compute it for a specified LQCI instance. With common specification formalisms such as DFAs and Boolean formulas, the number of possible improvisations can easily be exponential in the size of the problem instance. In this case, assigning probabilities to words one at a time as described above in the abstract construction would be highly impractical. Instead, the algorithms we present in the following sections are able to avoid enumerating exponentially-large sets by working with implicit representations to create distributions equal to or approximating the one produced by the greedy LQCI construction.

4   Exact LQCI for Automata Specifications

The greedy LQCI construction from Sect. 3 gives us a way to determine if an LQCI instance is feasible and, if so, to build an improvising distribution. Implementing the construction requires several operations—such as computing the size of the label/cost classes—which may or may not be tractable depending on the types of specification used in the instance. In this section, we will identify a sufficient list of operations which yield an efficient generic improvisation scheme for any class of LQCI instances with specifications supporting these operations. Then we will instantiate the scheme for two natural classes of specifications given by deterministic finite automata, obtaining efficient improvisation algorithms.

Following the description of the preceding section, we can see that for a given LQCI instance, the operations listed below are sufficient to complete the greedy LQCI construction and sample from the resulting distribution:

Definition 3. *(Sufficient Operations) Given an LQCI instance $\mathcal{C}$:*

1. *Compute the list of possible costs Θ.*
2. *For each $i \in \{1, \ldots, |\Omega|\}$ and $k \in \Theta$, compute $|I_{i,k}|$.*
3. *For each $i \in \{1, \ldots, |\Omega|\}$ and $k \in \Theta$, sample uniformly from $I_{i,k}$.*

If we can implement these operations in polynomial time, we can build a polynomial-time improvisation scheme in the sense of [16,17], i.e., an algorithm which solves the LQCI problem in polynomial time, and whose generated improvisers themselves run in polynomial (expected) time. To do this we first compute the list of possible costs and the size of each $I_{i,k}$. We then perform a modified version of the greedy construction which assigns probabilities to entire cost classes instead of individual words. As each word in a class has the same label and cost, we can satisfy our cost and randomness requirements with a distribution that assigns the same probability to every word within a class. Then to implement placing probability p on each word of $I_{i,k}$ without enumerating this potentially exponentially-large set, we simply choose the set with probability $p|I_{i,k}|$ and then sample uniformly from it (see the Appendix [21] for a detailed argument).

Theorem 2. *Suppose for a class of LQCI instances the operations in Definition 3 can be performed in polynomial time (in the size of the instance). Then there is a polynomial-time improvisation scheme for that class.*

One broad class of specifications to which this scheme can apply is deterministic finite automata (DFAs): for example, we can encode the specifications from our robotic planning example as DFAs. While a DFA can encode the hard specification $\mathcal{H}$ directly, encoding cost and label functions is not as clear. We consider two natural encodings: most simply, we can label each state of the DFA with an integer, assigning the associated label/cost to words ending at that state.

Theorem 3. *Consider the class of LQCI instances where $\mathcal{H}$ is a DFA, $\mathcal{K}$ and $\mathcal{L}$ are given by DFAs which output an integer cost/label associated with the state they end on, the length bounds are given in unary and all other numerical parameters in binary. This class has a polynomial-time improvisation scheme.*

Proof (Sketch). Operation (1) is trivial. For (2) and (3), we can easily construct DFAs accepting all improvisations with a given label and cost, then apply classical techniques for counting/sampling from the language of a DFA [23]. □

To capture cost functions like path length or mission time (as in our planning example), we consider a second encoding using weighted DFAs: states are again labeled with integers, but the cost is now given by *accumulating* costs from every state passed through. Here, the number of possible costs can grow linearly with the largest cost of a single state, and so be exponential in the size of the (binary) encoding; as a result we only obtain a *pseudopolynomial* improvisation scheme by applying Theorem 2. The algorithm can still be feasible, however, when the magnitude of possible costs is not too large, as we will see in Sect. 7.

Theorem 4. *Consider the class of LQCI instances as in Theorem 3 but where $\mathcal{K}$ is given by a weighted DFA, i.e. summing the integer costs associated with each state of a DFA accepting path (with multiplicity). This class has a pseudopolynomial improvisation scheme.*

Proof (Sketch). We can perform operation (1) by dynamic programming over the states and word lengths up to the length bound n. If the maximum cost of a state in the DFA for $\mathcal{K}$ is M, then the cost of an improvisation is at most $M(n+1)$; so for (2) and (3) we can build DFAs of size $poly(M, n)$ recognizing $I_{i,k}$ and then apply counting/sampling as above. If state costs were encoded in unary, the operations above would take polynomial time and Theorem 2 would apply. Converting from binary to unary yields a pseudopolynomial scheme.   □

5   Approximate LQCI for Symbolic Specifications

The LQCI algorithms for DFAs that we developed in the previous section cover many useful specifications; however, as we will see in Sect. 7, even fairly simple specifications can require very large automata when represented explicitly. In this section we propose an algorithm that avoids such blowup by working with *symbolic* specifications given by Boolean formulas. We cannot use our scheme of Theorem 2 directly, because counting the number of solutions of a Boolean formula is #P-hard. Nevertheless, we will show that by leveraging recent advances in SAT solving, we can *approximately* solve LQCI to any desired accuracy.

We consider LQCI instances with specifications given by Boolean formulas, whose variables encode traces and costs; for modeling convenience, we also allow a vector of auxiliary variables z. Specifically, we assume we are given:

- a conjunctive normal form (CNF) formula $h(x, z)$ such that $\exists z.h(x, z)$ holds if and only if the bitvector x encodes a trace satisfying the hard constraint;
- a CNF formula $\ell(x, y, z)$ such that $\exists z.\ell(x, y, z)$ holds if and only if trace x has the label encoded by the bitvector y;
- a CNF formula $k(x, y, z)$ such that $\exists z.k(x, y, z)$ holds iff trace x has cost y (a positive integer).

We further assume that the instance has only a polynomial number of labels, although there can be exponentially-many costs.

Given such an instance, we can readily build a CNF formula $\phi_i(x, y, z)$ which is satisfiable iff x encodes a word which has length between m and n, satisfies the hard constraint, belongs to label i, and has cost y. The solutions x for a particular choice of i and y comprise the associated cost class, so that the operations we need for the greedy construction are instances of the *model counting* and *uniform generation* problems for SAT.[2] Recent work has yielded practical algorithms based on SAT solvers which solve these problems approximately [7,27][3]:

---

[2] Since we do not want to count over the auxiliary variables z, we actually require *projected* counting/sampling, which the algorithms we use can also perform [7,17].

[3] We note that UniGen [6,7] is not strictly speaking an almost-uniform generator as in Definition 4 since it only supports sufficiently-large tolerances; for theoretical results, one can substitute the algorithm of [4] to do *exact* (projected) uniform sampling.

Definition 4. *([7])   An approximate counter is a probabilistic algorithm $\mathcal{C}$ which given a CNF formula F with set of solutions R_F, a tolerance $\tau > 0$, and a confidence $1 - \delta \in [0, 1)$ guarantees that*

$$\Pr\left[|R_F|/(1 + \tau) \leq \mathcal{C}(F, \tau, 1 - \delta) \leq (1 + \tau)|R_F|\right] \geq 1 - \delta.$$

An almost-uniform generator $\mathcal{G}$ *is a probabilistic algorithm that, given F as above and a tolerance $\epsilon > 0$, guarantees that for every $y \in R_F$, we have*

$$1/((1 + \epsilon)|R_F|) \leq \Pr[\mathcal{G}(F, \epsilon) = y] \leq (1 + \epsilon)/|R_F|.$$

We can modify our greedy construction to work with only approximate counting/sampling as follows. If the cost bitvector has $|y|$ bits, the cost of a word is between 1 and $2^{|y|}$. To avoid enumerating exponentially-many cost classes for label i, we group words into "cost buckets" by subdividing this interval into powers of r for some $r > 1$, i.e. $[1, r), [r, r^2), \ldots, [r^{b-1}, r^b)$. We will have $b = O(\log_r(2^{|y|})) = O(|y|/\log r)$ buckets, and we can estimate the size of bucket j by approximately counting solutions to $\exists z.[\phi_i(x, y, z) \wedge (r^j \leq y < r^{j+1})]$. We will then use these estimates to choose a distribution over buckets, following the intuition of the greedy cost construction that we should assign the most probability to buckets with lowest estimated cost, but with some adjustments to bound the error that approximate sampling introduces.

For each label class i with randomness parameters α and β, we apply a modified form of the greedy cost construction, shown in Algorithm 1. We start in lines 1–3 by using model counting as above (with a tolerance τ and confidence $1 - \delta$ to be specified later) to find estimates c_k of the size of each bucket k, and corresponding lower bounds p_k on how much probability the bucket would have received in the exact greedy construction (the extra $1 + \tau$ factor accounting for possibly overestimating the size of the bucket). If these lower bounds total more than 1, then we know there are too many improvisations for the instance to be feasible (assuming the model counts are within their tolerance) and we return false on line 4. Otherwise, on lines 5–7 we proceed as in the greedy construction, starting from the cheapest bucket, increasing the assigned probability per word to $(1 + \tau)\beta$ until a probability of 1 is reached. The factor of $1 + \tau$ ensures that, even if the model counts have underestimated the size of the cheaper buckets, we still assign them at least as much probability as the exact greedy construction would. Next, line 8 checks if there are too few improvisations, similarly to line 4. Finally, we return our distribution over buckets, as well as a lower bound on its expected cost that we will use next.

If Algorithm 1 does not return false for any label class, then we complete our approximate LQCI algorithm by running the greedy label construction from Sect. 3, using the lower bounds from Algorithm 1 as the expected cost of each label class. As before, we declare the instance infeasible if the construction fails or if its expected cost exceeds the cost bound c. Otherwise, we obtain a distribution over all the cost buckets; our improviser then simply chooses a bucket from this distribution and applies almost-uniform sampling to sample a word from it.

Choosing the bucket count and counting/sampling tolerances appropriately, our algorithm can approximate an improvising distribution to within arbitrarily-small multiplicative error, using polynomially-many calls to a SAT solver:

Algorithm 1. ApproximateGreedyCost($i, \alpha, \beta, r, b, \tau, \delta$)

1: **for** $k = 1$ to b **do**
2:      $c_k := \#SAT(\exists z.\phi_i(x, y, z) \wedge (r^{k-1} \leq y < r^k), \tau, 1 - \delta)$
3:      $p_k := \alpha c_k / (1 + \tau)$
4: **if** $\sum_{j=1}^{b} p_j > 1$ **then return** False
5: **for** $k = 1$ to b **do**
6:      $p_k := \min((1 + \tau)\beta c_k, 1 - \sum_{j \neq k} p_j)$
7:      **if** $\sum_{j=1}^{b} p_j = 1$ **then break**
8: **if** $\sum_{j=1}^{b} p_j < 1$ **then return** False
9: $Lo := \sum_{j=1}^{b} p_j r^{j-1}$
10: **return** $\{p_j\}_{j=1}^{b}, Lo$

Theorem 5. *There is an algorithm which, given a Boolean LQCI instance $\mathcal{C}$, a cost tolerance $\zeta > 0$, a randomness tolerance $\gamma > 0$, and a confidence $1 - \delta \in [0, 1)$, runs in $\text{poly}(|\mathcal{C}|, 1/\zeta, 1/\gamma, \log(1/\delta))$ time relative to an NP oracle and either returns $\perp$ or an algorithm sampling from a distribution $\widetilde{D}$ over words. With probability at least $1 - \delta$, if $\perp$ is returned then $\mathcal{C}$ is infeasible, and otherwise:*

1. **Hard Constraint:** $\Pr[\mathcal{H}(w) \mid w \leftarrow \widetilde{D}] = 1$
2. **Cost Constraint:** $E[\mathcal{K}(w) \mid w \leftarrow \widetilde{D}] \leq (1 + \zeta)c$
3. **Randomness over Labels:** $\forall i \in \{1, \ldots, |\Omega|\}, \ \lambda \leq \Pr[w \in I_i \mid w \leftarrow \widetilde{D}] \leq \rho$
4. **Randomness over Words:** $\forall i \in \{1, \ldots, |\Omega|\} \ \forall y \in I_i,$
   $\hat{\alpha}_i / (1 + \gamma) \leq \Pr[y = w \mid w \in I_i, w \leftarrow \widetilde{D}] \leq (1 + \gamma)\hat{\beta}_i$

6   Maximum-Entropy LQCI

Our LQCI definition requires providing conditional probability bounds for every label, which while allowing maximal control of the distribution, can be unwieldy to use. However, if we drop conditional bounds entirely, trivial solutions with unnecessarily-poor randomness can appear. For example, consider an LQCI instance with parameters $\lambda = 0.5$, $\rho = 0.5$, $\hat{\alpha} = (0, \ldots, 0)$, $\hat{\beta} = (1, \ldots, 1)$. With this choice, any distribution will satisfy the randomness over words constraint, and all labels have the same marginal probability of being selected. Then assume that we have two labels, costs $\Theta = (1, 2)$, and cost bound $c = 1.5$, along with the following cost class sizes: $|I_{1,1}| = 1$, $|I_{2,1}| = 1$, $|I_{1,2}| = 1000$, $|I_{2,2}| = 1000$. Now simply assigning 50% probability to $I_{1,1}$ and 50% probability to $I_{2,1}$ is an improvising distribution. Assigning 25% probability to all 4 classes is also an improvising distribution, and clearly preferable from the perspective of randomness. Unfortunately, without a nontrivial randomness over words constraint, we have no way to push the improviser to select the second distribution. To enforce this, we introduce the concept of entropy from information theory.

Definition 5. *Given a discrete random variable X with a set of outcomes Ω and probabilities $p : \Omega \to [0, 1]$, the entropy of X is $H(X) = -\sum_{x \in \Omega} p(x) \lg p(x)$.*

To obtain a problem formulation that maximizes randomness without requiring probability bounds for each class, we invoke the Principle of Maximum Entropy: amongst all improvising distributions (without a randomness over words constraint), we should select the one with the highest entropy (as first proposed for reactive CI in [30]). This yields a notion of Maximum-Entropy LQCI:

Definition 6. *A* Maximum-Entropy LQCI (MELQCI) *instance is an LQCI instance where* $\hat{\alpha} = (0, \ldots, 0)$ *and* $\hat{\beta} = (1, \ldots, 1)$. *A* τ-improviser *for a MELQCI instance* $\mathcal{C}$ *is an improviser (as in LQCI) whose output distribution has entropy at most* τ *less than the maximum-entropy improvising distribution for* $\mathcal{C}$. *We define the* MELQCI problem *as, given an instance* $\mathcal{C}$ *and* $\tau > 0$, *determining if* $\mathcal{C}$ *is feasible, and, if so, generating a* τ-improviser for $\mathcal{C}$.

We can solve MELQCI efficiently in the same cases as LQCI:

Theorem 6. *Given a class of MELQCI instances for which one can perform the operations in Definition 3 in polynomial time, there is a polynomial-time algorithm which given an instance from the class and a* $\tau > 0$, *computes a* τ-*improviser.*

Proof. (Sketch). Once cost class sizes have been computed as in Theorem 2, the search for the desired distribution over cost classes can be formulated as an optimization problem with a separable convex objective (the entropy of the distribution) and linear constraints (improviser constraints). This problem can be solved in time polynomial in the size of the instance and $\log(1/\tau)$ [10].

As in Sect. 4, we can transform this algorithm into a *pseudopolynomial* scheme for accumulated-cost DFA specifications.

7   Experiments

We ran several experiments on the robotic planning problems from Sect. 2 (code available at [20]). These experiments aim to demonstrate that we can encode practical problems as LQCI instances solvable using our algorithms, highlight the relative advantages/disadvantages of our exact/approximate algorithms, and show the necessity of the label function in ensuring meaningful randomness.

As a minimal experiment, we used a 6×6 grid world with a small range of costs (0–3 per cell, 8–39 for paths); we compared against a 7×7 grid world with a much larger range of costs (0–9 per cell, 38–137 for paths).[4] We encoded the specifications in Sect. 2 both as DFAs for our exact LQCI and MELQCI algorithms, and as Boolean formulas for our approximate LQCI algorithm. The Boolean encodings were obtained by formulating the specifications in the SMT theory of bitvectors, and bit-blasting them with Z3 [26]; the resulting formulas had several thousand variables and tens of thousands of clauses. We used UniGen3 [7,27] for uniform generation with its default tolerance[5] of 17, and an

---

[4] A larger 8×8 map exceeded our 24-hour wallclock timeout for all exact and approximate experiments.

[5] UniGen3 cannot guarantee a multiplicative error of less than 7.48 [6]; see footnote 3.

Table 1. Experiment parameters and improviser construction times (in minutes).

Map	Problem Type	(λ, ρ)	$(\hat{\alpha}_i, \hat{\beta}_i)$	r	γ	δ	Wall Time	CPU Time
	Exact QCI	(0, 3e-5)	(1, 1)				540	5568
	Exact LQCI	(0, 1e-5)	(0.3, 0.4)		N/A		444	6102
6×6	Exact MELQCI	N/A	(0.3, 0.4)				444[a]	6102
	Approx. LQCI	(0, 1e-5)	(0.3, 0.4)	1.2	10^2	0.2	23.7 ± 0.6	93.3 ± 1.4
	Approx. LQCI	(0, 1e-5)	(0.3, 0.4)	1.2	10^3	0.2	21.2 ± 0.7	81.5 ± 1.1
	Approx. LQCI	(0, 1e-5)	(0.3, 0.4)	1.2	10^4	0.2	20.2 ± 0.7	78.4 ± 3.4
	Exact QCI	(0, 3e-5)	(1, 1)					
	Exact LQCI	(0, 1e-5)	(0.3, 0.4)		N/A		Timed out	
7×7	Exact MELQCI	N/A	(0.3, 0.4)				(24-hour wall time)	
	Approx. LQCI	(0, 1e-5)	(0.3, 0.4)	1.2	10^2	0.2	42.8 ± 2.1	186.1 ± 3.9
	Approx. LQCI	(0, 1e-5)	(0.3, 0.4)	1.2	10^3	0.2	38.8 ± 8.8	152.6 ± 9.0
	Approx. LQCI	(0, 1e-5)	(0.3, 0.4)	1.2	10^4	0.2	38.8 ± 9.7	145.5 ± 9.5

[a] The LQCI/MELQCI runtimes were nearly identical, since MELQCI reuses the LQCI computations and adds a convex optimization step, which took negligible time.

in-development version of `ApproxMC` [8,27,28] for approximate model counting with tolerances of 1.4, 6.7, and 23.25, so that the overall γ values were 10^2, 10^3, and 10^4. To put these values into context, the small/large maps had on the order of $10^7/10^9$ improvisations, and we required that no word have $> \rho = 10^{-5}$ probability of being selected. Therefore, with our tightest/loosest γ we are guaranteed that no word will be more than 0.1%/10% of the distribution respectively. The confidence was set to 0.8 ($\delta = 0.2$), ApproxMC's default confidence. Each model counting call however required a much higher confidence to achieve an overall δ of 0.2.

For the small/large maps respectively we used length bounds of (1,25)/(1,30) and cost bounds of 30/50. We used label probability bounds of (0.3, 0.4) throughout, except for unlabeled "QCI" experiments. The experiments were run on a 64-core machine with 188 GB of RAM; we used 62 parallel threads, unless this exhausted RAM, in which case we used 16 threads. The experiments are summarized in Table 1; due to significant runtime variability for the approximate experiments, we report means and standard deviations over 10 repetitions. For all exact experiments which completed within the 24-h wallclock timeout, RAM usage was ≤ 6 GB per thread, and the average time to sample an improvisation was ≤ 1 ms; all approximate experiments required ≤ 250 MB RAM per thread and took ~ 20 s to sample an improvisation.

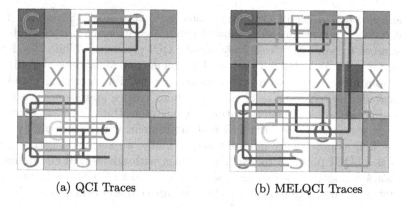

(a) QCI Traces   (b) MELQCI Traces

Fig. 3. Randomly-selected traces generated by the QCI/MELQCI improvisers for the 6×6 map. Note that all the QCI traces use the same charging station.

We can draw several conclusions from these results. Improviser construction with the exact algorithm is significantly more expensive than with the approximate algorithm, in both CPU time and RAM. This is not surprising, as the exact encodings resulted in enormous DFAs which, for the large map, approached 10^{10} states. Conversely, sampling is much faster for the exact algorithm, with no SAT queries required. We can also see that the approximate algorithm can be used to practically solve problems that are infeasible to solve exactly, such as the large-map problem. We expect new developments in the relatively young field of approximate model counting/sampling will further speed up our algorithm.

Visualizing several randomly-chosen traces from our exact QCI and MELQCI experiments in Fig. 3, we can see the importance of labels. In unlabeled QCI, the robot always charged at the substation near the main road due to the lower expected cost of such paths. In contrast, MELQCI yielded a near-uniform distribution over the charging stations. This increase in diversity was not free, with the average cost rising to 21.4 for MELQCI from 8.7 for QCI. This trade-off demonstrates how LQCI allows us to balance the need for control over our improvisations with the need for meaningful diversity (not merely randomness) by choosing appropriate label functions.

8 Conclusion

In this paper, we introduced *labelled quantitative control improvisation* as a framework allowing correct-by-construction synthesis of randomized systems whose behavior must be diverse with respect to a label function and near-optimal with respect to a cost function. We studied the theory of LQCI problems and developed algorithms for solving them for broad classes of specifications encoded as finite automata or Boolean formulas. Our experiments demonstrated how our framework can be used to formalize and solve realistic robotic planning problems.

There are a number of clear directions for future work. Scalability is an evident concern: our experiments show that our algorithms can require substantial resources to solve even relatively small LQCI problems. While LQCI with Boolean formulas is a difficult #P-hard problem, our algorithms will directly benefit from future progress in model counting; our DFA algorithms could also be improved through the use of abstraction to reduce state-space explosion. We also plan to explore generalizations of our algorithms, such as extending our approximate scheme to MELQCI and to problems with exponentially-many labels, as well as potentially infinite traces. Finally, we are investigating extensions of the LQCI problem to *reactive* settings with adversarial environments, and to *black-box* settings for design-space exploration and other problems where we do not have complete models for the cost function and other constraints.

Acknowledgements. The authors thank Skyler Stewart for designing Fig. 2, and several anonymous reviewers for their helpful comments. This work was supported in part by DARPA contract FA8750-20-C-0156 (SDCPS).

References

1. Akkaya, I., Fremont, D.J., Valle, R., Donzé, A., Lee, E.A., Seshia, S.A.: Control improvisation with probabilistic temporal specifications. In: First IEEE International Conference on Internet-of-Things Design and Implementation, IoTDI 2016, Berlin, Germany, 4–8 April 2016, pp. 187–198. IEEE Computer Society (2016). https://doi.org/10.1109/IoTDI.2015.33, https://doi.org/10.1109/IoTDI.2015.33
2. Almagor, S., Kupferman, O.: High-quality synthesis against stochastic environments. In: Talbot, J.M., Regnier, L. (eds.) 25th EACSL Annual Conference on Computer Science Logic (CSL 2016). Leibniz International Proceedings in Informatics (LIPIcs), vol. 62, pp. 28:1–28:17. Schloss Dagstuhl-Leibniz-Zentrum für Informatik, Dagstuhl, Germany (2016). https://doi.org/10.4230/LIPIcs.CSL.2016.28, http://drops.dagstuhl.de/opus/volltexte/2016/6568
3. Baier, C., Brázdil, T., Größer, M., Kučera, A.: Stochastic game logic. Acta informatica pp. 1–22 (2012)
4. Bellare, M., Goldreich, O., Petrank, E.: Uniform generation of NP-witnesses using an NP-oracle. Inf. Comput. **163**(2), 510–526 (2000)
5. Bloem, R., Galler, S., Jobstmann, B., Piterman, N., Pnueli, A., Weiglhofer, M.: Specify, compile, run: hardware from PSL. In: Proceedings of the 6th International Workshop on Compiler Optimization meets Compiler Verification (COCV 2007). Electronic Notes in Theoretical Computer Science, vol. 190, pp. 3–16. Elsevier (2007). https://doi.org/10.1016/j.entcs.2007.09.004, http://www.sciencedirect.com/science/article/pii/S157106610700583X
6. Chakraborty, S., Fremont, D.J., Meel, K.S., Seshia, S.A., Vardi, M.Y.: On parallel scalable uniform SAT witness generator. In: Proceedings of Tools and Algorithms for the Construction and Analysis of Systems (TACAS), pp. 304–319 (4 2015)
7. Chakraborty, S., Meel, K.S., Vardi, M.Y.: Balancing scalability and uniformity in sat-witness generator. In: Proceedings of Design Automation Conference (DAC), pp. 60:1–60:6, June 2014

8. Chakraborty, S., Meel, K.S., Vardi, M.Y.: Algorithmic improvements in approximate counting for probabilistic inference: from linear to logarithmic sat calls. In: Proceedings of International Joint Conference on Artificial Intelligence (IJCAI), July 2016

9. Chen, T., Forejt, V., Kwiatkowska, M., Simaitis, A., Wiltsche, C.: On stochastic games with multiple objectives. In: Chatterjee, K., Sgall, J. (eds.) MFCS 2013. LNCS, vol. 8087, pp. 266–277. Springer, Heidelberg (2013). https://doi.org/10.1007/978-3-642-40313-2_25

10. Chubanov, S.: A polynomial-time descent method for separable convex optimization problems with linear constraints. SIAM J. Optim. **26**(1), 856–889 (2016). https://doi.org/10.1137/14098524x

11. Denise, A., Gaudel, M.C., Gouraud, S.D., Lassaigne, R., Oudinet, J., Peyronnet, S.: Coverage-biased random exploration of large models and application to testing. Int. J. Softw. Tools Technol. Transfer **14**(1), 73–93 (2011). https://doi.org/10.1007/s10009-011-0190-1

12. Donze, A., Libkind, S., Seshia, S.A., Wessel, D.: Control improvisation with application to music. Tech. Rep. UCB/EECS-2013-183, EECS Department, University of California, Berkeley (Nov 2013). http://www2.eecs.berkeley.edu/Pubs/TechRpts/2013/EECS-2013-183.html

13. Donzé, A., Valle, R., Akkaya, I., Libkind, S., Seshia, S.A., Wessel, D.: Machine improvisation with formal specifications. In: Music Technology meets Philosophy - From Digital Echos to Virtual Ethos: Joint Proceedings of the 40th International Computer Music Conference, ICMC 2014, and the 11th Sound and Music Computing Conference, SMC 2014, Athens, Greece, 14–20 September 2014. Michigan Publishing (2014). http://hdl.handle.net/2027/spo.bbp2372.2014.196

14. Finkbeiner, B.: Synthesis of reactive systems. In: Esparza, J., Grumberg, O., Sickert, S. (eds.) Dependable Software Systems Engineering. NATO Science for Peace and Security Series, D: Information and Communication Security, vol. 45, pp. 72–98. IOS Press, Amsterdam (2016)

15. Fremont, D.J.: Algorithmic improvisation. Thesis (2019). https://www2.eecs.berkeley.edu/Pubs/TechRpts/2019/EECS-2019-133.pdf

16. Fremont, D.J., Donzé, A., Seshia, S.A., Wessel, D.: Control improvisation. In: Harsha, P., Ramalingam, G. (eds.) 35th IARCS Annual Conference on Foundations of Software Technology and Theoretical Computer Science (FSTTCS 2015). Leibniz International Proceedings in Informatics (LIPIcs), vol. 45, pp. 463–474. Schloss Dagstuhl-Leibniz-Zentrum fuer Informatik, Dagstuhl, Germany (2015). https://doi.org/10.4230/LIPIcs.FSTTCS.2015.463, http://drops.dagstuhl.de/opus/volltexte/2015/5659

17. Fremont, D.J., Donzé, A., Seshia, S.A.: Control improvisation (2017). https://arxiv.org/abs/1704.06319

18. Fremont, D.J., Dreossi, T., Ghosh, S., Yue, X., Sangiovanni-Vincentelli, A.L., Seshia, S.A.: Scenic: a language for scenario specification and scene generation. In: McKinley, K.S., Fisher, K. (eds.) Proceedings of the 40th ACM SIGPLAN Conference on Programming Language Design and Implementation, PLDI 2019, Phoenix, AZ, USA, 22–26 June 2019, pp. 63–78. ACM (2019). https://doi.org/10.1145/3314221.3314633, https://doi.org/10.1145/3314221.3314633

19. Fremont, D.J., Seshia, S.A.: Reactive control improvisation. In: Chockler, H., Weissenbacher, G. (eds.) CAV 2018. LNCS, vol. 10981, pp. 307–326. Springer, Cham (2018). https://doi.org/10.1007/978-3-319-96145-3_17

20. Gittis, A., Vin, E., Fremont, D.J.: Randomized synthesis for diversity and cost constraints with control improvisation (artifact). https://doi.org/10.5281/zenodo.6558391

21. Gittis, A., Vin, E., Fremont, D.J.: Randomized synthesis for diversity and cost constraints with control improvisation (2022). https://arxiv.org/abs/2206.02775

22. Hansson, H., Jonsson, B.: A logic for reasoning about time and reliability. Formal Aspects Comput. **6**(5), 512–535 (1994)

23. Hickey, T., Cohen, J.: Uniform random generation of strings in a context-free language. SIAM J. Comput. **12**(4), 645–655 (1983). https://doi.org/10.1137/0212044

24. Kozierok, C.M.: The TCP/IP guide. http://tcpipguide.com/free/t_TCPOperationalOverviewandtheTCPFiniteStateMachineF-2.htm, (Accessed Jan 21 2022)

25. Kress-Gazit, H., Fainekos, G.E., Pappas, G.J.: Temporal-logic-based reactive mission and motion planning. IEEE Trans. Rob. **25**(6), 1370–1381 (2009)

26. de Moura, L., Bjørner, N.: Z3: an efficient SMT solver. In: Ramakrishnan, C.R., Rehof, J. (eds.) TACAS 2008. LNCS, vol. 4963, pp. 337–340. Springer, Heidelberg (2008). https://doi.org/10.1007/978-3-540-78800-3_24

27. Soos, M., Gocht, S., Meel, K.S.: Tinted, detached, and lazy CNF-XOR solving and its applications to counting and sampling. In: Proceedings of International Conference on Computer-Aided Verification (CAV), July 2020

28. Soos, M., Meel, K.S.: Arjun: an efficient independent support computation technique and its applications to counting and sampling. CoRR abs/2110.09026 (2021). https://arxiv.org/abs/2110.09026

29. Sutton, M., Greene, A., Amini, P.: Fuzzing: Brute Force Vulnerability Discovery. Addison-Wesley (2007)

30. Vazquez-Chanlatte, M., Junges, S., Fremont, D.J., Seshia, S.: Entropy-guided control improvisation (2021). https://doi.org/10.15607/RSS.2021.XVII.051, https://doi.org/10.15607/RSS.2021.XVII.051

Author Index

Printed in the United States
by Baker & Taylor Publisher Services